D1300906

Rebecca West

A LIFE

CARL ROLLYSON

SCRIBNER

SCRIBNER
1230 Avenue of the Americas
New York, NY 10020

First published in Great Britain by Hodder and Stoughton

SCRIBNER and design are trademarks of Simon & Schuster Inc.

Set in Goudy Oldstyle

DESIGNED BY ERICH HOBBING

Manufactured in the United States of America

1   3   5   7   9   10   8   6   4   2

Library of Congress Cataloging-in-Publication Data

Rollyson, Carl E.
Rebecca West: a life/Carl Rollyson.
p.   cm.
Includes bibliographical references and index.
1. West, Rebecca, Dame—Biography. 2. Women novelists, English—20th century—Biography.
3. Women journalists—Great Britain—Biography. 4. West, Rebbeca, Dame. I. Title.
PR6045.E8Z85   1996
828'.91209—dc20   96–24231
[B]   CIP

ISBN 0-684-19430-9

Published in Great Britain as *Rebecca West: A Saga of the Century*.

To Lisa

Today I've been glancing thro John Rosseles's Shakespeare's Country in which I came across the following reference: "In 1649 a witch was hanged at Worcester, a witch whose obstinate skill in argument was the terror of her examiners; and the name of this witch was Rebecca West."

JOHN RODGERS TO REBECCA WEST, March 5, 1942

It seems to me that personal relationships presented themselves to Rebecca like those angular figures in books of optical illusions, which on some involuntary switch of perception suddenly change from ascending to descending stairs. As an artist she gave much attention to the fact that the significance of relationships is often not simply (or perhaps truly) apparent in their first aspect. But she could be feverishly deluded . . . by the sudden transformation of the shadows on a hospital wall into the church of the Madonna dell 'Orto in Venice; an imaginative achievement in which there is no truth or insight at all.

NORMAN MACLEOD

If Rebecca ever came back . . . it would be as a firework.

ALISON MACLEOD

Contents

Preface

IF YOU ARE READING the biography of virtually any significant British or American writer—from say 1910 to 1980—you may find a reference to Rebecca West. The biographer will probably be quoting from one of her book reviews or reminiscences, for she was among the finest critics and raconteurs of her age, and indeed of any age. Virginia Woolf once wrote to her "as an admirer who actually drove 8 miles the other day to buy a copy of the *Daily Telegraph* in order not to miss your article. This is not an effort I am in the habit of making, but a proof of the great admiration with which I hold your work." The entry on Rebecca West in the Columbia Encyclopedia contains the succinct verdict: "one of the finest writers of prose in twentieth-century Britain."

Part Scottish, part Anglo-Irish, a product of genteel poverty, dark complected and self-conscious about her appearance, Rebecca West was at home in a world of minorities struggling for self-determination, and an arch opponent of communism and of every orthodoxy that denied human differences and individual autonomy. She was a marriage of contradictions, a feminist, a mistress, and a dutiful wife. Her affairs with H.G. Wells and Lord Beaverbrook are the stuff of legend. Her novel, *The Return of the Soldier,* is one of the defining works of World War I. Her biography of St. Augustine is a penetrating study of the religious mind and what she calls the first modern man. Her reports on the Nuremberg trials in *A Train of Powder* and on traitors in *The Meaning of Treason* are modern classics, and she practically invented the form of the nonfiction novel in *Black Lamb and Grey Falcon,* one of the masterpieces of world literature.

Historian, biographer, novelist, critic, and journalist—Rebecca West's versatility is astonishing. Yet she has not received sustained critical or biographical attention. Compare her to the other major literary figures of her generation: The shortage of first-rate commentary is striking.

In his introduction to *Rebecca West: A Celebration,* Samuel Hynes explains why critics have been slow to reckon with her achievement.

"Few writers can match her range, or her steady moral seriousness," he concludes, lauding her "intellectual toughness." As she admitted in *Black Lamb and Grey Falcon* her multifaceted work "could not fuse to make a picture of a writer, since the interstices were too wide." Publishers also had trouble promoting her. Jonathan Cape wanted to build her up as a novelist, but she did not produce fiction at regular intervals, and the style of each successive novel was different, making it difficult for her to catch on with a popular audience—although two of her novels, *The Fountain Overflows* and *The Birds Fall Down*, were best-sellers.

The few introductory studies of Rebecca West tend to chop her up, assigning separate chapters to the different genres of her work. Consequently the development of her career, and the way her fiction and non-fiction relate to each other, have barely begun to be understood. A biography can help fill her interstices and follow the evolution of her oeuvre.

Victoria Glendinning, Rebecca West's choice to write a short biography, initiated the process of putting West in her proper context, but Glendinning did not have access to some of West's important Yale archive, restricted until the death of Rebecca's son, Anthony West. The Yale collection includes correspondence between Rebecca and her husband, Henry Andrews, H. G. Wells's vibrant love letters, and many other important letters, papers, and manuscripts. In the 1970s, Gordon Ray obtained special permission from West to use the Yale archive, but only for the purpose of studying Wells's letters. She prevented Ray from quoting H.G.'s sexier letters and exerted considerable influence on how the biographer told his story.

Glendinning curtailed the last part of her biography, reasoning that Stanley Olson, designated by West to write a long biography of her, would do justice to her later career. But Olson died before he could begin a draft of his biography. He was forty-two years old, my age when I first began this biography in 1990 after discovering that Anthony West's death had allowed Yale to open its archive.

I knew no one in Rebecca West's family. I had the sanction of no one to write this biography. I began by immersing myself in the Yale archive, and also writing to and interviewing people whose letters turned up at Yale. One of them, historian Arthur Schlesinger, put me in touch with Anthony's second wife, Lily. She helped me to contact Kitty West, Anthony's first wife, and his children by Kitty, Caroline and Edmund West. My agent in London, Rivers Scott, who had been one of Rebecca's *Sunday Telegraph* editors, put me in touch with many other sources of information, including Alan Maclean, Rebecca's editor at *Macmillan*.

Maclean recommended me to Rebecca's nephew, Dr. Norman Macleod, who opened up still more avenues of research.

The acknowledgments reveal the extraordinary record of cooperation I have received from all sides. I have tried to tell as many of their stories as will fit into a capacious narrative. Yet I have left much out, aspects of Rebecca West that will surely emerge in the forthcoming editions of her letters, essays, and reviews. I will miss writing about her. As so many of her friends have told me, in her company you felt you had a story worth telling. Even better, she made you feel you were helping her tell her story. She needed an audience to complete her plots, and she conveniently left a huge paper trail; easily ten thousand letters and more, not to mention her diaries and manuscript notebooks. Rebecca had a rough tongue. She could take your breath away, but she would also give you her last breath, the gift of life. A biographer could hardly ask for more.

Rebecca West

A LIFE

CHAPTER I

The Family Romance

I
(1895)

TWO-YEAR-OLD Cicily Fairfield toddles into the sea. Letitia and Winifred, her two older sisters, do not notice her staggering in the waves, and they do not come to her rescue. Cicily gets quite far out before her father Charles catches up with her, whooping and gathering her up into his great strength. In later years, after she has adopted the pen name Rebecca West, the water breaking over her becomes associated with her first sense of danger and death, mitigated by her father's forceful embrace. She discovers that this is what she wants: a "physical male-ness." It is what any child wants from a father, she supposes—"a sort of thing that can save one physically, in a very simple way."

Charles Fairfield was good at dramatic gestures. Isabella, Rebecca's mother, liked to describe how her husband had jumped from her side into a rough sea—the only seaside visitor answering a call for volunteers to aid a sinking ship. Charles had the good looks of a storybook hero: dark flashing eyes, high cheekbones, a chiseled jawline, and an erect, slim, soldierly bearing. He had been a gunnery instructor in the second Rifle Brigade, the "Prince Consort's Own," seen service in Canada, and witnessed American Civil War battles—at one point being pressed into action as a stretcherbearer. He had run a sawmill in Virginia and a mine in Colorado. He exuded an air of adventure and of the Wild West—not only to his youngest daughter, but to his family and friends. It seemed that Charles Fairfield had been everywhere and done everything. "The cleverest, best informed and interesting man I ever knew," said an old friend.

Sharp-witted and amusing, Charles captivated men and women alike. He had an artist's eye and was adept with his hands. One friend fondly remembered a doll's house Charles had made for him, which had been passed from hand to hand in the family until it had fallen to pieces. He told Rebecca her father had been the most fascinating man he had ever met.

17

Rebecca admired her father but realized he had a repugnant side. Aloof and arrogant, he spent days barely speaking to anyone, except on superficial matters. He risked the rent money on commodities market speculations. Rebecca traced his recklessness to his upbringing in County Kerry, Ireland. He modeled himself after his feckless father, Major Charles George Fairfield, a lifelong gambler who squandered two small inherited fortunes.

Major Fairfield righted himself, marrying an heiress, Frances Crosbie. With only a life interest in her property he could not leave it to his second wife, Arabella Rowan, whom he married in 1833. When he died in 1853, twelve-year-old Charles and his three brothers (Digby, Arthur, and Edward) lost their idyllic country estate, moving to smaller quarters in Dublin. Charles resented the change, regarding the Crosbie estate as his natural domain—illustrated charmingly in his brother Digby's sketch of him, at about age ten, galloping on his pony.

Arabella Rowan, tall and beautiful with the look of an eagle, turned her son into a "Dublin snob." A descendant of the Dennys, Blennerhassetts, Ropers, Masseys, and other distinguished families, she raised Charles to regard himself as a member of the Protestant Irish governing class and educated him in hate: "My grandmother refused to go to Dublin Castle because the Viceroy had refused to pardon a Protestant servant of hers for what she considered the trifling offence of murdering a Catholic," Rebecca told George Bernard Shaw. Arabella devoted herself to an austere religious sect, the Plymouth Brethren, plastering her Dublin house with "huge notices about the Blood of the Lamb."

Arabella allayed her fanaticism by what Rebecca called "an error of genius." Arabella hired a French tutor, Elysée Reclus, supposing that he must be a Protestant fleeing persecution. In fact Reclus and his brother Elie were famous anarchists, involved in both the republican movement of 1848 and the French Commune of 1871. They imbued in Charles and his brothers an enduring interest in ideas that smoothed their progress in a London cram school, where Digby and Charles prepared for the army and Arthur and Edward for the Civil Service.

Digby died at twenty-five on leave from India; Arthur found a place at the Board of Trade; and Charles received his military commission from Queen Victoria in a private audience at Buckingham Palace, a mark of royal favor rumored to be an acknowledgment that Charles's father was the illegitimate son of a royal duke. Charles Fairfield entertained his family with stories about standing transfixed in front of a "stout woman going into middle-age" with a "peony-red face" and a "carpish mouth" speaking in the "silvery, prim-voweled voice of a schoolgirl." He also spoke of her as a great figure—someone who belonged in the company of Charlemagne or Henry VIII—treating her with some delicacy, as though she were snared in a predicament she should not have been required to cope with until she grew up. Charles Fairfield brought history home, mesmerizing his family.

Yet his shortcomings made him seem to Rebecca a failed hero. In one of her bitterest judgments, thirty-year-old Rebecca concluded, "More and more did his proceedings fail to crystallize into achievements, more and more did his personal life become a discontinuous string of episodes that were hardly events. In every company he was always, for the moment at any rate, recognized as the superior of all present; and except for this duty of establishing his superiority he had not a moral idea in the world." Set the house on fire, and he would put out the flames—but he could not be counted on to rebuild it.

2
(1883)

REBECCA'S PARENTS met aboard ship en route to Australia. Charles had just left Colorado and his position as a mine manager to escort the seven-year-old son of Australian friends who had been killed in a buggy accident. It was like Charles to take up the cause of another's life, even to the detriment of his own. Isabella had been sent by her mother, Janet Campbell Mackenzie, to check on the health of her brother, Johnnie. He had gone to Australia seeking a cure for his tubercular condition. The trip resulted in another interruption of Isabella's promising career as a pianist. She wanted to rebel against her mother's instructions. She disliked the way the male's well-being was always put first. She had a strong mind of her own. As Rebecca once put it: "My mother was like a whiplash." Possessed of a shrewd temperament verging on the cynical, she attacked life with vehemence. But she loved her brother and could not bear the thought of him as a sickly exile, even though she worried that she might suffer the same fate. (After landing in Australia, she discovered that Johnnie, though disposed to too much drinking, had regained his health and found his niche as an itinerant musician, traveling with his faithful wife Lizzie.)

Isabella gave concerts aboard ship and drew Charles's attention. To her, he appeared a mysterious figure with dazzling black eyes that seemed incongruous with his tender regard for women and his elders. His vigorous dark hair, mustache, straight nose, tanned skin, and gaunt figure made him look "exotic, romantic, and a zealot." Isabella was an equally intriguing figure. A "black Highlander"—called so because of her dark-haired and dark-eyed Mediterranean look—she moved and spoke nimbly, in a birdlike way that Rebecca compared extravagantly to the sight of "eagles flying high over Delphi."

Charles courted Isabella after they landed in Australia. She had never known such an adventurous man, although her mother Janet had done the romantic thing, disobeying her father by eloping with a musician. When her husband died, she had heroically refused the community's charity in favor of establishing her own lace shop in George Street, one of the best locations in Edinburgh.

The widowed Janet and her family—Janet's sister Isa and her sons (Joey, Johnnie, and Willie)—deferred to Janet's eldest son, Alexander. He became an important composer, conductor, and musical administrator, and President of the Royal Academy of Music in London from 1888 to 1924. Alexander provided his family with the fruits of his growing reputation.

The destruction of this thriving household occurred when one of Isabella's brothers offended Alexander, treating his fiancée as an interloper at a family supper. Alexander walked out of the Mackenzie home forever, and the family never recovered from his loss. The estrangement especially devastated Isabella. She and Alexander had developed as musicians in each other's company—he was an important support for her because as a woman she lacked the performing opportunities available to him. Now he avoided her, and she had to rely on the loving but feckless Joey and Johnnie, pale shades of the iron-willed Alexander. Her brother Willie, an alcoholic painter, proved useless.

Isabella and her diffident sister Jessie were dowerless. "In her middle twenties, within call, or rather wail, of the thirties," what was Isabella to do? She met few unmarried men, the only eligible suitor was an artist who "seemed never to have heard of a proposal of marriage." She had broken off an engagement to a wealthy man after a picnic when he so fussed over a lost umbrella that she realized (with some regret) she would not be able to endure his "unromantic and philistine security."

Somehow Jessie managed to marry. Isabella's cousin Jessie Watson Campbell found a place for herself as a governess in France. Joey died in Canada of lockjaw, the consequence of an injury sustained in a runaway wagon accident. Johnnie sailed to Australia. Then Janet Campbell Mackenzie's health deteriorated, and Isabella had it broken to her that her family could no longer afford to live in Heriot Row, the city's finest residential street. Apparently there had been irregularities in the handling of Janet Campbell Mackenzie's legacies and business, and she would have to sell her comfortable home. (A similar problem with rent collection from her properties had deprived Charles Fairfield's mother of much of her income.) Isabella's mother and aunt settled into new and decidedly inferior quarters in Duncan Street outside the New Town, where they had always lived. Isabella found a place as music governess with the Heinemanns, who had been delighted with her piano playing.

The Heinemanns later told Rebecca about a man of "superior station" who courted Isabella but withdrew his suit when his family opposed the match. An irritated Isabella heard her mother say, "you are well out of it. His family might well have condescended to you."

Shortly afterwards, she sailed for Australia. Like her mother, she did the romantic thing. On December 17, 1883, she married Charles Fairfield, also an exile from his native land.

3

(1884–1887)

THE FIRST YEARS of the marriage were happy. To Isabella, it seemed as though they might "live happily ever after, and that meant Australia," a generous, abundant land such as she had never seen at home, a haven of "second chances," where "fortune and forgiveness" could shine down "like the Australian sunshine." Her husband brought home painters, poets, journalists, and politicians; they would spend the night in good-natured argument.

Charles Fairfield prospered in Melbourne, writing articles for *The Argus* and developing formidable expertise in public finance. He put no great stock in democracy or in labor unions. Some matters seemed best handled by an elite. He scorned women's rights. He rejected Socialism. Social legislation meant "molly-coddling." Not that he had any illusions about the "governing class": "To-day, greatly given to cigarette-smoking, pigeon-shooting, dry champagne, and new ways indescribable, that class no longer believes in itself: if it still possesses the genius of command, it has more than once shown itself wanting in the loyalty to follow a capable leader, and courage to assert its constitutional position."

Charles's uncompromising and unpopular positions angered both his employers and his readers. They did not like it when he predicted a business downturn or when he defended the rights of Catholics to have their own schools. The family left Melbourne under a cloud, after which it was said a woman threw herself into Melbourne harbor for love of Charles.

4
(1885–1906)

THE FAIRFIELDS' FIRST CHILD, Letitia, born in 1885, delighted Charles. He named her after his adored sister (herself named after an ancestress, Lady Letitia Coningsby). Letitia had died at the age of seven, leaving Charles and his brothers bereft. When Isabella wrote to her mother about Charles's devotion to his daughter, Janet Campbell Mackenzie replied: "He puts me in mind of the Italian gentlemen who were so fond of their Babies." In her memoirs, Rebecca could not imagine a happier age for Lettie or her father, who doted on this "very pretty little girl with golden hair and blue-grey eyes, an exquisite complexion, a sweet and serious voice and a gentle air which captivated adults."

Two years later, Winifred was born. At first she was a slight disappointment, for her parents wanted a boy, but then she made a surprising success, Rebecca said, as a girl. Compared to the fair Lettie, Winnie had a dark complexion like her mother's and much of her parents' intense personalities.

Shortly after Winnie's birth, the Fairfields moved to Scotland, where Charles found a job writing for the *Glasgow Herald*. He struck a colleague as "perhaps a little nervous and excitable," with a reputation for fast writing and stubborn adherence to his ideas. His controversial reputation thwarted his chances of succeeding to the paper's editorship. Irish blood accounted for Charles's contrariness, a colleague speculated. In her memoirs, Rebecca pictured her forty-seven-year-old father as an exile "too old to make his mark," except for a minor reputation as an extraordinary orator in the antisocialist cause.

When Isabella's health deteriorated, Charles moved his family to south London, where she could give birth to her last child, born on December 21, 1892, and christened Cicely Isabel (she adopted the spelling of Cicily). She quickly became the focus of Fairfield affection, particularly to her mother, as she was the product of an attempt at reconciliation between husband and wife, who had been "more or less living apart." But the estrangement continued after Rebecca's birth—a fact brought home to Winnie in an embarrassing moment at school. Some girls asked her where everybody slept in their house; when she told them, they said, "Well why don't your mother and father sleep together?"

Lettie and Winnie called their baby sister Anne, an abbreviation of Anne Telloppy, because eight-year-old Rebecca insisted, with her usual knowing air, that her pronunciation of antelope was the proper one. She sometimes signed herself Anne in letters to her sisters, and called Lettie and Winnie Frisk and Podge—names she had invented as a little child.

Virtually everyone in the household seemed a parental figure to Rebecca. She felt overprotected, but also teased and censured. Family pets can feel grievously wounded at slights, and nurse grievances. Eight years separated Rebecca from Lettie, and Rebecca resented Lettie's experience and authority; she did not enjoy being kidded and scolded.

Winnie sympathized with Rebecca, for Winnie had also suffered Lettie's chastisement. And Rebecca was even more excitable, rebellious, and untidy than Winnie; she was a trial for her eldest sister, whose immaculate sense of form and obedience rankled with Rebecca. Lettie dismissed Rebecca's outbursts at Lettie's bossiness as "childish resentment." Winnie comforted Rebecca with poetry, reciting "The Lady of Shalott" and other verses, teaching Rebecca that "personal sorrows could be relieved by a beautiful picture, which could be as vivid if it were written down on paper in words as if it were painted on canvas, and would be fixed in the memory, to be returned to for comfort or sheer pleasure." Winnie had, in fact, made a "powerful medicine" of literature, becoming "Rebecca's muse."

In her romantic moods, Rebecca remembered the house at 21 Streatham Place as graceful, with well-shaped rooms, a lawn ending in a grove of chestnut trees, and a garden. In her memoirs, the turn-of-the-century city flowered during idyllic strolls along pathways strewn with pale pink petals the color of candy. She loved the fragrant flowers and plants and the visits with her father to a farm, where she had fresh Jersey milk. When she wanted her older sister to revisit the neighborhood with her in 1950, Lettie resisted, calling their childhood home a "dreadful little hovel" in squalid surroundings. In 1923, a less sentimental Rebecca called Streatham "one of the drearier suburbs in South London." The family's straitened circumstances showed in the unkempt garden, the gas lamp in the hall which remained unlit when Charles Fairfield was away, the threadbare Regency dining room chairs, the darned towels and bed linen, and their shabby clothing. They found cleaning curtains and cushions a costly expense but managed to employ an all-purpose maid willing to work for paltry wages in a decent and lively home.

In 1898, five-year-old Rebecca moved with her family to Richmond-on-Thames, on London's outer edge. Father took them for wonderful walks up Richmond Hill to see the view of the "green vale through which the silver Thames meanders towards Windsor Castle." On the summit, in the midst of neo-classical mansions with gleaming windows, brilliant gold paint, and flawless pilasters, Charles Fairfield reminisced about his privileged Irish childhood on the Crosbie estate, explaining to his three daughters the "fine points of a horse." In their "starched pinafores" the

Fairfield sisters demonstrated the drill their father had taught them, using walking sticks instead of rifles.

Rebecca cherished every sign of her father's special favor. One autumn afternoon he asked her why she was digging up conkers (horse chestnuts) she had buried in the garden. "I am God," she explained, "and they are people, and I made them die, and now I am resurrecting them." As he continued to watch her, her father asked: "But why did you make the people die if you meant to dig them up again? Why didn't you just leave them alone?" She replied: "Well, that would have been all right for them. But it would have been no fun for me." It puzzled her to see him gazing at her with so much relish until she realized that "he must be watching me simply because he loved me." With a swelling heart she ran to embrace him. Later she learned he had repeated her conversation to her mother, predicting a great future for her "rather on the lines of the atheist Popes of the middle ages."

Rebecca glowed when her father confided in her. He drew pictures for her of the people he had known as a boy in Ireland. He talked about ideas incessantly, and she could not remember a time when she did not have a "rough idea of what was meant by capitalism, socialism, individualism, anarchism, liberalism, and conservatism." She grew up quickly, absorbing his facility with words, writing "first-person sagas about animals" by the age of seven.

Rebecca's love of words, she later insisted, also came from her mother. Like her husband, Isabella told stories well, taking wry pleasure in life's vagaries and in the human quest to impose order. Human beings were so odd and complicated, there was no telling how one of Isabella's or Charles's stories might end. Their tales had the unpredictable quality of life itself.

Rebecca credited her family with shaping her novelist's voice. They had peculiar friends, eccentrics like themselves, with funds of unusual anecdotes. Strangers entered their lives right off the street—like a Russian-Jewish family who stood outside the Fairfields' garden railing, listening to Isabella's piano playing until they were invited into the house. Isabella manifested her power by putting a "high polish on anything."

Rebecca was only six years old when her father told her the sad story of her uncle Edward, a Colonial Office administrator. One night, shortly after Edward's death in 1898, Rebecca awoke and became agitated by the shadows that haunt children's bedrooms. Her father said she should not be frightened, and then he drew back the curtains, and lay down on the bed next to hers looking out at the stars. He hummed a song, fell silent, and in the darkness his daughter watched him cry. Two years earlier Charles's brother Edward had been made a scapegoat for the abortive Jameson Raid (December 29, 1895), a foray made by volunteers into the Boer colony of Transvaal, led by Sir Leander Starr Jameson. An associate of Cecil Rhodes, Jameson supported a rebellion of mainly British settlers scheming to create a united South Africa. To protect the guilty government minister, Joseph Chamberlain, Edward was charged with sending Colonial Office approval for the raid. In fact, he had condemned it as "unlawful and inexpedient." The accusation felled him. He never recovered from a subsequent stroke and died at the age of thirty-nine.

Uncle Edward's persecution, and with it the idea that one could become the victim of a conspiracy, haunted Rebecca. She never forgot her family's discussion of the Dreyfus Affair, centering on a French general staff officer, Captain Alfred Dreyfus, an Alsatian Jew wrongly convicted of treason in 1894, a victim of the anti-Semitism that permeated the army. Not until 1906 was Dreyfus exonerated, after a decade of violent debate among his attackers and defenders. Edward Fairfield's reputation would not be fully rehabilitated until the 1970s, late in Rebecca's life.

Charles Fairfield was the man who brought the news home, the family's standard-bearer in the outer world. He proved so essential to Rebecca that she would seek ways to rationalize his errant behavior, to make him a victim of circumstances—perhaps of a plot to besmirch his character—even as she lashed out at his betrayal of his wife and family. She sensed her father's powerful sexuality and saw the smirking look of a man who knew women found him attractive. She was too young to know anything about sex, yet his flirtations angered her. Later she learned of his frenetic involvements with family servants and prostitutes, and expressed her rage at him in her memoirs.

In 1901, sixty-year-old Charles Fairfield abandoned his family for Africa. Rebecca never discovered a satisfying explanation for his shocking departure. Sometimes she called it a gallant effort to recoup the family's fortunes; sometimes it represented "a wildgoose chase." Eight-year-old Rebecca reacted with a love poem that ends by expressing the "anguish of a soul/that finds its twin has faithless been."

Even on his return to England a few years later, Charles did not rejoin his family, instead dying in Liverpool in 1906 when Rebecca was thirteen. Sent to bury her husband, Isabella returned home with his last words scrawled on a "scrap of paper," expressing his love for his children. Nothing else remained, not even his watch, studs, or cuff links. "Even his old dressingcase had gone. If he had been found dead in a hedgerow he could not have been more picked bare of possessions. If he had not left his regimental badge at home when he went to Africa, we would have nothing of him," lamented Rebecca.

Rebecca would spend a lifetime trying to reclaim her father, probing his family history for signs of his fate, making the story of her parents' marriage the centerpiece of the memoirs she could never quite finish, but which she constantly revised, hoping to fix once and for all the meaning of their lives and lay to rest her own anxieties about her place in the world.

The years between the ages of eight and thirteen—between her father's absence and death—were hard for Rebecca. High-strung and given to storms of weeping, she looked for someone to blame. She directed most of her fire at Lettie. Some of it engulfed her mother, but Mrs. Fairfield, struggling to hold her family together, hardly seemed sporting game. To get angry at Lettie, then, was like opening a safety valve, saving Rebecca the guilt of hurting her mother or denigrating her father. Lettie became a whipping post to which Rebecca resorted frequently.

For many families the clock stops in childhood, and the smallest, seemingly trivial incidents take on cosmic significance. Rebecca's petty criticisms of Lettie derived from her sense of having had a deprived childhood. To Rebecca, Lettie had usurped her father's role and had assumed an unwholesome authority over both of her sisters, complaining about their incivility at school, and defending the family's honor from the offenses of her wayward siblings. Lettie came down hard on Rebecca with Isabella's approval, so that she would be neither spoiled nor conceited. Rebecca realized her mother and sister were proud of her, but their seemingly constant criticism nurtured her indignation. Her effort to establish dominance, her feelings of inadequacy—all that familial approval and disapproval—kept her reeling. She reacted violently to any reproach.

Rebecca's safest bond had been the earliest one with her parents. Like other bereaved children, she fiercely rejected help from anyone else, developing a festering sense of injustice and exhibiting a rancorous urge to prove how much she had been abused. These regressive emotions deprived her of any effective defense against her own enormous hostility. She often felt persecuted and accused others of persecution mania. She came to believe that the world was out to get her.

CHAPTER 2

The Young Rebecca
1901–1912

I

IN 1901 THE FAIRFIELDS moved to Edinburgh, where Isabella could nurse her ailing mother. This fatherless family of women had to reconstruct their lives among dour Scots who adopted, Rebecca later said, a "prudent despondency about life." Her mother had not lived in the city for thirty years and could not count on the resumption of old relationships. She earned a small income typing theses for university students.

Lettie found a "rather old fashioned" little house centrally located "on the corner of a rather slummy area but overlooking parkland." It had no basement or garden, but she liked the decently equipped kitchen, the three bedrooms, and a little drawing room. The rent was a reasonable sixteen pounds a year. In *The Judge* (1922), Rebecca described their street, Buccleuch Place, as a row of "tall houses separated by so insanely wide a cobbled roadway that it had none of the human, close-pressed quality of a street, but was desolate with the natural desolation of a ravine." Ten years later, she softened and simplified her view: the street had become lovely, bounded on one side by the Meadows and the other by the backs of George Square houses.

The plucky Isabella found scholarships for her three daughters, dragooning the world into giving them a decent education. She had a paltry income, yet found shillings so that Rebecca could attend plays and concerts. Isabella ate so little that Rebecca later said that her mother had been anorexic for several years. She looked haggard, dressed like a scarecrow, and kept herself going by drinking innumerable cups of tea.

Rebecca marveled that her mother never sent her daughters out to work as secretaries or shop assistants, for poverty was a very near thing. Rebecca remembered a "dreary diet of bread and butter, porridge and eggs and milk." When Isabella was hospitalized for diphtheria, Rebecca had to go to the landlord's office to explain that the rent would be late. The rent collector shouted at her and threatened to initiate eviction proceedings. Isabella recovered, but Rebecca never got over her humiliation.

Her shame increased because of her wealthy Aunt Sophie—married to Arthur Fairfield, one of Charles's brothers. Sophie told horrible stories about Charles's gambling and philandering even as she contributed to educating Lettie, her favorite. In her memoirs, Rebecca termed Sophie the "daughter of an aged scoundrel named Blew-Jones," who had exploited the "simple peasantry of the Far East," getting them to exchange "valuable objects . . . for objects perhaps not so valuable."

Rebecca portrayed Sophie as tyrannizing the Fairfield household, denouncing Winnie and herself as though they were pickpockets. Sophie lamented their poverty, pretending that only Lettie was "worth anything," and that Winnie and Rebecca were no help to her mother and probably expected Lettie to support them. Such comments, Rebecca insisted, encouraged Lettie to live in a "fantasy world" of superiority. Rebecca called the Blew-Jones family her "horrid rich relatives, who used to look at us as if we were puppies whom nobody had been strong enough to drown." When one of them tipped her, she waited until he left the room and then gave wicked imitations of him.

Aunt Sophie gave Lettie fifty pounds to purchase books when Lettie received a Carnegie Scholarship for medical school. Her sisters also had scholarships. Winnie attended the Cheltenham School, "a very good school in some ways but appallingly snobbish," Lettie thought. One of Rebecca's earliest letters reports that Winnie was "disconsolated at Chelt." It was a school for upper-class girls looking forward to their presentation at court, doing the London season, and getting married. Winnie felt "out of it," for few of them had to earn a living, though the Cheltenham degree prepared them for teaching careers. Nevertheless, Winnie did well, earning distinctions in History, Constitutional History, and French History in her 1903–1904 examinations.

In Edinburgh, Rebecca attended George Watson's, founded by an eighteenth-century merchant. With separate schools for boys and girls, it was one of several institutions established from the sixteenth to the nineteenth century by the respectable merchant class, which put a high value on education and wished to make it as widely available as possible.

The classes were large—an advantage, Rebecca thought, because teachers did not have the time to muck about with her character— except for Dr. Ainslie, the headmistress, who made her miserable. A pale and detached woman, she loathed Rebecca and regarded her as rather like a high explosive. When fourteen-year-old Rebecca published a spunky letter in *The Scotsman* on women's suffrage, Dr Ainslie summoned Mrs. Fairfield to an interview and asked her, "Can't you get your daughter not to do these extraordinary things?" An amused Isabella cautioned her daughter not to make herself "conspicuous," advice Rebecca found hard to take. Instead, she got into more trouble for composing in cooking class a poem, "The Death of God," which asked "why did you tell me nothing of life?" Dr. Ainslie chastised Rebecca in front of her other classmates. Even worse, the headmistress insulted Rebecca's mother, who sought Dr. Ainslie's advice about her daughter's future and asked to modify a plan recommended by her teachers. Dr. Ainslie said that since Rebecca was a scholarship student she ought to acquiesce to those who had been "generous enough" to support her education. Rebecca confessed, "I couldn't say a civil word about Dr. Ainslie if my life depended on it."

Rebecca bitterly resented schoolmates who were "most unpleasant about my poverty." At thirteen, she and Winnie called on Mrs. Heinemann, their mother's benefactress, who stared rudely at her shabby clothes and treated her as the "child of an unimportant person." Such indignities could not be forgotten.

In 1906–1907, her last year at George Watson's, Cicily Fairfield was listed as a distinguished pupil and awarded a prize for the best essay. At sixteen, tuberculosis abruptly ended her schooling. "It was rather dramatic," she later declared. The disease did no lasting damage; she spent much of her time reading in the Carnegie Library, forming a lifelong devotion to Henry James, and she recovered her health by working for a year outside Edinburgh in a market garden, taking the only cure available for her ailment: fresh air and rest. A relieved Rebecca escaped dusty chalkboard learning and teachers who had no passion for their subjects. "How is it that you never went to university?" a family member once asked Rebecca. "Well, what do you think the university could have done for me?" she replied.

2

LETTIE PROVED more of an education for Rebecca than any formal school training. She was the trailblazer. Rebecca once suggested to her that "as there was no boy in the family," she was "looked upon as a substitute." Lettie involved her sisters in the activities of Fabian socialists such as Sidney and Beatrice Webb, who pioneered the concept of the welfare state. Industrialization and the demands of the Empire were making new demands on women, and Lettie saw herself as part of a new professional class of women who could help change the world.

All three Fairfield sisters became suffragettes and socialists—repudiating their father's politics and resenting his treatment of their mother. Fifteen-year-old Rebecca put her hair up, pretending to be a grown-up lady in order to sell copies of the suffragette paper at a meeting where Lettie was speaking. Lettie's stage presence, strong voice, and blonde and beautiful, ladylike appearance were persuasive, though they did not protect her from assault. Selling *Votes for Women*, she offered one to a sedate-looking old lady in rustling black silk and a widow's bonnet, who brought her umbrella smartly down on Lettie's head, exclaiming, "Thank God, I am a womanly woman." In Rebecca's own skirmish, a policeman hit her in the throat; striking dock workers pelted her with herrings.

Rebecca sent reports to Lettie (now working in London) about Edinburgh demonstrations for the vote. "We're just settling down now after the rush for Sir Edward Grey [Liberal Party Foreign Secretary]." In Leith, a sympathetic crowd, watching the police drive a leading suffragette into retreat, had lifted her up and forward, and then Rebecca watched how

> the police beat her back and struck her again and again in the face. Then two plain clothes men arrested her and one kept hitting her across the windpipe, so she gripped him by the throat until he promised not to do it again. In a minute the crowd rescued her . . . and this time the police led a baton charge. It was a disgusting sight—one man had his head cut open from ear to ear, and several people were covered with blood.

Rebecca stood outside a polling place from ten until eight and shouted, "Keep the Liberal out!" Liberal women called her "a hooligan and a silly fool and other pretty names." One Liberal man menaced her, but a policeman intervened. She was later warned not to stand by herself, for the Liberal women would scratch her eyes out. One Liberal man amused her with the coaxing gambit, "stop shouting, my dear, and come and have some tea in town!"

3

AT SEVENTEEN, Rebecca began writing autobiographical fiction. She drew herself in an abortive novel, "Adela": seventeen, with brown eyes "as melting as the antelope's" and the "face of a young panther." She is a "whirlpool of primitive passions" with a "ravenous intellect" and a "hunger for academic fame." Adela has won a scholarship to study science in the university, but she and her mother, deserted by the father, are so poor that they must apply to a rich male relative, the industrialist Tom Motley, for additional financial support, which he refuses them. Like Mrs. Fairfield, Adela's mother works as a typist. Other than accepting employment from Motley or marrying a rich, older man, there seems no way for Adela to achieve security. But she disdains these solutions. She has a "passion for work. She was abandoned to it as any nun to prayer: the inkstains on her fingers were her stigmata." She believes that not to be a scientist is tantamount to not living, and as a "secret member of the Saltgreave branch of the British Socialist Party," she scorns her wealthy, snobbish relatives, and feels humiliated by asking for their help. What is worse, her derelict father, who has "gambled away his patrimony in the pursuit of copper-mines," returns home to a forgiving wife who expects her daughter to forsake her education and help support him:

> Adela felt as if she had suddenly become ten years old again. That delicate voice with its perpetual undertone of offended taste had terrorized her childhood into unnatural quietness. From the moment of her birth she had been warned that any rough word or gesture might bring upon her plebeian mother and herself the appalling spectacle of an aristocrat repelled to tears and shame.

Adela believes her condescending father has always hated her. (Winnie once told Rebecca that their father did not like her.) Determined to desert her home's stifling atmosphere, Adela visits her Aunt Olga, whose family holds stuffy middle-class ideas that are no improvement on Motley's demeaning offer to hire her. Here the novel ends, a promising work with sharp observations and a surprisingly mature style, though stuck in its author's inability to imagine Adela's escape route.

4

FOR REBECCA, the stage offered a point of departure. At school, she had loved playing Sir Peter Teazle in Sheridan's *School for Scandal.* That she obtained the best parts in plays and "got hell" from her schoolmates only made her more determined to pursue a theatrical career. The theater offered her a platform on which she hoped to shed conventionality. Sarah Bernhardt had enchanted her by "pythoning about" in *La Dame aux Camelias* but she chafed at the ordeal of playing in old-fashioned drawing room dramas "bristling with 'asides' " and infantile behavior.

Rosina Filippi, a renowned acting teacher, spotted Rebecca's work at a charity show and invited her to audition at the Academy of Dramatic Art in London. Rebecca had a gift for comedy, and she saw the stage as the perfect way of expressing what she felt about life. She would like nothing better than to throw herself into as many different roles as possible.

Isabella decided to move the family home to London, so that Rebecca could begin her acting career. In the suburb of Hampstead Garden, they picked out a cottage, naming it Fairliehope, in memory of a splendid old farm in the Pentland hills overlooking the Clyde. Winnie took charge of the garden, planting roses and wallflowers. Rebecca demanded a lilac bush and an almond tree.

5

REBECCA FAINTED in the tube station on her way to audition at the Academy of Dramatic Art. Three women bent over her and asked if she had anyone to look after her—a sister perhaps? "No," Rebecca replied, "a theatrical manager." Closing her eyes she heard one whisper: "Poor child—an actress! I'll pay for the brandy!" Of the judges at her audition Rebecca remarked "Oh, the 'manner'! They all sat and looked 'brilliant.'" She had to admit, however, that they were kind and made allowances for the fatigue that resulted in her faint.

By her own admission, Rebecca was a young woman who had been "an irritating child," one who "revolted against all authority." At ADA, she put the wrong foot forward immediately by expressing regret that her sponsor had left the school. Rosina Filippi had quarreled with the staff and the principal, Kenneth Barnes. Although he promised to help Rebecca, she got old men's parts. She was unlucky: while playing Antonio in *The Merchant of Venice,* half of her false mustache fell off.

Rebecca suspected Barnes of deliberately sabotaging her. Like Dr. Ainslie, he humiliated her publicly. Her fellow students were cruel, realizing that Barnes disliked her. She made herself even more unpopular by asking her teachers why they did plays that were such rubbish. She persisted for three terms, hoping that the fourth and final term, which included a public performance, might yield a good role, but she was not promoted.

According to Rebecca, Kenneth Barnes remarked that she had "no personality." It seems a perverse thing to say, but he may have been referring to an inability to project herself on stage. Lettie called Rebecca curiously stiff in performance. Winnie thought a twitch (a condition that plagued Rebecca periodically) disqualified her for the theater. She was short (under five feet three inches), and she lacked conventional beauty.

Her striking broad brow and riveting eyes were not matched by the lower half of her face, which fell apart at her asymmetrical mouth and slightly protruding teeth.

Out of a pride still wounded at sixty-five, Rebecca would say, "I do not think I should have failed, for I had dramatic gifts." She learned to develop and to control her voice while removing every trace of an Edinburgh accent. This command of her instrument, as actors call it, enhanced the dramatic appeal of her personality. To biographer Lovat Dickson, she confided that even "decades afterwards" she would pass the RADA building (it had become the Royal Academy of Dramatic Art) in tears.

6

IN THE SPRING OF 1911, a defeated Rebecca left drama school. She had not forsaken the theater, contacting stage managers for word of new productions, but she was not hopeful, believing that only the beauties and the well-connected got jobs. She said that Lettie treated her failure as an actress as evidence of her ridiculous ambition and hectored her to seek a civil service job: "Don't you think, dear, that you'd better realize that your looks are against you, and try to get into the Post Office?"

Since everyone in Rebecca's family wrote—she would often say it seemed as natural as breathing—she decided to contact one of her father's Fleet Street editors. But he dismissed her: "Oh, I think you'll find something more suitable to do than writing." When an *Evening Standard* reviewer mentioned he could not attend a matinee, she offered: "I'll write the notice if you'll give me the tickets." The paper liked the review and gave her temporary work.

As a committed suffragist, Rebecca thought of writing for the cause. The movement's leaders were beautiful women—not the plain lookers their male opponents alleged them to be. Rebecca admired Mrs. Pankhurst's small and delicate figure on which clothes hung so well, and her daughter Christabel's graceful movements ("like a ballet dancer"), and Mary Gawthorpe "that irresistible combination—very pretty and very funny; one laughed and admired at the same time." Had these women been on the stage, "they would have been a riotous success, with infatuated young men waiting at the stage door," Rebecca asserted.

She admired their physical courage and could not imagine submitting herself to imprisonment and forced feeding. Prison would prove not merely unpleasant, it would violate every principle of a rigid class society and expose women to a frightening association with the "underworld," "a descent into the depths" that a properly brought up young woman would regard with horror. Rebecca came close to this descent during a riot outside the House of Commons. In the grip of two policemen, each with an arm on her loose coat, she slipped to her knees and crawled through a crowd, letting down her hair and reversing her hat, thus eluding the two mystified policemen.

All three Fairfield sisters sympathized with the Women's Social and Political Union (WSPU), founded on October 10, 1903 by Mrs. Emmeline Pankhurst after she discovered that male support for feminism—even among her allies in the Labour Party—was "lukewarm." But the WSPU's exclusive focus on votes for women troubled Rebecca and other feminists such as her new friend Dora Marsden, a diminutive woman of "exquisite beauty," a "perfectly proportioned fairy," so "flowerlike." A heroine of the suffrage movement, Dora was also a harsh opponent of the WSPU's autocratic leadership. In 1911 she established a new feminist journal, *The Freewoman*, promulgating radical thought on a vast range of issues, from politics to morality to sexuality, from the pens of leading writers, women and men.

Dora and Rebecca shared certain searing family experiences. Dora's father had left his family when she was eight, after years of a strained marriage, causing extreme financial hardship that led Mrs. Marsden to work as a seamstress. He had been an unreliable provider who compared poorly with his stalwart wife, the "saviour of the family." Like Isabella, Hannah, "a quiet, gentle, kind woman," eschewed any public advocacy of women's rights, while supporting her daughter's desire for a career.

In the next two years, Rebecca worked at *The Freewoman* in various capacities, including literary editor and assistant editor. Her zest stimulated the staff, especially Grace Jardine, Dora's close collaborator, and Rona Robinson, whom Rebecca called a "glorious red-haired bachelor of science, who had been in and out of jail for the cause." Of a *Freewoman* discussion circle Rebecca said, "Everyone behaved beautifully—it's like being in Church, except Miss Robinson and myself. Barbara Low has spoken very seriously to me about it." Rebecca argued with Barbara, who did not appreciate her irreverent wit, and Barbara seemed to Rebecca a "muddler" who wrecked the discussion circle and wrote poorly. Rebecca adamantly insisted that the paper become more literary and less tedious in its attacks on the WSPU.

The Freewoman caused a rift at home; its candor about sex offended Rebecca's mother, who had been "deeply shocked when Zola came to England with a mistress." As H. G. Wells quipped, the journal "existed it seemed chiefly to mention everything a young lady should never dream of mentioning." Lettie made it worse for Rebecca by remarking to her mother, "She'll never get on to a decent paper."

As Cicily Fairfield, Rebecca published her first article in *The Free-woman* on November 30, 1911, less than a month before her nineteenth birthday. In her debut performance, she reviewed a book on women in Indian life, declaring in her first sentence, "There are two kinds of imperialists—imperialists and bloody imperialists." The tone, of course, is striking: clipped, authoritative, brash, and meant to shock—"bloody" reflecting the indelicacy her mother deplored.

Mrs. Fairfield did not read *The Freewoman,* but when Rebecca learned that her article would be featured on a poster, she sought a pen name. She asked at least one friend for suggestions, but hurriedly settled on "Rebecca West," the name of the fiery character who commits suicide in Ibsen's *Rosmersholm.* As with most things, she was of two minds about her name change. Cicily Fairfield seemed an impossibly genteel name; no one would take her seriously. But "Rebecca West" seemed a harsh alternative.

Ibsen's Rebecca West is an outspoken advocate for emancipation, an enemy of tradition, and an outcast. Kroll, a friend of the Rosmers, accuses her of bewitching Rosmer, a descendant of a distinguished family. She has made him into a free thinker, traducing his ancestral beliefs.

Kroll alludes to Rebecca's alluring sexuality, which (she implies) Kroll himself has enjoyed. She confesses to coveting Rosmer and to contriving his wife's suicide. Undermining her confidence, Kroll claims that she is illegitimate. He also insinuates that her supposed stepfather and former lover, Dr. West, is her father. Finally, he reveals an ambivalence at the heart of Rebecca West that would mark the career of the literary figure who adopted her name:

> I don't think this so-called Emancipation of yours goes very deep! You've steeped yourself in a lot of new ideas and new opinions. You've picked up a lot of theories out of books—theories that claim to overthrow certain irrefutable and unassailable principles—principles that form the bulwark of our Society. But this has been no more than a superficial, intellectual exercise, Miss West. It has never really been absorbed into your bloodstream.

Did Cicily Fairfield hear the antisocialist, antifeminist voice of her father in Kroll's words? "Most people's minds are divided, it seems to me," concludes Ibsen's Rebecca West. The words certainly apply to Cicily Fairfield—outspoken yet wishing to respect her mother's sensibilities, angry at her father and yet desperately wanting to believe that he loved and approved of her. In *Rosmersholm*, Rebecca West's attachment to her older lover Rosmer can be interpreted (as Freud did) as an extension of the incest she has committed with her father. In the 1920s, her real-life counterpart would undergo a psychoanalysis that uncovered her sexual fantasies about her father. Of course, she need not have been conscious of these parallels between herself and Ibsen's heroine—any more than an actress needs to be aware of all the reasons why a particular role fits her well. When her second *Freewoman* article appeared, she memorialized the date in a scrapbook: "Rebecca West born February 15, 1912."

7

IT TOOK less than a year for Rebecca West to make a name for herself. She began by attacking in *The Freewoman* Mrs. Humphrey Ward, "the grand old woman of English letters and the formidable figurehead of the Tory antisuffrage campaign," and ended by demolishing H. G. Wells, seeing in him not the freethinking, iconoclastic, and scandalous figure of English intellectual life, but instead a purveyor of "spinsterish gossip."

Rebecca West seemed to have a mind quicker than any of her contemporaries, exhibiting an ease of expression, a stinging jab of a style, and a droll sense of the occasion equivalent to a great actor's timing. She knew when to take out the stops or to arrest her audience with a contrary opinion: "Writers on the subject of August Strindberg have hitherto omitted to mention that he could not write."

Who else but Rebecca West could dispose of the foremost dramatist of her day in two sentences? "Shaw never brought anything so anarchic as an unmarried mother on to his stage. Although he cultivates the flower of argument so well, he does not like the fruit of action." She often put her case in eighteenth-century sentences, composed of antitheses, that gave an epigrammatic quality to her arguments: "Our upper classes are impotent by reason of their soft living. Our lower classes have had their vitality sweated out of them by their filthy labours." Accustomed to male condescension, Rebecca West reversed it and mimicked its superior tone: "Mr Harold Owen is a natural slave, having no conception of liberty nor any use for it. So, as a Freewoman, I review his antifeminist thesis, *Woman Adrift*, with chivalrous reluctance, feeling that a steam engine ought not to crush a butterfly."

She had a superb ability to capture opinions in images: "Arnold Bennett, with all his faculty for seeing through brick walls, is never completely successful in portraying young women. Always his young women have the slightly vulgar air of a conjurer trying to make an impressive mystery out of a commonplace trick with a bowl of goldfish and a couple of rabbits." In a sentence she could work up a complex of thought and feeling better than any other book reviewer of her day, or perhaps of any day: "The baldness and badness of popular novels is as touching as the ugliness of a cherished rag-doll."

She took hackneyed terms and made them vivid again: "spinsterhood is not necessarily a feminine quality. It is the limitation of experience to one's own sex, and consequently the regard of the other sex from an idealist point of view." To her, Bennett and Wells were spinsters: they had no deep imaginative experience of women and thus presented figures out of touch with reality.

Rebecca's early journalism came at a time when the feminist movement had lost the attention and sympathy of the British public, busy "earning its living all day and interested in gardening in the evening." She argued that feminism had to be promulgated across the classes—as it had been in 1905, when the WSPU "started on its great work of rebellion." Then its "collection of teachers, mill-girls, shop assistants and workers of all descriptions" had mounted an effective protest movement. Unfortunately, the WSPU had become divorced from its base and had trained a "new army of detached suffragist organizers," becoming perceived as simply a political group in opposition to the Establishment male politicians. "The window-smashing of last March [1912] was not effective," Rebecca maintained, though "it might have been had they been smashed from inside the drapery shop and not outside; if each stone had been a declaration that one of the wage-slaves in these bird-cages of servitude had decided to revolt." She believed in fighting words: "For certainly we need rebellion. Unless woman is going to make trouble she had better not seek her emancipation."

Since *The Freewoman* represented itself as not only anti-status quo and feminist, but also radically individualistic, Rebecca was able to indulge in mock-autobiography:

> I must confess that the passage in Mr Kennedy's book, which gives me the most tranquil pleasure is an entry in the index: "Sex, the unimportance of, p. 224." This is Napoleonic. One yearns to grovel just a little. This clarion note re-echoes in the letter-press when Mr Kennedy exclaims: "Even at the present day there are men, though their number may be relatively small, who would . . . willingly see the whole female sex at the bottom of the sea if they thought for a minute it would tend to interfere with their ambitious designs." That thrills me. It is just how I feel about the male sex. I greet Mr Kennedy as a kindred spirit.

This sort of writing amounted to a flirtation with readers, and it could be taken as a challenge by the men Rebecca dispatched with such *savoir faire*. To her *Freewoman* colleague Grace Jardine, she wrote: "I have had a playful but passionate letter from J. M. Kennedy, which I have answered with maidenly reserve." Her reply enticed her male pursuer, who wrote her a six-page letter with "another fervent invitation to meet him and talk over the many problems which etc." This time Rebecca called on help from Rona Robinson: "So I'd better let him let off steam. Can I tell him to meet me at your office on Wednesday afternoon? . . . You might let me know if this is convenient! It is an odd request but, knowing J. M. Kennedy, (and knowing me) you may understand!" He knew her family and had sent her a present for her nineteenth birthday. She found him a very ugly man who reminded her of a poached egg. In his mid-thirties, "plump and sprightly," he bore a slight resemblance to Oscar Wilde.

Rebecca found a less resistible suitor in *The Daily Herald*. It had seduced her, she told Dora Marsden, into editing the woman's page. "They are tired of baby-clothes, they say, and want 'hot Gospel' talks to women. I fear this means trials for sedition, so I may not long be free." Rebecca remained at liberty, but she became involved with an editor, Rowland Kenney, an ex-railway worker turned socialist journalist. He shared her conviction that upper-class women had co-opted a potentially working-class movement. A great talker, dark-haired and slim, with penetrating, smoldering eyes, and a ruddy complexion, thirty-year-old Rowland greatly appealed to Rebecca but he was married, and she found her love for him "damnable." Calling her his "darling girl," he pleaded with her not to make him feel that their relationship was "such a calamity." He wanted to believe he could help her. "*Don't* talk of the 'hideousness' of it again dear. My love is not such a hideous thing surely." If some things were denied to them, surely they could meet and talk. They did not have to think they would "make a ruin either of our lives or our love." They apparently stopped just short of sexual intimacy, and they weathered the crisis. Rebecca wrote to Grace Jardine: "Don't repeat my gossip about Rowland Kenney wishing to leave *The Daily Herald*. He doesn't really want to—very much the reverse—but his wife rather wishes it."

8

In September 1912, in a *Freewoman* review, Rebecca brought herself to the attention of H. G. Wells, a regular reader of the paper and an occasional contributor, by making fun of his style:

Mr Wells's mannerisms are more infuriating than ever in *Marriage*. One knows at once that Marjorie is speaking in a crisis of wedded chastity when she says at regular intervals, "Oh, my dear! . . . Oh, my dear!" or at moments of ecstasy, "Oh, my *dear!* My *dear!*" For Mr Wells's heroines who are loving under legal difficulties say "My man!" or "Master!" Of course he is the old maid among novelists; even the sex obsession that lay clotted on *Ann Veronica* and *The New Machiavelli* like cold white sauce was merely old maid's mania, the reaction towards the flesh of a mind too long absorbed in airships and colloids.

This provocative dismissal turned H.G. on his head, for the forty-six-year-old novelist and social thinker had become notorious as an advocate and practitioner of free love. He stayed married to his second wife, Jane, while conducting affairs with young girls less than half his age, members of the "Fabian nursery," daughters of prominent socialists who had invited H.G., the man of new ideas, into their homes and then ostracized him, aghast at their daughters' pursuit of him. One of them, the Pre-Raphaelite beauty Amber Reeves, had borne H.G. a child after more than a year of chasing him. (George Bernard Shaw marveled that H.G. had held out for as long as he did.) Hubert Bland, the father of another of H.G.'s mistresses, punched H.G. in the nose and snatched his daughter out of a train just as she and H.G. were embarking on an amour. Amber's outraged father, pistol at his side, showed up at H.G.'s club. H.G. avoided gunfire, but his club forced him to resign. He was a sexual magnet, the most exciting man of his generation. He had conducted a three-year affair with the novelist Dorothy Richardson, who had miscarried his child. There had been a fling with novelist Violet Hunt, and he was currently making love to another novelist, Elizabeth von Arnim—to mention only the most prominent of his liaisons.

Rebecca had heard sensational stories about H.G. at the Fabian summer schools she attended. Yet she did not seek him out. Indeed, she suggested that his ideas and his fiction were stodgy. And she said it so well. When he invited her to visit him, she did not respond with "maidenly reserve," or seek a chaperon in the good offices of *The Freewoman*.

CHAPTER 3

The New Woman and the Old Man
1912–1913

I

REBECCA ARRIVED for lunch at Easton Glebe, H.G.'s country home, on September 27, 1912. She was not yet twenty years old. H.G. liked her daring and amusing articles but suspected that she did not know quite as much as her aggressive words implied. He disavowed a sexual interest in her and saw himself as making a "generous gesture" to a young writer. In person, she struck him as "a mixture of maturity and infantilism":

> She had a fine broad brow and dark expressive eyes; she had a big soft mouth and a small chin; she talked well and she had evidently read voraciously—with an excellent memory. We argued and she stood up to my opinions very stoutly but very reasonably. I had never met anything quite like her before, and I doubt if there ever was anything like her before. Or ever will be.

Between the brow and the eyes, the mouth and the chin, H.G. limns a countenance built upon antitheses, a mixture of dark and light, expansive and concentrated. The small chin suggests infantilism, but it is set within a face that is simultaneously sensual and intellectual, dominated by the "big soft mouth" he watched in wonder, for it expressed an appetite as large as his own.

Rebecca thought H.G. the most interesting man she had ever met. At forty-six, he was old enough to be her father. Short and heavyset with a high-pitched voice, he impressed himself on an observer as "so commonplace looking that in a crowd he manages to resemble everybody else and is quite indistinguishable." He had short arms, a shapeless torso and tiny feet, but his piercing blue eyes, massive forehead and animated speech were captivating. In more intimate encounters, a woman would find that he had "exceptionally smooth skin," a honeyed scent, and a rather large penis. He had a mental and physical swagger which Rebecca compared to the "walk of the matador into the centre of the arena when he is going to fight the bull to the finish."

At their first meeting, he talked almost nonstop for five hours, filling Rebecca's afternoon with his "immense vitality and a kind of hunger for ideas." He had flattered her and the *Freewoman* staff, saying that they were the "noblest work of God." After their initial encounter, they exchanged notes. Between the fall of 1912 and the spring of 1913, they met frequently. She expected him to make love to her; instead, she had to settle for "watching his quick mind splashing about in the infinite."

H.G. was not so quick to debauch Rebecca because he had barely recovered from his notorious affair with Amber Reeves. After the Fabians had abjured him, he published *Ann Veronica* (1909), a thinly disguised novel about himself and Amber, causing a public scandal. Out of deference to his wife Jane he was trying to avoid entanglements with aggressive young women.

Jane had been with H.G. since 1894. One of his science students in the days just before he was to make his reputation as a writer, she had been eager to learn and exhibited a composure and sophistication sorely lacking in his first wife Isabel. H.G. and Jane had begun an affair while H.G. was still married—not the first time he had committed adultery. He had already seduced one of Isabel's friends. Jane's family was outraged when H.G. left his wife to live with Jane, but she stuck by him through his divorce and married him on October 27, 1895, just at the moment when he had achieved his first great success with *The Time Machine*. She realized early on that she could not satisfy her husband's sexual appetites or compete with his restless, teeming mind. Beatrice Webb, one of the leading Fabian socialists, said Jane had a "small nature" and bored H.G. He said that she had "every virtue, every charm, *only* she's dead as a herring." Yet she had contrived an indispensable role for herself as his helpmate—keeping track of his business affairs, confidently raising his two sons, George (Gip) and Frank, and presiding over an efficiently run household. H.G. reveled in family life, playing rollicking games with his sons and lavishly entertaining friends at Easton Glebe parties—at which Jane shone as an excellent hostess, good sport, and fetching mimic. Sometime after the birth of their second son, H.G. and Jane had made a pact: he could pursue other women so long as he told her and avoided public embarrassment. If she ever resented his affairs, she never let on. Even when his liaisons did excite public notice, she carried on as if nothing were amiss. She permitted nothing to interfere with her part as the steadfast Mrs. H. G. Wells.

Rebecca met Jane on her first visit to H.G. and thought her a "delight-fully pretty woman." She had prim, regular features, a neat figure, and a voice like a "very soft bird call." Rebecca thought her "charming but a little effaced." Jane stayed in the background. She kept to herself what she really thought.

Besides Jane, H.G. had his mistress, Elizabeth von Arnim, to consider. A woman his age, she formed part of a pleasant, comfortable relationship that Jane tolerated because it did not disturb her family life. H.G. admired Elizabeth's petite figure and perky personality. This aristocrat, popular novelist, and risqué conversationalist flattered and entertained him effortlessly. She had sought him out, supposing that he was just like his hero in *The New Machiavelli*—"an innocent outcast whose wife was about to divorce him." Elizabeth soon learned that Jane had no plans to jettison H.G., but she still fancied herself as his savior. One can see why. The Wells personae of his novels are all simple and unaffected men who suffer because they lack the love of a good resourceful woman. Neither H.G. nor his fictional surrogates ever see the havoc and the hurt they inflict on others, and the performance of the ingenuous Wells hero is so well executed that many women embrace it. With two mature women attending to his needs, why should H.G. risk this cosy arrangement for an untested Rebecca? He had talked things over with Jane and she agreed that exchanging Rebecca for Elizabeth would upset their stable tripartite alliance.

It was up to Rebecca to change H.G.'s mind. She wanted to meet men and to escape a home life that had become stifling. She felt her mother had rejected her, for Isabella had not reconciled herself to Rebecca's flamboyant style. Lettie only made matters worse, scoffing at her younger sister's ambitions. Rebecca still felt her father's departure and death as a "loss of fortune." She longed for the emotional satisfaction of a sexual relationship. She wanted a lover. She wanted to be married.

Rebecca scorned *Ann Veronica*, but it did present H.G.'s fictional counterpart as saved by a much younger woman, who endows him with the energy and moral courage to defy society's staid dictates. *Ann Veronica* exhibits extraordinary sympathy for the suffragettes and captures beautifully its heroine's spirited desire to change things. "The world was in some stupid and obvious way *wrong*," thinks Ann Veronica—as did Amber Reeves and Rebecca West. Ann Veronica is independent, a radical but not a group follower, and as soon as Capes, an older scientist, awakens her sensuality she openly declares her passion. "What do you want?" he asks her bluntly. "You!" is her immediate reply. Capes warns Ann Veronica that their affair will "spoil" her life, and she retorts, "It will make it." Indeed, Ann Veronica's biography echoes Amber Reeves's and anticipates Rebecca West's: a stifling home life, participation in militant suffragism, a growing sense of independence, and then a love affair with an older man.

Rebecca could remain hopeful because H.G. came calling at the Fairfield home in Hampstead, writing afterward to Rebecca: "You consider me an entirely generous and sympathetic brother in all your arrangements." His bravura performance caused her to gush: "Our drawing room was hallowed yesterday by the presence of Wells, who dropped in suddenly and stayed 2 ½ hours! Wasn't it glorious?" H.G. charmed even Isabella. She saw him as a great man taking a paternal interest in her daughter.

But by the beginning of 1913, Mrs. Fairfield had become suspicious. Rebecca had written to H.G. in Switzerland concerning proofs of an article about him, saying she could not meet his deadline. Then one morning, during her bath, Isabella knocked on the door, announcing a telegram for her. Rebecca asked her mother to read it. After a long pause, Isabella read, icily, "No hurry about the artichoke, Wells." Of course the word should have been "article," not "artichoke," but Mrs. Fairfield was not amused.

One day in February or March, in the midst of their literary talk, Rebecca and H.G. suddenly paused and kissed each other. Rebecca declared her love. She confronted H.G. with the meaning of his kiss— surely it gave promise of greater intimacy. She wanted none of the "commonplace lovemaking with her contemporaries." He admitted he was "greatly drawn" to her, but he balked at the idea of an affair, and she withdrew, suffering a nervous collapse that lasted several weeks.

When Rebecca resumed work in late April 1913, her articles in the socialist newspaper, *The Clarion*, became increasingly militant. In "The Sex War" (April 18, 1913), she appended to her attack the refrain: "Men are poor stuff.... Men are very poor stuff.... Oh, men are very poor stuff indeed.... Oh, men are miserably poor stuff!" She did not write another article for two months. She wrote to Dora Marsden: "I've been too unwell to do anything as yet—even writing letters is beyond me ... I've had an awful quarrel with Wells. I don't think we shall ever speak or write again! I'm longing to slaughter him."

2

IN MAY 1913, Rebecca and her mother departed for a month in France and Spain, a trip meant to take her mind off H.G. The journey may also have been decided upon for Mrs. Fairfield's health. On May 4, Rebecca wrote to Winnie: "I hate Paris. The people are hideous and atrociously dressed and the proportions of the buildings are vile." She was as angry at herself as she was at H.G., admitting that her plight was "both tragic and ludicrous" and "entirely my own fault." Four days later she sent Dora Marsden a note from Spain: "I am feeling better but I'm not well yet." Madrid was a "ripping place," full of jolly people who sang loudly and spit on the streets. Rebecca was sleeping better and hoped to resume her writing when she returned to England.

In *The New Freewoman*, Rebecca published two pieces about her Spanish sojourn, "Trees of Gold" and "At Valladolid," which dramatize her "tragic and ludicrous" state of mind. Her autobiographical protagonist leaves London in a fatigue that easily gives way to frenzy. Spain's "violent and courageous beauty" revives her, but it also intensifies her hysteria. Indeed, the country's wildness provokes two suicide attempts. A doctor is summoned to attend a gunshot wound under her left breast, and he learns that she has also taken sixty grains of veronal. She confesses to him, "They say I'm like a black cat. Perhaps there is a feline type in which consciousness is a most persistent disease. Life has planted itself in all our nerves: we can't root it up. And it was an agony!" The cause of this agony has been a lover who "left my body chaste" but "seduced my soul: he mingled himself with me till he was more myself than I am and then he left me." She renounces the idea of suicide, however, because of her mother and sisters, who gather around her and make her realize they have made "an interesting life out of our uneasy circumstances." In a way, suicide would be a "destruction of my mother's substance," and thus would also be a "damnable sin. Virtue imprisons me in life. But pain easily unlooses the leash of virtue and I spend every night in tears."

Rebecca later termed her prose "an externalization of internal events in my life." She had not shot herself or taken veronal but she also suggested that she made attempts on her life: "I think it would have been a miracle if they had succeeded, although I meant them to, in the double-think way of youth."

In early June 1913, Rebecca wrote H.G. a letter of appeal and recrimination. Only a typewritten draft survives; exactly what he received cannot be ascertained, but the draft eloquently coincides with the superheated drama of her *New Freewoman* pieces:

> Dear H.G.,
> In the next few days I shall either put a bullet through my head or commit something more shattering to myself than death. At any

rate I shall be quite a different person. I refuse to be cheated out of my deathbed scene.

I don't understand why you wanted me three months ago and don't want me now. I wish I knew why that were so. It's something I can't understand, something I despise. And the worst of it is that if I despise you I rage because you stand between me and peace. Of course you're quite right. I haven't anything to give you. You have only a passion for excitement and comfort. You don't want any more excitement and I do not give people comfort. I never nurse them except when they're very ill. I carry this to excess. On reflection I can imagine that the occasion on which my mother found me most helpful to live with was when I helped her out of a burning house.

I always knew that you would hurt me to death some day, but I hoped to choose the time and place. You've always been unconsciously hostile to me and I haven't tried to conciliate you by hacking away at my love for you, cutting it down to the little thing that was the most you wanted. I am always at a loss when I meet hostility, because I can love and I can do practically nothing else. I was the wrong sort of person for you to have to do with. You want a world of people falling over each other like puppies, people to quarrel and play with, people who rage and ache instead of people who burn. You can't conceive a person resenting the humiliation of an emotional failure so much that they twice tried to kill themselves: that seems silly to you. I can't conceive of a person who runs about lighting bonfires and yet nourishes a dislike of flame: that seems silly to me.

You've literally ruined me. I'm burned down to my foundations. I may build myself again or I may not. You say obsessions are curable. They are. But people like me swing themselves from one passion to another, and if they miss smash down somewhere where there aren't any passions at all but only bare boards and sawdust. You have done for me utterly. You know it. That's why you are trying to persuade yourself that I am a coarse, sprawling, boneless creature, and so it doesn't matter. When you said, "You've been talking unwisely, Rebecca," you said it with a certain brightness: you felt that you had really caught me at it. I don't think you're right about this. But I know you will derive immense satisfaction from thinking of me as an unbalanced young female who flopped about in your drawing-room in an unnecessary heart-attack.

That is subtle flattery. But I hate you when you try to cheapen things I did honestly and clearly. You did it once before when you wrote me of "your—much more precious than you imagine it to be—self." That suggests that I projected a weekend at the Brighton Metropole with Horatio Bottomley. Whereas I had written to say I loved you. You did it again on Friday when you said that what I wanted was some decent fun and that my mind had been, not exactly corrupted but excited, by people who talked in an ugly way about things that are really beautiful. That was a vile thing to say. You once found my willingness to love you a beautiful and coura- geous thing. I still think it was. Your spinsterishness makes you feel that a woman desperately and hopelessly in love with a man is an indecent spectacle and a reversal of the natural order of things. But you should have been too fine to feel like that.

I would give my whole life to feel your arms round me again.

I wish you had loved me. I wish you liked me.

> Yours
> Rebecca

Don't leave me utterly alone. If I live write to me now and then. You like me enough for that. At least I pretend to myself you do.

Whatever the final form of Rebecca's letter to H.G. (he destroyed nearly all of her correspondence to him), he replied:

> How can I be your friend to this accompaniment? I don't see that I can be of any use or help to you at all. You have my entire sympathy—but until we can meet on a reasonable basis, Goodbye.
>
> Yours
> H. G. Wells

I shall look for your work in *The Clarion* and *The New Free-woman.*

The postscript was not an idle promise. It could not have been many weeks between his curt dismissal of her and this encouraging note: "You are writing gorgeously again." She had realized, H.G. told her, that she could not get a "pure deep draught of excitement and complete living" out of him. He contended that he had been generous and self-denying in refusing to let her squander her flare-up on him—"one only burns well once—on my cinders." "Nana" (July 1, 1913) is one of Rebecca's pieces that excited H.G.'s admiration:

I remembered how I once saw the sun beating on the great marbled loins and furrowed back of a grey Clydesdale and watched the backward thrust of its thigh twitch with power. I was then too interpenetrated with interests of the soul and the intellect to understand the message of that happy carcass: if my earliest childhood had realized that the mere framework of life is so imperishable and delicious that with all else lost it is worth living for, I had forgotten it.

Here was evidence, H.G. affirmed, of her recovery, that she could be "as wise as God" when she wrote, and not the "tortured, untidy . . . little disaster of a girl who can't even manage the most elementary trick of her sex."

Apparently Rebecca made no attempt to contact H.G.—though his destruction of her correspondence makes it difficult to be certain. Instead she alluded to him in *The New Freewoman* (July 15, 1913), classing Galsworthy and Wells as examples respectively of "The Melancholy Bloke" and "The Cheerful Cove." She had wanted more than friendship from him, and she found a way of saying why by associating the pleasures of the flesh with the sense of personal immortality: "the force liberated by one mass of matter may ensoul another mass of matter, and perhaps it may be so with the ecstasy made by our bodies." Suicide, she speculated, was not just an urge for annihilation but an expression of the magnitude of one's feelings snared in the "limitation of one's own humanity." Suicide might be the self's paradoxical attempt to expand, like a "too-tightly-stretched canvas . . . ruined by cracks and veinings of the paint." Thus "it may be that one gets the expansion of the self that is necessary before all experience is endurable by submitting to a process that is its apparent elimination." Was this not a way of telling H.G.—and herself, of course—that her suicide attempts were the prelude to rebirth and growth?

In the autumn of 1913, Rebecca reviewed H.G.'s novel, *The Passionate Friends*. She praised Stephen Stratton and Lady Mary Christian, who had "the love of coevals, who had been playmates and intimate companions, and of whom the woman was certainly as capable and willful as the man . . ." She endorsed H.G.'s comments on the role of labor and on the need for women to find socially useful work. Nevertheless, she found the novel troubling. He had Lady Mary abandon Stratton because he was poor and unable to support her with the "material perquisites of aristocracy." Why should H.G. think this craving for comfort "a symptom of modern womanhood"? Why did he think in such conventional categories and make his characters renounce their "rash defiances"? Why did he tolerate their "flinching and weakness," and subordinate their "quick personal wisdom" to the "slow collective wisdom"? Rebecca implied that the defects of the characters stemmed from defects in their author, provocatively adding: "The woman who is acting the principal part in her own ambitious play is unlikely to weep because she is not playing the principal part in some man's no more ambitious play." Three days after the review, H.G. wrote to Rebecca that it was "first rate."

By November 1913, his affair with Elizabeth von Arnim had soured. Jealous of Jane's unshakable hold on H.G., Elizabeth turned hostile, inventing cruel nicknames for H.G.'s wife, whom she now wanted to displace. At the beginning of her romance with H.G., the aristocratic von Arnim had been disposed to overlook his "common accent and bad table manners." But, given his final comment on her rejection of him, he evidently resented her noblesse oblige: "It's because I'm common, isn't it?" H.G.'s son, Anthony, later commented: "I think he saw himself through her eyes . . . and read a judgement on him that he couldn't take there: 'You're perfect in broad comedy, but for gahds sake don't ever try to play Strindberg, you haven't the figure for it.' "

H.G.'s life needed a fresh turn. Sometime between November and December he got it, for by December 6, he was writing to Rebecca:

> My dear,
>
> You have written me the most beautiful love letter in *The Clarion* to say that you are happy and that you are a panfer—I think alone. Of course we hunt alone, dear panfer, and come padding back to the lair with the blood of dogs round our mouths, dogs we amuse ourselves killing. All my heart to you Panther dear.
>
> Jaguar

The article to which H.G. referred ("Some Race Prejudice," December 5, 1913) contained some of Rebecca's most lyrical writing, conveying her pleasure in "London unregenerated": "That little canal in Maida Vale which made a shabby Venice of the village garden's stucco balustrades; that cliff of houses in the Harrow Road that looks down on the red and green lights burning on a wide barren space mossy with darkness where trains run screaming like the wind all night." She was describing where she lived now; H.G. would be one of a handful of her readers who would know that she had recently moved out of Fairliehope, her family's Hampstead home, and was on her own. Doubtless Rebecca, considering her affinity for cats, invented their animal names. In *The Research Magnificent* (1915) H.G. endows Amanda (clearly modeled on Rebecca) with a "gift for nicknames and pretty fancies." She calls herself Leopard and intimates the color for her is black. Benham (H.G.) is Cheetah, or the hunting leopard, "the only beast that has an upcast face and dreams and looks at you with absentminded eyes like a man. She laced their journeys with a fantastic monologue telling in the third person what the Leopard and the Cheetah were thinking and seeing and doing." In *H. G. Wells in Love*, H.G. recounts with relish Rebecca's fables of the Pussteads, "two melancholy but furry and eccentric animals." But it was the image of them as ruthless outsiders with blood around their mouths that excited him. After all, Rebecca had chafed him several times for his conventionality. Now he would expunge the spinster in him and worship his wild thing:

December 2, 1913
Dearest Panfer
There is NO Panfer but Panfer, and she is the Prophet of the most High Jaguar which is Bliss and Perfect Being.

CHAPTER 4

Panther and Jaguar
1913–1915

I

H.G. AND REBECCA pursued a furtive love affair, as H.G. did not want publicity. He told Jane immediately that Rebecca had become his lover, and she reacted with her usual aplomb, accommodating her husband's desires and making no fuss. This excited H.G.'s desire to make the most of his new liaison.

Rebecca felt guilty defying her mother's standards of propriety; she felt angry that those standards forced her to hide her lover. She had nursed her mother through various illnesses; Graves' disease had made Isabella irritable and had given her sharp tongue an extra edge. Rebecca also withheld the news of her new passion from her sisters, increasing her sense of isolation.

Rebecca and H.G. met often at his London flat. They were a good fit, and she relished their mental and physical rapport. Like Rebecca, H.G. was the precocious, spoiled, youngest child of the family, with two older brothers who, he later realized, showed great forbearance in not completely smothering him with the pillows they used to silence his incessant, annoying chatter. He, too, had a feckless father, who would rather play cricket or "clear off" than run a business and support his family. His mother, a loving and devoted parent, was also a devout Christian who verged on religious mania, expecting her husband and children to be correct and conventional—a less sophisticated version, it appears, of Rebecca's own caring but rigid and traditional mother. Both writers knew what it meant to be caught in a family that embodied within it the extremes of raffishness and rectitude.

The sheer power of sex overwhelmed Rebecca. As H.G. put it in *The New Machiavelli*: "sex marches into the life of an intelligent girl with demands and challenges far more urgent than the mere call of curiosity and satiable desire that comes to a young man." But Rebecca was not a sexual adventuress. She preferred the conventional positions and resisted what she called H.G.'s "sexual hiccups"—her term for some of the unconventional sexual practices he favored, such as anal intercourse.

Neither H.G. nor Rebecca wanted her to become pregnant. It would complicate his life intolerably. Jane had given him two sons. Amber Reeves had wanted his child and had produced a daughter for him. He had willingly conceived these offspring. They were now growing up; he did not wish to begin fatherhood once more. Saddling Rebecca with a child would hardly make her life easier or endear her to him. Indeed, their affair thrived on freedom from responsibility.

Rebecca had every reason to avoid a pregnancy. Coming into her own as a writer, she had moved from feminist and socialist circles to Fleet Street's *Daily News & Leader*. The journalist S. K. Ratcliffe had recommended her to Robert Lynd, the paper's editor. A neighbor of Rebecca's mother, Ratcliffe had befriended Rebecca and her sisters at Fabian summer schools. She liked Robert's "slow but . . . delicious humour," and admired his wife Sylvia's beauty and grace. Rebecca relied on Sylvia, a fellow writer and great hostess, renowned for her quick wit, good nature, and her youthful, "fresh and silvery" laugh.

But Rebecca had more than journalistic ambitions to fulfill. She was writing fiction and had come under the influence of a powerful literary couple, Violet Hunt and Ford Madox Hueffer (he changed his last name to Ford after World War I). Rebecca reviewed his novel, *The New Humpty Dumpty*, published under the pseudonym of Daniel Chaucer. She saw no reason to respect his "absurd nom de plume" and shrewdly assessed his uneven oeuvre, observing that his latest work was "an unfriendly companion volume" to *The New Machiavelli*, Wells's attempt in novel form to write a new primer for the government of the modern world, focusing on the political and erotic adventures of Richard Remington, a genius from the lower middle class remarkably like H.G. himself. In reply, Ford had created Count Sergius Mihailovitch Macdonald, a Russian aristocrat drawn as "the perfect gentleman, the true servant of the Prince." Rebecca skewered Ford's conservatism, which prevented him from seeing that genius might well be a chaotic force expressing itself not in gentlemen but in scoundrels, who act upon their intuition. She declared her vote for Remington (Wells) with his "hot, irritable fumbling at ideas."

Rebecca's handling of *The New Humpty Dumpty* recalls her review of *Marriage*. It produced a similar result: Ford and Violet extended an invitation to a prodigy they hoped to make their protégée. Violet was forty-six, H.G.'s age, when Rebecca met her. Like him, she had had many lovers, including H.G. himself. Rebecca thought Violet showed signs of wear—the strain of so many assignations—but she retained remnants of her beauty. Rebecca admired her exquisite bone structure and "tungsten-tough fragility." "Hollow-cheeked and wistful," with a slender body, Violet had a flickering radiance, and a voice Rebecca compared to the fluting of an owl. Deeply read in English literature, Violet was also the author of several novels Rebecca respected—although she did not think them great literature.

Rebecca revered Ford's powers as a novelist and praised his efforts as a mentor to young writers. She would soon be writing reviews for the *English Review*, the journal he edited. But he was indiscriminate about women and apt to "roll the eye at all God had created female." She compared him to a pink whale, but without "cetacean firmness." He more closely resembled a dying pig "a minute after the beginning of his collapse." He had a mouth full of crowded, misplaced teeth, and adenoids that made it difficult for him to breathe. Out of his perpetually open mouth his voice issued with strange sound effects. Rebecca remembered him talking to the artist Wyndham Lewis about the decoration of a mantelpiece: "I find it, whoof, so restful, honk." He had prominent blue eyes and hair that was like chicken down. He moved very slowly, "as if his limbs and torso were so many sacks of chaff held together by a flimsy covering."

To Violet, Rebecca first appeared in a pink dress and "large, wide-brimmed, country-girlish straw hat that hid her splendid liquid eyes." Rebecca seems to have been a little wary of this advanced couple, for Violet noticed she "kept her feet planted very regularly and firmly together" during the interview. Rebecca suspected that they wanted her to keep quiet about Ford's authorship of *The New Humpty Dumpty*, in order to avoid paying a percentage of the royalties to his estranged wife Elsie.

Violet remarked that Rebecca was "sweet and reasonable, but not to be kidded." A good listener, she was all "milk and honey" with a voice that reminded Violet of "something mellifluous, soothing, like sweet bells rung in tune. And quite superiorly, ostentatiously young—the ineffable schoolgirl!" Ford later told a friend he found Rebecca "great fun . . . but promising."

Violet said that she and Ford told Rebecca stories about *The New Humpty Dumpty* during their first meeting. Did Ford divulge that his novel contained in the character of Herbert Pett, "an egotistical little man," an attack on H.G., who had reneged on his promise to help edit and finance *The English Review?* The acute Rebecca might easily have seen it for herself.

Like H.G., Ford and Violet were celebrated and scandalous. A wonderful gossip, Violet delighted in the drama of sexual intrigue. Ford was often the life of the party, inventing delightful games and entertainments. On one occasion he had Rebecca and several others scissoring silhouettes with undreamed-of panache. Another time he had his guests standing up and improvising a passable aria out of King Arthur's dying words. He treated friends to his incomparable stories, endless and exquisite, a complex filigree of fiction forming and reforming itself in a "lively iridescent confusion." He swore they were the truth, but the stories floated past his guests like a largesse of light and cloud until the fairytale hour was over.

In Violet's London home, South Lodge on Campden Hill, Rebecca met many contributors to *The English Review* (which she would later call "the most impressive periodical ever to appear in our language") and many other writers and fashionable people. Wyndham Lewis remembered meeting Rebecca, "a dark young maenad," at Violet's, and the stir her late arrival caused as she "burst through the dining-room door . . . like a thunderbolt." For Rebecca, it was a "coming out" in the literary world. A mother's domestic life was the last thing she wanted. H.G. had shown her an American newspaper column lauding her work and comparing her to Emerson. "Fame!" she exulted to one of her confidants.

2

Rebecca's pregnancy caught everyone by surprise. It had been the result of a hurried moment in H.G.'s London flat when it seemed they were about to be interrupted by a valet. As the more experienced lover, H.G. put the blame on himself. He had been using no birth control devices, relying only on withdrawal. At the critical moment he had "slipped" and lost control.

Once again, H.G. confided in Jane and secured her pledge to help him manage this unfortunate accident. He would keep her abreast of every development; this would be a crisis they would manage together. When H.G. announced at his own table among his intimates that Rebecca was pregnant, Jane calmly observed that Rebecca would need help in coping with her new condition.

H.G. cautioned Rebecca to confide in no one while they decided what to do. Abortions were illegal and hazardous. They agreed that Rebecca would have the baby and then put it up for adoption. They both clung to the idea that childbirth would change nothing between them.

Of course, it changed everything. H.G. resolved to whisk Rebecca away from London, where her pregnancy would arouse gossip. In early December 1913, they started meeting in the London home of H.G.'s friend, Mrs. Carrie Townshend, while he formulated his plans. Rebecca relied on his resources, for her income as a journalist would not cover the expenses involved in setting her up outside the city with household help and a nurse—essential to her if she was to go on writing.

Rebecca brooded on the restrictions of her condition. H.G. recommended a holiday at Violet Hunt's Sussex cottage. Rebecca complied, but she felt ill and helpless. It did nothing to improve her spirits that H.G. remained with Jane at their Essex home. Rebecca West had published articles condemning the shameful treatment of unwed mothers and illegitimate children; now she found herself shuttled about to suit her married lover's convenience. He provided every comfort to ease her plight, promised to "run up for Monday afternoon or Tuesday lunch" at Violet's cottage, but her isolation depressed her—especially after she acceded to his request not to confide in the sympathetic Violet, who was famous for broadcasting secrets.

In January 1913, with H.G.'s assent, Rebecca told Winnie about her pregnancy. Winnie viewed it as the result of a love match and was sympathetic. Then Rebecca told Lettie, who deplored H.G.'s behavior but stood by her sister. Then Rebecca told her mother. The conventional Isabella, shocked that a married man who visited her home had taken advantage of her daughter, flung his letters into the fire, saying his paternal talk at her Hampstead home had been an elaborate ruse. Rebecca never got over her mother's disapproval. It created an enduring heartache she acknowledged in old age: "I found . . . a photograph of my mother, which shows her very good-looking and very noble looking—her head held very well . . . How I wish I could have made her happy by marrying early and never meeting H.G."

H.G. met Winnie and appreciated her kindness. Her voice reminded him of Rebecca's. Winnie worried, however, that Rebecca would not be "discreet enough." What an appalling predicament for Rebecca West, whose very identity turned on her candor.

Perhaps Rebecca would have balked at carrying on with H.G. if Jane had lodged a protest, if H.G. had been less ardent, or not quite so proficient in engineering their affair. He told her that she had revitalized him; it was the "most wonderful thing living clean and simple again. You don't know the ugly creases you have taken out of my mind." He dreamed of her as he dreamed of love when he was a boy. He loved her as he had never loved anyone else. He was "glad beyond gladness that we are to

have a child." He could not wait to see her "dear swelling boddy again."*
He kissed her feet, her shoulders, and the soft side of her body. He was
even becoming fat, out of sympathy, he supposed, for her condition.

Rebecca was getting her first taste of long periods without H.G. His
letters convey their closeness, but his words also reflect his campaign to
mollify her. She craved more of his company than he wished to give. He
let nothing interfere with his traveling and family life with Jane and his
two boys. He wrote to Rebecca frequently throughout January and early
February of 1914, describing his trip to Russia: "St. Petersburg is more
like Rebecca than any capital I have seen, alive and dark & untidy (but
trying to be better) and mysteriously beautiful." He recommended that
she find a place in Llandudno, a Welsh resort with excellent rail connections to London, and he made all this scheming sound like a scenario got
up for their entertainment. She would be Mrs. West, and he would be
Mr. West, employed in the movie business. She should let no one call her
"Miss." He sent her a check to purchase warm clothing for the winter in
Wales. He advised her not to give anyone her address. "Keep up a legend
that you are going to live in the hinterlands, use that as your address and
make vague promises to people to see them. . . . It will leave us far freer
with each other and it will save Jane enormous embarrassment."

Rebecca detested H.G.'s concern for Jane—a hardboiled conniver, in
Rebecca's view. She was sure that Jane resented her. Rebecca believed
Jane hid behind her respectability, secretly enjoying Rebecca's trials, and
always holding the better hand because H.G. did nothing without her
counsel. They were still very much a couple and showed no signs of a
breakup.

Yet H.G.'s ardor thrilled Rebecca. His letters from Europe reveal in
graphic detail their cozy and cuddly relationship, as well as his raw sexual
hunger. He professed to be abashed by his "unspirituality," but he could
not wait to "lay hands" on her. He wanted to use his "delicious" woman.
He loved the sweet smell of her body. He craved her legs and could only
tickle her feebly with a pen, kissing her "metaphorical feet." Although
he urged her to burn such letters at once, she saved them.

H.G. coupled his erotic notes with evocations of Rebecca as his soul-
mate: "You are the woman mind I used to dream about and which I have
been looking for all my life. You are my sister. I love your clear open hard-
hitting generous mind first of all and still I love it most of all, because it is
the most of you." Rebecca seemed to be the ideal woman who had

*In his correspondence, H.G. spelled body with two dees and usually omitted apostro-
phes in contractions.

stepped out of the pages of *The New Machiavelli* and into his real life. Though he may have been mooning over Amber Reeves in the novel in Remington's depiction of Isabel Rivers, he could not have forecast Rebecca West any better: "Never before in my life had I known a girl of her age, or a woman of her quality. I had never dreamt there was such talk in the world." Remington is inspired by the "intellectual sympathy" he shares with Isabel, the "jolly march of our minds together." Even if she had been a "crippled old lady," Remington is sure they would have "hunted shoulder to shoulder"—words that resemble the Panther-Jaguar idiom in H.G.'s letters. Isabel always has something fresh to say, and she begins her writing career "not in that copious flood the undisciplined young woman of gifts is apt to produce, but in exactly the manner of an able young man, experimenting with forms, developing the phrasing of opinions, taking a definite line. She was of course tremendously discussed. She was disapproved of, but she was invited out to dinner." She goes through Remington's writing with a "keen investigatory scalpel. Her talk puts me in mind of a steel blade. Her writing became rapidly very good; she had a wit and a turn of phrase that was all her own."

No wonder H.G. thought that Rebecca had become his words made flesh, for she joined him in what Richard Remington calls his "amazing *lark*," the "thrill of adventure, the curious bright sense of defiance, the joy of having dared." In *The New Machiavelli*, love is called "a supreme synthesis," raising lovers to "a new level of life," and this is also the tenor of H.G.'s loving missives from Russia to Rebecca. His month away gave him the time to create the myth he and Rebecca were to embody.

Writing from Moscow on February 9, 1914, the day before he would start for home, H.G. schooled Rebecca in the pattern of their lives. He would take her to Llandudno where he wanted to be naked with her ("never since I was first married have I so pent myself as I have since we parted in Warwick Street"), but she would then have to endure seven weeks alone as he resumed his family life in Essex.

By mid-February, they had changed locations for their "lair"—as H.G. called it—preferring Hunstanton on the Norfolk coast because he could get to it easier from Easton Glebe. He suggested that she get some books from the *Daily News*, which she apparently did, for her reviews continued to appear until a week before she gave birth. But she was merely "playing scales"—to borrow her phrase for Arnold Bennett's book reviews.

By March she was settled in Hunstanton, and H.G. continued his flying visits and amorous correspondence to his "delightful bedmate," "sweet eyes," "darling colleague," and purring Panther. Apart from her he was bored. He missed the noises she made, and his love was all consuming:

[April 14, 1914 postmark]

I shall lay my paw upon you this Wednesday night and snuff under your chin and bite your breast and lick your flank and proceed to other familiarities. I shall roll you over and do what I like with you. I shall make you pant and bite back. Then I shall give you a shake to quiet you and go to sleep all over you and if I snore, I snore. Your Lord. The Jaguar.

So H.G. managed to caper about between home and his "dens" with his "dusky" Panther, until a hockey accident at his home in late May kept him away from Rebecca for several weeks.

By late July, Rebecca was coming to full term. She missed London's literary life and had to lie about her feelings to Violet Hunt, saying that a lung inflammation required several weeks of nursing in the country. She needed complete rest and could not see anyone. Some last-minute complication alarmed H.G., for on August 4, 1914, the day England declared war on Germany, and the day before Anthony Panther West was born, Jane cabled H.G.: "I am full of misery at your telegram. It isn't Rebecca herself is it who is in danger. I try to think the message might mean the child—not her. This is horrible. Give her my dear love if you can." The telegram reveals how implicated Jane had become in every twist of H.G.'s life.

Whatever trouble Jane feared, it proved temporary. The next day H.G. announced to Rebecca: "I am radiant this morning. With difficulty I refrain from going about giving people large tips. I am so delighted to have a manchild in the world—of yours. I will get the world tidy for him." He had been writing about "national catastrophes," which he punctuated with whistling as he thought of his love for her and the "Great Man" he expected his son to become. "Lie and purr with it and I will manage the world part for a bit."

Soon after Anthony's birth, Rebecca realized that she had fallen in love with him and could not give him up. She felt fiercely protective— an emotion she attributed partly to the start of the war. She adored watching him sleep; his quiet dignity soothed her. Lettie, Mrs. Townshend, and Wilma Meikle, a suffragist friend, attended Rebecca during her painful recovery—made worse by an infection neglected by a country doctor. Mrs. Townshend, impressed with the bond between Rebecca and her baby, told H.G. that it would be a pity to separate mother and child. Remembering the nerve-wracked Rebecca, Mrs. Townshend observed: "Suckling is a wonderful calmant." She also corrected his assertion that Rebecca wanted a "young man's life." No "bachelor-woman," she acted like a wife, not an advocate of free love, and unlike H.G. she did not keep sex in a "water-tight compartment." She longed for a home and family, and with such an establishment she would improve as a writer, Mrs. Townshend thought. Rebecca would settle for a fifth of H.G. "better than the whole of anyone else." H.G. conceded that mother and child should not be parted, saying to Lettie: "Well, I'm a rich man and can give her that. At least I can let Rebecca keep her baby."

Mrs. Fairfield also visited. She wanted Rebecca to bring Anthony home, even though it would mean publicly acknowledging Rebecca's unwed status. Rebecca refused. She wanted her own home and her boy with her. Her decision widened the breach with her mother, who had such a strong objection to H.G. that she stopped visiting her daughter lest she encounter him. Winnie and Lettie continued their visits to their sister. H.G. lauded the way Lettie backed Rebecca, noting that Lettie wrote "swaggeringly" about his "little Cub."

H.G. worried that Rebecca would soon tire of domesticity, especially since his visits were brief and sporadic. He lined up writing jobs for her. He got Walter Lippmann, founder of a new periodical, *The New Republic*, and a devout admirer of H.G. as the prophet of a new age, to make Rebecca a contributing editor. Soon she was writing on literary and social topics. But journalism was only a temporary relief for Rebecca's depression. H.G. diverted her with volleys of cheerful chat, but her spirits sank as one cold succeeded another. She seemed in disarray, having to placate servants, who were hard to secure in wartime, and to scrounge for scarce necessities such as milk, which sometimes came watered, so that Anthony's plump and rosy flesh became "suddenly froglike and unfriendly," hostile to the touch.

In late September, H.G. engineered her move to a rented farmhouse in Braughing, a Hertfordshire village, only thirty miles outside of London but far enough away from her literary capital to do nothing to relieve her disheartening quarantine. She took some comfort in wonderful views of a nearby valley, of a hawthorn tree in front of her house, and other pleasant sights in her country habitat. But she was still playing according to H.G.'s farcical script—this time representing her as Mrs. Rebecca West whose husband was a roving journalist. It is telling that when Rebecca gave a disguised account of this period in an article, "Women of England" (*Atlantic Monthly*, January 1916), she referred to herself as a married woman, "the Lady," adopting a title in fiction she did not possess in fact.

H.G.'s charm rarely flagged. He called himself her "old beasty," who wanted to stick his nose under her armpit and "crawl about & gossip and make love for a week or ten days." They would "play with each other just delicious" with "bits of fur flying." It made him "*fat*" with love for her. Usually, he came only for the weekends. They went on what he called "honeymoon" expeditions in his new automobile, Gladys. Candid about his recreational need for her—he called it a "boddy cure"—she marveled that his weekend visits, when he came to her fatigued and in need of comfort, strangely revived their relationship.

In these early war days, Rebecca had to cope not only with various shortages but, for about ten days, with billeting soldiers—eleven Hampshire men whose commissariat had fallen behind them in their trek from the West Country. Yet the opportunity to participate in the war effort energized her. She compared her rejuvenation to H.G.'s coming home one morning "completely breakfastless, with the big milk-can swinging against his legs, and the knobby little tins rattling in his pockets, and arguments against the hoarding of gold boiling over in his head." It was not unusual to have to walk six miles for essential supplies (deliveries could not be counted on), yet this intellectual man was "possessed by a white flame of tranquillity. Exaltation poured through his veins like light."

3

IN THE SPRING OF 1915, a disaffected servant complained of Rebecca at Braughing Rectory and turned up in London threatening to expose her. H.G. consulted his solicitor, E.S.P. Haynes, and wrote to reassure Rebecca that the troublemaker had been silenced. He told her not to worry, but how could she relax when he also admonished her: "Please don't let the new cook see too much of our ingoing or outgoing letters."

These domestic difficulties led to quarrels. H.G. conceded that they had recently been "ragging" their love "all to pieces," fretting over household details that neither of them could handle competently and that were consuming Rebecca's time and spirits. She should have a nurse and an infant companion for Anthony, quarters in London where she could be Miss West and have her books, typewriter, teas, and access to a club—to be supplemented by a convenient lodging or "house of call" for "Mr and Mrs West," or some other arrangement where the "widow West" could receive her friend (H.G.). It would be managed soon, he vowed. H.G. took care to sketch these possibilities, for Rebecca had proposed staying with Violet Hunt. The notoriety sure to follow Rebecca's removal to South Lodge in London bothered him: "Do you think you could endure V.H.'s questions constantly?"

Rebecca spent a dreadful June and July in Maidenhead, in a Thameside hotel, a "place of grimed plush hangings and gilt cornices," with poor service its excuse for a "franker filth." Her anger alarmed H.G. and he sought reassurance: "When I come away from you I am always more in love with you than ever. I hope you do keep on being in love with me. We never either of us met anyone who was so naturally ours as each other and we never shall." He entreated her to "keep your rump up and the work moving." She had been downhearted about her "persistent inability to work," and grateful for a letter from Ellery Sedgwick, editor of the *Atlantic Monthly*, requesting work.

H.G. was making good progress on a novel, *Mr. Britling Sees It Through* (1916). Mr. Britling, one of H.G.'s many self-portraits, is a "strange, fitful, animated man" with a wife who approximates Jane. He admires his wife's "practical capacity" and her devotion to their two little boys. But he relegates her to the company of "rather fastidious, rather unenterprising women who have turned for their happiness to secondary things," like their homes and gardens. Such a wife cannot satisfy Britling, a "Pilgrim of Love" off in search of the perfect mate. Rebecca figures in the novel as Cecily Corner. She is not Britling's ideal love—that character is Mrs. Harrowdean, modeled on Elizabeth von Arnim—but a lovely young girl with a sister named Letty. With "something in her soft bright brown eye—like the movement of some quick little bird," Cissie is drawn as a dreamer, old-fashioned in her desire for an exemplary romance: "he and she were always to be absolutely in the right (and, if the story needed it, the world in the wrong)."

When H.G. foundered in the writing of *Britling* in the fall of 1915, he showed it to Rebecca, who gave him the impetus to complete the novel: "It does no end of good to get you into my work. I was frightfully *tired* of the old book and now it's alive and fresh again. All because old Panther has read it." He was also gratified by her defense of *The Research Magnificent* in "The Novel of Ideas" (*The New Republic*, November 20, 1915). She attacked his critics for supposing that fiction was incompatible with the presentation of ideas and for despising his greatest attribute, the intellect, "which we are told should be taken from the hot grasp of the artist and left to the cold hands of the professor." She believed that art, like life, existed on all levels simultaneously: "Today every one of us moves at the same time in the personal world of passions and desire for comfort, and the impersonal world of ideas, as the swimmer gives his body at once to the air and the sea."

In her first book, *Henry James* (1916), Rebecca argued for an attachment to ideas as passionate as that which the majority of people reserve for personal relationships, so that a concept could be felt with the "sensitive fingertips of affection." Her brief study (begun in the autumn of 1915 and completed about a month after James died on February 28, 1916) was one of the first efforts to assess his whole career. She credited him with several masterpieces, including *Daisy Miller, Washington Square, The Wings of the Dove,* and *The Ambassadors.* The early work revealed faults of characterization, when James had not yet found his true subject, the international theme, which he virtually invented, discovering rich emotional possibilities in his American characters who sought a more complex identity in Europe. James sometimes tired of this theme, or did not know how to do it full justice—even in such a considerable achievement as *The Portrait of a Lady,* because the conduct invented for its heroine, Isabel Archer, is "so inconsistent and so suggestive of the nincompoop." Rebecca objected to Isabel's motive for marrying the impecunious aristocrat Osmond—that somehow the marriage would remove the vulgarity from her inheritance of seventy thousand pounds—and to Isabel's decision to return to Osmond after she perceives he is a scoundrel who married her for her money. Such behavior proved Isabel to be not a "paragon of ladies but merely very ladylike." James's women did not *think;* they were presented as sexual objects who behaved by the most conventional standards and exhibited no sense of their own.

Henry James appeared a year after Wells published his attack on James in *Boon.* Rebecca echoed H.G.'s principal indictment of James: an absence of ideas and a devotion to art exclusively for its own sake.

4

BY THE END OF 1915, H.G. and Rebecca had perfected their myth—best evoked in H.G.'s letters: "your jaguar comes with his red tongue out and his tail sunshiny, pad, pad, pad, through the jungle." H.G. adored Rebecca because, like a great actress, she could play any role: "Dear bed girl with the elfin face. Dear beautiful woman. Dear slut. . . . Darling carnivore. Sweet boddy." When met with silence, he exploded: "No letter from you! . . . Have you murdered the dear Cub? Have you been unfaithful?" Then he made it up to her: "I have it very much on my mind that I was rather cruel to you this morning. Dear little Panther I didnt *mean* to knock you about. But I *did* knock you about. But olways I love you truly below these irritations."

CHAPTER 5

Sons and Lovers
1915–1918

I

IN THE FALL OF 1915, H.G. installed Rebecca in a house in Hatch End, a London suburb. With a nurse, two general servants, and her friend, Wilma Meikle, as housekeeper-companion, she now became "Miss West" and one-year-old Anthony, her nephew. "I hate domesticity," Rebecca declared. She pined for "ROMANCE. Something with a white face and a slight natural wave in dark hair and a large grey touring-car is what I really need." Stuck in the house, she was sometimes an irritable mother. One of Anthony's earliest memories (he was about three) had to do with eating his supper and Rebecca coming in with a friend to look at him. He had a Scotch nurse named Peary and he remembered Peary saying to Rebecca, "Will you no wait and see wee Anthony eat his strawberries?" "I will not," she replied, and out she went.

With London nearby, she struck up new friendships, "chumming" with Ibsen's translator, William Archer, "a dear creature" and "one of the real internationalising forces in English letters." She and H.G. dined with friends like the historian Philip Guedella. She enjoyed the company of women novelists like Tennyson Jesse and May Sinclair. With H.G. and William Archer, she had dinner with John Galsworthy. She loved films and went to them with H.G. and others, meeting the great film director D. W. Griffith at a showing of his epic, *Intolerance*. She kept up her interest in the theater, occasionally attending rehearsals and going to parties with the producer Nigel Playfair. She amused Shaw, who said he embarked on a "precipitous flirtation" with her, acknowledging that she could wield a "pen as brilliantly as I ever could, and much more savagely. We fell into each other's arms intellectually and artistically."

2

BY THE MIDDLE OF 1915, Rebecca had conceived the plot of her novel, *The Return of the Soldier*. In early 1916, she had reached the last chapter. It had cost her "buckets of blood and sweat," she assured S. K. Ratcliffe, her mentor, but it was a "masterpiece:" "what *verve!* what *brio!* what an instrument!" Her confidence proved short-lived, for she had considerable trouble finding the right tone for the opening and concluding chapters. While she struggled to write fiction, in 1916 and 1917 she continued her contributions to the *Daily News*, *Daily Chronicle*, and *The New Republic*, reviewing contemporary fiction and books on feminism, socialism, women workers, and the war. She pursued a campaign against male authors, like Arnold Bennett, who did not give women their due. Of the women working in explosives factories, Rebecca observed: "Surely, never before in modern history can women have lived a life so completely parallel to that of the regular Army." Perhaps the most impressive feature of these articles is not their style but the author's painstaking effort to render the precise nature of work: how women wound strands of cordite into charges on bright brass wheels, while others sat at sewing machines, fashioning covers for these charges, or hammering the cordite filling into cartridges.

The war had caused her to reconsider her commitment to socialism. She denounced trade unions who saw things only in terms of class struggle, ignoring the German invasion of Belgium and the threat to England. Her disparaging comment on the "orgiastic loquacity" of the revolutionary movement in Russia suggests she held out little hope for it.

3

IN 1916 PANTHER SAW her Jaguar (as he always signed himself) sporadically. They had their usual fun and fights, with H.G. writing humorous, angry, then apologetic letters, sent from Easton Glebe, London, or the Continent. She complained, "I ates being separated from my Jaguar. Do you realize you were away from me for a month and that I have only seen you twice since."

Rebecca grabbed glimpses of the fitful "Great Man" in public places, she told S. K. Ratcliffe. There were moments when she felt their lack of a steady, everyday relationship, was unbearable. She found solace in her affection for Anthony, but she was afraid of growing old (she was now twenty-four) and worried that there would be "no more peacocks and sunsets" for her. "I suppose there always were only a limited number. But how one wants them all!" she confessed to SKR, as she usually addressed him. Nevertheless, she suspected her "misery is going to be good for literature."

In January and February of 1917, Rebecca struggled to complete *The Return of the Soldier*. For the first part of January, she kept Anthony, who had a bad cold, in her room while she wrote. She made occasional visits to London, where she took in films and facial massages, and met H.G. at a flat in Claverton Street he had secured for the purpose. She dined with H.G. and his close friend, Arnold Bennett, whom she immediately disliked. He had the "swelling quality of a balloon" and moved with the stiffness of a pachyderm, habitually retracting his head, "as if some one was flourishing a fist in his face and he was dealing with the situation by cool rigidity of bearing." His "cockatoo crest" of graying hair and his mannered flamboyance put her off, especially his penchant for attending the opera in a "shirt front embroidered with green fleur-de-lys." Altogether he was an antique piece, "cumbrous and ornate, rather like English Empire furniture." She found him portentous and pontifical and must have enjoyed H.G.'s reference to old Arnold's fob as "gastric jewellery."

Rebecca also dined with H.G. and a new friend, Sara (Sally) Tugander, the confidential secretary of Bonar Law, leader of the Conservative Party. H.G. came to Hatch End for brief visits, sometimes staying a few nights. Lettie and Winnie visited for a day or two, as did Violet Hunt and the novelist G. B. Stern (Peter to her friends), whom Rebecca had met at a South Lodge party. Violet, Peter and Sally formed an alternative to the erratic H.G. and to her difficult domestic state, which never quite settled as she tried to balance the demands of being a mother, a writer, and a lover. Sometimes H.G. was solicitous: "I am sorry and perplexed about Alderton [her home in Hatch End]. Sooner or later we'll find the perfect ménage." Sometimes he lost his patience and issued ultimatums: "Clear Wilma out." Exactly why H.G. objected to Wilma Meikle, Rebecca's housekeeper companion, is not clear, but he often took a dislike to Rebecca's friends and thought a change of scene and household staff would recapture their early carefree days of love.

4

When Wilma did clear out in late February 1917, Rebecca moved to Leigh-on-Sea in Essex. She took possession of a house, Southcliffe, on March 9 in a snowstorm, with no coal or gas, and the pipes frozen. On Marine Parade, the house had a magnificent view of the Thames estuary.

Peter had replaced Wilma. The new arrangement pleased Rebecca as she watched the blinds being put up and arranged the curtains. She saw a good deal of Sally Tugander and liked walking with her on the seawall. She continued her peripatetic schedule—shuttling back and forth to London for teas, dinners, films, and facial massages.

Nearly three years old, Anthony played on his scooter, running on the Promenade and enjoying the public garden across from his house. He delighted in a spacious world of lawns and bowling greens. A main walk took him out to the bluff above old Leigh, where he enjoyed looking at the estuary's expanse.

Rebecca spent a good deal of time with Anthony, but to him she seemed distracted. She had a habit of caressing him in an absentminded way. Years later, he found the words for what her abstracted gestures signified to him: "What have I done? What am I going to do?" She had lost precious time during her pregnancy and her time away from London; playing catch-up, she was not sure she would succeed. H.G. tried to help her, urging his American agent, Paul Reynolds, to represent her. But he did not think a *New Republic* writer would command substantial commissions. In retrospect, Anthony concluded: "She had come to believe, as people whose hopes have been too rudely dashed often do, that she was an unlucky person. And then, too, she was haunted by a sense that she had an ambiguous reputation." If Anthony had read his mother's diaries, he would have felt vindicated by her constant reiteration of the feeling that fate was against her. Her belief that she had an "ambiguous reputation," as well, made her thin-skinned and subject to frequent mental and physical upsets. Her nature was "defiant," H.G. pointed out in his autobiography, but her sense of propriety and family loyalty was "instinctive." She was both a "formalist and a rebel," he concluded.

In the spring of 1917, a visit to Fairliehope, her mother's Hampstead home, eased Rebecca's anxiety. She brought Anthony with her, and Isabella fell in love with him. Rebecca made at least nine visits to Fairliehope in 1917, taking Anthony with her several times. His grandmother doted on him.

In spite of her beautiful surroundings, a bored Rebecca pined for H.G. Zeppelins flew overhead, contributing to her growing nervousness, although at first she and Anthony welcomed the excitement. They had spectacular views of thunderous air raids from their windows. " '*Prrretty* aeroplanes!' said Anthony. '*Lovely* guns!' " Violet Hunt visited on Sunday, May 20, and commented in her diary: "Oh the sadness and wisdom of Rebecca! The boy is like Gyp [H.G.'s older son, christened George Philip]—spoilt and sad and soft—more like his mother."

When H.G. told Rebecca in early June about his trip to Russia, she exploded. He tried to divert her with a trip to their favorite hideaway, Monkey Island, a tiny spot on the Thames. It made no difference. She remained irritable. In the autumn he began sending her scolding letters. She had dulled his passion. He deplored her behavior during air raids. He could not stand her constant "oh God!" which only made things worse. He preferred to ignore the disagreeable, not to wallow in it as she did. A shadow had blackened everything he loved about her. He would always put his optimistic temperament over a resistant world, and she was just the opposite: "every disagreeable impression is welcome to your mind, it grows there." He and Rebecca were incurably incompatible: "It is your nature to darken your world and blacken every memory. So long as I love you you will darken mine." He knew that she had not meant to do so, but there it was. He would stick by her in the "most essential things," but he would not pretend any longer that she made him happy. "The Panther and Jaguar are beasts of two different species and the Jaguar's natural habitat is up cheerful trees."

Rebecca's reply took H.G. aback. If he expected her to be conciliatory, he was mistaken. She said that her passion for him had also diminished. Confronted with her vehemence, he proposed that they continue to see each other while they sorted out how much love might be left in their liaison. Rebecca assented and almost immediately felt better. By the end of September she announced to friends her reconciliation with H.G. He vowed: "so long as you stick to me, I sticks to you dear Panther."

5

SEPTEMBER 28-30, 1917: Three more air raids in quick succession, four hours of constant gunfire, and a bomb that fell about seventy yards from Rebecca's house. From the Promenade, Anthony saw a field with a bomb crater and dead cows. A battery of antiaircraft guns jarred the house at night with their slamming concussions. While the guns reloaded, Anthony could smell the burning cordite, and began to cry. Rebecca took him into her bed and held him tightly, but he continued crying.

Rebecca resolved that he should be moved to London, where the bombs had not yet reached. She shopped with him to prepare for the Montessori School he would attend there and then accompanied him to the city a week before he started school on October 11, 1917, just past his third birthday. It pleased Rebecca to see that he enjoyed his first day. She wrote to one of her friends: "He is indulging in much speculative thought; he told Lettie the other day that a mouse has a curly tail because it eats hard things. 'It's what you eat gives you curly locks.' "

Later in the year, when London proved unsafe, the school was moved to Wokingham in the country, where Anthony seemed to enjoy the farm animals, reporting to Rebecca his delight in the "very sweet" twelve baby black chickens. There were ponies to ride, young calves he watched grow, and various sports.

When Anthony's schoolmates asked him about his parents, he did not know what to say. H.G. detested the ruse of calling Rebecca "Auntie Panther," saying he wanted her to be frank with her servants. But Rebecca could not afford to be candid since H.G. did not openly acknowledge that he was Anthony's father. Consequently, Anthony was told nothing. H.G. appeared to his three-year-old son as "someone enormously buoyant, cheerful and energetic, who blew in and out of my already sufficiently bewildering existence, quite inexplicably and unpredictably." Anthony quickly took refuge in stories he could not keep straight about his family, provoking his playmates' ridicule. He had no remedy for lying because he did not have enough truth to tell.

Ostracized by his fellow students because he was so vague and evasive about his family, Anthony felt humiliated. He became sullen and hostile, expressing an aversion to schoolwork. Lettie noticed that he became quite aggressive with other children, agreeing to take part in games, then dropping out, even though his behavior "spoiled it for others." Lettie and Rebecca worried that he had no friends his age. Rebecca found him less affectionate. He developed a mania about not being kissed or caressed. He would recoil and say, "You hurt me."

Though Rebecca visited him often, and brought him home frequently, Anthony would later look on her behavior as virtual abandonment. In his own words, he had been used to the "private world of sensibility and intense feeling" of his mother and her female friends and servants. He liked living with his "pretty, brown-eyed, almost black-haired and very cuddly Aunty Panther." Going away to school had put an end to his cozy existence.

Rebecca discounted his complaints that his teachers mistreated him. She knew the headmistress, Miss Hillyard, very well, and she believed in the Montessori method, which recognized that children suffered "continual agonies from the frustration of their will to power." Rather than inhibiting children with games that kept them "childlike children," and reinforced their sense of inferiority, Montessori teachers guided them to maturity and to a sense of their own power. But when Rebecca went to school, she was accorded a "very cold reception," because, she later learned, Anthony had been saying that she and her housekeeper went out at night and left him alone.

Remembering these early days with his mother in his autobiographical novel, *Heritage,* Anthony observed: "Our life together was to me full of mysteries." Rebecca rejoined that "Anthony always knew I was his mother and Wellsie [Anthony's name for H.G.] his father." But Anthony was not encouraged to speak their true names, to address them as mother and father. The game of calling them "Auntie" and "Wellsie" deeply troubled him, for he had to play a false part, and he saw his mother pretending in public. She was a performer, never quite real or genuine to him. He never quite trusted in her as his mother. He also thought she put him out of the way, as though he were an embarrassment or an inconvenience. Preoccupied with her work, she did not make him feel wanted. Then she would take him up again as her pet, but to him it seemed a "toy-cupboard life."

Anthony saw little of H.G.—never more than three days at a time, except for holidays that might stretch into a week or ten days. He cherished his father's visits because H.G. had the "successful amorist's gift of concentrating his whole attention on the person he wanted to charm." Absorbed in Anthony's games, he would invent variations that the child could work out during his father's absences. H.G. also commemorated their times together in charming and comical drawings with captions that transformed their visits and outings into children's stories. He drew Anthony's nurse Peary as a guardian angel bidding him good night; he drew Anthony as a great pirate, Captain Anthony Bones, engaged in great adventures, escaping from soldiers, jumping into a river and swimming across it to a safe haven in his cave. He pictured Anthony riding a large horse, a camel, and a mythical creature called a Deinotherium. Rebecca tried to compete with H.G., inventing a long story, "The Time Book," her version of a science fiction fantasy, but it lacked H.G.'s verve.

Only later did Anthony understand how emotionally starved he was. Rebecca eventually admitted that sending Anthony away to school at the age of three had been a mistake; nevertheless, she had done it to protect him, and she had taken him to plays, the zoo, the beach, and done most of the things that mothers do with their children. But Anthony missed her continuous presence, and he grew to resent the dramatic and hasty departures and returns. He disliked being hurried through his childhood.

Anthony did not complain about a life that bewildered him, because his mother never let down her guard, never gave any indication that something was wrong. Instead, he played a game with servants, trying to get them to admit that his aunt was really his mother. Anthony's own duplicity, his childish willingness to play his mother's game, made it easier for her to delude herself that all was well. She wrote to Sally Tugander Melville: "I hope Major Melville [Sally's husband] was not shocked by my calm allusions to Anthony, but I've been with Anthony for three years now and I have got so thoroughly accustomed to him that I can't realise that he's an unusual fact. He's a very nice one, any way. Particularly now that he's been Montessoried." Yet Rebecca realized he was bored, and that his nurse could not cope with his active mind and body. With him out of the house, she confided to S. K. Ratcliffe, she could get on with her new novel, *The Judge,* and "the copy will really begin to rip."

6

On September 20, 1917, *Century* magazine cabled Rebecca that they were buying her first completed novel, *The Return of the Soldier,* for serialization. It had been inspired by a medical journal article describing the case of an older factory employee who had fallen down a staircase on his head and revived thinking he was a twenty-year-old. He then rejected his anguished wife and sought out an old sweetheart. This, in short, is the plot of her novel. Thirty-five-year-old Chris Baldry, suffering from shell shock, is shipped home from the front under the illusion that he is twenty. He does not recognize his wife Kitty or remember his life at Baldry Court. He asks to see his former lover, Margaret Allington. Neither Kitty nor her companion Jenny (Chris's cousin) had known about Margaret, whose shabby clothes and lower-class manners they find repellent.

Margaret was based on Mrs. Vernon, Rebecca's former landlady, whose sweet and noble temper had much impressed her. Chris Baldry's fate hinges on Margaret's behavior, for she has the power to continue his blessed idyll of youth or to bring him back to reality, which means restoring him not only to his wife but to his place as a soldier. Jenny, the novel's narrator, gradually realizes that Chris's life on the family estate has not been so wonderful; rather it has been an illusion as false as his amnesiac belief that he is twenty, not thirty-five. Margaret makes Jenny see that Chris has craved a passionate, caring, even maternal love that Kitty, a cold, doll-like beauty, cannot supply. Everything appears perfect in Kitty's fastidious household, but all is sterile, and Chris yearns for the untidy but ebullient and motherly Margaret to nurse his starved sensibility.

Kitty is one of those "secondary women" that Wells defines in *Mr. Britling Sees It Through,* preoccupied with the material perfection of their lives, which are flawless but lifeless, and so cannot nourish love. Kitty reminded biographer Gordon Ray of Rebecca's view of Jane Wells, a malevolent, controlling force in H.G.'s life, a "lady," who "frightened" him, representing "gentility to him."

Just as H.G. turned to his untidy but ebullient and motherly Rebecca for love, so Chris Baldry turns to Margaret. Margaret is an idealized love, what H.G. liked to call a "lover shadow," the male's perfect mate. Margaret has the nobility that Rebecca admired in her landlady Mrs. Vernon, who had been to Monkey Island, the setting for Rebecca's and H.G.'s loving excursions and for Chris Baldry's trysts with Margaret five years before he married Kitty. Margaret's unqualified love contrasts with Kitty's possessiveness, which is accentuated by her rattling jewelry.

Chris's amnesia allows him to forget Kitty and to enjoy Margaret without guilt. This absolute separation of one life from another was also the ideal H.G. sought and which troubled Rebecca, because it was not real. They simply could not go on in such a way, any more than Margaret and Chris can in the novel. Chris is childish, not only during his amnesia but in his prewar behavior; it is revealed that at twenty he broke with Margaret because he saw her rowing a boat with Bert Wells. "Here I am, coming to say good-bye because I must go away tonight, and I find you larking with that bounder." It is an inside joke, of course, for H.G.'s childhood name had been Bertie, and in a novel, *Joan and Peter*, published the same year as *The Return of the Soldier*, he refers to himself as a "counter-jumper." But what is not so funny is that Chris rejects Margaret because of Bert. "He wasn't trusting me as he would trust a girl of his own class, and I told him so, and he went on being cruel," Margaret confesses to Jenny. Not only did Rebecca's novel remind H.G. of his lower-class origins, she was also making a telling point about the jealousy that H.G. always said got in the way of relationships. In the grip of the usual double standard, he worried about her being unfaithful to him, but that did not stop him from being unfaithful to her. The only safe woman was someone like Jane—a name he had literally invented for his wife, whose real name was Catherine. The only safe woman for Chris is Kitty, a woman who will not cuckold him because her modus vivendi is as mistress of the manor. Rebecca despised H.G. for playing it safe, even as she loathed Jane for being so good at it.

Margaret does not want to hurt Chris, but she eventually realizes he cannot remain fixated on his youth, and she cooperates with the psychiatrist who successfully guides Chris back to reality. Dr. Anderson quickly diagnoses Chris as the product of an older father, a little envious of him, and a mother who would have preferred him to be stupid. Interviewing the three women, the psychiatrist softly comments that "like a hunter setting a snare," Chris turned to sex "with a peculiar need." Margaret answers immediately: "Yes, he was always very dependent." The family background is a sketch of H.G.'s, who wanted sex but also mothering, whose letters to Rebecca were childlike and needy.

7

THE ANNUAL REGISTER put *The Return of the Soldier* on its short list of distinguished work in all artistic fields. The book established Rebecca's reputation as a novelist; its elegant prose was much admired and the novel still compels admiration as a "small masterpiece." For its time, *The Return of the Soldier* was a daring departure, unabashedly employing the Freudian ideas that had begun to emerge in Rebecca's literary criticism. Well reviewed in both America and Britain, it went into a second printing and was later adapted for the stage. Rebecca lived to see the film of it in 1981, with Alan Bates, Julie Christie, and Glenda Jackson.

CHAPTER 6

The Judge
1917–1921

I

BY CHRISTMAS 1917, Rebecca had written half of a new novel, *The Judge*. She found it slow going. H.G. contended that her "whale of a book" was formless.

Rebecca fitted the novel with an epigraph: "Every mother is a judge who sentences the children for the sins of the father." *The Judge* has two mothers, Mrs. Melville and Mrs. Yaverland. Mrs. Melville, the mother of the novel's Edinburgh heroine, Ellen, has been abandoned by her husband, who, like Charles Fairfield, dies away from home. Ellen dismisses her Irish father: "he was just an expense" and as "dreadful as Iago." She has been taught to be wary of men and resolves not to marry until she achieves some greatness. Yet her anger against men and their "loathsome maleness" is actually an indication of how much she expects from them. Mrs. Melville instills the male principle in Ellen, who becomes a substitute for her only son, who died of influenza. Ellen is drawn to Richard Yaverland, a strong, tall man who looks to her "like a king."

Like Rebecca, Ellen is a spunky suffragette who knows how to make life "a fair picnic for my tongue." The novel's first half reflects her triumphant sense of life, which is no less impressive than the young Rebecca's exuberance. Ellen craves drama. Sarah Bernhardt's performances have enchanted her. Rebecca spoke of Ellen as "one of my favourite creations."

Ellen succumbs to Richard Yaverland's advances, agrees to marry him and live in an Essex village, the site of his family home, Yaverland's End, presided over by his mother, Marion. Ellen undergoes a shocking change, as abrupt as Rebecca's confinement and isolation during her pregnancy. Competing with Marion for Richard's affections, she becomes part of a demented love triangle, inspired by Rebecca's nearly suicidal passion for H.G. As she told critic Jane Marcus, "I damned near found myself in the millrace."

Marion treats her illegitimate son like a substitute for the local squire who deserted her. At the same time, she rejects her legitimate son, Roger, born after her lover's butler has raped her. Richard, fiercely protective of his mother and contemptuous of the weak-willed Roger, will pay heavily—like Ellen—for becoming a projection of his mother's longings.

How to conclude the novel and to link the two stories—Richard's and Ellen's—baffled Rebecca. Both mothers must die: Richard must murder his brother Roger and be hanged. Only then, she thought, could the really exciting part of the novel begin.

2

WHILE H.G. FRETTED that Rebecca was failing to build herself up as a novelist, her provocative reviews had made her name. In *The Egoist* (October 1918), Dora Marsden suggested that "in the public eye Rebecca West's wit has continued to exhaust the conception of Rebecca West. For it she is just the highbrowed reviewer of books who removes the skin of her victims to the accompaniment of a happy laugh." Max Beerbohm called her "La Femme Shaw." Frank Harris was less complimentary, saying that she acted "as if she were the spouse of God and I a blackbeetle who had happened to cross her path—silly bitch!"

H. M. Tomlinson, a neglected writer whom Rebecca had reviewed favorably, wrote to her: "How scared and respectful they are of you. They'd argue with me for years; but one look from you is enough to keep them quiet." After reading a July 1920 *New Statesman* review of hers directly attacking Allen and Unwin for publishing a novel about "large, pure, platitudinous women who live in a world remote from reality and incomparably more unpleasant," Shaw cautioned her about the libel laws, giving her a three page lecture on the subject.

In *The Georgian Scene* (1934), Frank Swinnerton extolled Rebecca's work in *The New Statesman*: "I doubt whether any such brilliant reviews were ever seen before; they certainly have not been seen since. . . . She amused, she stung; but she held fast to her own standard of quality."

From April 1920 to December 1922, Rebecca wrote fifty-five two-thousand word reviews of 136 novels. With so many works to consider, she took vivid short cuts: "It is diligent, it is sober, it is in good taste, but it differs from a good book even as a canal differs from a river." She made readers feel they were taking part in a tradition of criticism, noting, for example, that

Henry James had said the "essential thing about D'Annunzio in his *Notes on Novelists*. With exquisite refinement and many thousands of words he conveyed that they may be a magnificent palace, but there is something wrong with the drains." Faced with six unremarkable novels, she discovered one "bright and pretty, the literary equivalent of cheerful wallpaper," while in "each of the other books a commonplace mind turns out its pockets with relentless thoroughness." Sometimes she was indignant on behalf of great literature: "It is intolerable to think that this sort of meritless verbosity should be compared to the work of that great artist, Anthony Trollope; there ought to be a literary Blasphemy Act." When she had only one or two novels to review, she might indulge herself in intellectual sport, calling a character in an E. M. Delafield novel, "a certain kind of female fool who is perhaps the penalty we pay for the Reformation."

She consistently reviewed D. H. Lawrence's novels as the products of a genius, but this did not stop her from seeing many flaws and absurdities in his work. She thought his notion of the relationship between men and women "pugilistic and exhausting. . . . One is as surprised when one reads of Aaron's love affairs as one would be if one opened a book on physiology and found an account of asthma purporting to be a description of the normal respiratory process." Similarly, of the new generation of American writers, Sherwood Anderson "is the one we have most reason to envy," yet "his stories are monotonously full of young girls coming back to their home towns with a suitcase and a psychosis, of middle-aged men corked by inhibitions."

Rebecca thought her female contemporaries—such as G. B. Stern, Sheila Kaye-Smith, Mary Webb, Rose Macaulay, E. M. Delafield, Dorothy Richardson, Virginia Woolf, Katherine Mansfield—had done most of the good work in minor fiction, but she also believed they had not yet equalled the work of the major male writers. In a feminist age, women confronted unusual problems that made them self-conscious and perhaps not as free to express themselves as men. Their "special relationship with society . . . is rubbed into them." Women were news in a way that men were not. However a woman novelist created her characters, she would be judged as though she were showing either an acceptance or rejection of society's ideas about a woman's place.

3

IN THE WINTER OF 1919–1920 Rebecca moved to a spacious flat off Queen's Gate in South Kensington. It marked her emergence from

H.G.'s years of rationing her time in the city. It was also a happier period for five-year-old Anthony, who attended a day school, and saw more of H.G., who visited two or three times a month loaded with playthings, especially toy soldiers, which he employed in elaborate floor games for his son.

For Rebecca 1919–1920 proved to be a disaster. It took her months to recover from a case of pneumonia. During an evening visit to friends in Cornwall she had fallen into a water tank. In a bruised and shaken state, she had nursed her mother through a bout of bronchitis. Then she had succumbed to measles, ptomaine poisoning, seborrhea, and tonsillitis. In a nursing home in South Cornwall because of a carbuncle—a painful, disfiguring, and pus-producing skin infection—she had insisted that H.G. stay away. He scoffed at her sensitivity, but in early September 1920 he conceded "you must have had a frightful time." He had been reading about carbuncles in the *Encyclopedia Britannica* and had to admit he had not realized "they were anything so bad."

H.G. became irritable when Rebecca was ill and treated her misfortunes merely as inconveniences to him. In one of their heated arguments he had admitted that on a recent trip to Russia he had had a brief affair with Moura von Benckendorff (later Budberg), Maxim Gorky's twenty-seven-year-old secretary. He alluded to others, including Margaret Sanger, an American leader of the birth control movement. Rebecca, who had been faithful to H.G., retorted that she now felt free to take other lovers.

One seemed to present himself when the writer Compton Mackenzie invited Rebecca to recuperate at his cottage in Capri. He was grateful for her *Time and Tide* (July 16, 1920) review of his novel, *The Vanity Girl*, which other critics had savaged. Rebecca said that Monty (as his friends called him) made "violent love" to her for a week, assuring her that he was about to separate from his wife. His encouraging words about *The Judge* heartened her. She found him "beautiful and ethereal"—a "young Shelley"—though she knew he was thirty-seven years old. She wanted to believe in his love and thought that perhaps the trip to Capri might be a means of effecting a break with H.G.

Monty's biographer tells a different story: Rebecca made a "dead set" for Monty, who found her physically unappealing. Dismayed that she had taken his flattery so seriously, he retreated to a friend's house. Frank Swinnerton said he saw Rebecca striding out in the garden after Monty, who crouched down to avoid her notice and hid behind a garden wall.

Rebecca gave up on Monty, who set off on a South Seas voyage. She turned to his wife Faith, "beautiful beyond belief," and clever and good-natured as well. Faith secured a tenant for Rebecca's flat during her months in Capri. Rebecca arranged for six-year-old Anthony to be boarded at school and to spend the Christmas holidays with Winnie, now married and nursing her first child, Alison. The separation upset Anthony, just getting used to life with Rebecca in London. He took one resentful look at Alison and said: "Why can't she be kept in the kitchen?"

In Capri, Rebecca flourished, writing for a week without becoming sick, a record she could not remember equaling in the past eighteen months. She planned to finish *The Judge* by April 1921. She loved working in the open air, her writing pad resting on hot marble and baking in the sun. The Mackenzies had a tiled balcony with carnations in earthenware pots growing everywhere. The good weather restored her resistance. Often subject to stomach upsets, she exclaimed: "my tummy blossoms like the rose."

Rebecca's self-confident tone alarmed H.G. By late October, his letters took on an imploring tone:

> Please love me and be faithful to me. It is much bitterer and more humiliating for the male and I can't bear the thought of it. I love you and want to keep you anyhow, but I know that in spite of myself I shan't be able to endure your unfaithfulness. I am horribly afraid now of losing you. It will be a disaster for both of us.

Rebecca was cultivating her "pidgin Italian," enjoying the male and female company in Capri, and writing chatty letters to her mother, while H.G. felt "overworked and bored." He was lonely and down on himself, confessing he had "trampled on people" and had almost tried to lose Rebecca. He realized he had treated her "so's I've got no right to you any more." She would not be in Capri when he came, he said, working himself up into a towering state of self-pity, looking for "a breast and a kind boddy" and finally bemoaning:

> God has no thighs. . . . When one calls to him in the silence of the night he doesnt turn over and say, "What is the trouble Dear?". . . . Have I ever got into your arms to cry? I would like to do that now. (Though I believe we should presently forget about the crying in our mooshal efforts to comfort each other.)

Gradually, the idyll in Capri turned into a nightmare. Shortly after they had arrived, Faith got the flu. With the servants gone for the evening, Rebecca spent most of the night nursing her friend. Faith recovered but then became depressed, suffered several hemorrhages, and became irascible. She accused Rebecca of refusing to leave the house and of spreading stories about Monty. A doctor and nurse visited during the day, treating Faith for a gynecological disorder, but Rebecca was left in an isolated house at night, not feeling competent to take care of an invalid, whose family ignored Rebecca's letters importuning them to see to Faith's care.

When an "exhausted and horrified" Rebecca got away from Capri in late January after a three-month stay, H.G. met her in Naples, presenting himself as a friendly companion. They took up quarters for a month in the Hotel Cappucinni in Amalfi, then moved on to Florence. H.G. remained his fitful self, sometimes rude, sometimes "a perfect angel," Rebecca wrote. He left her to enjoy herself in Florence.

Rebecca met Alice Keppel, one of King Edward VII's mistresses, and her daughter, Violet Trefusis. Rebecca thought Alice beautifully dressed and "carefully good-looking," Violet on the heavy side but "redeemed by her splendid lion-coloured hair and her splendid bearing. She swaggered like the three Musketeers in one." Violet was trying to get over her love affair with Vita Sackville-West, which had almost destroyed Vita's marriage to Harold Nicolson and Violet's to Denys Trefusis.

Violet missed Rebecca when she left Florence, saying that Rebecca was the "only person worth speaking to in Florence, and one of the most human, genuine people I have ever come across—brilliantly clever, with the only true conception of cleverness—namely, that it is of such secondary importance, and that one's emotions matter infinitely more." Rebecca could tell that Violet was "desperately unhappy," but Violet did not feel free to tell her why. They would remain lifelong friends, and after Violet's death Rebecca would remember her fondly, praising her literary talent and her superb understanding of art.

In Florence, Rebecca had her only meeting with D. H. Lawrence, later described in her essay "Elegy." She had spotted the value of his work early on, and his fiction, particularly *Sons and Lovers*, clearly had an impact on *The Judge*, where mothers wield such magical influence. Two of her friends, Reginald Turner and Norman Douglas, took her to meet Lawrence, who had just arrived and was already writing an article about the city. She remembered his very white skin and bright eyes, with hair and a beard of a "luminous red." He moved quickly and joyously like an angelic figure: "His body was very thin, and because of the flimsiness of his build it seemed as if a groove ran down the centre of his chest and his spine, so that his shoulder blades stood out in a pair of almost winglike projections." She was much taken with the man, whom she regarded as

something of a saint of modern literature, uncorrupted by competition
with his literary contemporaries, deliberately eschewing the kinds of
comforts she valued in her travels so that he might gauge the true state
of modern man's soul. He was the one writer the age had produced with
the "earnestness of the patristic writers," a modern St. Augustine intent
on revealing the spirituality of human beings even as the England of his
day was "swamped in naturalism." She was attracted to the way he found
pleasure in any intense feeling, and to his observation of nature. His discovery of a "filemot-coloured flower that he had not seen since he found
it on Mount Olympus" riveted her attention, for in bending over it "his
face grew nearly as tender as a mother bending over her child." She compared his otherworldly, lithe body to that of an "elongated elf." He was,
in short, her embodiment of the ideal artist before whom she acknowledged her lesser self.

Rebecca visited Giotto's Tower, the Bargello (her favorite), and other
famous sites. She worried about her ailing mother and wrote letters to
her inquiring about her health and providing a running account of her
activities—always excluding news of H.G. She was homesick and she
wanted to see Anthony very badly. She had sent him postcards from
Capri, telling him about things that might intrigue him—like the blue
lizards on the Faraglioni rocks, found nowhere else in the world, and
caves where the people of Capri used to hide from pirates. He was her
darling who pleased her by writing a letter with his own "paw. . . . Get
Aunt Winnie to give you a big hug. You're a dear good Anthony."

4

Rebecca arrived home in the spring of 1921 to find her mother dying,
wasting away from Graves' disease, a condition that Isabella knew made
her look "hideous, with staring eyes." In tears, she had instructed Lettie
not to bring Anthony to visit her anymore: She was afraid that her
strange appearance would frighten him, and she wanted him to remember her as she used to be. Isabella loved Anthony dearly, and he reciprocated, expressing the fondest feelings for his Grannie. To her cousin,
Jessie Campbell, who had criticized Rebecca for her liaison with H.G.,
Isabella left this deathbed message: "Tell Jessie that there is never a word
of reproach to be said to Cissie or the little precious, because he has
brought such joy and happiness to me."

Anthony later wrote a far less sentimental ending to his grandmother's life. He was brought to London at her dying request. For the

first time, Rebecca explained to her six-year-old son that she used to be called Cissie and that her last name was Fairfield. But her real name was West, and his real name was Anthony West. He immediately asked her about H.G. Anthony had witnessed some of the quarreling between Rebecca and H.G., and he realized that the "contestants were more than just friends." Was H.G. also a West? Anthony asked Rebecca. She answered no, and put him off, saying that he was not ready to hear about his father, and she was not ready to tell him.

Anthony had already put similar questions to Lettie. "Was his Panther . . . his aunt or his mother? Was H.G. his father?" Lettie raised Anthony's concerns with H.G., and she received from him an uncharacteristically rude response. He told her that he knew more about children than she did, and that a "boy had no natural desire to know about his parents." Her notion was bourgeois, and he dismissed it. There would only be trouble if other people worried Anthony about it. So she was to "please leave the matter alone." Lettie could not help wondering "whether H.G. was the cleverest man in England or a silly little fool."

Anthony wanted assurance from Rebecca that she really was his mother, and she gave it, emphasizing how happy she had been to have him, but asking him to continue calling her Auntie Panther for a little longer. Anthony's reaction was relief and joy at having his mother acknowledge him, but also frustration at having to maintain a fiction, since everyone he met seemed to know the truth about his relationship with Auntie Panther.

Anthony remembered his last meeting with his nearly delirious, hysterical grandmother as traumatic. Isabella called for her nurse, for some reason frightened that she had been left alone with Rebecca's "bastard." Observing the tension between Rebecca and her two sisters, Anthony blurted out that he was glad he was not a Fairfield. He said they were all horrid and beasts. He watched Lettie "flushed with terrible joy." She knew that she could never be expected or even asked to forgive Rebecca for what Rebecca had done, because Rebecca had almost killed her mother with shame and disgrace by bringing him into the world, and had now killed her by bringing him into the house. For Anthony, the discovery of his bastardy was overwhelming: He had found out what he was and learned that everybody knew. He had seen a boy beaten at his school for calling another boy a bastard, and he knew the word was used as a weapon to hurt people. But the price he had to pay, if Auntie Panther was to be transformed into his mother, was the admission that the word bastard described him. The adult Anthony was not sure how much he realized then and asked himself: Did he know that the word would crawl like a snake between himself and his mother, as the years went on, to make Fairfields of them, "cherishers of the injury we have inflicted upon each other by being of one blood?"

Rebecca and Lettie denied that anything like this scene happened. Lettie remembered that after her mother's funeral, she joined Rebecca and Anthony at their summer cottage in Norfolk. Anthony insisted on knowing where his Grannie was. Rebecca tactfully told him that "Grannie's body had been buried in the ground because it had got too old to be any more use to her." Anthony indignantly replied, "She should have been loved more."

Rebecca wrote to H.G. shortly after her mother's death: "I realise how terribly I loved her—what a queer passionate genius she was and how all through me I belong to her. I only quarrelled with her more than most people do with their mothers because we loved each other so much more. I can't bear her to be dead." In those last hours of her mother's life, Rebecca was consoled by the "one or two bright times when she talked of Anthony." H.G.'s letters were a comfort: "Thank you for being such a good husband—I will try to be a good wife to you. I am aghast to think what I would feel like if I hadn't you." She assured him that her mother's was "the most generous and natural nature that ever lived—and if it was an egotist that was only because its wicked husband never gave its ego any rights as you've given me. I am so grateful to you when you told me I didn't mean all the things I said about the old lady when I was cross with her."

Lettie, who had carried most of the burden of her mother's last ailing months, elicited H.G.'s sympathy: "Lettie is my dear sister and whatever I can do for her please let me do. You know that I care for her very warmly." Rebecca worried about Lettie staying on alone at Fairliehope. "It must be awful without the old Lady." After her mother's death, Lettie moved to a flat in Gray's Inn Square and began studying for the bar while continuing her duties as a doctor. A year later, she became a Roman Catholic, much to her sisters' dismay. Nevertheless, Rebecca wrote to Winnie: "Do be tender with her. She was so dominated by Mother that she was bound to go to pieces after Mother's death."

5

H.G. SPENT TIME with Anthony in the summer of 1921, taking him and Rebecca on motor trips and composing a poem, in Anthony's voice, for his seventh birthday, complete with illustrations, including one of Anthony riding a bike put next to the lines "When I've learnt to read and sum/Wellsie says he'll give me one." H.G. cautioned Rebecca that their son had to be handled carefully: "Don't talk about him or let Peary talk about him, in front of him. He hears everything." Then he was off to the United States on another one of his journalistic jaunts—this time to report on a Washington peace conference.

6

IN DECEMBER 1921, Rebecca completed *The Judge*, dedicating it to the memory of her mother. In the novel's final pages Ellen's mother, Mrs. Melville, increasingly intrudes into Ellen's mind, "especially in moments of loneliness or uncertainty." Similarly, Richard Yaverland clings to his mother Marion in an almost infantile fashion. Richard murders his brother Roger, insanely angry because the feckless Roger has come home to spoil Richard's reunion with Marion, who has gone out to commit suicide, hoping that her final desperate act will release her son to Ellen's love.

Trained by her mother to seek a man who would be her king, Ellen replaces Marion, who had imagined she was giving birth to a "king of life." The novel concludes with Ellen's decision to conceive Richard's child before he is arrested for murder. Thus she repeats Marion's "sin" of producing an illegitimate child.

Rebecca knew that a mother's love, the most natural thing in the world, could become unnatural and tyrannical. Perhaps Ellen is strong enough to resist the mother's sentencing of her child for the sins of the father. The first half of the novel certainly conveys her inner strength. Yet it is difficult not to second critic Elaine Showalter's conclusion: "Women are punished in this novel, punished for their innocence, for their self-betrayal, for their willingness to become victims."

Rebecca rejected critic Raymond Mortimer's suggestion that the theme of *The Judge* was due to "a fashionable absorption in Freud," yet she admitted "I was inspired to do this book by consideration of the relationship between my father and my grandmother—who went in for religious passions instead of Marion's sexual ones." Unfortunately she did not explain how the mother/son nexus contributed to Charles's overbearing but magnetic personality and to the creation of Richard Yaverland. Perhaps Charles Fairfield's inability to give himself wholly to his wife and daughters was traceable, in Rebecca's view, to an unnatural closeness to his mother and to his earliest years on the Crosbie estate, a self-contained world that fed his ego like no other environment could, just as Yaverland's End feeds Richard's.

7

SOMERSET MAUGHAM complimented Rebecca on her gorgeous use of language in *The Judge*. He also warned her that striking metaphors interrupted the narrative and drew attention to the author. Critics began to suggest that Rebecca's critical brilliance undermined her characters and bloated her fiction. Virginia Woolf remarked that *The Judge* was a "stout, generous, lively voluminous novel," but she had given up on it because it "burst like an over-stuffed sausage." Reviewers praised her elegant "pictorial" prose but deplored the novel's lengthy, diffuse, and rather lugubrious second half. Christopher Ward paid her the painful compliment of a parody mocking her mandarin style and "illustrating the influence of Henry James upon an otherwise perfectly good novelist."

The End of My Youth
1922–1923

I

REBECCA HAD MADE herself ill over *The Judge*. She had kept at it while reviewing books for *The New Statesman* and plays for *Time and Tide*. Off in America in the autumn of 1921, H.G. worried that he might lose her: "Are you still being a good faithful Panther and loving your Jaguar good and steady?" Her diary reveals that his letters cheered her. She still wanted him. On January 13, 1922 she wrote: "Going to meet darling Jaguar." They were to rendezvous in Spain, a virile country, "raw, unfinished, striving." On the fifteenth, she had more dreams of him aboard her ship, the *Macedonia*. "Heart breaking fast with love," she wrote on the seventeenth as she caught the five o'clock boat to Algeciras, where she met H.G. and they walked to their hotel, the Reina Cristina, probably the best in Europe, Rebecca thought.

In Algeciras, Rebecca's reunion with H.G. floundered. She was tired from traveling in fog and storm in a terribly cold boat, which made her ache because she had not brought enough warm clothing. H.G. was bedeviled by a serious nosebleed that had to be cauterized. They managed only a few walks on the beach and visits to local sites before he became peevish and bedridden. Rebecca said her fifty-five-year-old lover acted like a "whimpering and squealing" baby. The doctor did not think H.G. seriously ill, but H.G. kept Rebecca busy nursing him, which irritated her because he had taken her own illnesses with such ill grace. She knew that during her prolonged period of ill health the year before, he had embarked on an affair with Margaret Sanger, a prominent feminist and pioneer advocate of birth control. He had met her in 1920 and resumed their relationship on his last American trip, even while writing Rebecca loving letters and pleas for her to be faithful.

In her late thirties, Margaret suited H.G.'s brand of feminist lover—

"very beautiful, with wide-apart grey eyes and a crown of auburn hair."
Like Rebecca, she was romantic and rebellious, but she had another
quality Rebecca rarely displayed: a serene and gracious confidence. H.G.
continued to write to Margaret, seeing her even after she married an oil
millionaire in November 1922. Like H.G.'s Jane, Margaret's husband
allowed her extraordinary latitude in pursuing a very active social and
political life. Rebecca would not have known all the details of H.G.'s far-
flung romantic life, but he had been angry enough once before to let her
know that she had competition. He had come back from America having been spoiled by *someone*.

H.G. had been lionized there, and though he had claimed to be too
old for such lavish attention and bored with it, his letters to Rebecca suggest that it gratified him: "I am famous here, people turn round in the
street and when I went to a play . . . the other night the house stood up
and clapped." Now he felt let down and expected Rebecca to revive him.
She wanted fun, expecting him to rejuvenate her.

H.G. knew to a remarkable degree what Rebecca was thinking, and he
admitted to himself that he had disappointed her. He had spread himself
too thin, devoting his energies to too many writing projects, trips, and
lovers. He was on the verge of a nervous breakdown, and he realized that
it was wrong to expect her to minister to him in his deteriorated condition. He also knew that because Jane had his confidence, Rebecca
resented having to play the wife without getting his full attention or
acknowledgment as his partner and the mother of his son.

Yet H.G. could not seem to help himself. She irritated him because
she was "maddeningly receptive to every infection." Sickness seemed to
haunt her. It seemed incredible to him that, of all things, she had developed a carbuncle the year before. Nobody would ever think of having
such a strange, disfiguring thing! H.G. understood it was a painful malady and that Rebecca could not very well help it, yet he sputtered that it
was a "perfectly aimless, useless illness." Actually, Sir Richmond Hardy
does this sputtering in *The Secret Places of the Heart*. But the character is
the thinnest of H.G.'s disguises. H.G. was honest enough to have
another character pronounce a judgment that applied equally to H.G.
and his fictional surrogate: "The amazing selfishness of his attitude! I do
not think that once—not once—has he judged any woman except as a
contributor to his energy and peace of mind."

Only one woman was spared this egotism—Sir Richmond's wife, who,
like Jane, craves a respectability that her husband honors because he
married her before his freewheeling ideas were developed. Other women
were sexual therapy for H.G., and when they got sick, they were no use

to him. Rebecca became an especially difficult problem for him because like Sir Richmond's lover, Martin Leeds, she combined hypochondria with a demon will for work: "Nothing stops that though everything seems to interfere with it."

H.G. conceded that Rebecca had had a tough time with servants, who tried to bully her in ways they would never try with a man. Any little thing could upset her nervous temperament. Yet they had shared so many lovely times together, and she could be so domestic and wifely. His term for Martin Leeds fits Rebecca perfectly: "emotionally adhesive." She bonded to him, and he felt more bonded to her than he had desired. Part of what made him angry at her was that she could make him feel so much. They had been on the verge of breaking off their affair many times, yet they had always reunited, the "old habits of association" proving to be too strongly ingrained.

H.G. felt that he and Rebecca had reached an impasse. Rebecca told him that she had given him everything, and the trouble with H.G. was that he did not "love enough." He had Martin Leeds say these words, but they are allowed to stand unchallenged, and Sir Richmond Hardy dies from exhaustion, unable to resolve his contradictions. Instead, he has a distraught, untidy Martin (Rebecca) weep over his coffin and exclaim: "It is as if someone had suddenly turned out the light." It is also as if H.G. killed off his fictional alter ego for the pleasure of seeing Rebecca's novelized self provide an obituary—not only for him but herself: "There is nothing left in me now to love anyone else—for ever. . . . Who is there to laugh with me now and jest?"

H.G. got away with as much as he did with Rebecca because he could make any woman feel she was indispensable to him. Sir Richmond Hardy observes: "There are times when the love of women seems the only real thing in the world to me. . . . Before life can talk to me and say anything that matters a woman must be present as a medium." For all her fury at H.G., Rebecca still regarded herself as his medium.

Exhausted in Spain, H.G. could well imagine dying, and he cast Rebecca in the role of chief mourner—as in his fiction. In fact, Rebecca decided to hang on in Algeciras, hoping for an improvement in his condition. It occurred on January 26, when he rose from his sickbed to accompany her on several walks. Four days later, a "very naughty" Jaguar was playing the devil and would not be pacified until they made love.

Then Pat Dansey, a confidante of Violet Trefusis, and Pat's friend, Joan Campbell, turned up. They provided a welcome break from H.G.'s demanding company. Rebecca later admitted that Pat acted as a "buffer" between her and H.G. His recovery continued, and they moved on to

Ronda, relishing several walks and a visit to the cathedral. H.G. liked the place. "I think it will be all right," she wrote to Lettie. The glorious sunshine, clean air, wildly beautiful mountains, the amazing marigolds, Spanish iris, and narcissus rejuvenated Rebecca. Their hotel sat on the edge of a cliff a thousand feet high, from which they looked down on a wonderful valley decked with young wheat and golden stone farmhouses.

Rebecca sent Anthony postcards, explaining that Wellsie was ill with a nosebleed. She presented her son with vignettes of her vacation:

> Today there's a wind coming from the West over the Atlantic and a wind coming from the East over the Mediterranean—and they meet just here! And the waves in the Bay can't break on the shore but are blown backwards! And the sun shines in the spray so that the whole bay looks covered with rainbows. Love, Panther

Rebecca counted on Lettie to keep a watch over Anthony and sent her a postcard: "How good you are being to Anthony!"

For another month Rebecca and H.G. toured Seville, Madrid, and Paris. He oscillated between being a darling and a brute. He caught a cold and argued with a tour guide in the Alhambra. On their return to England, Rebecca took to her bed with a cold and sent a letter to him complaining about his insufferable conduct. He was an egotist. Friends of hers they had met on their Spanish tour complained of his obnoxious behavior. If he continued to make public scenes, there would be a scandal. He had turned into a nag. He replied on March 20, affecting a comic style that made light of his ornery behavior: "The old male Pusted has read her letter attentively and declines to plead guilty to an Enlarged Egotism. He objects to the Better Jaguar Movement." He had dropped his own campaign to improve her behavior after their Italian trip, though he admitted to hectoring her about completing *The Judge* because he wanted it out of the way for their Spanish holiday. Now he was through with trying to change her. She could do as she liked. He was not going to worry about what other people thought and saw no scandal simmering, except in her own mind. He resolved to treat her with "courtly politeness" and would never again order her around like a servant. Writing in the third person, he added: "A barrier of respect shall be set up between them." He would just have to stay away when he did not "feel up to being improved by Panther and her friends."

2

IN THE SPRING and summer of 1922, Rebecca decided to take up "furious riding" to relieve the heavy weather of her mood. Her "dramatic instinct" made her look like an accomplished rider. One stable gave her the "bloodiest of all their blood hunters," and she had bolted along in terror for three miles, so impressing those who saw her that they invited her to follow the staghounds the next day, over treacherous ground they were sure she could handle. She predicted death for herself one day in foxhunting country, but she rode again and again without incident.

Rebecca had a few lunches and dinners with H.G., and they took an excursion in late July to Glastonbury and Avebury. He visited Anthony, living with his mother in South Kensington and attending a day school. For Anthony's eighth birthday, H.G. sent him a message: "Go on being as nice as you are now and go on loving Auntie Panther and Pearie and everyone who loves you." He urged his son to learn all he could, to draw, to swim, "learn to do and make things." They would pick out a birthday present together and lunch at the Criterion. For the first time, he signed himself "your very affectionate Daddy Wellsie."

H.G. was troubled about Anthony's education, expressing his alarm to Winnie that Anthony could not read and seeking her advice: "He's naturally a very bright little animal and it is really damnable that he should be made into that most desolate and unhappy gloomy thing, a *backward* boy." Perhaps taking him out of school and employing a governess might be best, H.G. proposed. He would pay for one, if he was convinced there was value in it. Rebecca had made inquiries about a governess for her eight-year-old "nephew," a bright but "lazy boy." She had decided to take him out of school because a neurotic class mistress had created a bad atmosphere. She hired a tutor in arithmetic and French, who also took Anthony to museums and introduced him to the arts.

Rebecca was still casting about for a way to break with H.G.—a fact he acknowledged in several letters sent to her in August expressing his annoyance, but still searching for a formula that would effect a reconciliation while not pressing her too hard. She had called him a "nagging schoolmaster," "pompous ass," and "swine." He apologized and promised not to bother her anymore. But he felt that their separation was a tragedy. Face-to-face with him she would realize this. He would come immediately in response to her telegram. When she failed to respond, preferring to enjoy the company of friends in Porlock (a picturesque village on the Somerset shore), he leveled several preposterous charges at her: She had been unfaithful; she was losing control of her life; her writing was deteriorating. Each letter became more abusive. On August 28, Rebecca recorded in her diary: "Another awful letter from HG. Received two letters in afternoon from HG accepting break. The end of my youth."

Rebecca decided to meet H.G. in early September to formalize their break and to make sure he would make provision for child support. She rightly predicted that her decision would provoke him to another round of apologies and placation, but she planned to be firm and to refuse another effort at reconciliation. Throughout September H.G. wrote and wrote to Rebecca—encomiums to her "noble heart" and reminders of their good times together. London was wretched without her. He could not sleep. He had been unfaithful to her, he admitted, and he could find consolation with another woman, but he loved her intensely. "You have the most wonderful brain I have ever met, the sweetest heart, the most loving and delightful humour, wit abounding, on ten thousand occasions you have been supremely beautiful to me." H.G.'s provocative mixture of confession and cajolery softened Rebecca. She still wanted a separation, but he made it difficult to achieve a clean break, proposing that they dine with friends in order to keep their emotions in check.

Rebecca dined with H.G. and a friend on October 19. He inched his way back into her life. She saw him at least once in December before departing with him for a week of rest in Paris, where they saw Violet Trefusis and welcomed the new year with her friends. He dined with her twice in mid-January after their return from Paris. On January 28, 1923, he sent her a note confirming their understanding that he would dine with her on the thirtieth and stay the night at her flat; her diary entry for that day shows that he came to tea, stayed for dinner, and spent the night with her. The frequency of his visits increased in February and included a motor trip to Hampton Court.

H.G. thought he was making progress with Rebecca, but a letter to him in late March broke it off between them. It is likely that she had lost all patience after receiving his letter of March 21. She had complained to him about a woman in Boston who had raised Rebecca's name in connection with H.G. It was exactly the kind of incident she had always feared would embarrass her and spoil her plans for an American lecture tour. H.G. belittled her concern with a perfunctory "I'm sorry" and a blasé comment: "Something of the sort happens about most people who go to America." Then he griped about

> this growing mania of yours about the injustice of my treatment
> of you in not murdering Jane. The thing goes on and on with you
> and I am tired to death of it. I do regret very bitterly that I ever met

you but I have done what I could to make some sort of tolerable life
for us. I can do no more than I have done. It's your business, in my
idea, to disregard these fool scandals and go to America and succeed, as you certainly will do if you go, in spite of them. It's not your
business, it's not playing the game, to lacerate me about it. For ten
years I've shaped my life mainly to repair the carelessness of one
moment. It has been no good and I am tired of it.

The letter's dismissive tone infuriated Rebecca, who maintained she
had been a most "wifely wife"—another hit at Jane, who had left Rebecca
to nurse H.G. In spite of H.G.'s many tributes to Jane's fidelity and
housewifery, Rebecca alleged that his portrait of his wife was a myth
that he put over not only on his friends and family but on his biographers.

Rebecca called Jane a "greedy, unscrupulous, sadistic woman with a
curious delight in deception." Jane liked the good life H.G. provided, and
his sexual intrigues titillated her. Behind the scenes she could help him
manipulate his various women, exercising control while masquerading as
the long-suffering wife. The more H.G. misbehaved, the more he owed
Jane for backing him up. She cleverly played on his indebtedness to her,
realizing that sooner or later he would return home. When he got into
one of his nervous breakdowns, she relied on mistresses to put him back
together. Jane actually cared very little for H.G. as a man—indeed
neglected his needs—Rebecca concluded.

Rebecca's portrait of Jane derived from just a few meetings and was
based on speculations derived from H.G.'s statements to her and from his
novels. An intriguing passage in *The Secret Places of the Heart* expresses
exactly the idea of Jane which Rebecca worked up in her own mind. Sir
Richmond Hardy says of his wife: "she detests me. Reasonably enough.
From her angle I'm entirely detestable. But she won't admit it, won't know
of it. She never will. To the end of my life, always, she will keep that detes-
tation unconfessed. She puts a face on the matter. We both do." When
Rebecca summoned her own evidence, it was exceedingly impressionis-
tic—indeed novelistic in its evocation of Jane's sullen and resentful face,
as though Rebecca wanted to rip away her rival's mask of propriety.

Rebecca saw herself as the love slave sacrificed on the altar of the
"Virgin Mother," a patently literary invention of the dark siren versus
the blonde heroine. This myth is key to understanding why Rebecca felt
so humiliated. The myth required inflicting pain on Rebecca, the sexual
object. Rebecca said she remembered, for example, a party to which she
wore an inexpensive evening dress. Jane and H.G. entered the room, and
Rebecca soon left. The next day H.G. said to her, "Are you sure you're

expected to wear evening dress like other women?" Rebecca gathered that Jane had raised the question with him. What a "strange situation," Rebecca recollected, "The Socialist thinker, the humanist, the humanitarian was upholding the double standard and the conventional attitude to the adultery of a husband."

3

APPARENTLY CONCEDING the finality of Rebecca's feelings, H.G. replied on March 22 to her letter renouncing him: *"So be it."* Perhaps she was right to think her life would be better without him. He would see to Anthony's support, including insurance money and school bills, and he would provide her with five hundred pounds a year for household expenses pending a complete settlement of their affairs. He was still "stunned," and concluded, "you have been a dear delightful wonderful friend at times and you have been a terrible tie and servitude to me. When I pick myself up presently I shall feel terribly lonely but I shall be free." He had decided not to see Anthony anymore, believing it was better to surrender him entirely to Rebecca. He knew that would sound "very cold and hard. I suppose most love in the world is an artificial thing that needs the care of both the people who carry it."

As in all their crises, the letters continued to flow, with H.G. reiterating throughout the rest of March that divorcing Jane and marrying Rebecca would not work. Could she really put up with the press his divorce proceedings would engender? Would she want Jane's job of paying the bills, seeing to the business of his translations, his income tax returns, and so on? Would she get the respect that she craved of the household servants and of the world? Or would she criticize him for having gotten his divorce too late, and gotten it in the wrong way? Wouldn't there be endless quarrels about the servants and household management?

But H.G. does not seem to have been playing a straight game with Rebecca so far as eight-year-old Anthony was concerned. He knew how much it meant to her for Anthony to have contact with his father, and to regain Rebecca, H.G. resorted to emotional blackmail: "Separation means separating from Anthony for me. He'll have no father to stand by him. He can have, if we live together without a divorce. A divorce will oblige Anthony to leave his present school." Rebecca always contended that H.G. cared rather less for Anthony, especially when Anthony was very young, than H.G. professed he did, and the tone of H.G.'s letters in March of 1923 appears to ratify her feeling.

At this point, Anthony was merely another pawn in H.G.'s love game. In spite of his supposed acceptance of a break, H.G. really wanted Rebecca back. He wrote that he desired her "almost intolerably." He was again suggesting excursions together so that they might thrash things out. His desire for her was laced with self-pity, a down-in-the-mouth mood calculated, perhaps, to appeal to her maternal side:

> You know you must face certain facts about me. It is a most important thing for you to understand how persistently I doubt the possibility of anyone loving me. I dislike myself as an inadequate instrument. I am maddened by my fluctuation of will and mood. I think I am ill looking. I am not amused at myself in any way. I cannot understand anyone loving me. I can understand your being intensely loved or my boys being loved. But not this hard, strained inconsistent thing with a sort of greatness and a voice and a life that jangles.

The humbled H.G. concluded: "I dont know Panther. I havent the face to ask you to try again."

Rebecca appeared to relent somewhat. Winnie destroyed H.G.'s letters proposing marriage to Rebecca in a last desperate effort to win her back. He claimed in his autobiography that early on Rebecca's family pressured her into demanding marriage to make her respectable—a dubious allegation, since Isabella would not have considered H.G. a desirable match for her daughter. Lettie, who would soon convert to Catholicism, would not have regarded marriage to H.G. as a proper union, and Winnie appreciated his charm—and was on good terms with him—but she never said he was a suitable husband. Rebecca later claimed to biographer Gordon Ray that she dreaded a marriage to H.G. because Jane and her friends would mount a campaign against her. When Rebecca finally insisted on marriage, she said she did so on the advice of an attorney as a way to force H.G. to a decision about their relationship: "Marry me or give me three thousand pounds a year or leave me." Until then, he had given her various sums, but there was no legal, permanent financial arrangement.

In the spring of 1923, with matters unresolved, Rebecca and H.G. declared a truce. Newspaper magnate Max Beaverbrook wrote to H.G., inviting him to dinner: "Miss W. will be here. She knows I am asking you." Rebecca's presence for a weekend at Max's home, Cherkley, and other meetings in May indicate a growing fascination with him, first stimulated when she met Max in H.G.'s company. They were sexually

attracted to each other. He had a mischievous look that probably
appealed to her. Like H.G., he was short—but with a much trimmer
body, a very large head and a wide mouth. He had an impish grin and a
wicked tongue that reveled in gossip, drama, and political scheming. He
had the enormous energy of a self-made man, and was essentially an outsider—like H.G.—who enjoyed stirring the pot. He had been the champion and the confidant of the Conservative Prime Minister, Bonar Law,
who employed Rebecca's friend, Sally Tugander Melville, and he had
amassed a great fortune in his native Canada, won a seat in Parliament,
and served in the Cabinet during the First World War. Through his
newspapers, the *Daily Express* and *Evening Standard*, he had become a
dominant force in shaping public opinion. In comparison to the plucky
Max, H.G. may have seemed like a spent force—at least this is how
Rebecca would characterize her feelings in her incomplete novel, *Sunflower*, which she would begin to write in 1925.

One night in the spring of 1923, Max asked Rebecca to become his
lover. They agreed to meet the next day to talk things over. In the morning Rebecca awoke full of joy, realizing she was in love with Max. The
only thing that marred her mood was the thought that she would have to
tell H.G., brave his wrath, and protect Max from his vindictiveness.
Then Max sent her a message saying he had to go away and could not see
her. A stunned Rebecca did not know what to do. Then events seemed
to decide things for her: H.G. and Rebecca were thrown together again
on June 20, 1923 in "the Gatternigg horror."

4

WHILE PLYING Rebecca with his penitent letters in the spring of 1923,
H.G. had begun an affair with an Austrian journalist, Hedwig Verena
Gatternigg, who had translated several of his works. A beauty with big
brown eyes, delicate features, and a slim figure, she had a fetching
fragility, accentuated by her curling lashes and glistening dark hair. He
compared her face to the Mona Lisa's. She was a soothing diversion from
his troubles with Rebecca, and from his misgiving that she was enjoying
Sinclair Lewis's attentions. Rebecca had recently met him, and H.G.
knew that they admired each other's work. Later in the year she would
hail *Babbitt* in *The New Statesman* (October 21, 1923) for being "saturated with America's vitality . . . Mr Lewis has an individual gift of
humour, a curiously sage devotion to craftsmanship, and a poetic passion
for his own, new country."

Hedwig Verena meant little to H.G., and after several assignations, he dropped her. Obsessed with H.G. and suicidal, she arrived at his London flat wearing only her shoes and stockings under a raincoat, which she flung open, declaring: "You must love me or I will kill myself. I have poison. I have a razor." Fearing a frightful scene, H.G. opened a door and instructed a maid to fetch the hall porter. As he did so, she slashed herself across the wrists and armpits with a razor. He treated the wounds with cold water, and with the assistance of the porter had her taken off to Charing Cross Hospital, where she recovered.

To squelch a scandal, H.G. consulted with Beaverbrook and Rothermere, who made certain no account of the incident was published in their papers. There were a few stories published elsewhere, but H.G. managed to elude an exposé. To Rebecca, he lied about his affair and about the circumstances of the suicide attempt, saying Hedwig Verena had overdosed herself with sleeping pills while Jane was with him in his London flat. Rebecca stood by him, even though Hedwig Verena had visited her the day before her suicide, accusing H.G. of seducing her. Rebecca suspected her of desiring a love triangle and of wanting to stage a scene.

The day after the suicide attempt, H.G. and Rebecca met in Kensington Gardens and H.G. thought they got on well. But the incident had involved her in precisely the kind of scandal that she dreaded would down her. She also resented that H.G. was simply using her for his protection. She would have been furious had she known about all the lies he had told her. Only many years later, after biographer Gordon Ray investigated the incident, did she become aware of the extent of H.G.'s deception.

5

H.G. THOUGHT he had recaptured Rebecca. They spent the early summer of 1923 together in Marienbad. But their love remained a series of "bright flashes" interrupted by fights. She was his darling; she was a silly inconsiderate bitch. He proposed collaborating on projects since she could see and describe better than he could but lacked his gift for constructing plots and lively dialogue. She was his indispensable lover: "Put me back between your legs and keep me there and talk to me more than you have done and take care of me because I have to be taken care of and no one can do it but you." Exhausted and irritable after the Gatternigg affair, he seemed close to a nervous breakdown. Rebecca planned to depart in October, an all-expenses paid American lecture tour—the beginning of her new life.

In early August, Rebecca settled Anthony and his governess into a furnished house in Swanage. She thought a country setting would do him good after his poor and gloomy performance at school in the city. She had decided to board him at St. Piran's, located between Marlow and Maidenhead in Berkshire. Nine-year-old Anthony seemed to have behavioral problems.

Winnie's three-year-old daughter Alison was terrified of her older cousin: he beat her up. Rebecca rejected Winnie's concerns, though, instead confiding to Lettie her qualms about Alison, "who is incredibly beautiful but also incredibly evil." To Rebecca, what Alison said couldn't be true, not after what Rebecca had been through to have Anthony and to keep him with her; he had to be perfect. Only after decades of trouble with Anthony did she admit: "people often told me there was something wrong with Anthony, I never believed them."

At Swanage, Rebecca complained of a jealous and quarrelsome H.G. trying to monopolize her time now that he realized she really meant to go to America. She was miserable and had no time to prepare her lectures, and she felt depleted. H.G. was trying to lure her back by promising to leave Anthony as much money as his other boys. He seemed almost ready to divorce Jane, she thought, but she felt it was too late for that. She had wanted to write another book, a study of feminism, but her personal life had made it impossible, and she continued writing reviews and articles.

In the autumn, H.G. hungered for her and wanted to know when she was coming back to him. "Nobody licks his fur properly 'cept her. Nobody yowls back same as she does. Wants to take Handsful of her dear soft hair and stroke her Magnificent Flanks and———. Ssh!" H.G. wrote her pathetic letters and telegrams after she had again demanded he make definite arrangements for their parting. By mid-September, she found herself nursing him through another one of his neurasthenic attacks.

There would be no final dramatic scene, no final forswearing of love. Rebecca sailed for America on October 20, 1923 taking the only way out she deemed feasible. "I ought to have liberated her," H.G. admitted in his autobiography. "I realize I got much the best of our relationship; but there was no one to take her place with me, and she was fond of me as well as resentful and there was no one ready to take my place with her. . . . The effective break came from her."

CHAPTER 8

The New World
1923–1925

I

REBECCA'S OCEAN LINER docked in New York on October 26, 1923. Met by her English agent Andrew Dakers and several reporters, she had to fend off two journalists who pried into her relationship with H.G. She changed the subject. Nevertheless, they referred to her in print as H.G.'s protégée; his huge reputation in America contributed to the curiosity about her. Already a romantic legend was forming.

Her striking physical presence—dominated by her broad brow and widely set brown eyes—captivated reporters. She made an interesting study in paradox: Her fashionable shingled, dark hair tumbling squarely backward seemed at odds with her baby mouth, brazen little nose, and the nick in one of her front teeth. With a chin and throat dominated by soft, childish curves, she talked and ate with extraordinary gusto.

Rebecca's romantic buildup was evidently too much for her agent Andrew Dakers. During her first fortnight in America he suddenly flung himself on her hotel room sofa, buried his head in the cushions, and began to make sick cowlike noises. To her concerned query, he replied that he had been in love with her for five years; she was so wonderful he couldn't stand it any longer. He writhed and panted and kept kissing her hands, once giving himself an awful jab with her ring, before a visitor interrupted them. She made sure not to get caught with him alone again.

Rebecca began her American tour in Springfield, Massachusetts, on October 30, 1923, with stops in Philadelphia, Chicago, Indianapolis, St. Louis, and other midwestern cities before returning to New York City in mid-December for a breather. In January she would head to the West Coast. Her lectures on the modern novel and feminism drew sizeable attendance and rave reviews. One audience member commented on her "extremely mobile face" which seemed to mirror her every thought and

95

the lightning changes of her emotions. An exuberant Rebecca declared she loved America; she never wanted to go home.

Of course, she was also critical and puzzled by things American. Why did so many women wear hair nets and carry themselves so sloppily? Why were American men so slow? Their machines whirled, the hotel service was superb, but their minds and bodies dragged.

Chicago proved to be one of her favorite cities. She had a magnificent view of Lake Shore Drive from her hotel room and marveled at the sunsets. But she deplored the city's raucous and violent Prohibition atmosphere. She was curious about its literary life; figures like Carl Sandburg fascinated her, and she enjoyed meeting Harriet Monroe, founder of the influential magazine, *Poetry*. But she had already given up her idea of settling there with Anthony, finding the corruption and the American attitude toward the law appalling, not to mention the lack of moral, intellectual, and aesthetic standards. She was astonished to find herself at a party with bootleggers, real outlaws who made $500 a day and bragged about bribing public officials. Rebecca soon realized she was unprepared for the illicit, potent liquor one of her hosts offered her before a lecture. She liked to tell her family the story of starting one talk as a black veil descended over her eyes. She came to sometime later to find herself on the platform talking, with some of her audience in tears. She had no idea why. Someone said to her afterward, "What a moving and stirring lecture. But I don't understand how it related to the topic."

2

REBECCA REALIZED that American men found her attractive, but hard to fathom. Lawrence Langner, of the Theater Guild in New York City, called her "an odd mixture of beauty, unconventionality and respectability." He wrote her half-joking, half-serious love letters, saying he had suffered over her more than she realized. She did not respond to his advances.

A Jewish businessman proposed to her; a Philadelphia attorney courted her. She found plenty of eligible men, but none that excited her until she met John Gunther. At six feet two and 190 pounds, blonde and blue-eyed, neatly dressed and with a keen, quick mind, John had considerable appeal to women. They soon discovered that he liked their company. He was only twenty-two when he interviewed Rebecca (almost thirty-one) for the *Chicago Daily News*. Rebecca looked at this slender, tall, and golden-haired figure and pronounced him a "Gothic angel . . . with the vitality of seven carthorses." John showed her his fiction. It was awful,

Rebecca told him. Although he continued to write stories and novels, he followed her advice and obtained a post as a foreign correspondent, eventually becoming world-renowned for his "Inside" books on Europe and other continents. Rebecca left John in Chicago and did not see him again until he visited London a year later, where they became lovers.

She met another lover, Charlie Chaplin, in Hollywood, where she was "entertained to death by film actors." (She had first encountered him in H.G.'s company in 1921.) Writing to Rebecca on April 10, 1924, near the end of her American tour, Lawrence Langner supposed she had "vamped half California." She did find it "glorious beyond one's dreams" and wished she could live there. Langner warned her: "Do be careful how you handle Charlie Chaplin—they say he has quite a way with you intellectual women!" She often reminisced about how he romanced her on both coasts. One night in New York City, they broke into the Central Park boathouse and were arrested. The police would only let them go after he did some of his famous routines.

Many years later Chaplin bragged about his conquest of Rebecca to fellow writer William Saroyan: "Bill, she was a piece of cake," Charlie assured him. An astonished Bill claimed to have chased her around a bed for four hours before quitting in disgust. "Dear Boy," Charlie instructed him, "that is not how it is done. You do not chase anyone around the bed. You do it from the moment you say 'How do you do?' "

But Rebecca treated her times with Chaplin as set pieces she liked to elaborate for entertainment purposes. In her private reveries, he became—after H.G. and Max—the third in a trio of small male lovers: nimble, voluble, and romantic. Their powerful personalities and their exercise of power over masses of people intrigued her. If Chaplin disturbed her less than the other two, it was because he pursued nubile girls. He might play at courting her, but she knew they could never make a match.

3

IN A MATTER OF MONTHS, Rebecca met many Americans who would form enduring relationships with her. Writer and photographer Carl Van Vechten shepherded her through the cultural milieus of Greenwich Village and Harlem. One of the Algonquin Round Table stalwarts, the radio personality and critic Alexander Woollcott, adopted Rebecca as his cause. Rebecca conceded that the owlish, corpulent Aleck could be prickly, but no one had been kinder or more loyal to her, she claimed. To him, she was always "the incomparable Rebecca," whom he had first read in *The New*

Republic, one of the few writers who could make him laugh out loud. He introduced her to Irita Van Doren, editor of *The New York Herald Tribune,* which would eventually finance her stays in America and feature her as a book reviewer. Rebecca resumed her friendships with writers she had first met in London. Novelist Fannie Hurst, "a Jewess of the most opulent oriental type," represented to Rebecca a homey warmth and protectiveness that often helped to soothe Rebecca's easily frayed nerves. Doris Stevens, an American feminist writer Rebecca had reviewed in *Time and Tide* (March 24, 1922), had a straightforward and seemingly endless energy that bolstered Rebecca and relieved her tensions.

Appalling scenes and misunderstandings drove Rebecca nearly mad. Invited to an F. Scott Fitzgerald party, she expected him to pick her up. When he did not arrive, she spent a fruitless evening trying to locate him. Afterward, she heard he had made fun of her in front of his amused guests. At a party in New York, writer Heywood Broun's wife suddenly declared to her:

> Rebecca West, we are all disappointed in you. You have put an end to a great illusion. We thought of you as an independent woman, but here you are, looking down in the mouth, because you relied on a man to give you all you wanted and now that you have to turn out and fend for yourself you are bellyaching about it. I believe Wells treated you too darn well, he gave you money, and jewels and everything you wanted and if you live with a man on those terms you must expect to get turned out when he gets tired of you.

During her hectic tour, a depleted Rebecca often suffered coughing spells and colitis. Her short temper sometimes made her seem snooty. She detected "much anti-English feeling" among Americans, who prided themselves on their informality and regarded English reserve as an example of "high and mighty bad manners."

4

IN NOVEMBER and December 1923, H.G. wrote Rebecca self-pitying and goading letters, complaining about her silences and her gadding about. He proffered advice and affection. Her replies have not survived, but his reveal that he had lured her into the old debate about Jane and marriage. Then he abruptly announced that he was thinking of adopting nine-year-old Anthony. "A boy ought to have a man in his life." He had told Gip, his older son, about Anthony and would soon tell Frank, his younger one, as well.

It is unlikely that Rebecca took H.G.'s adoption plans seriously. He had never shown that degree of interest in Anthony before, and her letters to others reflect no anxiety that H.G. would actually assert his parental rights. She sent Anthony postcards from the Midwest, telling him about the wide expanse of the Mississippi, the prairie, the "miles and miles" of "comfy houses" and woods, the "funny" food ("usually chicken or turkey—which doesn't seem right as it isn't Christmas!"), and the mince pie eaten year round in Iowa ("This is an Indian name and the people call it 'Ioway' ").

On January 4, 1924, on his way to Portugal, H.G. wrote to his "dearly beloved Anthony" to say that he was the "dearest little boy alive" and to express how much he had treasured their day together and the opportunity they had to talk. He was sorry that Anthony was being bullied at school but that he had to "stick out that sort of thing." Anthony cried easily and proved a tempting target for his tormenters. H.G. advised resistance. Anthony would get bigger and stronger, and he should look out for allies. This is what H.G. had done when he had been bullied at school. He had found a friend who stood by him, and the attacks on him had stopped. Anthony should know that his Daddy Wellsie wanted to help him in his troubles, and he asked Anthony to do some pictures for him and to write to him.

Realizing that he had not secured Rebecca with his comments about adopting Anthony, H.G.'s January and February letters adopted a lighter, more playful tone as he experienced a "wave of feeling" for her, and he enjoyed his visits with Anthony, "one of the dearest little beasts in the world. We mixed very well then whatever we have done since." But H.G. was plainly jealous of the good time he imagined Rebecca to be having in America, and he tried to make her feel guilty, calling her a "Black Panther" and insinuating that she was courting disaster: "Dont forget Mr. A. P. West altogether or else I shall steal him." An unmoved Rebecca sent H.G. a sarcastic reply.

5

IN NEW YORK CITY for Christmas, an astonished Rebecca received a message that Max Beaverbrook had been looking for her. In London, he had dropped her so abruptly that she had no expectations of seeing him again. He had humiliated her. Why would he want to resume a relationship? she asked herself. Yet his attentions flattered her. She told friends about how his secretaries had sought her out—and then Max arrived and made love to her at her hotel, apparently picking up from where they had left off as if their separation had meant nothing to him. He seemed to her to be a man very much in love, and he won her over. Then he called her one evening, putting off a trip they had planned and saying their life together in London would be impossible. "It was torturing for him to see me," Rebecca confided to Fannie Hurst. "He's going to call me up tomorrow morning at eleven but I've no hope. I think this is going to be the standard attitude. I do wish to God he hadn't come. The poor old donkey."

After a fortnight, he vanished, leaving her to wonder what it had all meant. She thought that she had something worthwhile to give him, and that something good could be derived from their relationship. When she returned to London in May 1924, she sent him brief messages, addressing him as "sweetheart" and "my pet lamb." How he took this encouragement is unknown, for he was careful to destroy virtually all the evidence of their affair with the help of his authorized biographer, A. J. P. Taylor.

One surviving item is a playful but grisly fable Rebecca sent to Max about a "wicked newspaper proprietor." He busily fends off his four wives (Rebecca lists herself as one of them) and a "pure young enemy—whom he laughs to scorn and dismisses." When each wife arrives with a baby, Max instructs his "familiars," a butler and a Negro to park the babies in a row on the lawn. The wives are then poisoned with cocktails on the terrace, removed by the Negro and butler and dumped into a flowerbed with their feet sticking out. The pure young enemy returns, observes the familiars doing their evil work, and runs for help. Meanwhile the adult corpses are taken in a wheelbarrow and strewn in the drive as Max explains to the investigating officer that he accidentally ran them over speeding in his car. Panic ensues when it is discovered that all the corpses have been insured with Max's paper, the *Daily Express*, and will draw the million pound benefit, thus bankrupting him. A desperate Max commits suicide in his pond as the pure young enemy returns with a concoction that revives the corpses. The pure young enemy then announces he is a Mormon and will take them all to Salt Lake City. "So to the great open spaces where men are Mormons," Rebecca concludes.

Perhaps only another intimate of Max could explain the intensity of Rebecca's almost perverse interest in his polygamous personality. To outsiders, he seemed a rogue. Rebecca speculated that "it must have been something evil in me that loved him." Yet he continued to attract the devotion of formidable women and men throughout his long career. Max knew so many people in high places that any new protégé of his was likely to be bowled over. He could make you feel at the "centre of things, in the very signal box from which all the wires were pulled and the signals flashed the wide world over."

To Rebecca, who loved clothes and always noticed how people dressed and carried themselves, Max's "careless elegance," his vanity about his delicate hands, and his attention to his "meticulously well-shod feet" must have been especially appealing. Like her, he was a profound listener with a remarkable memory that made him a superb raconteur—the best novelist Arnold Bennett ever heard, and Bennett, a crony of both H.G. and Max, was in the best of positions to make such a judgment.

In January 1924, after Max abruptly departed from her life, Rebecca collapsed in her New York hotel with an attack of colitis. Her West Coast lecture tour had to be put off for a month.

This gave her time to see more of New York City. She marveled at Manhattan's design, dwelling on its two great streets, Fifth Avenue and Park Avenue, and expressing a fondness for Washington Square, which had "a quaint Bloomsbury touch about it, and a little brother of the Marble Arch." Yet her feeling about the city would always be ambivalent; it was as monotonous as it was dazzling. Much of New York, despite its great architecture, seemed quite pedestrian and run-down. She missed London garden spots such as Campden Hill and St. John's Wood. "New York is the essence of all towns, the supreme defiance of nature," she observed in "The Magician of Pell Street," her first story with an American setting.

6

"TWO VERY PATHETIC" letters from Anthony in early March convinced Rebecca to cut her American visit short:

> Dear Panther
>   Please write to me soon . . . When are you coming back from America? First you said in March, but now you are starting a tour on March 6th.

> Dear Panther
>   I want to become a Catholic, for I admire the Catholic religion . . . all Catholic's have been nice to me and helped me . . . specily Aunt Lettie.*

---

*I have not corrected Anthony's misspellings and grammatical errors in this and subsequent letters.

Rebecca occasionally attended Catholic services, finding in ritual "a picture of spiritual facts which human language still finds it difficult to express adequately." She admired the spiritual discipline the church inculcated in its members. She advised Anthony to write to Lettie. Rebecca feared it would "raise an awful dust" with H.G., but she felt obligated to write to him as well. Anthony was also writing him letters, saying Major Bryant, St. Piran's headmaster, wanted to see him.

On March 17, Major Bryant had written to Lettie: "Anthony's latest escapade is to cut his sheets with a pair of scissors." He was an "extraordinary youth who needs firm handling at the moment." Anthony wrote to Lettie about a dream that troubled him: "I felt a wiehght on my chest and I looked down and saw some thing whyte and gleaming, on a cross. I can still feel a weight there now." She sent him books about the mass. He secured his headmaster's permission to go to church on Sundays.

H.G. was outraged. Anthony later remembered his father spending three successive days at St. Piran's with the headmaster and with Anthony, presenting in direct, plain, but tactful terms the "rationalist case for treasuring intellectual freedom and steering clear of authoritarian systems of thought that tended to limit or abridge it." It was a decent thing to do, an older Anthony averred, but it did nothing to alleviate his suffering, exacerbated by an alcoholic and incompetent headmaster. How could H.G. have ignored Major Bryant's blotched face and trembling hands? Why couldn't H.G. see that Anthony was "numb with misery and apprehension" about what would happen to him next in that "squalidly demoralised institution"? Why hadn't H.G. realized, in Anthony's words, that "what I really needed help with was the problem of how to live comfortably with my newly acquired knowledge that I was his bastard, and for that reason a scandalous and disgraceful object?" His parents, sad to say, were not prepared to understand the depth of their son's anguish.

From St. Piran's Anthony had written to Lettie: "Only twelve more days and Panther may be back!" He needed her desperately, but she had been reluctant to return. Calling a halt to her tour was "terribly inconvenient," she wrote to Lettie, in an accent that sounds callous, because she expresses no sympathy for him other than acknowledging he is miserable. She thought of herself, of course, as establishing a career in America, making sure that she had the means to live independently and to provide him with a comfortable life. But what did this mean to him? He was going through what is now called separation anxiety at the very time when he needed his mother's support in his strides toward independence. Like other children in similar circumstances, he accepted mothering from whomever was nearest—in his case, from Lettie, to whom he wrote several letters, obviously seeking her affection and approval.

Rebecca's trip to America seems to have been the dividing point in her life with Anthony. As far as he was concerned, she returned home a different person. She had become a celebrity and was turning her whole life into a performance. Anthony felt estranged, watching Rebecca consort with "well groomed, expensively dressed people," who had not intruded on their early days. Now they were received as though they held the "key to life."

Rebecca kept a scrapbook of the enormous press she received between 1923 and 1929, reports of her lectures and interviews in American and British newspapers, some of which Anthony saw and mentioned in his letters to her from school. She subscribed to a clipping service that sent her hundreds of items. On a single day (May 6, 1925), for example, there were articles in three newspapers headlined: "Lady Novelist's Attack on Mr. Churchill." "Lady Novelist on Man's Failure," and "Miss Rebecca West Opposes Duff Cooper." *Radio Times* called her "Bernard Shaw in Skirts!" announcing a radio interview with the "most brilliant literary critic of her sex now before the public. She is also one of the most scintillating conversationalists of our time." Many of these newspaper articles contained flattering photographs of her, and for Anthony they had the effect of taking her away from him.

After Rebecca returned home in the spring of 1924, Anthony gave her a good looking over. He stole glimpses of her standing in front of a mirror appraising herself carefully. She inhaled, raised her chin and dropped her shoulders slightly, straightening her back. These subtle adjustments seemed to lengthen her neck and arms. She had achieved the pose he had studied in her photographs. When he protested this transformation, she replied, "It's just a game . . . It's all such fun, being a success, becoming a new person, being worshipped." But she reassured him: "The game of being Somebody is to do with my career—it won't change anything between us." But the game troubled Anthony. He wanted it to stop so that they could "start living as we really are." He wanted to whisper the "forbidden words, *Mother, Mamma, Mummy* into her ear." But he did not, realizing that the word mother would evoke her dark, complicated, unhappy past, and she would become "inexplicably uneasy and evasive."

At St. Piran's, Anthony had struggled to maintain his "cover story": that his parents were dead and he was being brought up by an aunt. Now he confronted her, stating that he simply had to know the truth about her and H.G. She plainly acknowledged that she and H.G. were his parents, but she made him promise not to tell anyone until he was an adult. Ordinary people would not understand his situation, and it would embarrass his father, she explained. To Anthony, this only made things worse; it was a "dangerous secret" he was sure he could not keep from the badgering boys at school.

7

IN EARLY JUNE, Rebecca spent a day alone with Max Beaverbrook. After lunch, they walked in the garden of his home at Fulham. He laughed off their earlier lovemaking, implying that he had been drunk during their first tryst in London; then he had felt awkward when he realized she had taken him seriously. A puzzled Rebecca observed that his explanation did not take into account their meeting in New York. Later that day she learned he had been making love to a young actress. She doubted his story about being drunk with her and wondered if he was simply running away from her because of ambivalent feelings. If what he said was true, he was vile; he was just as vile if it was not true. She felt he had soiled their love and made her feel foul—so humiliated that she would never feel clean again. Max's third abrupt withdrawal from Rebecca stimulated in her a desperate mood akin to the one H.G. aroused when he first spurned her. She spent a sleepless night and felt suicidal. She relieved some of the tension by writing a long account of her feelings to Fannie Hurst, and by thinking about how much Anthony needed her.

On July 31, 1924, Rebecca sent Max a telegram:

HAVE FORGOTTEN YOUR TELEPHONE NUMBER SO COULD NOT CALL BACK YOUR SECRETARY TO TELL HER THAT IF YOU PUT ME NEXT WELLS AT DINNER I WILL WRING YOUR NECK MANY OF YOUR FRIENDS ARE DEADLY BUT AT LEAST I HAVE NOT LIVED WITH THEM FOR TEN YEARS. REBECCA

Throughout the spring and summer, Max descended on her at approximately three-week intervals, each meeting becoming more hysterical and unpleasant. Rebecca's friend, Doris Stevens, speculated that Max's bizarre behavior might be due to impotence. Rebecca told Doris that Max's doctor had told her as much. Armed with this information, Rebecca staged a final scene with him, declaring to Doris that she had driven him into the night. She had acquired more confidence and more control of her feelings about him. She felt sorry for him, and she could not help adoring him, but he was quite angry with her now.

Rebecca believed that she had had rather hard luck with men. Since she had returned from America, H.G. had been haunting her London flat with more proposals of marriage. She had rejected him harshly just to get rid of him. They met by accident in a theater, and by the end of the month he was importunate: "I know I shall be your lover to the day of my death."

In August 1924, she took Anthony to Austria for a holiday—still trailed by H.G.'s loving missives. Her harsh treatment only seemed to augment his ardor: "Panther is my lost love and a black hole in my heart." When she did not melt, and she refused his offer to have her and Anthony join him in Montpelier for the winter, he threatened her: "I dont think it's much use my going on seeing the small boy if that's all you want to see me for. You've taken yourself away from me and you'd better take him too." Almost immediately he was apologizing: "I wrote rather a hard letter to you this morning. I'm sorry. I'll get used to the separation as time goes on and then we will work out some way of dealing with the boy."

In the autumn, H.G. carried on his mating dance around the figure of Anthony: "It's hard to think what good I can be to him unless we live together." Other letters announced that H.G. was going off to the south of France to live with a "body slave," and that meant he probably would not see Anthony for years. H.G. saw only impediments ahead. What point was there in his writing letters to Anthony? "What is there to write about now? We've broken. Am I to tell him that?" At any rate, he warned that if there was any "Roman Catholic fooling" with Anthony's mind, he would "cut him right out of my life and he will have to work out his destiny in the rich aimless Fairfield way." (Anthony did not become a Catholic.)

Rebecca said that her troubles with H.G. and Max were signs that she was "hounded by a malevolent fate." She found both men appealing, but devils had possessed them. Other men gazed at her adoringly, talked rapturously about her at parties, and then dropped her. Obviously men found her terrifying, but why? She wanted to know. She loathed life without a man.

8

IN THE AUTUMN OF 1924, Rebecca welcomed another outsider into her circle. The anarchist Emma Goldman had arrived in England on September 23, 1924, intending to organize a campaign against Bolshevik tyranny. In New York, Rebecca had met and liked Emma's niece, Stella

Ballantine, and Rebecca held the highest opinion of Emma's campaigns in the United States for freedom of speech. She responded warmly to Emma's letters and invited her to tea. Rebecca remembered meeting a "solid thickset woman with heavy glasses" in her mid-fifties with a "rollicking sense of fun but for the most part sad because she had no outlet for her gifts." By the end of October, Rebecca had arranged meetings for Emma with editors, writers, and publishers.

Goldman arrived at a pivotal time in British politics. The Labor Party had opposed British intervention in the Russian civil war. When Labor took power in February 1924, it had made efforts to normalize relations with the Soviet Union, thus calling down upon it the fury of the conservative press. Public opinion was virulently anti-Communist, and in the election of late October, the Labor Party and the policy of normalization were defeated. Thus Goldman was initiating her campaign at the very moment that anti-Communism was closely associated with a Conservative victory. She recognized that her attacks on the Soviet Union put her uncomfortably on the side of reactionaries, but she persisted—as did Rebecca, who pointed out that to "reject a conclusion simply because it is held by the Conservative party is to be snobbish as the suburban mistress who gives up wearing a hat or dress because her servant has one like it." To pretend that the Soviet Union was a "conscientious experiment in Communism," was sentimental rubbish, Rebecca declared, and Socialists who shut their eyes to its evils degraded the Socialist movement, which would rot from within, she predicted, if it did not oppose a government that deprived its citizens of the "elementary rights of free speech and assembly." Neither Emma nor Rebecca advocated intervention in Soviet affairs: "We must let each people seek God in its own way," Rebecca proposed. Her concern was, rather, that in propping up the Soviet Union as a positive model Socialists would lose their credibility, their ability to reckon with "real facts," and become "tedious liars about life."

Initially H.G., Bertrand Russell, and others welcomed Emma Goldman's campaign. Both Wells and Russell had visited the Soviet Union and issued critical reports. She also tried to win over such influential Labor Party opinion makers as Professor Harold Laski. But virtually everyone, except Rebecca, eventually backed away from Emma, because she refused to separate her attack on the Soviet Union per se from its treatment of political prisoners and other instances of injustice and anti-democratic activity. Russell's reservations about Goldman's position were typical: he had no alternative to the Bolshevik government, and he objected to her determinism, which contended that the evils of Bolshevism were inherent in its ideology—in other words, it could not have developed in any way other than it did. For Rebecca, this determinism was not a problem because she saw the commissars duplicating the tyranny of the tsars.

Rebecca went on to analyze the attitude of the Labor Party in a way sure to win her few friends. She suggested that the Party's "flight into sentimentality" over the Soviet Union was connected to its brief, uneasy period in power. It had always been in the minority and enjoyed the position of a small boy confronting a bully; Labor could always be sure of its martyrdom. To suddenly have to fight to win, to be treated as an equal, robbed it of its "halo of static moral superiority." Adopting the unpopular position of supporting Soviet Russia, then, opened a route back to the "comfortable place of opposition," where principles did not have to be put into practice.

Rebecca called herself a "Menshevik or Social Democrat." The Mensheviks had wanted a loosely organized mass party, but they had been defeated by Lenin's Bolsheviks, who argued for a small, tightly disciplined cadre of professional revolutionaries. To Rebecca, this distinction between Bolshevik and Menshevik was absolutely fundamental; it meant the difference between democracy and tyranny, between genuine social change and forced social planning. As a feminist, she had argued for the incorporation of all classes of women in the movement, and against the dominance of middle-class professional organizers. The narrower the leadership, the surer it was that a movement would lose touch with the people it purported to serve.

Rebecca ridiculed her Western colleagues who returned with positive reports from their brief trips to the Soviet Union or who palliated its problems. She observed that Goldman "is a Russian and speaks Russian as her native language. This equipment has been felt to be in the worst possible taste by other investigators of the Russian problem who lacked it." Moreover, Rebecca was not afraid to stake her opinion on a personal judgment: "Emma Goldman is one of the great people of the world. She is a mountain of integrity." This claim testifies not merely to her affection for Emma but also to a bond they shared as women and as thinkers.

Rebecca pressed Emma's cause for nearly a year and apologized to Emma for not being more effective. Emma gradually became almost as disillusioned with the English as she had become with the Russians. The English were a cold, standoffish people. Deeply depressed by the summer of 1925, she felt she had suffered a "disastrous defeat." In her bitterness, not even Rebecca escaped judgment. Emma thought that she radiated "light but not warmth" and that they had never gone beyond the intimacy established at their first meeting.

9

REBECCA INCLUDED John Gunther in one of her dinners for Emma Gold-man. Soon she and John were a loving couple. He saw her in the summer of 1925 in Italy, and in other places, visits he commemorated in a love letter in early December 1925:

> I remember how after loving you in moonlight in Diano Marino—and then having to return to London—how for days and days I lay sleeping with my arms open, and fell asleep pretending your lovely body was there—how in fact in an extraordinary way there was an actual perfume of you in me, in my skin, in my bed. And then that divine week-end in Paris, and the London nights before the fire: and the day in Antibes when you had more of me than anyone ever had had before. But you know—it's curious— I've never been a good lover to you—oh yes—never. I can't tell why. But I know it's true. I suppose it is because I want to save for myself some final and eventual illusion of myself—why have every-thing now?—what hell it would be—not to be able to dream.
>
> Lord—how I wanted you in Paris last month—. . . . How is Sun-flower?

This letter ratifies what Rebecca felt about her intimacies with men. Even at their most loving they withheld something from her. She had started a novel that dealt with this male ambivalence. It was about an actress who is torn between two men who are clearly modeled on H.G. and Max. The actress is called Sunflower.

CHAPTER 9

Sunflower
1925–1927

I

REBECCA SPENT the first part of her summer 1925 holidays with Anthony
in the South of France. She admired his swimming and thought he was
happy. In August, she took him to a cottage in Cornwall, owned by Mrs.
C. A. Dawson Scott ("Sappho"), Rebecca's colleague in PEN, the international writers organization. Sappho observed that Rebecca seemed a
"curiously gentle and yet penetrating person and Anthony has the same
qualities." Rebecca acknowledged that the separations had been hard on
both of them. She was no doting mother, she admitted, but they had to
establish a reasonable life together if he was not to grow away from her.

2

IN MID-DECEMBER 1925, Rebecca sailed for a six-week stay in New York
City, where she hoped to clinch a deal to dramatize *The Return of the Soldier*. She expected to be home by the end of March for Anthony's Easter
holidays. In the meantime, he would have to remain at St. Piran's for
another term.

Almost immediately things went wrong. Plans for dramatizing her
novel ran foul of arguments about rights and percentages and about who
would manage the production. Rebecca used her time to work on *Sunflower*, now grown to more than 70,000 words. It felt like an "incubus"
that she estimated would reach 120,000 words before she was through.
Wrangling over her play and cultivating business relationships
exhausted her. She had expected to live in the comfort and sympathy of
Fannie Hurst's home, but she had to move to a hotel room when Fannie's mother visited her.

A suitor from Philadelphia arrived in a sad state after his sister had died suddenly. She confessed to him that she was in love with a younger man (John Gunther). It was "achingly painful," she wrote to John. Lettie was complaining with "an air of Christian martyrdom" about going down to see Anthony on his visiting day. "I realise that I have not a soul in the world to back me—to take one ounce of trouble to spare me and help me. Oh, wow *wow!*" Rebecca complained to John. She wrote to Lettie, thanking her for visiting Anthony but disputing his complaints against her: "I had very few nonbusiness dates and he could have seen much more of me if he hadn't insisted on always going upstairs when there was anybody else." To Anthony, of course, this was the question: Why couldn't he see his mother *alone?*

The New York weather was unspeakable, with the roads frozen and snowdrifts in Central Park as high as fifteen feet. John Gunther had come for a weekend, but his bronchitis confined him to bed until his hasty departure for Chicago, where she hoped to join him in early March. The agent Carl Brandt had divined that Rebecca and John were in love, and he promised not to tell anyone. "Not that I'd mind if he did, for I'm very proud of you, my *dear,*" she assured John.

In late March, seeing no resolution to *The Return of the Soldier* production problems, Rebecca regretfully wired John that she was returning to England.

3

FOR THE 1926 SPRING HOLIDAY, Rebecca took Anthony to Italy. They settled comfortably at the Hotel Miramar in Diano Marino. Anthony seemed fine; they enjoyed bathing off a breakwater in a "bright blue but ice-cold Mediterranean." Then she took him home to complete his summer term at St. Piran's, which she visited on prize-giving day. Anthony was agitated, and Rebecca consulted with H.G., urging him to think of a new school to which they might transfer him at Christmas. Then she read in the *Evening Standard* that Major Bryant had been convicted of a drunken driving charge. Canceling her Italian trip, she hurriedly hunted for a new school, doing it by herself since H.G. was off on a motor trip in France. He sent her a message acknowledging the trouble without any concrete suggestions. She eventually found a place for the next term at The Hall in Hampstead, recommended to her by the author Naomi Mitchison.

After his summer term, Rebecca took Anthony again to Antibes, where he enjoyed more swimming and canoeing. But an uneasy Rebecca had to deal with another complication in her son's upbringing. Major Bryant had shown Lettie a letter of Rebecca's in which she mentioned certain problems with Lettie. Rebecca wrote to her saying she had not had the courage to bring them up, but now she thought it best to say that although Lettie was the "best and sweetest person in the world," she had grown into a "fault of manner" stemming from the "degree of authority" their mother had allowed her to exercise over Rebecca and Winnie.

To John Gunther, Rebecca was far more brutal, alleging that Lettie "hasn't a thought about me that goes more than two centimetres below the surface which isn't dislike and shame. She wishes I didn't exist." Lettie criticized her appearance and suggested that her career had foundered. She had found fault with the book on Henry James, expressing the hope that it would not offend his relatives; she worried that the owners of the inn at Monkey Island would be offended by *The Return of the Soldier;* her only comment on *The Judge* had to do with her disgust that Rebecca could create such a character as Richard Yaverland's mawkish brother Roger. Rebecca's manners, her conversation—all of it embarrassed Lettie. Lettie treated Anthony like an "appalling freak." She was actually experiencing delusions about him, claiming that his complexion was so dark that he would be discriminated against for being part colored. Rebecca claimed that this constant abuse had caused her to have a nervous breakdown, fighting back tears for nearly a fortnight, but she had gradually righted herself, cheered by the company of Lloyd Morris, an American book reviewer and lecturer at Columbia University.

Lloyd found Rebecca's "dark loveliness" dazzling. She had a luminous quality that lingered long after he left her. He thought of her as an allegorical figure of "Twilight" in an early nineteenth-century Romantic painting, framed by the "somber cloud of her hair," great dark eyes, and lips parted in a tender and sometimes sad smile. She had resonance, an afterimage that was "all light—quivering, incandescent, volatile." No matter what the activity—a lazy day at the beach, a shopping foray to Cannes, a trip to Nice just to sample the ices, a jaunt through an Italian frescoed arcade, dinner at a new bistro—the simplest excursions became celebrations of her spirit. She seemed to hold nothing back. Lloyd watched her perfecting each moment, investing incredible energy and intelligence. He unashamedly portrayed her as a kind of priestess and called her friendship "benedictory." Rebecca craved acolytes, and Lloyd obliged.

Rebecca's brief rendezvous with John Gunther also proved restorative. A few months later she wrote to him: "You are a good sweet thing, and what you've been to me in the last two years I can't begin to tell you."

4

WITH ANTHONY SETTLED in his new school in Hampstead for the 1926 autumn term, Rebecca sailed back to New York. She was met at the dock by Lloyd Morris and his mother, who brought her to the Hotel Majestic on West 72nd Street. She was provided with marvelous rooms at the minimum rate "all because I'm a celebrity," she wrote to Lettie. Irita Van Doren, the new book review editor of the *New York Herald Tribune,* had given her an eight hundred dollar contract for four reviews, plus weekly expense money. But almost immediately she took ill, finding it hard to sleep and to eat. She felt exhausted all the time. After a series of tests, nothing more serious than anemia was diagnosed. A week of "rather heroic treatment" revived her. Anthony's letters cheered her: "I rather imagine that he is getting on better than we think," she suggested to Lettie.

With the dramatization of *The Return of the Soldier* still stymied, and her income low, she put aside work on *Sunflower* to ghost an autobiographical novel, a four-part serial, about a war nurse. The offer of $10,000 from *Cosmopolitan* magazine, a Hearst publication, soothed her nerves and provided enough money, she estimated, for a year. For two weeks she had hardly left her room, producing 15,000 words and the first of her reviews for *The New York Herald Tribune*—another 3,500 words by early November.

Rebecca disowned *War Nurse* as hack work and got the publisher to remove her name from the title page when it was published as a book in 1930. Not fully developed fiction, it has little dialogue and few dramatic scenes; the first-person narration is sometimes monotonous. It is a rush job that reveals Rebecca's uncertain grasp of American slang and her occasional use of British expressions. Publicity for the novel stated it had been developed from a diary, though Rebecca said she took the story down as notes for a novel which proved useless.

In spite of *War Nurse*'s limitations, it is a narrative of some power. The novel's heroine is Corinne Andrews (not the nurse's real name), who comes from a wealthy New York family and volunteers for service in World War I. She goes on an odyssey which—whatever its basis in fact—Rebecca cast as a quest for values, in which a young woman forsakes her family's Puritanism and materialism and forges her own identity. There are passages that step outside of Corinne's straightforward narrative, in which she speaks of the "sex antagonism" which makes women side with women and men side with men. Her curious combination of conventional and unconventional attitudes—her willingness to sleep with a married man, but her essentially monogamous nature—reflects similar divisions in Rebecca.

Rebecca was having an affair with Stephen Martin, a handsome California banker. Although he was not a literary person, he loved poetry. He had been a casual acquaintance she had first met in 1923, but they had been lovers during her last three weeks in New York. He was a speculator, broke one day and a millionaire the next, and she had no idea if their love would last. Certainly it was far different from what she felt for Max, and she dreaded she would return to New York in January and find her new love "just a dull man with a drawl." But he sounded like Max, and she wanted it to be "real and lasting." She would not tell John his name, though she had told her new lover about John. She was not considering marriage, and she remained on friendly terms with John, always grateful for his kindness. He had become involved with another woman who would shortly become his wife.

5

THE HEARST PEOPLE at *Cosmopolitan* had suggested that Rebecca bring Anthony over to New York for the Christmas holidays, but she felt it was "no town for a child," and she was on board the *Berengaria* in mid-December. Dining with Rebecca and Anthony in London on December 21, Sappho observed Rebecca's nervous behavior while eleven-year-old Anthony went out for a walk with a friend. When the friend returned at about eight P.M., saying Anthony had decided on a longer excursion around Hyde Park, Rebecca became very agitated. Fortunately, he soon returned and they had a quiet dinner.

Anthony was sent out of the room when friends like Greta Mortimer visited. Greta had met Rebecca at drama school in London, but they had lost track of each other until Anthony was about four, when Greta accidentally encountered mother and son after the performance of a play. A puzzled Greta wondered who Anthony was, and Rebecca did not explain. Greta would become a great comfort for Rebecca, because she stood apart from the literary world and the general run of people Rebecca knew: Greta's daughter, Rosalind Burdon-Taylor, sensed that it was a relief to Rebecca to talk very frankly with her mother.

6

IMMEDIATELY AFTER Anthony started school in Hampstead on January 20, 1927, Rebecca returned to New York City. In a two-month stint, she finished her work on *War Nurse,* did another batch of reviews for *The New York Herald Tribune,* and nursed Stephen Martin who had become fatally ill. In the early spring she wrote to John Gunther, "My poor Steve died just before I left New York. I am much better now, although for about a month I had the most curious neurotic symptom. I went stone deaf! It was just a physical manifestation of my desire to hear no more bad news, I suppose."

A young movie executive approached her about writing a script. They talked in her sitting room at the Hotel Majestic until midnight and then he left. An hour later, he was at her door declaring he had been obsessed with her ever since he had seen her photograph. After meeting her, he had felt destroyed. She had made him impotent, he claimed. He had been walking in Central Park, and had come back to kill her, he said, immediately striking out at her. They struggled in the dark, and he began to strangle her. Just as she was about to lose consciousness, he fell on his knees to the floor in a kind of fit, and she rushed out of the room, made her way down a corridor, and locked herself in a bathroom. She feared a scandal and decided not to fetch anyone, instead waiting until it was light. By then he had departed.

The man's confession of impotence reminded her of Max and of a painful scene with Charlie Chaplin a fortnight earlier. Charlie claimed to have made passionate love to her because he suspected she had made him impotent and he wanted to discover if it were so. What was it about her that seemed to emasculate men? She decided to undergo psychoanalytic therapy.

7

FROM APRIL to the middle of July 1927, Rebecca resided at the Villa le Rose in Florence, writing *Sunflower* and producing six *Herald Tribune* reviews. She engaged an American lay analyst, Mary Wilshire, whom she probably met in Los Angeles during her first American tour. Rebecca thought Mary a genius, and Mary believed Rebecca made rapid progress in intensive psychotherapy, sessions lasting about two hours at first, and then developing into marathons of four hours and more. Rebecca probed her unresolved feelings and fantasies about her father. Over the course of one three-day period she gradually uncovered a "Father Violation Memory." On the first day, she summoned up a scene of weeping over her father's death. It disturbed her to recall how she had loved him and turned hostile toward her mother. This "moderately painful memory" engendered another: a scene in which her mother made some gesture checking the infant Rebecca's masturbation. The first day's session ended with Rebecca remembering her father exposing his penis to her through the bars of her cot. By the end of the third day, she had retrieved an "extremely painful" memory of her father offering the tip of his penis to her mouth and called out "Mamma. Mamma. Mamma!" Later, when her mother had applied a mustard plaster to an ailing Rebecca, the child had interpreted her mother's action as a cruel punishment for some offense committed by or against her father. Rebecca had afterward developed hysterical symptoms, in which railway carriages triggered her father violation memory. The noise of the locomotives seemed to beat on her head and body indiscriminately. Reduced to a completely helpless state of infancy, faced with an overwhelming experience that somehow brought back the "overarching" figure of her father at her crib, she would be "hauled into the railway carriage in a state of dripping misery which nobody understood."

Charles Fairfield had perverted her love with his *droit de seigneur* attitude toward women and with his ruthless disregard of the consequences of his actions. Yet Rebecca could not gainsay his power, which manifested itself in what she called an "animal fantasy." She had connected an image of her father urinating in a grove with the happy unconsciousness of animals who also urinated outside. Lettie's "face of concern" suddenly appeared in Rebecca's fantasy, as Rebecca mused on the way animals were free from the taboos of sex and concluded: "if my father and I were animals we would be free to enjoy each other."

Rebecca was angry at what she could not have, angry at her father for having the power to show her what she could not have, and angry at her mother and Lettie who dominated her reveries as so many superegos. Rebecca's notes on her analysis read like "short-circuited flashes," exhibiting the delayed, fragmentary reactions common in cases of sexual abuse, which have a kind of "sleeper effect" on the victims. But she skirted the issue of what actually happened between herself and her father. She called it a case of a "latent highly disguised sexual fantasy." But this formulation derives from her old age when her attitude toward her father had softened considerably.

8

REBECCA CALLED the other subject of her psychoanalysis her "Max complex." On a single page, in two columns, she schematized their essential traits. His sadism she interpreted as a "transferred pleasure due to impotence." Her masochism she termed a kind of expiation stemming from "guilt due to transfer of libido to father." Picking Max as a lover ensured that she would be "deprived of what I wanted"—the love affair as a form of self-punishment. She traced their interest in oral eroticism and masturbation to infantile experiences—in her case a desire for a "detached non entering penis." They were also united in a Jehovah Complex—she found his money and power attractive; he found her gifts alluring and a sign of her power. Her infatuation gratified him enormously. "His consciousness of penis answered to my penis fantasy," but "his inferiority intellectually and morally" had made him impotent. He had proved a poor substitute for the "bond between me and my father—purely sexual," Rebecca concluded.

This drawing of columns and categorization of feelings and complexes makes Rebecca's involvement with men seem allegorical, as if they were all representations of her father. What she sought was an all-embracing relationship with a man, whom she could regard as her superior, as a kind of sovereign who would be deserving of her complete devotion.

In *Sunflower,* Rebecca's heroine searches for such a sovereign. Sunflower's lover is Lord Essington, for he is Rebecca's version of H.G., of Sir Richmond in *The Secret Places of the Heart,* of the noble identity H.G. had conferred upon himself in his published fiction and in their love life as Lord Jaguar. Essington, a Liberal Party politician who has recently lost his high government office, follows H.G.'s program of acting as his young mistress's mentor and protector, while compartmentalizing her life, expecting her to cater to his whims and to baby him through his bad moods. Just turned thirty and having spent most of her twenties with him, Sunflower never wavers in her belief that Essington is a great man. But she has reached the point of wanting to leave him because he proves incapable of giving all of his heart to her and because he cannot force her to submit. Like the frustrated Wells, who never was able to convince his contemporaries about the necessity of the world state he wrote about with so much élan in his essays and novels, Essington grows increasingly fretful and aged as his views become outmoded.

Sunflower longs for a simpler existence—without the abstractions and institutions by which her friends and lover are guided. Essington calls Sunflower stupid, but her sensitivity and great humanity is itself a form of intelligence that neither Essington nor Sunflower herself (cowed by his constant criticism) recognize. It is quite clear, for example, that she is maturing as an actress—a fact Essington begrudges her but which others repeatedly acknowledge. This merging of her talent and humanity is what makes her so attractive to Francis Pitt, who seems to her to be exactly the lover she has always wanted.

Pitt, an Australian millionaire, is a surrogate for Beaverbrook. Pitt represents precisely those qualities that Essington and Wells lack. Sunflower craves Pitt's "rich and appetizing voice" like the "smell of good food cooking." He has an ape's mouth, an over-large head, and over-broad shoulders that suggest an almost pre-human personality that is appealing because it is direct and unfiltered, somehow purer than the "tangle of transmuted sweetness kindliness and sensitiveness" that distinguishes the refined Essington, who is a "more recent, more edited kind of man" than Pitt. Pitt's lion color, earthy skin, and tawny hair, the deep lines in his face that remind Sunflower of the folds in an animal's hide, his broad paw-like hands and feet, his growling sounds of pleasure, convey an elemental quality that she luxuriates in after Essington's tortuous intellectuality. Sunflower is entranced by an extraordinary scene in which he crams his hands in a glass of port while his Borzois clamber over him, licking the drops from his fingers. In short, Pitt has the animal magnetism that pervaded Rebecca's sexual fantasies.

Pitt's energy, his way of surrounding himself with all kinds of men and women, his behind-the-scenes politicking, his way of focusing on and practically burglarizing other people's personalities is a faithful rendering of what Rebecca found so fascinating about Beaverbrook. "Surely a man who loved one like that was God to one, for he made one. He gave one life," Sunflower concludes.

Of course, Rebecca's idealization of Beaverbrook was rudely ravaged by his abrupt shift away from her, and in a part of the novel Rebecca had outlined but did not develop,* Sunflower was to experience a similar rebuff. She would then tour America, entertain other suitors, try to recover her sense of humanity among Negroes and the poor while plaguing herself about Pitt's real feelings. In a note to herself, Rebecca remarked: "My treatment of the theme is weak. I must go for it boldly. He does love Sybil Fassendyll [Sunflower]—but he is afraid of her, as Charlie Chaplin was afraid of Marie Doro. She finds out that he looked for her—and dare not tell him so."

Sunflower thinks of the differences between Essington and Pitt as a "thrilling drama." Indeed, they dramatize Rebecca's feeling that she was

---

*Rebecca eventually abandoned *Sunflower*, unable to imagine a convincing conclusion and fearful of Beaverbrook's reaction. (He had sent word through novelist William Gerhardie that he was not pleased at the idea of her basing a character on him.) The incomplete novel was published in 1986.

constantly poised between two alternatives that opened up a gap she could never quite close in her writing or in her life. These options seemed not merely personal but evolutionary, and the sundering of the sexes a problem for civilization itself. Her notes for *Sunflower* read:

The Theme of the Book is
I. Women have remained close to their primitive type because doing the same job—wifehood and motherhood. Men have departed from the primitive type because they are doing utterly different jobs.
II. The type of civilisation men have produced demands great men— greatness that presses too hardly on the men. They are bound to buckle under the strain.

In a debate with Duff Cooper about whether the woman's place was in the home, a part of which was printed in *The New York Times* (September 20, 1925), Rebecca contended that there was a "great war going on today between the primitive self of man and his modern environment." No longer a hunter or agriculturalist who encountered conditions in which his courage was constantly challenged, modern man confronted mechanical and machinelike work, and his resulting passivity produced instability and hysteria. Like the notes on her psychoanalysis, *Sunflower* projects a division of the sexes she would continue to explore for the rest of her career.

CHAPTER 10

The Strange Necessity
1927–1928

I

IN THE AUTUMN OF 1927, Rebecca moved into a new flat at 80 Onslow Gardens in South Kensington. It cost no more than her Queen's Gate flat (275 pounds a year), but it was newer and roomier, with a first and second floor. Her light and airy surroundings included a large roof garden, and a living room with French windows that gave it a lofty atmosphere. She decorated her attractive siting room in soothing green and ivory colors, featuring a carved marble mantelpiece, a Chinese lacquer screen, and lots of books.

Rebecca's psychoanalysis rejuvenated her. "I feel marvelous," she wrote her American agent, George Bye, "if you hear of riots raised in Paris by the American Legion it is really me—though all in innocent playfulness." She had interrupted work on *Sunflower* to complete a book of criticism, *The Strange Necessity,* and to fulfill a lucrative contract with *T.P.'s Weekly* to write about whatever she wanted. She tossed off several articles for the *Daily Express* and *Evening News* on women's issues and social policy. She was in superb form as a public speaker, the *Yorkshire Post* (December 9, 1927) calling her "by far the most interesting woman speaker of the day. . . . What is so striking about her now is the harmony between this quiet, reflective manner, and the thing that she wants to say. She has stopped being 'clever.' " She had a searching mind and did not rely on superficial ready-made remarks—like so many British writers who had toured America and had come home to pontificate. In *The Observer* (December 11, 1927), Cecil Lewis was dazzled by her range of topics—from the making of Hollywood movies, to the theater in Bath, to the distressing economic state of Great Britain. *Truth* (December 14, 1927) reported Rebecca taking the chair at a PEN meeting, "wearing superior white satin and jade beads." Sappho heard her speak at a Claridge's tea on December 9 and then dined with her, "the most fascinating woman in London."

Rebecca complained of overwork and fatigue, which resulted in painful colitis. She coped with thirteen-year-old Anthony's illnesses, such as chicken pox. He seemed terribly tall and thin to her. He had exhibited an interest in art, and she admired his drawings, believing that he showed real promise as an artist.

Rebecca had been on reasonably good terms with H.G. for some time. A remorseful H.G. had nursed Jane through her last days suffering from cancer. When she died in October 1927, he set about collecting and editing her own writing—modestly written, oblique short fiction that reflected her elusive personality. H.G.'s introduction reaffirmed her central role in his life and how her death had devastated him. Feeling vulnerable, H.G. seemed to take more of an interest in Anthony's education. He wanted to meet with Rebecca and discuss in detail their plans for him. He was also eager to have his older son Gip meet Anthony (Gip took Anthony to the zoo), and H.G. invited Anthony to Easton Glebe for Christmas.

H.G.'s renewed interest in Anthony peeved Rebecca and made her anxious. She was used to spending her holidays with Anthony. What is more, Mrs. Wilshire had treated Anthony in Antibes and diagnosed a "terrible mother fixation," which contributed to his infantile behavior and problems at school. She believed he felt "horribly overshadowed" by H.G. and consequently inept in intellectual matters; under Rebecca's care, he had adapted as well as possible to his abnormal circumstances. A happy Anthony did spend his holidays with H.G., but Rebecca did not like it.

On January 3, 1928, H.G. wrote to Rebecca: "Evidently it is no longer possible for us to correspond . . . I see no advantage and every possibility of friction in dealing with or about him through you." Rebecca replied in kind. There would be no more letters between them. H.G. would be able to see Anthony "as before" and she would be glad if H.G. continued to promote the friendship between Anthony and his half brothers.

Anthony was being coached for a new school, Stowe. H.G. concurred in the decision, writing in April: "Anthony is going to be a very charming and worthwhile young man and it will be a pity if his prospects are injured by our bad temper. Will you let me know precisely how he stands at Stowe? Is he known to be your son? My son? Who knows what?" Once Anthony was settled there, H.G. proposed to visit him in May.

Anthony had been scheduled to enter Stowe after the first of the year, but it had been put off because of an attack of conjunctivitis. Then in the early spring of 1928 he developed a cough. Examinations indicated tuberculosis. A frightened Rebecca predicted the worst, fearing that he would not survive the disease. But his case proved mild and her concern shifted to the psychological damage he would incur as a result of being shut up in a dreary sanatorium with dying people. He had been looking forward to attending his new school, and he had adjusted well to her new flat. Now she would have to separate him from his new pet, a "disreputable Sealyham."

It was a sad period for Anthony. In May, shortly before his removal to a sanatorium in Norfolk, a grave H.G. and Gip showed up at the Onslow Gardens flat. Seeing Gip, his older half brother, who was already married, made Anthony morose over the gulf between himself and his father's other life. His quarantine in the sanatorium did nothing, of course, to relieve his sense of isolation. H.G. commiserated with Rebecca: "This misfortune of yours reopens all sorts of shut-down tendernesses and I feel like your dear brother and your best friend and your father and your once (and not quite forgetting it) lover. Count on me for any help you need." Rebecca railed against his "fake cheerfulness and his acted concern and utter heartlessness."

Rebecca spent several days in a hotel in Cromer to be near Anthony, relieved to see him looking healthy in the open air. She praised him as an "angel of patience and pluck." He wrote her cheerful letters, saying he felt well and enjoyed his pleasant fellow patients. Toward the end of his stay in the sanatorium, he became bored and restless, and Rebecca found it difficult to find a tutor to satisfy his longing for lessons. She felt constrained by the two-hour limit on her visits, which were allowed only every other day. As she feared, he became attached to two charming patients who suddenly died. H.G. visited him only once—at Rebecca's request—and he left her to pay the substantial bill of over two hundred pounds.

2

IN EARLY JUNE 1928, the success of John Van Druten's stage production of *The Return of the Soldier* cheered Rebecca. She had admired his earlier play, *Young Woodley* (1925), which she called one of "three first-rate plays written by young Englishmen since the war." He and Rebecca had met on the *Berengaria* in December 1926 sailing to England. In the summer of 1928 John joined novelists Beverly Nichols and G. B. Stern as part of Rebecca's circle at the Villa Mysto, situated between St. Raphael and Cannes.

Rebecca had fallen in love with this spot, a coastline of rose-colored rocks cutting into a turquoise sea. Enchanted with its coves and creeks, she compared swimming there to "bathing in the Book of Revelation." Her "golden playground" could be approached only by a narrow coastal road with hairpin turns. On arrival, one was greeted by a huge oleander, "pink-and-white, and full-blown," which sent out clouds of scent. A gate opened to an avenue of palms that made Rebecca think she was nearing an Oriental palace. The nights were cool; in the moonlight the dark leaves of the trees cut scimitar-shaped patterns and the trunks gleamed, standing forth like "armed giants, sinister and splendid." She drank her morning coffee on the balcony watching the "Mediterranean blue between the golden branches of mimosa" and thinking over her work. Delighted with her superb cook and a parlor maid, Rebecca spent the most contented three months of her life. She wrote every morning and read copiously at night.

Beverly Nichols had become devoted to Rebecca after suffering the "salutary crack" of her whip. He adopted her as his "invisible censor," envisioning the "mockery in her beautiful eyes" forcing him to scrap his self-indulgent prose. Rebecca remembered the young Beverly as "exceedingly handsome in the style of Sir Joshua Reynolds's Infant Samuel." Brash and gay, he "recited passages from [her] review with charming bursts of happy laughter. Nobody but a reviewer can imagine how this gets one down," she later commented.

Beverly liked watching Rebecca sunbathe, remarking that for him she blocked out all other bodies in the neighborhood. G. B. Stern remembered that Rebecca had never been in better form—full of salacious gossip, outrageous wit, and delightful silliness. Like the simplest child, she would blurt blunt truths and then turn to her friends and say, "I wasn't *rude*, was I?" G. B. Stern had known Rebecca when she was a disheveled young upstart who used to comb her hair "to a frenzy" with her agitated fingers. Now her dress, like her sitting room, exuded order. But there was a nagging problem, Stern conceded. Rebecca's detractors, miffed by the continual references to her as the "most brilliant and witty tongue of her generation," asked "Well, tell me what she has *done*? Only two novels and some journalism?"

3

IN LATE JULY 1928, Jonathan Cape published *The Strange Necessity*, a collection of essays and reviews—Rebecca's bid to consolidate her literary position, to take the measure of the best literature of her time and simultaneously to display her own quality. The title piece is an autobiographical, intricate, informal, and meandering essay, allusive, oblique, and repetitive—a new form of writing for her, not easy to follow. It had grown from six thousand to over thirty thousand words, she explained to Jonathan Cape, to whom she provided a précis that cannot be bettered for its brevity:

> It begins with a discussion of James Joyce's *Ulysses* which is probably the first estimate to be done neither praying nor vomiting. In it I come to the conclusion that though it is ugly and incompetent it is a work of art. That is to say it is *necessary*. Then I go on to discuss what is this strange necessity, art which is so inclusive of opposites?—as for instance the paintings of Ingres and the books of James Joyce? This leads to an analysis of literature, and the discovery of a double and vital function it fulfils [sic] for men. Firstly it makes a collective external brain for man; secondly it presents certain formal relations to man which suggest a universe more easy in certain respects than the one he knows.

In a subsequent letter, she asked Cape if he could see to it that *The Strange Necessity* was "treated as a technical, high brow book? Reviewable really as a book on psychology." She might have added that she had written a work of criticism and aesthetics in the form of a novel, for in it she portrays the personality of the critic, herself, in scenes and in her version of stream of consciousness writing that is itself a tribute to Joyce and even more to Marcel Proust, whom she considered Joyce's superior.

The essay's first paragraph presents a scene. Rebecca has just closed the door of a bookshop and is walking down the street toward the Boulevard St. Germain in the "best of all cities." She is exhilarated not only because of where she is, but also because she has been sold a little volume "not exactly pretentiously, indeed with a matter-of-fact briskness, yet with a sense of there being something on hand different from an ordinary commercial transaction: as they sell pious whatnots in a cathedral porch. Suddenly she stops, exclaims "Ah!" and smiles "up into the clean French light." She spies a dove "bridging the tall houses by its flight," and she feels an "interior agreement with its grace," a "delighted participation in its experience." The city, the bookshop, the book, the bird, the day—all conspire to make her spirit soar, all make up her aesthetic sense of life, the beauty that derives from the harmony human beings fashion out of their surroundings. Art is the word for that harmony; criticism is the word for the consciousness of that art.

Her first paragraph constitutes, in miniature, her entire argument: Art is what makes her whole and gives her character its integrity. What is more, art does the same for the world at large; it is a steady, cumulative fund of knowledge that is a kind of science, with each great book a type of experiment, in which the artist explores certain facets of human character—like a scientist tests hypotheses.

The first paragraph is also representative of the essay in that neither the bookshop nor the book is named, and why the book should be sold in a matter-of-fact but devout manner is not explained. Often her points are withheld, and a reader not attuned to her reason for doing so will be irritated as she recycles her scenes. Why doesn't she say it all at once? Because she is implying she does not know it all at once. She is writing, in other words, as she thinks, as she is formulating her ideas, which are based on her experience on this day in Paris. To apprehend *how* she has arrived at her position on art she must be accompanied on her day, just as one follows the characters in *Ulysses* on their day in Dublin, just as one parses Proust's long sentences to understand the grammar, the structure of human consciousness. Understanding art is not a matter of drawing a straight line between points.

It would be tedious to recapitulate paragraph by paragraph an essay that extends over two hundred printed pages—indeed, Rebecca's Proustian inventiveness sometimes flags as *The Strange Necessity* veers perilously close to a pretentious exercise. She has to work terribly hard at showing how Pavlov's experiments with dogs resemble the artist's experiments with humanity, since each, she believes, carries on a methodical inquiry into the mind that has advanced knowledge.

Rebecca concludes that art is nothing less than the organ of pleasure that ties the world together for human beings. This is why, she reminds us in the last ten pages of the essay, she found so much pleasure on her day in Paris in what she finally names as Sylvia Beach's bookshop, closing one of the many circles in her argument. Literature has helped her to establish herself in the universe, to understand why it is better to live than to die. This last point is a curious one, evolving out of her Freudian sense that human beings are caught between their conflicting impulses to live and to die, and out of an even more personal conviction that "life has treated me as all the children of man like a dog from the day I was born." *The Strange Necessity* ends on a symphonic note:

> And that I should feel this transcendent joy simply because I have been helped to go on living suggests that I know something I have not yet told my mind, that within me I hold some assurance regarding the value of life, which makes my fate different from what it appears, different, not lamentable, grandiose.

As she said of *Ulysses*, her own essay is a daring, extraordinary effort, for all its faults. That grandiose can be defined as both pompous and magnificent suggests the risk she knew she was taking in setting forth herself as an exemplar of her ideas.

4

THE STRANGE NECESSITY received mixed to negative reviews. On August 9, 1928, Arnold Bennett—one of her "uncles," as she termed Wells, Shaw, and Galsworthy in *The Strange Necessity*—published a review of her book in the *Evening Standard*. Under the title, "My Brilliant But Bewildering 'Niece,' " he lauded her acuity and facility but deplored her need to perform. "She must be odd," and it led her into "irresponsible silliness." In effect, he accused her of being arbitrary in words that were perhaps meant as a tit-for-tat, since she had remarked in her essay "Uncle Bennett" that "there are innumerable occasions when one suspects that he writes, not because he has something to say, but because of that abstract desire to write, which is hardly ever the progenitor of good writing."

In *The Bookman* (August 1929), Conrad Aiken said of *The Strange Necessity*, "she writes very badly. . . . If she could somehow manage to treat her audience a little less as if it were gathered for tea and her writers a little less as if they were dilapidated lions collected for the occasion to have their manes combed and their tails pulled—one might be surer of her future position. As it is, one feels that perhaps her future years are numbered." In *Transition* (1929), William Carlos Williams admired her exposition, conceding the validity of several of her points, but he objected to her "hieratical assurance," alleging that she had misread Joyce. His full-scale defense of Joyce only convinced her that she now had become the target of Joyce's adherents. In *The Saturday Review of Literature* (November 10, 1928), Edward Garnett seconded her view of Joyce, but added: "Miss West struggles with Professor Pavlov and her materialistic confusions remind one of an enterprising baby with a bucket of tar. Everything round gets horribly smeared."

In *The New York Times* (December 2, 1928), Hugh Walpole praised Rebecca's method even as he took exception to many of her judgments, citing the "completeness of her investigatory power that is not to be found in many critics. The reader knows why and how she achieves her particular positions, for there are no blurred edges to her processes." Wyndham Lewis, who had attacked Joyce in *Time and Western Man* on similar lines, sent her his compliments. She was gratified to receive a long letter (it has not survived) from Havelock Ellis, evincing a detailed understanding of her argument. George Bernard Shaw did not react to her treatment of him in her essay on her literary uncles (his mind was marvelous and shining but too thin), except to drop a sociable note, signing himself "your too affectionate uncle G. Bernard Shaw."

Always a faithful courtier, Alexander Woollcott complimented her, expressing special enthusiasm for *The Strange Necessity*, which encouraged her to detail how her feelings had been rubbed raw: "most of the reviews are declarations of personal dislike against me by people I have never met, chiefly on the ground that I am a society butterfly who ought not to occupy myself with these serious questions."

Rebecca took H.G.'s initial response in July to *The Strange Necessity* as a jab: "Dear Ex Panther, *The Strange Necessity* is marvellous. It ought to have music by Stravinsky." He tried again: "Dear Pussy. I didn't dislike *The Strange Necessity*. I only said it ought to have music by Stravinsky. Can't I tickle you in the ribs when you dig into mine?" Nettled by her treatment of him as Uncle Wells, and her invention of a character, Queenie, to satirize the mawkish love affairs in his novels, he called her a "lazy Panther" repeating her "cherished delusions. There never was a Queenie but you've said it so often you've got to believe it." His next letter whined: "it sets people who havent read me against my books." By August, he was bringing in the big artillery:

The Strange Necessity only does for your critical side what the Judge did for your pretensions as a novelist. You have a most elaborate, intricate and elusive style which is admirably adapted for a personal humorous novel. It can convey the finest shades of sympathy, ridicule and laughter. It is no good whatever for a philosophical discourse any more than it was for a great romance about the tragedy and injustice of life. You are ambitious and pretentious and you do not know the quality & measure of your powers. Some of the Return of the Soldier though the style is Conrad-haunted is admirable. Chunks of the Judge are magnificent. As a whole it is a sham. So is this book a sham. It is a beautiful voice and a keen and sensitive mind doing "Big thinks" to the utmost of its ability— which is nil. God gave you all the gifts needed for a fine and precious artist and he left out humility. And humility in the artist is what charity is in the saint.

There my dear Pussy is some more stuff for your little behind. You sit down on it and think.

H.G. did not mention it, but part of his anger was surely aroused by the personal images of him found in *The Strange Necessity*, shut up in a drawing room, putting out all the lights except a single lamp with a "pink silk shade," and sitting at the piano having a "lovely time warbling in too fruity a tenor." She continued this demasculinization in her comment on the "passages where his prose suddenly loses its firmness and begins to shake like blanc-mange."

Rebecca may have been miffed that he was still using her as a model for his characters. In *The World of William Clissold* (1926), she appears as the fearless Helen, who is disposed of with smug superiority. Helen is not a malign portrait—indeed she embodies many of Rebecca's wonderful, social qualities—but Rebecca resented his characterization of their "selfish fellowship" and her fictional transformation into a successful actress devoted to the business of exploiting her personality.

5

REBECCA FELT beleaguered by the reviews of *The Strange Necessity* and her jousting with H.G., who sent her insulting letters by "every post." To Lettie she cried: "All men are mad." Through psychoanalysis, she had come to realize that she was full of guilt and possessed of a disposition which in less favorable circumstances would have disposed her to believe she had sinned against the Holy Ghost. Because her family had been hypercritical of her, her sense of guilt had increased, while also inducing a great measure of hostility in her which she feared she expressed in writing "apt to strike people as unsympathetic."

But Rebecca had started another novel, *Harriet Hume*, which she hoped to finish by Christmas 1928. Perhaps it would compensate for what she glumly supposed others were calling a "sterile and erratic career."

CHAPTER II

Sex Antagonism
1928–1929

I

ON SEPTEMBER 23, 1928, Rebecca sailed for New York City. She would stay for little more than a month, gathering material for short stories that would eventually be published in *The Harsh Voice* (1935), and continuing her reviewing for *The New York Herald Tribune*. Anthony had made a full recovery from tuberculosis and would enter Stowe soon. But Rebecca had had such a scare during the agonizing months of May and June that she did not want to leave him any longer.

The pieces Rebecca wrote in the fall of 1928 are unremarkable, except for her *Herald Tribune* review of Virginia Woolf's fantasy novel, *Orlando*. Rebecca called it a "poetic masterpiece." Orlando, born in the Elizabethan period and still alive, exemplified the development of civilization and of both sexes. Especially intrigued by the passages in which Orlando undergoes a sex change from male to female, Rebecca maintained that they were the heart of the book because Woolf was "debating . . . how far one's sex is like a pair of faulty glasses on one's nose; where one looks at the universe, how true it is that to be a woman is to have a blind spot on the North Northwest, to be a man is to see light as darkness East by South."

The review was one of those fortuitous instances of great minds thinking alike, for Rebecca herself was close to finishing a novel, *Harriet Hume*, which she would subtitle a "London fantasy," and which explored the differences between the sexes, demonstrating what would happen to a woman who could actually enter a man's mind and think his thoughts. Virginia Woolf wrote to Rebecca in appreciation: "I can't tell you how it exhilarates me to feel your mind running along where mine tried to go (what a lot more you have guessed of my meaning than anybody else!) and expanding and understanding and making everything ten times more important than it seemed before."

2

By MID-NOVEMBER 1928, Rebecca had returned to London, happy to find fourteen-year-old Anthony in good form and about to enter Stowe. She intended to remain at home until the spring, except for ten days with Anthony in Paris for Christmas. She was keeping it from H.G.—"a man of scrambled domesticities"—to scotch an anticipated invitation to Christmas dinner with H.G. and Odette Keun, his current mistress.

Since 1925, H.G. had been spending part of the year in the South of France at Grasse with Odette, the daughter of Dutch and Italian parents, a volatile personality with a salty tongue. Like H.G.'s other women, she had pursued him, pledged her devotion to him, then became maddened by his waywardness. Rebecca liked her. They shared a jolly cynicism: At the funeral of one of H.G.'s mistresses, Rebecca is supposed to have turned to Odette and remarked, "Well, I guess we can all move one up."

Odette was kind to Anthony when he visited her and H.G. but Rebecca worried about his campaign to see more of his son, inviting Anthony for weekends at Easton Glebe, and announcing: "I'd like him to take a place here." The predictable skirmish over the holidays occurred on schedule: "I think your refusal to let Anthony go to Easton for Christmas one of the most malicious things you have ever done. He loses the chance of getting upon jolly terms with his half brothers, he loses a bright time. For a mere whim of yours," H.G. declared.

It was no mere whim. She was reliving the terrible times when Anthony had not been received at Easton Glebe, when Jane was still alive and H.G.'s bastard son would have been an embarrassment to her. Now with Jane out of the way, H.G.'s path was clear. He thought only of himself—not of all those years when he had kept Rebecca and Anthony on the sidelines. Now that Anthony was of an age when H.G. could act as mentor to him, when Anthony had bright things to say and could amuse his father, Rebecca felt exploited and robbed of the reward of enjoying her son.

Alarmed that Anthony's growing affection for his father jeopardized her position as his custodian, Rebecca sought the advice of an attorney, Theobald Mathew. Their correspondence reveals that she came to rely heavily on his counsel and developed great affection for him, remarking many years later that he was the "nearest thing to a brother I've ever had in my life." Following Mathew's instruction, she instituted an action to adopt Anthony. She intended to spare her son the embarrassment of producing a birth certificate on which no father had been specified. Mathew also suggested the possibility that Anthony be made a "Ward of Court," in case H.G. "did in the future make any effort to interfere in any way."

Rebecca treated H.G.'s outrage at these legal maneuvers as irrational, and the efforts of his lawyers to thwart them as mean-spirited; she vented her grievances over the occasions when he had not troubled himself about his son and she had carried all the emotional burden. Yet H.G., however tardily, was asserting a father's rights; the impact on Anthony was palpable: "Every day there was something new and exciting to do, and everything we did was made to seem amusing." Getting his father's attention was gratifying, even though in a few years Anthony would show that he too harbored hostility over H.G.'s years of neglect. Rebecca did not see the damage she was doing herself by insisting on the adoption, that in time Anthony would conclude she had done her best to separate him from his father, while professing to be concerned only about his welfare. When Anthony returned home refreshed from his Easton Glebe visits, he sensed that his mother considered him disloyal, and that in some way he was his father's "accomplice." Rebecca suspected that H.G. was "up to something," but she could not imagine what. She never asked her son about his visits to his father, and thus left him wondering: "What is it all supposed to be about?" It had taken him years to read her expressions, to decipher that "slightly glazed look" that preceded her histrionics. She played the "wronged mother," in a "scene of tenderness with her only son who misunderstood her." He detected a "hint of music in her voice"—a sure sign she was calculating the "effect of her words and not speaking entirely naturally." Rebecca had overreacted to H.G.'s overtures to Anthony, to what she considered the caprices of a fickle father—a type she knew too well. She would never be able to see it from Anthony's side, that he was willing to take such love as H.G. had it in him to give. For her, that kind of love had never been enough. Why should it be good enough for her son?

3

ANTHONY FOUND the adjustment to Stowe difficult: "in response to a wail of agony . . . I will have to give Anthony a Latin tutor in the holidays. He is, of course, dreadfully backward owing to his long absence from school," Rebecca wrote to Winnie on March 7, 1929. Rebecca had visited him and had been impressed with the openness of the school and the happy faces of the children. Stowe was relatively new, having been established six years earlier by J. F. Roxburgh, who had set out to reform the public school as he had known it in his boyhood. It would still offer an education for gentlemen, but it would be less regimented and the curriculum more open to modern literature, the visual arts, and nature than its nineteenth-century models. Instead of simply learning from a pre-scribed reading list, the boys would be encouraged to draw and to paint, and to move beyond "set books." Above all, Roxburgh wanted to give his boys "freedom in their daily lives." There were to be no petty rules "about dress or about who could walk where."

When Rebecca visited Anthony in late March, she reported to Win-nie that he was "quite well." But he was not happy. However grand and caring Stowe might have been, it did not suit him. For Roxburgh had only been partially successful in remedying the worst features of the pub-lic school. He had not abolished fagging, the system by which a younger boy waits upon and serves an older boy, and he had not ensured that the boys would be free from beating when they failed in their prescribed duties or disobeyed the rules. That these beatings were often inflicted by the older boys once again put Anthony at risk, because he had never been able to withstand bullying.

One other factor put the finishing touch on Anthony's two-year career at Stowe. Noel Annan, who was Anthony's junior by two years and who had a splendid time at Stowe, recalls that Anthony had the "misfortune of having this narrow-minded, authoritarian housemaster." A housemaster is a very important figure in a boy's life at public school, particularly in the early years, and it was obvious to Annan that Anthony had crossed his housemaster. He was miserable, a sour, unhappy boy who treated his fellows rudely. H.G. visited Anthony, sud-denly putting him into an adult world for four or five hours, but then he would be returned to the awful grind and to a censorious housemaster who did not approve of H.G.'s visits. No matter how liberal Stowe might be by public school standards, it would seem a confining place for Anthony.

Rebecca wanted to believe that he had finally settled down, and the surviving letters he wrote to her from Stowe seem light-hearted. He reported progress in his drawing and writing, and his letters were some-times illustrated and decorated with doggerel. But he was guarded: "I have had a spell of thought lately . . . The thoughts won't be seen by you as they aren't of a sufficiently mature or considered nature." Anthony later remembered an indulgent but detached mother, who left an order at Fortnum and Mason to send him a pound of strawberries a week as soon as they were in season. His judgment would have shocked Rebecca, because she communicated frequently with Roxburgh and his staff and visited Anthony virtually every fortnight during his first term at Stowe.

4

In June, Rebecca settled her legal battle with H.G. She prevailed with the adoption, but the terms set out by a judge required her to consult H.G. about Anthony's education, to permit Anthony to spend part of his holidays with his father, and to name H.G. as Anthony's guardian should she die. She remained uneasy, and the wrangles over travel arrangements and times for Anthony's visits to H.G. continued. She wanted Anthony to spend the end of the summer with her at Agay, in the South of France, after he completed his term at Stowe, whereas H.G. wanted him at Easton Glebe. From the Villa Mysto in Agay, on July 23, Rebecca instructed Anthony: "Write to H.G.—THIS IS IMPORTANT—and say I have told you he wants you to go to Easton with a tutor in September that I would like to have the tutor here because you don't want to miss the swimming. If you like tell him you would rather go in the Christmas or Easter holidays than now." Anthony did come to the Villa Mysto, but H.G. also had him for part of September.

Roxburgh had written to her about Anthony's deficiencies in mathematics and in the classics, suggesting the need for a tutor, and she planned to employ one while Anthony enjoyed the company of people friendly to him. To Agay, Rebecca had invited Lady Rhondda, the owner of *Time and Tide* (Rebecca was a frequent contributor), the Melvilles (friends since her days at Leigh-on-Sea), and a new companion, twenty-year-old Pamela Frankau, daughter of the novelist Gilbert Frankau and a promising writer herself. Rebecca once described her as a "Jewish gazelle," and at another time as "beautiful in the manner of Disney's Bambi."

Pamela already knew several of Rebecca's confidants, especially G. B. Stern and John Van Druten. Pamela had been apprehensive about her first meeting with Rebecca, expecting the "cleverest woman in the world" to have a "brilliant, hawklike face with some form of oriental turban above it." She was surprised to greet a thirty-six-year-old woman smaller than herself, who held her head high and moved and spoke with light, rapid movements. Rebecca broke down whatever reserve there might have been between them by making Pamela laugh until tears ran. In this early phase of the relationship, Pamela worshipped Rebecca. Much later, Pamela described Rebecca as a woman of "passionate, whirling loyalties" that made Pamela a little afraid of her.

Rebecca's summers in Agay with Pamela and G. B. Stern (recently divorced from her husband) proved a wonderful refuge, a kind of "female Republic" that enchanted the maturing Anthony, who had never before been exposed to so many women's bodies "baking in the sun." To Lettie, Rebecca explained: "I daren't have any men here for fear of H.G. which is a pity for Anthony, but it can't be helped." Not surprisingly, Pamela became Anthony's focus of attention, and they spent hours talking—often about sex. "The way I had been brought up had given me the idea that a woman was the thing to be, and that I had somehow done wrong by being a male," Anthony later told Victoria Glendinning. He appreciated that Pamela treated him as an equal, that she cared for him, and seemed to listen so attentively to his confused ideas. Observing the "wonderful swims" Pamela and Anthony took together, Rebecca delighted in their companionship. Pamela continued their friendship by visiting him at Stowe, visits he facilitated by requesting from Rebecca spending money for lunches with her. On one occasion, he asked his mother to hire a car for Pamela's trip to Stowe. "I doubt if even/Helen of Troy/Could my Pamela's/Charm destroy," reads one of Anthony's verses.

In Agay, Pamela introduced Rebecca to Pat Wallace Frere. (The daughter of the writer Edgar Wallace, she married the publisher A. S. Frere in 1932.) A great admirer of Rebecca's work, Pat, like Pamela, anticipated meeting Rebecca with some trepidation. But over lunch they divided their acquaintances between puffingers and pussingers, a game Rebecca often played with her intimates and which immediately endeared her to Pat. Rebecca also invented an elaborate fantasy about Lady Mary, a formidable figure who owned a summer house along the dangerous narrow coast road leading to the Villa Mysto. From a car all one could see were the steep drops to the sea. Driving past a part of the road that had a wall with wire netting above it Rebecca asked Pat, "Did you see that? There must have been a gate there." Naturally it had to be Lady Mary's. "Ring the bell and drop a thousand feet," Rebecca announced. Her cozy little jokes surprised Pat. She had not expected Rebecca West to have such a nice and silly side, so pleasure giving and affectionate. Pat thought of herself as a "peripheral bore," yet Rebecca never treated her to a captious or cross word.

5

IN MID-AUGUST, Rebecca described H.G. as perpetually making her life a "burden by attempts to take Anthony away from me." She claimed that in court his lawyer had tried to prove her an "undesirable person unfit to have charge of him." (Actually, H.G.'s lawyer had cast aspersions on Rebecca's character to her lawyer, Theobald Mathew, not to the judge.)

Suspecting that H.G. would foment some new disturbance if she resumed her fall book reviewing in New York for the *Herald Tribune*, she wanted to stay put and do her reviews in London.

The legal fees from Charles Russell, Theobald Mathew's firm, came to over ninety pounds for the period January to July 1929, and an edgy Rebecca was still communicating with Mathew on September 11 about how to hand Anthony over to H.G. later that month: "I cannot tell you how maddening it has been to hunt for the tutor and not hear when H.G. was going to be back. To say nothing of Anthony's disappointment because H.G. would neither come to stay here nor travel with him."

At this point, a desperate Rebecca wrote to Bertrand Russell, whom she had first met at the age of seventeen. She had grown up hearing about his distinguished family from her mother and father, and he had always been kind to her. She recapitulated her story of H.G.'s bad behavior since she had left him in 1923, highlighting his cruelty to Anthony, and rather going over the top in making her case: "He was furious if I devoted any time to the child, and he loved exposing the child to strangers by advertising he was his illegitimate child. . . . He has never in his life seen Anthony except at my suggestion." One provision in their recent court settlement nettled her, that she had to make H.G. Anthony's guardian in her will. H.G. now seemed insane to her, possessed of an "anti-sex complex like Tolstoy's—you punish the female who evokes your lust." He was doing it now to Odette, who had actually bragged about it to Rebecca, saying H.G. frequently hit her and gave her black eyes. H.G. had also gone down to Stowe at the end of last term and created trouble. Now he had taken Anthony away from her lovely summer villa for the last three weeks of his holidays, and she was chagrined to admit that the "boy adores him. I've always brought him up to do so, which I rather regret now." She could not bear to think what would happen to Anthony if she died and H.G. became bored, getting his fun by "frustrating him at any crisis." Would Russell, therefore, act as Anthony's testamentary guardian also? She knew of no other man who could act on her behalf, and her sisters were "silly and inexperienced." She did not trust any of her friends to know enough about children to act wisely. She would see to it in her will that Russell would incur no expense. There was no one else of his stature to whom she could appeal, and "H.G. is afraid of you and wouldn't dare to oppose you, or do anything in your sight that was manifestly reactionary." She realized it was a lot to ask, but she counted on Russell's compassion.

Russell equivocated, and Rebecca sent a reassuring letter in late September, saying "you are one of the few people whose good opinion he

[H.G.] desires. That is why I particularly want you to do the job." She attributed H.G.'s "frenzy" to Jane's death, which broke up their conspiracy to "persecute the sexual woman." Russell responded on October 9 with a sympathetic but noncommittal letter, noting he had no trouble accepting her interpretation of H.G.'s behavior. "I took a dislike to him in 1905 when he visited me for the week-end. This dislike was increased during the Amber episode, and not diminished by his attack on me [for Russell's pacifism] during the war. However, since then he has gone out of his way to be nice to me. I do not know anything of his attitude about you and Anthony." Russell suggested that after the death of Jane, H.G. became hostile toward any woman who had once attracted him sexually. But he doubted her thesis about an "anti-sex complex." Ambition and vanity seemed quite enough to describe H.G.: "WOMAN tempts him to acts which are ill thought of not which he thinks ill of." Although Rebecca was quite willing to accept Russell's offer to see her attorney, in the end he backed away from involvement in Rebecca's affairs, and she decided to appoint Mathew as Anthony's guardian.

6

THROUGHOUT HER TROUBLES with H.G., Rebecca spoke of "sex antagonism," of her doubts that men and women could get along. Harriet Hume was another attempt to explain why. It reads almost like a replacement for Sunflower, the novel she did not know how to complete. Harriet Hume, a pianist, is the artist who by reading her lover's mind strips him of his self-deceptions. She is a "white witch" who, in the words of the novel's epigraph, is "mischievously good." Arnold Condorex, a politician whose name suggests both his scheming, predatory side and his kingly, even noble qualities, is confronted by Harriet on the eve of his ruin. She is his better half, his conscience, whom he rejects but continues to confront on every occasion he sees her. Angered by her exposure of his plotting (he has become a government minister through various intrigues), he ends up trying to murder her for standing against his ambition to dominate and to move up in the world.

Condorex is a self-made man who finds his position precarious because he has not been born to wealth, class, or position. He has had to scramble for everything and thinks in terms of the power he is gaining or losing in every turn of the political wheel. In love with Harriet, he nevertheless rejects her as abruptly as Max rejected Rebecca, because Arnold sees that Harriet's love is all-enveloping; it penetrates deep within him, and it is not something he can control. To invite her into his life as an equal is to lay bare thoughts to which even his closest confederates have not been privy. Every time Arnold meets Harriet, he falls under the spell of her exquisite art; every time she provides evidence of her prescience he flees.

Harriet is like a work of art looking for a body in which to incarnate herself. She is attracted to Arnold because of his immersion in the social and political life of Westminster, the seat of government. She is a creature of her South Kensington flat, which conforms in basic details to Rebecca's 80 Onslow Gardens, and she is pictured as a goddess in her garden awakened to life by Arnold as Adam, whom she is quite willing to make the first man in her life, just as he is in her thoughts. Her power to invade his mind, exposing the conniving world he actually lives in, enrages him because he has to examine himself and consider the implications of his actions. He knows that what he is thinking appears only a second later in Harriet's mind. But that it is a second later is what makes it art, not life. As Harriet laments, "I know it, yet I know it a second too late! 'Tis the artist's special quality and defect!" Art can only master itself—not compete with the world in which Arnold wants to be king.

Arnold, like Max, has it in him to think like an artist and to appreciate art. "How like you are to me," Harriet tells Arnold. She assures him that had he wanted to, he could also read her mind. But the last thing Arnold and his prototype Max wanted to do was to enclose themselves in a woman's private world—as enticing as Harriet's flat and Rebecca's 80 Onslow Gardens had been for their lovers. If Rebecca felt she was rejected as a woman, Harriet is the principle of femininity itself which Arnold rejects, for he declares that he has "never known a woman with more exquisite understanding of the female person." Because he so wants to feel superior he spurns even Harriet's compassion.

As an embodiment of art, as still as a tree in her immovable grace, Harriet represents everything that Arnold cannot manipulate; she becomes for him a strange necessity which he confronts at the end of the novel. He regards her as his "malign opposite," and he tries to treat her like a political opponent who must be gotten out of the way. But as she says earlier in the novel, she refuses to die, and she invokes the aid of two policemen who (it is gradually revealed by their use of the past tense) are dead. There is a hint that Arnold has shot himself and that this last scene of stalking Harriet occurs in a spectral realm on the edge of eternity, the point at which the couple can be reconciled, since both are beyond the contest of individual wills.

The style of *Harriet Hume* is arch. The prim and formal quality critic

Joseph Warren Beach admires has put off some readers. Virginia Woolf thought it "tight and affected and occasionally foppish beyond endurance, but then it is a convention and she does it deliberately, and it helps her to manufacture some pretty little China ornaments for the mantelpiece." The style helped distance Rebecca from the anguish of *Sunflower,* while remaining faithful to the earlier work's themes. *Harriet Hume* does somehow have the quality of Mozart—as Beach suggests— the music Rebecca often played to calm herself. It also reflects her versatility, for it is as different from *The Judge* as that novel is from *The Return of the Soldier. Harriet Hume* has some of the poetry, founded on sharp observation, that Rebecca lauded in *Orlando:* Harriet observes the chaperones at a party dozing in their "corsets like jellies left overnight in their moulds."

The novel's best sentences carry the rhythm of a fantasy, a self-enclosed world. At its finest moments *Harriet Hume* demonstrates how politics can become a species of fantasy, a matter of words in a game agreed upon by its participants that bears little connection to reality. The joke in *Harriet Hume* is that Arnold has received his title of Lord Mondh by writing about and championing an obscure Far Eastern country, Mondh, that does not exist. His title—indeed his whole reputation—is built upon nothing. But he speaks so learnedly of Mondh that his words are treated as facts. Of an old, decrepit politician Harriet remarks: "Though he himself is not quite a living man, his faltered words and shaken gestures reflected, like an old and clouded mirror, the speech and carriage of a living man." The circularity of the sentence apes the circularity of the political world, palsied and corrupt, and a mere shadow play of the real world it purports to reflect. *Harriet Hume* is a satire, a biting account of the futility of political factions, of the way every seemingly sly grab at power rebounds viciously on itself. Yet the mood at the end of the novel is one of conciliation—not that the conflict between men and women has been resolved—but rather that the warring sides of an argument have conceded each other's good points without relinquishing their dispute. For Harriet does not know what eternity has in store for them as a couple; what she does know is that there is such a thing as an amity of opposites.

H.G. concurred. On September 13, he wrote to Rebecca, calling *Harriet Hume* "charming. It's more your stuff than anything you have ever written hitherto. You've got your distinctive fantasy and humour into it and it gives play for just the peculiar intricate wittiness which is one of your most delightful and inimitable characteristics." He saluted her as a writer who had wakened from her "intellectual trances. It's a joy to praise you unreservedly. Homage and admiration." He recommended that she read Jung, because she was "driving at the same thing in the love-antagonism of Harriet and Arnold. To use Jung's slang she is Arnold's *anima*." H.G.'s praise did not mollify her: "I got a letter from H.G. praising *Harriet Hume* but expressing wonder that I should have been capable of writing it in my state of deplorable abandonment to sloth and bad habits," she wrote to G. B. Stern.

CHAPTER 12

Rebecca Cicily
1929–1930

I

REBECCA YEARNED for male companionship and marriage. Then in the autumn of 1929, she met a banker, thirty-five-year-old Henry Andrews. Thoroughly versed in Rebecca's work, he had seen the dramatization of *The Return of the Soldier* six times. He had been wanting to meet her. They were introduced at the writer Vera Brittain's home. Rebecca admired Vera for her "dogged" intellectual and moral qualities, and the stoicism that had served her well as a nurse during the gruesome war years. Vera gave Henry her warmest endorsement. He had been a New College, Oxford, contemporary of George Catlin, her husband, having returned to the university from an internment in Germany that had lasted for the duration of the war. Vera observed that the experience had "developed in him a measure of kindness and tolerant wisdom considerably beyond the unexacting standards of the average Englishman."

For two hours Henry sat on a floor cushion at the feet of the usually restless Rebecca. He was one of those gallant men who had a "wonderful knack of making you feel the only woman in the world." They discovered a mutual passion for France, and Rebecca confided to Henry that at Vezelay she had experienced the "greatest aesthetic emotion" of her life, when she had climbed the steep street and looked across the square at Christ and his Apostles over the portal of the Abbey of St. Mary Magdalen. Henry accompanied her home afterward. He sent her flowers and came calling at her flat.

At a party Rebecca pointed out Henry to her friend Pat Wallace Frere: "You see that man with sides but no back to his head. That's Henry." Immediately christened the Elk, his tall and robust mother naturally became the "Elk Dame." Pat liked Henry's beautiful eyes. "They were bluer than blue. Sympathetic, but not cold banker's eyes." Pat did not think Henry handsome, but something in the manner of this tall, thin, plain man, who addressed the volatile Rebecca as "Cicily, dear child," kept her friends "in stitches." Unlike some friends, Pat did not find Henry dull: "You had to take a little trouble. If you're very fond of someone, as I was of Rebecca, and they love somebody, then you're fascinated why."

Impeccably well-mannered and steeped in European art and literature, Henry seemed a godsend. He knew at once the kind of tone to take with Rebecca, and she responded graciously. Their courtship did not begin in earnest until early 1930, when she returned from another month-long stay in New York City, where she had continued her book reviews for the *Herald Tribune* and wrote a literary column for *The Bookman*.

2

REVIEWING THE REPORT of Anthony's poor performance at Stowe, H.G. wrote to Rebecca on January 1, 1930: "It means we have neglected the formal education of our exceptionally brilliant boy so that he figures as a backward one." H.G. was appalled at Anthony's lack of preparation in science ("he's over fifteen!"), and he scoffed at the report's suggestion that his son had a "block" over Latin. He simply had not done enough.

Rebecca replied with a correction: "I am afraid you've got the facts about Anthony's education rather dark in your mind." The trouble had begun at St. Piran's where "he learned nothing." But she had done her best since then with tutors that coached him during every break from school. Every master who had taught him Latin believed he had a block, so there was no point in saying he had not had enough of it. She found it insufferable for him to suggest "we have neglected" his education. Her anger interrupted her work.

Henry Andrews did his best to console Rebecca, who now had put her confidence in him. "Please, please don't think any more about the HG worry," she wrote to him in mid-January in Berlin, where he was employed by the German banking firm, Schroder's. She had always been able to triumph in her fights with H.G., she assured Henry, and her good fortune in having supportive friends canceled out H.G.'s cruelty. Henry's sympathy, in particular, had "made the difference between heaven and hell!" A few days later, Rebecca sent a letter to his Swiss address: "It has been so lovely waking up every morning and getting a guarantee that you're really as interesting (among other things) as I remember you." He was a good lover, she later noted, "he was everything I could have hoped for in lovingness and passion."

Throughout their courtship in 1930, she signed her letters to him Rebecca Cicily. For she was simultaneously the writer he respected and the woman who revealed her family troubles and sought his protection. She had rehearsed for him the history of the "implacable hostility" and sadism H.G. and Max had practiced upon her, and she presented herself as "terrified and defeated." He became her "darling," her champion, her knight. Now thirty-seven and a little tired, she wanted calm. "In the evening I dined with Evelyn Waugh and a covey of Bright Young People, which wasn't so good," she told Henry. This woman of the world craved a quieter, less demanding, and sheltering relationship.

Rebecca Cicily dined with Henry whenever he was in London, and he called her from Germany throughout the first months of 1930. They were considering marriage. She sought Henry's advice about Anthony. After a talk with Roxburgh, Anthony's headmaster at Stowe, she was beginning to think he was "ineducable." Recently Anthony had asked Roxburgh to be excused from attendance at chapel because he objected to Christianity. He especially rejected the Bishop's views on birth control. Yet Rebecca thought he was well liked at school and that his drawing showed promise, even if it lacked finish.

Emily Hahn, a young writer and friend of John Gunther's visiting London, got a glimpse of Anthony and Rebecca together. The malicious talk about other people startled Emily. When Rebecca made a scathing remark about someone, Anthony seemed eager to say something equally cutting. "He sneered. A sixteen-year-old boy sneering," Emily marveled.

A genial H.G. visited a perplexed Rebecca, who told Winnie that he had behaved as though there had been no acrimony between them. The next day he wrote to apologize for having worried and wounded her. He would try to be more considerate. He was shocked at how little they had laughed together the previous evening. "I think you have rather an exceptional power of diffusing highly refractive mists about you and seeing things in the wrong proportions." He asked her to think about how much he had loved her and how bitter it had been to end their companionship. He had felt humiliated and exasperated and she had made him "suffer pretty badly. Even now not to see you well distresses me. When you score any success I say, which is absurd, " 'That's my Panther.' " She had been shocked at his making jokes over D. H. Lawrence's recent death. Her diary entry on his visit reads: "Absolutely mad."

3

ON MAY 1, 1930, Rebecca settled in again at the Villa Mysto in Agay, having spent much of April in Paris and in the south visiting cathedrals and museums. Henry visited Agay, but work kept him away most of the time. June Head Fenby, Rebecca's friend and secretary, thought Rebecca was happy with Henry, "except that she was never happy with anyone really." June found him hard to fathom: "a person to himself." Rebecca later described Henry as "odd to look at," a sort of giraffe of a man, but gentle and "beautifully dressed." Emily Hahn, who had not met Henry yet, asked Rebecca about him. What was he like? What did he look like? Was he handsome? "Yes," Rebecca said, "from the neck down." Winnie destroyed letters in which Rebecca referred to Henry in less than romantic terms. Winnie's daughter Alison remembered one in which Rebecca said she "fancied" Henry very much. "She didn't go so far as to say she loved him."

Rebecca sent Henry ardent letters and stories about her spring and summer in France. He replied with several letters and telegrams each week, calling Rebecca his "loving delight." He looked in on Anthony, monitored his progress at school, and took him to lunch, reporting that Anthony spoke of her sweetly and expressed a hopeful attitude about schoolwork. Henry encouraged her to finish her work on *Ending in Earnest*, a collection of her *Bookman* articles, and otherwise to rest herself.

It was generally assumed that Henry was a wealthy man—not only because he was a banker, but also because of his penchant for lavishing gifts on his friends. Certainly Anthony's earliest impressions were that Henry had money. In fact, Henry had lost a good deal of it in the stock market crash, having bought heavily on margin, and was now relying on his salary. Rebecca suggested that they pool their resources and go forward with their marriage plans. She was making enough from her writing, so he need not worry about supporting her.

Spurred by her generosity, Henry took the next step. In mid-August, he consulted his formidable Uncle Ernest, his father's brother, who had taken up Henry with a heavy hand after the early death of Henry's father, Louis, in 1908, when Henry was fourteen. A relieved and delighted Henry reported that his uncle approved of their plans and would help Henry financially after they married. Henry now felt their uncertainty at an end. It was a great moment, since his uncle had been a father to him.

Rebecca would not learn the full story of Henry's background until several years into their marriage. But even his admission of financial difficulties signaled that in many ways he would need her protection as much as she required his. Eventually she would elaborate a biography of Henry that would rival her own in its lament for a childhood blighted by a father's early death. Like her, Henry could be mistaken for the very embodiment of the English tradition, and yet like her, much of his background was anything but English. They were a team of transplants, never certain of how they would take to new soil, ever alert for signs of rejection. While Rebecca prided herself on being exotic, Henry took being English to its highest power; together they assembled a coalition of contradictory qualities that made for a trying yet enduring marriage.

The Andrews family had its roots in Scotland, but in the early nineteenth century one of them, a horse dealer, married a Danish Jew on a business trip and settled in Schleswig-Holstein, a duchy then allied to Denmark but annexed by Prussia in 1866. The family continued, however, to think of itself as British and to send its children to Scotland and to England for their education. Henry's father, Lewis, and his two brothers, Ernest and Willy, were polyglots (speaking English, German, and Danish fluently) and successful in the import-export business, which took Lewis to Burma, where Henry was born in 1894.

While Lewis was visiting relatives in Hamburg, he met and married Mary Chavatsky, of Lithuanian, Irish, and English extraction, who became a British subject when she married Lewis. The couple planned to return to Rangoon, Lewis's base of operations, but they remained in Hamburg after he was diagnosed with Graves' disease, the same affliction which had shortened Mrs. Fairfield's life. He had been a generous man, a great gift-giver, cheerful, and a "playful and comradely father," as Rebecca puts it in her family memoirs. Now he became harsh and irritable, hypercritical and sensitive. He could not bear any kind of noise, and his home took on the "hush of a clinic." His boys were often banished to a courtyard and commanded to play well out of sight of the home. When Lewis died, he had lost much of his fortune, and his wife Mary, used to comfortable existence, found herself beholden to Lewis's dour brother, Ernest. Bewildered by her plight, she looked to him to educate her two sons, Henry and Ernest, in the expensive Andrews tradition.

Henry, still a boy, seems not to have taken in the full implications of the new situation and what his dependence on his Uncle Ernest would come to mean. His earliest letters to his uncle—dating from 1912 when he was eighteen—reveal a conscientious young man eager to impress his uncle and to secure his approval. In her family memoirs, Rebecca feels aggrieved for Henry—having had her own experience with rich relatives on whose kindness she did not like to rely. When Rebecca met Henry, she was appalled at his subservience to his uncle, but realizing that Henry's happiness depended on it, she played along, addressing elaborately courteous letters to him and signing herself Cicily Fairfield.

In 1914, at the end of an exhausting Oxford term, Henry accompanied his mother to Hamburg to sell a house belonging to the family. Evidently relieved to be abroad, Henry ignored the signs of impending war, and enjoyed running about town as he liked—in the words of Rebecca's family memoirs, "pursuing academic knowledge." He had a gift, she noted, of being able to concentrate on his own thoughts in a way that amounted to a "state of ecstasy" as he indulged in an "orgy of reading," especially the works of poets and philosophers. In this intellectually dazed condition, he soon found himself interned by the Germans for the duration of the war in a camp called Ruhleben, "Peaceful Living." A friend of Mary Andrews conveyed to Uncle Ernest the message that Mary and Henry had remained "staunchly English" and rebuffed attempts to make them German. "In fact, Henry, whom we saw the evening before we left, said he would rather have shared the fate of the other British, than be one of the few exceptions."

In spite of this dreary incarceration, Henry managed to create the equivalent of a university inside the camp of four thousand prisoners—a discussion circle in which he and others presented academic papers. Henry was particularly proud of his work on Joan of Arc, which reflected a belief in women that Rebecca rarely found in men. "It sounds like an old fashioned phrase but he took a delight in women. I can always imagine him as a sort of Middle Eastern potentate—very kindly with a huge harem," said a friend of the older Henry.

Henry's letters to his mother and uncle during his internment are often moving testimonials to his enterprise and touching belief in the power of art and ideas. His mother rightly saw the value of the letters and had them published in In Ruhleben by Richard Roe. Although Uncle Ernest was sympathetic to Henry's plight and sent him packages, he found much of Henry's philosophizing stale beer, and even Rebecca had to admit that his poetry was pretty bad—the product of a tin ear.

If Ruhleben strengthened Henry by forcing him to fall back on his own resources, it also intensified his solitude. Rebecca thought of him as "hopelessly rootless." His mother had largely neglected him during her husband's terrifying illness. Then the move to London and to Uncle Ernest's begrudging shelter did further damage. "Oh, it's *such* a story!" Rebecca cried while trying to explain it after Henry's death to his friends: "I have never known anybody so isolated as Henry . . . I have never known anybody who struck me at once as so uncared for." Henry seemed to have all the equipment to be great, the machinery was in place, but he did not "tick over."

On December 1, 1918, Mary wrote to Ernest: "Seeing the boy and watching him, one can't help noticing the signs of past suffering. His nervous system and sensitive excitable mind will have to be taken in hand and built up again." Ernest responded generously, for he was moved by what detention had done to Henry: "at first I felt as if I had a stranger in the house but he seems to be gradually getting his former self again and it will perhaps not be long when he will be able to start on some definite and regular work as that will probably more than anything else assist him to forget his experiences during the war." (Henry later told Rebecca that he had been like other released prisoners of war, in a "state of hating the world that had gone on while their lives had been smashed.")

Ernest referred to this period as Henry's "years of absence"—a telling phrase, for there was indeed a gap in Henry's development that he could never quite fill. During detention, he had been accidently struck in the head by a German guard. Rebecca would come to believe that this severe blow contributed to the erratic behavior Henry began to exhibit after the first years of their marriage.

Henry and his uncle quarreled about his health. Ernest suspected that if Henry attended Oxford again he would overwork himself just as he had before the war. Henry's friends found him "seared by the long ordeal of Ruhleben . . . withdrawn and ultrasensitive." Looking "drawn and older than his years," his "light, musical voice" and measured words had a "melancholy tinge." But Henry persisted in his desire to return to university and assured his uncle that he was happy and calm and would need only a term or so to recover his full powers. He was only twenty-four, he pointed out: "My own time has obviously not come yet." But he felt he had a mission, and that he had to articulate his credo:

> What we, what Englishmen, need now is philosophy, some background of thought, some principles of action, some purpose of more than personal value. Fifty years ago we were the leaders of Europe, now we are the laggards.

From January to June 1919, Henry applied himself diligently to his studies. On June 26, he reported to Uncle Ernest that he had failed to get the B.A. that would qualify him for a John Locke philosophy scholarship: "I am not really robust enough to keep up the strain. This has at any rate got me into good working form and I am not at all depressed. It means that I shall pursue the same plan that was formed last term, and maybe go in for the John Locke next year. Nothing has been wasted." Ernest's reply encapsulates their differences:

I am sorry all your labours did not bring you the reward at which you were aiming but I am not surprised. It is many years since I wrote to Mr. Jones that I saw nothing but a huge superstructure built on wholly insufficient foundations and this, I think, still holds good today.

In these circumstances I cannot get myself to share your anticipations of success in the future and to me you seem to be lost completely in words, words, words, oceans of meaningless words.

Henry's poor performance baffled friends. Douglas Woodruff, one of Henry's closest friends, wrote in his memoirs:

He was the only man I knew to have completely failed in Greats, which was the examiners' way of showing their displeasure at the way he had completely ignored the set books, Republic of Plato and Ethics of Aristotle, while on the other papers he had written eloquently and revealed a mind constantly dwelling on philosophical themes.

On the eve of exams, Roy Harrod (later a distinguished economist and biographer of Keynes) confided to his friend Douglas: "I wrote him [Henry] a long and as it now appears tactless letter on the day before. I have written again." It seemed inconceivable to Roy that a man of Henry's quality could fail when others not nearly in his class passed. On August 9, Roy tried once more with Henry: "for more than eight months I have been watching you, awaiting events, fearing the worst!" Roy attempted to come to terms with Henry's sense of failure: "Disappointment in yourself and cowardice are your two troubles, you told me the other day. You are no longer inspired, on the preach, no longer a true and mighty prophet." Roy wrote not merely in sympathy but to tell Henry that his struggle to conquer his fears and revive his inspiration constituted a labor not merely for himself but for all men. Henry had become convoluted, tied up in his own thoughts, the "this's and that's of your life have become so complicated. But this doesn't really matter; when the need arises you will turn over a new leaf and say the simple thing. The important fact is that even now when you say the complicated or meaningless thing you move us to ecstasy. I hope this description, such as it is, isn't hurtful. It surely ought to make you hopeful." Henry answered that he was hopeful, but Roy continued to worry that his friend would not persevere.

Roy Harrod's long letter is extravagant in its praise of Henry and emotional in its attachment to him. Rebecca thought the two men were lovers: "His [Henry's] Oxford friendship gave him the first contact with the educated sensitivity, which he admired more than any other human quality perhaps because there had been none of it in his own home."

Oxford enchanted Henry: "he ached for its privileges." Rebecca mused: "sometimes I thought that much of his eccentricity was assumed, fabricated in a dream of being the Warden of New College or All Souls, and a famous Oxford character, walking in an obvious daze down the Broad or the High, while undergraduates told their parents with affectionate smiles, 'That's old Andrews.'" Henry once confessed to her in the "blackness of desolation": "I would have liked to spend my whole life at New College, but they did not want me." He had to settle for a postwar pass degree.

After a brief, unsuccessful position at Barclays, where he was judged not to have the "essential clerical virtues" or a mind befitting a "useful executive," Henry found a place for himself at Schroder's, having at Oxford befriended Henry Schroder, who found Henry's fluent German and French invaluable and started him as a correspondence clerk. (One of Henry's great triumphs after the war had been to give the "finest speech of the day" as Oxford's representative at the reopening of the university in Strassburg.) He proved to be a superb negotiator and Schroder quickly promoted him. Douglas Woodruff liked to tell the story of Henry's first raise of twenty pounds. He promptly returned it, saying he was not the sort of person who watched the clock and waited for a twenty-pound raise.

4

ON SEPTEMBER 11, 1930, Henry wrote Rebecca to say he would be at the station in London awaiting her arrival from France. They were about to begin a new epoch, he announced, signing himself: "Yours for ever Henry." On October 7, he presented her with an engagement ring. Rebecca told George Bye, her American agent, "He says he's going to look after me and let me write, so it ought to be grand." Four days later she went to see her cousin, the Reverend Sir Henry Denny, about officiating at her wedding in his village church (Abinger, near Dorking, Surrey). The couple visited Uncle Ernest and Mary Andrews, Lettie and Winnie. At tea with Henry's mother on October 24, there was "serious talk" about Henry's business. The next day, Rebecca tried on her wedding dress and ordered a hat.

On November 1, 1930, Rebecca West and Henry Andrews were married. She came quickly up the aisle in honey-beige velvet and a matching close hat, carrying a sheaf of lilies and red flowers. Several friends wondered at the Anglican ceremony, since the couple did not attend church.

It seemed more like Rebecca to dash off to a Registry office one foggy day or be abducted by a man who insisted on marrying her "willy-nilly!" said one friend. Rebecca confidently intoned the solemnities of the marriage service, but the word obey had been omitted from the bride's vows, and the bridegroom promised not to endow but to share with his bride his worldly goods. Rebecca looked well and very happy, and Henry appeared "a man of substance and humility, the proper backdrop for a novelist's stage."

Lettie sent a warm welcoming note to Henry: "I feel sure that it is exactly as my dear mother, who adored her Baby so, would have wished . . . I am so glad to think she is going to be loved and cared for, as she deserves. All the days I have known her I have never come to the end of her sweetness and wit and goodness of heart and I am sure you never will." Lettie was thrilled to see Rebecca settled and respectable. Winnie was less enthusiastic, mainly because Rebecca's and Henry's determination to live well seemed excessive, and she disliked ostentation.

The couple honeymooned in Genoa. Rebecca sent Lettie a note thanking her for her help with the wedding and remarking that Henry was an absolute dream to travel with. Rebecca had been doing for herself and others for so long that she luxuriated in the way he spoiled her. Her secretary, June Head Fenby, had remarked as they were leaving the church: "At least she is going away with someone who will buy her railway ticket. Hitherto, she has bought everyone else's."

CHAPTER 13

Ric and Rac and Comus
1930–1933

I

IN LONDON, Rebecca and Henry found a "magnificent flat" in 15 Orchard Court. Dividing the expenses between them, they found they could afford the price (four hundred pounds a year)—reduced because of a failure to rent the block of flats in a depressed real estate market. Normally these flats would have gone for anywhere from between five and thirteen hundred pounds a year.

Adjacent to Portman Square and full of light, their flat overlooked Regent's Park. Rebecca liked living high up—a change from her garden-level home in Kensington. In Onslow Gardens she could "no more grasp the city as a whole than a caterpillar can grasp the form of a cabbage as it wriggles through its leaves." Now she had London before her like a map, or like "an aspic jelly with human beings embedded in it instead of prawns."

Henry traveled often to Germany on business, which he found engrossing, and Rebecca sent him affectionate letters, reporting on her activities and on the refurbishment of the flat. She was excited, busy, and happy. They called themselves Ric and Rac (the names of two dogs in a French comic strip). They were a loving, chummy couple. This kind of fun with a man had been absent from Rebecca's life for a long, long time.

On July 1, 1931, on the eve of a summer holiday in Switzerland, Henry revised his will, stipulating that it should be handed unopened to his wife after his death. He left everything to her, asking only that she make provision for the support of his mother. In an attached letter to her, he added:

No words can express what I owe to you. All the best that life gave me until I met you, all generous thoughts and efforts, seemed

149

to find their true value in whatever ability they gave me to understand you and to love you. If ever you should feel lonely or disheartened I hope you will recall how when I was lonely your work recalled me to the ideals and enthusiasms of my youth and gave me strength not to compromise.

Your Ric

2

ANTHONY WAS AWAY at Stowe when Rebecca and Henry married, but he had seen enough of Henry to form a disapproving and even contemptuous impression. He resented Henry and was jealous of this new man who had usurped his mother's attention. He disliked the way Henry smiled at Rebecca appreciatively. Everything about Henry's appearance irritated him: the immaculately polished shoes, the pearly and boyish smile—Henry was the kind that "wanted to be friends too soon." Anthony hated Henry's knowing air—enhanced by Rebecca's having told Henry so much about Anthony before Henry and Anthony met. Anthony felt an adolescent outrage at Henry's assuming an immediate intimacy to which Anthony felt he had no right. Even Henry's generosity made Anthony suspicious that he had been co-opted.

Henry would not do; he looked the opposite of H.G.: he was not Anthony's father—the only acceptable match for Rebecca. In his adolescent intolerance, Anthony found in Henry a fit image to vilify. Why had his mother chosen such an unsuitable husband? For his money, surely, and as a form of insurance, so to speak, in her battles with H.G. Anthony despised her calculating side and cynically decided he would accept whatever presents Henry lavished on him while scorning the pretentious life of Orchard Court. Anthony thought it especially suspicious that Henry had taken to calling his mother Cicily, as though at home, at least, she could disown what had gone before.

Henry's most appalling offense was that he had a "sort of Midas touch of boredom." As Anthony put it, he "bored for England." Henry had "a very deliberate way of talking, and everything was given a fuller e x p l a-n a t i o n." Leaning forward he would look at Anthony and start smacking his lips. Anthony knew something was building up inside of Henry, and Anthony longed for him to get on with it. Henry was full of depression-era lip-smacking advice that Anthony found ludicrous: "You know, Anthony . . . it's much more prudent to buy two pairs of very good shoes . . . because if you buy a single pair, they'll not last so long . . . and if you purchase two very good pairs and wear them on alternate days, look after them and see that they are polished, they'll last almost indefinitely." Yet Anthony understood that Henry's intentions were good. Henry really wanted to help him. He was a good and kind man, and Anthony felt ashamed of ridiculing and distrusting him. Yet he could not overcome his "instinctive revulsion."

For some time Anthony did not reveal to Rebecca the full extent of his feelings about Henry or about his continuing difficulties at school. If she sensed trouble, she did not let on. Her letters to Aleck Woollcott in the spring of 1931 seem exuberant. "Mr A is more than a success." Anthony, "bigger than ever," had become obsessed with drawing and read little, except for *The New Yorker.* She had taken to calling him Comus. Milton's masque had been performed at Stowe, and perhaps Rebecca meant to jolly him with the name of a Dionysian pagan god. Anthony sought a more sinister source: a character in Saki's story, "The Unbearable Bassington," whose mother, Victoria Glendinning notes, has such a "love of possessions and gracious living . . . that she will sacrifice her son rather than part with a painting."

3

BY THE END OF OCTOBER 1931, Anthony failed Latin and was asked to leave Stowe by Christmas. He told H.G. he wanted to get on with the rest of his life. He would become a painter, and there was a girl he was in love with. An angry H.G. dismissed these schoolboy sufferings, saying Anthony was still a child and had better forget about love, considering that he had just failed his examinations. Anthony had looked to H.G. as his savior, and H.G. had let him down. Anthony retaliated, using many of the same terms Rebecca had been applying to H.G. for years:

Dear Mr Wells

(or should I say dear father) I think my mother is very well equipped to control my future with out [sic] your help. Why you consider that you have any interest in the matter I can't think; you've treated mother like dirt ever since I was born and you have almost entirely neglected me—£100 per annum for my education, food, board, clothing, munificent—you only came to see me to get Panther when I was small and now you have the impertinence to imagine that you can take me from her, and listen, little sadist sweetheart, not only are you wrong but you've made me realise

what a little wart you are. Telling me how wonderfully you've done
for me! But for public scandal you would have given me the works
as you did Ann Reeves and all the other poor creatures that have
been fools enough to believe in you.

I think you an ace wart and, god, how I loathe you.

Your loving son
Anthony P[anther] West

H.G. acknowledged this outburst with a curt note, mentioning that
he had been "quite ready and willing to concern myself with your
affairs," but he saw no reason to do so without Anthony's request.
"Apparently now you want to be left to your mother (with whom you
have temperamentally much in common) and Pamela [Frankau]. Very
well. So be it." He had considered speaking with Pamela but had decided
it was none of his business. Anthony had to go his own way. To Rebecca,
H.G. concluded that Anthony was "very *young* and extremely silly." He
was also very likeable, but H.G. was not going to chase after him. "If ever
I get a chance to meet him I shall call him Anthony and behave accordingly and I hope he will comport himself in the same spirit."

Rebecca employed Humphrey House, a distinguished scholar, to tutor
Anthony. Eventually Anthony improved in all areas, but he failed his
entrance examinations for Oxford.

With H.G. out of the picture, Rebecca counted on Pamela to help
moderate Anthony's extreme feelings, although she began to suspect
Pamela of turning into Anthony's ally and conspiring against her, for
Pamela had urged Rebecca months earlier to remove Anthony from
Stowe before Rebecca had been ready to acknowledge its unsuitability.

When Anthony's emotional health did not improve, Rebecca consulted a psychiatrist, Hanns Sachs, whom Rebecca called the "best practising psychiatrist in Europe." Unfortunately, Sachs was about to leave
for an appointment at Harvard in the fall of 1932. He began treating
Anthony and advised Rebecca on September 7 that it might be necessary for Anthony to follow him to Boston if he could find no one at home
with whom he might form a satisfactory transference. Sachs said his
main aim was to ease Anthony's high tension: "He is high strung to the
point of danger in his emotional as well as in his intellectual activity. In
other words, to keep him out of harm would be my aim more than to do
positive good." Still in England on September 21, the psychiatrist gave a
preliminary evaluation: Anthony was hesitant to enter the world of men.
Even before his break with H.G., it had been difficult to form any sort of
bond with males, who in Anthony's experience were seen only as school-

boys and masters. He viewed such types as merely separating him from his mother. Consequently, he felt quite helpless and inhibited. That he had taken up boxing and painting and was in robust health marked a transition to a less stifled state.

4

A NERVOUS REBECCA saw Anthony off to America at the end of September. Henry took his Cicily to Switzerland. She enjoyed traveling with such an attentive man, but she could not overcome her nervous exhaustion. She had also suffered an ectopic pregnancy, undergone a therapeutic abortion, and a hysterectomy. Henry had wanted a child, and Rebecca later said she felt sad about not being able to give him one. But she did not dwell on her operations or seem to regret, for her own part, her inability to have another child.

In November, after a series of fainting fits, she took refuge in Bad Weisser Hirsch, a sanatorium near Dresden, taking the complete cure— outdoor exercise, including walks in the forest and the village—and learning German. She felt invigorated in air she compared to wine and was pleased to have lost weight. At night she crawled into bed with *Time and Tide* or one of the other papers Henry thoughtfully sent her.

Rebecca continued to worry about Anthony, expressing to Henry "silly fears about his safety." Anthony had broken off communication with her; he did not answer her letters. Trying to calm herself she assured Henry: "I can wait till it resolves. Let us just ignore the whole thing till then." But of course she could not do that and began almost immediately discussing Anthony's case with the doctors in the sanatorium, because she feared he might be suicidal.

He had sent her a letter which she interpreted as his farewell, quoting part of it for Henry: "So sorry I have been a worry to you, my dearest pussinger. I hope you've forgiven me." She tried to respond in the philosophical manner of Dr. Lahmann, the head of the sanatorium, who remarked: "Ach, eighteen years, it wouldn't be heissy if he wasn't thinking of suiciding himself." She counted on Henry to see her through: "I cannot tell you how much I appreciate the way you've dealt with the situation [he had called Anthony to be sure he was all right]—oh my angel Ric, how wonderful you are! So sensible when it's needed, and so insensible when that's needed—but Rac has rolled right over and is lying with her paws in the air gasping with admiration. But really you know how deeply, almost achingly grateful, I am."

Henry had tracked down Anthony, who was in New York City staying with Emanie Sachs, one of Rebecca's close friends. She had enjoyed entertaining him, and he had behaved like a darling, requiring no special mothering from her. Anthony did not tell Emanie what had happened to him, except for a vague reference to a relationship with a Boston girl that had gone badly. Anthony had been an impeccable guest, fitting in well with Emanie's company. "Often he reminded me of you so acutely that it wasn't funny," Emanie wrote to Rebecca. What Rebecca thought of Emanie's impressions has not survived.

Anthony wrote his mother a reconciling letter: "We are adept at misunderstanding but I feel so much improved since this last month that I don't think I shall find it so easy to misunderstand you again. You're a greatly loved Pussinger though in the past I have sometimes seen you through a glass darkly."

5

ANTHONY RETURNED home from Boston in April 1933. Rebecca found him so adolescent that he stuck out in "Byronic humps." But the "clumsy and melancholic calf" had continued painting well. She favored his intense, even savage, murals. One of St. John the Baptist struck Rebecca as especially promising. Anthony wanted to study art and enrolled in the Slade in London. He rebuffed her advice and Henry's when they tried to counsel him about a career and to explain that his settlement would not produce a living for him.

Life with Rebecca at her Portman Square flat always included high drama. Anthony cut his hand to the bone with a razor and fainted on the bathroom floor. Rebecca rushed in to bandage him but fainted as soon as he revived. He took one look at her and fainted again. It was all "very Russian," Rebecca confided to her diary. Anthony decided to find a place of his own.

He did not consult Rebecca or Henry when he picked out a pretty house called "Quarry Farm" in Tisbury, Wiltshire. Nevertheless, Rebecca managed to convince herself that things were more or less on an even keel with Anthony, writing to H.G. that Comus had entertained her the previous evening. He had "broken with his girl and this is unfortunate because she did the cooking . . . Jesus the male is helpless." If H.G. would visit Anthony in his new home, she promised to cook them a meal, and perhaps H.G. would want Anthony to make copies of his murals. Even if H.G. did not visit (there is no evidence that he did), father and son were certainly reconciled by the summer of 1933 when Anthony turned nineteen. Anthony later said his hostility to H.G. vanished during his months in America.

Rebecca was disappointed when Anthony dropped out of the Slade. Lettie had the idea that there had been some kind of trouble there with Anthony and mentioned it to Rebecca. A fearful row ensued. "You do like to meddle, don't you?" Rebecca said, effectively checking any further discussion. It troubled her greatly that Anthony did not want to work.

CHAPTER 14

Anticipating the Apocalypse
1933–1935

I

ON MAY 13, 1933, within three months of Hitler's taking power, Henry had written a memorandum accurately assessing the menace of the new regime. He had attended a board meeting of the Berlin Power and Light Company. Jews were being dismissed from management positions, and he protested, pointing out: "all the foreign interests would take a serious view if the management were interfered with for motives which had nothing to do with the commercial interests of the Company." Henry was appalled that "men of sober judgment in important positions, whom I had come to know and like and trust in the course of difficult negotiations," spoke the language of Hitler's anti-Semitism. It amounted to a "deliberate lowering of the intellectual level of the country." He noticed that these men deluded themselves by employing words with "philosophical implications" and a "romantic tinge." "Gleichschaltung," meaning equalization, came to stand for bringing all of Germany—its principal organizations and businesses—into line with the central government. The term rationalized the campaign to squeeze out the Jews. Henry bluntly told one of his business colleagues that the anti-Jewish activities were a "gigantic piece of jobbery, designed to get places for one's friends or to help one's friends by ruining their competitors." This colleague replied that there might be something to Henry's observation, but that "there was also something beyond this," for they were "trying to re-introduce principles of decency," to keep faith "Treue halten" and that therefore "He must begin by keeping faith with those who had assisted him in the past. (It is the habit to talk of the Chancellor as 'He'.)" It disgusted Henry that a sophisticated colleague would use " 'Treue halten,' with all the associations that the lovely German word 'Treue' has to an educated German, and apply it to what he acknowl-

156

edged to be jobbery and for him to shut his eyes to the obvious fact that there can be no principle of keeping faith which involves wrecking everyone else's contract!"

Henry estimated that three million people in Germany had Jewish ancestry, even though a much smaller number identified themselves as Jews. The persecution of such large numbers would rend the fabric of society. Academic life would be ruined: "It is already clear that not only psychiatry, but also the studies of economics, the social sciences and anthropology in Germany will for the time being be all but suppressed."

One of Henry's most charming friends believed in the "ideals of the movement" and was shocked and troubled at the attitude of the rest of the world. It devastated Henry to find almost no one able or willing to see the disaster of Hitler's hegemony. One of the few Germans who agreed with Henry told him he did not have the power to "interfere." The final words of Henry's memorandum served to strengthen Rebecca's dread of an apocalypse: "Hitler is essentially an orator, swayed by his movement as much as he sways them, the danger of a situation in which victories are required is very great indeed."

Henry began a program of helping individuals under direct threat, such as Edith Jacobson, a Jewish psychoanalyst, who had been arrested and interrogated. Rebecca wrote to Ruth Lowinsky, a friend, who also knew Edith Jacobson. Could Ruth write a letter to Edith, saying she knew about her arrest and could provide evidence of her existence should the Nazis deny any knowledge of her or her whereabouts? Henry was in Germany, and Rebecca was concerned for his safety. "Will you leave my name out all the time because of Henry?" Rebecca would later write of Henry: "He risked his life again and again to get people and their money out of Germany, never giving way to fear."

2

REBECCA TRAVELED in Germany with Henry and observed the people's increasing arrogance and contempt for other countries. She wrote about her growing sense of the apocalypse in newspaper columns for *The New York American* (1931–1933), alerting her readers to tyranny in both the Soviet Union and Nazi Germany, and recommending her friend Dorothy Thompson's book, *I Saw Hitler.*

In *Letter to a Grandfather* (1931), Rebecca implied that the sadism and masochism that grew like tumors on sexual relationships had corresponding cancers in the political and religious realms. Nazism and communism appealed to people looking for absolute truths, a form of revelation traditionally supplied by religion. People yearned to accept authority, even without revelation, so long as it brought order.

Rebecca shared her contemporaries' anxiety and quest for authority, finding her own touchstone in St. Augustine, the great Church father whom she had been reading since her teens. In *St. Augustine* (1933), her emphasis on his restless travels, obsession with sex, ruthless self-criticism, strong mother, and hatred of his father makes him a figure resembling her own Richard Yaverland in *The Judge*. But she also treats Augustine as a powerful father figure. He is the first modern man, Rebecca claims—a precursor of great artists such as D. H. Lawrence and Proust. He has the twentieth-century artist's preoccupation with time and with how human beings perceive it. She might have titled her biography, *St. Augustine, Our Contemporary*, for she demonstrates that he was born at a time when the world seemed to be deteriorating, when the Roman Empire was crumbling, when nature itself—as one Church father wrote—was apparently exhausted. The earth seemed to lose its fruitfulness and sense of possibility. The Church itself was beset by various heresies just as divisive as the warring political creeds of her own time.

Rebecca employed Augustine's belief in original sin as a symbol of the neuroses that made a mockery of free will. The individual could not break free through independent efforts. Paradoxically, one's freedom depended on tradition, on conserving what the human race had learned from history. Everywhere she saw communists and fascists arguing revolution—not the painstaking, often interrupted progress that Rebecca associated with liberalism.

3

WITH HITLER'S ADVENT, Henry was beginning what Rebecca called his "death dance" with Schroder's. Henry and Rebecca realized that given his political views he would be fired. When he did lose his job a year later, it was over the dismissal of a Jew Henry had chosen to run a hydroelectric power station, part of his reorganization plan for the Berlin Power and Light Company. The Jew had been replaced with a Nazi. "I can't serve with a man like that," Henry said. "In that case, you cannot work for Schroder's," he was told.

Rebecca and Henry seemed to be living the good life. In truth, they lived at the outer limits of their means—with Rebecca supplying much of the money for the extras that made them appear wealthy and extravagant. She wrote reviews for the *Daily Telegraph* at fifteen guineas each, continued her column for *The New York American,* sold short stories to well-paying magazines such as *The Saturday Evening Post,* turned out quickie projects—such as *The Modern Rake's Progress,* her collaboration with illustrator David Low. She tried to write a play, *Goodbye Nicholas,* which she intended for The Theatre Guild in New York but which never got produced—chiefly because of a very lame third act. She was often exhausted and worried about Henry's traveling back and forth between Berlin and London and putting in twelve-hour days. There is a hint of hysteria in her letters from this period, a terrible dread that her life with Henry might come to an abrupt end through some political and economic reverse.

This is the fate of her fictional characters in *The Harsh Voice* (1935), who worry about money and whose lives are set against the background of the 1929 crash and the ensuing worldwide depression. Like Rebecca's American lover, Stephen Martin, Sam Hartley in "The Abiding Vision" has his ups and downs in business. Just when he is about to be destroyed by a congressional committee investigating his companies, he resurrects himself with the ringing phrase: "I am an American and I took risks." Walking out on the congressional committee, he becomes an overnight sensation on the strength of press reports. What saves Sam from becoming merely the cruel engine of an economic system seems to be the power of love—the devotion of both his wife and his mistress, who admire him for his manly risk taking. The women in this story exercise a humanizing influence that Rebecca rarely imagined possible before meeting Henry.

On Henry, Rebecca had pinned exorbitant hopes. He would rescue her from the world's atrocities. Rebecca could do things for herself, but oh what a pleasure to have Henry do them for her, especially with such loving grace. She told an interviewer: "my husband can do anything—everything that I can, better than I can, except perhaps the technical side of writing. It's a great satisfaction to me, and I think I probably recognise in that the emotion I had about my father."

4

IN SPITE OF HENRY'S calming company, Rebecca could not shake off a growing irritability and periods of depression which had begun in the autumn of 1933 and continued into the spring of 1934. She experienced excruciating pain from gall bladder and appendicitis attacks and eleven tooth extractions. Anthony announced his intention to leave for America (he did not). He and Henry quarreled about money, with Henry urging the virtue of "thrift in Comus." Then Anthony became ill with rheumatic fever, and a frightened Rebecca watched over him, taking his temperature. He recovered but remained depressed and ungracious.

Henry tried to divert Rebecca with a skiing holiday in January 1934. An excellent skier, he enjoyed himself. Rebecca had to be dug out of snowdrifts. Back in London, she took up dancing lessons and dined out with her favorite friends. Nothing worked. In April she briefly resumed seeing a psychiatrist, and seemed to pull herself together by working hard, starting a novel, *The Thinking Reed.*

On September 9, Rebecca fell down some steps, feeling ill, and by the end of the month she was in a clinic to have her appendix out.

CHAPTER 15

The Return of the Father
1934–1935

I

ONE OF REBECCA'S *Daily Telegraph* reviews (June 24, 1932) resulted in a new friendship with a young French woman, an aspiring writer also married to a banker. She claimed that D. H. Lawrence had been "discussed more brilliantly and profoundly than ever before in a book by a lady with the fascinating name of Anaïs Nin." Anaïs had been flattered by Rebecca's attention: "Do you know what touched me? It was Rebecca West, who asked if she could meet me—not I who asked her." They met several times in Paris—becoming so wrapped up in one conversation that they got lost in the St. Germain woods.

Anaïs extolled Rebecca for her "love of life and keen perceptions . . . I think you are like Harriet Hume and that you can transcend one's thoughts." Rebecca was, indeed, the Renaissance woman: "in possession of an intricate and graceful culture, the woman who struggled and knew the darkness of life, the generous Mother, and the living force, for I see you like that, swift and ever in movement keen and compassionate."

They shared not merely an admiration for Lawrence but a desire to plumb the depths of the psyche uncovered by Freud and to go beyond his rather limited view of women. In a review of *New Introductory Lectures on Psychoanalysis* in *The Daily Telegraph* (November 30, 1933), Rebecca hailed him as the "most tough-minded man of his time, who has done more than any other to scotch sentimental prejudices in himself and others." But he "suddenly goes into the keepsake plane," she declared, when he spoke of woman as a "riddle" and an "enigma," and turned her into a passive entity for whom "to be loved is a stronger need than to love." She dismissed his remark that a "marriage is not firmly assured until the woman has succeeded in making her husband into her child and in acting the part of a mother toward him." She called this a "horrible recrudescence of Peter Pan where one least expects him. . . . Perhaps it would be a good thing if the sexes were forbidden to refer to each other in written matter."

Anaïs had written to Rebecca about her therapy with Otto Rank, once one of Freud's closest disciples and now a dissenter. Anaïs contemplated becoming a therapist and promoted Rank's efforts to escape from the "formulas of conventional psychoanalysis," which seemed too passive and deterministic. Rank believed in "emotional shock treatment." Anaïs had undergone short, intensive treatments lasting about two months—similar to the total immersion Rebecca herself experienced in Florence in 1927.

Anaïs's analysis was bound up in unresolved feelings about her father, who had deserted the family when she was ten, and who rivaled Rebecca's father in his Don Juanism. Anaïs hated him for his unfaithfulness, but she was also drawn to him sexually. Rank had written about the "return of the father," and of his powerful impact on the woman's consciousness. Anaïs claimed to have "lived out his writings" in November 1933 by staging a final encounter with her father and having intercourse with him.

Both women had fantasies about submitting to men, of finding, in Anaïs's words, the "joy of her femaleness expanding in strong arms." Henry Miller wrote to Anaïs, "prepare to be raped." No comparable message from any of Rebecca's lovers has survived, but note how many times she claimed to have been assaulted by men and complained of their sadism. One of her appointment diaries has a bit of doggerel that is a rape fantasy: "Violate me in the violet time/ In the vilest way you know/ Ruin me, savage me/ Brutally, savagely./ On me no mercy show."

Neither Rebecca nor Anaïs liked what they termed weak men. Rebecca was especially harsh on what she called "pansies." Anaïs craved the experience of seduction and submission. As Erica Jong concludes: "Her multitudinous seductions were all incestuous at heart. She was forever wooing and winning her mythic father by mimicking his behavior. He was the Zeus who ruled her mental universe." The last thing Rebecca wanted to do was mimic her father, even if she desired men with some of his characteristics, and she had a sensibility some women found masculine. As Virginia Woolf observed: "R's great point is her tenacious and muscular mind, and all her difficulty comes from the weals and scars left by the hoofmarks of Wells."

In the spring of 1934, Anaïs visited Rebecca at Orchard Court. They enjoyed a "dainty, formal lunch" with Anthony, but Anaïs disapproved of the "*encaustique*" and "*grande monde*" atmosphere." Rebecca seemed most real when she didn't talk, when Anaïs had time to observe her glow, her "earthy hands." Wearing the "wrong shade of green" Rebecca seemed out of place in this "beautifully decorated house which does not reflect any particular individual soul." Rebecca reminded Anaïs of herself in her "pre-Rank epoch, a little abstracted, a little uneasy, wanting to shine exclusively yet too timid deep down to do so, nervous and talking far less well than she writes."

At their second lunch, Anaïs found this disharmony deepening, admitting in her diary to disillusionment with *Saint Augustine* and with a hostess who now seemed sexless and entirely domestic. "When I give her my novel, it is Rebecca West the emotional woman I want to touch." She thought that Henry Miller had led her to repudiate the intellectual Rebecca. It did not surprise her to find that Rebecca rejected Miller's *Black Spring* and favored his book on Lawrence. Anaïs was disappointed that Rebecca had liked her writing so much better than Miller's, for it had been her mission to tout his work in London and to have Rebecca recommend it to publishers. Rebecca showed it around, but without much enthusiasm.

Their third meeting proved most satisfying to Anaïs, for they discussed their lives, their fathers, their education. "I made myself. My father disappeared when I was nine, abandoned us," Rebecca told her. This new, spontaneous Rebecca delighted Anaïs: "Her past and mine created one of those arrowlike routes, and in one instant we stood where it takes others years to stand." They kissed and parted with great affection, Anaïs noting that Rebecca had switched to a low Irish voice. "You did not meet your Father again. I wonder what it would have done to you," Anaïs wrote after her spring 1934 visit.

2

IN EARLY 1935, good to mixed reviews and accolades from Rebecca's colleagues greeted her collection of short stories, *The Harsh Voice*. Critics found her style excellent and her plot construction clever. They also chided her for certain meretricious and melodramatic tendencies which gave way to twist endings and heavily psychologized characterizations. Like her letters, these stories seethe with conflict and tension. *The Harsh Voice* proved popular. By late January, A. D. Peters (he had supplanted Andrew Dakers as Rebecca's agent) reported to Rebecca that almost ten thousand copies had been sold. It encouraged her English publisher, Cape, to hope that she could be built up "as an author, rather than as a writer of scattered books."

Virginia Woolf sent her praise of *The Harsh Voice* to Rebecca, as did
H.G., who called the volume exciting and "extraordinarily good." It
filled him with "immense RESPECT" for her. He admired the "magnificent workmanship," and he expressed his gratitude that in "Life Sentence" Rebecca had "killed Letty. If she had been killed ages ago the
world might have been very different." (In the story Lettie's surrogate,
Alice Pemberton, a sort of sadistic saint, is always at people to improve
their lives and becomes so insufferable that her husband murders her.)
He was now entirely philosophical about their breakup: "Our intellectual quality is so different that I should always have nagged you by trying
to clip your extravagant black pinions. . . . You have a richness. I am simplicity. That is why I came off artistically from the beginning and got
slovenly later and why you had to begin with such a spate of undisciplined imagination in the Judge before you got to the MASTERY of
these stories."

He was not complimentary about "The Addict," which had just
appeared in *Nash's Magazine* (February 1935). Not "so very good," he
complained, and a "trifle cattish." Harsh might have been his word for
this thinly disguised dressing-down of Humbert Wolfe. Rebecca had
been appalled to watch her beloved Pamela Frankau abandon herself to
the clutches of what Rebecca considered to be an inferior poet who
sponged on women. In the story, he is called Claude Cambray, an invet-
erate liar who uses his dark good looks to romance women without ever
consummating his affairs. He is both a writer and a lover manqué, so
pathetic in his addiction to making women fall in love with him that it is
intriguing that Rebecca would spend 20,000 words elaborating the life of
such a trifler.

Pamela's biographer, Diana Raymond, is surely right in concluding
that the story is driven by Rebecca's hatred; the more she thought about
Humbert the more of a monster he became and the more it seemed
incumbent on her to expose him. That he seemed so unworthy of
Pamela, and so much less of a figure than Rebecca herself, fueled
Rebecca's rage and jealousy. There is no evidence that Rebecca had a
lesbian attachment to Pamela, even though Pamela later engaged in lesbian relationships and confessed that in the summers at Agay: "Of
course I must have been in love with Rebecca." Yet Rebecca's vehement
dislike of homosexuality is cause for investigation. G. B. Stern once
wrote to Rebecca of her love for her, carefully separating her feelings
from the sexual implications her words might have aroused: "Don't misunderstand me: I'm not that way about you and it wouldn't be nice if I
was." Apparently none of Pamela's female friends knew what she had

vouchsafed to Anthony West during their Agay summers—that she was struggling with this very question of her sexual identity, but the astute Rebecca who spoke of Pamela's extreme youth may have guessed at and been revolted by her suspicion. Pamela's close friend, Pat Wallace Frere, remembered talking to Rebecca about a scene with Pamela (years after their summers in Agay), in which Pamela confessed her lesbianism. Pat discovered that she and Rebecca "both shared this real distaste."

In "The Addict," Claude Cambray, like Humbert Wolfe, is not a real man. He is a safe type a woman might pick who is not sure that she wants to commit herself to a man. Indeed, he engages in fantastic tales in order to avoid intercourse with women who are sheltered or so young that they are not yet sure of their sexual identity. Such is naive Agatha, who is clearly modeled on Pamela. Like Humbert, who was old enough to be Pamela's father, Claude plays the feckless fatherly role with Agatha— just the kind of relationship that had seduced and tormented Rebecca.

Through "The Addict" Rebecca aimed to take charge again, to *show* Pamela what her liaison to Humbert Wolfe looked like, to present Pamela with her own face. As Diana Raymond notes, Claude's "physical as well as personal likenesses to Humbert are exactly drawn." Similarly Agatha Marley has Pamela's "smooth dark head held with the timid courage of a deer." No one, as H.G. implied, could miss identifying the real-life prototypes for Rebecca's "cattish" story.

Before securing publication, Rebecca realized that this story would not redound to her credit. Swearing her friends to secrecy, she showed them the manuscript. One of them persuaded her to change a detail that too clearly linked Humbert and Claude, but as is usual in such literary attacks most of them "sat and twittered," as Pamela later put it in *Pen to Paper*, in which she gave a highly disguised account of this episode. Rebecca initially planned to sell the story to an American magazine, thus dampening its effect in London, but when it was not sold there she could not resist having it published in a large-circulation English periodical.

A week before publication, Rebecca finally clued Pamela into what was about to hit her and Humbert. She emphasized the story's humor, saying that it took from Humbert only the most obvious and well-known characteristics. Everyone knew, Rebecca said, about Humbert's lying and his tale about the tragic death of one of his children—he had been sent by his wife for the doctor and he had interrupted his mission by sitting down to write a poem, completely forgetting about the doctor. In fact, his family was thriving. Pamela greeted this nervous chatter with silence, then said: "You put that in?" Rebecca looked startled as Pamela said, "It happened to him—surely you knew it." It had gone on being

Humbert's "worst haunt, the death of those two babies." An aghast Rebecca swore that she had no idea that the incident had been true. Now she looked "haggard and haunted." It was too late to change the story. Rebecca wanted Pamela to cushion the blow by having her show the story to Humbert. Pamela refused and broke off her friendship with Rebecca as soon as she saw how "deeply hurt" Humbert was: "he sat like a stunned child."

Pamela wrote to Rebecca, expressing her shock at realizing they were poles apart. Rebecca had had such a profound influence on her that before the appearance of "The Addict" she had belittled Rebecca's dislike of Humbert. But he remained the "most important factor" in her life. Rebecca had recently written a review of one of Pamela's novels, and Pamela confessed that "your understanding of me in that column and your sympathy for the book make me weep." This acknowledgment of how painful their parting was did not move Rebecca—or if it did, her attitude changed and hardened over the years, for sometime later she annotated Pamela's letter: "she had read the story she pretends to object to and told me I could publish it. And it's quite an excuse and self deception to do that *and* write this letter."

Pamela took her revenge four years later in a novel, *The Devil We Know* (1939). She portrays Rebecca in the guise of Jennifer Nash, whose "sharp eye for money" leads her to marry the boring, orthodox Simon Flood, a middle-aged man with a "marketproof bank balance" after she has experienced the youthful torments of "haphazard love." Lawrence (Anthony) is Jennifer's troubled young son who has a "straight uncompromising eye" and cannot abide Simon. When Jennifer marries him, Lawrence exclaims: "He doesn't agree with any of our things!" Much more attractive to Lawrence is his wayward, charismatic father: "Absent fathers are inclined to resemble forbidden fruit," Jennifer is reminded as she frets over Lawrence's decision to live with his father. Before publication Pamela was persuaded to remove the intimate references to Rebecca, though Pamela could not resist observations such as, "Her voice had an obsessing quality; its light peevish cadences would be easily remembered."

In *Pen to Paper*, Pamela admits that her portrait of Rebecca in *The Devil We Know* is as marred by hatred as is Rebecca's of Humbert Wolfe in "The Addict." Both story and novel are meant to exact the maximum cruelty. Like *The Strange Necessity*, *Pen to Paper* is part autobiography, part aesthetic treatise, in which Pamela explains that art cannot be forced to serve meretricious ends; the details of actual lives cannot simply be grafted on to literature. Jennifer Nash and Claude Cambray do not live as fully realized characters.

"The Addict" speaks to Rebecca's sense of the apocalyptic. She may have convinced herself that by writing the story she was saving Pamela from the delusion and doom of caring for a false father/lover, an impotent, aging Byronic figure, who would abuse, not protect her. Pamela's Humbert was as much Pamela's fictional creation as Claude Cambray was Rebecca's. Rebecca was determined to expose him and kill him off just as she had done to Lettie in "The Salt of the Earth." But at the back of "The Addict" lurked an even greater fear. Henry was showing the first signs of infidelity that made Rebecca question her own choice of a male standard-bearer.

CHAPTER 16

The Difference
Between Men and Women
1935–1936

I

AFTER THE FIRST YEARS of her marriage, Rebecca began to notice that
Henry developed crushes on young women. He liked to ply them with
chocolates and flowers and squire them around. He was partial to
dancers. Dancer and choreographer, Agnes de Mille, realized quickly
that Henry was taking a sexual interest in her, but she fended him off: "I
did not take it personally, because Henry was interested in all the girls."
Agnes had first met Rebecca in California in the early 1920s, and then
Henry and Rebecca had opened their home to her when she visited England in 1934. She adored Rebecca and became fond of Henry, regarding
his pursuit of young women as a way of flexing his muscles. She felt he
had made such an effort to remain in Rebecca's shadow that he needed
an outlet. But one of Henry's closest male friends observes that Henry
just seemed to like bedding women; they were part of his insatiable
appetite for chocolates and wine. He was an enthusiast of affairs and
loved to gush over women like a silly gourmand. Indeed, Agnes saw him
more than once engulfed with a schoolboyish giddiness over a ballerina.

It took years for Rebecca to sort out Henry's motivations, and she was
never confident that she had plumbed his character. In the first phase,
1933–1935, she noticed a gradual lessening of his sexual interest in her.
He was as loving and attentive as ever but they made love infrequently.
She treated his flirtations with other women as just that—flirtations.
Rebecca later attributed her blindness to Henry's affairs to a ridiculous
vanity and to a mistaken impression that he had become impotent—just
like some of her other lovers.

In her unpublished memoirs, Rebecca's gift for drama and for making events cohere into a myth took over as she elaborated a thesis that Henry was "working out a fantasy that was the opposite of H.G.'s." Henry was not sacrificing the sexual woman to the Virgin Mother; instead, he was sacrificing the intellectual, faithful woman to the "mindless prostitute in many incarnations." Rebecca named names. Henry had affairs with distinguished figures in the arts and with common prostitutes. It took her the better part of the 1930s to realize that he was not merely indulging in "sentimental friendships."

Not until after his death in 1968 did she cast herself as a victim of her intellectual and sexual success. She had given men intense physical pleasure, she insisted, yet they had abused her, behaving with "a kind of fury" and holding grudges beyond her power to remedy. She did not think herself unique; many successful women must have annoyed men into similar efforts to reject and humiliate their wives and lovers. Given Henry's insatiable sexual appetite, he could have satisfied both his wife and his mistresses, Rebecca asserted. That he did not, only confirmed her belief that he had deliberately meant to hurt her.

None of these later interpretations of Henry's behavior are to be found in Rebecca's 1930s correspondence, although she did begin to share with female friends her puzzlement over long periods when Henry did not have sex with her. She was mystified but hopeful that their physical relations would resume. But she was also hurt and sometimes felt rejected—leaving her open to the advances of other men.

2

IN EARLY 1935, Rebecca was recovering from an operation on her breasts, which had become swollen and painful—a condition she called mastitis, in which cystic nodules develop, giving the breasts a lumpy appearance. Removal of the affected tissue relieved her physical suffering, but she fell in love with her surgeon, Pomfret Kilner. "He and I spent one night together and were perfectly happy, then he broke it off," she explained in an unpublished memoir. She understood that for "safety's sake," the affair had to end, but she had hoped they could see each other occasionally, for she was "mad with loneliness." Rebecca went to Pat Wallace Frere and in floods of tears confessed her great love. "It was too much for me," Pat admitted. "I tried to make light of it. I said, 'Everyone, my dear, every woman falls in love with her surgeon. It's nonsense.' She said, 'No, but it's true.' Poor man, he ran for cover."

Lloyd Morris, an American friend, noticed Rebecca's depression and felt guilty about not being able to cheer her up. She tried to immerse herself in her work and complete her novel, *The Thinking Reed*, which had begun so well. But the novel stalled, and she accepted a commission to write a series of articles on the New Deal for British and American journals, sailing in late March and looking forward to reunions with old friends.

Aboard ship she wrote to Henry that the sea voyage would do her good. "I have felt miserable the last few weeks, utterly springless and incapable of concentration." She had not told him about her lover, and away from Henry, she recovered much of her old feeling for him. She asked his forgiveness if she had failed him—"oh, darling, I am an *ass!*" He had been supportive, even though she had not been very good company. She proffered tender admonishment: "Be a good Ric; sleep a lot *in bed* not in a hall armchair: *not too much wine,* Ric (it really isn't good for his tummy). Rac has had one cocktail during the voyage and feels much the better for this abstinence." She wrote Henry constantly throughout her American sojourn, sharing her pleasures and adventures, repairing as best she could her feelings for him. Henry showed no sign of any estrangement between them, and when Rebecca returned home in May, she resumed an affectionate relationship with him even while longing for her surgeon.

3

REBECCA AND HENRY traveled in France in the summer of 1935, dining in Paris with Anaïs Nin, her husband Hugo Guiler, and Henry Miller. Rebecca and Henry also visited Anaïs and Hugo at their home in Louveciennes. They took a drive, with Henry and Hugo sitting in the front and behaving like responsible bankers while Anaïs and Rebecca enjoyed a sharp and comical conversation. Obviously pleased that she could keep up with her witty friend, Anaïs really let go. To her diary, she confided her observation that Rebecca had lost confidence in herself. Any sort of criticism agitated her. Yet the next day Rebecca recovered herself, and they had a rollicking shopping spree, talking nonsense and discussing lipsticks. Anaïs painted Rebecca's eyelashes, Rebecca wore a copy of Anaïs's white hat and her nail polish. Then in Anaïs's room the talk became intense as they delved into their lives, and the turmoil of Rebecca's childhood. Rebecca said that Anaïs was stronger than she was. The visit ended with the foursome going off to Rouen for several days.

Rebecca and Henry continued on to Switzerland. She wrote to Uncle

Ernest that the trip had been a "marvellous success for Henry," curing him of his poor appetite and insomnia. They had been hiking. "I did 20 km including a rise of 4000 feet yesterday—not bad for my tough old age," she boasted to her American friend Doris Stevens. Even so she was "feeling grim. With Europe folding up before Germany and Italy I feel one must go Communist, and Lord how I hate that religion."

Rebecca elaborated on this theme in an essay, "The Necessity and Grandeur of the International Ideal." Since the war Europe had behaved like a person "shattered by a traumatic experience: capricious, distracted, given to violence toward the self and others, careless of their environment, and incapable of carrying on a normal constructive life." Fascism had appealed to infantile emotions, the quest for an ideal childhood, in which the dictator as "all-powerful father" provided protection and provision. Organizing the state on "nursery lines" gave many people a "degree of emotional satisfaction far greater than they would receive from participation in political activities, and puts them in an exalted state, comparable to that of young persons in love, when the merest trifles seem of tremendous and delicious significance." In normal times, would people take such satisfaction in the fact that the trains ran on time in Fascist countries?

The notion of the "all-powerful father" prods the biographer not only to think of Rebecca's own childhood, but the way in which she personalized and psychologized virtually everything. Her approach to reality was, indeed, biographical—in the sense that she gave it a personality that could be analyzed. The biographical mode endowed her with enormous explanatory power over events that others might consider too complex, too confused, too chaotic to reduce to the form of a plot, a conspiracy, or a psychological theory. It was based, of course, on the projection of her own feelings, which might lead her away from her subject, but which also might meet and elicit from her subject a significance that a less projective personality would never come close to fathoming. She could be wildly wrong about a person, a people, an incident; she could also be extraordinarily prescient.

4

THE ROUEN EXCURSION provided Rebecca with the stimulus to complete *The Thinking Reed*. It is set in France, which Rebecca said she "loved more than any other country." She had to exercise considerable discipline in order to "axe half a Baedeker-full of descriptions." The setting also provided her with an international theme, the marriage of a young, wealthy American of French descent to a French-Jewish automobile manufacturer. In her book on Henry James, she had complained that he had not given his heroine, Isabel Archer, the moral intelligence of an adult. In Isabelle Terry, Rebecca set out to right James, to rewrite, in a way, *The Portrait of a Lady*.

Isabelle, who has studied at the Sorbonne, has a "competent steely mind." But since her aviator husband's death she has found herself involved in an affair with Andre de Verviers, who likes to make passionate scenes. Isabelle detects a masochistic streak in herself, one that is akin to Sunflower's, and of course to Rebecca's. She stages a violent scene, publicly grinding his flowers into the ground, demonstrating that she will be more dangerous than Andre's game playing can tolerate. Unfortunately, the fastidious Lawrence Vernon, the suitor Isabelle favors, witnesses the incident and stops courting her.

To disguise her humiliation Isabelle marries Marc Sallafranque, "a clown possessed of industrial genius, a charming disposition, a grotesque appearance, and no self-control," Rebecca remarks in a synopsis of the novel. Isabelle learns to love Marc. He uses the language Ric and Rac reserved for themselves when he says to Isabelle: "I thought you'd rest all the morning, and I would sit by you and lick your hand and wag my tail." He shows no trace of the sadism she has come to expect in men, "only tenderness and pity." With Marc at hand, Isabelle is able to see her "priggish and censorious" nature. He helps Isabelle recover her purpose, just as Henry helped Rebecca—which she acknowledged by dedicating the novel to him. Nevertheless, it is Rebecca, it is Isabelle, who must watch over their wayward mates. For Rebecca, it meant negotiating matters with prickly Uncle Ernest, which she found humiliating; for Isabelle it requires keeping Marc away from the gaming tables, where his huge losses have jeopardized his relationship with the government which helped to establish his business after the war.

Isabelle and Marc seem to lose their way among the trifling rich, who "treat life so that it would never form any pattern, to rub down each phenomenon till it became indistinguishable from all others of its kind." As in her baffling attraction to Andre de Verviers, she finds it "odd that she and Marc should find themselves among such ridiculous people." Marc has known only the discipline of his work as an industrialist; outside of that he is immune to criticism and unable to see the consequences of his imprudence. He is sulky and nihilistic: "This damned life, it makes us all the same," he complains to Isabelle.

To save him from a night at the gaming tables that she is sure will ruin his career, Isabelle stages another violent scene, screaming at Marc in the casino, accusing him of infidelity and fainting. In the event, she does reclaim Marc's sensible side, but at the price of losing her child. Her miscarriage, she reflects, "formed part of a society that was itself a miscarriage, that had not cohered into a culture or civilization, that could not cohere into the simplest sort of pattern." This lacerating self-criticism, joined to Isabelle's understanding of the world at large, is what Rebecca had found lacking in James's not quite adult Isabel.

The Thinking Reed is a dramatization of the capricious and infantile world that Rebecca deplores in "The Necessity and Grandeur of the International Ideal." It is a world she knew firsthand. "I do not for one moment put Isabelle and Marc as admirable people," Rebecca notes, but they deserve respect, she might have added, because of their ability to think—however fitfully.

Isabelle almost loses this ability after her miscarriage. She blames Marc entirely for the loss of her child. She even requests a divorce, supposing that a more fastidious man—the bland, second-rate artist, Alan Fielding—would suit her better. But when she sees Alan's bad paintings, from which (he acknowledges) something is missing, she returns home to Marc, realizing that her hatred of him has been sheer self-indulgence: "I got the maximum sensation out of hurting Marc . . . I gave way to that impulse without restraint, because I am a rich woman and have never been disciplined." As Rebecca puts it in her synopsis, Isabelle "reflects that the tiresomeness in the male has something to do with his power, that Marc's violence has something to do with his industrial genius, and that power and genius are what a woman wants in a man." Like her notes on *Sunflower*, which spelled out its two themes, Rebecca states in her synopsis that the two themes of *The Thinking Reed* are the "effect of riches on people, and the effect of men on women, both forms of slavery, of forced adaptation, against which the individual with a sense of individuality is bound to struggle."

At the end of *The Thinking Reed*, Isabelle says to Marc: "I want to think of you as being better than I am in every way." Isabelle is immediately taken aback by her avowal, admitting "that sounds abject, but it is not. I want to feel that way about you not because you are a man and I am a woman, but because you are you and I am I. If we were different people and I were really better than you, I should be quite content to think it, it should be possible for a wife to feel that her husband is not superior to her and for the marriage to be all right." Marc protests the compliment, alleging that Isabelle is superior to him and can no more see it than she can see her whole face. "I have often thought in loving you I love a woman of whom you have never heard, of whom you have not the slightest idea, who is nevertheless entirely real."

Neither husband nor wife is entirely convinced of the other's feelings. If Isabelle's reconciliation with Marc is complete, it is nonetheless one between enemies—as men must necessarily be to women, Isabelle believes. Like Rebecca, she has finally found rest with a man after ricocheting from her other lovers, but she cannot help thinking about what Marc has done to her. Resignation more than celebration marks Isabelle's attitude: "Had you not better learn to put up with men, since there is no third sex here on earth? Or have you made arrangements for traveling to some other planet where there is a greater variety?" The novel's final two sentences unify Rebecca's vision of the male and the female, the personal and the public, the individual and society:

> It struck her that the difference between men and women is the rock on which civilization will split before it can reach any goal that could justify its expenditure of effort. She knew also that her life would not be tolerable if he were not always there to crush gently her smooth hands with his strong fingers.

5

IN THE *New Statesman and Nation* (April 11, 1936), Elizabeth Bowen called *The Thinking Reed* a "classic novel [with] almost no imperfections. . . . It is impossible to think beyond it." In *The World's Body* (1938), the distinguished American poet and critic John Crowe Ransom said the novel was "perfect in a form so rare that hundreds of efforts must fail in order that one may be successful." *Time* (March 9, 1936) considered it "among the best novels in the short memory of man." Reviewers saw *The Thinking Reed* as a comedy of manners with a sharp satirical edge. They admired the sensuous evocations of Paris, Antibes, Le Touquet, and her figures of speech—both concise and extravagant. In *The New Republic* (March 11, 1936), Malcolm Cowley cited the description of Isabelle's face, which had the "pasteurized look of a wealthy orphan," and the description of the gold-digging Poots, who has a habit of drooping her eyelids in an expression that "made her face look like an unmade bed." Nearly all critics acclaimed her gallery of minor characters, especially Aunt Agatha, Alan Fielding's formidable relative (reminiscent of Uncle Ernest), to whom he and everyone else abase themselves.

This extraordinary critical success, plus handsome advertisements announcing "Rebecca West's first novel in seven years," should have encouraged her to write more fiction, for it could be viewed as solidifying her reputation as a novelist. Yet she continued to be dogged by charges that she was more of a critic than a novelist, and that *The Thinking Reed* was actually more of an essay than a novel. In *The New York Times Book Review* (March 8, 1936), Louis Kronenberger, one of her most thoughtful readers, suggested that even the most brilliant and climactic scene in the novel—the dinner party at Le Touquet followed by a night at the Casino—was "at once unreal and overreal, at once too theatrical and too intellectual—the same scene that enthralls us as spectators dissatisfies us as thinking beings." What it amounted to was a "fabulous amount of melodrama."

The mixed reviews are symptomatic of Rebecca West's problematic place as a novelist. Few reviewers or even her later critics have taken sufficient cognizance of her effort to write novels—each one quite different from the other—which do not easily situate themselves in the English and American tradition. Her brief against James was that he had not been enough of a critic, and that there should be a way to combine what was called essay and novel writing in one form. The French had found it in Proust, and she was exploring his form in *The Thinking Reed,* making both her characters' mentalities and their social scene her subject. Malcolm Cowley came closest to recognizing her ambition by singling out a passage concerning Poots, whom Rebecca called in a short essay, "A Novelist's Dilemma," the "crystallization of a lifetime's hatred." But Cowley's introduction of the passage, saying it is an example of the novel's "wise and picturesque generalities," does not do justice to Rebecca West's unification of the social and the psychological:

> [Poots] had the voice which had been fashionable among Englishwomen for some years, a tired and timbreless gabble which made a curious claim to sense, which pretended that though the speaker was late, or in debt, or taken in adultery, it was the very contrary of her fault, since she had been besieged by people inferior to herself, who had urged upon her a delay so great, a financial policy so extravagant, a sexual habit so profuse, that the lesser figure of her actual fault made it appear by contrast a virtue, or at least an unusually practical and restrained way of dealing with the situation.

The Proustian length of her sentences make extraordinary demands on the reader, but that is because the clauses are like so many layers of social observation the writer must both summon and analyze. The long sentence captures a complex of societal forces working through an individual: Poots is in a class of people who refuse to take responsibility for their own actions. The novelist demonstrates a political sensibility of genius, which can argue not only ideas but can show how, on a daily basis, people can deny the consequences of their own actions and still live quite well, free and clear of any obligation to rectify their own chaos.

CHAPTER 17

Love and Marriage
1935–1936

I

IN THE AUTUMN OF 1935, Rebecca accepted the British Council's invitation to lecture in the Scandinavian and Baltic countries. Finland, in particular, seemed a "beautiful example of a small nation threatened by the great powers," and she resolved to write a book about its "struggle for independence." But the grammar and the pronunciation of Finnish defeated her, and she suspended her writing project in the spring of 1936, when the British Council invited her to lecture in Yugoslavia.

Starting in Vienna, she had an exhausting tour of Lyublyana, Zagreb, Split, Dubrovnik, Sarajevo, Belgrade—with stops also in Sofia and Athens. The trains were often dirty, smelly, noisy, poorly equipped, and poorly ventilated. On one segment of her journey she had to sit upright for thirteen hours on a "hard and narrow seat in a tiny compartment with three other travelers in a train that rocked and bumped" ceaselessly. She often found herself lecturing to people who barely could understand English, and "listening to Balkan French and replying to it is a form of physical torture only to be compared with the bastinado." Through what she deemed lack of communication and incompetence, she often spent fruitless, fatiguing hours traveling and waiting. "Jugoslavia is distinctly a country where one has to be in a state to deal with the unexpected," she reported to Colonel Bridge of the British Council. Yet almost immediately, she realized she had to drop Finland, for Yugoslavia was a "more picturesque and convenient example of the political thesis I wanted to expound." She knew that it would be "overrun either by Germany or, under Russian direction, by Communism; which would destroy its character, blot out its inheritance from Byzantium."

On April 22, 1936, Rebecca sent Henry a long letter about her lecture tour, concentrating on a ten-hour journey to Skopje she had taken in the company of a poet, Stanislav Vinaver ("half Polish Jew, half Serb"). This "extraordinary person" was Press Bureau Chief for the Yugoslav government. She relished reciting his biography to Henry. Readers of Black Lamb and Grey Falcon would know him as Constantine—a name well chosen for the representative of a world that recalled for Rebecca the early church. At the Easter ceremony—"you know, candles and three processions round the church," she told Henry—she marveled at how it was "so like Augustine." The ancient frescoes in monasteries, an "angelic old priest," the mosques, the villages with "Rics and Racs dancing in their lovely clothes," the evening cabarets—she had discovered the paradise of her imagination. She had lunch with the Bishop of Ochrid in the porch of a church he especially liked because he had rid it of a poltergeist, which used to "snatch the marriage crowns from the heads of people being married there." Elected "honorary guest for next Easter," Rebecca apprised Henry so that he should be ready to travel. "I am much more interested in life here than I am in England, and I feel so ashamed of our national policy. If only we were solid with the French we could have filled this part of the world with light."

Stanislav told Rebecca about his "beautiful German wife." Rebecca met her and learned about her history: "she's put her head in a gas oven and wanted to kill the children because he is half-Jewish. She has been in an asylum several times since the Nazis came in." This "dotty" woman, as Rebecca called her, became the infamous Gerda of Black Lamb and Grey Falcon.

Stanislav was forty-five, short and fat, "like a Jewish Mr Pickwick, with a head like a cone with the apex cut off thatched with coarse black curls." For ten hours on the train he had talked incessantly. "It was quite abnormal," Rebecca reported to Henry. Later, after the Easter ceremony, Stanislav had become anxious. At the hotel, he "jumped up on poor Rac." Politely fending off his advances was not enough: "I got violent, then I got frightened." She had learned during the day that her guide was a "hard case." She had heard a story that he had been caught in Russia during the revolution, sentenced to death, but had saved himself by turning Bolshevik, serving as a Commissar from 1918–1921. She decided she would rather die than submit to this thug: "It came to a stand-up fight in my bedroom we rolled over and over. I hammered him with my fists, and finally maneuvered him out of my bedroom, in a scene that was funny at the end . . . I then locked the door and reflected that I was in a fairly bad way." She had little Yugoslav money—having been summoned to her trip before she could change currencies—but she would try to cable the British Legation. If that failed, she figured she had enough money for a bus. She knew this all sounded improbable, but her fears had been aroused by staying at a hotel which took no notice of the frightful noises she and Stanislav were making. He was an important official, and she was without her passport, having given it to the hotel-keeper. How could she leave without being questioned? The military police interrogated all travelers. Feeling stymied, she went to bed, exhausted.

Stanislav greeted her the next morning, apologizing for the night's struggle but refusing to return her to Skopje. He would have her stopped if she tried to travel alone. He had to protect her, he said, because of her "bourgeois prudishness," which would prevent her from seeing southern Serbia's beauties. At night there was a rematch: "I fought and fought and fought for about two hours." His ardor cooled when his colleagues joined him and the hotels seemed, to Rebecca, more proper. He threw one more romantic fit after she got the flu, bursting into her room, declaring his love that gave him no fear of infection. While she sneezed and gasped, he stamped his feet and raved and blustered for three hours. The next day he courted her with "flowers, papers, fruit," remonstrating "But you don't understand, you treat my love as England treated Lord Byron." Aggravated by lack of sleep, Rebecca moved toward the window, deciding to throw herself on a beautiful chestnut tree's branches. Then an English acquaintance, Joel Balfour, came to her rescue, "though I looked as if a hyena had clawed half my face." Her case was worse than she had supposed, for she had been diagnosed with erysipelas, followed by low blood pressure and anemia. She had deep lines in her face and her hair had become grayer.

Rebecca believed that Vinaver "meant to be kind, but was just a stupid uncivilized brute, and one can do nothing whatsoever about it, because if he was my enemy I would never dare go back into or through Serbia." She needed him for her book. Even as she attacked him, she was rehabilitating him, saying there was "some excuse for him in one way— apparently all French women journalists sleep with the officials of the Pressburo, and at first he was genuinely amazed to find I didn't intend to be agreeable." This divided view of Stanislav is more than a little reminiscent of her take on H.G. and her other sadistic suitors. Did Henry smile when Rebecca asked him not to worry about anything? *Don't write to Balfour about it*—all English letters are read, and anything to do with me or the people I was connected with will be read for some time to come." Balfour might have conveyed a very different view of the situation, one less in keeping with her mythmaking. The letter also provided cover and served as a diversionary tactic. Neither Henry nor Stanislav knew that Rebecca had resumed a romance with an old roué, Antoine Bibesco, during her evenings in Belgrade.

Antoine, a Rumanian prince, had first made love to Rebecca in Paris in 1927. They had quarreled in an extravagant parting scene the following morning in bed. Dressed in his "famous black crepe-de-chine garment," he got off some superb lines. Rebecca thought she would never see him again. But in Belgrade, he still looked like the handsomest man she had ever met, and he was just as witty in English as in French. A man with a resourceful vocabulary and a persuasive tongue, he amused and flattered Rebecca, and she relented.

2

REBECCA SPENT a good part of May 1936 recovering in an Austrian sanatorium from the rigors of her journey and brooding on Stanislav Vinaver, who began all his declarations "Tu est ni belle ni jeune mas mais je t'aime." Not really encouraging, Rebecca observed. He wrote to Rebecca in mid-June, when she had returned to London. She baffled him, and he admitted that he had not found the right tone for his letter. He thought of her often but had trouble fashioning a clear idea of her. It seemed to him that she had a capricious personality, but he conceded a tendency to complicate things too much. After a month traveling with her he felt he knew her less well than when they had commenced their journey. He signed himself her dear and devoted friend.

In July, Rebecca's affair with Pomfret Kilner briefly revived. He had written her and arranged to meet in June, then six weeks passed without a word from him. Finally he responded: "He took me in his arms and said he loved me and hated it all being too dangerous, and asked me to see him again and write to him." She did, and again he had turned silent. The unresolved nature of their affair continued to upset her.

Yet Henry remained Rebecca's prince, and she worried about his health. In July 1936, Uncle Ernest died. It had been a "grim business," Rebecca wrote to an American friend, Emanie Sachs. The doctors had predicted a quiet, peaceful death, but he had struggled and lingered for three months, exhausting Henry in the process. He had some kind of strange attack or seizure, Rebecca was never quite sure what it was. Years later, when he was diagnosed with cerebral arteriosclerosis (a gradual shrinking of the brain), she thought of this episode and suspected he suffered brain damage. It was at Crawley, Uncle Ernest's country home, that Henry told her that his father had committed suicide, and that one of his uncles had been in a lunatic asylum. She went upstairs to her room "turning round and round as I mounted the staircase because I thought someone was going to hit me from somewhere." From then on, she thought of Henry as her charge as much as he thought she was his. It did not prevent her from railing at him, or from being unfaithful—any more than his deep devotion to her precluded liaisons with other women—but he had also evoked her deep sympathy and desire to make life comfortable for him.

Although they had always expected Henry would inherit his uncle's estate, the size of it (the figure ranges in Rebecca's accounts from £140,000 to £170,000) surprised them. They were now rich—although Rebecca was quick to catalogue Henry's list of family dependents and fret over his penchant for unwise investments that, she thought, brought them several times near ruin.

3

IN FEBRUARY 1936, twenty-one-year-old Anthony surprised everyone by getting married. He had met Katharine Church, a painter, at a party just before Christmas 1935. "It was very romantic," she remembered. All her friends were there, people like the sculptor Henry Moore and the critic William Empson. There was also a gloomy young man. He wouldn't dance. He looked rather ugly and physically awkward. He just sort of stood there and glared at her. Kitty wanted to dance. She was having a glorious time. Just as she was going home, he said: "May I take you to the Ivy for lunch tomorrow?" She said, "I don't go out to lunch. I'm a painter." Then she relented: "I've got a bit of cold stew, and if you like you can come out about one o'clock and we can have lunch in my studio." Over that lunch he said, "Will you marry me?" She said, "Rubbish, you only saw me last night. This is the most ridiculous thing I ever heard." She thought "thank God I'm going off skiing in a week's time." Anthony must have learned the time she was departing from Victoria Station, because when she arrived, there he was standing on the platform.

Anthony floundered on the beginner slopes. "We were in a hotel annex. I came back one teatime and I found a note from Anthony: 'Can't stand any more of this I'm going to Paris will you join me?' " "Well," she thought. "I'm not going to waste half my holiday. Of course I won't." Every night someone climbed across the snow to the annex and said "Miss Church is wanted on the telephone." Anthony said, "Come and join me in Paris." She said, "I'm going to finish my skiing." But she did join him in Paris, and he kept on about getting married. "We moved into each other's arms, as it were, in Paris. And he moved into my flat and liked it there. I kept saying, 'We're all right like this.' "

Kitty knew that marriage would make painting more difficult, if not impossible. But he broke down her defenses with a spoiled child's determination to have his own way. The struggle suddenly didn't seem worth the hassle, and she gave in. She did not expect their love to be for life. This hope—never a certainty—came later. "Why he insisted on the legal vows I can't imagine. I suppose it made him feel safer? . . . I know what it was. He wanted to be saved. He was saved. . . . He needed a mother and a wife. I was [five years] older."

Anthony took Kitty to Orchard Court to meet his mother. Kitty had already heard stories about his terrible childhood. "I must have been prejudiced, but I think Rebecca broke this down by the warmth of her personality and reception." Rebecca took to her and made it obvious, treating her with kindness and respect, as "one artist to another"— which Kitty had not expected and which she valued, even though she was

> puffed with pride and the confidence of youth . . . I can't remember what she was wearing. She was never elegant but always obviously expensively dressed and with a kind of vulgarity and carelessness—what I think makes Virginia Woolf allude to as her gypsy quality. She generally wore a lot of jewelry, which in those days I took to be "costume" but was probably real. There was a string of uncut emeralds for instance—which looked like ordinary craftsmen's beads and on someone else could have been the acme of sophisticated understated distinction, but I think she lacked the taste to aim for that.

Kitty remembered the spacious flat, the art (Maurice Lambert's Fish on a round glass table), the good food elegantly served, wine in the right glasses, avocados as starters. Kitty had never tasted them. Rebecca reacted with the amazement of the Lady of the Manor.

"Rebecca certainly enjoyed money and luxury and made it clear she did—in fact not only couldn't she imagine that anyone would *not* but would have thought such an attitude deliberately priggish and puritan (which perhaps it is?)." They were waited on by a manservant, and Kitty learned that Henry insisted on this as he had to have a man to brush his clothes. (She and Anthony later joked about the "brushin' room.")

Rebecca was as nice about the proposed wedding as Kitty's mother was *not*. "My mother—the soul of respectability—could hardly bring herself to be civil to Rebecca and naturally assumed that I must have been pregnant as did all her friends who commiserated with her." Kitty's mother, "quite grand and well bred," came from a wealthy and well-born family, the Lyles, and it disgusted her to have a daughter married to a boy born on the wrong side of the blanket.

Kitty appreciated H.G.'s decency. He took them home after their wedding for a celebration lunch. Rebecca came and she gave them a "biggish cheque" which they rashly spent on the down payment for a gorgeous large Dufy cornfield. After living with it for six months, they realized it was outside their means and took it back. (Rebecca would later cite this episode as evidence of Kitty's and Anthony's improvidence.)

Anthony and Kitty saw a lot of Rebecca when they were in London. But Kitty always took her cue from Anthony. She never quite trusted Rebecca or wanted to confide in her.

Kitty, a dominant personality and gifted painter, had urged her husband to give up painting, certain that he would not produce first-rate work and dreading the consequences of living with an artist who was not her equal. "I'm sure I stopped him. I'm sure I said, 'Why do you paint? You're no bloody good.' Not in those words, but I'm sure I did." Kitty was just as sure that Anthony had great talent as a writer, and with her encouragement he was making a difficult transition to a new identity.

Rebecca responded with misgiving to Anthony's change of course, believing he had talent as a painter. But she did not contest his plans to write, preferring to let him find his own way. His first efforts would be seconded by Raymond Mortimer, one of Rebecca's literary colleagues and a friend, who helped Anthony secure a niche as a book reviewer at *The New Statesman.*

Rebecca and Kitty got on remarkably well. To a friend, Rebecca wrote: "Anthony up and married a pretty blonde after my own heart— Scotch, dogged, a fine painter, and very funny. It's so good I'm hanging onto my thumbs."

Even though Kitty remembered Rebecca's generosity quite well, she freely admitted she never liked her:

> Of course it was mostly because of what she did to Anthony. But also I suddenly conclude to my great surprise it was partly because I *disapproved* of her so much! (Just as my mother did.) I always thought of myself as an infinitely tolerant and broad minded woman! But the combination of her extreme extravagance and self-indulgence shocked me with my frugal (almost mean) Scottish nature.

Kitty was hardly alone in her reaction to Rebecca's excesses. "All my life Winnie has been going on and on about my extravagance—it is a fixed idea," Rebecca wrote to Lettie. Winnie's daughter, Alison, had made it a chorus: "When I mentioned once I had found a nice fur coat (squirrel for £15.15.0 at Barkers) Alison immediately said, 'I expect it's the dearest in London.' "

CHAPTER 18

Gone with the Balkans
1936–1938

I

REBECCA RETURNED from Yugoslavia in June of 1936 feeling even more convinced that the fate of civilization itself was at stake, and that English pacifists were wrong to oppose rearmament. Canon Sheppard had founded a Peace Pledge Union, sponsored by Aldous Huxley, Rose Macaulay, Storm Jameson, Vera Brittain, Siegfried Sasson, and other writers. Lord Robert Cecil had promoted a peace ballot that received more than ten million votes. In *Nash's Magazine* (August 1935) Huxley and Sheppard presented their peace platform and collected 100,000 signatures. In the June 25, 1936 *Nash's*, Rebecca replied: "Do you believe that you are going to abolish cancer if you get 100,000 people to sign a pledge that they do not intend to have Cancer?" Peace pledges might have done some good in the nineteenth century, when England was an aggressive power, but now they were unrealistic. She did not suppose England had turned "angelic"; rather, depleted by the last war and "thanks to democracy," it had a population that would not stand for an aggressive Great Britain.

Because the next war would put the whole population at risk through aerial warfare, the conscientious objector "as a factor in modern pacifism is out-of-date as an arquebus in modern warfare." There would be no time for interposing the pacifist view between warring powers—the "same whiff of gas may waft us up to the Golden Gates." The poorer countries in Europe—such as Yugoslavia—were depending on strong countries like England to keep out of German arms. "Representatives of every shade of opinion" in Yugoslavia had told her so this past spring.

Attempting to sway Nazis with pacifists' arguments would be like relying on the "power of the cross to subdue a fanatical Moslem." Nineteenth-century wars had been different. Treaties had been signed, tempered by the "democratic and humanitarian ideas formed by Western Europe during the last hundred and fifty years. But it is precisely these ideas that the Nazis and Fascists have thrown overboard." To imagine what it would be like to be conquered by Germany one had to remember what the Finns and Estonians had suffered under Czarist Russia or what the old Turkish Empire had done to Serbia, Bulgaria, and Greece. These conquerors had taxed and extracted the resources of the defeated. Did the members of the Peace Pledge Movement think the Germans and Italians would act otherwise? Rebecca then quoted an Italian nobleman who spoke to her in Vienna three months earlier: "You English are so rich and we are so poor! And we are going to get rich, by taking whatever colonies we like!" Henry had recorded a similar sentiment in his notes on Hitler's accession to power, expressing his wonder that Germans should think they had been the only ones to suffer during the Depression.

Rebecca concluded by acknowledging that her message was not as attractive as Canon Sheppard's. She could not offer a "single, splendid, magic gesture like the signing of a pledge." She knew that trying to rebuild the League of Nations and to pool defenses that would suppress aggression was a heartbreaking task, which "must meet failure again and again, and cannot know the joy of banishing violence from its arsenal." But such a plan was the only way to keep the idea of pacifism alive and "force it to take its opportunities when they arise." The Peace Pledge Movement, on the other hand, constituted "nothing but the suicide of that idea, touching and graceful, but death nonetheless."

2

In July 1936, General Franco began his revolt against the Spanish Republic. In September, Rebecca wrote an article expressing her dismay at the press reports and public opinion:

It is assumed that the rebel forces in Spain are a white-souled band of patriots, rather like the cavaliers in old-fashioned novels for school-girls, who are fighting for the preservation of law and order against blood-thirsty barbarians, and who wish only for the perpetuation of a harmonious society in which a benevolent aristocracy lived but to nurture and protect a simple peasantry.

Her own travels in Spain led her to the opposite conclusion: The aristocratic and propertied classes and the military had done nothing to "promote law, or order, or benevolence." Never had she found a "wealthy people so entirely free from any feeling that they had any debt to repay to the society that had given them their privileges." Only the republican government had made an effort to improve the lot of its people. Foreign residents in Spain had complained constantly about the irresponsibility and corruption of the upper classes. One altruistic Spanish nobleman Rebecca had known had been thwarted by members of his own class. It was outrageous that the British government refused to allow the Republic to purchase arms to protect itself; it was tantamount to siding with the rebels and to supporting the "flag of anarchy. It is yet one more proof that the real Reds in this country, who hate society and who would let in on us blood and famine and slaughter for no other reason than to satisfy an appetite, are those that howl against the Reds."

3

IN LATE MARCH 1937, Anthony and Kitty came to Orchard Court for a jolly farewell lunch. Rebecca and Henry were about to depart for Yugoslavia, guided by Stanislav Vinaver, who had planned an extensive itinerary in Croatia, Bosnia, Montenegro, and Serbia. Rebecca complained about the amount of luggage Henry was taking. Anthony laughed when he heard Rebecca say that Stanislav would meet them at the frontier and remarked: "Vinaver will say, 'In this country leather suitcases that size are not allowed,' or perhaps if he feels very ardent, 'In this country men called Henry Andrews are not allowed!' "

Rebecca kept a diary of the Yugoslav trip, using their pet names Ric and Rac. It formed the core of *Black Lamb and Grey Falcon*, especially her emphasis on a journey that was also a portrait of a marriage. The diary is more personal and intimate than the book, but also less profound, less historical and seasoned, not yet brewed in Rebecca's mind as a work of literature, but extraordinarily valuable as a first draft of the experience that she would sift and expand in her masterpiece.

On the train to Zagreb, Croatia, Rebecca and Henry sat in a first-class compartment full of Germans. Middle-aged and overweight, they complained of the heavy burden of taxes Hitler had imposed on businessmen. As Henry well knew, business life in Germany had become difficult because Nazis got the jobs whether they were competent or not. Private citizens had lost their liberties; even public officials had no authority unless they were Nazis. But the young people were solidly for Hitler; the Nazis had cultivated and pampered them. The plight of these Germans would be fully dramatized in the first section of *Black Lamb and Grey Fal-*

con, for Rebecca wanted to emphasize the enormous gap between German tyranny and Balkan liberty.

Stanislav introduced Rebecca to Serb and Croat writers, who debated the merits of their peoples and revealed just how difficult it had been to form a union of the south Slavs. Stanislav talked fondly of his wife and seemed to take no notice that his anecdotes revealed a woman whom Rebecca thought was mad—a woman who rushed down a volcano simply because she believed she was at the spot where Goethe had slipped. Rebecca appreciated Stanislav's solicitude for her, but she was still morose about her fitful affair with K. (Pomfret Kilner). She perked up when they attended a Catholic service in a Croatian church. How odd to hear the Catholic mass sung with such gusto, Rebecca thought. But "wait till you see the Serbs," she urged her Ric.

The meals were sumptuous. At lunch lots of wine, the first dish pancakes stuffed with mushrooms and chicken liver, the second dish fried chicken with superb rice and potatoes, then a wonderful compote with peaches, cherries, and quince, accompanied by heavenly biscuits, then superb coffee. The Germans on the train said she would find no good food in Yugoslavia! Everyone got drunk. Rebecca had to bully her Ric to behave himself. He had become hostile to Stanislav. The Yugoslavs saw the tension between these two men vying for the lady and laughed. The meals, but not Ric's rowdiness, appeared in *Black Lamb*. In literature, Henry would be presented as the perfect husband.

Rebecca had liked Henry's spirit, though, and got fonder of him as they walked about. It lessened her hurt over K., who had, she alleged, sadistically used her to quench his sexual desire. He was not a giving person. "Only Ric can give. His spirit is fine generosity," Rebecca recorded in her diary.

The good feeling did not last. Arriving in Split (on the Dalmatian coast) melancholy overpowered her. It was early April and the city looked very handsome and Italian, but Rebecca felt quarrelsome, a mood not improved by a visit from Elsa, Vinaver's wife, whom Rebecca deemed self-satisfied and ugly. Henry was even more horrified than Rebecca when Elsa insisted on accompanying them on their travels. He saw in her the worst kind of German. He had told her "The Serbs [who] hold the Austrians had no right to bombard Belgrade, as it was an open unfortified town. Does your husband think so?" Elsa had replied: "Yes, he would say so, but then he is a good official." Henry regarded her attitude as disloyalty to her husband and the sentiments of a Nazi who held the Slavs in contempt. There followed several days of gloomy travel with "unamiable Mrs V." She contradicted Stanislav when he expounded his theory, delivered with his usual ebullience, that all women are possessed by their husbands. Finally, Henry and Rebecca insisted that Elsa be put on a bus because the car was too small for all of them plus the driver.

In Ochrid, Ric and Rac stayed in the same rooms where Stanislav had attempted Rebecca's virtue. She extolled Stanislav's exuberant acceptance of Balkan life in all of its diversity. "Yes," Henry replied, giving her a theme she would expound brilliantly in *Black Lamb*: "But they are not really different, there is a unity. If you have one of a family that is a priest and another that is a brigand, they are quite different but they may also be the same."

When Henry went out to get sweets for tea, Rebecca sulked over K. When Henry failed to return promptly, she worried about Henry and forgot about K. Rebecca overheard a young wife in the hotel say: "This is very curious. She is very anxious, but one always reads that English wives are so cold with their husbands." When Henry finally returned, it amused the young wife that Henry and Rebecca sat so close to each other. Elsa ate Rebecca's roll with "an air of demanding colonies." Ric was peeved.

The next day he was playful, but Rac could not get K. out of her mind. She napped. Ric returned, having "angelically bought some rolls." She loved the way he catered to her, showing his kindness from day to day.

Rebecca took Henry to visit Bishop Nikolai, one of *Black Lamb*'s major characters—the most remarkable man she had ever met. The power of his eyes, his theatrical manner fascinated her, although she suspected he did not trust her or Stanislav, whom he thought an "awful ass." Bishop Nikolai celebrated Easter mass like a command performance, thrilling Rebecca with the words "Christ is Risen!" The congregation regarded him as a saint. Then Mrs V. committed an unpardonable sin and actually took over the distribution of Easter eggs to the children. Henry and Rebecca watched in horror as she crassly intervened, with a sentimental expression on her face. She had desecrated a living faith, trampled on the spirits of a people who celebrated in Easter the tragic conception of life. This scene would serve as one of the climaxes of *Black Lamb*, in which Elsa (renamed Gerda) acted out the denial of life and Stanislav (Constantine) the submission to evil, so that in his defeat he might remain innocent.

Overcome by the church and chapel at the monastery of Sveti Naum, Rebecca pardoned K. She walked outside and beheld a lake silver against a horizon of deep black-blue and violet hills, on the right side a dark cloud hovering over a snow mountain. Poised over the upper ranges a "Niagara of cloud" appeared as a "dense white light." These clouds swirling over the peaks, and below the foothills shadowed in dark green through twilight, impressed her as the most romantic scene she had ever gazed on.

Rebecca awoke the next morning dreaming of having been in someone's arms; she heard a sweet male voice say, "Do you know why you still love K.?. . . . Because you are soft as he is." Then Ric was at her side saying it was after six and they must be going. She spent the day puzzling out the dream. Its surface meaning seemed to be that she and K. had the same cuddly quality, but then the psychological meaning of soft struck her unhappily. She was being told she was as infantile as K., and as sexually defective as he was, and as mad as he was. Rebecca watched her mind trip its circuits over and over again: "I feel oddly wretched and discontented and apprehensive, while at the same time extremely intellectually happy and interested." It was her perpetual state of mind; Yugoslavia merely took it to a higher power.

Rebecca's driver, called Dragutin in *Black Lamb*, amused and terrified her. He swerved the car to kill a snake. She told him she had rather hoped the sports of driving and snake killing could be kept apart. Later he did the same thing, even stopping the car to smash in the snake's head with a tool. He leaped around yodelling, frightfully pleased with himself, and Stanislav joined him. Rebecca examined the snake, admiring its black lattice embroidery. Dragutin's powerful desire to kill and his lively and attractive personality are one of the human paradoxes Rebecca poses in *Black Lamb*. Immediately after this scene, Dragutin expresses his affinity for nature by discovering the herb field, in which Rebecca and Stanislav roll with abandon.

The next day, Henry outpaced everyone running up the top of a hill. Stanislav protested they had no time for hijinks if they were to stick to their itinerary. "Sheer rot," Rebecca thought. Stanislav's imbecile solemnity had been provoked by jealousy of Henry's strength. At dinner Stanislav reported a conversation between himself and Dragutin at the site of a great Serb military victory. "Ah, if we could bring 1000 Croats up here and show them how liberty is won." The genial Dragutin replied: "Yes, show them how liberty is won, and then hang the lot of them."

Along the way Henry and Rebecca had been buying peasant dresses. At a market Henry slung several over his arm. Two women came up and started fingering the fabrics. He thought they were complimenting him on his purchases, but Rebecca was amused to discover that they thought Henry was an itinerant salesman.

Another day, another dream. She had forgotten most of it on waking but she had heard abundant waters flowing in the distance and heard herself saying: "The trouble is, I want a new lover and I'm 44." There had been a scene in a maternity hospital; she had just had a baby. She feared it had died and worried because Ric had not come to visit her. She asked herself what it meant. Would her book turn out badly and Ric not love her?

At dinner Rebecca provoked Stanislav by denying Goethe's greatness. She admired his brilliance, but she could see he was poisoned with German thought. Stanislav said Goethe had opened up the classical world, Rome, and the very meaning of culture not only to Germans but to all of Europe. Rebecca rejected Goethe as an impostor and extolled Gibbon. Goethe had had a terrible influence on Napoleon. She was miffed when Henry sided with Stanislav. "Tolstoy and Goethe—these are the sacred icons of our modern world," she sneered.

Rebecca found the frescos in Byzantine churches ravishing: an angel giving a sharp military command, Mary shrinking as she accepted it, the Blake-like fresco of St. Elias in a cave. There were two little stylized trees one each side of his tortured feet projecting from a cave. He was dressed in a yellow robe covered with a sheepskin mantle, with his hand clenched under his beard. She could hardly bear to leave.

The trip had begun in late March and by the middle of May the travelers had seen a little too much of each other. Rebecca and Henry had had a bad scare. They had almost been killed following a Montenegran on a narrow mountain path—the incident is used in Black Lamb to underscore the Slav fervor that embraces death as passionately as life. Dragutin and Stanislav were fighting, and Stanislav was becoming almost as rude and ungracious as his wife. Rebecca excused him, believing he was ill.

4

WITH THE TRIP almost over in late May, Rebecca dreaded going home. Budapest, Vienna, and her trip back through Croatia reminded her of the materialistic culture that was the enemy of the spirit she had found in Yugoslavia, especially in Serbia and Montenegro. Austrian food was wretched, and she slumped back into gloomy thoughts about K. Everything seemed stupid and superfluous after Yugoslavia. But Henry remained a dear, and they rounded out the circle of their sojourn by a pleasant Orchard Court dinner with Anthony and Kitty.

Rebecca resolved to bury herself in her book. It was the only alternative to torturing herself about her love life, or lack of one. Writing was the best antidote to her feeling that her talent had been stymied by the hateful emotions she provoked in people she most loved. She had, in other words, her own life-and-death struggle to master.

In short order, of course, the Yugoslav trip became a great adventure. The morose grumbling of the diary gave way to nostalgia: "I suppose I'm tired, we did run about," Rebecca wrote to an American friend, "but oh! it was grand, and we had front seats all the way, we were in a Croat riot on our last morning, which I do call enjoying oneself to the last."

Rebecca never became fluent in Serbo-Croatian, but her exercise books reveal a painstaking effort to learn grammar, vocabulary, and phonetic changes. She worked on lists of verbs, the use of tenses and nouns, and on various reading and writing exercises. In a pocket-sized notebook, she drew maps and made rudimentary drawings of landscapes and buildings, and sketches of Byzantine art (Pantocraters, Madonnas, and angels).

Working on what she loosely called her "Jugoslavian diary," Rebecca originally conceived of it as a short book, perhaps to be included in a revised edition of *Ending in Earnest* (1931), a collection of essays that had not been published in England. After her first Yugoslav trip, she had asked her agent, A. D. Peters, to approach Macmillan about publishing it, saying it would be a "snap book," ready by the autumn. Peters thought the timing for a book of essays just right, since *The Thinking Reed* would be "going very strong right through the summer."

The second Yugoslav trip proved that Rebecca's book would not be a snap. Four months later, she was writing her friends about a "wretched, complicated book that won't interest anybody." She could not resist bemoaning that her sexual life with Henry was over, and that "it never began, and I howl my eyes out." Rebecca claimed that her "physical relations [with Henry] terminated totally from about 1937." They still shared a double bed, and she felt they still shared great intimacy, enjoying their long walks and travels together. He had satisfied her sexually and she thought she had satisfied him. He never offered an explanation of his sexual withdrawal. Once, lying beside him in bed, she had cried out: "Why don't you make love to me anymore?" Henry said nothing.

To members of Rebecca's family, her story of Henry's sexual withdrawal seems incredible. Her nephew, Norman Macleod (Winnie's son), always found them a very loving couple. He visited them frequently and saw no signs of strain or tension. His sister Alison is even more emphatic: "I don't believe it." Visiting Rebecca and Henry for a weekend in 1939 she witnessed Rebecca "fondly rubbing up against Henry, like a cat. He seemed responsive." Could Rebecca really live with a man for so many years who did not respond to her advances? Alison thought Rebecca and her two sisters rarely told the truth about sex; "they'd been brought up in an age when girls didn't."

That Rebecca and Henry were physically affectionate does not, of course, prove that they were sexually active. Certainly Rebecca, in her mid-forties, craved sexual partners—as did Henry. In late 1939, Rebecca wrote to Emanie Sachs about Henry's "mild infatuation" with a Finnish soprano. "She's lovely and has a voice like a dream." In the same letter, however, Rebecca admitted: "I can't understand Henry. There seems to be great devotion but he hasn't made love to me for at least three months. I just don't understand it." K. had reappeared "in a very odd way" in early November 1938: "He and H.G. and I sat round the dinner table and talked over our situation! In H.G.'s house. But K. won't be my lover—he's too scared. This is tough luck because I admire his little podgy person as I've never adored anyone else."

5

ON DECEMBER 13, 1937 Rebecca sent a note to Peters: "I am plowing on with the book—but my God it's long!" By February 1938, it had turned into a two-volume work, the first part of which had reached 200,000 words. She told her publisher, Harold Macmillan, that he must be feeling "something near panic at the length." (The firm had given her only a two hundred pound advance.) She did not think the book would be ready before June. The Yugoslav government delayed sending her information; she had turned to the time-consuming process of getting private individuals to answer her questions. In July, Henry wrote to Anica Savic-Rebac, one of Rebecca's Yugoslav friends and advisers, that Rebecca hoped to have a first draft finished by August.

She yearned for a final trip to Yugoslavia to see one more Easter and her "poor darling Slavs, how I love them." She deemed it likely that war would soon destroy the country. Rebecca had little of her usual gossip to report, she said, apologizing to one of her correspondents. Life had been quiet during this period of intensive writing, as she churned out a manuscript that she thought might be called "Gone with the Balkans."

CHAPTER 19

War
1938–1941

I

BY APRIL 27, 1938, when Rebecca left for her third trip to Yugoslavia, to be present once more at the Orthodox Easter, Hitler had absorbed Austria into the Third Reich and Czechoslovakia was threatened. Rebecca headed for Macedonia to write the last section of her book "on the spot," feeling the urgent need to capture a world soon to disappear.

As usual, traveling proved arduous, and Rebecca was only beginning to feel rested when she wrote to Henry on May 8. The exquisite and enormous meals made her feel like a "tightly stuffed black sausage Rac." She spent the afternoon with her friend, Anica Savic-Rebac. Attractive, bright-eyed, and clear voiced, the learned Anica, about the same age as Rebecca, had a Ph.D. in philosophy; she was a superb classical scholar and linguist, speaking English, French, German, Italian, Hungarian, and Russian. She taught at a Moslem college and embodied an extraordinary range of European culture that Rebecca knew the Nazis would destroy. They discussed "the universe" and did "little shoppings," spending the evening walking along the Varda and in cafés drinking coffee and wine, nibbling little bits of sausage on skewers, and talking with the local politicians and teachers.

Rebecca did not find the central scene of her book, set in a sheep field, until her third trip to Yugoslavia. She and Anica had been looking for a festival, but Rebecca was grateful that it had concluded by the time they arrived at the seven-foot flat rock, "shining with blood." All through the night infertile women and men with barren fields had been slaughtering lambs and cocks on the top of the rock, sticking candles in the rock's holes and crevices, and swathing it with red and white wool as they walked around it three times. Around the greasy rock she saw fragments of jars women had thrown from the top. "You cannot imagine anything *more messy*," she assured Henry. There were only a dozen or so people left, but Rebecca saw two lambs slaughtered and a child's forehead marked with the blood of both in a circle. The smell sickened her. Rebecca described the scene but did not editorialize: "as yet I am only taking notes."

On the way home, Rebecca rested in Venice. Henry sent her a guidebook letter, addressing her as "my sweet" and recommending that if she were not too tired she should see various monuments, museums, and churches. His taste for Titian's *Ascension of the Virgin* seemed of a piece with his reverence for Rebecca: "that fine figure of a woman standing on a cloud with all the philosophers below raising their hands in wonder. Next door you will then see Tintoretto's painting of the same subject— angels swirling round in concentric circles in the midst of which is the spirit of the mother of God whom they are heaving aloft." Rebecca wanted something a little more earthy from Henry, but another part of her never failed to appreciate his worship. He thought she should rest herself with a gondola ride out to Torcello, "small but beautifully proportioned and with two mosaics of great importance. I think that coming from your visit to the Macedonian churches this might be well worthwhile."

Henry wrote to Hugh Seton Watson (a British expert on the Balkans) about Rebecca's trip, reporting that she had encountered a "frightful Nazi," who had "screamed" at her about Czechoslovakia. To Hugh, Henry recommended Franz Borkenau's book on Austria. Franz and Henry were friends, and Henry endorsed Borkenau's judgment that "the future of Europe will to some extent depend on the answer to the question whether Germany is capable of drawing the line anywhere." Henry had his answer. Too many men of influence in Germany had become Nazi propagandists; they had no work to return to as industrial managers or administrators. Sitting pretty meant losing their livelihood.

2

THE END OF SEPTEMBER 1938 brought Munich and Chamberlain's capitulation to Hitler, with the false claim of "peace in our time." Just before the agreement on September 29, Anica wrote to Henry quoting his words: "I hope England will do the right thing." He had said them with "such a sad expression" that she had realized his doubts. "I see very well that Chamberlain's politics must be as bitter for England as it is for us," she concluded. To Aleck Woollcott, Rebecca wrote: "We have ordered steel shutters for our bedroom . . . Munich made a spring war inevitable."

They continued to help people fleeing from Nazi tyranny, securing employment for them and going to extraordinary lengths to get them settled even when the quota for German immigrants in the United States had been used up. Soliciting information from refugees, Henry wrote memoranda on the state of German public opinion and military preparedness, especially in the aviation industry.

Rebecca had watched the ghastly buildup to Munich with loathing. "The country is split from top to bottom," she explained to another American friend. No dinner party was complete without a huffy scene. Her friends, Ruth and Tommy Lowinsky, for example, were on opposite sides—he for Chamberlain and she against him. In Sussex, where she and Henry had rented a summer house, Rebecca went around asking questions about how to handle the refugees she was sure she would have to house. "Nobody knew anything." The government seemed paralyzed. "It looks to my cold cynical eye as if the Government did not want us to fight Germany and wanted to scare us." She was repelled by the "hysterical joy and gratitude to Neville Chamberlain" that first greeted the Munich agreement, effectively dismembering Czechoslovakia and consolidating German gains.

By the end of November, a heartened Rebecca announced that public opinion had "stiffened," but she feared that the country might already be ruined "beyond repair." She found it difficult to "preserve any equanimity in the face of all these dreary political events. . . . It's the poisoning of the whole of life by the spread of the Nazi spirit, which is something that you come up against every day in every department of your life."

3

ON SEPTEMBER 1, 1939, Germany invaded Poland. Two days later England and France declared war. Rebecca thought it quite possible that they would all die, but "in the meantime there's this awful slow motion and remoteness." These were the winter months of the "phony war," when England and France did no more than blockade Germany by sea while Hitler and Stalin partitioned Poland. Like many people in England, she persevered, in Naomi Mitchison's words, "planning on something like the existing basis" while supposing that England might be invaded and conquered as Denmark and Norway were in the spring of 1940. "I feel like a female elephant undergoing her three years pregnancy as a result of intercourse over the radio," Rebecca declared to Aleck Woollcott. Everyone was waiting for action and feeling the strain.

Rebecca wanted Anthony and Kitty to sail for America. She called them to say she had bought tickets on the *Queen Mary* so that they could emigrate. Anthony and Kitty were offended and refused to leave England. Rebecca did not ask whether they really wanted to go to America. "She always knew best how other people should live their lives," a resentful Kitty concluded.

At first, Rebecca supposed Anthony might be spared military service because of his "damaged lung and irregular heart action." But "there was never any question of that," said Kitty West. Anthony was in excellent physical shape. Frances Partridge, who got to know Anthony and Kitty before the war, observed that Anthony was like a "cat on hot bricks" about the call-up, and that he and his mother had had words about it— she suggesting that he would be something less than a red-blooded male if he shirked his duty. As a lifelong pacifist, Frances found attitudes such as Rebecca's shocking.

Rebecca later recalled a lunch with Anthony at the Ivy, where he blithely told her that he would let other men do the fighting. To Rebecca, his behavior was unconscionable; she told him he was being immoral. Anthony reacted in surprise to her attitude, she claimed. But how could he be unaware of her antipacifist position? she wondered. Like so many other issues, mother and son saw each other—as Anthony had said earlier—through a glass darkly. It is clear, however, that Rebecca never came to terms with her son's complex attitudes toward the war.

Anthony confided not in Rebecca, but in Frances and her husband Ralph who took an immediate liking to Anthony and Kitty; this "charming, delightful couple" lived only six or so miles from Ham Spray, the Partridges' Wiltshire home. Frances's compassion for Anthony may have been colored by a meeting with Rebecca several years earlier, when Anthony was in his mid-teens: "I do happen to remember her talking about her boy, and I wondered what he was like. He sounded like rather a problem. She was saying she thought he had now settled to something." Anthony's warm personality and looks—his dark hair and shining white teeth—appealed to Frances and Ralph. "I think we realized pretty soon that he had had a very difficult childhood. He would talk about it quite freely. He was always very obliging in conversation." But he was also volatile: "He could go off at a touch as though a match had been set to him. He could be wonderful, amusing, equable. Then something would get at him. His whole face changed and he became slightly out of control. Neurotic." Such moments would pass quickly, but they reflected an unstable, wayward element in Anthony's personality. One of Kitty's other friends noticed that with the mention of the word "bastard" a shadow would come across Anthony's face. Frances felt sorry for Anthony as he struggled to define himself, confronted with a mother, "frightfully successful as a social figure, a novelist," who had made a fortunate marriage, and held views of the war so different from her son's. He had the air of someone tossed out into the world too soon.

Anthony often sought the older Ralph's advice. Ralph soon discovered that Anthony had a dishonest streak, especially about money, borrowing and spending it without any sense of responsibility—behavior that embarrassed and troubled Kitty on several occasions. He would lie about his purchases of expensive art works and household items—virtually anything that caught his fancy—grossly underestimating their cost. The post would come and Kitty would discover that they were terribly overdrawn. She found it frightful and said to him: "You must promise me not to spend any more money. This is awful." He went straight to the telephone and he bought an eighty piece dinner service. "I don't think Anthony knew what money meant. He thought it was an amoral thing," remarked Frances. And somehow his behavior was all connected in the Partridges' minds with his pampered and yet deprived childhood, in which he had had the best of everything except his mother's love. He acted as though he expected money to be available to him. Anthony seemed to look to friends like the Partridges not only for sympathy, but for an intimacy he had never established with his mother.

Ralph had distinguished himself in military action in World War I, but the slaughter revolted him, and he became a staunch pacifist. His Wiltshire home became a center of discussion about the war. Frances watched Anthony's fluctuating attitudes. He declared himself a conscientious objector, but he wanted to prove he was no coward by volunteering for hazardous duty on a mine sweeper. Yet Anthony wavered. Conscientious objectors were not allowed to serve on mine sweepers. Frances realized that "with this subject one broaches a source of misery." Anthony was in a "frightful muddle and hated talking about the war."

Rebecca had made it both intolerably easy and hard for Anthony—first offering him safe passage to America, then criticizing him for not staying to fight on her terms. He felt he should do something for his country, yet he had not made up his mind what it should be. His mother tried to make it up for him, provoking him into anger and guilt about his indecision.

Rebecca had not only publicly declared where she stood, she had exposed the contradictory thinking that had left Anthony at an impasse. In a long letter to *Time and Tide* (December 16, 1939), she issued her "Challenge to the Left," responding to a series of letters from Naomi Mitchison and others. Rebecca had no patience with Socialists who caviled about going to war, harping on its horrors and decrying the narrowness of patriotic nationalism that only strengthened the capitalist state: "to tuck this attitude under one's Left-Wing was hardly consistent with the admiration felt by Mrs Mitchison and her friends for Russia and the Red Army, and the idea that the workers may claim their rights by armed insurrection." So what if the war was about "power domination, access to cheap raw materials and markets for the finished products"—as one antiwar correspondent put it. "May a nation then never defend itself against another that wants too big a whack of power domination?" Rebecca asked. Her pointed questions mercilessly exposed the addled thinking of such left-wingers, who never confronted the consequences of their thinking, who never said: "Rather than fight I would face the prospect of living under the Nazis, taxed to the last farthing, spied on and brutalized, with a concentration camp round every corner." Instead they said, " 'I would rather not fight, fighting is horrible.' They say it with an imbecile priggishness, as if everybody did not know that war is an obscenity."

It seemed to Rebecca that in the war they had "arrived at a crisis when the forces of capitalism are due to receive the greatest blow aimed at them since the beginning of history." Surely the objective should be to win the war and create a Socialist majority and state "based on the principles of liberty, equality, and fraternity." (History proved the soundness of her judgment with the Labor Party's victory after the war.)

Rebecca knew that war offered terrible choices, but she could not abide those on the Left who excluded themselves from making such choices. Even H.G. acted peculiarly, alleging that "we have been rude and unkind to Stalin—as if that bird had ever cared what we did," Rebecca told Aleck Woollcott. She knew that her side did not have clean hands, but the other side's were dirtier: "I insist we must defend what is thirty per cent good against what is only fifteen per cent good," she declared in another letter to Time and Tide (January 6, 1940).

Anthony finally decided on farming, which provided him with an exemption from military service. Kitty felt a little ashamed—her father had died in World War I—but Anthony made a success of it, getting up at 4:30 in the morning to get the milk out. He also spent part of the week in London working for the BBC. Rebecca seemed relieved that he had found worthwhile employment and the tension between them subsided.

Anthony continued his writing. Rebecca reported to H.G.: "Anthony has done 18,000 words of a novel. God help us all." Anthony's note to Rebecca says all that is needed to convey his momentous decision:

Dear Rac,

In fear and trembling—an uncorrected proof—let me have it back fairly soon. Don't be too fierce—Henry may read it if he can be bothered. I only have feelings of secretiveness and inadequacy faced with you.

All my love and all our loves
Anthony

4

"THE GREAT BORE WAR," as Rebecca called it, dragged on. She hated both the calm and the uncertainty but still worked on her "wretched book on Yugoslavia." Harold Guinzberg, her American publisher, sent encouraging words, allaying her fears about its length. He had read 429 pages of manuscript and had heard that she had informed Aleck Woollcott it would be 320,000 words. "No matter, for it makes good reading with its variety of subject—history, anecdote, flora and fauna, duly spiced with your personality. . . . It seems to me you have created a new and fascinating method of presenting history."

Rebecca stayed at Possingworth Manor in Sussex in the autumn of 1939 as Henry went back and forth to London, working "like a dog" for the Ministry of Economic Warfare. The blackout in London was terrible. Lettie had been evacuated from her flat and had been sleeping in her London County Council office. Winnie and her civil servant husband Norman had been evacuated to Bath and were housed in billets. Everyone was living miles away from where they usually did, so that life seemed to have lost its "connective tissue." Rebecca felt cut off from her friends and had few guests. Henry worried about her, telling his mother that Rebecca had not been really healthy for about eighteen months. Her book had taken a tremendous toll on her nerves, but she had the consolation of a country house with a beautiful view, far from the village and close to the woods, where she could write in quiet.

Rebecca admitted to Aleck Woollcott that she had adjusted to wartime conditions rather easily; she was neither too old to really suffer nor too young to react to it as an intrusion. She felt "cheerful but bewildered. One feels awfully like an actress who turns up for a big show and finds they haven't got her part written for her." She and Henry had decided to look for a large country house to buy.

5

By December 7, 1939, Rebecca and Henry had found their country estate. Done in the Regency style, Ibstone House had nice rooms, and except for some horrible wallpapers was fit to be occupied immediately. They would do their "pretties" after the war if they and the house were still standing. It had a small farm with cattle and pigs, and a circular walled garden. Near Stokenchurch, overlooking a lovely valley and the Chiltern Hills, it was less than an hour's drive from London. Rebecca relished acquiring the property for six thousand pounds from a bank with an insolvent client. "They can't get anything like what they hoped for out of it," she confided to G. B. Stern. At the bank Rebecca overheard it said: " 'We can't help feeling that Mr. and Mrs. Andrews know our position and are pressing us.' It was A BANK said that. Little Panther laffed and laffed and laffed."

But various ailments and misfortunes continued to plague her, including a bout of jaundice in January 1940, which had taken her from shades of "daffodil to mimosa and from primrose to beige," and now "off-white." At the end of February, the son of Greta Mortimer, Rebecca's old friend from drama school days, died in an air crash. Rebecca had been close to him and thought of him as Anthony's younger brother, enjoying his development into the "most charming dashing creature with golden hair and twinkling blue gray eyes." It exasperated her to see the male family members giving way to grief and saying they could not face it. Even the doctor nearly fainted in the mortuary. All of the funeral arrangements devolved to her and heartbroken Greta. "MEN ARE NO DAMN USE FOR ANYTHING," Rebecca fumed.

Rebecca liked to do for people, but in the case of her own family she overdid it, expecting them to be grateful for her advice and financial support, and never suspecting that it would be judged interfering and a form of control. Winnie's daughter, Alison, was a favorite target: "She always appears to think of herself as a Communist missionary, and to talk to people as if she was the first Communist they had ever met . . . I don't like to attack her about this because I can't get on terms with her mind. She seems not to have a single Fairfield or Mackenzie characteristic." This was only one of Allison's many faults Rebecca totted up for Winnie in their correspondence.

Alison and Rebecca argued about Clifford Odets's rousing play, *Waiting for Lefty*, which actively involves the audience in a union meeting deciding on a strike. No doubt Alison's defense of the play seemed tiresome to Rebecca, who could not have relished her niece's lecture that the meaning of culture was "not an opportunity of expression for some (more or less) interesting personality, not something fed to the ignorant from above, but a living, developing force arising from the needs of common people." The scenes that bored Rebecca would have meant "a whole lot to a working class audience," Alison assured her. Not at all daunted by her formidable aunt, Alison charged: "You are apt to imagine that because a question has been settled in your own mind it has been settled everywhere." Appalled by the pact Stalin had signed with Hitler in August 1939, Rebecca had become a virulent anti-Communist. The news that the "Russian Communist State, built on the gospel of the Jew Marx, had joined hands with anti-Communist, anti-Semitic Germany" had sickened her the morning it was announced. She compared it to going into a church and seeing the celebration of a Black Mass. Alison joined the Communist Party in early 1939. She was not quite nineteen years old. In May 1940, Rebecca resigned her vice-presidency of The National Council for Civil Liberties, charging that it was now acting "on instructions from the Communist Party"—an accusation which its secretary, Ronald Kidd, vehemently denied.

Rebecca had a sense of gloom about the war, but she tended to take it out on her family, and she had to be humored. In one of his letters to Rebecca, H.G. sounds as though he is playing the part of the gentle, mollifying husband. Replying to Rebecca's irritation over Anthony's neglect of her, and over his manners and business affairs, H.G. remarked that the "cub is self-centered, careless and uncouth. He never explains. He has that hatred of writing letters all writers share. He feels that a letter ought to have at least one bright remark and accordingly he never sends a brief and businesslike note." But she should not think her son acted out of "malice aforethought" or let these lapses in good form trouble her too much. Anthony regarded anything that demanded prompt attention from him as "fussy. A rather distraught young man and young woman, very intent, both of them, upon what is really good work" deserved sympathy. "We have to stand it," H.G. urged her.

Rebecca never saw herself as the aggressor. Quite the contrary, as she explained to a friend, she expected her family to do her in: "Anything that brings me in contact with my sister Lettie is literally murderous for me. I just feel life isn't worth living if any mind so gifted can be so utterly destructive." When Lettie got flooded out and became ill, she repaired to Ibstone to recuperate, and ruffled Rebecca.

Rebecca expressed her exasperation in "Around Us the Wail of Sirens," a *Saturday Evening Post* article (February 8, 1941). Lettie is transformed into Eva, a cousin who afflicts Rebecca's household with an oafish German refugee, one of her protégés, or "lame dogs," as she calls them—though Rebecca reacts to them as "lame cobras, or even lame skunks." Eva is in the tradition of Dickens's characters, looking past Rebecca and "everyone closely connected with her, to the distant objects of her charity." Eva has acquired this habit since the days she was allowed to "bully her juniors in the nursery," running about the world "seeking for opportunities to make people do what they would prefer to leave undone." It is hopeless to try stopping her: "To prove her wrong would be to strike at the roots of her being, to annihilate all there is of her, so nobody ever does it." She is the dethroned spoiled child attempting to reconstitute her kingdom through a passion for good works. Even Henry finds her officiousness disturbing, and domestic bliss is not recovered until Rebecca installs the refugee in a hotel room.

The *Saturday Evening Post* article is one of several Rebecca published in American magazines about the period between May and August 1940 that became known as the "Battle of Britain," when the Royal Air Force beat back a Nazi attack meant to soften up the country for an invasion. Rebecca provided vivid portraits of a people under siege, with humorous and hardy comments from her servants ("The Bright Face of Danger," *Readers Digest*, October 1940), glimpses of life underground in the London shelters ("Shocking," *Saturday Evening Post*, October 26, 1940), and the hazards of running a household ("Housewife's Nightmare," *The New Yorker*, December 14, 1940). If the bombing of London terrified and saddened people, it also bored them, as they became accustomed to the underground shelters and awaited the bombers arrival. "The air, only theoretically refreshed by a conditioning machine, beats with a faint pulse which slows down one's own. People look brownish, moving through a brown mist, to the tired eye. The mind swings loose of the present."

Shuttling back and forth between her new country house and Orchard Court, Rebecca felt safe if cramped in her apartment house's shelter. Yet a high explosive bomb bursting at least three hundred yards away from her was like a tooth extraction with "insufficient local anaesthetic, a tooth with roots all over my body." She pitied the poor in shelters that were no more than "a sheet of iron plastered over with earth." But in the main these articles seem self-contented; she conveys the impression that she enjoyed the war. She sent a bellicose note to Aleck Woollcott shortly after Churchill replaced Chamberlain:

> We are all going about our business, with one eye on the map and a certain amount of curious feeling about the bowels. I have never felt so coldly ferocious in my life, and optimistically carry a

couple of linoleum knives wherever I go. . . . We do feel a wild exhilaration in what our Air Force has done. Really, we are the same people as the Elizabethans and doesn't it show more now that we have got rid of the abominable Neville!

To Irita van Doren she exclaimed: "You can't think how exhilarating it is to live with a firework attached to one's tail! It lends a real sporting interest to life." Rebecca ached for her friends, though, and for a couple of good shopping days in New York.

Drawing up a will, dated August 8, 1940, she named her attorney Theobald Mathew and Henry as executors, and left Ibstone to Henry and her remaining estate to Anthony, who would also inherit Ibstone after Henry's death. If both Henry and Anthony died, Ibstone would be Kitty's.

One of Rebecca's mainstays during the war was her secretary, Margaret Hodges. A Cambridge graduate, with a degree in French and German and a knowledge of shorthand, Margaret had been employed first by Henry, when he set himself up in London in the mid-1930s. Then she moved to Ibstone, where she typed draft after draft of *Black Lamb and Grey Falcon*, and became Rebecca's companion and comfort. Rebecca regarded Margaret as a daughter, really. They had a similar sense of humor; they cooked together—making jam at half past ten at night in the kitchen; they took long walks in the woods and talked about everything, including Henry. To Margaret and Rebecca, Henry sometimes figured as a cartoonish character, the bumbling Daddy, forgetful, querulous and deaf, announcing, "This is the first I've heard of it." Rebecca was called the long-suffering Simpkin. Margaret worked for Rebecca for four years, but they remained lifelong friends.

Rebecca's letters during this period are full of the high drama of her skirmishes with servants, which became a staple of her correspondence for the rest of her life, constituting her invention of a new minor genre—the servant mystery story, verging on the Gothic, the romantic, and sometimes the theater of the absurd. She had a Welsh cook who was a "half-wit," succeeded by an Irishwoman who was "quite mad," and got madder, barring her bedroom door because people eight feet tall and half-naked were going through the house all night. Things settled down with a French cook, but unfortunately her speciality was fashion, not food. Throughout this changing of the cook brigade, Rebecca and Henry suffered through various illnesses, culminating in the diagnosis of his duodenal ulcer—just in time for the arrival of a Portuguese cook who "could speak no English and could cook nothing but very hot savoury rice."

Rebecca called her mad Irish cook, Bridget, "Little Horror of War," and commemorated her in an article, "The Man Who Came to Dinner," in honor of Aleck Woollcott's wartime visit to Ibstone. Rebecca had admonished Bridget three times not to indulge in her penchant for bay leaves—liberally thrown into every course, including dessert. But the disaster was worse than that, for instead of cooking dinner for Woollcott, Bridget had overcooked fifteen pounds of prime sausage Rebecca had been saving for herself and her neighbors. In a panic, Rebecca began cooking chops and commandeered everyone in the house to gather items from the grounds at Ibstone for a salad. Rushing into the kitchen they came to halt before Bridget at the stove, throwing leaves into a pot of soup, leaves "green and smooth and exquisitely veined, with dark-red stems. Leaves from the Portuguese laurel, which grows in the courtyard; leaves that are deadly poison." Rebecca groaned and asked Bridget what she was doing. "Making soup for Mr. Woollcott," she replied.

The dinner came off well, but not without considerable anxiety that Bridget had put leaves in some of the other food. "We ate bite for bite with Aleck so that he should not go down to the dark waters alone." There was one moment of terror, when he suddenly seemed convulsed, but it had to do with thinking of a former friend of theirs who had become an isolationist. Rebecca remembered the dinner for Aleck's "hundred happy phrases." On leave from the army, John Hodges, Margaret's husband, recalls the party going on and on. In the end, chain-smoking Aleck and Rebecca talked for about two hours—on every conceivable subject. John was absolutely exhausted when he went to bed. Aleck was so alive, and Rebecca so responsive. "And there would be old Henry, the husband, sitting there at the end of the table, very owl-like with his glasses, a very tall man looking down on this and that."

Rebecca said little about her married life during the turbulent war years, although Henry was obviously her anchor. She seemed too caught up in the furor of the war and her household to measure what he meant to her. In articles and letters Rebecca poured out her love for her country home. They had put the farm in working order, and she derived from this restoration of a derelict land "an access of dynamic force which has carried me through some very disagreeable wartime experiences." Ibstone had once been a large, square Georgian house, which an eccentric owner had pulled down, except for its fourth wing. Rebecca reveled in the clean-up, in preserving fruit and growing vegetables, in the two Jersey cows, fourteen Polled Angus steers, and five calves. She claimed to have fulfilled a childhood fantasy, having recently discovered an old photograph of a house where her mother had spent her happiest years, and that house was "as like my new possession as one pin to another." Milking a cow gave her "an agreeable sense of power," Rebecca enthused.

"It's so difficult now doing concentrated artistic work that it's a relief to have absorbing work ready to turn to," Rebecca admitted. "The funny thing about war is that you work till you drop whether you're doing war work or not—and you eat enormously. After an air-raid you want a good slice of bread and jam." Henry buoyed her; he just plodded on, "looking like a patient old mule, with bombs dropping fore and aft, never giving a damn, and being extremely funny about it all."

Rebecca admired Henry's work at the Ministry of Economic Warfare because he was thinking so hard about the postwar world and how it could be put together. He also revered her total immersion in *Black Lamb and Grey Falcon*. It was now over 400,000 words long, providing a "complete explanation of the course of history, but that course will completely prevent anyone from having time to read it," Rebecca lamented. The book was almost done, but she found the epilogue a struggle to write. She sent part of her book to Aleck Woollcott, who remarked, "I had meant merely to glance at it but the sweep of it carried me out to sea. . . . You've gone in this wise, rich book far, far beyond anything you ever reached before."

6

ON JANUARY 8, 1941 Henry wrote to Harold Guinzberg at the Viking Press to say that Rebecca was finishing her epilogue and cutting parts of her book, fashioning an extraordinarily long narrative (now 500,000 words) with "breathers by the interweaving of light and shade." She had been interrupted by the war and by settling in the new house, and, unfortunately, she was scheduled to have a major operation in February. Busy in London, Henry had not been as helpful to her as he would have liked, but now he was prepared to shepherd the book through publication, emphasizing to Harold the importance of a first-class index for a work that would be used as a reference as well as read as a narrative, and of two detailed maps, which identified the important place names so that the reader would not get lost in the geography of the country. Both Viking and Macmillan followed his detailed suggestions, including his idea that the maps be put on the inside covers of both volumes. Indeed, no item seemed to escape his loving care, including meticulous attention to the spelling of Slav names and a painstaking review of the galleys.

Rebecca complained of fatigue and wisecracked about her forthcoming operation: "Yes, I am going to be disembowled once again, I never pass a fishmonger without exchanging a sympathetic glance with the kippers." She had a tumor that was now "slightly larger than myself." The operation had been put off because of her persistent anemia.

A relieved Henry was able to cable friends on February 16: "REBECCA'S OPERATION PERFORMED THIS MORNING WITH COMPLETE SUCCESS." She had finished the epilogue just before admission to the hospital, and by February 25 felt well enough to make some minor changes. Henry admired her "unusual concentration and strength of will." Nevertheless, she faced complications from surgery and was making a slow recovery with "two bad setbacks"—Henry reported to Harold Guinzberg on April 8. Rebecca joked about it to the American novelist, Joseph Hergesheimer: her surgeon had leaned over her saying, "She loves me, she loves me not," plucking organ after organ. The truth was, she confessed, she had to rest most of the day.

On April 6, Germany launched a successful attack on Yugoslavia, which had refused to bow to Hitler's pressure. Rebecca worried about her friends, especially Anica Savic-Rebac and Stanislav Vinaver. Later she learned that three monks she had befriended had been murdered and that thirty thousand people in Macedonia had been packed into trains and transported out of the country.

The first exhilarating days of the Battle of Britain were over. Winnie had received a "heartbreaking letter from Lettie," and in Bath, where Winnie and her family still lived, homes and lives had been destroyed— the "dull murderous thuds go on and on. The town is almost a total ruin. The walls stand up and as you approach it looks just like a city of the living. People are going mad, you see them leaning against the walls muttering." Such letters made Rebecca mutter about Winnie's "provoking pessimism." Yet she admitted the war news was "unbearable."

The Yugoslavian book now seemed a "preternatural event." Why should she have been moved in 1936 to devote five years of her life, "at great financial sacrifice" and to the utter exhaustion of her mind and body, to an "inventory of a country down to its last vest-button, in a form insane from any ordinary artistic or commercial point of view"—a country which then ceased to exist? She found the hair rising on her scalp at the "extraordinary usefulness of this utterly futile act." Reading her proofs proved difficult. She might confront the same fate as her Yugoslav friends, but she could not stand to contemplate it.

Both her British and American publishers saw the book's greatness. To Rebecca's letter, abjectly apologizing for all the delays, and expressing her prayer that she would write a novel for Viking that would make it a lot of money, Harold Guinzberg replied that he could not predict how her book would sell, but he was not worried about the "ultimate fate of *Black Lamb*." He was certain that it was a "monumental achievement and a brilliant addition to the ranks of lasting books, and that sooner or later a great many people will want to own and read it." At Macmillan, her British editor, Lovat Dickson, later remembered that the bombing of London had disrupted publishing and paper was strictly rationed. At precisely this moment Rebecca had delivered her manuscript. "A smaller publisher, smaller in outlook as well as in size, might well have been appalled at the prospect of publishing at this time a work of such remote scholarship and forbidding length, at what would necessarily be a high price." Yet Daniel and Harold Macmillan did not hesitate, for they were fascinated with the book. "Who would not be," Dickson asks, "by a book which demonstrated by its argument that the East End of London would not then be lying in ruins if the Balkan Christian powers had not been defeated by the Turks in 1389?"

CHAPTER 20

Black Lamb and Grey Falcon:
A Modern Scheherazade

I

In 1941, Yugoslavia no longer existed; its people had lost their freedom in the German invasion. Rebecca dedicated her book to the Yugoslavs, sounding a nostalgic note when she expressed her hope they would recover the "Fatherland of their desire" and become again "citizens of Paradise." She structured her book as one continuous journey through Croatia, Dalmatia, Herzegovina, Bosnia, Serbia, Macedonia, Old Serbia, and Montenegro, a tour of history, which was also her journey, the story of a writer who constantly sought her own heaven on earth.

Black Lamb and Grey Falcon interweaves characters, dramatic scenes, dialogue, description, reportage, autobiography, literary criticism, philosophy, theology, and feminism; her insights are grounded in the colloquial as much as they are in art history and figurative language. Her book has been used as a travel guide; it is also a primer on how to take the modern world. She provides an account of civilization and its discontents. The book might seem tiresome and pretentious if it were not punctuated by story after story, each reflecting on the teller and the told. Some of the stories she tells at her own expense; she is not afraid to reveal her most deep-seated prejudices. But there are so many stories— enough for a thousand and one nights—that no single opinion she offers should be viewed in isolation, no thesis need mar her novel of history. She writes, in short, a self-correcting masterpiece.

In her prologue, Rebecca, like Proust, explores each phase of her feelings by delving further and further into the past and then reeling it back into the present. Her prologue is comparable to the "overture" in *Remembrance of Things Past*, in which Proust's method, themes, and characters are encapsulated. She recalls an evening in October 1934 in a London nursing home recovering from an operation to remove a tumor.

Restless, she tries to amuse herself by listening to music on the radio, switching from program to program until a wrong turn of the knob brings her the announcement that the King of Yugoslavia has been assassinated in the streets of Marseille that morning. Ringing for her nurse she demands a telephone so that she can call her husband and talk to him about the terrible news. How dreadful, the nurse responds, asking Rebecca if she knew the king. When Rebecca says she did not, the nurse wonders why Rebecca thinks the assassination so terrible.

That only a person's private world matters to the nurse reminds Rebecca that the word "idiot" is derived from a Greek root meaning private person. Rebecca explains to her nurse that assassinations lead to other dire events—indeed to 1914, to other wars, to humanity's apparently willful destruction of itself that might very well issue, this time, in her own death, in the global catastrophe that she knows would sooner or later overtake her generation. It is no use, however, for the nurse cannot grasp her patient's argument, and Rebecca recognizes that idiocy is a female fault; women are cut off from the world at large and cannot imagine how great events will engulf them. Men are no better, of course: They concentrate on public affairs but their preoccupation with large issues dims their vision, and they do not see the details that make up everyday reality.

Black Lamb and Grey Falcon is Rebecca West's effort to comprehend a world out of balance, a world of divergent sexes, a world that can only be saved by a marriage of opposites, of a husband and wife making up between them a whole vision of history. Only by telling her husband about the assassination, only by having him accompany her on her second trip to Yugoslavia, can she get history right—explain to herself and the world why what happens in Central Europe affects the core of Western identity. She speaks to her husband in the prologue of *Black Lamb and Grey Falcon*, but she is addressing her readers as well when she remarks that she knows he does not want to travel to Yugoslavia but that once there he will discover the importance of the journey.

Rebecca explains that thirty-six years earlier, when she was five, her mother and cousin had stood beside each other reading a newspaper with consternation because the Empress Elizabeth of Austria had been assassinated. This early childhood memory—joined five years later on June 11, 1903 by the assassination of the King of Serbia and his wife—remained more vivid to Rebecca than the murder of Franz Ferdinand in 1914. From the earliest age, it seemed to her that human beings were as much in love with death as with life.

Rebecca quotes Pascal's sentiment that man is a thinking reed who knows he will die and whose consciousness of death is nobler than the universe that would crush him. Pascal's words, she writes, inspire her to explore the dangers that threaten human existence. She believes that the Balkans will help to explain to her why she feels so personally threatened by her anticipation of another world war.

Rebecca also explains her affinity for Yugoslavs, whom she cherishes for their intense polyglot intellectual curiosity, which she contrasts to the standoffish, tepid reception visitors receive in England, which does not realize how much it owes to the Slavs who slowed and then stopped the spread of the Turks into the West. The Balkans allow Rebecca to see the conflicts of history in the open and not in the blurred and false optimism of the British Empire or the diffuseness of life in modern towns. Urban life actually covers up what people need to know if they are to survive.

Rebecca acknowledges a romantic—one might say a Balkan—strain in her blood that tends to intensify every insight, creating as much a fiction of Yugoslavia as a fact by including at strategic intervals her husband's sensible English advice: dispense with apocalyptic revelations, for if they were to come true she would not like it. Without Henry Andrews to test out her observations, to ask pointed questions, to respond with as much intelligence as emotion, the narrative of Black Lamb and Grey Falcon might not have achieved its balance between thought and feeling, fact and imagination, which is also the equilibrium of Rebecca's marriage.

It is Rebecca's contention that what occurs on the world stage is connected to the private heart. History must be brought home and made our own. How is it that Europe has come to suffer its Second World War and the triumphs of fascism even as her own country and most of Europe remain supine? What accounts for this passivity not only in her culture but in herself?

In Macedonia, in a sheep's field, she witnesses the sacrifice of a black lamb. Disgusted at the sight of the greasy and blood-drenched rock, reeking with the guts of life, she recognizes a ritual meant to purge people of sin. A little girl is brought to watch a man slit the black lamb's throat, catching in the spurt of blood enough to make a circle on the child's forehead. Rebecca rejects this ceremony, and the idea that such sacrifice is necessary. She is especially enraged that the little girl will be brought up to believe that such cruelty is required and will associate the act of childbearing with sin and pain.

Life divides for Rebecca right then between people who embrace and reject this notion of sacrifice, which she links to the great Serbian poem (recited to her by Constantine, himself a symbol of a defeated people). Tsar Lazar is visited by a gray falcon (Saint Elijah) offering him the choice of two kingdoms: heaven and earth. Lazar chooses heaven (eternal salvation) rather than earth and accepts the sacrifice of his soldiers and his kingdom in the battle against the Turks. Lazar's choice is the desire to be pure, to make a sacrifice of oneself, rather than be implicated in the evils of the earth. Rebecca rejects the thesis of the poem, that Lazar could redeem himself without considering the fate of his people, for his redemption meant five hundred years of domination by the Turks. In her own time, appeasing Hitler means consigning millions of people to slavery.

In the epilogue Rebecca charges that England in 1939 resembles the defeated Lazar at Kosovo in 1389, retreating from the superior force of the Turks. A conservative, mediocre England has forgotten what it means to fight for survival. This does not change until Churchill's leadership, when the country finally decides to reject its defeatist policy and to engage the Axis in a fight for freedom, to seek its kingdom of heaven on earth—the same one the Yugoslavs are fighting to preserve in the Second World War.

2

IN *The New York Times Book Review* (October 26, 1941) Katherine Woods hailed *Black Lamb and Grey Falcon* as the "apotheosis" of the travel book form. Clifton Fadiman's review in *The New Yorker* (October 25, 1941) pronounced *Black Lamb* "one of the great books of spiritual revolt against the twentieth century." His one reservation had to do with the book's size: "there is a little too much of everything." Rebecca agreed. "But what was I to do?" she asked him. She thought of herself as writing for the "historian of the future . . . or for that matter anybody who will have any say in European affairs after the war—or any artist." She herself had reviewed huge books and complained "this just is too damn much to be known, it can't be presented, it can't be apprehended. I still feel this is a real difficulty . . . in the way of man making anything of the universe."

The more critical reviewers rejected Rebecca's romanticism. In *The New Republic* (December 1, 1941), Nigel Dennis identified her journey through Yugoslavia as the "retelling of a tale we know all too well; the quest of the frustrated Western intellectual for a Nirvana of vitality and self-expression." Only when the "full swell and pageantry of these volumes take hold" did she leave her "small dogmatisms" and apply her "full powers to the story of centuries of tyranny and rebellion." This is a common misreading of *Black Lamb and Grey Falcon*, which overlooks the book's cunning strategy, its author's simultaneous presentation of herself as a character and a historian, a traveler and a novelist, prejudiced and objective at the same time.

In *The Nation* (June 8, 1941) Stoyan Pribichevich identified Constantine as Stanislav Vinaver and excoriated Rebecca for accepting his point of view. In effect, she had become a stooge for the government press bureau in Belgrade and had naively transmitted its propaganda for a unified and centralized Yugoslav state. She would have been better off writing a simpler travel book, sticking to her wonderful descriptions of the physical surface of things. His condescending attitude ignored her copious reading in Balkan history, her travels without Vinaver, and the plot of her book which dramatizes what Clifton Fadiman noticed as the "disintegration of Constantine." He is both "hero and victim, Churchill and Chamberlain," concludes critic Clare Colquitt.

Pribichevich censured her inattention to the peasantry. It is true that she is enamored of monarchs and heroes. (Critic Harold Orel notes, for example, that the bureaucratic Diocletian whose red tape helped strangle the Roman Empire is nowhere to be seen in Rebecca's "wonderworking and larger than life-size Emperor.") Pribichevich fails to see that her driver, Dragutin, gradually supplants Constantine as an authoritative voice in the book, a voice of earthy peasant wisdom, humor, kindness, but also ferocity. She is anything but naive when she quotes Dragutin shouting: "Hey Croat! You're a brave fellow. How do you like us Serbs?" When the Croat boy (who has been working with Serbs) answers that he likes Serbs very well, smiles, and admits "I had thought you were my enemies," Dragutin responds by twisting the boy's ear and saying "We'll kill you all some day." The boy wriggles and laughs, but the menacing quality is chilling and, as critic Richard Tillinghast observes, "prophetic." Rebecca West was hardly a dupe. She loves Dragutin for his closeness to nature, his reverent attitude toward water and animals, which she made touching and humorous at the same time. She finds him sitting on the automobile "trying to teach a tortoise he had just picked up on the road to lick a piece of chocolate. 'Why always grass, grass, grass?' he was asking." Later she has to explain to Dragutin that the tortoise's bowels "would immediately act if it was carried in an automobile." He is a complex human being. He loves to kill snakes; he is in fact a lover and a killer—another example of her view of human beings who sway between love of life and death.

Richard Tillinghast, a sympathetic critic, challenges "West's sanguine view of the Byzantine Empire, not shared by many modern historians," and he finds her view of the Turks "cartoonish." Especially foolish is her claim that there is no word in Turkish for interesting. "Anyone with even a basic knowledge of Turkish will often have used the verb *ilgilenmek*, 'to be interested in,' the adjective *ilgine*, 'interesting,' and a dozen other related words." The Turks can seem so disproportionally evil only in a writer who is ignorant of the Byzantine ruling classes who regularly employed "assassination, castration, blinding of enemies" and were "anything but decent and dignified." They were guilty of precisely the corruption and excessive taxation that she attributes to the Turks. Her ignorance of Islam, Tillinghast concludes, is "appalling."

Nearly all the negative judgments of *Black Lamb and Grey Falcon* take issue with its politics and feminism (or lack of it), paying virtually no attention to the implications of its novelistic form.

Critics like Lesley Chamberlain characterize some of the dialogue between Henry and Rebecca as "starchy and stylised." Mary Ellman makes contemptuous fun of the dialogues, dubbing Rebecca the balloon ("given over to piercing perceptions and lightning intuitions") and Henry the ballast (thinking "sound, solid, careful thoughts"). There is truth in this division, but it won't do because, as critic Dale Marie Urie notes, Henry's great monologue on the idea of process is "remarkably like the thought processes of West herself." It is well to remember that all the words in *Black Lamb and Grey Falcon* are Rebecca's own, even when she is quoting others. Henry does double duty, to use a cliché, as her other half. As in most intimate or long marriages, he sounds both like himself and like his wife. Critic Peter Wolfe says it best: "she does not consult him on every decision; nor does she ask the reader to share her high opinion of him. So little is clutching and forced in the Andrews' relationship, in fact, that *Black Lamb and Grey Falcon*, in addition to its other services, could do duty as a marriage manual."

When A.J.P. Taylor wrote to *Time and Tide* to protest an unfavorable review of *Black Lamb and Grey Falcon*, he and Rebecca became fast friends. She did not know that he had written at the instigation of historian Lewis Namier, a friend of Rebecca's whom she admired for his "pellucid" and "debonair" style. Taylor had no doubt that Rebecca was a brilliant writer, even though he later had doubts about *Black Lamb* and thought her a "strange mixture of penetration and wrong headedness"— a remarkable judgment coming from a scholar often accused of exhibiting a similar division of mind. Shortly after their correspondence began, he confided to Rebecca that her inaccuracies did not have any effect "on the picture you were making."

Rebecca responded to Namier's review of *Black Lamb* gratefully, though she objected to his view of her:

artlessness! You say, "There is no more system or completeness in it than in the colour-scheme of wild flowers in a field." How I worked to get that effect. I wanted people, not the great and good, but just people—to learn what the South Slav situation is and its importance to them. They couldn't learn anything about that situation without following a long, complicated story, making many more demands on their powers of concentration and their patience than they were accustomed to concede. To get them to go the way I wanted them I deliberately gave the story the loose attractiveness of various pleasant things in life—such as wild flowers in a field. Again and again I broke sequences and relaxed tension to get the lethargic attention of the ordinary reader along the road.

The language Rebecca employs, especially in her last sentence, conveys how much she wanted her book not only to be about a journey but to convey the sense of presenting itself as a journey. Several sections, for example, are entitled "Road." Journalist/travelers still rely on her guidance: "I would rather have lost my passport and money than my heavily thumbed copy and annotated copy of *Black Lamb and Grey Falcon*," writes Robert D. Kaplan in *Balkan Ghosts*.

3

BLACK LAMB AND GREY FALCON is still the book to read on the Balkans. It renders vividly the tensions between Croats, Serbs, and Muslims, and the inability of the great powers to understand or to promote a unified Yugoslavia. The extraordinary vibrancy of the south Slavs that Rebecca evokes so well continues to mesmerize such unromantic reporters as Misha Glenny in his award-winning book, *The Fall of Yugoslavia*. Glenny is far more skeptical of Serb pretensions than Rebecca. Her pro-Serb bias would surely have made her an unpopular commentator today among those who condemn Serbian aggression. Yet her book explains better than any other why Serbs led in founding Yugoslavia after World War I, just as the Prussians led in establishing a unified Germany and the Piedmont led in Italy. Serbs had the strongest tradition of self-rule, and that tradition—Rebecca would have pointed out—was stifled and perverted during Tito's Communist rule, which promoted a bogus internationalism and suppressed differences between Serbs, Croats, and Muslims that were bound to emerge once Communism proved itself a sham. In *Serbs and Croats: The Struggle in Yugoslavia*, Alex N. Dragnich has recently reaffirmed Rebecca's attack on Tito, who weakened the Serbs (the largest ethnic group in Yugoslavia) by assimilating them into different republics in a Soviet-style federalism. Tito falsely claimed that he had solved the nationality problem and unified the Yugoslav state. In fact, he had merely postponed the day of reckoning, when the Serbs would reclaim the vanguard role they played in pre-World War II Yugoslavia. Tito had made it impossible to address the unresolved issues left over from the war by denying the concept of national political rights—not only for Serbs, Croats, and Muslims but for Macedonians, Albanians, Hungarians, Italians, and Slovenes. The Third Balkan War (as Glenny calls it) hardly vindicates Rebecca's partiality to Serbs, but it does confirm her view that national, ethnic, and local identities should not be summarily subsumed by any ideology.

CHAPTER 21

Blocked and Abandoned
1941–1945

I

BETWEEN OCTOBER 1941 and the end of 1944, Rebecca struggled to complete her "Russian novel," provisionally entitled *Cockcrow*. Set in 1908, it focuses on fourteen-year-old Laura Rowan, the daughter of a Russian mother, Tania, and an English father, Edward. Laura accompanies her mother to Paris on a visit to her grandparents, the Diakonovs. Nikolai Diakonov, a Tsarist minister, is living in Paris in disgrace, unjustly suspected of divulging information that led to the assassinations of several government officials. When Laura accompanies Nikolai on a train excursion into the Parisian countryside, they are accosted in their carriage by Chubinov, a revolutionary who announces to Nikolai that his trusted friend and aide, Kamensky, has been a double agent, betraying both the government and the revolutionaries. The shock proves too much for Nikolai, who dies before returning to Paris and to Russia, where he had hoped to submit himself to the Tsar's judgment, even at the risk of dying first at Kamensky's hands.

Laura witnesses the male public world Rebecca West criticizes in *Black Lamb*. Although Nikolai treats Kamensky as a trusted subordinate and even condescends occasionally to show Kamensky some affection, he has not really known his man; he misses the details that make Kamensky not only an individual but a traitor. The inquisitive Laura picks up Kamensky's spectacles, sees that they are made of clear glass, and concludes he is a pretender. Her discovery provides one of the details that convinces Nikolai that Chubinov has correctly identified Kamensky as a double agent, whom Chubinov knows as the master revolutionary, Gorin. (Ford Madox Ford told Rebecca of such a case, of the double agent Azeff, whose story is the inspiration for the novel.)

It devolves on Laura to see that Kamensky/Gorin has loved and betrayed Nikolai just as he has loved and betrayed Chubinov and the other revolutionaries. As Gorin he is a father figure to Russian radicals, and Chubinov's attitude toward him is nothing less than reverential. At the same time, Chubinov is the son of one of Nikolai's oldest friends, and although Chubinov detests Nikolai's politics, he comes to warn Nikolai and to confess that he has regarded Nikolai as a father figure. Thus treachery is deeply imbedded in family relations. Although it seems incredible that Kamensky/Gorin could endear himself to opposite sides of the political spectrum, in fact those opposites are kin to each other—just as in *Black Lamb and Grey Falcon* the Serbs and Croats argue against each other but use the same accents and gestures.

Both Nikolai and Edward Rowan are reminiscent of Rebecca's autocratic Anglo-Irish father, whose mother's name was Arabella Rowan. Like Charles Fairfield, Edward Rowan is a snob: "his voice always sounded as if he were making fun of someone." Nikolai regards himself as a "pillar" holding up the Tsar's kingdom. Edward Rowan is "strongly and slenderly built." Laura admires him as a "symbol of calm," but he is "too arrogant," and prone to "Irish malice." He stands with "too artificial an alertness," in a position appropriate only to a "fencer in play." In fact, he establishes his authority by verbal fencing: "Her father liked to play at tyranny, it was his nature to argue." Nikolai never accepts anyone's opinion without an argument. He is "like a mad king out of a play." Indeed, he is Rebecca West's version of King Lear, blind to the treachery in his own family. Laura's mother Tania has chosen to marry a tyrant similar to her father. In many respects, Edward Rowan establishes a household with a brilliant but submissive wife, resembling Charles Fairfield's own household. Edward Rowan even comes from County Kerry. He has grown up in a privileged home Laura hears about but never gets to visit, and in her deprived state she deplores his "cold pedantry and lack of ordinary feelings." Edward Rowan is also an adulterer, another kind of family traitor.

Rebecca's novel stalled when she tried to project Laura Rowan's life beyond the duel between Chubinov and Nikolai. She did not yet see that their train journey, like her journey to Yugoslavia, had to encompass the novel. Attempting to write past the logical conclusion of her novel, she finally had to stop, having taken a wrong turn.

2

IN JANUARY 1944, Churchill changed horses on Yugoslavia, provoking an eruption in Rebecca's life with aftershocks that lasted almost to the day she died. Since April 1941, when Yugoslavia was attacked, he had been supporting General Mihailović, the leader of the loyalists, often referred to as the Chetniks,* supporters of King Peter and the Yugoslav government-in-exile in London. It had been the natural choice for Churchill, a fervent anti-Communist before the war—although he did not want to upset the Soviets, his valuable ally, by appearing to oppose Communists in Yugoslavia. The other option had been to back Tito, head of the Yugoslav Communist Party since 1937 and leader of the resistance (the Partisans) in the western part of the country. Before the war, the Yugoslav Communist Party had a negligible following. A paid Soviet agent, Tito had followed Stalin's line slavishly, even approving the Hitler–Stalin pact in 1939 and calling the war a British imperialist enterprise that Communists should shun.

For over two years Churchill had stood by Mihailović, even though he received reports that Tito was engaging in an effective guerilla campaign against the Germans. Mihailović, hampered by lack of supplies and arms, conducted fewer attacks on the Germans; there were reports from the SOE (Special Operations Executive) in Cairo that he was collaborating with the Germans and the Italians although British and American officers who were with the loyalists saw no evidence of this.

Richard Lamb, in *Churchill as War Leader* and David Martin in *Web of Disinformation: Churchill's Yugoslav Blunder,* take a position close to Rebecca's, condemning Churchill for going over to the Communists. Franklin Lindsay, in *Beacons of the Night,* provides a first-hand view of Tito and the Partisans and argues that Churchill was right. Boris Todorovich, a member of Mihailović's forces, and Michael Lees, a British liaison officer with a Mihailović unit, and others, have published memoirs defending his policies and claiming that his refusal to fight stemmed from strategic and humane considerations (Germans killed one hundred Serb hostages for every German killed) and that his failures to engage the enemy were exaggerated. One of the key arguments of Milhailović's defenders is that Communist infiltration of the British services, including the Foreign Office, SOE, and BBC, ensured that Tito's successes were overstated and Milhailović's were underplayed, and after 1942 often knowingly maligned. In August 1943, Sir George Rendel, British ambassador for the Yugoslav government-in-exile, became disturbed at the anti-Mihailović tone "creeping into any discussion we had on Yugoslavia." By 1943, the British had found it easier to send supplies and

---

*The Serb-Croat spelling is Cetniks, but Chetnik has entered English usage. Otherwise, I use the Yugoslav ć rather than spelling it out as tch.

arms to Tito than it had ever been able to do for Mihailović. Support for Tito, Rendel noted in his memoirs, had more to do with seconding the efforts of Britain's Russian allies, now touted in the British Left's campaign for Tito.

Rebecca believed in Mihailović's staunch anti-Fascist record before the war, and even if he had parlayed with the Germans, she said it would have been for temporary tactical purposes. Such shifting of position was common fare in Balkan history, she emphasized. She relied on reports from Yugoslav friends and a considerable flow of correspondence from Slavs who admired *Black Lamb and Grey Falcon* and wanted to apprise her of what was happening to their country. She also had access to information from contacts in the Foreign Office.

Rebecca's friends R. W. Seton-Watson and A.J.P. Taylor, historians of the Austro-Hungarian empire and of the Balkans, questioned Mihailović's motivations. Seton-Watson wrote to *Time and Tide* (July 24, 1943): "It is not a service to the Yugoslav cause to exaggerate his role or to treat him as one who can unite all Yugoslavs behind him." Reports of Mihailović's collaboration with the Italians and of his forces' burning of Croat villages disturbed Seton-Watson. Tito had contributed at least as much to the resistance as Mihailović, and he had the "active sympathy of our Russian allies," Seton-Watson concluded. But he made no mention of the massacre of thousands of Serbs by Croat and Moslem Ustase (Fascist collaborators).

A.J.P. Taylor put the case directly to Rebecca: "You don't seem to have made up your mind whether Mike [Mihailović] is right because he is trying to preserve Yugoslavia or whether he is right because he has despaired of Yugoslavia and is going back to great Serbia. All you insist on is that somehow he is right, but you can't have it both ways." Taylor predicted that the post-World War I effort to combine Slavs into multiethnic national states was doomed to failure. The Serbs would be better off without the Croats because federations of Slavs would never be stable enough to defend themselves from the great powers. Russian influence was inevitable in the Balkans, and Rebecca should make her peace with it. There is no record of her reply to Taylor's letters, but she would surely have scoffed at this sentence: "The Russians are not democratic now, but there is a chance they may become so; there's not much chance for us." She wanted Russians to become defenders of Western virtues, Taylor alleged, virtues the British were "too corrupt and feeble to do anything about." In a passage that could only have maddened her, he deplored Russian ruthlessness while excusing it as an inevitable historical process, one that Great Britain itself had done much to promulgate: "The peasant must disappear; that is the lesson of all civilization. Nasty for him, but it can't be helped. And, in the long run, the Russian way of liquidating him is no worse than our way in the eighteenth century, which has made us the civilized people we are." Rebecca had made it clear in *Black Lamb and Grey Falcon* that British imperialism, as bad as it had been, was not anywhere near as evil as Nazism and Communism. To relativize all forms of imperialism in this way was to lose one's moral compass—which is what she saw happening in the move from Mihailović to Tito.

To Rebecca, Churchill had decided, before the end of the war, to consign Yugoslavia to Communist tyranny. She had predicted before Munich that either the Nazis or the Communists would dominate the small countries in Central and Eastern Europe. By picking Tito, Churchill had made his choice. His short-term goal might be winning the war, which meant supporting Stalin and Tito, but in the long term he had already lost the peace. By the end of January 1944, she had completed a satirical story, "Madame Sara's Magical Crystal," which exposed Churchill's crime. In effect, she implied, he had replicated Munich, handing over a country's destiny to a dictator. For patriotic reasons, she did not publish the story, accepting the word of Sir Orme Sargent of the Foreign Office that the switch had been made to Tito for purely practical purposes, so that the war against Hitler could be won as quickly as possible. But she never changed her support for Mihailović and the Yugoslav government-in-exile.

3

MILAN GAVRILOVIĆ, head of the Peasant Party in Yugoslavia before the war and then a minister in the London government-in-exile, wrote Rebecca a note about *Black Lamb and Grey Falcon* shortly after its British publication in early 1942 (it had appeared in America several months earlier). He liked the book very much, although he pointed out errors he hoped she would correct in a second edition. He shared her views of the Austro-Hungarian empire and of the dangers of Communism. She met him and his wife, Lela, at an official function, and they soon became friends. Rebecca often visited them at their home, befriending their children, Kosara (Kosa), Voya, and Darinka (Soza), as well as Aleksa when he joined the family in London at the end of October 1945.

The bond between Rebecca and the Gavrilovićs became especially profound because she identified with their exile. She told Milan Gavrilović a story that convinced him and his family that her anti-Tito attitudes had put her in jeopardy. In early January 1944 Rebecca had had lunch with Herbert Morrison, a Labor Party minister in the War Cabinet, and with Kenneth Pickthorn, a Conservative MP for Cambridge and a staunch supporter of Mihailović. After lunch with Morrison and a discussion with cabinet minister Anthony Eden, Pickthorn had become disturbed at how the government apparently viewed his and Rebecca's efforts on Mihailović's behalf. He turned to Rebecca and said, "You and I could easily find ourselves in prison for a year if we continue our activity." Milan's son, Aleksa, believed that the pro-Titoists would never forgive Rebecca for her views: "The Right wouldn't say Churchill was wrong, and the Left followed their own policies." She felt herself to be a pariah. "There were others who were sympathetic to her position but kept quiet," Aleksa avowed.

Kosa believed that the ostracism Rebecca felt sealed her commitment to the Gavrilović family into a love/hate affair corresponding to her divided nature. Certainly for better or worse she treated them like family, except for Milan himself, who was spared her paranoic reactions.

Kosa observed that Rebecca seemed incapable of truly giving her affection to someone without feeling threatened by the gift and diminished by her own generosity. It was like giving away a part of herself that she could not reclaim. She would send what Kosa called "gift-catalogue letters," enumerating all the things Rebecca had done for her. Kosa realized that Rebecca expected her to be eternally grateful. This demand for appreciation became exasperating, even though Rebecca deserved it. She could make a claim on someone that was annihilating.

Yet for Kosa there is no doubt that "we loved Rebecca and she loved us." She was enormously, spontaneously entertaining, and took great joy in the Gavrilović family. On a visit to the Gavrilovićs, Rebecca sat in their mother Lela's chair and happened to feel something Lela had stuck under the cushion when she had gotten up to answer the doorbell. Rebecca said: "The public is kindly requested not to remove cushions of chairs because the family laundry is kept there." The Gavrilovićs found a second home at Ibstone while visiting during the air raids. Kosa used to help in the kitchen, and one day spilled the entire lunch on the floor. Rebecca said, "Pick it up. They won't know what happened to it." She had a way of bustling life along.

Rebecca wrote a letter to Myra Curtis, Kosa's principal at Newnham College, revealing how upsetting and yet how grand she found the Gavrilovićs. They were not to be regarded as "ordinary human beings." It would be like applying "plain geometry to gases, or trying to make a sunset fill in a ration card." She could not satisfy Curtis's inquiry about their financial position: "Possibly prayer is the only method by which we could be given this information." She expected Kosa to "go on being wafted to Cambridge on a Gavrilović tide," motivated by "considerations that would be recognised as valid by the characters of Homer." Rebecca reported herself ready for any crisis, "as these people are really angelic in character and full of genius."

The Gavrilovićs of the letter are Rebecca's own overstated creation, true in spirit perhaps, if not always faithful to fact—like *Black Lamb and Grey Falcon* itself, Kosa remarked. But then everything was overblown with Rebecca. Kosa remembered Henry mentioning some very fine antique furniture he had wanted to buy. He had not done so because he knew Rebecca would make a scene. "ME, MAKE A SCENE, ME!" shouted Rebecca, making a scene. She seemed to Kosa the consummate actress, saying what she felt at the moment, and feeling its absolute truth. There was nothing behind this phenomenon; she was simply absorbed in her role.

All of the Gavrilovićs admired Henry enormously. Aleksa appreciated the intellectual rapport between husband and wife. Although Henry took an unassuming role, he worked closely with Czech leader Jan Masaryk and other Central European leaders, planning for the economic reconstruction of Europe after the war. Kosa, Soza, and Voya adored Henry as the perfect English gentleman. Soza showed him some of her youthful poetry. He was charming about it; only afterward did she appreciate his criticism: "It is very beautiful, my dear, but you know you must not just fall in love with words. They must mean something." Kosa found him a "tall and sparse and somewhat ascetic looking figure. He was gentle in speech, but precise and a little fastidious." Voya thought Henry the pokiest driver in England: "The light would change and Henry would not move the car. Then instead of accelerating, he would get out of his car and apologize to the driver behind him—by which time the light had changed again."

The Gavrilovićs saw that Rebecca was Henry's queen, he her *chevalier servant*. The French medieval analogy reveals what went wrong with the marriage and why Henry supplied both succor and disappointment. As Kosa suggested, "at the first sign of danger, at the slightest threat to her reputation, her peace of mind, her mere comfort, Henry would enter the lists, his lady's colours flying high. But, when the danger came from within, as at times it did, he would be driven to distraction by his impotence. How could he protect Rebecca from Rebecca?" The inner demons are, by definition, elusive. Knights are not psychiatrists, nor are most husbands.

But Henry did his best, trying to spare both Rebecca and Lela Gavrilović the results of Rebecca's storms. Lela had unwittingly offended Rebecca with a story. At the age of eleven or twelve, Lela had collided with a waiter one disastrous afternoon in Abbazia's most elegant pastry shop. An enormous tray of pastry, pots of tea, cups of cappuccino, and hot chocolate topped with whipped cream, glasses of mineral water, dishes of ice cream, and other delicacies descended on Lela and on her exquisite suit with a pleated skirt of white flannel. Nothing so calamitous had happened since the fall of the Austro-Hungarian empire. Lela had worn the suit to show off to her mother and her friends, but Lela had created such a spectacular mess that her mother, usually a woman of great courage, ran out of the shop.

Lela had told this story many times, impressing her children with her juvenile excesses, working on their admiration and curiosity by leaving out details she knew they would press for: How had she coped with the situation? Who cleaned up? Who paid for the smashed porcelain? How did Lela feel? But Rebecca was horrified at one thing: the white flannel suit with the pleated skirt. At eleven and twelve, Rebecca was a shabbily dressed figure of genteel poverty—as she describes herself in "A Visit to a Godmother." That Lela could make such a joke of the dress appalled Rebecca. Lela was surprised, replying to Rebecca in her poor but fluent and often eloquent English: "But Rebecca, you must have had dozens of vite flannel suits or somessing like vite flannel suits, ennyvey, since zen." Yes, but "not then, not when it mattered. Not when I wanted it. Not when you did." Lela's efforts to placate Rebecca only made it worse: "Ach, vant it, vant it. I did not really vant it . . . I just remember ze mess. Ze funny faces." Rebecca's rage increased: "And she didn't buy it simply because she couldn't, because it was *one of a kind*? And you ruined it. . . . And forgot about?" Lela said reasonably, "Vell, Rebecca. I have *not* forgotten. After all, I am telling you ze story."

What for Lela was a story became for Rebecca a parable of the rich. Lela had been relatively wealthy, now she was poor. The change in status did not seem to spoil her enjoyment of the here and now; she allowed nothing to interfere with her happiness. Lela would say, "I cannot help it, and if I cannot help it, I shall not think about it." Lela's attitude maddened Rebecca, who determined to set her right.

One morning at half past six the doorbell rang at the Gavrilovićs' London flat. It was Henry, looking ghastly in a crumpled suit—a remarkable appearance for such a fastidious man. "Iss Rebecca ill?" Lela inquired. "Perhaps," he muttered oddly. "May I come in?" he asked in front of Kosa and Voya, who were gaping at him and blocking his way.

"Of course. Please," they immediately responded in soothing accents, offering tea to this kind man they loved so much. It was awkward. Nothing was said for a while. Then with the tea, Lela (looking at his disheveled figure) asked, "Did you stay at your club?" Henry shook his head. He had spent the night in his Rolls. He just sat there, his elbows leaning on his thighs, his hands hanging limply between his knees. He never moved. Finally Lela said very softly, "Henry." Startled, he looked at Lela with such unspeakable misery that Kosa thought Rebecca must be dead.

"I came to ask . . ."

"Anyssing, Henry."

"Cicily wrote you a letter. I asked her not to send it. She refused. I have come to ask you not to read it."

"Of course."

"I thought I would wait here with you for the postman . . ."

"Of course."

"She loves you very much."

"Of course."

"She has not been able to write, you know. It is very hard for her."

"Of course."

"When it is all over, she will be different. I mean, she will be the same as she was . . ."

The morning post brought a heavy, long letter. Henry took it from Lela. "May I?" he asked her. Lela barely nodded and he tore the letter across and threw it in the stove.

Other letters came, and Lela, warned by Henry, destroyed them unopened. Henry was right, of course. Rebecca did return to her old self. She never abandoned the Gavrilovićs. Indeed, there would be several jolly postwar reunions, when Rebecca visited the sisters Gavrilović, resettled in America, or when they visited her. When she finally did finish her Russian novel, *The Birds Fall Down* (1966), she dedicated it to Milan and Lela Gavrilović, "whom I love and honor." When Milan died in 1976, she wrote in *The Washington Star* that he was one of Europe's wise men, whose wisdom had been rejected. "He was the very image of the day we threw away when we decided to stay in the night."

CHAPTER 22

"And How I See the Drama Go On" 1944–1945

I

DURING THE LAST TWO YEARS of the war, life continued at Ibstone with its usual assortment of troubled household staff and farm laborers, illnesses, visitors, and refugees. Rebecca complained of chronic fatigue, but she worked with the Woman's Institute in her village, traveled to London for meetings of the Scenario Institute (discovering scripts), reached the 75,000 word mark of her Russian novel, wrote articles for *Time and Tide* and other journals, attended a reception at Buckingham Palace where she met the Queen, and "put in a hell of a lot of time wiping the eyes of the bewildered Yugoslavs."

Rebecca took great joy in the visits of her grandchildren Caroline (born October 7, 1941) and Edmund (born March 16, 1943). Rebecca admired Caroline's "great glowing brown eyes." She was sure to have her mother's "grace and fine build." Edmund was so big and blond and Nordic-looking that Rebecca could not imagine how he had gotten into the family. She admired the hard work Anthony put in on the farm, ably assisted by his "gay and capable" Kitty, a "perfect mother." Rebecca reported to her American friend Doris Stevens: "Anthony says in an awed way, 'I have done well for myself,' which is indeed the voice of love!"

Less than a month later, in April 1944, Rebecca's vision of Anthony's happiness, and her own, collapsed. Her anxieties began with the haunting conviction that H.G. was dying. He had progressively deteriorated in the first months of 1944. Anthony rang Rebecca to say that it was liver cancer and that H.G. would be dead within a year. There might be a brief remission. H.G. might feel better before he got worse, but because of his growing suspicions, Anthony said it was best to tell him the truth. Anthony had wanted to have this conversation with his mother in person but could not get away from London, where he was working part-time for the BBC. Rebecca said, "I suppose you did not want to tell me over the telephone because you must be feeling dreadful." He surprised her by replying, "No, it was because I thought you would be feeling dreadful." In her diary, she claimed her "chief anxiety" was that Anthony would not be "hit too hard." She had made her peace with H.G. She had not forgotten any of his cruel treatment of her, but she emphasized that "our affection is real and living."

A few days after Anthony's call, Marjorie Wells (the wife of H.G.'s eldest son, Gip) telephoned, prompting Rebecca to visit H.G. She found him "pitifully miserable and afraid," fretting about his illness and about his doctor's refusal to tell him exactly when he would die. He cried and said he didn't want to die. An incensed Rebecca deplored Gip's and Anthony's decision to tell H.G. he was dying. It had led to a breach with Lord Horder, who was not only H.G.'s doctor, but an old friend and H.G.'s pupil in the period before he became a writer. Rebecca listened to H.G.'s fond comments on Horder and believed H.G. missed him terribly, for Horder was not only a good doctor but the "greatest of Nannies," adept at holding people's hands when they were afraid. H.G. asked her to write to Horder and to intercede on his behalf. Overcome by H.G.'s helplessness, Rebecca confessed that she felt as if "he were my child and people had tortured him." She went home to Ibstone to walk in the woods and weep.

Her reaction put her in opposition not only to Anthony but to the rest of H.G.'s family. They believed in him as a great man who always defended and demanded the truth. Surely he would want to be informed of his approaching death. He said as much in one of his letters, decrying the "humming and hawing" of his doctors. It was exasperating not to be given a "plain answer." But Rebecca scoffed at his devotion to truth (calling him a big liar) and dismissed the family out of hand, saying they were stupid and silly to frighten him during his last days. She talked with Horder, whom she understood as refusing to be more definite with H.G. about his condition because his enlarged liver was not yet cancerous. To Anthony and Gip, however, it was simply a matter of time—a few years at best—before H.G. succumbed; they felt uncomfortable ducking his pointed questions.

In mid-April, Rebecca and Anthony met at the Lansdowne, her London club, to discuss H.G. She was angry with Anthony for confederating with the Wells family. To her, he appeared obstinate, uncomfortable, with a "swollen and stupid" face, the opposite of her "tough, sensible, mature" Anthony, who would soon be thirty. She disliked his bogus self-importance. It irritated Rebecca to have Anthony point out that H.G.'s mistress, Moura Budberg, was a Soviet spy, and that H.G. had no one to depend on but Gip and Marjorie. Rebecca knew that rather better than Anthony, she thought. She found him "curiously melodramatic" when he took her hand (" 'ponging it,' as actors say") and declared in a nasal voice that he did not mean to be cruel—he would rather do anything than hurt her—but she had to know the truth. It had been a long time since she had been the center of H.G.'s life, and she had better reconcile herself to the fact that he was much closer to Gip than to her. An outraged Rebecca retorted: "Don't talk such nonsense, it's some years since I took firm steps not to be the centre of H.G.'s life. . . . What are you putting on this show for?"

But Rebecca's own reactions answer her question. She may have made her peace with H.G., but she felt entitled to regard the entire Wells family as fools and Anthony as speaking in that "sweetish humbug which was the style of the Wells household." Hadn't she, in her own words, characterized her feeling for H.G. as that of a mother for a child? Wasn't she rejecting Anthony in those passages in her diary that commented on "something so queer about Anthony's face, so fat and animal." Although she portrayed him as turning against her, undoubtedly to Anthony her attitude and demeanor signaled a rejection of him. He may have come off as rather artificial and stagy in his approach to his mother, but his acting was a kind of reverse image of hers, a form of role-playing he had learned from her. Yet to Rebecca, Anthony's behavior was an example of emotional excess of a piece with his monetary extravagance, now in evidence in his habit of keeping a taxi ticking outside during his appointments in wartime London.

Rebecca seems to have been too upset to have realized that there may have been some gallantry in Anthony's treatment of her; he was tactfully trying to tell her not to interfere in the Wells family. As he got into the cab she called out, "I bought this hat this morning. Is it too young?" Anthony laughed and shouted, "Of course not, you've got fifty years before you." She makes no comment on this parting in her diary; it is a keepsake of love that neither mother nor son knew how to treasure.

Less than a month later, in May, Rebecca received a note from Kitty announcing that Anthony had asked her for a divorce. He had been seeing a twenty-four-year-old woman at the BBC, and he wanted to marry her. "That's a pity, my love, as you are married to me," Kitty replied. A shocked Kitty was unprepared for his request and initially thought he was joking. She told Rebecca: "Last month has been as happy as any other in the last eight and a half years of my life which is saying a lot." Since this had been Rebecca's impression of the marriage as well, she was very angry at Anthony and aggrieved for Kitty, whom Rebecca "loved like a daughter."

In late May, Rebecca wrote to H.G. of the "shattering blow" Anthony's behavior had given her, made worse because he had seemed to her "completely stabilised. And he certainly had shown signs of remarkable practical ability. I had thought him sure of a happy life." What a pity H.G. had to cope with this trouble while he was ill, but she ended on a cheering note: "as one who has known the furry carcass for over thirty years it strikes me the doctors have all been wrong, and you need not worry at the moment about removal to another sphere of usefulness? controversy? whatever. Much love, Panther."

An astounded Rebecca learned that Anthony expected Kitty to keep the farm going while he pursued his affair and work in London. This calamity overturned Rebecca's world. "I can't tell you what I felt like," she wrote a friend, "because I suddenly found—to an extent I hadn't grasped and can't quite explain—that my happiness in my life was dependent on Anthony's happiness—and more still on Caroline and Edmund's happiness. That my son should spoil these glorious children's prospects—their psyches' prospects, I mean, just can't be borne. This goes deeper than anything." Rebecca had noticed the especially close bond between Caroline and Anthony, and she feared that her "intelligent and sensitive" granddaughter would be "maimed by this tragedy." Rebecca was also thinking of her own closeness to her father and the grief his abandonment had caused her.

Rebecca wanted to ensure the financial security of Kitty and the children. She went to H.G.'s house to say that if he planned to leave money to Anthony, it had better go instead to his wife and children. Gip came down the stairs looking "so like his abominable mother" that Rebecca could hardly bear it. She asked him if he thought H.G. well enough to tolerate such a discussion. Gip blinked at her like an owl and said she must use her own discretion. "I realise it will be very painful," she said. "Yes," he replied, "but of course Anthony hasn't really had any chance, has he? I mean he's had no sort of bringing up, has he? I mean, he had no sort of regular education, had he? I mean, he was put down here and put down there, wasn't he?" It was almost enough to make Rebecca cry. Trying to remain calm she referred to extenuating circumstances—his year in the sanatorium and later a heart infection. "Ah, yes! Ah, yes!" was all Gip said.

H.G. behaved remarkably well, considering his own poor health and his son's troubles. His words had a soothing impact on Rebecca: "Rebecca, I must tell you that Anthony has told me he wants to leave Kitty. I have done everything to dissuade him." He then talked to her for about ten minutes, kindly, wisely, and lovingly, which Rebecca gratefully received in her characteristically divided way: "I remembered again what had once been between us, what he had stood on and dragged round the house by its hair and thrown into the canal with a brick round its neck—but what was still a living thing." H.G. sent for Kitty and told her he was changing his will to leave something for her and the children. He did it gently, making none of the fuss about Anthony that marked Rebecca's dealing with Kitty.

The next week, Rebecca visited H.G. again, and he told her about his long talks with Anthony. He agreed with her that their cub was silly, theatrical, and childish. He found Anthony confused and repetitive, but he urged her not to worry so much about Anthony's affairs. There was bound to be much about him that they did not understand; he did not explain himself very well. Nevertheless, H.G. did not intend to lose confidence in him.

At first, Kitty welcomed Rebecca's fervent support and thanked her for a "wise and kind and helpful letter." After Anthony had left her, she had read over everything he had written, realizing that nearly all of it was autobiographical. He had forbidden her to read his manuscripts, because she had a knack for discovering those evasive or dishonest aspects of his work, causing him to destroy it and rush away from her into his "secret shell of despair and fury." In her happiness with him she had been able to ignore "this barrier of reserve and secrecy." Now the barrier had been broken, and they had said things to each other which should have been said long ago. She still loved him and would not relinquish him easily just because he asked her. There had been too much of that in her marriage already. She did not care to have the farm without him, yet she would not move out just to please him and his new love. The farm was something she and Anthony had built together, and she could no more imagine handing it over to another woman than Rebecca could imagine consigning Ibstone to Henry and another.

Kitty's initial reaction to Anthony's request for a divorce impressed Rebecca, particularly Kitty's remark that Anthony seemed to feel the "idea of parting with the farm almost more than parting with the babies!" It was an appalling thought to Kitty, who had surprised herself by loving motherhood. That Anthony, a devoted father when at home, was reverting to his adolescence (Rebecca's pet theory), seemed confirmed by

Kitty's report that Anthony had said his new love was "himself at 18. You know better what that means than I do," Kitty told Rebecca, "but in any case it seems to me a most perverted fancy. I can't think of anything personally that would attract me less." Even Kitty's willingness to wink at Anthony's affairs (she was to learn he had had others) so long as he did not smash all that they had coincided with Rebecca's acknowledgment in her diary that Anthony had been unfaithful, but she had hoped he would not use a trifling affair to break up his marriage.

Rebecca speculated that Anthony was a reincarnation of her father. Was he to become a "shiftless, queer, dishonest, vagabond" like Charles Fairfield, a man whose "great gifts were of no avail"? It was as if Anthony were not "living his own life, but were forced to re-enact the destinies of the damned precursors." Rebecca tied her Gothic knot even tighter by musing that Anthony's actions also mimicked H.G.'s, "who is really only a successful version of my father." H.G. had left his "sweet and kind first wife when he was about Anthony's age and went off with Jane who was a bar between him and all honesty."

Rebecca could scarcely admit that she had contributed to Anthony's troubles: "Sometimes in Anthony's childhood I failed him—I can see where I could have been more loving—but I was so tired and tormented—and I don't think I failed him often. I have tried to make up for those failures." Rebecca knew that for all her demonizing of H.G., she would be blamed for Anthony's misadventures. A son may attack his father for not being close, but he will condemn his mother for not giving him the love and security he craves. It is the "maternal paradox: because the mother is at the center of her son's life, he comes to believe in her omnipotence—a belief that only dooms her to disappoint him." Rebecca's reaction to her responsibility was to become a more intrusive part of Anthony's life. The more she tried to redeem her failures the more Anthony and Kitty regarded her as perpetuating them. Every move Rebecca made to express her love also came loaded with hostility, for "sons do seem to create problems for women who are trying to balance their love for a particular male child with their own accumulated resentments toward men." There is nothing unusual in Rebecca's linking her son to her father, except that her literary sensibility transformed this link into a plot as powerful as her fiction. "I am having a really bad time," she wrote to G. B. Stern, "Second Part of The Judge and all that."

Rebecca began calling Anthony's and Kitty's friends. One of them told her that he had been restless for months; it was surprising that Kitty had not noticed it. But to Kitty, Anthony had always been restless; they had moved every eighteen months or so during their marriage. Rebecca wrote to Anthony's psychiatrist, the English Freudian, Edward Glover, giving her view of Anthony's childhood and explaining her recent dealings with Anthony and Kitty. She wrote to Anthony, pointing out that it would weigh heavily on his conscience if he abandoned his children. He had only to think of the damage done himself. Her greatest regrets, she told him, were those occasions when she had failed him. She asked Anthony to meet with Henry, who had been a wonderful source of support throughout her ordeal, and whom Anthony trusted. Anthony agreed but then canceled the appointment.

Rebecca wrote to Kitty, saying that even if Kitty parted from Anthony, Rebecca hoped Kitty would not divorce her. Rebecca expressed her love and admiration for her daughter-in-law, but also rehashed in offensive detail all her reasons for thinking Anthony had gone mad and why Kitty should pity her. She treated Kitty to her theories about the unreliability of men; she conceded Anthony's "appalling childhood" (due mainly to H.G.'s weakness and Jane's wickedness), her lack of friends, money, and wretched health, and sending Anthony away to school at too early an age so that she could do her work. Naturally he assumed that his mother could not be bothered with him. It was not true, but it was understandable that Anthony should feel this way, Rebecca admitted. Because Anthony had been bullied at school and gone through that terrible period in the sanatorium, she had been reluctant to discipline him. Rebecca was deeply sorry that her "failure" had created this problem for Kitty; she confessed that she often misjudged Anthony because he looked so much like her, and she expected him to think just like her. Rebecca believed that Anthony was seeking love but that he had a tendency to "snarl at it, worry it, and chase it in a corner, which is a torment to himself and the persons he loves." No one could have coped better with this situation than Kitty, and sooner or later Anthony would realize it. Rebecca was putting a good deal of trust in H.G. just now because he was helping Anthony to get on good terms not only with his life but with his writing. Rebecca concluded her appeal: "Please, *please* hang on."

Rebecca spoke several times on the phone with Anthony, each time feeling that his tone toward her and Kitty became more belligerent. She had concluded he was on the verge of a major breakdown. There had been a particularly nasty telephone exchange over his new love, whom Rebecca insisted on meeting—so as to eliminate any difficulties in the divorce case she told a suspicious and surly Anthony. When he flatly refused, she replied: "You're very independent, aren't you? But really you'd better come and see me." He told her she was making mischief in his life, and she hung up on him. She now believed that Anthony had determined to set everyone against her, and that she could do nothing to make him happy. As she later dramatized it for Lettie, "There was a feeling of murderous evil, of brooding wickedness, that simply made my blood run cold."

In some desperation, Anthony reached out to one of Rebecca's friends, Joyce Seligman, who lived in Ibstone village. Rebecca was very fond of Joyce and her husband, Hugh, a banker. Like Rebecca's other friend, Ruth Lowinsky, Joyce represented all that was kind and loving in friendship; she would often be included in Rebecca's catalogues of those who had stood by her and cherished her. Anthony happened to see Joyce in Paddington Station, putting her son on a train to Eton. Could they talk for a moment? Anthony asked her. "He spun a long tale," Joyce remembered, and he asked whether she could not "do something with Rebecca. Tell my mother I am not damnable, and my heart's better than she thinks." Daunted by the complications of his life and supportive of Rebecca, Joyce replied: "I don't think I'm of any use to you at all. And I don't want you to upset your mother. I think you're being a bit cruel to her." Joyce recommended that Anthony speak with Rebecca's secretary, Margaret Hodges, who had become very close to her. Later Joyce spoke to Rebecca about the scene at Paddington, saying Anthony looked "extremely ill." Rebecca dismissed his effort as another one of his ridiculous and melodramatic maneuvers.

2

THE ESTRANGEMENT between Rebecca and Anthony took a bizarre turn in late June. Anthony suspected Rebecca of planting an awful story in H.G.'s mind that Anthony had become involved in traitorous activity. Rebecca had warned Anthony that she had heard rumors about his pacifist sympathies, and that he might become the scapegoat in a Communist plot against her, engineered by Tito sympathizers in the Foreign Office. She said she had received word that she would be discredited by luring Anthony into a political movement that would make him liable to prosecution. Sensitive about his failure to get into active service during the war, Anthony imagined that his mother had somehow twisted the story and intimated to H.G. that his son was disloyal. Kitty came to believe in Anthony's suspicions as well: "I do think Rebecca made the most of it."

Anthony had come under suspicion in 1940. He and Kitty had had foreigners (friends of theirs) as visitors to their Wiltshire farm, and this had aroused doubts, especially when a window curtain flapping in the wind was taken as a signal to the enemy. It seems ridiculous now, but dozens of houses were searched in the part of Wiltshire where Anthony and Kitty lived. Fears ran high because of the fall of France and the possibility of a German invasion of Britain. The police searched his home for six hours, taking all his foreign books, maps, and guides. They opened the drawers in his desk. "What's all this?" a village policeman asked. Kitty said, "Well my husband reviews books for *The New Statesman* every week." "What does that mean, reviews books?" he asked. "You read the novel and you say if it's good or bad," she replied. Then they searched Anthony's pockets. They happened to find a letter from a friend saying: "I'm afraid this barge is not fit for foreign service." (Anthony was considering buying a boat.) He also had a paper on abstract art, entitled "Axis." The Rome–Berlin axis was the only axis the village policeman knew about. The crowning discovery was Anthony's toy soldiers, given to him by H.G., and hidden behind some books in the library. He had put them there after Kitty had said: "Come on, you can't play with soldiers. You ought to be earning money. Get down to it and write a book." In view of these suspicious circumstances, he was marched off to the police station. A terrified Kitty wondered if he would ever return home. In the police station, Anthony was interrogated and insulted by a hectoring chief of police who told him: "And by the way that's a pretty nasty shirt you're wearing." Anthony called Rebecca from the police station. "They think I'm a Nazi spy," he told his mother. "Oh, are you?" she replied. She meant to be funny, but there could be no joking with Anthony on this subject, especially not when he was getting the third degree.

Anthony was put under surveillance for three weeks as a suspected fifth columnist. Rebecca intervened, urging Harold Nicolson, Harold Laski, and others with influence in the government to relieve the pressure on Anthony. But in his darkest moments Anthony seemed to think his own mother had informed against him and spoiled his last days with H.G. As the V2 rockets pounded London at the end of the war, he sat with his dying father trying to find the right moment when H.G. would be lucid enough to hear Anthony's side of things, but the moment never came, and Anthony was left with his father's final, wearily muttered words: "I just don't understand you."

3

ANTHONY ARRANGED for Henry and Kitty to meet in London in early July 1944. Kitty arrived at the Carlton Grill, disconcerted to see that Rebecca was also present. Rebecca could not help admiring her perfectly beautiful looks, which Rebecca compared to a "wood-nymph, with really golden hair." But Rebecca was certain that Anthony had arranged Kitty's meeting with Henry just to put Rebecca in a bad light. They adjourned to the bar, where Kitty infuriated Rebecca by defending Anthony, saying things like "such things do happen—men fall in love." But Anthony was not behaving normally, Rebecca retorted, his telephone conversations with her proved that. "It's a funny thing that that's exactly what Anthony says about you," Kitty observed. When Rebecca tried to explain how Anthony had tried to alienate her from H.G., Kitty said she did not see why Rebecca should trouble herself with H.G.'s affairs at all. Rebecca watched Kitty put her head forward like a beautiful slender serpent and ask why Rebecca wrote to Anthony telling him he would regret leaving his children. It was an "unjustifiable interference." Taken aback, Rebecca asked Kitty if she had read her letter to Anthony. "Of course . . . Anthony showed it to me, he showed me all your letters. And let me say, I wish you hadn't asked Anthony to stay with Caroline . . . because it was for me to ask that, not you," Kitty told her. "But Anthony's my son," Rebecca rejoined, "surely I have a right to tell him if I think he'll regret deserting his children." Kitty was emphatic: "You have none at all, you have no right to say anything at all. This is a matter between Anthony and me." Trying to get some agreement out of Kitty, Rebecca suggested: "But mayn't I even offer an opinion?" Kitty said, "No, it's my business, not yours."

When they could not get a table for lunch at the Carlton, they took a taxi to the Ritz. On the way, Kitty told Rebecca she had great hope for Anthony and believed that he was maturing—an attitude quite different from what she expressed in her first letter to Rebecca after Anthony left her, and an attitude that now maddened Rebecca, who said she wished Anthony was dead. He was evil and vile and would bring nothing but suffering on everyone. Kitty flinched and grasped Henry's hand. Kitty defended Anthony, Rebecca repeated her wish that he was dead. Kitty remembered Rebecca screaming insults at her and Henry arranging for the head waiter to escort her out to a taxi. Rebecca remembered Kitty warning her not to interfere with her children: "I'm old enough to look after them." Rebecca departed, saying, "I'm sorry I simply cannot bear to have lunch with you. . . . My son is a villain and my daughter-in-law is a fool. What hope can I have in my grandchildren?" Henry stayed behind to have lunch with Kitty, learning from her what Anthony had said about his psychoanalysis, particularly his humiliating memories of when he was seventeen and his mother had let him see how disturbed and erratic she found his behavior. When Henry returned to Ibstone that evening, Rebecca was upset to learn that he thought she had made an unprovoked attack on Kitty, an impression Rebecca attributed to his deafness and his desire to see the goodness in Kitty. "Henry is a perfect angel, but he is not quick," Rebecca explained. Rebecca deemed Anthony's recollections of his childhood, which Kitty conveyed to Henry, "curious rubbish that had no conceivable basis in reality," full of a humbugging use of psychoanalytic jargon.

Telephoning one of Kitty's friends later, Rebecca admitted she had lost her temper. Even longer letters to Kitty ensued, alternately aggressive and defensive, expressing Rebecca's devastating realization that Kitty did not like her. The gloom of these letters surpasses *The Judge,* for in them Rebecca pronounces a sentence on Anthony as fearsome as that novel's epigraph: "I know that all our lives long there will be awful crises, when there is debt and rows and attempts at suicide and new starts . . . and never, never, *never* any way of making Anthony happy. And never any freedom from a desire to make him happy." Rebecca tried to repair her relationship with Kitty, confessing that she could not renounce her fondness for her and her love for the children. Kitty had been a wonderful mother and wife, and Rebecca deeply regretted they had quarreled, especially since Rebecca had roared at Kitty when she was exhausted and unhappy. She asked Kitty's forgiveness, for she realized that Kitty's unhappiness was far greater than her own.

In early July, Gip reported to Rebecca that H.G. had had at least one stormy confrontation with Anthony about his intention to divorce Kitty. (Rebecca later told Lettie that H.G. was shocked at Anthony's "cold cruelty" to Kitty.) Although Anthony appeared outwardly calm, Gip guessed that he was "wracked and overwrought by the whole affair." Anthony agreed that should it be H.G.'s intention to leave him money, it should be left to Kitty and the children instead. Gip's wife, Marjorie, also wrote to Rebecca the news of H.G.'s improving health and of their concern that further talk of Anthony's and Kitty's divorce would set him back just when he was beginning to regain his form.

Rebecca waited until September to tell Winnie and Lettie the full complicated story of Anthony's and Kitty's breakup. Rebecca felt the alarm over H.G. had triggered in Anthony a nervous breakdown—also brought on by four years of hard work on the farm during a war. But as H.G. got better, Anthony showed no improvement. Rebecca now interpreted Kitty's hostility to her as a transference of the anger she should have expressed against Anthony. Rebecca imagined it relieved Kitty to blame her and that it ingratiated Kitty with Anthony. Kitty had turned over to Henry a letter of Rebecca's warning Anthony about his political affiliations. Henry already knew about the letter and asked: "What about it?" Kitty suggested: "Well, isn't it rather like a detective story?" Rebecca interpreted this incident as a further effort to discredit her by suggesting she was mad. Rebecca thought Kitty so blind with love for Anthony that she could not see how reprehensible it was to show Rebecca's letter to Henry, especially when Kitty followed up with a letter to Henry saying she could not see Rebecca again but hoped that Henry would continue as the grandfather of her children. "It is a letter sickening in its insincerity and its obvious intention of driving a wedge between Henry and me," Rebecca told Lettie. Kitty's letter has not been found in Rebecca's archive, and it is not one Kitty can imagine having written to Henry, whom she treated politely but not with the warmth Rebecca attributes to her. What seems to have provoked Rebecca's attack on Kitty in this instance was Henry's sad reflection: "My dear, I am afraid you have made a gulf between yourself and the young people."

Neither Anthony nor Kitty was now communicating with Rebecca, and she felt completely helpless. Lettie came to Ibstone to console Rebecca, but Rebecca did not take much comfort in being solemnly told that the trouble with Anthony and Kitty stemmed from their being married in a registry office.

In mid-July, Pamela Frankau also came to stay at Ibstone. Humbert Wolfe had died in 1940, and Rebecca had asked Pamela to forgive her for having attacked Humbert in "The Addict." Pamela realized that her anger was spent: "But of course, I've forgiven you—ages ago." Pamela believed that the seat of Anthony's trouble was H.G.'s illness; it had caused him to question the strength of his tie to Kitty, and it exacerbated his anxieties about the war, which to Pamela fit with his adolescent rebellion against school, against any kind of discipline, indeed against authority itself. Pamela conceded she was indulging in amateurish analysis, but she did regard Anthony as regressing to his seventeenth year. Rebecca learned from Pamela a number of shocking things. Anthony had never valued the grand holidays Rebecca had given him or acknowledged how much she had done to make his life comfortable. On the contrary, "H.G. was everything to him," Rebecca concluded, comparing Anthony's attitude to her own early worship of her father and devaluation of her mother, a dynamic intensified by her father's absence in her life and H.G.'s absence in Anthony's. "And how I see the drama go on,"

Rebecca exclaimed. She predicted that Caroline and Edmund would now do the same—thinking too little of Kitty and adoring their father, who would look in on them at six-month intervals.

4

BY MID-OCTOBER 1944, the crisis over Anthony had subsided. After talking things over with H.G., Rebecca visited Anthony's garage flat in London, where he was recovering from jaundice. He no longer wanted to divorce Kitty. His affair with a BBC co-worker was over, and he hoped to resume his married life. Mother and son spoke reservedly. She found him less excitable. Kitty had a flat in Eccleston Square and was not doing badly.

Rebecca now blamed Kitty for having been a bullying wife who accused Anthony of preventing her from becoming a great painter. Like Jane Wells, Kitty had the "same capacity to build a graceful setting round herself in which she sits and quietly thinks out ways by which she can make the lot of others intolerable, the same delight in encouraging the worst in her husband while appearing gentle and detached, the same gift for duplicity." Rebecca feared that Caroline would not recover from this hiatus in her family life. Edmund seemed young enough not to have been injured by it. He was not like either of his parents, and she predicted he would be a "man of action, he has great power over his playmates."

Troubled by stomach upsets in the early part of 1945, Rebecca lost several working days in bed, blaming Kitty for turning Anthony—now "amiable but cold"—away from her. On a visit to Ibstone, Lettie nettled Rebecca by advising her to stop abusing Kitty. It did no good. Rebecca vowed never to trust her daughter-in-law again, calling her a "twisted and dangerous creature," and in the same breath acknowledging Kitty as a good and devoted mother.

Rebecca visited Anthony and Kitty in their London home shortly after they reconciled in mid-February. Rebecca marveled at how the children thrived under Kitty's care. Caroline had become "first-rate stuff, a comet" and Edmund a "roistering pirate." Rebecca hoped he would become "a broader, more generous, fuller H.G." Kitty's successful motherhood gradually healed the breach between her and Rebecca. "A complete reconciliation has happened between all our family," Rebecca reported to her solicitor, Gerald Russell. She instructed him that in the event of Anthony's death, she wanted his inheritance to be divided equally between Kitty, Caroline, and Edmund.

By the end of 1945, Rebecca was exulting in a visit from Anthony, Kitty, and the children. As she came down to breakfast Rebecca saw Edmund eyeing the large red engine she had bought for him. He then knocked on the breakfast room door. Henry opened it, and the two stood facing each other, Henry looking down from his great height and Edmund, somewhere at his knee, looking up. "Henry," Edmund asked, "may I borrow your engine?"

CHAPTER 23

Retribution and Treachery
1945–1946

I

REBECCA'S POLITICAL and personal world fractured as the governments-in-exile lost British backing and found it impossible to work with the communists in Central Europe. She had predicted these events in 1944, when she refused to join the National Committee for British-Soviet Unity, deploring Soviet Russia's tactless, doctrinaire actions which jeopardized the future peace of Europe. Immediately after the war, she was writing articles and prefaces to books assailing the Soviet Union for its appalling displacement of millions of people at the start of the war (1939–1941) before it became Britain's ally.

Concerned about her personal safety and security, Rebecca detected signs of treachery and sabotage everywhere. "This week I feel a growing fear of what the Communists may do to me personally," she recorded in her diary for January 31, 1945. Leaving the podium for a few minutes before delivering a speech on Yugoslavia, Rebecca returned to find most of the speech ripped out of her notebook. At home, a housekeeper and her husband went around Ibstone village asking people questions about Rebecca and Henry. Rebecca was certain her papers had been searched and speculated that her frequent bouts with gastroenteritis were the result of poisoning. She alerted her American friend Doris Stevens: should Doris learn of Rebecca's and Henry's suddenly committing suicide, she would know what to think.

The summer 1945 election campaign did little to lift Rebecca's spirits or allay her suspicions. She had voted Labor. Winston Churchill, a gallant war leader, had done the work of five men heroically, but a sixth man was needed, one who was not a throwback to the Edwardian period and the eighteenth century. Rebecca pinned her hopes on Labor Party ministers like Herbert Morrison and Ernest Bevin, who had a more realistic view of Russia. She admired the former's grasp of domestic issues and the latter's seasoned toughness in the trade union movement. But she doubted these two outstanding men could successfully surmount the difficulties of a Labor Party divided against itself.

2

AFTER THE WAR Harold Ross at *The New Yorker* cabled Rebecca requesting articles and stories from her. He warmly received her promise to send him an article on the treason trial of William Joyce, familiarly known as Lord Haw Haw, whose flamboyant, know-it-all radio broadcasts from Germany during the war fascinated and infuriated the British public. Rebecca's portrait of him in *The Meaning of Treason* (her study of the postwar treason trials) is the single best biography she was ever to write—a brilliantly perceptive study of a disaffected spirit.

William Joyce was the product of an Irish Roman Catholic father and an English Protestant mother and grew up in a home rife with religious conflict but devoted to the British Empire. William's father, Michael, had made himself most unpopular in his native Ireland because of his pro-Unionist politics, and William adopted his father's allegiance—even enlisting in the British army before he was of age. Dismissed after four months, William enrolled in classes at the University of London with the expectation of reenlisting after graduation.

There was something extraordinarily pure and touching about William's patriotism. During his brief army stint, his fellow recruits made sport of his earnestness by whistling "God Save the Queen," knowing that he would jump out of bed and stand to attention. Yet William knew there was something suspect in his family history that put into doubt his allegiance to the British Empire. He had been born in Brooklyn, New York, and feared that the British authorities would consider him an American citizen. It has never been proven whether or not William also knew that his father had become an American citizen, for Michael Joyce destroyed evidence of his American citizenship and claimed to be a British subject when he moved back to Ireland when William was still a young boy. William's treason trial would hinge on the issue of his citizenship. Did England have the right to try him after his American citizenship was established?

William's pro-British fervor revealed itself in a remarkable style. At the age of sixteen he wrote to army officials expressing his desire to draw his sword for the Empire. His patriotism had been sharpened by a bitter awareness that he was in the despised minority in his native land; a love of the British was tantamount to treason. A product of mixed parentage alienated from his native land, coming to London to make his mark, possessed of a sharp and eloquent tongue that often got him into fights—these qualities are reminiscent of Rebecca, a Rebecca gone awry, so to speak, by becoming involved with the British Fascists and indulging in a love for street fighting.

Rebecca's earliest memories of her father's conservatism, of reading writers such as Kipling, of revering the Royal Family (memories that came flooding back to her when she met the Queen during the war), equipped her to amplify William's biography, presenting him as a sincere soul, an excellent tutor of young children, who perverted his own desire for distinction into an identification with totalitarianism, made necessary when England did not recognize William Joyce's abilities, when its own Fascist leader, Oswald Mosley, failed to treat his deputy William with the respect William had worked so hard to earn. William turns on England as if on a lover who has spurned him, and Rebecca imagines him leaving England at the beginning of the war to serve Hitler as if seeking a way to return triumphantly to London.

Exactly how William Joyce transformed himself from British patriot to traitor, from a conservative to a fascist, has never been fully explained. Rebecca succeeded in her biography of him because she extrapolated with psychological brilliance a convincing narrative, in which she equates the intensity of his desire to be accepted by the British with the intensity of his fascism, a powerful new ideology that would restore an effete England to William Joyce's idealized and heroic version of it, a version England had failed to achieve during William's youth. As Rebecca said to Lettie, the entire Joyce family probably thought Hitler would "kindly restore England to its Victorian state."

In Rebecca's biography, Joyce becomes Britain's insidious alter ego, invading British homes with an intimate, cocksure radio voice. She heard a plaintive note of someone whom society had not taken to itself. In Joyce's voice, she heard, no doubt, the sounds of her own sense of rejection. His passionate ambition was to exercise authority. Rebecca's passion had always been to thwart the authority others seemed to exercise over her. She compared the grief of Joyce's followers during his trial with the mourning of the early Christians—a particularly apposite analogy, since she found in Joyce a saintly devotion to his cause even when he knew he was going to be executed.

For Rebecca, family life determines the individual, and in her evocation of William's background she remarks that he was being "strangled by the sheer tortuousness of his family destiny." For her, it is fated that this man's life should end on the gallows. His problem is that he wants to govern, not to be governed, Rebecca concludes, speaking again not only for Joyce but for herself and her vision of humanity which is constantly straining against authority. Like Rebecca, William was the "apple of his family's eye," and like her, he reacts to that confidence in his exceptional abilities with an extraordinary rebelliousness, as if his own genius is paradoxically inhibited by the family's claim on him. Joyce invested fascism with an international character, she argues, so that fascism sanctioned his betrayal of family and country in a way that other British Fascists, such as Mosley, could not allow.

Those passages in which Joyce's character hands over to Rebecca's are clearly apparent as she shifts to suppositions. She has him embarking for Germany: "One day his little feet twinkled up the area of his basement flat near Earl's Court. His eyes must have been dancing." Such passages are bereft of evidence but full of her utter identification with her subject, her ability to show what joy it must have been to Joyce to turn traitor. Her prose is infectious, making readers also speculate on what "must have been."

Rebecca calls William Joyce "the revolutionary," a term she uses to define one who both hates order and loves it, who will destroy so that he might create a superior order. It is here that Rebecca took her stand in the postwar world against revolution, reaffirming what she had said twenty years earlier about the Russian Revolution—that it was bound to restore the tyranny of tsardom. One cannot murder society in order to save it. That William Joyce is transformed into the quintessential Rebecca West character is revealed in a single sentence: "He was not going to be king." Every dynamic character in her fiction and nonfiction sooner or later is measured in the language of royalty. Joyce's kingly attributes suggest to Rebecca that he is a symbol of humanity, that he has it in him to want simultaneously to live and to die. Like one of Shakespeare's heroes, his struggle is tragic. His example is an "end to mediocrity."

It is an empathetic portrait, yet Rebecca affirms the court's decision that William Joyce must hang. All of her later writing is an effort to reconcile herself to authority and to study how badly things go wrong when those like Joyce will not submit to be governed. Even though he was not a British subject, she thought it right that he should be tried as a traitor. She carefully threaded her way through the legal arguments, affirming the rightness of the principle that allegiance draws protection and protection draws allegiance. William Joyce, in other words, conducted himself as a British subject, traveled abroad on a British passport, had a claim to be protected by British laws and the British government, and by the same token was liable to be tried by them.

The very lengths to which Rebecca goes to justify this conclusion, however, suggests that it was a near thing in her own mind, that her own sympathies and the court's judgment could have gone the other way—that is, a part of her also believed that the individual has a right to throw off allegiance, a matter the lawyers debated for days. Rebecca concedes at the end of *The Meaning of Treason* that there is a case for the traitor and that all men should have a drop of treason in their blood. Otherwise how can the status quo be challenged, how can a nation avoid the fatal complacency that would lead to its demise? Thus Rebecca presents herself as a hanging judge, with qualms.

Rebecca's ambivalence about Joyce also had to do with his Irishness. While covering the Joyce trial in September 1945, Rebecca wrote to Emanie Sachs: "God evidently felt about my sister Lettie as I do, and while she was in Ireland punished her for her treasonable affections by sending her a septic inflammation of the leg." She felt about the Irish as Southerners do about Negroes, Rebecca confided to Emanie: "they just seem to me a different and repellent breed, whom one could only like if they converted themselves into faithful servants."

Rebecca's painstaking defense of British justice in *The Meaning of Treason* stemmed from her awareness that others saw the Joyce trial quite differently. She was dismayed at the American newspaper correspondents who thought the legal case against Joyce weak but were also glad that he was hanged even if it was a frame-up. To Henry's mother, Mary, Rebecca described Joyce as a "little whippy jig-dancing sort of Irishman, quite ugly, but full of fight. He swaggered in and out of the dock, really very courageous indeed and made a very dignified appearance in court, on his appeal." This was the admiration of an adversary, but also of a woman struggling against her own Irishness, and a sense of isolation. "You may not realise, from outside, that a clue to her was that she was half-Scotch, half-Irish," A. L. Rowse said. "She was a big woman, a strong personality, very warm and generous (Irish)." She was actually a small woman, under five feet, three inches, but she projected a voice, a personality that, like Joyce's, transcended her diminutive size. No more than Joyce did she ever see herself as acceptable, an Establishment figure.

3

REBECCA'S ACCOUNT of the Joyce trial first appeared in *The New Yorker* in late September 1945, an astounding feat, since the trial had concluded in mid-September. The trial ended on a Thursday afternoon, and her cabled article arrived the next afternoon in *The New Yorker* office. "I know of only five or six writers in the whole world who could have written such a thorough and journalistically competent story in such a short time, and I know of no other who could have equalled it in literary excellence," Harold Ross told her. He was not exaggerating, for soon Rebecca and *The New Yorker* were swamped with fan mail from professional writers and readers. When her 6,700 word article came in, Ross immediately decided to make over the week's issue to accommodate her journalistic coup, hiring a special weekend crew of printers. A jubilant Ross practically gave her free reign over future stories. "WE WANT WHATEVER YOU WANT TO WRITE ON THE AMERY TRIAL," Ross cabled her.

John Amery was the perfect foil to William Joyce. The son of a distinguished father, a statesman and writer, John had conceived the idiotic scheme of a "Legion of St George," drawn from British prisoners of war who would fight alongside Germans against Russians to save Europe from bolshevism. Amery had been born with everything Joyce craved and had thrown it away, playing his life as farce to Joyce's tragedy. Yet Amery's story, Rebecca realized, had personal meaning for the British; one whom they had privileged had turned against them. It had been a painful case because his mother and father had been so much admired and because Amery seemed like a lunatic, even though there was no evidence to certify him as such. He had been in trouble since he was fifteen, when he had issued bogus prospectuses for a film company. His mother adored him, and he had been a devoted son, but he seemed completely out of touch with reality.

The isolation of Rebecca's traitors was also her own. Richard Crossman, a distinguished journalist, politician, and scholar, who had served with Henry in the Ministry of Economic Warfare, tried to explain how Rebecca had estranged herself from much of the Left in Britain. In early 1946, she was fighting with the editor of the *New Statesman*, Kingsley Martin, whom she considered no better than a Stalinist when he sided with Tito as the lesser evil. Contending with him put her in a lather, or as one of her interviewers put it, "I gather she used him as a quick emetic." Crossman argued that she seemed to dislike most Leftist intellectuals, and yet she was offended when they rejected her. He compared her to other great independent thinkers such as Plato, Hobbes, Dickens, Tolstoy, and Yeats, who had influenced the Left. But they had done so as individuals who could not abide coteries. Like them, she would have to be unpopular with contemporary coteries, although her very independence might mean she would be taken by a "coterie of to-morrow." But Rebecca wanted both—her individuality and her coterie, her independence and her family. It was a very human contradiction, and it involved her in the paradoxes she loved to puzzle out in the lives of traitors, many of whom were virtually indistinguishable to her from family members who had rejected her.

4

ON JULY 21, 1946, Rebecca attended the memorial service for General Mihailović in London. He had been captured, tried, and shot by Tito's government as a Nazi collaborationist. Rebecca regarded the execution as a crime, and pointed to Mihailović's fervent anti-Nazi activities, which she had first learned about in 1936 traveling through Yugoslavia. She revered him as a man of simple habits and upright character, done in by a communist conspiracy and the pusillanimity of her own government. Many allied soldiers had testified to Mihailović's Homeric courage and comradeship. His death seemed to Rebecca the death of another hero, another king.

CHAPTER 24

The Trials of Nuremberg
1946

I

REBECCA RECEIVED fan mail from America about her Joyce and Amery articles that far surpassed the response to anything else she had ever written. *Time* and *Life* were planning feature articles on her. She accepted Ross's offer to cover the Nuremberg war crimes proceedings, believing her report would yield a fitting conclusion to her book, *The Meaning of Treason*.

A Royal Air Force flight carrying Rebecca and several members of the British team of prosecutors arrived in Nuremberg on July 23. She went straight to the courthouse. There she renewed her acquaintance with one of the American prosecutors, Francis Biddle, who greeted her as an exciting diversion from the courtroom, which Rebecca called a "citadel of boredom." Now in its eleventh month, the trial had ground down the spirits of nearly everyone, so diminishing the personalities of the defendants that it was difficult to tell which was which.

Rebecca had first met Francis Biddle sometime in the 1920s on one of her trips to America, and then again in 1935 in Washington, where she reported on the New Deal. Attorney General in the Roosevelt administration, a gifted lawyer and an engaging man, the sixty-year-old Biddle had an ease about him that his colleagues admired. Like most of the lawyers at Nuremberg he was married. His wife Katherine had visited him in the spring of 1946, but she had returned to the States to care for their son Randolf, recovering from his wartime service. Most of the women on the Nuremberg staff were single. "This gave the society a relaxed, tolerant, and philanderous ambience which many of us found agreeable," recalled Telford Taylor, one of Biddle's colleagues. To Rebecca, it seemed that everyone was in love but with few places in which to consummate their passions because of the housing shortage.

Taylor found Biddle a "bit of a swell," suave and self-confident, the scion of a prestigious Philadelphia family. Rebecca remarked to one of Biddle's colleagues: "Isn't it curious that the only aristocrat on the bench is an American?" Biddle could be arrogant, impatient, and caustic, but his agile mind delighted Rebecca, who responded immediately to his frank interest in her and to his good looks. The more direct he became with her, the more she dropped her rather hurried cleverness, a ploy, he suspected, to disguise her diffidence.

Shaking his hand, Rebecca asked Francis about his charming wife. He complimented Rebecca about *Black Lamb and Grey Falcon*, saying he and Katherine had enjoyed reading it aloud to each other. What had happened to Constantine? he asked. Alas, he had become a communist, Rebecca replied, and was furious with her book. She shrugged. They talked all evening. It saddened him to see her arrive at the courthouse heavy, gray, and out of breath. Seeing her again after so many years apart reminded him that her mouth seemed, at first glance, a little cruel. But he liked her strong and capable hands. Her extraordinary eyes, her nice smile and voice captivated him. He startled Rebecca by saying: "Why have you let yourself go? You could be as wonderful as ever." She amazed him by reacting shyly, muttering something about getting old. Francis dismissed her concerns, suggesting a few improvements in her appearance, especially her hair. She had her hair done.

Francis found Rebecca strangely unsure of herself and sensitive to snubbing. Lady Lawrence, the wife of Sir Geoffrey Lawrence, Nuremberg's presiding judge, had received her with indifference, the way a middle-class country family might treat a great artist—"I don't see why all this fuss is being made over her." It amused Francis to watch Rebecca boil over as she used her "nice, clean, short Saxon words." He comforted her back into a smile and succeeded in absorbing all of her attention.

After a few days, Francis was amazed at her transformation. She looked rested and bloomed by his side at lunches, dinners, parties, and strolls in the woods and around the old town of Nuremberg. For Francis, the walks eased the long months of strain, and he enjoyed discussing H.G., a hero of his youth. H.G.'s novels had transported Francis beyond his narrow world. Francis liked to tease Rebecca. He embarrassed her, but she became more outgoing. Two days after her arrival, he invited her to spend the weekend at his impressive residence, the Villa Conradi, enclosed in a huge tract of land with an avenue of pines and birches, a park, a little lake, and a house full of heavy furniture and art of the Italian minor masters. He put her in a room with a "highly erotic" painting hanging over her bed. For a whirlwind ten days they were lovers—and gloriously happy. Without Rebecca's saying anything, Francis had divined her sexual troubles with Henry and set himself to remedy them, to show that there was nothing wrong with her. He told her that he knew she was a good match for him when they first met, and that they could always have been so. He had felt it for twenty years.

Rebecca realized, however, that this Nuremberg interlude would not have been possible if Francis's wife Katherine had been there, for Rebecca saw how he adored her. Things Francis told her about his sex life with Katherine—that she had refused to sleep with him for eighteen months after the birth of their second child—suggested to Rebecca that Katherine was manipulative and punitive. But Francis seemed to indulge Katherine and to consider her extravagant behavior nothing more than feminine oddity. "What chance have you and I when men love such alligators? What chance had I against Jane?" Rebecca moaned in a letter to a female friend. Rebecca later thought about putting both of the Biddles into a short story.

Rebecca paced herself by limiting her court appearances. She took copious notes on the trials, often organizing them at Biddle's villa. She reserved the writing of her article for her return home to Ibstone. When she departed for England on August 6, a bereft Biddle confessed to missing her, a "gay and amusing wench." Rebecca did not expect to see him again. "I'm fifty-three and I might as well put the shutters up. I had, but he made me take them down," Rebecca confessed, declaring that he would be her last lover.

Henry, Kitty, Edmund, and Caroline met Rebecca at the station in Croydon. They remarked on how well she looked. Lettie was also on hand that night at Ibstone, which made Rebecca wildly irritated. A week later, on August 13, Rebecca awoke feeling sick and apprehensive. To calm her agitation she had Henry drive her to the head of a valley three miles away so that she could walk home. On her return, Henry told her that Marjorie Wells had called to say that H.G. had died that afternoon. She had been planning to show him her photographs of Nuremberg. Now she felt desolated, grateful for his love and for thirty-four years of friendship, but still rueful about the way he played the devil with her. His tyranny was the other side of the medal, an incorrigible part of him that made their life together intolerable. Rebecca thought she had been good for him, but she conceded that he had got on pretty well without her. She asked his daughter-in-law, Marjorie, for a keepsake—nothing valuable, just something that he often used, perhaps from his writing desk. (Eventually she bought the carpet in the room where he worked for his last twenty years.) The more Rebecca thought about it, the gladder she

was that she and H.G. had never married. It might have ended her literary career, and that would have meant missing so much. Taking care of a
great man would have turned her into something like the custodian of a
museum.

Rebecca struggled to complete her Nuremberg account. Her head
was boiling. It now occurred to her that Henry's rejection of her as a
woman was the vital thing that had wrecked her life, not H.G. Yet she
admitted that Henry's love and care for her never faltered. "Oh God,
what a world," she cried out. She paced the house thinking of her love
affair in Nuremberg, occasionally standing stock still, utterly self-
absorbed, and crying out "Francis!" Rebecca's moods disconcerted her
new secretary, Anne Charles, a replacement for Rebecca's beloved Margaret Hodges, who had left Ibstone with her husband John (now out of
the army) to start a family and a teaching career.

Rebecca discerned a frightful symmetry in her first lover's death and
her involvement with her last. She did not want to give up Francis quite
as easily as she maintained in her letters to female friends. His loving letters described a villa haunted by her absence. He wanted word pictures
from her that described how she looked and where she walked. He had a
dream about them walking into a theater. He spoke to a passing woman,
distracted by her beauty, and Rebecca stopped to look at her. Annoyed,
he said sharply, "Aren't you coming, Rebecca?" She looked at him and
flowered into a smile. He knew in an instant that she was his. Filled with
happiness, he suddenly woke in the dark.

It was no fun without her, Francis wrote to Rebecca. Could she come
for a few days as they wrapped up the show in Nuremberg? He tried to
hear her laugh and could not, but then he recalled the way she would say
"lovely, Francis, lovely!" He wanted only her. It was a joy to be with a
woman who wanted to do exactly what you wanted to do and yet never
surrendered. She never quite gave all of herself, Francis realized. He
would hold back some of what he felt if he did not hear from her, but
what he really wanted was to show her the memoir of love he sat writing
between court sessions. She had opened such possibilities for him that he
tightened into misery and rebelled when she started to say: "if we never
meet again." He knew what she had intended to say—that their love
would continue, "even in a wilderness." He feared that he sounded silly
to her. But he continued his epistolary banter and signed one of his letters (on August 10, two days after she left Nuremberg) "your disrespect-
ful Francis."

He was immensely relieved to receive her first letter on August 16, a
charmingly indiscreet note that he called a magic carpet that could take

them anywhere. Should he send a plane to Paris to pick her up? He expected the final judgments to be rendered in mid-September. She could fly in then, and they could have a few days together and then fly to London. He found Rebecca so different from other women. She never said things like "tear up my letters." Francis wondered how H.G.'s death had affected her. Had it sent her thoughts "spinning back"? He wanted to call her but thought it might be inappropriate; he was having trouble writing the polite, innocuous little note she could show to Henry. Did she get the mail herself or did Henry, handing over a letter, say: "Another letter from Nuremberg, my dear." Francis worried that he was boring Rebecca, perhaps crowding her. He also worried that his wife Katherine suspected him of straying. In one of his letters to Katherine he had made a bad joke about making "English love" to Rebecca, and he must have realized that other letters contained all too much news about Rebecca, revealing his infatuation with her.

She responded to his letters somewhat cautiously but encouragingly. She told him about her great love for H.G., and then worried that her account would put him off. She suggested that once Nuremberg was over, he would have his fill of her. By the end of August, Francis was in agony awaiting Rebecca's next letter. He had had a vision of her settling to work on her novel, confining herself to the noble terrain of her art, and rejecting his intrusive letters.

Rebecca's next letter soothed Francis's fears and strengthened his love with her fine strong words. He was so crazy to see her that he proposed flying over to London in early September before the trial ended. He was ready to take her on any terms she offered.

There had never been more than three days between her letters, he thought, although it was hard to tell because she rarely dated hers. He especially cherished one that began: "I come to breakfast, full of you, in my body and your stars in my eyes, now there is a letter for me, and I open it breathlessly and it is not what I wanted but all about vermouth, and there are two worlds in which I love." She had sent him one "invincibly happy" letter. She had been watching her diet, Anthony had told her she looked pretty, and she had told Francis: "I could be anywhere that anybody who wanted to see me wanted me to be."

Rebecca embarked from London for Berlin in late September, on her way back to Nuremberg to cover the last days of the trials, intent on quenching Francis's request for "one last lovely fling."

2

REBECCA ARRIVED at the London airport late at night for her dawn departure. Finding the terminal almost deserted, she nudged a man sleeping
on a bench. He gazed up at a motherly-looking woman, dressed in the
drab clothes that had become familiar to him after five years of war. She
was very apologetic about waking him and asked gently: "Can you tell
me if this is the right place to get the plane to Berlin and Nuremberg?" If
it wasn't, then they were both in the wrong place, said Joseph Laitin, an
American correspondent assigned by Reuters to join a wire service team
covering the trials. Uncomfortable in the cavernous terminal, Rebecca
obviously wanted to talk and introduced herself as Mrs. Andrews of the
London *Telegraph*. This led to an awkward situation when the RAF
ticket agent showed up to validate credentials. He said Mrs. Andrews
did not check out as a *Telegraph* correspondent and asked her to step
aside while he ticketed the man from Reuters. Laitin went back to sleep
and was again awakened by a flustered Rebecca West, who explained to
the groggy Laitin that the contretemps was the result of a misunderstanding. "I'm actually going to Nuremberg for an American magazine,
but I always use the *Telegraph* in situations like this because so few people
ever heard of *The New Yorker*." But Laitin was an avid reader of the magazine and could not recall any pieces from London by an Andrews. "Oh,"
she said. "I use the name Rebecca West."

Rebecca liked Laitin and proposed they travel together. They boarded
an airport bus and sat together. As they pulled out, a man in a bowler hat
looking very much like a banker ran alongside the bus holding up an
umbrella and pointing at Rebecca. The bus stopped, and Henry handed
Rebecca the essential equipment. Arriving in Berlin, Rebecca suggested
they take a walking tour. Laitin felt adopted. She knew enough German
to help him deliver a food package to a man whose sister he had met in
London. In a heavily bombed area they walked up four flights of stairs
with no walls, the only address he had. Rebecca served as an interpreter
when Laitin inquired about the man's whereabouts. He was concerned
about leaving a large package of goodies with a woman who looked like
she could use several large meals. Rebecca observed: "I know this type of
woman. She'd starve to death before touching food that belonged to
someone else." Ashamed of himself, Laitin turned over the package, and
Rebecca pulled out a pack of Camels from her purse, emptied half of it
on the bare kitchen table, and they left. It was a generous gift, for
Rebecca knew that cigarettes were better than any currency. In Berlin, a
party of four could spend an evening at the best black market nightclub,

leave one American cigarette as a tip, and the waiter would feel well rewarded.

Laitin was impressed with Rebecca's understanding of the Germans. Although she was by no means fluent in the language, she was good enough to get by and negotiate her way through Berlin's rubble. It was a grim scene, made worse by the looks of hunger and hostility on people's faces. People sat in tea shops devoid of cakes, drinking ersatz coffee. "Not a smile anywhere," Rebecca wrote to Henry. The next day (September 26), Rebecca and Laitin took a plane to Nuremberg. They saw each other occasionally, but they were both too busy in those last hectic days of the trial to resume their friendship.

Francis had a car waiting for Rebecca at the Nuremberg airport, so that she could quickly pick up her press pass at the Palace of Justice and join him at the Villa Conradi. His sickly appearance alarmed her. He seemed to have aged. A shy Rebecca remarked that she was tired. The next day a frustrated Francis erupted when a colleague interrupted his tête à tête with Rebecca at the villa, calling him away for meetings with the Russians. Rebecca attended the court, typing up her notes during recess without enough time even to eat a sandwich, staying up until midnight, and producing eighteen hundred words a day. Not until Sunday, September 29, did she and Francis have a chance to relax and enjoy each other with a trip to look at the cathedral in Bamberg. They picnicked on a hillside near a castle and enjoyed walks in the woods with friends.

By October 2, Francis flew Rebecca (calling her "a Sabine woman") to Prague, the most beautiful city Rebecca had ever seen. The lovers walked on its famous bridges, marveling at the towers and spires and waterways, and admiring the farmlands, orchards, and a garden that looked about to fall down from the heights into the heart of the city. Their tryst was spoiled only by Francis's flu, which exhausted him and made him sleepy. That night they saw a film, *Brief Encounter.* Its story of strangers meeting in a train station drawn into a short and poignant amour is intense and unforgettable. Rebecca found it an agony to watch. For the next two days they enjoyed Prague, visiting churches and sitting in cafés. They returned to Nuremberg on October 4 for a last dinner at the Villa Conradi. Rebecca put on her best dress and said her good-byes to the staff.

The next day they flew to London. Rebecca expected Henry to pick her up, but he had not received her cable, and Francis became her chauffeur, accompanying her home to Ibstone. She found him cold to her in the car, and later attributed his aloofness to jealousy, for she had spent her time on the plane talking to a younger and more attractive man.

Francis seemed blank to her when they arrived at Ibstone, and a drink did nothing to soften him up. He departed and later rang her, missing her and leaving a message she interpreted as a brush-off.

Rebecca found home an utter letdown. Francis visited for a day, recovering his devoted and affectionate feelings for her. She expected their affair could not go on, except in some attenuated form. But even that seemed heavenly to her, although she was still fond of Henry and could not bear to think of separating from him.

After leaving London, Francis sent Rebecca letters from Paris. She worked on her Nuremberg article. He dined with Monica Stirling, a young writer Rebecca had befriended at the urging of another friend, the actress Margaret Rawlings. Monica described a dinner with Francis. She found him a charmer who wanted to talk about nothing but Rebecca. Monica had tied him up in "knots of tenderness" showing him one of Rebecca's poems.

By late October, however, Francis's letters stopped, and Rebecca complained of boredom. "Katherine has got him," Rebecca fretted, as she struggled over a letter to him. She had concluded he was a sentimentalist who liked to get hurt in affairs with women. She had fallen for him, even though his way of having an affair hurt her. She had come home to Henry, who was the "greatest darling in the world," even if he was pure hell to live with, behaving sometimes like a doddering old man feuding with the servants and messing up the household accounts.

There had been troubles with the farm bailiff and other members of the staff, whom Rebecca accused of cheating Henry by stripping the farm of its produce and profits. Henry seemed oblivious to their machinations and suffered periods of eccentricity, chiefly manifested in an incredible verbosity and in sudden odd statements.

On November 11, Rebecca received what she termed an outrageous letter from Francis, and she replied asking him not to write again. He cabled her two weeks later that he was deeply sorry and disturbed, and then he sent her another letter. She had thrown it in the coke furnace, deciding she did not want to be bothered with reading love letters bombarding her in ways that reminded her of her correspondence with H.G.—especially since Francis wrote so much about how brave Katherine was and how he did not want to do anything to hurt her. It revolted Rebecca to read Francis's comment that Katherine teased him about Rebecca "constantly and funnily, is never cruel nor mean, it is her sweet defense." "My God!" Rebecca exclaimed in disgust. She had had enough of the furtive rituals of his lovemaking.

When Rebecca decided it was over with Francis, she got sick, but she recovered quickly, admitting that in the old days such an affair would have made her wretched for months, perhaps even years. After the initial shock of realizing the affair had no future, she had ceased to care for Francis, expressing only a mild desire to meet him and snub him.

It still seemed to Rebecca that her involvement with Francis and Katherine Biddle was remarkably similar to her struggle with H.G. and Jane. Certainly if she had been able to read Francis's letters to Katherine, Rebecca would have felt vindicated. For if there is no evidence that Francis actually confided in Katherine about his amours, as H.G. trusted in Jane, Francis is remarkably casual in his letters to Katherine about describing his meetings with Rebecca, treating Rebecca as an episode in his married life with Katherine, so to speak. As she told an American friend: "Men are all filth . . . don't worry over Francis B. I'm doomed to have no luck. I shall just forget it, and get on with my work."

3

HOWEVER HURTFUL, the affair with Francis Biddle did rejuvenate Rebecca. She brought a new zest to her writing, which seemed to her like a modern Book of Revelations. She focused on the significance of the trials and the temper of the victors and the defeated. She provided vivid portraits of the defendants such as Goering, whose soft, feminine, and sometimes humorous qualities reminded Rebecca of a madam in a brothel. She marveled at the Allies' restraint, their sober accumulation and presentation of the war crimes evidence, their circumspect occupation of German cities, as though the conquerors were saying, "Pardon my mailed glove."

Rebecca transformed Nuremberg into the story of the German imagination, of its penchant for fairy tales and overbuilding, its Wagnerian dreams of grandeur, which contributed to the excesses of Nazism. In a Schloss, an old Victorian mansion, she found a metaphor for this Germanic need to overproduce and to dominate. She expected it to be like the English variety, "a desert place of shabby and unpainted staging, meagerly set out with a diminished store of seed boxes." Instead, it was neat, clean, full of plants, and perfect, flourishing in the hands of a crippled gardener's single-minded devotion prophetic of Germany's rebirth. When she came to revise her reports on postwar Germany for her book, *A Train of Powder,* she retitled them "Green House with Cyclamens," for the scene at the Nuremberg Schloss became Rebecca's own fairy tale— her tribute to and warning about the self-dedication and dynamism of

German culture, which she regarded as a great force for both good and evil. She knew that the Germans were perfectly capable of transforming their fairy-tale desire for a happy ending into "Lear's Kingdom of loss."

Rebecca believed that the trials made a profound statement, settling once and for all that crimes against humanity should be punished. Yet the Nuremberg judges, she realized, were compromised. Some of the indictable crimes, such as unrestricted submarine warfare, had also been committed by the Allies. American and British judicial procedures baffled the German attorneys, who did not understand the role of cross-examination or the relatively passive Allied judges, because German judges took a far more active role in questioning witnesses. "The trouble about Nuremberg was that it was so manifestly a part of life as it is lived; the trial had not sufficiently detached itself from the oddity of the world," she concluded.

"Green House with Cyclamens I," the first part of A Train of Powder, condenses the arc of Rebecca's own Nuremberg experience, beginning with her plane landing in Nuremberg, her interlude in Prague, her return to the trials, their aftermath and subsiding significance as people continue the task of rebuilding Europe. She even mentions Brief Encounter, using it to define the Czech estrangement from the British, who had let them down at Munich. The elliptical Britishisms of the lovers in the movie, who decided not to consummate their affair, left the Czechs cold. "Sexual renunciation on secular grounds is not a theme which Central Europe understands," Rebecca observes. Brief Encounter seemed a drab and inhibited little drama for a people desperately worried about the Russians looming over their land. During the film a drowsing American attorney from Nuremberg (it was Francis Biddle) suddenly woke up at the entrance of a minor character: "By God, that man looks just like Goering." Rebecca remarks that the lawyer was using the screen as a "palimpsest with the great tragedy imposed on the small." This was an example of her own tendency to conflate the great and the small, the public and the private, in her own life and career, reflecting on what her own renunciation and rebellions had cost her, and how what happened to her was a part of history writ large.

Rebecca's parents, Charles and Isabella Fairfield. Charles had the good looks of a storybook hero: dark flashing eyes, high cheekbones, a chiseled jawline, and an erect, slim, soldierly bearing. Isabella was a "black Highlander", called so because of her dark-haired and dark-eyed Mediterranean look – she moved and spoke nimbly, in a bird-like way that Rebecca compared extravagantly to the sight of "eagles flying high over Delphi." *Courtesy of Alison Macleod.*

Six-year-old Rebecca being fed blackberries on a country outing with her sisters Lettie (lower left), Winnie (upper left), and two cousins. *Courtesy of McFarlin Library, Special Collections, University of Tulsa.*

Winifred "Winnie" Fairfield, aged 18. Winnie had a dark complexion and much of her parents' intense personalities. She recited poems such as 'The Lady of Shalott' to her baby sister Rebecca. Winnie made a "powerful medicine" of literature, Rebecca remarked. In fact, Winnie became Rebecca's muse. *Courtesy of Norman Macleod.*

Young Rebecca New Year 1911. Just turned 19, she had already attempted a novel, drawing herself in the heroine, Adela, with brown eyes "as melting as the antelope's" and the "face of a young panther." *Courtesy of McFarlin Library, Special Collections, University of Tulsa.*

The Wells family and guests (H.G. Wells, Frank Wells, Jane Wells, Ella Hepworth Dixon, Wells's cousin Ruth Neale) at Easton Glebe about 1912 (just before H.G. met Rebecca). H.G. later deplored Rebecca's "growing mania" about Jane. Rebecca called her a "greedy, unscrupulous, sadistic woman with a curious delight in deception." *Courtesy of H.G. Wells Collection, University of Illinois.*

Rebecca and Anthony. Soon after Anthony's birth, Rebecca realized that she had fallen in love with him and could not give him up. She felt fiercely protective – an emotion she attributed partly to the start of the war.

BELOW. Rebecca and Ford Madox Ford, *c.* 1914. She revered his powers as a novelist and praised his efforts as a mentor to young writers. She found him indiscriminate about women, apt to "roll the eye at all God had created female." She compared him to a pink whale, but without "cetacean firmness." Out of his perpetually open mouth his voice issued with strange sound effects. Rebecca remembered him talking to the artist Wyndham Lewis about the decoration of a mantlepiece, "I find it, whoof, so restful, honk." *Courtesy of H.G. Wells Collection, University of Illinois.*

Lettie in her World War I uniform. She was the family trailblazer whom Rebecca resented for her bossiness, her experience and authority. *Courtesy of Alison Macleod.*

H.G. Wells, *c.* 1920. In the midst of his affair with Rebecca, he was now afraid of losing her, as she widened her circle of friends and threatened an interest in other men, "Please love me & be faithful to me. It is much bitterér & more humiliating for the male & I can't bear the thought of it." *Courtesy of J.R. Hammond.*

Rebecca at 31. Lawrence Langner of New York City's Theatre Guild called her "an odd mixture of beauty, unconventionality and respectability." *Courtesy of McFarlin Library, Special Collections, University of Tulsa.*

Newspaper magnate Max Beaverbrook, Rebecca's sometime lover. Short like H.G., he had a much trimmer body, a very large head, a wide mouth, and an impish grin. He reveled in gossip, drama, and political scheming. He had the enormous energy of a self-made man, and was essentially an outsider – like H.G. – who enjoyed stirring the pot. Champion and the confidant of the Conservative Prime Minister, Bonar Law, a dominant force in shaping public opinion. The plucky Max may have made H.G. look like a spent force – at least this is how Rebecca would characterize her feelings in her incomplete novel, *Sunflower*, which she would begin to write in 1925. *Courtesy of House of Lords Record Office.*

1922. Rebecca and her niece, Alison Macleod. "Rebecca is looking bored because she wasn't much interested in children," comments Alison. *Courtesy of Norman Macleod.*

c. 1925–1926. Anthony at eleven or twelve, a sad boy, bullied at school, missing his mother (off travelling in America), and craving more of his father's company – the entertaining Wellsie who played games with Anthony and drew him pictures. *Courtesy of Rosalind Burdon-Taylor.*

BELOW. One of Rebecca's lovers and a lifelong friend, Rebecca called the six foot two, 190 pound John Gunther a "gothic angel . . . with the vitality of seven cart horses." *Courtesy of McFarlin Library, Special Collections, University of Tulsa.*

Aerial view of Ibstone House and its grounds. Done in the Regency style, the house had a small farm, and a circular walled garden. The land looked over a lovely valley and the Chiltern Hills.

1938. Rebecca at 45. Still troubled by her aborted affair with her surgeon, Pomfret Kilner (K), she confided to her diary, "He and H.G. and I sat around the dinner table and talked over our situation! In H.G.'s house. But K. won't be my lover. He's too scared." *Courtesy of McFarlin Library, Special Collections, University of Tulsa.*

RIGHT. Rebecca with Yugoslav guide Constantine (Stanislav Vinaver). His rotund body reminded her of the "best known satyr in the Louvre." Their driver, Dragutin, becomes in her book the voice of the earthy Serb peasant, kind and ferocious. He twists the ear of a Croat boy and in a jolly voice says, "We'll kill you all someday." *Courtesy of McFarlin Library, Special Collections, University of Tulsa.*

RIGHT. In Herzegovina, Rebecca's feminist spirit rebelled against traditional costumes which wrapped women in overlarge men's coats with collars projecting forward like visors, hiding women's faces in veils, expressing the male solidarity with death, and their "special hatred for the instrument of birth." *Courtesy of McFarlin Library, Special Collections, University of Tulsa.*

Approaching the Dalmation city of Korchula, Rebecca praised it for its Balkan quality of visibility. Henry would see things so much more clearly in Yugoslavia, she assured him. *Courtesy of McFarlin Library, Special Collections, University of Tulsa.*

Rebecca rejoiced in Sarajevo. Like a woman, the city had resisted the Turks by yielding. "Plump in insubordination" it makes the sultans and viziers lament, "But when did we conquer these people?" *Courtesy of McFarlin Library, Special Collections, University of Tulsa.*

Caroline West. Rebecca admired Caroline's "great glowing brown eyes." She was sure to have her mother's "grace and fine build." *Courtesy of Kitty West.*

Edmund West and Lily West (Anthony's second wife). Only nine years older than Edmund, Lily was like a playmate for Anthony's children, Rebecca remarked. Edmund was so big and blond and Nordic looking that she could not imagine how he had gotten into the family. *Courtesy of Kitty West.*

Rebecca, Caroline, Kitty, and Edmund West. Rebecca enjoyed attending her grandchildren's school events. But she worried about Caroline, suspecting her granddaughter wanted to retreat from the adult world. An offended Caroline responded by studying hard, passing Cambridge's entrance exam, and winning the prestigious Girton Scholarship. *Courtesy of Kitty West.*

Anthony, Cheryl, Edmund, Kitty West. Shortly after Edmund's marriage to Cheryl (1976). Rebecca liked nothing about Cheryl – her looks, her voice, her manners, her clothes, her vocabulary, her posture – all were found wanting. *Courtesy of Kitty West.*

BELOW RIGHT. 1959. The year Rebecca was damed. She approached a dais, curtsied, took two steps forward and the Queen pinned her with a cross and a steel star. The Queen thanked her for doing so much good work. "Bless her heart," Rebecca thought, "so I have, but I doubt if she will ever know what it was. But it couldn't have been more prettily said." *Courtesy of McFarlin Library, Special Collections, University of Tulsa.*

Francis Biddle. Attorney General in the Roosevelt administration, he became Rebecca's lover at the Nuremberg trials. A gifted lawyer and an engaging man, the sixty-year-old Biddle had an ease about him that his colleagues admired. He liked Rebecca's strong capable hands, her extraordinary eyes – and her nice smile and voice captivated him. To Rebecca, he represented "one last lovely fling." *Courtesy of Franklin D. Roosevelt Library, Hyde Park, NY.*

Francis Biddle. Rebecca wrote in *The New Yorker* that he "looked like a highly intelligent swan, occasionally flexing down to commune with a smaller waterfowl." *Courtesy of Syracuse University Library, Department of Special Collections.*

Lettie, Henry, and Rebecca at the wedding of her nephew Norman Macleod. Rebecca and Norman's bride, Marion, exchange knowing looks. *Courtesy of Norman Macleod.*

Rebecca, Henry, Albert, and Mr. Briggs. Rebecca called her golden labrador a "very sentimental version of Don Juan," untrainable but a wonderful walking companion. *Courtesy of McFarlin Library, Special Collections, University of Tulsa.*

In Mexico, 1967. Henry developed a cold and wore his thickest clothes. Rebecca's once robust image of him dematerialized. He resembled a dying man-god, walking with a "hieratic delay." *Photograph by Rebecca West.*

BELOW LEFT. Rebecca at 79. Portrait by the late Chester Williams. *Courtesy of Chester Williams.*

BELOW RIGHT. Rebecca at 85. She was still writing fiction, a novel about Leonora, a woman her age, bedeviled with members of her love life and struggling with physical decay – relieved by trips to indoor swimming pools, "One got something of what one had got from love-making, from that first thrust into the water, the surrender of the whole body to an unusual element." *Courtesy of McFarlin Library, Special Collections, University of Tulsa.*

CHAPTER 25

"The Sibyl of Our Time"
1947–1948

I

JUNE 1947, GREENVILLE, South Carolina. Thirty-one white defendants stood accused of shooting dead a black man. He had been taken from the local jail, where he had been incarcerated pending a trial for murdering a white taxi driver. Rebecca sensed that Greenville, no less than Nuremberg, would make a riveting *New Yorker* study of the connections between culture and crime. Harold Ross concurred, jokingly telling her: "I suppose you'll be staying with the Judge after the first day."

Like many visitors to the South, she was overwhelmed by its lushness—wild bush roses, spectral tall lavender, brilliant purples—and its heat. She walked, dripping, all day long through the black section of town, admiring a "lovely dark severe girl in coffee coloured linen with a pale scarlet flower on her shoulder." Children in bright cottons were playing on a side street, and from a cabin she could hear a soft, lilting, repetitive voice: "You don't know an' you don't care. You don't know an' you don't care. And it's because you don't care that you don't know. That is what it is, you don't know because you don't care." In the white section she heard radios; in the black sections people singing. Southern oratory charmed her. She would title her article "Opera in Greenville."

Rebecca found the people in the local newspaper office sensitive and helpful; Germany had foundered for lack of such fine and fearless people. She admired the journalistic standards of the Charlotte and Greenville papers. She quickly made friends with the reporters and was invited into their homes. Although she was dead tired, their intrepid spirit revived her.

Inside the courtroom she listened to the dialect: "Co't of Lo—South Ca'o'ine." A witness said, "then they drug the negro out of the car." Drug was a better word than dragged, Rebecca observed. One of the alleged lynchers advised her to leave town, implying she was in some danger; outsiders and reporters were not welcome. Rebecca calmly said, "stay here," and went across the street into a shop and bought some chocolates. She returned, saying, "Take these to your children and never mind about me."

The gesture reflected her empathy for the men on trial. She did not excuse the crime, but she saw these thirty-one men as caught up on a rash murder that shamed their better selves, and she detected moments in the trial when they appeared repentant. She attacked their lawyers, who exploited the jury's prejudices and attributed the town's troubles to outside agitators, but she treated the trial as an event with profound implications for the South, predicting that in spite of the not guilty verdict lynching had been exposed as a crime the culture could no longer perpetuate. Rebecca offered few judgments on the society itself, but the tone of her article implied that she expected the South would eventually rectify its unjust and criminal behavior.

The warm response of most Southerners and Northerners to Rebecca's article in *The New Yorker* was extraordinary. Spared much of the vituperation that usually attended an outlander's report on the South, Rebecca was lauded for her objectivity. She did not condescend to Southerners—a particular failing of Northern journalists. She felt she had no call to pronounce judgment: "Lately Europe had not been really what any of us could call a peaceable community," she remarked. Measured by the violence in Europe, a lynching party was not that impressive; rather, it was important as an "indication of misery." When she thought of South Africa, of the breach between England and Ireland, she saw no reason for excoriating the South as peculiarly evil. Indeed, the trial, for all its shortcomings, had shown killing for what it is: "hideousness that begets hideousness." A black had murdered a white, so whites had murdered a black. She was confident that the accused white men sitting in the court with their families could see the senselessness of the slaughter and treat it as a "symptom of an abating disease."

Harry Ashmore, editor of *The Charlotte [North Carolina] News*, sent Rebecca a summary of Southern editorial reaction to her article. He challenged her interpretation of the defense lawyers, but he admired her exact and inspired characterizations. He thought she was kinder to the town and its people than they had any right to expect. Harold Ross told Rebecca about the volume of complimentary mail; only a few Southern ladies had written to ask if Southern men were really like that. The lack of dissent to her piece was "absolutely amazing."

2

IN LATE AUTUMN 1947, Rebecca returned home to write a series of articles for the *Evening Standard* on a small remnant of fascists fomenting anti-Semitism. She accused the Communists of street-fighting with the Fascists, mainly to further Communist propaganda and to gain the Jewish vote. She attacked both sides so vigorously that at the mention of her name the Fascists and the Communists would stop fighting to boo and hiss her. She attended some of the meetings incognito, impersonating a charlady, hobbling around on a stick, wearing a white wig and a bonnet. She put on a show for the Gavrilovićs, who admired how completely she transformed herself for this role. She had a lovely moment at a public meeting when a Fascist yelled, "As for Miss Rebecca West, she is the perfect example of the hack journalist." The Communists were of greater concern; she estimated that in London they outnumbered the Fascists ten to one.

Rebecca enjoyed working for the *Evening Standard* because of her editor, Charles Curran. A plain-spoken, well-read man, he loved retailing political gossip. She thought him ugly, yet she adored him. They fought over his Catholicism, which Rebecca abhorred. She wanted an affair, and when he demurred, she got angry. She disliked his obsessive talk about lust. But he was too good a man to lose, lending a sympathetic ear to her troubles but remaining robust in their disagreements and often rousing her out of self-pity. So she stopped pushing their relationship further than he had wanted it to go: "What an ass I am! How rude and narrow-minded and bigoted I've been! What does it matter to me what you think about love and lust and trigonometry, and what does it matter to you what I think about them!"

3

Rebecca's fame as a journalist came to a climax in early 1948 with the American reception of *The Meaning of Treason.* (The English publication was held up a year for legal reasons.) Her prominence made her more than ever eager to combat negative reviews, more certain of the communist conspiracy against her. *Time* magazine decided to do a cover story on her, and she invited reporters and photographers into her home. She became suspicious when a *Time* staffer requested a photograph of her and H.G. Then she mounted a campaign of protest against a paragraph describing her liaison with H.G., Anthony, and the appearance of his first novel, which had just won the Houghton Mifflin award. Rebecca worked through her agent A. D. Peters, Dorothy Thompson, and John Gunther, friends of Henry and Clare Booth Luce (*Time*'s owners), to get the paragraph suppressed. *Time* editor John Osborne wrote to Rebecca, acknowledging her point that she had been generous and helpful in the gathering of story material. But as a journalist he could not concede her argument that her cooperation obligated *Time* not to print any facts objectionable to her. He argued that the story of Rebecca West as artist and person could not be told without some reference to a relationship well-known for several years in the English and American literary communities. Rebecca felt that her hospitality had been abused and that she had been treated like a serf for *Time*'s convenience. "Oh, haven't you often done the same thing yourself as a journalist?" Osborne asked. An outraged Rebecca denied she had and maintained that her reputation depended on her not violating privacy.

Rebecca felt compromised as a reporter, having her life with H.G. publicized. She hated revealing an intricate story that no one would get right. She dreaded Lettie's reaction; Lettie had always been sensitive about Rebecca's reputation. Rebecca worried about offending H.G.'s family. Letters, cables, and phone calls went back and forth for weeks. Rebecca threatened to sue the magazine for invasion of privacy. Even Max Beaverbrook phoned a protest to *Time*. It capitulated in late November 1948, before going to press for the December 8 issue.

Time called her the "No. 1 Woman Writer," a graying, stocky figure with vestiges of her girlhood beauty showing through her mature, intelligent face. Some things had not changed. She still had an untidy appearance: "she often looks as if somebody had thrown her clothes on her as she rushed for the train." The piece caught the peculiar intellectual ground she occupied with the aphorism that she was a "Socialist by habit of mind, and a conservative by cell structure." It paid her the supreme compliment of ending the story by lauding her style, which in a prosy age continually strove toward a "condition of poetry, and comes to rest in a rhetoric that, at its best, is one of the most personal and eloquent idioms of our time."

The Meaning of Treason was a popular and critical success—thanks in part to the *Time* send-off. The book hit the 25,000 mark in sales before Christmas, a most impressive figure in a season of slumping sales. Even when reviewers dissented from her conclusions, they extolled the book's style and method. As Harold Ross told her, she had almost singlehandedly invented a way of covering trials that made them every bit as gripping as a play, a film, or a novel. Years later, Truman Capote would hail her as one of the inventors of the nonfiction novel—rightly so, because she had not only reported the trials, she had worked like a biographer and historian, reading copiously in government records and documents, and interviewing members of the traitors' families and their friends. She had had the advice, as well, of Theobald Mathew, her own solicitor and now Director of Public Prosecutions, who had first suggested the trials as a topic.

Lionel Trilling, Rebecca West's most thoughtful American reviewer, both admired and distrusted her style, calling attention to its "hectic flush," and lavish use of metaphor and allusion. She wrote an "anxious prose," he observed, bent on presenting the idea of the nation state with an "incantatory glorification of it." He understood why. Since the Russian Revolution, nationalism had been in bad odor with progressives, who had committed themselves to the international ideal which would break down narrow and partisan barriers between peoples. He associated Rebecca West with Edmund Burke, who viewed the nation as "an almost mystical entity of language, custom, history, and destiny." *The Meaning of Treason*'s fervor combatted ideology, which in her view subverted nationhood. Traitors, in other words, put their trust in communism, fascism, or some other doctrine, and betrayed their fealty to the age-old harmony of nation, family, and hearth.

Trilling realized that Rebecca had detected a flaw in liberalism: it ignored the "deep instinctual roots of man," and that ideas had powerful psychological origins. Liberals preferred to think that ideas developed and changed as a result of debate and conflict. Trilling himself wanted more discussion of ideas, less attention to personality per se, which tended to overwhelm the political issues, but he acknowledged her "special place in our intellectual life because she maintains a liberal democratic position together with a strong traditionalism."

Evelyn Hutchinson, a Yale professor who had become a champion of Rebecca's work, reinforced her sense of mission, avowing that she had a major, if difficult, role to play in contentious times: "You are the major prophetess, the sibyl of our time"; the Roman poet, Virgil, had explained how extremely unpleasant it was to be inspired, Evelyn informed her.

4

NINETEEN FORTY-EIGHT had been a sensational year. Rebecca reported on the Democratic, Republican, and Progressive Party conventions in Philadelphia. She earned the enmity of many American Leftists by scorning the Progressive Party presidential candidacy of Henry Wallace, whom she regarded as a Communist dupe. Abusive letters convinced her that a smear campaign had been arranged to make her seem anti-democratic, anti-Semitic, and anti-Negro. She confidently brushed aside her enemies. Her fellow reporter, William L. Shirer, found her "sexy and sardonic," even in the intensely humid heat of the Philadelphia summer in days before air conditioning. They spent a fruitless Sunday searching the city for a drink, but she never lost her verve. "I would have gone bananas without her," he remembered.

At Christmas, Rebecca welcomed Anthony, Kitty, and their children to a house wreathed in holly with a seven-foot Christmas tree. She was proudly recommending his award-winning novel to her friends. Anthony and Kitty had sold their house in London and moved to a Dorset village, Tarant Hinton, believing it would be healthier for the children, especially Caroline, who did not thrive in the city. Rebecca practically chirped with pleasure at their visit, petting and indulging them in every luxury, and giving them a gorgeous party. She thought of Caroline as an introverted beauty, difficult to fathom. The outgoing Edmund charmed her. On Christmas Day he brought her a toy he had got out of his stocking, a little figure of Puss in Boots. He wanted to know if she could fix it. He had heard it said she was clever. He explained that its tassel was on the wrong side, and he thought it must be terribly awkward for the poor creature to have that part of its body on a different side from its face. Rebecca took the incident as an example of his "kindly nature," and wondered if it presaged a reforming impulse that would set the world right.

CHAPTER 26

Richard III's Mother
1949

I

IN EARLY SEPTEMBER, Charles Curran rang Rebecca to say that the *Evening Standard* had just received an advertisement of Anthony's new novel, announcing that he was writing a full-length biography of his father, H. G. Wells. To Charles, it appeared that Anthony was exploiting his mother's liaison with H.G. to puff himself. One of Charles's colleagues deemed Anthony a "good for nothing" who had lived on his father and mother all his life and had "skunked out of military service." Charles advised Rebecca that the advertisement would do Anthony "endless harm." He urged her to put this point strongly to Anthony's publisher, Eyre and Spottiswoode.

In shock, Rebecca reviewed the sequence of events leading up to the advertisement. In May, she and Henry had visited Anthony and Kitty at their house in Dorset. As Rebecca picked up a book off the top of a low bookshelf, a letter from Anthony's American publisher fell out. She caught sight of a sentence with her name in it, saying that if Anthony permitted publication of a book jacket blurb revealing he was the son of H. G. Wells and Rebecca West, it would sell the book as nothing else. She spoke about it to Anthony immediately. He said that he had left the letter out for her to see, and that he did not think the publisher's proposal would appeal to her. Later that night, after Henry went to bed, Rebecca raised the issue again, assuming that Anthony shared her conviction that this was a crude and vulgar attempt to profit from their lives. She could see, however, that he very much wanted the blurb to be published. "I am not ashamed of either of my parents," he told her. That was not the point, Rebecca rejoined. She had never concealed the circumstances of his birth from her friends, but why give carte blanche to anybody who might want to write injurious things about her and H.G.? She found this invasion of privacy distasteful; it would weaken her effectiveness as a journalist if she became the focus of stories about her private life. She was controversial enough as it was. Anthony disagreed and doubted that her journalistic career would be jeopardized. It might even do some good to clear the air, scotching rumors and insinuations that would inevitably lead to a muckraking biography. To her, his comments implied that she was a coward not to risk criticism of her behavior. Then Anthony and Kitty cut off the conversation, stating they would defer to Rebecca in this matter and let her decide. She said that Anthony could identify himself as her son, but she preferred that he not mention H.G. She could see Anthony's disappointment, but she believed he had sulkily agreed to respect her wishes.

After Anthony had gone to bed, Rebecca stayed up to restate her concerns to a sympathetic Kitty. Rebecca could not honestly say that her affair with H.G. had been a triumph or that she had been happy; consequently, she was not comfortable lying about it or telling the truth. Either way she felt compromised and did H.G. no good. She knew Anthony saw it differently—that he had as much right to acknowledge the story of his father and mother as she had to suppress it. A few days later, Rebecca wrote to Anthony reiterating her attitude.

In late July, after Rebecca returned from Germany, Anthony visited Ibstone. He did not discuss the blurb, but he mentioned that an American journalist told him Rebecca had succeeded in expunging the reference to H.G. in the *Time* cover story. He looked ill to her, with that bloated look she associated with his mental crises. Curran's September phone call about the advertisement prompted her to write to Douglas Jerrold at Eyre and Spottiswoode, Anthony's British publisher. The reply from Jerrold, an old friend from Henry's Oxford days, "electrified us," as Rebecca put it, for Jerrold reported that Anthony had approved the announcement, assuring the publisher that "no one would take an exception." Admitting that he had been misled, Jerrold promised to omit any reference to H.G. in subsequent advertisements.

Consulting Gip and Marjorie Wells, Rebecca discovered that they too were disturbed about the advertisement and shared her feeling that it was tasteless and an invasion of privacy. They were also not prepared to see a public announcement of Anthony's forthcoming biography of H.G. It had been discussed with him, but no agreement had been reached yet. They were now anxious to reach some understanding with Anthony so as to avoid further embarrassment.

Because Anthony had deceived his publisher, Rebecca believed that he had never intended to show her the blurb mentioning her and H.G.

He had not raised the question of biographical details; she had had to confront him with it. His motivations perplexed her. Was he suffering from another mental breakdown, or behaving like a scoundrel? Was he counting on a large amount of money from the sale of his biography? She had been generous with Anthony, giving him a two hundred pounds a year allowance. In July, she had agreed to guarantee his three hundred pound overdraft. Was he using the biography to remove any need to depend on her and Henry financially?

Rebecca had always been uneasy about Anthony's proposed biography of H.G. She felt it was much too early to delve into certain events such as the Gatternigg affair, when a woman had attempted suicide in his London flat. She knew that H.G. had destroyed much of his private correspondence, including most of her letters, and she did not believe that he wanted a biography that included the details of his private life. She presumed that Anthony would be dealing with H.G.'s work and aspects of his public career. Anthony gave friends Ralph and Frances Partridge the impression that there would be very little mention of Rebecca. She did nothing to dissuade Anthony from doing the biography. In fact, she wrote to Max Beaverbrook, asking him to see Anthony for an interview about H.G. She counted on the Wells family—chiefly Gip and Marjorie—to negotiate a contract with Anthony that steered clear of the more personal elements of H.G.'s career. By her lights, she had been tactful and liberal with her son. But after the appearance of the advertisement in the *Times Literary Supplement* mentioning H.G., she let her exasperation with Anthony show to old friends like G. B. Stern: "Why the hell does it still matter so much to him?" It seemed a kind of weak leftist snobbery to her; she wished "he'd grow up and be a person."

Rebecca puzzled over what to do next, explaining to several friends the options that seemed available to her and asking for advice. Both she and Henry felt that it would be wrong simply to veto Anthony's desire to make his relationship with H.G. publicly known. Henry proposed to meet Anthony and tell him that he could go ahead with additional advertisements but at the price of a total severance from both of them, since he had disregarded his mother's wishes and acted unscrupulously with his publisher. Henry believed that if Anthony really felt so strongly about his father, he should be prepared to accept the consequences of a breach.

Before taking any other steps, Henry received a letter from Anthony, expressing his shock that "mother was ashamed of having loved my father and borne me." It saddened him not to be able to acknowledge Rebecca as his mother. Nothing could be done to persuade him to be ashamed of his father or to believe that his relationship with H.G. was a dishonorable one. If he could not say proudly who his father and mother were, his silence implied that their relationship was disgraceful. He could not remain quiet. He hoped that Henry would not ask him to do it. Then Anthony explained why it was so important to him that he should openly acknowledge his parents:

> Before I realised that my father and mother were great people and that I was honourably born vulgar and beastly people hurt me a great deal with the word bastard and more than half convinced me that I did not belong in the world of decent human beings. I hope that I am not going to meet those values again in the mouths of people I love. I love you both. For that reason I cannot bear it that you should suggest that my origins are shameful, that I am shameful, and that I must discreetly live my existence down, I hope you will not do so.

Anthony's letter eloquently evoked his pain; it did not acknowledge Rebecca's. Indeed, it accused her and Henry of making his life more painful and humiliating. It asserted his rights; it did not recognize that she had any. Henry took one look at the letter and realized that it was not written by a gentleman. Anthony had broken his word to respect his mother's wishes.

Rebecca showed Anthony's letter to Marjorie Wells, who vehemently rejected its sincerity, calling it an "exercise in literary composition." She thought him selfish and self-pitying, and "completely lacking in any sense of obligation toward his mother and father and the world at large, and determined to get his own way at any cost (to others, of course)." Having authorized the shameful advertisement, he was too stubborn to apologize. Her husband Gip took a more tolerant view, writing Anthony a sympathetic letter. Marjorie assured Rebecca that as literary executor, she would make certain Anthony submitted the manuscript of the biography to her before publication.

When Anthony realized that Rebecca had enlisted Marjorie Wells as her ally, he replied to Gip's letter, assuring his half-brother that he had intended to submit the manuscript of H.G.'s biography to him, and that Gip would have full editorial control, which meant suppressing any objectionable material. Anthony also sought to restore a reputation he believed his mother had gravely damaged: "I understand that it has been represented to you that I have recently broken various promises and undertakings and my word is not to be relied upon. The only thing I have to say on this subject is that I have not broken any words to anyone and that I hope I will hear no more of this gratuitous slander."

Then Henry visited Anthony, who treated his stepfather's arrival in a Rolls-Royce at his Dorset home as an ultimatum from the Lord of the Manor. Halfway up the front steps Henry stopped, declaring to Anthony and Kitty that he would not come into the house or impose himself as a guest until he had announced the purpose of his call. If Anthony did not swear to desist from publicizing the story of his parents, then Henry would have to consider changing his will, implying but not actually saying that Anthony was a major beneficiary of a considerable sum. Anthony could not see why he shouldn't acknowledge his father. "There's all the difference in the world between a private secret and a public secret," Henry pointed out. Henry turned to Kitty, imploring her to act as his ally and to think of the impact on her children if he changed his will. She turned her back on him and walked into the house. Anthony watched his stepfather's long face lengthen. He said he would give Anthony a week to reconsider, reminding him that a significant sum was at stake.

A shaken Henry returned to Ibstone to give Rebecca a full report of the meeting with Anthony and Kitty. Henry said Anthony held Rebecca responsible for persuading H.G. to leave two shares of his estate to Kitty and not to him. Anthony had also told Henry that Rebecca had a curious kink in her character: she hated the thought of Anthony's receiving money from H.G. She had even prevented H.G. from settling a great deal of money on him when he was a boy. Henry had scoffed. Why would a girl in her twenties in fitful health and with domestic difficulties reject a settlement? Anthony replied that in the papers Marjorie Wells had sent him for his biography of H.G. he had found one of Rebecca's letters revealing the awful truth. Henry wanted to see the letter. Anthony replied that the Wells family had burned it because it was such a "disgraceful document."

Rebecca denied Anthony's charges about the will, saying H.G. had told her he had done enough for Anthony. She refused to believe that any letter of hers to H.G. about Anthony's settlement would dishonor her.

Henry called Marjorie Wells. She knew nothing about the letter, and spoke of Rebecca with great affection. Henry called Anthony to say his allegations were false. Anthony said the letter still existed, but he had wanted to spare Henry's feelings. Rebecca's attitude toward H.G. was difficult to analyze and stemmed from a powerful unconscious need to stand between him and his father, Anthony alleged. He cited as proof a letter in which Rebecca proposed to H.G. that he give her a life interest in the five thousand pounds he intended to confer on Anthony:

It is going to be difficult if after A. comes of age I am dependent on him for the rent of the house. It's not a good or normal relationship. You know well that you can trust me to hand over properly. I've taken very good care of all his funds. Also its not good for him to feel I haven't anything.

To Anthony, the passage conveyed Rebecca's paranoia that he would someday be in a position to lord it over her. All she could think of, Anthony pointed out to Henry, was that money to Anthony might become a source of pain and humiliation to her. (Rebecca might well have retorted: "All Anthony can think of is what pains and humiliates him.")

Then Anthony struck a low blow, one that Henry would certainly consider ungentlemanly. Anthony enclosed one of Rebecca's letters to him, voicing her usual complaints about Henry's erratic and tiresome behavior, referring to his idiocy and silliness, his incompetent handling of the house and the farm, and even wondering if he had become prematurely senile. Once Henry read what Rebecca had said about him, Anthony suggested, perhaps he would realize that Rebecca did not always accurately represent those who loved her.

Rebecca did not think her letter to H.G. compromised her in the slightest. She had been sensible and prudent. As for Anthony's handing over her letter about Henry to Henry, that had been a mean thing to do. But she and Henry had an absolute trust in each other: Anthony could do nothing to divide them.

Rebecca recommended to Anthony that he show her letter to H.G. to a solicitor, who would put him right about it. She had been acting on the advice of her solicitor, Theobald Mathew, who had pointed out that young people were often careless about money and that a provision for the mother's income would put the relationship with the son on a sounder basis.

Rebecca's agent, A. D. Peters, had come to know mother and son fairly well. Anthony asked him to be his agent as well. Peters supported Rebecca, but he tried to make her see Anthony's case, how desperately he wanted it known to the world that H.G. was his father, and how determined Anthony was not to let anything—not even his mother's feelings—stand in the way of his desire. Echoing Henry, Peters concluded that Anthony did not understand the "difference between public and private knowledge of a fact that concerns him so closely."

One unintended result of this September controversy over the publisher's blurb was the strengthening of Rebecca's marriage. Henry had been marvelous, steady and loyal to her, and indefatigable in investigating Anthony's accusations. When Anthony had produced Rebecca's letter about Henry, Henry had turned to Rebecca and said that he knew she had been going through a bad patch and that he had given her an appalling time then.

By November 1949, Rebecca had worked out that there was a fundamental difference between her and Anthony. She lacked his self-consciousness. "When I catch sight of myself in a mirror I'm always surprised to know I look like that, I have the same sort of nescience about my own character and destiny," she told Charles Curran. Anthony, on the other hand, was "passionately aware of himself and his own destiny," and abetted by Kitty, who now seemed to Rebecca without any scruples whatsoever. Kitty and Anthony were joined in their "frozen attitudes of hate" toward her. But it would not do Kitty much good, Rebecca predicted. She expected that Anthony would leave Kitty again and had refrained so far because he did not want to injure his children as he had been injured when Rebecca left H.G.

Rebecca also thought Anthony envied her early start as a writer. He had often remarked upon it, and at thirty-five he was just beginning to make his reputation. Compared to Rebecca, Anthony had enormous doubts. Rebecca knew this, and that children of famous parents often lacked confidence. "He doubted everything about himself," his second wife Lily has said. It is easy to see how outgunned his mother made him feel, and how he attributed to her all sorts of powers and plots he could not foil. He could not assuage himself in work that was not yet mature, so he relieved himself in life, Rebecca speculated. This sense of inferiority accounted for the ruckus Anthony had stirred up during H.G.'s last two years, his incredible need to feel that *he* mattered most to his father and that Rebecca mattered almost not at all. In this sense, Rebecca acknowledged that she had indeed put herself in between father and son.

2

SOMETIME IN THE AUTUMN OF 1949, Anthony decided to emigrate to America. As he told his friends Frances and Ralph Partridge he would go first to "spy out the land," and bring Kitty and children a little later. Anthony did not say so, but Frances suspected that his quarrel with his mother about the *Times Literary Supplement* advertisement had something to do with his decision. Indeed, he wanted to put as much distance as possible between himself and his mother. Soon he would begin work on a novel, *Another Kind*, which projected a very gloomy future for Britain, overcome with labor strife and subject to a neo-Fascist takeover.

Rebecca learned of Anthony's planned emigration from Pamela Frankau, her old friend from summers in the South of France and some of Anthony's confidants. Pamela visited Ibstone and told Rebecca that he had asked for her help, since Houghton Mifflin, Anthony's American publisher, was hers as well, and she was living in America. Rebecca gathered that Anthony wanted to publicize his book and make a success similar to his mother's. She regarded his emigration not as a declaration of independence but as an act of rebellion and rivalry. Anthony had told Pamela: "My father's and my mother's accounts of their relationships don't match. I must see justice done."

Charles Curran urged Rebecca to seek a reconciliation with Anthony. She could not do that, she said, because their quarrel was not an isolated incident but part of a "long and horrid story," in which she felt like Richard III's mother. Now every good thing Anthony had done seemed like a record of deception. She had been delighted at Anthony's dedication of his novel to Henry, but now she realized it was part of a long pre-meditated plan to "rook and exploit" him. When Kitty sent a letter to Rebecca thanking her for Christmas presents and making no mention of their quarrel, Rebecca accused her of being insensitive and bad-mannered. She sent an eight-page, typed, single-spaced letter to Harold Ross, alerting him to Anthony's arrival in New York. She told him she loved her son and that he could be charming, witty, sensitive, original, and erudite, but he was also dishonest and unreliable about money. He often behaved like an ass. She hoped Anthony would cool off, but Ross should be prepared to hear some outrageous stories.

CHAPTER 27

The Medusa Head
1949–1952

1

IN DECEMBER 1949, Rebecca began writing about a mysterious trial involving the murder of a disreputable car dealer, Mr. Setty, and his alleged murderer, Mr. Hume, accused of cutting up and packaging the pieces of his victim and dropping them from an airplane into the sea. Like so much of Rebecca's reporting, the story had implications beyond its ostensible subject matter; it became an inquiry into human motives and crimes against humanity, centered on a study of family life that became an allegory of her obsession with Anthony.

Rebecca visited the large family of the fisherman, Mr. Tiffen, who had found Mr. Setty's remains. She was impressed at their healthy, happy, and good-tempered life. The grandmother told her: "I'm lucky, you know. Other people have family troubles, I've never had one, not a single one of my children but has turned out all right." Rebecca thought of her son and his resemblance to Donald Hume, the alleged murderer, born a bastard. "Illegitimacy does something to people. But I can't warn the world of that," Rebecca said. Anthony and Donald were alike in having winning personalities, in finding generous friends who adopted them and gave them money, and forgave them for defrauding them. Donald even had a beautiful wife like Kitty, who stood by her husband, and had nearly as much to do with the crime as Donald himself.

2

IN MID-JANUARY 1950, Rebecca visited Marjorie Wells, who asked her about Anthony. Rebecca alluded to his impending American journey. Marjorie knew nothing about it and became alarmed, because Anthony still possessed four suitcases full of H.G.'s uncatalogued and uninsured papers and a few of Rebecca's letters—an embarrassment to Marjorie, who had not examined the contents carefully or consulted Rebecca. Marjorie did not trust Anthony, and she suspected he meant to take the papers with him to America. Her concern intensified when she remembered meeting Kitty just a few days before Rebecca's visit. Kitty had said nothing about Anthony's trip. Suspecting she had been deceived, Marjorie demanded from Anthony immediate return of the papers. He promised she would have them after he sailed to America on January 24; to surrender them earlier would be to acknowledge that he had intended to remove them from the country without her consent. He felt he was being treated like a blackmailer; she felt she was making a reasonable request. Anthony had not bolstered his case by burning two of his mother's letters, claiming he did so because they put her in a bad light and he wanted to protect her. When Marjorie proved adamant about handing over the papers at once, he wrote an angry letter renouncing his title as authorized biographer and declaring himself a free agent who intended to honor his contracts with publishers, even though it would be difficult to write a biography without access to H.G.'s archive.

In New York, Harold Ross and journalist Dorothy Thompson conferred on what to do about Anthony. Thompson told Ross that she had first seen Anthony when he was nine, and Rebecca had introduced him as her nephew. Surely that was enough to arouse Anthony's resentment, Dorothy said. Rebecca thought she was the "sanest person in the world," but Dorothy knew better. They had become friends in Berlin in 1924; they had traveled together for a month in Germany in the spring of 1949. Rebecca was highly neurotic, Dorothy assured Ross. Healthy as a horse, she constantly complained of illness like a champion hypochondriac. Dorothy loved Rebecca, but after reading Rebecca's letter to Ross, Dorothy concluded: "I can understand her son's resentment and difficulties with his mother."

Harold Ross wrote a friendly note to Anthony shortly after his mid-February arrival in New York. When Anthony walked into *The New Yorker* office, he startled Ross, who expected to meet the scowling or solemn figure he had seen in publicity photographs. Instead, Anthony looked like a masculine version of Rebecca. They had a brief, somewhat awkward talk. If Ross wanted to help him, Anthony suggested he put in a good word for him with his mother. Ross agreed to do that, and asked Anthony when Rebecca might be coming to New York. Anthony replied that his mother did not think she would ever come again; she believed that by announcing himself as H.G.'s son, Anthony had made her position in America impossible.

After Anthony left to visit Dorothy Thompson, Ross wrote to Rebecca, arguing that she had vastly exaggerated the damage that Anthony or any journalist could do to her. Anthony's novel and his announcement that he was H.G.'s son had certainly drawn attention—his first novel was reviewed widely in important newspapers and magazines, and his picture appeared on the cover of *The Saturday Review*—but this attention had not harmed Rebecca in the slightest. Americans took people pretty much the way they were; Rebecca had little to fear. Indeed, the press had been very positive about Anthony and regarded him as a promising new novelist. Of course, there were columnists who loved to dig up dirt, but that kind of journalism discredited itself, Ross assured Rebecca. He felt good about Anthony and even patriotic about Anthony's decision to make America his home. Several of Rebecca's friends expressed similar feelings—nettling her, because she viewed Anthony as leaving his native land during a period of interesting social experimentation under the Labor government for the safe, soft, and conservative American climate.

The slightly condescending tone of Harold's letter—his effort to pacify a highly strung female who had gotten into a tizzy (his word)—made Rebecca resistant to his sensible advice. Although she had accused Anthony of melodramatics, she herself bridled when a friend suggested that she might be overdoing it. She interpreted Ross's letter as implying he believed Anthony's lies about her and that she had done badly by him. She realized that Ross was sweet and well-meaning, but he had been terribly unjust to her.

Diana Trilling met Anthony during his New York trip, at one of her friend Leo Lerman's big parties. She had spotted a tall young man standing by himself, apart from the crowd. It seemed obvious to Diana that he did not know anyone, and wanting to be friendly she came up to him. Pearl Kazin of *Harper's Bazaar* asked him for news about his mother. Anthony peered at her, looking down from his great height, and said, "My mother doesn't tell me anything. I don't know anything about my mother. You see, my mother didn't want me to come to America. She wrote to *The New Yorker* to get them to stop me." An aghast Diana (she had not met Rebecca) responded drily: "Why?" Anthony said: "Well, she didn't want people to know that she had ever had me. She's very successful in America, and she doesn't want her public to know about me." Diana said, "I'm a very great admirer of your mother, and what's more, I've just had a son of my own, and I feel as though someone is walking on my grave." Anthony replied: "Oh, I don't go around talking about this to everyone." "You certainly do," Diana shot back, "you're doing it." "Well, only because you have such a kind face," rejoined Anthony, who could not placate her. Diana rejoined, "Oh nonsense, I don't believe the things you're saying. I just don't believe it." But Anthony continued: "You don't believe me. You don't believe the story about how my mother responded when I was arrested during the war?" He told Diana the story about being picked up by the police as a suspected Fascist and calling his mother for help. He was still offended that she had asked him if he was a Fascist. Diana took Rebecca's question as a joke, the sort of thing a mother might say to diffuse a tense situation.

It was just like Anthony to blurt out some "wounded filial thing about his famous mum," said Lily Emmet, whom he would soon meet and make his second wife. She never found him calculating about his image, or very astute about how his behavior would be perceived. Lily remembered a phrase from one of Anthony's chess books that sums up his impulsiveness: " 'possibly not the wisest move.' Possibly not the wisest move was something Anthony never thought of, ahead of time. So he would do things like this with a complete stranger. There is no question he made his position more difficult than it needed to be."

Rebecca thanked Dorothy Thompson for looking after Anthony and asked her to send word of his progress in New York. Dorothy liked Anthony's novel and had given him her son Mike's room to live in. She sympathized with Anthony as the son of two famous parents, just as her own son Mike had to try to equal her and Sinclair Lewis. As a single mother, Rebecca had had an impossible job: She had to be protector, defender, disciplinarian—tender and stern—all at the same time. "I just think no woman can do it," Dorothy told Rebecca. Dorothy believed that her very existence constituted a discouragement to her son Mike, and that he loved her intensely only made it worse. Dorothy had seen the same reaction in Anthony. He adored his mother and Dorothy had observed how pleased he was to hear Rebecca praised. But Dorothy reminded Rebecca that she was an extraordinarily powerful woman: "you are the Medusa head to him, too." So of course Anthony would have a hell of a time with himself and with his mother. Dorothy concluded that Anthony absolutely had to make a public point about his father. It was a way of offsetting some of Rebecca's strength.

Rebecca worried about how Anthony would support himself in America since his money was tied up in England. But when he accepted a well-paying job at *Time*, she was annoyed. What was the point of doing unsigned reviews, when he had done so well with signed reviews in *The New Statesman*? Harold Ross found Anthony "pleasantly cynical" about *Time*, where he had to appear only once a week. He was going to move into a place in Stonington, Connecticut, where he expected to write his next two novels.

Rebecca's anger flared again when she got word that Anthony was saying she had prevented him from doing H.G.'s biography. She wrote to John Gunther, who had also befriended Anthony, asking him to defend her—then she wrote again asking John to leave the whole affair alone since her efforts had become self-defeating. "Just be good to Anthony," she concluded. She got her agent, A. D. Peters, to visit Anthony and emphasize that she wanted him and no one else to write H.G.'s life.

Rebecca feared that Anthony had won over friends she had for thirty years and subverted her own high standing with them. She vastly exaggerated his influence, and apparently did not see the contradictions in her own attitude, for she had told many of her friends to treat him well. Yet she was surprised that they should want to effect a reconciliation between mother and son. It did not mean that they believed everything Anthony said, but that is how Rebecca took their efforts.

Rebecca lunched with John Morris, Anthony's former boss at the BBC. He had found Anthony shifty, crooked about money, a womanizer, and too ready to trade on the reputations of his famous parents. John told Rebecca that Anthony had criticized her as mean, hysterical, and neurotic, a rich woman who would give him nothing. John advised her to cut her "emotional losses." Rebecca concluded from this meeting that Anthony had never outgrown his dependence on her. In things great and small, he was a case of "arrested development."

3

WHILE REBECCA'S American friends were giving Anthony's book rave reviews in the spring of 1950, Rebecca was getting cordial, chatty letters from Kitty. To Rebecca, the letters seemed dishonest and idiotic. Did Kitty really think she could smooth things over so easily? And why was she so stupid about not realizing that Anthony had abandoned her for a second time? To Kitty, the letters were an effort to keep open communication with her children's grandmother. Because Rebecca so clearly wanted to be a part of Edmund's and Caroline's lives, and because Rebecca continued to send gifts and presents, Kitty thought it appropriate to acknowledge Rebecca's generosity and to assure her that she still had a place in her grandchildren's lives. Kitty still loved Anthony and had faith in him. She wanted to believe that all would go well and that she and the children would join him shortly.

But soon Kitty's letters to Rebecca registered plaintive notes: "Still no word from Anthony . . . I'm beginning to think that everyone has completely forgotten my existence including Anthony. . . . No more news from Anthony. I am beginning to feel very fed up. I really don't see why he should be absolutely unable to answer any of my letters no matter how I entreat him." Anthony had left England in January 1950, and by April Kitty was having second thoughts about a life in America. She told Rebecca that she felt quite set on an English education for her children, and she wanted to instill a sense of "continuity and purpose in their lives which seems so sadly lacking in Anthony." Also, she did not believe that her husband's infatuation with the New World would last any longer than his other enthusiasms. She could not remember a single reason why he believed a move to America was important, except that it was a very beautiful country. But Kitty found the idea of a life without Anthony insupportable, and she proposed to take the children to visit him as soon as he could accommodate them.

Rebecca took a much grimmer view of Anthony's behavior. Where Kitty saw signs of thoughtlessness and became exasperated, Rebecca detected a cruel and irrational streak. It did not surprise Rebecca when Kitty wrote in late April to say that Anthony did not want her and the children to come out to him. He wanted a year by himself to think things over. To Rebecca, this was absurd. A man with a family did not have a year to spare. Kitty took Anthony's message "comparatively calmly," Rebecca observed, but then his leaving her once before had taken the chill off. Even the resilient and ever hopeful Kitty realized Anthony was probably leading up to a request for a divorce.

Rebecca likened Anthony to her father, an example of the "invincible amateur" spurning the gifted, professional woman. Rebecca had always admired Kitty's dedication to her own talent; they were alike in that respect. Indeed, Kitty had done something that neither Rebecca nor Rebecca's own mother had been able to do; she had created a happy home life without sacrificing her talent. Kitty had style, Rebecca remarked to Harold Ross, "she creates a pleasant aesthetic atmosphere round the place, so that there is a credit balance." That Anthony could wreck what Kitty had so superbly wrought devastated Rebecca and confirmed her decision to try to break away from Anthony emotionally: "I am not going to smoke at the head on his account," she declared to Dorothy Thompson.

Rebecca told several friends that she expected Anthony to divorce Kitty—it had not been a healthy marriage. Anthony had been too dominant, Kitty too abject. Rebecca thought the durable Kitty would remarry and continue to paint, and that the children were tough enough to cope with this disaster. Rebecca suggested to Kitty that she cut Anthony right out of her life and deny him access to the children. Kitty was horrified at the idea; even if there was a divorce, she had no intention of separating the children from their father. In spite of his many faults, Anthony had been a splendid father when he had been home. Kitty would never forgive Rebecca for proposing this complete rupture; indeed, it proved to Kitty that Rebecca did not love her own son.

Rebecca said that because eight-year-old Caroline was an egotist she would not notice that her Daddy had gone, and that because seven-year-old Edmund was not an egotist he would not feel that anything important had been denied him. Caroline was a quiet, self-absorbed child, difficult to engage in conversation, and found her grandmother intimidating and frightening. Ibstone seemed always full of people, visiting there was an event, and she rarely had moments alone with her grandmother, periods when she could feel entirely at ease. It was too much like being received at court. Caroline sensed that these visits were an ordeal for her mother. Kitty worried about the journey there and often got lost on their drives to Ibstone. It was hard for Caroline to relax in this grand atmosphere with servants and guests constantly about. Visits were great social occasions, and Caroline never got an everyday sense of her grandmother.

Edmund was less self-conscious and more outgoing—a combination that clearly appealed to Rebecca. For Edmund, Ibstone had a strange and magical atmosphere—like the double hatch with doors on both sides in the dining room. He'd hear a mysterious rattle and open the door, picking up his breakfast without making contact with any human being. He liked going through the back of the house into the yard, a wonderful spot on the ridge of a hill. The view dropped down deeply into a valley and then steeply up on the other side. Edmund liked the look of the dilapidated windmill on the ridge and had great fun poking around a dried-out pond looking for newts. There was a staircase and a beautiful stone balustrade leading down to the walled garden with another pool and more newts. He romped through the greenhouses with flowers and cucumbery things, and the garden full of sweet peas in rows and fruit trees. Below all that there was a real farm he could visit, where wheat was cut in the ancient way and piled to dry in tepeelike shapes called stooks.

Edmund found his grandmother wonderful and amusing. He enjoyed hearing her talk, though he could not recall her ever telling him stories. Rebecca may have been inhibited around him, for she often commented that both Edmund and Caroline seemed to show no interest in adults. As a young boy Edmund never saw the disagreeable side of Rebecca that his parents were always warning him about. He knew that his mother did not like being at Ibstone, that she thought Rebecca was manipulative about money, and ostentatious. Kitty viewed the numerous guests as hangers-on and toadies, and she disliked all the talk about servants and their problems. But all Edmund saw was a smoothly running establishment. His visits were almost always during the holidays when the atmosphere was festive.

Even though Rebecca was never as close to her grandchildren as she would have liked, she usually enjoyed their visits and wanted to continue them. She had dreaded Anthony's taking the family to America, expecting that he would abandon them in a remote village of the Ozarks or some other equally inaccessible place. But she wrote to him, saying she was pleased to hear such good things about him from Dorothy Thompson. Dorothy could tell that Anthony relished the letter, but she was disturbed by his moody temperament, which she attributed to his "complex about 'deserting' his children." Dorothy's letters to Rebecca eventually produced a softening in her and a confession that she did not know how to cope with his alternating states of affection and animosity.

Dorothy commiserated with Rebecca, noting from her own observation of Anthony's behavior in her home that he could be extremely polite and deferential or equally careless and inconsiderate, acting as if other people did not exist. He was remote and undependable, failed to show up for dinner engagements, and prone to sudden and exaggerated enthusiasms for people which subsided just as quickly. Dorothy's frustration with Anthony's elusiveness was echoed by his friend and attorney, Anthony Lousada: "I have no idea what is in Anthony's mind," he told Rebecca. Anthony had been evasive about his reasons for going to America, and Lousada found it difficult to say what the primary motive for the trip had been.

Rebecca consulted Richard Butler, her solicitor, about ways to help Kitty and to assure Anthony he had a clear title as H.G.'s authorized biographer, but Butler advised Rebecca against making any substantial amount available to her daughter-in-law and agreed with Rebecca that she should "adopt a policy of remote kindliness." To do more would involve Rebecca in difficulties she could not hope to resolve.

With moods as variable as Anthony's, Rebecca began to blame Kitty and absolve Anthony. When Kitty mentioned she was having some trouble paying the children's boarding schools fees, Rebecca promptly sent a check. But she treated Kitty's need for help as a long-term claim on her income, not as a temporary sum to tide her over while she straightened out the family finances (including income tax problems) that Anthony had neglected. Rebecca always exaggerated her money worries, and in this case accused Kitty of responding to the "threat of ruin" by acting extravagantly. Rebecca also disapproved of sending the children away to boarding school, deciding they should stay at home with Kitty while Kitty tried to resume her career as a painter.

Although Rebecca enjoyed a spring trip to the south of France and looked forward to resuming work on a new novel, *Cousin Rosamund*, she constantly spun her wheels, inventing new scenarios about Anthony's life based on letters from her New York friends. But real news of him was scarce. In June, he had moved to a place in Stonington, Connecticut, that kept him out of New York, except for his weekly trip to the *Time* office.

4

In late September 1950, Rebecca learned from Kitty that the incommunicative Anthony had finally sent a letter explaining himself. He felt he had come to the end of a miserable period that had made him want to hide. He had been in a foul mood, and it was just as well that Kitty had not seen it. He missed his family, calling them the other three parts of himself, and he realized that a life apart from them was pointless. He did not regret their separation, because when he gave into his weak side, Kitty's courage was more than he could bear. It troubled him that she might have to put up with more of these breaks in their family life, but he loved her and needed her comfort. He described his situation as desperate. He had lost his job at *Time* and was running short of money.

Rebecca thought that with Anthony's hopes of an American triumph dashed, he would return home and resume his English literary career. He seemed to be leaning that way in a friendly letter he sent to her. The writer V. S. Pritchett, who had known Anthony since the late 1930s when Anthony contributed reviews to *The New Statesman*, promised Rebecca to see what he could do about enticing Anthony to publish for English papers. Pritchett had not thought much of Anthony's American plans but found it useless to argue with him. It seemed inevitable to Pritchett that Anthony would have to suffer a crisis before he could emerge reintegrated and in control of himself. Anthony could be "maddening, difficult, and erratic," but also endearing in his "flashes of self-knowledge."

The new year brought news from Harold Ross that he had bought one of Anthony's stories, and that his second-in-command, William Shawn, had asked Anthony to do a book review. To Ross, Anthony looked well and sounded good. Rebecca told Ross that she was extremely pleased that Anthony had made the "*New Yorker* grade."

5

BY THE SUMMER OF 1951, Anthony had done several reviews for *The New Yorker*, and his financial concerns eased. Rebecca rejoiced in his work, calling it "first-rate stuff," revealing a deep absorption in literature. Harold Ross wrote to her saying Anthony had been a hit. He had finished revising his second novel, *Another Kind*, and had plans for two more, and felt he now had his "head above water." Rebecca did not like *Another Kind*, deploring the influence of Graham Greene (whom she had never liked), and Anthony's echoes and inversions of incidents in her own stories and novels. But she had great hopes for his third novel because he had shown great individuality and a wonderful sense of form in his earlier work.

John Gunther and Anthony West were now "fast friends." They often met in New York for drinks or tea. John thought Anthony had become much calmer in the past year, if still as stubbornly intelligent, pithy, and erudite. Anthony's merciless reviews reminded John of Rebecca. "What a delightful thing heredity is," he wrote her.

In mid-July, Anthony felt confident enough to invite Kitty and the children to visit him in Stonington, Connecticut. Rebecca made arrangements for their trip (including the purchase of first-class air tickets). But the prospect of the trip to America gave Rebecca no pleasure when she learned from Kitty that Anthony no longer loved her. He had written to her expressing a desire to see the children but making it clear that he considered their marriage over. When Kitty arrived, she discovered he had settled himself in Stonington in a large apartment, seven rooms with expensive furniture and kitchen equipment. It was obvious to her that someone had been living with Anthony. She could not reach him, and he reiterated his intention to divorce her. This was kept from the children. Indeed, they had a wonderful time. America seemed a paradise. There had been little fun in England during the war and immediately afterward: no toys, no sweets. In Stonington, Anthony had the sea and every sort of luxury. He had "bloody everything," Kitty thought. One day, Anthony said, "I think I will take you to the best beach of all."

He hired a plane and took them to Fisher's Island in New York. "Well that was a bit rotten. It made it difficult coming home," Kitty recalled.

Rebecca also thought Anthony's goodness to the children a mean thing to do, "so terribly like H.G." He was getting on their good side only to make trouble for Kitty. An outraged Rebecca demanded he pay his family's fare home, which he had deducted from his *New Yorker* salary. He had shared very little of his American income with his family, and this made Rebecca regard him as selfish and inhumane. Anthony's next step, she predicted, would be to marry a rich American wife. She had come a long way in almost two years of trouble with Anthony, only to enclose him in the circle of her own suffering.

6

ON DECEMBER 6, 1951, William Shawn cabled Rebecca from *The New Yorker* offices that Harold Ross, the magazine's founding editor, had died. Shawn wanted her to know that right to the end she had meant "so very much to Ross." His death brought her to her "lowest ebb." He had been endlessly kind and thoughtful, soliciting and supporting her work, and responding to her heartaches with sympathy and good cheer. Sometimes he had irritated her with his fussy attention to minutiae that kept her going over galleys for hours and hours (once until four in the morning), but in his *New Yorker* she had found the best home for her writing. The magazine had begun by "keeping a full diary for a great city," Rebecca remarked in her obituary of Ross. But its recruitment of great writers had transformed it into a "diary for the world." She admired its devotion to fact, noting that Ross had checked her report on the Greenville lynching trial by hiring a local reporter to verify her details and two attorneys (Northern and Southern) to debate her view of the case.

Harold Ross had been incredibly understanding and helpful about Anthony, and she had responded to him as an editor and friend—really as one of the family. "The trouble is that I should have been your mother," she once wrote him. "The thought of you eternally surrounded by proofs coiled like spaghetti, is just the way I would like a child of mine to be. A higher compliment, sir, I have never paid, and probably you have never received one on quite that plane."

Like Alexander Woollcott (another devoted friend who had died in January 1943), Harold Ross had a reputation for being a grouch, a real terror to writers. But from both these men Rebecca received almost nothing but love, fun, and succor. She defended their characters stoutly.

She admired Ross's fluent letters, his "clear, hard classical American style." She worried that her long letters had overtaxed him, but William Shawn assured her that to Ross they were never long enough and refreshed him during his last illness. Janet Flanner, a distinguished contributor to *The New Yorker*, told Rebecca she had changed Ross's middle age: "[Y]our writing constituted his last bouquet as an editor."

Rebecca regretted that she had not seen Ross for almost four years, and she blamed Anthony, feeling that she would surely have visited Ross had it not been for her feeling that she should stand by Kitty in England. Rebecca acted as though Anthony had taken Harold Ross and much else away from her, preventing her from completing *Cousin Rosamund*, which had grown to 150,000 words and needed extensive editing. In a helpless rage, she declared Anthony was the worst thing that had ever happened to her; she should have relinquished him to H.G., even though he would have had no sort of proper upbringing. She confessed that it hurt unspeakably to say these things, but Anthony had spoiled her work and her friendships. He haunted her like some horrible dwarf in a fairy tale.

Rebecca vilified Anthony because she had just learned from Kitty that he had interviewed Dorothy Richardson, one of H.G.'s mistresses. Rebecca fumed over the idea that her own son would consult this old literary relic without telling her, especially since Anthony had not questioned Rebecca about H.G. Rebecca doubted Dorothy's reliability and disliked Anthony's delving into intimacies. When Max Beaverbrook told her that Anthony had proposed selling the serial rights of his biography to him, and that Anthony had accepted Max's offer of eight thousand pounds, Rebecca concluded that Anthony was bent on producing a scandalous biography—at the very time he was writing pious book reviews that Rebecca deemed abominable and reminiscent of Lettie. She had successfully squelched the personal passages in Madame Vallentin's recent H.G. biography, but Vincent Brome's did contain the objectionable Dorothy Richardson material without making any direct reference to Rebecca.

Janet Flanner reported to Rebecca that Anthony was putting on a Byronic act in *The New Yorker* office that the staff found hard to take. He had his friends there, but he was temperamental. Edith Oliver, one of his colleagues, called him the "hard luck kid." He was difficult to handle. When he started to act up, she joshed him: "You promised you wouldn't be paranoid for at least six weeks."

In early May 1952, Rebecca accompanied Kitty to court to obtain her divorce. Rebecca watched her go into the box, still lovely and looking like such a poor dear. Rebecca pitied the judge, for he had to read several of Anthony's letters, the "sort our family occasionally produces," she told Winnie. Rebecca characterized them as "sullen, stupid, brutal, humourless, exhibitionist, heartless." The judge swelled with outrage: "These are the most offensive letters I have ever read, and sheer non-sense," he concluded, giving Kitty custody of the children and stipulating that Anthony would have to get special permission to have the children visit him in America. After court, Rebecca took Kitty out to the Savoy for lunch with Charles Curran. Then she bought Kitty a cardigan and sweater and sent her a check.

CHAPTER 28

The Communist Conspiracy
1952–1953

I

SINCE WORLD WAR II, Rebecca had poured out a steady stream of articles and reviews, purveying an anti-Communist reading of history that she considered in the best tradition of liberalism, but which estranged her from much of the Left, many of whose members accused her of shifting to the Right. Her position had changed, but not in an abrupt or superficial way. As early as 1916, she had criticized certain British Leftists for not supporting the war effort, and the next year she expressed concern that the democratic possibilities of the Russian Revolution had been crushed in the Bolsheviks' brutal hijacking of power. Emma Goldman's trip to England in 1924 had confirmed Rebecca's dark view of Russia and her scorn for its lackeys, and *Black Lamb and Grey Falcon* consolidated her critique of a Left that seemed impotent to combat Fascism and other forms of tyranny.

In a brief essay, "Goodness Doesn't Just Happen," Rebecca acknowledged the reversal in her thinking. She confessed that her younger self had not understood either the difficulty of love or the importance of law. She had grown up in a world that prized rebellion, and she had been a rebel. She supposed that human beings were naturally good and that the law was a cumbersome instrument that dealt harshly with people. Law would lose its sway when the revolution brought an end to poverty and evil. Two wars, the concentration camps, and totalitarian government convinced her that the good in people was not merely a quality to be brought out. It had to be created by an effort of love and a submission to the "Rule of Law."

Rebecca capitalized the phrase. She now associated goodness with something that transcended human values, with God. She recommended religion as a technique for getting in touch with God, but she confessed that she had not discovered the right religion for her.

In a series of articles for the *Evening Standard* (January 28–February 1, 1952), Rebecca presented her interpretation of Lenin, Stalin, the aftermath of the two world wars, and why opposing the Communist conspiracy ought to be the paramount political program of modern life. She observed that the Bolsheviks' triumphs over the Mensheviks proved to be the fatal turning point in history; it insured a Communist Party schooled in conspiratorial, anti-democratic, and totalitarian techniques. Lenin had crushed the Menshevik effort to create a broad-based social democratic Left and fashioned a party restricted to those who "personally and regularly participated in one of its organizations." Here in embryo was the concept of the Nomenklatura, by which the State would be controlled exclusively by a single party.

Rebecca then showed how Stalin had consolidated and expanded the Party's power. He came from Georgia, seething with nationalist discontent, a land of patriotism gone sour in its confrontation with imperial Russia. Stalin's parents sent their son, a bright pupil, to the best high school in Georgia, a seminary dedicated to producing Russian Orthodox priests in an attempt to control the unruly Georgians. Many of the Georgian pupils rejected the seminary, equating it with Russian tyranny. The pupils were spied on and, in turn, regarded their priests as traitors. The institution was rife with informants. Stalin rejected his religious training and embraced the logic of revolution and conspiracy—indeed the seminary schooled him in the techniques of subversion that made him a ready recruit for the Bolsheviks.

True to her biographical interpretation of history, Rebecca saw Communism as an extension of Stalin's career. Communism created him, so to speak; but Communism could not have survived without the drive of his plotting personality. It would not have dominated history merely as an ideology or as a party that won elections; it had to survive through the careerism of individuals, which in turn was tied to the careerism of the party.

Rebecca alleged that at Yalta, Roosevelt gave the store away to Stalin, ceding him Eastern Europe. Nowhere after the war had a single Communist Party contested for power using legal means. Conspiracy, force, and the threat of force got Communist officials their jobs.

In America, the Communists had used more subtle and covert means to acquire information, influence, and behind-the-scenes power. By the end of February 1950, Rebecca had concluded that Alger Hiss, a former American State department official, was guilty of passing confidential government documents to the Russians. He had been convicted of perjury in January, and Rebecca was amazed that so many American liberals

were convinced of his innocence and had begun a vigorous press campaign on his behalf. Indeed, she regarded the controversy over Hiss as
the equivalent of the Dreyfus case, with an "odd difference." The French
officer Alfred Dreyfus had been accused of spying for the Germans and
vast numbers of Frenchmen furiously demanded that he be presumed
guilty, whereas when Alger Hiss had been accused of espionage, numbers of Americans howled and shrieked for his acquittal even before the
full dimensions of his mysterious case had been explored. What bound
these two cases together was the atmosphere of hysteria and character
assassination surrounding them both. Dreyfus had been attacked
because he was a Jew. During the Hiss trial, the personal slurs on his
accuser, Whittaker Chambers, made even his corpulence a sign of his
turpitude.

Reading a book on Hiss by her colleague, Bert Andrews, chief of the
New York Herald Tribune's Washington press bureau, Rebecca thought
the case against him proven; she strongly suspected the criminal
involvement of Hiss's wife, Priscella, as well. For Rebecca, Andrews was
a particularly compelling source. She still did occasional articles for the
Tribune, and she knew him well. More importantly, he had a solid reputation for impartiality. A Pulitzer Prize winner, he had written a series of
articles on the state department's lax security procedures. He had also
recommended Alger Hiss for the top post at the Carnegie Endowment
for International Peace. Andrews had presumed Hiss innocent until
Congressman Richard Nixon, then serving on the House Committee on
Un-American Activities (HUAC), began showing him the mounting
evidence that exposed Hiss as a liar and a likely communist agent.
Andrews accompanied Nixon on a trip to Chambers's farm, where
Nixon allowed Andrews to grill Chambers, probing for weaknesses in
Chambers's character and in the case against Hiss. Andrews became
immersed in every crucial development of the Hiss case, and he is cred-
ited by Nixon biographer Stephen Ambrose for contributing substan-
tially to Hiss's conviction.

The Hiss case confirmed Rebecca's worst suspicions about the spread
of communism. As she made clear to her American friend Doris Stevens:
"Francis Biddle is certainly not a communist or a fellow-traveler, but a
damned fool, and he feels uncomfortable about the number of people he
cleared when he was A.G. [attorney general]." Rebecca suggested that at
Nuremberg Biddle had told her far more about Communist infiltration of
the bureaucracy and the Democratic administration's unwillingness to act
than she had ever printed. Hiss was not an isolated instance, but rather a
textbook example of how Communists infiltrated key positions and com-

manded the loyalty of important opinion makers. Hiss had advised Roosevelt at Yalta, he was a friend of two Supreme Court justices, close to two future secretaries of state, and he knew nearly everyone of importance in the State Department. He had been considered for the position of the first Secretary-General of the United Nations. It had also been rumored that his departure from the State Department had been the result of questions about his loyalty raised as early as 1939.

Rebecca did not have confidential government information about Communist subversion, but she had access to friends like CIA director Allen Dulles, who did. (Henry first met Allen, then a Wall Street lawyer, in the 1930s when Henry was considering a job on Wall Street. Allen had assisted Henry in spiriting anti-Nazis out of Germany.) Allen's brother, John Foster Dulles, later Eisenhower's secretary of state, had conveyed Nixon's impressive dossier against Hiss to Allen. Rebecca's connection to Allen Dulles convinced her of the high quality of the men involved in the anti-Communist crusade.

But Rebecca did not simply rely on reports from Allen Dulles and Bert Andrews. She had Doris Stevens send her HUAC reports, memoranda, and articles about communist espionage. At Rebecca's direction, Doris also interviewed Elizabeth Bentley, a courier for the Communist Party who had testified before HUAC. Doris had worked for the New Deal and had excellent contacts in Washington. She interviewed FBI agents and wrote in detail to Rebecca about their activities.

2

THE FULL EXTENT of Rebecca's anti-Communism was not appreciated until she published in the spring of 1953 a series of articles in the London Sunday *Times*, which were reprinted in *U.S. News and World Report* on May 22, 1953.

She warned that anti-American elements in Europe had exploited the myth of McCarthyism, persuading people that the country had become a McCarthy dictatorship. She compared this crude caricature of American political life to a Goebbels lie and the worst kind of Moscow invective. By turning McCarthy into such a daunting menace to the Republic, liberals had played right into Communist hands.

Rebecca dealt with events before McCarthy had grabbed the headlines as a communist hunter, especially the testimony of Elizabeth Bentley in 1945 and Whittaker Chambers in 1948. She traced Chambers's career, starting with his first efforts in 1939 to alert the federal government to a Communist spy ring. She showed how his charges had been ignored for almost ten years, until HUAC had investigated them. She admitted that the committee followed roving lines of inquiry and hearsay evidence that needed much corroboration before it could be believed, and she acknowledged her distaste for HUAC's style—but in a mild form, pointing out its "relatively unimportant flaws in investigatory manners." One of its members, she regretted to say, examined witnesses as though he were picking a Yale lock with a crowbar. But like the British tribunals of inquiry, HUAC was doing a valuable service by dealing with "exceptional and unforeseen assaults on society, not to be repelled by any oblivious and familiar applications of the law." HUAC confronted the Communist Party, a closed system, operating outside the law, functioning like a state within a state. HUAC also had to contend with a Truman administration defending the slipshod hiring practices of the Roosevelt administration.

Rebecca regretted that Chambers had been turned into a figure of fun because he had produced from a pumpkin on his farm microfilms of government documents in Hiss's handwriting. Chambers's evidence, however, was no joke, and his autobiography, which she termed an "unkempt masterpiece" should not be ignored.

Rebecca brusquely dismissed the hullabaloo around McCarthy without dealing with him directly, saying only that he had been attracted to the investigations of Communists like a wet dog to a man in white flannel trousers. She thought him a man of "enormous ambition and considerable ability, who has not the faintest idea how to use his gifts in harmony with the established practices of civilization, and who cannot understand the chill which lowers the temperature around him." Compared to the crimes Communists had committed, his sins seemed venial. McCarthy had not ordered the assassination of his opponents, as Stalin had ordered Trotsky's. Communists were not being executed in America or abroad; anti-Communists were. Within the American government's bureaucracy, the Communists had created a spoils systems, hiring their own, and then losing or submitting incomplete employment records so that HUAC had difficulty tracing the networks through which Communists gained employment.

Rebecca found it hard to believe in the widespread intimidation of teachers and other government employees because they were suspected of being Communists; she cited a counter example of a teacher forced to join and remain in a Communist dominated union. She thought it ridiculous that HUAC should be regarded as an evil force equivalent to its Communist foe.

Rebecca ended her articles in a way guaranteed to rile certain readers, recommending that it was time to get on with the task of recognizing honestly the "nature and prevalence of the antisocial forces our genera‑ tion has allowed to flourish." Her tone was similar to *Black Lamb and Grey Falcon.* By implication, she was saying the Left had let down its own side by making McCarthy a bugaboo. Her last sentence twisted the knife into those who thought that by attacking McCarthy they were asserting their integrity. That was the "easier, much more popular thing to do," engaging in the "middle‑class fashion of today," repeating what might or might not be true, but was "certainly irrelevant: that we are all much superior to Senator McCarthy."

Criticism exploded over Rebecca West for these articles. Arthur Schlesinger, Jr., spoke for many anti‑Communist liberals when he wrote Rebecca a four‑page, typed, single‑spaced letter, identifying himself as an admirer of her work but expressing his surprise and dismay over her arti‑ cles. He pressed on her his credentials as an anti‑Communist. He had, for example, interviewed Whittaker Chambers in 1946 and had published the first full‑length exposure and indictment of the American Communist Party in a national magazine after the war (*Life*, July 29, 1946). He was on record as supposing Alger Hiss to be guilty. He specified efforts by the Truman administration to combat the Communist threat and the fights liberals had undertaken to oust Communists from the CIO. Arthur objected to Rebecca's characterization of McCarthy as an "uncouth individual, gen‑ uinely devoted, if in a lamentably undisciplined way, to rooting Commu‑ nists out of positions of power." Not so, Arthur declared. McCarthy was no more a genuine anti‑Communist than Communists had been genuine anti‑ Fascists. McCarthy was merely an opportunist. Just look at the people he attacked—staunch anti‑Communist liberals such as Charles Bohlen in the State Department and the journalist James Wechsler. McCarthy's reckless and unscrupulous attacks had led to smears against General George C. Marshall. How could such "scatter‑gun" denunciations advance the cause of anti‑Communism? They were as scurrilous as anything Goebbels had instigated.

Rebecca cabled Arthur her rejection of his "grossly offensive" and impertinent letter. She was not defending McCarthy, only showing how the myth of McCarthyism had been used to fuel anti‑Americanism. She had not dealt with McCarthy because she did not have the official record of his investigations. So it was irrelevant to chastise her for not noticing that among McCarthy's victims had been such worthies as Bohlen and Wechsler. Schlesinger's allegation that she had excused McCarthy and his scatter‑gun attacks was a smear worthy of Goebbels, she concluded, throwing Arthur's terms back at him. As the heat rose off her cable, she closed by saying it had taken considerable effort to frame her cable in these "restrained terms."

Rebecca's friend at Yale, Professor Evelyn Hutchinson, wrote to her noting that Walter Winchell had used her article to support a pro-McCarthy position. Accepting Evelyn's advice she published a letter in the New York *Herald Tribune* reiterating the points she had made to Schlesinger. She also replied to him in a six-page letter objecting to his manner, which she compared to a "schoolmaster reproving a backward pupil." It had taken all the courage she possessed to write those articles, because she knew she would be attacked by "every fool who had got hold of the word 'liberalism' without knowing what it means, and of every knave who knows how that word can be misused to serve totalitarian interests." Arthur had insolently misrepresented her article; she had never discussed McCarthy's sincerity because it was not relevant to her thesis. The rest of his letter consisted of "turgid restatements of principles familiar to me since I was fourteen." She could do without his hackneyed phrases. He was so obsessed with attacking McCarthy that he failed to see that her article had come at the problem of ferreting out Communists from an entirely different point of view, one that tried to show the British people how skewed their view of American reality would be if they supposed Joseph McCarthy was now running the country.

Arthur thought he had written an extremely tactful and courteous letter to Rebecca. He complained to John Gunther about her vicious cable, which compared him to Goebbels. John laughed and promised to arrange a meeting between Rebecca and Arthur the next time she visited the country. (This John did, and it resulted in an amicable friendship between Rebecca and Arthur.)

Arthur showed his correspondence with Rebecca to several prominent liberal anti-Communist friends, including Richard Rovere, a writer with *The New Yorker*. Rovere sent Schlesinger a blind copy of his letter to Rebecca, writing at the top a note: "At a convention of liberals held here yesterday—Roveres, Kahns, Shafers, Joe Lashes—it was resolved that your letter was fine and that Becky is NUTS." Richard's letter to Rebecca was considerably more restrained. He professed himself an admirer of her work and thought her point well taken that Arthur did not "sufficiently take into account the fact that the articles were written for a special audience and in a special set of circumstances." Richard believed that Arthur had misread her to the same degree as she had misread him. Arthur was not attacking her, but the use to which her position would be put by McCarthy's defenders. Richard also supported

Arthur's account of the damage McCarthyism was doing to the body politic. He hoped Rebecca would not place Arthur in the Goebbels class, for he was as far from it as any American alive.

Rebecca would have none of this palliation. Arthur Schlesinger had written an "impudent and lying letter," she replied to Richard, and she was aggrieved that he should write on behalf of such a sewer rat. She shoved both Richard and Arthur into the anti-anti-Communist movement, which she branded a "form of mincing gentility, an effort at moral fastidiousness by people who are essentially coarse-grained." Richard had erred, involving himself with "matters far too grubby for your handling." She discounted the argument that the Right employed her words to their advantage. She reminded him that he had been misrepresented in the *New Statesman*, but she had not dreamed of reproaching him for what he could not help. Judging by her mail, very few McCarthyites supported her; instead, anti-McCarthyite anti-Communists vilified her for being pro-McCarthy.

Richard wrote again, pointing out that her fan mail did not adequately reveal how her articles had been exploited. She had been cited in the media and in Congress as supporting views he knew were alien to her. Even worse, the appearance of her articles in David Lawrence's *U.S. News and World Report*, a well-known pro-McCarthy organ, made it look like Rebecca had gone Right.

An exasperated Rebecca pointed out that her *Times* articles had been sold without asking her approval. She exerted no control over the reprint rights. More importantly, she defined the divide between her and American liberals which could not be bridged: "One of the most foolish sentences in Arthur Schlesinger's fatuous letter ran: 'In America today, the sentiments and emotions which McCarthy invites and symbolizes are far more dangerous to our freedom than any threat from the political action of American Communists.' " She simply could not accept that the reactionary persecution of liberals came anywhere near in the scale of things to Communist thuggery and totalitarian tactics. To her, McCarthyism was a provincial, certainly unfortunate development, but a sideshow on the world stage when compared to the international Communist conspiracy. If Schlesinger and Rovere really believed that the issue was not her actual views, but the fact that her views were being misrepresented as pro-McCarthy, then why were they not vigorously defending her from the smears she had had to endure?

Rebecca thought American liberals were soft, afraid of losing their jobs and of speaking out against Communists. She had lost a few jobs in her early days because of her radical politics and simply took the risk of being outspoken and told her disapproving employers to go to the devil. McCarthy would lose what power he had if liberals would confront him rather than simply complaining and feeling cowed by him. She held no brief for HUAC and was surprised that its procedures had not been reformed. But to think that American intellectuals were being persecuted as their counterparts in Europe had been by the Fascists was nonsense, though it might gratify American egos.

She was not swayed by old friends such as Irita Van Doren, an editor at the *Herald Tribune,* who echoed Schlesinger's position: "I agree with you that things are happening among us which need investigation, but not the McCarthy kind, which has almost disrupted normal intellectual, political and cultural life in this country. Come over and take a look at us!" Arnold Weissberger, Rebecca's friend and an attorney who advised her, supported her anti-Communism but stressed that people felt trapped, incriminated by their participation in Communist front activities of the 1930s. He asked her to imagine what it was like—suddenly being summoned to explain your politics to HUAC in the vastly different atmosphere of the 1950s. It was not so simple a matter of bravely expressing your views and finding another job if you were fired. The newspapers would blazon headlines: "Rebecca West Admits Membership in Communist Front Organizations." Magazines would refuse to print her articles, radio sponsors would cancel her broadcasts. "Everything great and good that you have done will be over-shadowed," he assured her. McCarthy was succeeding not in suppressing communism but in eradicating liberalism. She had to be there, on the spot, to feel the fear. "The fear is irrational—but most fears are irrational," another friend assured her. People did not know what to expect next, and it was this indefinite quality that seemed worst of all.

But Rebecca also had American allies. The novelist James T. Farrell seconded her view that non-Communists had been manipulated to view anyone appearing before HUAC as innocent. On the contrary, many of the HUAC witnesses had been Communists or had Communist connections, and Rebecca was right—this league of Communists and fellow travelers had been log-rolling since the 1930s. It had prevented, for example, the truth about the Moscow purge trials from being revealed; too many liberals had failed to heed the American philosopher John Dewey's conclusions about Stalinism, and this blindness had done incalculable harm to liberalism. Communists had committed several murders in America that liberals had ignored. Farrell had his disagreements with Chambers, but he believed that Chambers was "truly the victim of a moral lynching campaign."

David Riesman, the author of the groundbreaking study, *The Lonely Crowd* and Professor of Social Sciences at the University of Chicago, sent Rebecca a note of appreciation, and observed that a new "united front" seemed to be in the making against those like her and him who took a more "differentiated stand concerning the work of the various committees, or who defends people who have told the truth before such committees."

Replying to Rebecca's letter about the blubbering of liberals, Sol Levitas, editor of *The New Leader,* agreed with her that the anti-anti-Communists had blown up McCarthy and his methods of investigation in a way that contributed to anti-American sentiment in Europe. Levitas did not think much of Schlesinger and his group, and he confirmed Rebecca's judgment that he was "arrogant, intolerant and unfair," a practitioner of a "double-bookkeeping system for both events and personalities . . . inherited from the Bolsheviks." Dorothy Thompson added that he was self-righteous and vain, using McCarthy's own methods of character assassination and terrorization against anyone who disagreed with him. Bertram D. Wolfe, an authority on the Russian Revolution and Communism, wrote to thank Rebecca for her "able and balanced" articles and seconded Levitas's dim view of Schlesinger's ability and motivations.

By the end of July 1953, Rebecca possessed several transcripts of McCarthy's recent congressional hearings. She found most of them unobjectionable, though they were marred by his crude manners and sloppy case preparation. He had been portrayed in the press as something of a clown, but she believed he was "ideologically dangerous." He fed on the almost universal dislike of bureaucracy; his taunting of bureaucrats might give satisfaction, but it also made it difficult for the modern state to function. To her, his contempt for the civil service was far more disturbing than any harm he might inflict on the anti-Communist cause. She did not believe that McCarthy would last as a political phenomenon; he would exhaust the patience of the Republican Party machine (he was condemned by the Senate in 1956 and died a spent force in 1957). She saved her anger for Schlesinger and Rovere, two characters she would not want to have lurking around her back garden. She interpreted Schlesinger's retort to Rovere not as a friendly demonstration of good will but as a form of intimidation—a warning not to alienate publications for which she had written.

To Rebecca, Schlesinger, Rovere, and their kind were phony liberals. To accept criticism from them was to abase herself to her inferiors. As the defender of true liberalism, she stood squarely between the Communists and the Right. Rebecca never changed her position. When Tito broke with Stalin in 1948, she did not believe Tito's independence was genuine; even if it was, he was still a Communist and would get no support from her; he would use it to Communism's advantage. Communists had shown since the Popular Front days of the 1930s how easily they could make liberal positions seem like their own. This is why certain liberals as well as ex-Communists found themselves confronting HUAC. Rebecca understood that Communists would desert liberals whenever the Party and its Russian head directed them to do so. Thus any sort of cooperation with Communists, such as augmenting the Party's attack on McCarthy, would damage liberalism and promote Communist goals.

In 1978, Rebecca passed up the opportunity to review David Caute's *The Fellow Travellers* for *The Sunday Telegraph*. She explained to her editor, Nicholas Bagnall, that she had been viciously attacked as a pro-McCarthyite. She acknowledged that he had been "indeed responsible for many attacks on various people," but she reiterated the gist of her *U.S. News and World Report* articles. It was a "delicate matter," she observed, conceding that McCarthy had victimized innocent people, but asserting that she doubted there were quite as many as Caute alleged. It would involve considerable research to check Caute's claims, and if she made a mistake, she would open herself to a libel action. "I certainly would not risk it," she concluded.

CHAPTER 29

The Kafkas and the Brontës
1952–1954

I

IN LATE NOVEMBER 1952, Anthony upset his mother by marrying again. He had told her nothing about a romance, though she had heard from friends about a nineteen-year-old woman he was courting—just the kind of thing H.G. would do, she thought. It gave Rebecca the sulks, and she grumbled that no doubt many people preferred him to her. She spoke as though he were a rival for the American love that had forsaken her.

Anthony's new wife, Lily Emmet, attended Radcliffe. On her maternal side she was descended from an old Newport family. Her father's family, from Long Island, New York, and Cambridge, Massachusetts, were related to Robert Emmet, the Irish patriot. Lily had met Anthony during a vacation in New York City. Rebecca predicted he might be happy if he did not have children. He had been a good father up to a point—showing great self-sacrifice, patience, and charm—but she doubted that he could sustain his familial feelings. He lived in a sphere that Rebecca admitted she did not understand.

Dorothy Thompson and Emanie Arling, two of Rebecca's closest American friends, met Anthony and Lily shortly after their marriage. Dorothy described Lily as very tall—taller than Anthony—and handsome, with a "smoldering look." Emanie gave a plainer description of Lily's looks and said she dressed in the sloppy fashion of college students. Dorothy's husband, Maxim, thought Lily sexy. Emanie called the wedding reception a party of the "middle rich." Anthony seemed pleased to see Dorothy and told Emanie that he wished his mother would come over to see him. Then he blurted out: "Would Rebecca be frightened by all this?" They were interrupted before Emanie had an opportunity to plumb that provocative remark.

Rebecca turned to Kitty for comfort, declaring: "I cannot tell you

what a fool I think Anthony for turning his back on you and the children." Rebecca wanted to compensate for Anthony's loss by becoming
closer to Kitty, Caroline, and Edmund. But she felt rebuffed. They
almost never visited, except at holidays. And she never saw Kitty alone.
The children seemed to ignore Rebecca and appeared rude because they
never said please or thank you. They would walk out without saying
good-bye. This hurt Henry as much as it did her because he had no
immediate family and was fond of the children. When Rebecca wrote or
called Kitty's friends, she took their reserve as disapproval of her for
making a fuss. It baffled her.

She applied to Emily Hahn for advice. Emily had just moved to England with her English husband Charles Boxer, and her daughter Carola
was Caroline's playmate. What was the purpose of this Kafka world?
Rebecca asked Emily. What charge had been brought against her? Emily
had no ready answers, but she did try to allay Rebecca's concerns. Kitty
and Caroline, and perhaps Edmund as well, behaved oddly, Emily conceded. But Emily's own child also acted strangely at times and went
through phases that puzzled and irritated her. Kitty's friends had probably accepted her eccentricities long ago, and Kitty's foibles did not
bother Emily, although she could see how blood ties made the problem
more maddening for Rebecca. Emily ventured a guess that Rebecca's
conflicting feelings about Kitty and the children stemmed from
Rebecca's old-fashioned sense that they were her charges and she had to
support them. She should not be surprised that Kitty's friends were cool
or noncommittal when she approached them. They were not necessarily
rejecting Rebecca but instead were retreating from a family problem they
did not want to confront and possibly worsen. Emily asked Rebecca to
imagine how these friends would feel if they were quoted. Emily's shrewd
observations passed Rebecca by; she could see only her side of it, and
how being shut out wounded her and Henry. At such moments, she
would observe that Kitty closely resembled Jane Wells, especially in her
coloring, her "fluttering movements," and cold inhumanity. Kitty was
like some rare bird Rebecca could not catch.

Emily rightly supposed that what stood between Kitty and Rebecca
was Anthony. They had such different views of him, and of what to do
about him. Kitty told Rebecca she saw him as a Byronic figure, whom she
had to take for what he was. Rebecca considered it a damn fool thing to
let a man run over her that way. Rebecca's impulse was to fight back, and
she despised Kitty for merely wanting to roll over. Rebecca's friend and
Kitty's, the literary critic Raymond Mortimer, sympathized with
Rebecca, observing that Kitty could not remake her life so long as she

loved Anthony. She ought to marry again, Raymond thought, but "le coeur a ses raisons."

Kitty offended Rebecca by taking the children over to America to spend the summer holidays with Anthony and Lily. This "odd outfit" struck Rebecca as macabre. Only seven years older than Caroline, Lily was like a playmate for Anthony's children, Rebecca remarked.

2

REBECCA HAD an awful scare in November with Winnie, who was vomiting up blood. Rebecca feared stomach cancer and had Winnie sent to Ibstone in an ambulance. Rebecca later said that Winnie's nurse told her that Winnie's illness was mental and that she was punishing her younger sister out of jealousy for her literary success. Rebecca believed it and resented Winnie for keeping her running up and down the stairs for three solid weeks. Winnie took Rebecca's breath away when she opened her eyes one day, looked at Rebecca with intense hatred, and said: "Oh, yes, I am Anne Brontë;" Rebecca could hardly have missed the point. The most melancholy of the three Brontë sisters, who lived in the others' shadows. Rebecca fortified herself with a large gin. Winnie's remark pained her because she had always been devoted to Winnie—forgetting or perhaps not realizing how high-handed she had often been with her reclusive sister. What Rebecca really wanted to do—as she admitted—was hit Winnie on the head, for she deemed almost any interruption of her writing routine as an assault requiring retaliation. Lettie, of course, had a featured role in Winnie's crisis, providing an infuriated Rebecca with much unsolicited advice. On closer examination, Winnie proved not to have cancer or any other serious malady. She promptly recovered and went off on holiday in Bath, forsaking Rebecca, whose household catastrophes continued.

3

STUCK AT the three-quarter mark on her novel, *Cousin Rosamund*, Rebecca turned to revisions of her writing on Germany for a book of essays, *A Train of Powder*. She managed to complete the revisions at home in early 1954, but she decided that only a month of absolute quiet and intensive work alone in a Paris hotel would allow her to finish her novel. Worried about the impact of her absence on Henry, however, she formulated a plan to keep him busy while she was away.

Life had once again become intolerable at Ibstone. This time it was not Henry's fault or the staff's fault, but that of the German wife of his deceased cousin and her cruel nine-year-old child. Both of them made intolerable demands on Rebecca's time. It depressed Henry to admit Rebecca was right; these were not nice people, but their departure left both Henry and Rebecca feeling devastated and guilty. He had gone to endless trouble to help his German cousins, and he had exhausted himself. Henry badly needed another occupation, something more than the stock market, the farm, and the district council. She had argued they should sell Ibstone, but by the look on Henry's face, she could tell it still meant everything to him to play the country squire. In desperation, she wrote a long letter to Bernard Berenson, whom they had visited in December 1951 at his villa in Florence. She gave him a detailed account of Henry's history: his suffering in the prisoner-of-war camp, his inability to make his mark at Oxford, the shattering of his hopes to rebuild postwar Yugoslavia when Churchill declared for Tito, his relentless efforts on behalf of displaced persons, and his dedication to the reconstruction of Germany and its reconciliation with its enemies. Henry was sixty. He had wasted too many years on saintliness. Rebecca admitted that she had often failed him by her absorption in her own problems. She put it to Berenson that he might be able to help by suggesting a scholarly project to Henry. She could not do it, for he would regard it merely as a sign of affection. But Berenson would have the authority that might convince Henry, who needed reassurance. She apologized for making such an intrusive request, but Henry's plight deeply troubled her, and she knew Berenson valued Henry as "he ought to be valued." She proposed that Berenson invite Henry for a visit toward the end of her stay in Paris. Berenson wrote immediately and assented, suggesting it might do Henry good to share the company of his guests and friends. But in typical fashion, Henry's visit to Florence did not result in a scholarly project for him, but in a plan to assist Berenson in lodging his papers at Harvard. Disgusted with Berenson, Rebecca recommended that Henry get what he could out of him but not to trust him or take the lead in any projects involving Berenson and his entourage.

In March, Rebecca retired to France in defeat, sending Henry detailed letters averaging a complaint a day about her health and offering advice on household matters: "I don't know if it will be safe to use a pressure-cooker at Ibstone, with our capacity for the dramatic." Henry took advantage of her absence by setting up the library the way *he* wanted it, informing her that he had bought several bookcases, shelves, and a mantelpiece that would enhance the value of the house.

4

REBECCA RETURNED to Ibstone from her month in Paris but departed again almost immediately for Yorkshire to give an address to the Brontë Society. Marvelous *Wuthering Heights* weather greeted her: an orange and slate blue stormy sky, sudden driving rain, and occasional lulls of silvery light streaming down on a landscape with huge, bright daffodils. There was an appropriate Brontë-like graveyard with gray tombstones laid out like tables for a banquet of ghosts. Rebecca's talk emphasized the artistry of *Wuthering Heights*, that it was no mere lucky stroke of romanticism, but indeed a critique of romanticism. She conceded Heathcliff's appeal but argued that the novel "repudiated the Byronic man." Heathcliff represented the nostalgia for the unfettered passions of childhood, but she dismissed the adult Heathcliff's "nerveless ranting." She consigned those smitten by him to the "millions more who have found evidence for the lovability of the beloved in remarkably odd places." His deeds were not magnificent; they were mean and cruel. Emily Brontë allowed him no dignity in death.

As early as her essay on Caroline Lamb in the 1920s, Rebecca had declared her opposition to Byronism. It revolted her when Kitty admired it in Anthony. By the time Rebecca's American friend Kit Wright first met Anthony in the 1950s, she had heard many tales of his Byronic treachery. When Kit met Anthony, she reacted against his vulpine appearance, especially his large white teeth. Her impression of him contrasts vividly with that of Frances Partridge. She first met Anthony after his marriage to Kitty and made friends without any connection to Rebecca. She liked his sudden flares of animation, "becoming all flashing white teeth, snapping black eyes and rumbles of suppressed amusement."

Rebecca ended her address to the Brontë Society praising all three sisters for resisting Byronism, noting that Charlotte had not ascribed to Mr. Rochester any very remarkable deeds. In both *Jane Eyre* and *Wuthering Heights* there were no heroes, only heroines. "Jane and the two Catherines have all the quality of magnificence which Emily Brontë refused to concede to Heathcliff. They have great courage; they are chivalrous and incorrupt." Rebecca's ever-lengthening novel, *Cousin Rosamund*, would also herald heroines, the rock on which civilization is built. She could not let go of Anthony, could not resist contesting his stories of their lives together, any more than she could abandon a novel like *Wuthering Heights* to its misguided readers, infatuated with a bogus hero.

CHAPTER 30

Heritage
1955–1956

I

ANTHONY AND LILY visited Rebecca and Henry in the late summer of
1955. Lily's impressions of Ibstone House and its inhabitants were remarkably similar to Kitty's. Rebecca seemed to relish the role of the banker's
wife living in an eighteenth-century manor house in the green belt near
London. This establishment almost seemed to have bubbles coming out
of it, making the effervescent statement: "Look, folks, we're rich."
Rebecca greeted them in her best imitation of the Lady of the Manor.

On the way to Ibstone, Lily raised the subject of Anthony's novel,
Heritage: "You know, this is rather autobiographical. Don't you think you
ought to say something about it to Mum?" He said, "Hm." He never
mentioned it to Rebecca. When she asked him what he was working on,
he replied "a light novel." An angry Rebecca later said that Lily "laughed
uncontrollably" at Anthony's remark. At the time, Rebecca thought Lily
was remembering the humorous passages in the book. Lily recalled that
their visit went off well. Rebecca thought so too, especially a picnic with
them and her two grandchildren. Lily had charming manners—an
improvement over Kitty, whom Rebecca had taken to calling "that
dreary form of refrigeration."

2

IN LATE SEPTEMBER, Rebecca got word that Anthony's novel was a disguised attack on her: she figured as a "glamorous actress who neglects
her darling little boy." She was thinking of writing a novel in which a
glamorous actress drowned her darling little boy. She resented Anthony
for visiting them, aping affection, and lifting two hundred pounds off of

300

Henry. In fact, the money was a delayed wedding present, but it became part of her recasting of their visit. At the picnic, for instance, she now remembered how Anthony and Lily had looked at her "as if they were marine creatures in an aquarium tank sliding away from me."

Rebecca's tack, in dozens of letters to friends over the next two years, was to refute the novel point-by-point, as though it were Anthony's literal rendering of their life together. In lawyerlike fashion, she assembled a massive brief—hundreds of pages of exculpation. Editor Michael Bessie saw one of her letters and thought, "Only someone that big could be that small." Her correspondence also constituted an attack on Anthony's integrity, portraying him as an unstable, shiftless, money-grubbing, ungrateful son who never acknowledged the sacrifices she had made for him. She alleged that he had expected to profit from a *Daily Express* serialization of his H.G. biography, but because his relations with H.G.'s executors had soured, he had turned to *Heritage* as a way of recouping his losses.

Rebecca's counterattack convinced Anthony that his mother meant to do him harm. By the time he published his father's biography in 1984, he had concluded that she had begun plotting against him when he first showed a preference for H.G. Similarly, Rebecca concluded that in late adolescence, he had begun to work up his pitiful story about being a neglected bastard and to make a career of it. In other words, mother and son played into each other's hands, and neither seemed to realize the damage they inflicted on themselves by accusing each other of perfidy.

Anthony named his fictional surrogate Richard Savage, after the eighteenth-century minor poet, the subject of Samuel Johnson's famous biography. Savage, a bastard, claimed that his mother, Lady Macclesfield, had ruined his life, refusing to acknowledge him or to provide him with the place in society he deserved. She had persecuted him and connived to get him hanged.

In an introduction to the reissue of *Heritage* in 1984, Anthony admitted he had been angry with his mother and that choosing the name of Savage for his hero was a case of "taking up a bludgeon to do what a stiletto would have done more neatly." He suggested that her hostility stemmed from her own father's abandonment of her as she was approaching adolescence and about to menstruate. Anthony remembered how she had surrounded herself with women—especially during his adolescence and those summers in southern France. Her revenge on him, Anthony implied, was her revenge on the male animal. He all but quoted the epigraph to *The Judge:* "Every mother is a judge who sentences the children for the sins of the father." Of the motivation behind *Heritage,* Rebecca wrote: "There is something in the male objection to a woman who can work. Ellen Terry and Sarah Bernhardt both had the hell of a time with their sons." Rebecca recalled the case of a man who blew up a plane because his mother was on it. Anthony would do something like that, she asserted.

Did Anthony grasp the irony of calling his fictional counterpart Richard Savage? Even in Samuel Johnson's sympathetic account, Richard Savage is a scoundrel, a sponger, a liar, and a spendthrift; he commits nearly every offense with which Rebecca charged Anthony. Unlike Savage, Anthony did not commit a murder, but Rebecca eventually feared that he would kill her. Like Richard Savage, Anthony West had friends who believed in his grievances and adopted the poor bastard thrown out of his home and disinherited by his powerful mother, soon to become Dame Rebecca. When he spoke of his mother "queering his pitch" in America, he was believed, because he so obviously wanted an understanding mother. To some women, this proved irresistible—as it had to Kitty. When Anthony moved to Stonington, Connecticut, he was befriended by Ann Fuller, who gave him a home and indulged him. When he ran up a huge telephone bill and stuffed it under a carpet so that she would not see it, she laughed off this childish ruse and found it endearing. "Of course after that I loved him more than ever—the way you do the naughty boys." When Ann later met Rebecca by accident at a party in Paris, and Rebecca introduced herself as Anthony's mother, Ann replied: "When he is in America, I like to think of myself as his mother." Ann found herself backpedalling through two rooms as Rebecca became a fountain of indignation, spraying Ann with spit as she effused her side of the story. Naturally, Ann thought her repulsive, the harsh mother Anthony had pictured.

Emily Hahn, Rebecca's friend and Anthony's colleague at *The New Yorker*, tried to calm Rebecca, suggesting that Anthony and Lily had not meant to mock her by their visit. It would have been hard for them not to visit her, and Anthony presumably did not want to think about the novel while he was there. Both of them probably felt guilty about it. Lily's reaction at the mention of *Heritage* was merely a "nervous laugh."

Rebecca treated the novel's appearance as a public degradation— even cabling Evelyn Hutchinson that she would understand if Yale canceled the lectures she had been invited to give in the spring of 1956. She alerted Max Beaverbrook to the anxiety the novel caused her. He replied that only a few people who knew the intimate details of her life would read the novel as autobiography; she was not to worry. If he meant to console her, he had the opposite effect: "I saw him not long ago. He is a remarkable young man. He is sure to go very far."

Rebecca speculated that Anthony had not written his book alone. Her enemies had fed him vulgar material. She claimed to detect variations in the book's style, even while saying she could not bear to read it at all. She had worried during the war that Fascist agents had got hold of him, or at least made it look as though they had. Perhaps the Communists had now played upon his sense of grievance. Such a hypothesis, preposterous as it seems, did fit quite well her view of the world. For she believed that the Communists recruited middle-class types who had failed to attain their rightful place, types who blamed society and its most powerful members for denying them recognition.

Rebecca had recently been publishing articles about the Communist spies Guy Burgess and Donald Maclean, emphasizing that these British foreign service officers had come from good families—aided by their fellow homosexuals and establishment figures, who could not believe that these Cambridge men could be disloyal. In Maclean's case, he had deceived his family for over twenty years. Both men had shown an immaturity that should have led to their dismissal, and yet they had been pampered until the very day they had forsaken England for the Soviet Union. Perhaps the puerile Anthony had unwittingly given himself over to similar subversive forces. The Macleans and Burgesses knew how to manipulate disaffected family members for political purposes.

For Rebecca, Communist subversion encompassed most aspects of private and public life. Communists sought to embarrass democratic governments and to drive wedges of distrust between them. Thus Burgess and Maclean had ostentatiously left behind copious evidence of their flight, making the most of their disloyalty so as to show the United States that Britain was an unreliable ally, because it was so unwitting about the traitors in its midst. Similar means would be employed to humiliate the staunchest anti-Communists. Consequently, Rebecca took the strongest means available to protect herself: through her agents, A. D. Peters and Odette Arnaud, she threatened to sue for libel any publisher in England or France who published *Heritage* (it did not appear in England until after her death).

Rebecca's friends who had known Anthony as an adolescent were ambivalent about *Heritage*. They deplored Rebecca's undressing in public: "Not your Mother, my boy. NOT you Mother," said John Van Druten, who had befriended Anthony during his summers in the South of France. John thought Anthony spiteful to give the Wells character, Max Town, the first name of Rebecca's other major lover. But John relished the novel's style and its images of Rebecca: "the first description of her waking up in a bad mood, with her hair looking like a sea-wreck was superb." Michael Arlen, admittedly an ex-friend, told John that Rebecca was "bound to get it, as all people who had hurt other people were always bound to get it." John thought Anthony had captured Henry perfectly; it had inspired John to perform his Henry Andrews impression for several friends. Doris Stevens remembered seeing Anthony in Rebecca's company in southern France, in London, during a visit to one of his schools, and through all of it Rebecca had been a doting parent, full of "tender concern" for her son. To her, *Heritage* was a fraud. Rebecca's cousin, David Ogilvy, voiced similar sentiments, calling the novel a "villainous mistake" and recollecting that Anthony's adolescent affection for his mother embarrassed him because members of his family always pretended to detest each other. Vyvyan Holland, an old friend from the 1920s, remembered Rebecca's sacrifices with special compassion, for she and Henry had recently undertaken (along with her friend Margaret Rawlings and her husband, Sir Robert Barlow) to finance the schooling of his son, Merlin. Vyvyan knew about family scandals; he was Oscar Wilde's son.

Harold Nicolson wrote Rebecca a gallant letter: "You have always to me seemed like a three masted schooner battling against wind and tide, and beautiful and deft in all your movements." He assured her that he spoke for her friends: "when something goes wrong and the ropes snap and the deck is soiled, we have not only the ordinary feelings of sympathy and indignation, but also a special feeling of aesthetic disgust."

But Rebecca, a connoisseur of literary gossip, realized that *Heritage* would stimulate parodies of herself and Henry. Pamela Frankau saw in Anthony's turning on his mother a repetition of her feud with Rebecca over "The Addict." Pamela had seen Anthony in New York just before his summer visit to his mother. "Shall you be seeing Rebecca?" Pamela asked. "That depends," said Anthony, giggling and giving her a slanted look. "On what?" "On whether she gets to hear about my novel." Pamela asked him about it. He responded cagily, not surrendering much information, except to say he intended it to be funny. Pamela remembered that Rebecca had said the same thing about her portrait of Humbert Wolfe in "The Addict." In *Heritage,* the "wheel had come full circle," Pamela concluded, with Anthony doing to his mother what she had done to Pamela. Pamela reflected that her own novel scoring off Rebecca, Rebecca's assault on Humbert, and Anthony's assault on Rebecca were all debilitated by failing to create whole human beings. Conceived in malice, their fiction resembled old snapshots in an album, not authentic flesh and blood.

3

DURING THE TUMULT over *Heritage*, Rebecca and Henry celebrated their silver anniversary on November 1, 1955 at the Dorchester Hotel in London in the company of forty-two guests. Rebecca enjoyed herself enormously. She continued her complaints about Henry's eccentric behavior, but she was grateful to him for seeing her through yet another crisis with Anthony and bouts of ill-health (including a jaw operation) and the usual domestic disasters at Ibstone. She wanted him at her side when she delivered her lectures at Yale in the spring, for there was no telling what cantrips Anthony had in store for her. She began to position her siege equipment in letters to friends like John Gunther, predicting that Anthony would try to trap her in some incident with the press. Henry wrote to John, expressing his outrage at Lily, a well-bred young woman, who had colluded with Anthony's "low nastiness." Neither Henry nor Rebecca credited John's belief that Anthony would not intentionally hurt his mother.

In the early months of 1956, friends wrote Rebecca that the buzz about *Heritage* had subsided. Inconsolable, she said the novel shaded her life like an upas tree, which yielded a juice used for poison arrows. Charles Curran's advice enraged her: treat *Heritage* as yesterday's news and concede that Anthony was bound to blame her, considering the wretched circumstances of his birth. Why give the novel legs by continuing to talk about it?

To Rebecca, the unkindest cut came from Dorothy Thompson. Before reading *Heritage*, Dorothy remarked that Anthony directed all his fire at Rebecca because H.G. was dead and could be safely canonized. She warned Rebecca that a son might have ambivalent feelings about his mother, but the mother would do herself incalculable harm if she hated her son. (Rebecca had already vowed never to see Anthony again.) She must learn to humor, even to forgive, Anthony's outrageous behavior. Rebecca was great enough and sovereign enough to do it. She should not bring herself down to his level. Dorothy quoted her husband's reaction to *Heritage*: "My God, can't that man forget—how long ago was it? Must have been the only interesting thing in his life. Who doesn't have an unhappy childhood?"

After reading *Heritage*, Dorothy wrote again stressing that after all it was a novel and the mother emerged as a "great and moody artist, fully alive only in her work, harassed by cares, and plagued by a responsibility which she is not, by nature, fitted to bear." This was an honest and accurate response—but not one Rebecca wanted to hear, especially when Dorothy exhorted her: "Dear Rebecca, stop having fits, and stop being wounded in your respectability. You are not, you never have been, and you never will be 'respectable.' " Dorothy had fingered the contradictory impulses in her friend's character that H.G. had identified in his autobiography. Couldn't Rebecca see that her life had been a triumph? "Jesus, who do you want to be?" Dorothy asked. Anthony had paid her the tribute of giving him a "wonderful (if highly unconventional) life." Dorothy admitted she would have been embarrassed if her own troubled son had written such a book, but she would also be thrilled at the compliment to a woman of genius. Born to be neither a mother nor a squire's lady, Naomi Savage (Rebecca's fictional counterpart) had not let these roles stifle her destiny as a great artist.

An outraged Rebecca annotated Dorothy's letter: "How different were her letters to me when her son went off the rails." Rebecca called Dorothy's advice rude and silly: "If you were not my dearly loved friend of many years I would never speak to you again." Did Dorothy really think Anthony could do Rebecca no harm in America? Did Dorothy remember how she had been "quietly edged out of New York" and lost her column at the *New York Post?* Anthony had been telling stories against Rebecca from the first day he had met Harold Ross. Anthony was "terribly plausible." She was certain the worst review of *A Train of Powder* had been influenced by his malicious stories. The novel's publication had occasioned many letters to her and conversations revealing that Anthony had been blackening her reputation for years. In *Heritage,* he had also libeled Odette Keun and presented a portrait of the Wells family that hurt them terribly. H.G.'s youngest son, Frank, called it a "wicked book," and expressed the family's solidarity with Rebecca. Marjorie Wells said the family would take whatever legal means were necessary to stop the book's publication in England.

Dorothy's next letter took a more Rebecca-like tone. Dorothy reported she had read sixty-eight reviews of *Heritage* and discovered that several mentioned the novel's autobiographical elements, some implying that Anthony might be justified in striking back at his mother. "This, of course, is *very* damaging to you," Dorothy admitted. It gave aid and comfort to Rebecca's political enemies. Now Dorothy could see the subtle treachery of the novel, especially its greatest lie, that as Dickie Savage, Anthony had reached "mature understanding and reconciliation. If he had, of course, he would never have written the book." Seconding Rebecca, Dorothy concluded: "Maybe Treason is the outstanding character of the epoch and the Meaning of Our Times." The novel appealed to the "psychopathology of the left," which enjoyed saving humanity while murdering its friends and exercising no private conscience whatsoever.

Charles Curran told a friend that Rebecca was incapable of letting go of *Heritage,* because she had "several skins fewer than any other human being, it's a kind of psychological hemophilia, which is one reason why she writes so well, and also why she is so vulnerable." Rebecca might still be sovereign, but she indulged the feeling of a conquered army, informing Evelyn and Margaret Hutchinson that they should not expect much from her spring lectures at Yale: "I have been defeated by forces that were too strong for me." When Kitty showed Rebecca one of Anthony's letters arguing that he had a right—even an obligation—to draw on his experience for his fiction, Rebecca would have none of it, noting that his version of the truth *always* put her in a bad light. He was a monster, and that was an end to it.

Replying to one of Rebecca's vehement letters about *Heritage,* Vita Sackville-West, no stranger to rumors and publicity about her private life, cautioned Rebecca not to invest too heavily in her depiction of Anthony's malice. "Do you really believe in malice?" Vita asked her. Of course it existed, but often what seemed malice was no more than human silliness, misunderstanding, and busybodiness. Certainly it was more amusing to be malicious than charitable, but an obsession with malice, when allowed to grow, got into the "beams of one's life like the death-watch beadle ticking away in the roof of an ancient church." Vita wanted to shake Rebecca and shout "pull yourself together!" In the boxing ring of contemporary literature, Rebecca had to expect hard knocks. 'Haven't you ever given any in return?' Vita asked. Rebecca's reply to this question, if there is one, has not been found.

Although Rebecca raged against Anthony, she did not want to cut all ties to him—especially through friends like the critic Raymond Mortimer. Raymond had written to Anthony expressing his outrage at *Heritage*'s cruelty. Raymond expected a furious reply from the touchy Anthony, but he had taken the criticism well. Raymond believed Anthony had constructed an elaborate fantasy about his mother: "Nothing he says, or writes, on the subject commands my belief." It amounted not to lies but to a streak of madness: "I have never been unaware of the unbalanced part of his nature." Rebecca remonstrated with Raymond as a man of sensitivity and character, to whom she bore much affection, to stick by Anthony. Raymond said he would. To others, she allowed that Anthony might still snap out of this deranged phase. But her predominant mood was not hopeful: "The first shock is over. I made up my mind to be realistic about it and not conceal the fact from myself that he is quite intractable material."

CHAPTER 31

The Family Politic
1956

I

IN EARLY APRIL, Rebecca and Henry journeyed to New Haven, Connecticut, for a series of lectures at Yale which proved to be a triumph. She proudly wrote to Lettie that the turn out at the first two talks had been so large that she had been moved into a larger hall. She began with a bang, contesting centuries of Shakespeare criticism. *Hamlet,* she contended, was not a sympathetic psychological study of a sensitive, introspective man, but rather a stern and pessimistic revelation of humanity's imperfections embodied in Hamlet's crass behavior. Ophelia did not love Hamlet and she did not kill herself. Where was the line in the play in which Ophelia expressed this love? Polonius and Claudius had used her as a pawn. As Queen Gertrude said, Ophelia's drowning had been an accident, provoked no doubt by Ophelia's great distraction and fear. Now that Hamlet had killed her father, she had no protector at court and the cruel Claudius had no use for her. Critics had missed the point: *Hamlet* was about politics and power.

Rebecca attacked a favorite target, Goethe, who treated Hamlet like a romantic hero with a conscience. Rebecca again put the boot to Byronism, which located the seat of power in the individual—whom Augustine had proven (using himself as a case history) was so base. Hamlet had no delicate feelings and killed without compunction. Like a prosecuting attorney, she overlooked the dramatic action that contradicted her case.

Shakespeare became, in good measure, Rebecca West. In one of her letters, she asserts:

> Shakespeare loathed Hamlet . . . thought Othello a fool, he obviously didn't care for the Macbeths a bit, I think he thought poorly of everybody in *King Lear* except Edgar, and didn't have the

affection for Cordelia that everybody assumes he had. *The Tempest* shows what he thought about the creator—Prospero made his land quite uninhabitable for normal people with those inventions of his, Ariel and Caliban, and he had been exiled to the island for behaving as intolerably in his kingdom.

The image of a king in exile, banished from his kingdom, longing for a Paradise Lost is also the image of Charles Fairfield. Virtually every powerful male figure in Rebecca's work is described as a king. A king is what Rebecca wanted, but he is also what she rejected. She wanted to submit to authority; she wanted to rebel against it. She was attracted to Rousseau's version of the natural man, and she admired the trappings and ceremonies of power. She yearned for the simpler dichotomies of earlier ages and saw her own family members as usurpers and tyrants in a world not much different from that of *Richard III*.

The Court and the Castle (1957), Rebecca's revision of her Yale lectures, is full of waspish asides. She can almost be heard thinking of Anthony or Lettie and relating their roles to the fate of the blocked writer and of western civilization:

> Freud gave sadists a new weapon by enabling them to disguise themselves as hurt children . . . the courtiers who blocked the staircase. . . . They are the circumstances of family life, the terrifying father, the embarrassing sister; the disabling sickness.

The courtiers blocking the staircase are the false claimants to the throne, threatening the writer's sovereignty, her efforts to reach the castle—the term Rebecca uses for the seat of religious revelation, the realm of magic that would settle all contradictions. To Rebecca, the Gerdas and Letties of the world are constantly spoiling revelation, as Gerda does in *Black Lamb and Grey Falcon* by usurping Bishop Nikolai's role in distributing Easter eggs; as Lettie did, Rebecca supposed, by taking up a career as a writer late in life just to tweak Rebecca. Rebecca even gives the name of Gerda to one of her fictional portraits of Lettie, "Short Life of a Saint," in which Lettie's religious quest and conversion to Catholicism are interpreted as her flight from a humanity she desperately wants to love but cannot quite embrace.

At Yale, Rebecca reaffirmed that she had thrown off the influence of her early mentors, Shaw and Wells, who believed in the perfectibility of man and of society, in revolutions which could raze society and build it again better from the ground up. Rebecca had become a disciple of Edmund Burke, who believed in reform not revolution, and argued that tearing down time-honored institutions did more harm than good, because it destroyed the partial regard for human rights painfully gained over the ages.

Rebecca suggested that in Trollope, for example, social institutions, no matter how unjust they might be to certain classes of citizens, were absolutely necessary to civilization's survival. Even bureaucracy, the bane of Kafka's life, was also his mainstay. It could crush individuals, level illogical and unjust charges against K. in *The Trial*, but society could not function without bureaucracy. Kafka knew this very well, having been trained in the Hapsburg Empire's bureaucracy.

The Court and the Castle is one of Rebecca West's most impressive books, the fountaining of a lifetime's thinking about history, literature, and politics. Frank Kermode, one of the century's most distinguished critics, extolled her power, the "full pressure" of intelligence and experience rarely seen in literary criticism. He thought her Trollope chapter "exceptionally fine" and the ones on Proust and Kafka the best he had ever read. But he admitted his "discomfort" with the alien mode of her thinking. Like many reviewers, he took issue with her "Calvinist *Hamlet.*"

Reviewer John Wain concluded that *The Court and the Castle* "is too profound and densely packed for me to be able to assess it until I have had time to live with it, to keep it beside me as a companion to my reading, as one keeps *The Sacred Wood* or *Countries of the Mind* or *The Wound and the Bow.*" It constantly challenges the way we read—a "book with a bite," as critic Peter Wolfe says. It is exciting and nimble. Rebecca at sixty-four was every bit as bracing as she was at nineteen.

Yale professor Cleanth Brooks happened to visit Rebecca shortly before one of her lectures and got a glimpse of her gusto. He discovered "the great lady," on the floor, energetically polishing her shoes. He found it endearing: "I'm sure she thought nothing of it, having grown up a woman who had always taken care of herself, who had her share of servants, but would not think it stooping to put a shine on her shoes." Literary agent Tom Wallace, then a student at Yale, got an entirely different impression of her. He greatly admired her work, but he remembers his disappointed view of her at a social gathering. She seemed to be putting on a show, and she had all the mannerisms of the self-absorbed, unapproachable celebrity.

2

REBECCA'S BRAVURA performance at Yale dovetailed with the completion of *The Fountain Overflows*, the first part of her Aubrey family trilogy, entitled *Cousin Rosamund*. Charles Fairfield makes his appearance in the novel as the journalist Piers Aubrey, a magnificent monarch of a father, an aloof but dazzlingly Byronic figure, brooding over the great events of his day, exciting both the reverence and the irritation of his colleagues, who do not know how to cope with this brilliant yet irascible and profligate man, who is a gambler and a spendthrift.

Rebecca often said she had Edmund Burke in mind when she created Piers Aubrey. As a child she had heard her father in argument honor Burke as though he were a god, and she claimed kinship with him through one of her great-grandmothers. She had grown up with this prophetic figure in the back of her mind. Like Burke, Aubrey is opposed to revolution and reveres tradition. Completely out of sympathy with the modern world, however, he is an isolated figure. He rues the fact that he is widely and respectfully read and yet exerts no influence.

Piers and his wife Clare (a physical and mental ringer for Isabella Fairfield) dominate their daughter Rose's consciousness. She is the novel's narrator, portraying her parents as Olympian figures with the same "eagle look about them" which prevents them from living on easy terms with their fellow human beings. Clare, for example, is at a loss as to how to treat Miss Beevor, her eldest daughter Cordelia's violin teacher, who has ludicrous musical standards. Because Clare exists in an aesthetic realm so far above what Miss Beevor or Cordelia could contemplate, she inevitably hurts their feelings. Unlike her husband Piers, however, Clare has compassion for those whom she estranges, and she practices a tolerance and decency that Piers can exercise only in the abstract, when he is defending political principles, or taking up the cause of a woman accused of murder. It is as if his interest in humanity can never focus narrowly enough to take in the plight of individuals unless some great issue is involved—in this instance a judge's abuse of power. Much is made of the way he handmakes Christmas presents for his children, because it is one of the few signs of affection he displays—aside from his stimulating conversations with them.

Cordelia, the prize student, hectors her younger sisters, Mary and Rose. Her wonderfully eccentric mentor, Miss Beevor, is surely a gift to Rebecca from the ghost of Charles Dickens. It is a musical family. Rose and Mary are protégées of their mother, a brilliant pianist. Cordelia saws away on the violin, an acute embarrassment to her mother and sisters, who are plagued by her insufferable blindness to her lack of talent.

Rose, Rebecca's stand-in, exhibits more compassion for Cordelia than Rebecca ever showed Lettie. Cordelia has Lettie's sense of propriety; she dreads that her unconventional family will embarrass her. Like Dickens, Rebecca uses the *bildungsroman* to surmount a painful past, recreating it in more charming terms.

Rebecca's choice of the name Cordelia seems odd for this self-absorbed, snobbish character—unless the choice is interpreted as ironic. Rebecca's Cordelia lacks the virtues of Shakespeare's heroine—or rather, Rebecca's Cordelia is a fool who thinks that she exemplifies the family virtues, when in fact her dictatorial attitudes are destructive of them.

But Rebecca had an iconoclastic view of Shakespeare's characters: "Cordelia I think a poisonous creature—clinging to the mean, mad father and leaving the King of France." The Cordelias of this world protest their loyalty and self-sacrifice a deal too much for Rebecca's taste. In *The Fountain Overflows* Cordelia is always reminding her mother and sisters of how she has struggled to make them a respectable family.

Although Rose and her sister Mary have promising musical careers, they remain fixated on their father—as Rebecca and Winnie were on Charles Fairfield. Like Charles, Piers is his children's greatest joy and their profoundest disappointment. Or as Rose says, "I had a glorious father. I had no father at all." The family kindles in his presence, and his wife exclaims: "We are all less than Piers." He fills his daughters with stimulating ideas, but he also fails to bring them up in a world to which they belong. He is as much myth as he is man: "He walked as if he had no weight, as if no limitation affected him." Father can walk this way in memory, especially for a child who feels favored: "For it was I whom he had loved the best," Rose assures herself, after Piers abandons his family.

Exactly why he does so is never made explicit—any more than Rebecca was ever certain why her father left home. Both Piers Aubrey and Charles Fairfield seem world-weary; there is an air of hopelessness about them. Though Charles painted watercolors that Rebecca treasured all her life and occasionally wrote about art exhibitions, she believed that he grew contemptuous of her mother's dedication to music, and that his coarsened and corrupted nature rejected the life of art to which Isabella remained committed. This is a very grave sin, since art is a means of salvation in a flawed world. As Clare puts it, "life is as extraordinary as music says it is." Human beings who deny the art in them—like Uncle Jock, who plays the flute beautifully but assumes a vulgar demeanor and tongue—perversely reject their own redemption. Rose speaks of her mother's "access to the vein of imagination in my father which he was now repudiating, but which must have been what made him fall in love with her in spite of her inconvenient genius and integrity." This wonderful sentence encapsulates the idea that in Clare, Piers fell in love with the best in himself, his imagination. When he leaves Clare, it is tantamount to a repudiation of his best self, the one he leaves at home, so to speak, in the care of his children. He flees, in other words, before they can witness his final degradation, his utter loss of hope for himself and the world. Rebecca could never know if her own father had reached such a low point, but fiction provided her with a way of filling the gap left by his absence, of endowing it with an Augustinian significance which did not ease her pain but at least made some sense of it.

Rebecca professed surprise that readers wondered why Piers Aubrey went away. She seconded Professor Anthony Cockshut's view that the subject of her novel is the difficulty of leading an artist's life. Although not an artist, Piers had an artist's vision, seeing "more of the truth than is convenient." Consequently, "he could not live at all. . . . He just could not bear life, and his family was part of it." The same could be said of Rebecca: She could not bear life, and her family was part of it.

Rebecca routs the anti-artist, Aunt Sophie, in her depiction of Aunt Theodora. The mention of her name darkens Clare Aubrey's face. Pretending to offer aid with a "rollicking bonhomie," Aunt Theodora reacts to Clare's expression of gratitude for a gift of a large sum of money with the intimation that the thanks had come "too late and was inadequate." Summoned to Aunt Theodora's house, the family has to put up with her "impudent exhortations," and Rose berates her mother for having accepted help: "I am ashamed to think I have been living on Aunt Theodora's money!"

Authority figures such as Aunt Theodora interfere with Rose's vision of her mother and father and of that early paradise of family life. Near the end of the novel Rose announces:

> I could not face the task of being a human being, because I did not fully exist. It was my father and mother who existed. I could see them as two springs, bursting from a stony cliff, and rushing down a mountainside torrent, and joining to flow through the world as a great river. I was so inferior that it did not matter if I should be prudent and escape the ruin to which my father had dedicated himself. His ruin, I saw, was nearer salvation than my small safety could ever come.

Her parents are literally the fountain of her inspiration, Rose emphasizes—as did Rebecca in an article about her parents, published six years after her novel:

My parents were superior to me physically and mentally, and I would have had to be more of a fool than I am not to notice it. I count it as one of the most lovable achievements that they somehow kept me from being humiliated by my inferiority and made it possible for me to enjoy their superiority without resentment.

The pleasure I derived from my father's combination of subtlety and simplicity, and all the other qualities which set him above my level, means that our relationship has gone on long after his death. I often think of him when other people above my level tell me something I did not know before.

It is significant that throughout the many years of writing her family memoirs, Rebecca never got beyond the time between her father's departure and death, between the ages of eight and thirteen. As Rose confesses later in *Cousin Rosamund,* the last volume of the never completed trilogy: "My father's desertion of me had never ceased to happen."

In *The Fountain Overflows,* Rose Aubrey laments "The waste of time before I was born," musing over all those years that preceded hers—like the years of Charles Fairfield's life that Rebecca tried to reconstruct in her family memoirs. In the daughter's mind the father's fate became linked to hers: He was a victim of circumstances, unable to control the conditions determining his sorry fate, just as she (at a tender age) could not correct the crooked destiny, the Byzantine world of childhood, that hemmed her in. Like Rebecca, Rose never accepts the fact of childhood, calling children "adults handicapped by a humiliating disguise."

The Fountain Overflows is a book about the struggle to grow up, and about the forbidding realization of impending disaster. Piers divines that the twentieth century will be a calamity. He rejects the Edwardian faith in a "law of progress." One of his colleagues tells Clare: "Your husband puts down in black and white the idea that we're not going forward, we're going backward. He says that civilisation's going to collapse. It's going to shrink instead of spreading. He says that country after country is going to be taken over by common criminals."

Rose has some of the gift of prophecy herself, which she displays at a party by placing her hands on children's foreheads and reading their minds. Poltergeists assault the house of Rose's cousin, Rosamund, who becomes the focal character of the trilogy, destined to experience the century's worst atrocities, including the concentration camp. Rebecca's trilogy is Pauline in its occult portrayal of the world as seen through a glass darkly. In notes for her projected trilogy (eventually she thought it might be four novels), Rebecca listed her characters according to their prophetic roles. Thus Piers "saw only a little way prophetically." Clare actually saw more but "got confused in life." Richard Quin, the perfect brother Rose and Mary dote on—and the idealized brother Rebecca never had, based on Isabella's brother, Joey, who died in his twenties—is described as lacking ambition because he knows he will be killed in World War I. Cordelia is "denied her gift of prophecy." Rosamund will become the "perfect priestess" and also the most enigmatic character— in part because she is powerless to prevent the awful vision of the holocaust she harbors. She is compared, in one passage, to an elusive, immobile Greek goddess.

In her multi-volume family saga, Rebecca set herself nearly an impossible task: to resolve her feelings about her own family, while integrating those feelings into her interpretation of the twentieth century. She had an ambition worthy of Augustine, who also used autobiography to express his understanding of God and man and to reveal the meaning of history.

3

WINNIE SPOTTED the real-life sources of *The Fountain Overflows*. She told her daughter Alison that Rebecca had romanticized much. As the youngest, Rebecca had been shielded from the worst aspects of Charles Fairfield's behavior. To Rebecca, Winnie wrote in praise of the novel, saying it would become a classic, and ratifying Rebecca's sense of the occult. Winnie remembered the stamping of horses at Streatham Place—a scene in the novel puts the Aubrey house above the site where horses once were stabled, and where their ghosts could still be heard stamping in their stalls.

An embarrassed Lettie found herself telling friends she had never played the violin. She was gracious about the novel, though she found Richard Quin, the darling little brother, an unsuccessful character, except as a baby. Rebecca was the only musical member of the family, Lettie emphasized, and also the one with the greatest imagination. Lettie remembered how real Rebecca could make her imaginary world, getting Lettie to pick her up to pat an imaginary horse. The portrait of Clare Aubrey, including her nervous disposition, captured Isabella Fairfield's personality perfectly, Lettie concluded.

Lettie told Rebecca she felt deeply hurt by the novel. Rebecca responded with an apology and a denial. Cordelia was not based on Lettie, and she was sorry to discover her sister thought so. "Of course I love you dearly and am, as well, very grateful to you for your constant kindness and affection." Except for a few minor details—such as Cordelia's affection for Aunt Theodora, which was like Lettie's for Aunt Sophie—Cordelia and Lettie had nothing in common, Rebecca alleged. But her autobiographical notes leave no doubt that she consciously regarded Lettie as Cordelia's prototype.

Anthony noted Rebecca's demolition of Lettie, and Rebecca as quickly denied it, claiming: "Nobody in the family is anything but delighted with the book." Was Rebecca having her mordant fun by dedicating the novel "to my sister Letitia Fairfield"?

The novel was a popular and critical success, doing much to rehabilitate Rebecca's reputation as a novelist; it had been twenty years since the publication of her last novel, *The Thinking Reed*. One reviewer called her "today's finest English stylist." Several reviewers recorded their pleasure at reading a novel so packed with characters and incidents worthy of Dickens and of the great Edwardian novelists, Wells and Bennett. By the middle of March 1957, over fifty thousand copies of *The Fountain Overflows* had been sold in America and close to 40,000 in England. It had been serialized in *The Ladies' Home Journal*. Fan mail inundated Rebecca and prompted her to observe: "the number of people who either were deserted by their fathers or who had a relative who *would* play the violin seems to be enormous."

CHAPTER 32

Lamentations
1956–1959

I

BY THE AUTUMN OF 1956, Rebecca was within two chapters of completing *This Real Night*, the second part of her family chronicle. To get the job done without interruption, she reverted to her frequent refuge: the south of France. Henry accompanied her, going to endless trouble for her comfort, settling her into the Hotel Gray and D'Albion in Cannes. When he left her to complete her work, she wrote thanking him. Never had she loved her Ric more, signing one of her notes "yours ever, with much agitation of the muzzle." She sent him charming, playful letters: "Rac ordered fresh sardines and waved her tail over them, as good as any I ever ate." Nevertheless, she had attacks of self-doubt, disliked the "porridgy" beginning of *This Real Night*, and feared she might not be able to push herself up the hill again—which seemed an awesome task after the success of *The Fountain Overflows*. The second novel might not have the same texture as the first. Winnie had said a sequel would be a mistake.

Just when Rebecca began to feel restored, her left leg and ankle swelled up, "white and shiny and hard like a motor-tyre"—a severe case of varicose veins. "Why was I born to look solid and squalidly robust when I am shot to hell"? she wondered. She was confined to bed for six weeks. Henry returned to do her many kind services; she repaid him with enchanting behavior. But it maddened and depressed her to stop work.

Then Winnie's health broke. An exhausted seventy-two-year-old Lettie tried to care for her, causing Rebecca, who never trusted Lettie to do the right thing, to fret. Rebecca's nephew Norman wrote, assuring his aunt that Lettie "rose magnificently to the first emergency," whatever her subsequent eccentricities may have cost Rebecca. By the autumn, Rebecca had rightly concluded that Winnie had lost her wits and was dying. It was a slow process, taking more than a year, and it unraveled

317

Rebecca, who had to watch her beloved sister become a "travesty of humanity."

Rebecca relived her childhood, charging that Lettie showed a lack of sympathy for her dying sister—even staging diversionary illnesses of her own.

2

IN HER MID-SIXTIES, Rebecca worried constantly about her own health, suffering a mild heart attack and two vascular spasms in the spring and summer of 1958, one of which left her prostrate on her bathroom floor. When Lettie visited Ibstone for a weekend in May 1958, she remarked on the contrast between Henry, looking fit, and Rebecca, who seemed under a strain.

Rebecca mourned the estrangements and deaths of old friends, many of them confidants from the 1920s. Invited to a luncheon honoring Paul Robeson, she decided not to attend lest her presence imply support of his Communist politics and embarrass her. When Lady Rhondda, the founder of *Time and Tide,* died in July 1958, Pamela Frankau wrote to Rebecca reminiscing about their wonderful days in the south of France. Rebecca replied: "Yes, wasn't Margaret nice at Agay! But she grew megalomaniac, and fantastic after that. She made the strangest demands of one and was outraged if one couldn't satisfy them, if only for her sake—and behaved as if one had refused her a glass of water." Rebecca had remained fond of John Van Druten, another Agay alumnus, who died in December 1957, but she rightly sensed that he had decided she was "something untrustworthy or dangerous." He had gravitated toward G. B. Stern, whose friendship with Rebecca had been strained when she had not shown the proper degree of distress over Anthony's treatment of Rebecca in *Heritage.*

Why did Rebecca seem "untrustworthy or dangerous"? One of Rebecca's protégées, the writer Monica Sterling, paid an uneasy visit to Ibstone in the summer of 1960 and remarked: "Rebecca's witch-like aspect makes her so incalculable and I can't shake off a feeling that anything she says may be recorded against me." Rebecca had ripped into the drama critic Kenneth Tynan, Pamela Frankau—Monica's dear friend—and several others. Around an element of truth Rebecca would draw the most fantastic arabesques. Monica gave the actress Margaret Rawlings, her friend and Rebecca's, a hypothetical example. Rebecca would say that Margaret was interested in novelist Lawrence Durrell, but the truth was that her daughter Jane was having an affair with him. The only element of truth in the gossip would be that Margaret admired Durrell. It was as if "some exchange were missing," some mechanism that prevented Rebecca from making a local call to reality and instead put her immediately onto some far-fetched explanation of events. When Pamela told Monica and Odette Arnaud, Rebecca's French agent, about how Rebecca reacted to her as a young girl and tried to interfere in her romance with Humbert Wolfe, Odette turned green and later said to Monica: "Pamela cannot lie—did you realize Rebecca could be like that? I'll never feel the same toward her." Monica concluded that in spite of her talent, success, and money, Rebecca was "deeply frustrated and of course it takes a fine and also a simpler character to accept that without taking it out on other people."

When Rebecca eulogized departed friends, she singled out their absolute loyalty to her. Their absence amounted to a rent in her defenses, and the worst was yet to come. In mid-January 1958, Rebecca and her closest friend, Ruth Lowinsky, had a "matey" morning conversation about where to go to dinner that evening. ("Roley-poley" Ruth, the author of several cookbooks, was a gourmet cook.) After lunch Henry stopped off at his London club and received the message from Justin, Ruth's son, that she had died that morning of a coronary thrombosis after telephoning to Rebecca. She had known Ruth for thirty years. They had gone to picture galleries, concerts, dress shows, and traveled together. Never envious of Rebecca, Ruth fiercely identified with Rebecca's conception of herself, and like Henry, defended Rebecca against all comers. Rebecca cherished Ruth's outspoken and impulsive side, her blunt but sympathetic articulation of home truths. Once after a party at Ibstone, she had said to Rebecca: "You have a terrible time running things here, with Henry countermanding every order you give and not hearing half of anything that anybody says." Ruth never spoke of it again, but Rebecca felt less lonely because her friend understood. The unconventional Ruth was always "willing to play." Only five days older than Rebecca, Ruth was her "twin," a vigorous woman with the energy of a forty-year-old. Rebecca cried in fits she had trouble controlling. Her leg swelled up like a bolster. She had strange, indecipherable dreams, suffered spells when she could not remember Ruth's first name, and had trouble spelling simple words such as persuade, which came out as "purswade."

Raymond Mortimer, close to Ruth, wrote Rebecca a consoling letter. Ruth had nursed him through a long illness and convalescence, and he regarded her as a sister, valuing her sympathy and practical advice. She might be less adroit than others in hiding her faults, but her friends loved her spontaneity.

Thinking she might be next, Rebecca typed out a short outline of the main events of her life and sent it off to Yale University, where she had decided to deposit her papers. She hoped to add to the outline at a later date, and to formalize the agreement with Yale, but for now she stipulated that the Yale archive would be closed during her lifetime and until the death of her husband and son. After that, Yale could make any use of the papers that it pleased. She wrote to friends asking them to send letters from her to Yale.

"The friends I have lost this year are beyond belief. But my enemies all seem awfully well," Rebecca lamented. She pictured Anthony at the head of them. She had concluded that *Heritage* represented his long-term plan to blacken her name. Now she realized that his destroying two or three of her letters to H.G. had not been an impulsive, perverse act—and certainly not some chivalric effort to destroy the evidence against her—but rather a plot to eradicate any testimony that might contradict his novel's portrait of her. Anthony lacked gallantry—unlike Henry, who would defend his lady whatever her shortcomings.

Instead, Anthony had *Heritage* published in France. Rebecca wanted to sue, but her attorney advised against it, assuring her that legal action would bring her more trouble and expense than satisfaction. Instead she undertook to have the Wells estate issue a statement clearing her of responsibility for putting a stop to Anthony's biography of his father. (Eventually Gip and Majorie Wells drafted a statement that proved unsatisfactory to Rebecca because it did not repudiate strongly enough Anthony's charges against her.)

3

IN EARLY NOVEMBER 1958, another death—this time of Rose Macaulay, a beloved literary colleague of "abundant charity and enthusiasms"—disconcerted Rebecca. Several reporters accosted her at the memorial service, one of whom blurted out: "I expect you will miss Dame Macaulay very much. Well, we're all hoping you will be the next." As his appalled colleagues stared, the scarlet-faced reporter spluttered: "I mean we're all hoping you'll be the next Dame."

By the end of November 1958, Rebecca had accepted the honor of Dame of the British Empire. 1959 began with congratulatory cables, letters, and calls responding to the official announcement of Rebecca's DBE. Charles Curran cabled: "Publish and be damed!" Rebecca told several friends that she never expected the honor: "I never sought to be teacher's pet and Bloomsbury loathed me." After her last three years of agony with Anthony, she admitted that "conventional respect means something." It disturbed Rebecca that, other than from friends like Noël Coward and Beverly Nichols, she received few acknowledgments from male writers, although she was astonished to get one from her nemesis, T. S. Eliot. Rebecca detected in Lettie an insinuation that Rebecca had somehow pulled strings to get the recognition. Winnie had one of her better moments when she heard of the award, and a relieved Rebecca saw that her sister was happy for her.

Henry, Lettie, and Rebecca's grandson Edmund accompanied her to the investiture on February 14, 1959. It was preceded by a luncheon at which Rebecca relished long conversations with the Queen and Princess Margaret. The ceremony itself lasted less than a minute. Wearing a black hat, coat, and skirt designed especially for the occasion, Rebecca approached a dais, curtsied, took two steps forward, and the Queen leaned over and pinned her with two "pretties"—a cross and a steel star. The Queen gave Rebecca the conventional thanks for doing so much "good work." "Bless her heart," Rebecca thought, "so I have, but I doubt if she will ever know what it was. But it couldn't have been more prettily said." They shook hands, and Rebecca stepped back and curtsied (not an easy maneuver in high heels). Then the Queen mentioned in a lower, confidential tone how much she had enjoyed their luncheon—a personal compliment that pleased Rebecca very much.

Rebecca found the renewed interest in her work, and resulting requests for interviews and speeches, fatiguing, and in the spring of 1959 retreated, once again, to the south of France, staying with Ralph and Anne Carlisle at their chateau in Cannes. Ralph, a retired banker, had been in the Ruhleben internment camp with Henry. Rebecca found Ralph's wife, Anne, a painter, a sympathetic and charming companion. At work on *This Real Night*, Rebecca was within a few pages of completing it, and yet something held her back—not just the interruptions she never ceased deploring, nor the book reviews and related articles she poured out by the score each year, but some reluctance to move on to the adult years of her characters. In a manuscript notebook, she remarked: "THE AGONY—getting back to the book in May 1959. If I can do this I can do anything. But I fear I can't." A colitis attack, then a commission to write on Madame de Staël, put the novel out of reach again. She picked it up in June during yet another French sojourn, making only a little headway.

Since the publication of *The Fountain Overflows*, Rebecca had managed to complete only one work of fiction, a late masterpiece, "Parthenope," which marked her last appearance in *The New Yorker*. Like *The Fountain*

Overflows, "Parthenope" is an account of a childhood, revealing the difficulty of surmounting its hurts, and of imagining a transition to adult life that would truly satisfy a restless and creative mind. The story's narrator is a woman who fondly recalls her Uncle Arthur and his fascination with Parthenope, a woman he spied in a garden with her beautiful, birdlike sisters. Uncle Arthur, Rebecca revealed to her editor at *The New Yorker,* was based on her Uncle Arthur, Charles Fairfield's brother, who had stopped just short of success in the civil service. The story's Uncle Arthur is a childlike man, who blurts out home truths to his superiors, impeding his career. "He often made discoveries such as a schoolchild might make, and shared them with an enthusiasm as little adult," states the story's narrator, who knew Uncle Arthur as a young girl.

Uncle Arthur becomes fascinated with Parthenope and her sisters because they wish to wall themselves up in the garden of their childhood. They have been married off by their sea captain father—who has given them the names of Greek goddesses—but they continually return to their childhood home. When Arthur invents an excuse to meet them, he is frightened by their fascination with his red hair and their treatment of him as some exotic creature. It eventually dawns on him that they are all mad, except for Parthenope, the one adult who empathizes with them and tries to protect them from brutal husbands who marry them for their beauty but abuse them when the women cannot function in the adult world. The sisters are, in fact, perfect examples of women as idiots, which Rebecca defined in *Black Lamb and Grey Falcon,* as women whose reality consists completely of their own society and personal relationships. They are entirely self-contented, virgin goddesses in spite of their marriages, the products of a sort of mental parthenogenesis, for they can do without the male sex altogether.

The import of such a story for Rebecca was obvious. She once created something like a society of women at Agay, but having done so regretted it as one by one her "sisters"—G. B. Stern, Pamela Frankau, Pat Wallace (who married the publisher A. S. Frere), and June Head (who married Charles Fenby) drifted away. On the one hand, Rebecca, a worldly woman—*Time* called her a "news hen" when she received her DBE—understood all about leaving the nest, about engaging with public life; on the other hand, like Rose in *The Fountain Overflows,* no world beyond the confines of her home ever seemed quite as complete, as self-contained as the womblike dream of childhood. For this reason Rebecca titled her sequel to *The Fountain Overflows This Real Night*—taken from a line in James Thomson's poem, *City of Dreadful Night:* "I wake from daydreams to this real night."

Parthenope's solution to prolonging the paradise of childhood is to spirit her sisters off to France, where she stages a holdup in which they are purportedly robbed and murdered. Many years later, Arthur discovers the ruse quite by accident during his travels through France and visits Parthenope, who tells him of her efforts to shield her helpless sisters. She returns them to what the narrator calls a "nursery happiness," a revealing phrase similar to one in a letter where Rebecca refers to her nursery anger over Lettie's interference in her life. Parthenope is, in fact, Lettie inverted, an elder, truly protective sister. Parthenope is also Rebecca, in that she is both the child and the adult, understanding both her infantile sisters and the world that would crush them. Parthenope is the artist who has created a fiction which has fostered her sisters' lives.

Parthenope speaks in Rebecca's accents when she asks Uncle Arthur: "Why should you have found me here, I wonder? It can't be that, after all, there is some meaning in the things that happen?" Rebecca was always searching for such a meaning—in seances, in travel, in politics, in family life, and most of all, in fiction. She was always asking why men treated women so unfairly and brutally. Uncle Arthur observes to Parthenope that she has the strength and intelligence of her sea captain father, and then he articulates a view of women that Rebecca could only express in fiction, when she was portraying not only her own suffering, but the conditions in which most men encounter women:

> And you know quite well that if you were a man you would regard all women as incapable. You see, men of the better kind want to protect the women they love, and there is so much stupidity in the male nature and the circumstances of life are generally so confused that they end up thinking they must look after women because women cannot look after themselves. It is only very seldom that a man meets a woman so strong and wise that he cannot doubt her strength and wisdom, and realizes that his desire to protect her is really the same as his desire to gather her into his arms and partake of her glory.

His words are a feminist parable on the stupidity of males, and a mature reflection on how life stimulates that stupidity. The words are also Rebecca's clearest explanation to herself of why men rejected her, of how difficult it was for them to accept a woman who would appreciate their help but did not really need it except as a way of partaking in her glory. It might have been Henry speaking in that last sentence, for he was the only man Rebecca had found who recognized that his desire to protect her and to partake of her glory were one and the same thing.

Parthenope knows that there is something mad about her quest to recover the garden of childhood. Are not staging a sham robbery, lying and plotting—all in her effort to rescue her sisters' madness—a form of madness itself? she asks. She confesses to Uncle Arthur that she has not acted for her sisters alone, but also in repudiation of a world she believes has rejected her. Here one detects Rebecca filling the envelope of her character, the details of Parthenope's plotting, with her own feelings:

> Something has happened which can only be explained by supposing that God hates you with merciless hatred, and nobody will admit it. The people nearest you stand round you saying that you must ignore this extraordinary event, you must—what were the words I was always hearing?—"keep you sense of proportion," "not brood on things." They do not understand that they are asking you to deny your experiences, which is to pretend that you do not exist and never have existed.

To Rebecca, to deny her "paranoia," her belief that the world had it in for her, was to suppress what she most prized: her perceptions, her art, her self.

Parthenope constitutes Uncle Arthur's lamentation for the lost child-hood he paradoxically carries within himself, a childhood he imaginatively recreates for the narrator of the story, herself a young woman when he imparts it to her, telling her about it "very often during the five years that passed before his death." But Rebecca saw the story as much more of a tragic lament, and Parthenope, like herself, as an isolated, even ridiculed figure, plagued by insane sisters, looking for a companion like herself:

> The first thing she [Parthenope] reveals is a desperate desire to play like a child, not to get involved in adult schemes or in the imbecile gambols of her insane sisters, but just to have leisure and enjoy herself—which puts her on terms with the child Arthur. The second thing she reveals is that it is funny in the eyes of the world to be tragic, and the person afflicted by tragedy knows this.

"Parthenope" constitutes Rebecca's argument with herself, with the conflicting demands and desires of the child's and the adult's worlds so beautifully evoked in *The Fountain Overflows*. Art objectified these con-flicting demands and desires, whereas their appearance in her life fright-ened and angered her. When her granddaughter Caroline, now approaching the age of eighteen, wrote to her, expressing her doubts about going on to university, Rebecca panicked. Caroline's headmistress, Miss Galton, had expressed some qualms about whether Caroline would pass the highly competitive entrance exams, and Rebecca reacted by treating her granddaughter's anxieties as a retreat from the adult world.

It looked to Rebecca suspiciously like a repetition of Anthony's failure to get into Oxford. Rebecca had observed the strong bond between father and daughter with increasing dread. She criticized Caroline for spending so much time with Anthony during the interval between school and university, believing that Caroline should occupy herself with studying languages and going to France. Rebecca feared that Anthony and Kitty had, consciously or unconsciously, imparted their "curiously ambivalent attitude toward material success."

Rebecca wrote to Caroline, questioning her gloomy assessment of England: "horribly shadowed and complicated" in ways that made a successful career undesirable. Things did not seem to Rebecca any more grim (even with the H-bomb) than they had been for most of recorded history. The point was to do as well as one could for oneself—not because one competed with others. Caroline's pessimism, Rebecca suggested to her, must have its roots in other problems Caroline was not ready to confront.

Rebecca had conceded to Miss Galton that she might be "over anxious" about Caroline. Rebecca remembered that at sixteen her bout with tuberculosis had sapped her of any desire to attend university. Did Miss Galton think Caroline might be ill? Caroline was not ill. But unable to allow Caroline to work things out for herself, Rebecca concocted a plan to get Caroline into a backup school, a sort of "emergency door" to Oxford or Cambridge. An offended Caroline responded by studying hard and passing the entrance exam to Cambridge and winning the prestigious Girton scholarship.

Rebecca seemed to understand that her zealous efforts to help her family might be self-defeating, but she could not control her negative feelings about them or check her assurance that it was her mission to save them. In one mood, she sloughed off her sense of obligation, declaring to Dorothy Thompson: "It is a feminist work we have to perform. In the past women subscribed to the legend that the mother was always wrong, and gave themselves up to the sense of guilt. We have to refuse to go under." In another mood, she capitulated to the idea that "motherhood is a strange thing, it can be like being one's Trojan horse." She had received a "long and lacerating" letter identifying Anthony as an "amalgam of the two sons of Marion in *The Judge*." It was as though she were punished for the sins of her imagination. One of her letters to Emily Hahn during this period begins: "Let me be a croaking raven once more."

CHAPTER 33

In the Cauldron of South Africa
1960–1961

I

ON JANUARY 6, 1960, an excited Rebecca took flight for a three-month tour of South Africa. She told Henry she might not come back to him. She had accepted a *Sunday Times* offer to report on the apartheid regime of Dr. Verwoerd, encouraged by her doctor and attorney, who believed she needed a complete change of scene. It had all been so sudden—the call from the *Times*—and when Rebecca learned she would have a thousand pounds in expenses for her clothes, she did a sort of dervish dance and had the Rolls readied for a shopping trip.

Rebecca had been stuck on *This Real Night*, the sequel to *The Fountain Overflows*, for more than six months, troubled by various illnesses and mishaps (including a severe case of food poisoning, recurrent colitis, and a fainting fit), and by battles with Henry over his inept management of Isbtone and its farm. Henry had repeatedly resisted her attacks on her secretaries, which had begun after the war with the departure of the revered Margaret Hodges. Rebecca thought most of them incompetent and untrustworthy—which usually meant they failed to organize and keep up-to-date her enormous volume of correspondence and manuscripts, misplacing items and even reading her private and confidential letters. She suspected one of poisoning her. At the same time, Henry commandeered secretaries for correspondence Rebecca termed inconsequential or for assistance with books he never got around to writing. When one of the women became infatuated with him, Rebecca suspected him of trifling with her affections and putting Rebecca in the position of an inferior, catering to her secretary's physical and emotional needs. When Rebecca's most recent secretary had a complete collapse, manifesting both physical and mental symptoms (including partial paralysis, hip pain, delirium, and memory loss), Rebecca concluded that she had gone mad. Henry protested, saying it was only a case of being "a little overtired." Rebecca had had enough and made a violent scene. Indeed, she regarded this most recent incident as a symbol of the "madness that has been allowed to invade my life even by people who care for me."

Rebecca could tell Henry was shaken by the announcement of her departure. He had reluctantly sacked the secretary, then lavished on Rebecca birthday and Christmas gifts (including an expensive camera and a handsome set of luggage). Through a friend at Barclays Bank he arranged for meetings with important South African businessmen and industrialists. At the airport, there had been some problem with the plane. In the VIP lounge, Henry slipped a large tip to an airline official and told Rebecca, "It will be all right, my dear. I've just seen the pilot." Of course, it was not the pilot. This incident was typical of Henry, who had a "vision of air travel that might have been appropriate thirty or forty years before."

Rebecca complained to friends that she did not want to undertake an exhausting tour of Africa, but she needed a destination where Henry was not likely to follow. She was nearly seventy years old and realized it was time to get on with her fiction. But she was also proud of her journalism, and she realized that South Africa was at a pivotal point in its history.

Under Dr. Verwoerd, the country was extending the institutionalization of apartheid even as its majority black population mobilized to oppose it in organizations such as the African National Congress and the Pan Africanist Congress. Verwoerd's National Party had a huge Parliamentary majority, which overwhelmed a weak, irresolute United Party, the official opposition, and a new, small Progressive Party. Through the use of the infamous "Pass Laws" the government restricted the movement of urban blacks, requiring them to carry identity cards at all times and separating commuting males from their families, terming them "migrant bachelors." Verwoerd planned to eradicate the "black spots" in the cities, and drive blacks into Bantustans or rural enclaves, which lacked or were poorly equipped with basic community services.

Rebecca realized that Verwoerd's fanatical personality and policies fostered revolutionary politics. (Allister Sparks, a historian of South Africa, has called Verwoerd the "Lenin of apartheid.") Verwoerd had hijacked the National Party and fed on its Afrikaner sense of grievance against the British and much of the rest of the world which opposed apartheid. Rebecca's fourpart series for the *Sunday Times* branded apartheid immoral and impractical. As a rapidly industrializing country, South Africa would find that it could not do without its urban blacks, especially since the government refused to tax its white citizenry to provide the transportation and the infrastructure to support the massive removals of blacks from the cities. Sooner or later, the whites—sixty-five percent of whom were Afrikaners—would have to strike a deal with the blacks providing equal rights and economic opportunities. But would there be time to work out an agreement?, Rebecca wondered, for the National Party's disastrous extremism would be answered by black militancy and the machinations of the Communist Party.

On January 7, 1960, a bleary-eyed and swollen-legged Rebecca arrived in South Africa after an arduous twenty-hour flight, with stops in Rome and Khartoum. She had trouble adjusting to the altitude (6,000 feet), which made her feel like a "piece of stretched elastic" by the end of the day. Sarah Gertrude Millin, one of the few South African writers to have become famous in Britain and other parts of the world, met Rebecca at the airport. Gertrude had visited Rebecca in England, and Rebecca had read her books. One of South Africa's most formidable monologists, the widow of a judge and quite wealthy, Gertrude overwhelmed the jet-lagged Rebecca with a welter of observations Rebecca could barely hear, let alone absorb.

Rebecca later reflected on how Gertrude had a "stocky power," enabling her to "drag huge situations over the threshold of her novels and there control them." Rebecca found herself being fed on by this literary incubus. Gertrude doubted that Rebecca would be able to grasp the country's complexity and went on and on about it, first installing Rebecca at a hotel; then calling her in the early morning hours, trumpeting her solos. Rebecca took Gertrude's agitation as symptomatic of a whole country aroused by apartheid. In earlier days, Gertrude had been a happy woman in England when speaking of her country; now she sounded like a cello in her darker moods, and she became for Rebecca a metaphor for the outsider's difficulty in penetrating and identifying with an alien culture in turmoil.

Exhausted to the point of tears and longing to sleep during her first days in Johannesburg, Rebecca nevertheless could not help noticing the landscape. She had thought of South Africa as a tragic country like Spain, "a stage setting of doom and sacrifice," but the veld looked like Salisbury Plain, "it rose and fell like a rough sea but was serene as a calm lake." The distant mountains, the many trees—acacias, poplars, and willows—when drenched in the pure light, had a robust innocence about them. The days were hot, the rains hard, the evenings cool.

Rebecca kept a journal and sent Henry long letters about the country and its people, jotting down dialogue and descriptions. Soon after her arrival, an interviewer from South African radio leaned over and asked,

"Now tell me, Dame Sybil, why have you come to South Africa?" An overjoyed Rebecca gave her Dame Sybil Thorndyke impression. It charmed the press. In Johannesburg, her first stop, she noticed that only blacks walked on the street in the heat, which had cracked her Ferragamo shoes. Whites drove and lived in the suburbs, which she compared to Chislehurst—except the villas and gardens were larger and built at enormous expense to cover the rock and red gravel. She found little to impress her in middle-class homes, which she said were dully decorated and presided over by badly dressed women. She liked the fruits and vegetables, but she found the main courses were abominably prepared and almost inedible. When she went out to buy some stationery, she was advised not to hold her purse by its strap but to carry it under her arm. Africans were adept at sidling up to foreigners and expertly emptying handbags of their contents, even in full daylight. As Rebecca was watching a disturbed woman screaming in the street, she felt her bag, which she was hugging under her arm, being gently drawn backward. She turned and saw a young African standing behind her, dressed in a neat tobacco brown suit. Embarrassed, she smiled at him, and he reciprocated with a sweet and gay smile that relieved her anxiety. But the murder rate in Johannesburg was over five times that of London, and in her opinion the police were not professionally trained or reliable. None of them walked a beat; they directed traffic and drove around in cars. She was advised not to walk alone at night—not even to stroll from her hotel to a restaurant.

"Everybody, everybody, everybody is full of bitterness about the political situation," Rebecca reported to Henry. Curious, she went into a black shop to buy some fruit from an agitated clerk. "But when you saw what it was didn't you know you ought to walk straight out?" an amazed journalist asked her. Rebecca watched multitudes of blacks standing in line for buses, their brown faces emotionless, like washing hung on a line. Their infinite patience impressed her.

South African novelist Nadine Gordimer invited Rebecca for a friendly dinner, pleased that Rebecca had announced to the press that Nadine was at the top of her list of people to see. Nadine had visited Ibstone two years earlier and had enjoyed Rebecca's hospitality. She liked Rebecca's "deep, slightly throaty voice," and her reassuring, straightforward way of speaking. Rebecca was open, friendly, and self-possessed without seeming authoritarian or prickly. Nadine was impressed with her tolerance of Henry's rather dull remarks, realizing only much later that he was "suitable ballast for her temperament."

Rebecca was eager to renew their acquaintance, although she did not hold with Nadine's view of economic sanctions. The country needed capital to develop. She also thought Nadine was obsessed with white guilt and tried too hard to establish friendships with blacks, unlikely to thrive in the current atmosphere. But she had enormous faith in Nadine as a writer and expected her to "ultimately come through."

Rebecca saw no virtue in economic boycotts that would impoverish blacks before helping them. As she put it in her journal, it was the intellectuals who were "proud of their poverty or ashamed of their riches." Rebecca thought many of the liberals were phonies and Communist dupes, and she attacked the small Liberal Party for its advocacy of a universal franchise, because she believed that as in England voting rights should be extended gradually as the black population became more literate. She argued the point with the impressive Zulu chief Albert Luthuli, winner of the Nobel Peace Prize, a man with the "face of an apostle," and one of the defendants in the treason trial Rebecca attended.

Rebecca met several exceptional figures, such as Sydney Kentridge, a defense counsel at the trial. He drove her around Johannesburg one evening discussing South African politics. She thought him brilliant and attractive; he later became a friend and adviser, seeing her when he visited England the following year. She met Harry Oppenheimer, the millionaire son of the mining magnate, "modest and self-effacing," who as a member of Parliament had fostered the liberal wing of the United Party. "Johannesburg is as exciting as Berlin in time of blockade," Rebecca offered. Harry disagreed but wished people were that excited. Rebecca concluded that people like the Oppenheimers hoped to keep the machine of government ticking "until the rest of Africa comes together after falling apart."

At the treason trial Rebecca observed that there were so many black defendants (thirty) there were not enough places for them to sit in the old Jewish synagogue converted into a courtroom. It had been going on for an incredible three and a half years when she arrived. Initially there had been over one hundred fifty defendants. Some of them had been dismissed without explanation; others had been kept in custody or had their lives disrupted by interminable proceedings that made a mockery of justice. Rebecca attended some of the trial. She observed that one of the defendants employed a cane, an instrument of magic. When he held it to his ear, he wished his counsel's words to go straight into the judge's brain; when he made circles with it on his forehead, he wished the prosecutor's words to reach the judge in a garbled state. Eventually all of the defendants were acquitted, but some, like Albert Luthuli, were confined to limited areas and prohibited from attending meetings or making speeches.

During Rebecca's first month in Africa, Henry sent her news of home and offered to send her funds if her *Sunday Times* expense account did not cover everything she wanted to do. They did not say much about the problems that had contributed to Rebecca's departure until late January when Rebecca, brooding on her return home, sent Henry a long complaining telegram, which he answered in similar terms. They each rehashed grievances. Henry was unusually frank in suggesting that Rebecca did not respect his interests or his friends and had hurt his feelings on many occasions when his only thought was to help her. She excoriated him for not even mentioning that his erratic behavior had made it difficult to work, and that he humiliated her when he took the side of her secretaries. She concluded: "I really do not know what to do. I am devoted to you. . . . We live the life you want to live, and I have never grudged any sacrifice which seemed likely to make you happy. I have not done enough for you but I have done what I can. Nothing seems worth while any more." She wrote to Margaret Hodges that she felt "terribly like not going back to Ibstone, and resigning myself to be lonely in my old age." She asked Margaret to set Henry straight if he should seek out her consolation. Rebecca even looked to Lettie for support, writing a long letter explaining her estrangement from Henry. Then she sent Henry another letter which did not disclose her meeting with Harold Macmillan, who had just made his famous "wind of change" speech in the South African parliament, acknowledging the inevitability of the African liberation movements. She no longer took any pleasure in sharing things with Henry. "I am considering what can be done," she concluded.

Henry was not cowed this time. He found her suspicions of him and of her last secretary unfounded, indeed absurd and "divorced from reality." She could not really doubt that he had made her the center of his life, Henry asserted, ending his letter, "My dear dear Rac I love you so. Your Ric."

At an impasse, Rebecca decided to drop her attack and did not write to Henry for another two weeks, by which time she had ensconced herself in Cape Town. Before leaving England, she had confided in her attorney, Richard Butler, about her troubles with Henry. Henry had also been in touch with Butler and persuaded him that Rebecca had jumped to far too many conclusions. The tactful Butler wrote to Rebecca, advising a reconciliation. Rebecca, tired of arguing, received it gratefully.

In Cape Town, Rebecca met and admired the novelist Mary Renault, who introduced her to Zach de Beer, a Progressive Party leader. Mary found Dame Rebecca a "great lady" who turned out to be "very unpompous." Lady Joy Packer, a novelist and wife of a British admiral,

also liked Rebecca's forthright manner, expressed in her "limpid observant eyes." On a tour of the squatter slums, Joyce Newton Thompson,
Cape Town's mayor, asked Rebecca if she wanted to take photographs.
Rebecca covered her eyes and said, "Oh, no, no! That's always being
done." "That's why I asked," the mayor said. Joy noted how difficult it
was for strangers to South Africa to understand that the "entire country
was not established all in one piece at one and the same time." The
mayor had tensed for the conventional photo opportunity, but her face
cleared when she understood that Rebecca wanted something more. Joy
was especially impressed with Rebecca's dedication because Rebecca
had contracted "apricot sickness," a form of dysentery, and yet took no
short cuts in investigating a complex multiracial society new to her. The
mayor introduced Rebecca to Margaret Ballinger, who represented the
blacks in Parliament, and who won Rebecca's instant admiration for her
staunch but unsentimental support of her constituents.

Rebecca had her share of mishaps, chiefly with the phone system. At
one hotel, a befuddled switchboard operator, who noticed that Rebecca
was getting a number of calls, began directing any call for anybody with a
complicated name to her. At another hotel, she became the victim of a
breakdown the repairman said was unparalleled in his experience: every
call to the hotel was put through to her room for a period of twelve
hours. When she took her phone off the hook, it "fizzed like a firework."
The camera Henry had given her was so complicated she was not able to
load it with film. It took her an hour just to decipher the directions.

In Cape Town an eighty-seven-year old doctor, a "moth-eaten old
blackguard," said to Rebecca: "I hope you haven't come out to sob on
the necks of these black fellows. I've treated lots of them and done lots of
postmortems on them and they're no more like human beings than
zebras. They can't think. And you know the American Negro—it's all
very well till something happens, and out of it all comes all the primitive,
you know, cannibalism and all that!" She was astonished at C. R. Swart,
the Governor General, who emphasized the extraordinary difficulties
Afrikaners had had to face in the past fifty years. Were they really that
unique? she asked him, thinking of the wars that had devastated Europe.
Had Afrikaner history been as difficult as, say, Polish history? Swart
refused to concede first place in suffering, and Rebecca presented a
sharply etched picture of him in one of her *Sunday Times* articles, a conscientious but narrow-minded and chauvinistic official.

But Rebecca was by no means prejudiced against Afrikaners. Indeed,
she had the same affinity for them as for the American Southerners she
portrayed in "Opera in Greenville." She believed that Afrikaners were

morally superior to their government, which was controlled by a small band of men who had dedicated their lives to politics. She compared the government's condition with America in the late-nineteenth century during its first period of rapid industrial expansion, when the level of government officials was far below that of the people who elected them. She saw in everyday Afrikaners a humanity largely lacking in their National Party.

Rebecca reported on one Afrikaner who swore he had never gone to a doctor in his life, having always been treated by a black herbalist. He spoke Xhosa and wanted to bring up his son with a "pickaninny" companion. "Illegal," Rebecca pointed out. The startled Afrikaner reacted like a child deprived of its toy, "But how, what do you mean?" She explained that the man lived in a white area and no child under twelve was allowed to live in servants' quarters. But the child would not work, he would be a playmate, the Afrikaner protested. "It is illegal," Rebecca said cruelly. "Look it up." He denied it, but she could see he was beginning to have his doubts.

Rebecca became fond of an Afrikaner farmer, who got excited and bellowed like a bull about his land: "DAON'T YEW THINK THET IS A MOWST BEEYUTIFUL MAOUNTAIN!" He thought Rebecca had come to write a love story about the Transkei. He shepherded her around the countryside, relishing talks with the natives and deploring the missionaries who would not allow the bare-breasted Tembu women into church in their native clothing. Rebecca agreed that they were incomparably beautiful, although she regarded their faces, smeared with white chalk or ochre, as lurid. The women had oval faces, refined lips, beautifully molded cheeks, chins, and jaws, slender necks and perfectly proportioned shoulders, straight spines and coffee-brown to purple-black complexions like "so many Toulouse-Lautrecs." They smoked long pipes that looked like flutes. Rebecca thought African tribal life abysmal; it simply did not engage her imagination.

In mid-March Rebecca journeyed to Basutoland (now Botswana). She visited the Roman Catholic university, Roma, and spoke with several students and faculty members. She found African students obsessed with one issue: "one man one vote." She did not think it advisable to revolutionize the country as quickly as they wished, or that it was realistic to think that all of South Africa's problems were due to whites and to apartheid. "I do not see what is gained by shutting our eyes to various disagreeable facts about African life," she remarked in her journal, as she considered black-on-black violence and the absurd power of the witch doctors. She thought lasting change in Africa could only come about in gradual, evolutionary fashion. In Durban, she was impressed with the Indian population and worried that it would be overwhelmed in a state designed exclusively on the principle of one man, one vote.

On March 19, Rebecca returned to Johannesburg to begin writing her four *Sunday Times* articles, "In the Cauldron of South Africa." She craved quiet and peace of mind, so that she could order the massive material she had collected in her two and a half months of travel. She dreaded staying in another hotel, where she was sure to be pestered by Sarah Gertrude Millin and others, and she had had her fill of greasy and overcooked breakfasts. She found refuge with Lulu Friedman, a translator of Baudelaire and a member of the writers' organization, International PEN. She had stayed with Lulu during her initial visit to Johannesburg, and they quickly became friends, sharing an acerbic wit and love of gossip. Lulu once gave this arresting description of her houseguest to Nadine Gordimer: "She said that Rebecca had two faces in one: not divided vertically—most of us have a right-side profile that differs from the left-side one—but horizontally. The upper part of her face, the brow and magnificent eyes, was intensely spiritual; the lower half, forward-jutting, thick-lipped mouth and chin, was brutally sensual."

Lulu protected Rebecca's privacy when she returned to the city to write her articles, and installed her in comfortable surroundings with access to her well-stocked library. Lulu owned a large beautiful home called "Tall Trees" with a magnificent two-acre garden featuring double rows of immensely tall pine trees and an avenue of Spanish Cork Oaks. The two women commiserated with each other about their problem children; they saw each other several times in England and corresponded until Lulu's death in 1977.

Lulu's husband, Dr. Bernard Friedman, had resigned his United Party seat in Parliament in 1955, protesting his party leader's refusal to commit himself to restore the franchise to Coloreds in the Cape. (The National Party majority in Parliament had disenfranchised the Coloreds as part of its white supremacist program.) Bernard Friedman had been active in the establishment of the Progressive Party, which Rebecca called in her articles the only "contemporary" party in South Africa, dedicated to eradicating apartheid and to developing a nonracial government. Friedman was steeped in South African history. He later wrote a book about Jan Smuts, accounting for the demise of the United Party, and although he had lost his seat in Parliament, he was still called upon for advice and policy making. Rebecca delighted in his lucid explanations of events and personalities and found his conversation charming and erudite.

Rebecca had not gone to South Africa to do spot reporting—that is, dispatches on late-breaking events—but she could not very well avoid commenting on the March 21 riots in Sharpeville. Robert Sobukwe, the Pan Africanist Congress leader, had called for a pass-burning protest. In Langa, a black township south of Cape Town, blacks and police clashed violently. In Sharpeville, south of Johannesburg, a large crowd of unarmed blacks approached a police station with the intention of turning in their passbooks. A policeman panicked and fired into the crowd. Sixty-nine blacks were killed and more than one hundred eighty injured. Photographs of the slaughter were published around the world. As Helen Suzman, a founding member of the Progressive Party states: "Never had South Africa been more unpopular abroad." Inside the country there were more riots, and the resulting tension led to a declaration of a state of emergency on April 21 and the banning of the Pan Africanist Congress and the African National Congress.

Rebecca reacted powerfully to Sharpeville, telling Janet Flanner of *The New Yorker*: "you can hardly disguise a certain excitement which springs up when you are conscious that you may be arrested by white Africans at two in the morning or massacred by justly irritated black Africans at any hour of the day." Writing an article immediately after the riots, Rebecca struck exactly the right note in her lead paragraph, emphasizing both her outsider's view and her unequivocal judgment of history:

> The traveller in South Africa is not surprised by the riots in the African townships, because they are part of the pattern imposed on this unhappy country by Dr Verwoerd's Government. They are not a breakdown of the system, but its fulfillment.

As in her Greenville report, she did not condemn the white majority. Indeed, she praised the many conscientious civil servants who had tried to inject humanity and common sense into an evil policy. Her phrase "unhappy country" empathized with all citizens, white and black, who had to suffer the administration of laws by a cruel, idiotic leader. In her experience, there were few leaders indeed who did not have some virtues, however awful their policies. Dr. Verwoerd was the "exceptional candidate who scores zero." Sooner or later it would be realized that he had "no real affinity with the stoutly sensible Afrikaners."

Rebecca made this last point, not to placate the white majority, whose party controlled Parliament, but to recognize their humanity, which their own representatives had ignored. Similarly, her comments on the civil service were a recognition of the bureaucracy, which she knew was needed to govern modern nations. Even though many South African laws were unjust, she did not want to encourage distrust for the law as such. Her reporting, in other words, supported the positions she had staked out in *The Meaning of Treason* and *The Court and the Castle*.

When Dr. Verwoerd was shot in the head at close range at the Johannesburg Agricultural Show, Rebecca happened to be there. She heard the "crack-crack" of the gun, she saw Verwoerd's head disappear backward as if his chair had been pushed over. The assassin, a white man, apparently lost in thought, stood in front of Verwoerd. (Confined to a mental hospital, the assassin committed suicide.) Verwoerd recovered remarkably fast, his mental faculties unimpaired. Helen Suzman joked rather grimly that the bullet had only cleared his sinuses. Rebecca implied in her on-the-spot report that the assassination came at a moment when Dr. Verwoerd's political strength was subsiding. His speech at the agricultural show had been greeted without much enthusiasm—even by the Afrikaners, who did not seem to relish his defiance of the international community or his scorn for its good will. A second assassination attempt succeeded in September 1966.

Henry wrote to Rebecca, full of concern for her safety and advising her to make sure her friends always knew of her whereabouts. A woman journalist had been arrested, and Rebecca thought the police might take her and the Friedmans into custody, but the police seemed more interested in white fellow travelers and Communists. Henry knew he could trust her to be careful and that she had a better reading of the danger than he could have, but he reiterated: "Rac darling, I want you back."

On her return to Johannesburg, Rebecca noticed that some of her South African acquaintances treated her coldly, and she hypothesized that the Communists had been spreading the word against her. She had had a fight with Nadine Gordimer, who suggested that a British diplomat, Sir John Maud, had plotted on behalf of the Nationalist government—a suggestion Rebecca found preposterous. She had met Maud and been impressed with his anti-apartheid stance. When Gordimer did not attend Rebecca's farewell party, Rebecca took it as further evidence of a change in the political climate—that the Communists were trying to discredit anti-Communists in order to usurp the anti-Apartheid movement. She distinguished between the South African Left, which she supported, and the Far Left—"liars and intriguers," although she later conceded that the harsh Afrikaner government had driven many people from the Left into the Far Left.

2

REBECCA RETURNED home on April 12, 1960. She worked on the last two of her four articles. It had been an exhilarating trip. "It is fifty years since I got my first cheque for writing," Rebecca remarked. "How interesting that after half a century it has brought me this further thing, which it really did me good to go through." On Edward R. Murrow's television interview program, she rendered a smashing indictment of apartheid. The *Sunday Times* advertised her articles in electric lights in Picadilly Circus. She hoped to expand them and her South African diary into a book.

In early May, shortly after Rebecca's last South African article appeared in the *Sunday Times*, Justice Kennedy, one of the presiding judges at the treason trial, wrote a letter to the newspaper denying the words Rebecca attributed to him and calling them libelous. A confident Rebecca brushed the judge's letter aside, saying she had the corroboration of three witnesses, including Lulu Friedman. She awaited a transcript of the trial to confirm her version.

In early September a *Sunday Times* attorney reported that the trial record did not support Rebecca's version of Justice Kennedy's remarks. She cabled Sydney Kentridge for help. A week later, she learned that it was Justice Bekker who put the questions she attributed to Kennedy. Was it libelous to get her judges mixed up? she asked Kentridge. He replied that the trouble came in when Rebecca stated that Justice Kennedy's line of questioning filled in a breach in the Crown's case, for she ascribed a motive which could not be "established even against the judge who really put the questions." In his opinion, her words were defamatory, though a British lawyer should be the one to advise about libel. But he went on to damn her version of things by saying that although Kennedy's questions occasionally seemed weighted in favor of the Crown, his overall performance had not shown such a bias. Kentridge emphasized that he was not speaking out of "conventional respect for a judge," and he wished he had spotted her error more quickly. "It would appear some correction and apology is unavoidable," he concluded. The issue dragged on for nearly another year, with Rebecca desperately seeking some way out. When Lettie suggested Rebecca should own up and get the embarrassing matter out of the way, Rebecca hardly spoke to her for more than a year. Justice Kennedy sued for sixteen thousand pounds in damages but finally settled for £3,500 and an apology from Rebecca and the newspaper.

How could Rebecca have made such a blunder? Sydney Kentridge suggests that it was hard to hear testimony in court—especially from high up in the gallery, where Rebecca sat with her friends, instead of at the press table. In letters to friends she complained about troubles with her hearing, worsened by the high altitude. She turned to Lulu Friedman at the fatal moment and asked her which judge was asking questions. She had trusted a friend and had been misinformed.

Sydney Kentridge, who advised Rebecca throughout her ordeal, and who visited her several times in England, witnessed her mortification over this blow to her reputation: "I got the impression that she thought it was one of the worst things that ever happened to her." He told her that one slip should not ruin her otherwise brilliant articles. Given her standing, he was astonished that she should take her mistake so much to heart, but she felt she had let down the *Sunday Times*. Later, when they met again, he could see that she wanted to expunge the entire episode from her mind. In letters to friends, she turned things completely around, accusing the *Sunday Times* of letting her down, condemning her English lawyer as incompetent, and branding Kennedy as part of the South African government's conspiracy against her, which included a falsification of the court record. She felt she had been treated shabbily by the *Sunday Times* lawyers, and she prolonged their effort to settle by endless speculation on how she could not have gotten things wrong. After the settlement she met with the paper's owner, Roy Thomson, who pointed out to her that if she had acted promptly and issued an apology, Judge Kennedy would not have brought his action. Thomson told her that she was considered "a difficult lady." She gaped, since it seemed to her she had been at the mercy of the *Times*'s attorney. Nevertheless, Thomson said he hoped she would continue writing for them. To Rebecca that seemed like an "invitation to bathe whenever I liked in a crocodile pool."

3

WINNIE DIED on May 31, 1960, shortly after Rebecca returned from South Africa, and she was inconsolable, writing to Lulu Friedman that Winnie was "Big Sister" who had protected her against "Bigger Sister." She remembered Winnie's love of poetry, regretted she had not had a writing career, and mourned the "refined beauty" of her youth. Few of Rebecca's friends ever got to know Winnie; she resembled rather a myth Rebecca had fashioned—similar to the "Lady of Shalott," which Winnie had recited to her baby sister. To Rebecca, Winnie was the lady living in the mirrored world of her own fantasies. She had taken to her bed, refused reality, and died. Rebecca's former secretary, Anne Charles McBurney, who did see something of Winnie, missed her sweet face and gentle wit. Rebecca portrayed herself as Winnie's chief mourner.

Dorothy Thompson's death in February 1961 also undid Rebecca, who for a few months considered dropping everything to edit a collection of Dorothy's letters. Dorothy had suffered a major heart attack and been in ill-health for more than a year. Shortly before she died, she wrote Rebecca a long letter detailing her misery over her son and praising Rebecca for overcoming the "horrid streak of masochism" that bedeviled women who took their troubles with husbands and children too much to heart. She lauded Rebecca as a woman who was not "a prisoner of her maternity, and who still possesses the power of indignation, not only impersonally, but on her own behalf." Rebecca had known Dorothy for forty-one years. They had met when Dorothy was a "singularly composed girl in her twenties, whom nothing it seemed would disconcert." Later, she had exhibited extraordinary resilience during a horrible marriage to Sinclair Lewis and its aftermath. She had been part of the "structure of life, like the Maine coast or the cliffs of Dover."

Henry tried to distract Rebecca from her mourning. He plied her with gifts, spending close to three thousand pounds on an aquamarine necklace, a diamond brooch, and two lead sphinxes of Madame Pompadour and Madame Du Barry, with "lovely coiffures, and ravishing decolletages, and paws crossed in front of them on cushions." They were set out on the new terrace at Ibstone. Rebecca treasured them, but she continued grieving. Even Henry gave up when she said his gifts were not what she wanted. If she felt like that, he said, they had better separate. He would take a flat in town. She asked him to give up the idea, still feeling fond of him—and loyal and responsible for him. She also dreaded what people would think. He had such good press as the doting husband. "Let it pass," she said. Two days later she went into his room while he was dressing and overheard him say to himself, as he was adjusting his tie in the mirror, "Rac, I've *tried* and *tried* to make you happy. . . ." She thought she might "crack and fly."

CHAPTER 34

Cross Fire
1960–1966

I

REBECCA DID NOT crack and fly. She stayed home and played the piano, "solidly working through Bach's *Six Little Preludes*." At breakfast, Rebecca liked to go to the window and watch the cats and pheasants "apparently expressing views on the weather." She had a new pet, a golden Labrador, Albert, named after the Prince Consort. She called him a "very sentimental version of Don Juan," untrainable but a wonderful walking companion. When he howled around the house, she translated: "but I want to marry the girl!" Rebecca's cat, Mr. Briggs, hissed at Albert, disapproving (Rebecca asserted) of Albert's disheveled appearance.

Albert was a magnificent beast, but a BEAST. Busy Rebecca counted on servants to give him a good walk, but he did not always get enough exercise. He got bored and chewed his plastic dish. When Rebecca took him out in her garden, he would chase the rabbits. "Aren't you ashamed of yourself?" she would ask him. One morning in the drawing room, while Rebecca sat in a beautiful Dior suit reading the newspaper, a cup of coffee on her lap, Albert entered, wanting to be stroked. So he just put his big head in her lap, spilling the coffee all over her. Henry's visiting cousin, Irene Garthwaite, became upset, thinking of that expensive silk suit. Rebecca said, "Irene, don't worry. Albert is in such dear need of love. Albert, I should have stroked you before I took this coffee."

Worried about Lettie, now in her mid-seventies, Rebecca carried on a correspondence with Lettie's neighbors, Vera Watson and Maboth Mosley, who were very fond of the perky and intellectually vigorous Lettie and somewhat confused by Rebecca's vehement protestations that her older sister needed so much looking after. Rebecca feared that the generous Lettie would give all her money away. "For goodness' sake," she exhorted her niece Alison, "take the money Lettie offered for Cathy's

340

[Alison's daughter] holiday lest it go either to the Blew-Joneses [Aunt Sophie's side of the family] or to the Society for the Preservation of Catholic Macaws on the Upper Amazon."

Rebecca also worried that Henry would do something reckless that would ruin them. He could not remember what she told him, replying with his usual refrain: "this is the first I've heard of it." He would leave home without money and once had to borrow some from his farm bailiff. He would promise to take Rebecca to the city or to the airport and then disappear—off to collect the morning papers and mail because he could not wait for them to be delivered, and then to stop in town to chat up a female clerk at a shop counter. On one occasion, Rebecca gave up on Henry and was about to depart, having asked her farm bailiff, Harold Tomlinson, to drive her to the airport. Henry finally appeared. "She could sweat a bit," Harold remembered. John Hodges had once seen her beat with both hands on an unflappable Henry's chest.

Rebecca claimed that even after twenty years in the country Henry could barely tell the difference between a rose and a tulip. Harold Tomlinson observed him walking around in city suits: "I don't think he owned a pair of rubber boots." But Henry thought of himself as a gentleman farmer and liked to give guests the benefit of his agricultural knowledge, which in fact was negligible. On one of their visits to Ibstone, Norman Macleod's wife, Marion, mentioned how much her children had enjoyed Ibstone's strawberries the previous year. Henry's gardener told him that unfortunately the current crop had not been good. But the next day Henry found a farmer nearby with exquisite strawberries and bought several pounds. He asked the man where they had come from. "Oh, from Ibstone," he replied. Henry said nothing. But he returned home and immediately sacked the gardener.

2

IN EARLY JANUARY 1962, Rebecca and Henry sailed for Barbados. She hoped it would alleviate her chronic bronchitis. She told Marshall Best, her editor at Viking, that the trip represented a "desperate effort to get a short story written." Gwenda David, Viking's representative in London, had suggested a holiday to Henry, for it was obvious that Rebecca could no longer work at home. Gwenda, Rebecca's confidante, did much to soothe Rebecca over the recent death of her devoted publisher, Harold Guinzberg.

After extraordinary mishaps boarding the ship, delays in airline connections, illnesses and mechanical breakdowns, Rebecca and Henry arrived in Barbados and settled into the Sandy Lane Hotel, the haunt of millionaires who seemed delighted that each room had a toaster. With such high prices, each room ought to be equipped with a guided missile, Rebecca remarked, and crabbily observed it was no better than going to Bournemouth. The food was mediocre, but the bathing could not have been better. In an improved mood, she called Barbados "like a piece of the West Country, which has drifted out to sea."

Rebecca spotted an ailing T. S. Eliot and his new young wife, Valerie. Rebecca admired Valerie's beauty and the touching way she led her enfeebled husband by the hand. They had a ground-floor room and sat on the veranda playing patience. The Eliots invited the Andrews for a round of drinks. Tom croaked to Rebecca about thrillers, sharing her liking for Simenon. Later at dinner, in a restaurant Eliot selected, Rebecca bridled at his exhibition of suffering over the noisy orchestra—as if *she* had chosen their rendezvous. Rebecca read the menu and said, "I see there's some good white burgundy"—in her opinion, the only passable wine on the list. She took Eliot's reply as a rebuke: "Had we better not wait till we see what we are going to *eat* before we think of what we are going to *drink?*" Rebecca refrained from picking the lamp up off the table and giving him a tap with it. Instead she quizzed him on his reading, realized it was superficial and decided, "I do not see anything in this man but the charlatan I have always seen." She and Henry dined again with Eliot in November 1963 at his London flat, which was full of paintings and drawings of him, of his framed poetry, diplomas and awards. "[A]n awful man," Rebecca concluded.

Three lovely weeks in Barbados and a month in New York without Henry restored Rebecca's zest. She reminisced with old friends—Emanie Arling, Doris Stevens, Evelyn Hutchinson, Alice Guinzberg (Harold's widow), and Bruce and Beatrice Gould of the *Ladies' Home Journal.* She visited Virginia Salomon, a new friend picked up in Barbados. Rebecca found Virginia's sweet, agreeable temper soothing. They went to Virginia's dancing class where sixty-nine-year-old Rebecca, instructed by a Puerto Rican teacher called "Killer Joe," enjoyed applying herself to the Twist. She met Katherine Anne Porter, "a giggling idiot of a Southern beauty . . . dressed in a ridiculous skimpy dress with an orchid corsage as worn by presidents of women's clubs." How could this farcical character be a writer? Yet she spoke beautiful French. Rebecca had two pleasant lunches with H.G.'s authorized biographer, Gordon Ray, whom she supposed was "cultivating my acquaintance." Or was she cultivating him? She confessed she had a "warm liking" for Gordon and wanted to give him access to H.G.'s letters to her so as to counteract *Heritage*'s portrait of her.

Rebecca gave a lecture at Columbia University, interrupted by a drunk who hollered: "Bull, shut up, it's all bull." He had the look of an angry god as conceived by William Blake. He stood in a white mackintosh in the middle of the lecture hall. Rebecca looked out at the shocked faces, laughed, and fell off the reading stand. The Blake-looking prophet made a splendid sweeping gesture and disappeared. After that, she found the audience all hers. She could do "anything with them."

Sailing home in late March, Rebecca enjoyed meeting Mary McCarthy aboard ship. Mary paid tribute to Rebecca's sparking conversation but thought her "cracked . . . she imagines that various authors are alluding to her and all her relations under disguises in their books."

3

IN THE SPRING OF 1962, Rebecca returned home to another crisis. Sound asleep on the A40 Henry had driven on the wrong side of the road and charged into a truck, completely demolishing his Daimler but fortunately harming no one—not even himself. He had always been a reckless driver, waving his arms about as he talked to other people in the car, grinding the gears and swerving into oncoming traffic. Lately, he had also begun to nod off as well—in the car, at home, anywhere. Rebecca had complained to the local doctor, who thought she was exaggerating. Now Henry would be prosecuted for dangerous driving.

After extensive medical tests, Dr. Michael Kremer told Rebecca that Henry was suffering from "atrophy of the brain" or cerebral arteriosclerosis. Winnie had succumbed to a similar disease and had withdrawn from Rebecca, as Henry now seemed to be doing—looking older and locked away in his own world. His intelligence had not been affected, but his temperament, sight, hearing, and impaired gait revealed brain damage. Kremer told Rebecca it was extremely rare for a person to have two relatives, themselves unrelated, with this affliction. It was "very bad luck," he said. Rebecca called it her destiny. Henry was not aware of it, but his mind was shrinking. Dr. Kremer gave Henry two, perhaps as many as four or five years to live. The degeneration had probably been going on for twenty years, predisposing Henry to act illogically. Kremer added: "I can see this is a great tragedy, he evidently had a fine mind and a fine physique." A stunned Rebecca began reevaluating the past two decades; she felt guilty about the blame she had heaped on Henry. She agreed with Kremer that Henry was not to know. Nothing much could be done about the condition. Henry would not notice that anything was wrong; it was pointless to tell him. A relieved Rebecca heard Dr. Kremer say Henry should not drive again. Yet until his last illness Henry continued to drive—against all advice and in the wake of a court case in which he narrowly missed serious conviction. It was one of those circumstances that proved to Rebecca that the gods were against her. With any luck at all, she should have been relieved of the anxiety of his driving, and Ibstone should have been sold. She could not enforce either outcome because she knew it would deprive Henry of his two greatest pleasures. It would also rob her of any influence she had over him. He would not listen to her at all if she insisted on revoking the things that made his day.

Although Rebecca lamented her plight, she also saw the absurd humor of it, of Henry as a kind of Mr. Magoo cartoon figure who kept walking through life oblivious of the mayhem he caused. Events conspired to smooth a path through the wreckage for him. In court, she was astonished to hear Henry's lawyer praise him as a prominent man, a contributor to various charities, a pillar of the community, and so on. She was outraged. Henry was let off with a thirty guinea fine and kept his driving license. Afterward she confronted his counsel. How could he describe Henry in such false terms? How could he square his conscience with his defense of such a reckless driver? The abashed lawyer looked down at his notes and cried out: "My God, I've mixed up my cases and defended the wrong man!" Henry celebrated by purchasing a Lancia.

The story is apposite to what life was like with Henry. Rebecca's nephew Norman once accompanied Henry on a motor trip during which Henry cannoned into the car ahead of him. There was a tinkle of glass. As the driver quitted his car, angered and shaken, the tall Henry approached the aggrieved party, stood over him, pulled out a huge roll of notes, and began to peel them off, saying, "So sorry." Then Henry went on his way; he always went on his way. Much to Rebecca's incredulity, he was "completely unperturbed." In fact, he was "perfectly cheerful, indeed quite debonair." He had been slowly declining for twenty-five years, yet no one seemed to notice it but her. Henry said he felt fine.

Rebecca yearned for the services of a "reliable witch doctor," for she had been doing a "tour of several different sorts of hells." Still hoping to finish a short story, a gallbladder attack felled her; then a new pear-shaped secretary in stiletto heels, who did no work—as if expecting any moment she would topple over—impeded her. Rebecca replaced another secretary who sat over the typewriter in "architectural immobility." When Rebecca found one that suited her, Henry disliked the woman, and Rebecca—caught in the "cross fire"—had to let her go.

4

IN LATE SUMMER 1962, Rebecca participated in a forum on censorship at the Edinburgh Festival. She called it "an indescribable orgy of bad taste, vulgarity, and bad criticism, with homosexuality of the vulgarest sort, pornography, and drug-taking exalted as the perfect recreations of the artist and his inspiration too." Although the press gave Mary McCarthy high marks for her firm chairmanship, Rebecca called her a "spavined Sacred Cow" for lending herself to this spurious crowd of litterateurs. After the fourth day, Rebecca swept out, pronouncing an anathema on the assembly. Back at her billet (a well-staffed Victorian house) she found a Corgi had eaten her favorite red shoes. Off to dinner at her nephew Norman's she was surprised to find Lettie answering the door and announcing: "I was at the Conference this afternoon, I could have made a far better speech than you did."

Rebecca had been incensed at the appearance of Henry Miller, that "odious old phoney," and the lizardlike William Burroughs, author of *Naked Lunch*, a book of "unparalleled filth." Next to the degenerate Miller, that "idiot gorilla" Norman Mailer looked like a "wholesome farm boy." Mailer's idea of conversation was "oafish and ragging." Rebecca dismissed Miller's friend, Lawrence Durrell, as a "squat little thing." These grotesques were worse than a sideshow at a carney. Stephen Spender was practically the only sane one there. Everyone else was more concerned with their sexual habits than with writing. Some writers like Muriel Spark seemed to enjoy the conference; others were nearly as caustic as Rebecca.

She objected to literature that was no more than a form of materialism. This is what sex amounted to in *Lolita*, and it is what vitiated that brilliant book, she believed. She was against censorship, but she objected to literature that had no moral standard or redeeming value. She had given evidence in favor of D. H. Lawrence in the *Lady Chatterly's Lover* trial, contending that the novel was not "obscene at all," that it demonstrated that "sex without love was of no service to anybody whatsoever." She thought Lawrence's use of four-letter words "foolish" but a minor blemish. He supposed he could deprive the words of their obscene value by using them frequently, but you might as well say that if you coshed people on the head sufficiently, it would stop hurting.

In Rebecca's estimation, the sexual freedom male authors advocated degraded women. She reported on the trial of Dr. Stephen Ward, who had pimped for a Cabinet minister, introducing John Profumo to call girl Christine Keeler. Ward had also befriended a Soviet agent, though it was doubtful that there had been any significant breach in government security. Rebecca was aghast at how little sympathy Christine Keeler and her confederate Mandy Rice-Davies received: "Here were a number of girls whose beauty ought to have aroused tenderness and sweetness who were used by men only to be beaten. . . . It wouldn't matter if there wasn't this alliance with literature, with Norman Mailer and Laurence Durrell and Nabokov." She took issue with the Labor opposition leader, Harold Wilson, who lamented that harlots were paid twenty-five times more than prime ministers and 250 times as much as members of Parliament. "Nobody sensible would go to a nightclub to see members of Parliament coming down staircases dressed in sequins and tail-feathers unless there were at least 250 of them; you need a lot, as market-gardeners cunningly say when they are selling plants, to make a show." Dr. Stephen Ward, she concluded, represented a society that used women as commodities. Look at the way he had taken home a prostitute simply because he had spotted her standing next to a cigarette machine, Rebecca emphasized, "two machines standing side by side, waiting for custom." It made her look at the men in the courtroom as so many marionettes. Alarmed, she saw that the Profumo case involved not only a government minister, but the law as well; the case impugned the integrity of society itself. Rebecca found that women mobbed Christine and Mandy in the streets, as though they were the "fruition of sex!" The women Rebecca met at cocktail parties also envied the pair of them. A disgusted Rebecca cracked that Christine and Mandy were the "only girls too bright not to marry peers." Offered "vast sums" to write a book on Christine Keeler, Rebecca was tempted but declined, still hoping to write more fiction but, as usual, complaining of the interruptions that prevented her from doing so.

Instead she revised *The Meaning of Treason*. She added new material on Communist spies and on the Profumo affair, reshaping her earlier pieces on Joyce and Amery, and making Joyce a symbol throughout the book of the decline of the amateur traitor, who betrayed his country as a matter of conviction, not profession. Marshall Best at Viking won her approval of a new title, *The New Meaning of Treason*, which alluded not only to the new version of her book but also the changing meaning of treason—now pursued not so much for the principle of the thing as for gain. The Ward trial demonstrated how degenerate and almost apolitical traitors had become; they merely flirted with the fringes of power. Many of the professional spies, like John Vassall, had blended into the British government; their discovery not only alerted the public to lax security procedures, it called into question the government's ability to maintain its integrity. This compromising of the British nation was as damaging as any secrets Vassall handed over to the Russians.

The New Meaning of Treason became a critical and popular success. "God doesn't love women writers. But I've had good reviews from his creatures, I must say," Rebecca admitted. She had a windfall of $30,000 when the Book of the Month Club decided to adopt *The New Meaning of Treason* as a main selection.

5

REBECCA'S MAJOR MEDIUM of expression in the early 1960s was *The Sunday Telegraph*, which offered her a regular spot for thirty-five guineas a review every three weeks. She liked to keep her hand in, making it a little more difficult, she thought, for reviewers to treat her badly when her books appeared. Reviewing also kept her abreast of her rivals, including her son Anthony. She read his reviews assiduously in *The New Yorker*— praising some for their learning and wit, blaming others for their stupidity and superficiality. When his opinions differed from hers, she regarded them as personal attacks—which they were.

When Anthony denigrated Christopher Herald's positive portrait of Madame de Staël, pointedly treating her as an actress in love with amateur theatricals, Rebecca wrote two reviews, one in the *Times Literary Supplement* and another in *Encounter*, defending Madame de Staël's personality and politics. To Anthony, Madame de Staël was a phony, a meddling, selfish, power-mad woman whose life and writing were vastly overrated. To Rebecca, Madame de Staël was one of the key personalities and writers who had resisted Napoleon and spoken up staunchly for human liberty. Anthony contended that Madame de Staël had wanted to marry Napoleon and had turned against him only when Napoleon rejected her. This interpretation came very close in its nuances to Rebecca's love/hate affair with Max Beaverbrook. Rebecca, for her part, suspected that Max helped to finance Anthony's career.

Anthony surprised Rebecca in the summer of 1961 with a letter apologizing for any hurt he had caused her. She reacted cautiously. In mid-August, she began a long letter to him, expressing regret over their estrangement for the past six years and wishing to end the separation between them. She never finished the letter, attempting at least four drafts before she abandoned it. It was an agony to rehash for Anthony her life with H.G., and there were private things she would never tell him, just as she would never expect him to confide in her the intimate aspects of his personal life. One draft noted that she had not replied to his bid for reconciliation sooner because she had not been able to write with his simplicity. In another draft, she explained her hesitancy as an inability to decide whether to accept his offer of peace and happiness, or to voice the doubts that troubled her. She contested the idea that she was a cold, unfeeling mother. On the contrary, because she would never have chosen to inflict on a child the disadvantages of illegitimacy, she felt for him a "particular poignancy." She explained the extenuating circumstances that made her less than an ideal mother, and she did not doubt that she had failed her son on many occasions. But she could not believe that she deserved *Heritage*, and when it was published her inclination was to explain nothing to him. She disputed many of Anthony's recollections of his childhood but gave up the effort, apparently a victim of her vacillation.

Lettie told Rebecca's nephew Norman that Henry had advised against making it up with Anthony, for Henry believed that Anthony only wanted to smooth the way for the English publication of *Heritage*. Neither mother nor son could disguise or abate the sense of shame each felt the other had caused them. In another exchange of letters they reiterated their grievances, with Rebecca complaining to Kitty about Anthony's "Mr Chadband tone."

Rebecca saw Anthony the next year in New York. She had sent no advance word of her arrival, not certain that she should see him. Anthony's feelings were also mixed; he had had a disturbing premonition of her coming. Mother and son were not only alike temperamentally, they shared an interest in the occult. They thought of themselves as Celts—anything but stolid English people. One night at about four, just before first light, Anthony and Lily suddenly awoke and could not get back to sleep. Later that day a friend told them Rebecca was in town—in fact her ship had docked the moment they had awakened.

Anthony's talk was pleasant but superficial. Rebecca complained about one of his autobiographical stories in *The New Yorker*. Then she asked him: "Why did you tell people that I had prevented you from writing Wells's biography?" Anthony denied it: "Who told you that lie?" Rebecca said, "Ross, to name one among many." Anthony shrugged her off: "Well, you know what Ross was." He changed the subject, saying he wanted her and Lily to be friends. She suspected him of turning the tables on her, inventing a situation that would pit one woman against another. She found him "uneasy, tongue-tied, untruthful."

A fragile reconciliation developed over the next few years, with Anthony and Lily visiting Rebecca a few times during their vacations in England. An apprehensive Rebecca disapproved of his desire to resettle in England. The literary landscape had changed so much she did not see how he could fit in. She also wondered whether he might not be devising some nefarious plot against her that required getting her into closer range. The birth of Anthony's daughter gave her no joy. She regarded it as another family entanglement, especially since she was named Sophie, reminding Rebecca of her abhorred aunt. "As for Lily," Rebecca vouchsafed to Kitty, "I think she may be nice but she's also a grinning idiot."

When Rebecca's grandson Edmund decided to attend medical school in America, she suspected that Anthony would not be able to pay Edmund's tuition (perhaps five times as great as it would be in England), and it would be left to her to support her grandson. Rebecca blamed Kitty for encouraging Edmund to look to America. In fact, it had been Edmund's idea to stay in the United States. He thoroughly enjoyed summers at his father's home in Stonington and planned to settle there.

Anthony had expressed some concern to Rebecca about the costs of Edmund's medical education, but he hoped to solve that problem with Kitty's help: their marriage settlement allowed the use of certain sums for their children's education. He told Rebecca he resented her effort to recall Edmund to England, as well as her campaign to get Edmund to consult with her nephew Norman, whom Anthony dismissed as a stranger who could not possibly be in a position to advise his son. Anthony and Edmund had consulted several English and American doctors and were not acting in the dark, as Rebecca supposed: "If you had any conception of the lavish scale of equipment, the scale of operation, and the variety and intensity of medical experience offered by an American teaching hospital I am sure that you would not be able to compare the costs of English and American medical education in the simplistic terms which you employ." Rebecca took her rebuff as another instance of Anthony's folly and bad faith. His response made her dread the appearance of a sequel to *Heritage*. When he wrote again, trying to keep an avenue open to his mother, she scornfully quoted his "horrible Chadband" sentence to Kitty: "Dear Rac, we love you so much but you make it so difficult for us to love you."

Rebecca did not see Anthony again until the spring of 1965, when Edmund received his undergraduate degree in biology from New York University and she was awarded an honorary doctorate. Edmund had just been accepted into the George Washington University medical school. Rebecca met and liked his new wife, Vita, whom she thought pretty, sensible, and chic. Edmund and Vita invited her to their Roman Catholic wedding, arranged after their civil ceremony to please Vita's mother and her family.

Accompanied by Bruce Gould of *The Ladies' Home Journal*, seventy-two-year old Rebecca breezed into the wedding reception in a regal manner, flushed with the excitement of a ride in a hot-air balloon that had just missed grazing power lines. As Vita listened to the breathless account, it seemed to her that Rebecca had welcomed the danger because it made such a good story.

Rebecca met Vita's widowed mother and other members of her Italian immigrant family, whom Rebecca admired for their good manners, hardy integrity, and neat home. She did not recognize Anthony at first, for he had grown fat, seemed to have lost his chin, and looked altogether like a has-been ham actor. She thought Anthony's teasing of his eyebrows an attempt to ape H.G.'s bushy ones. Vita thought the eyebrows made him look Faustian. To Rebecca, Edmund seemed a normal and happy young man, unaware of his father's troubles. To Vita, Edmund was merely pursuing a lifelong strategy of keeping his own counsel, refusing to be drawn into the family's cross fire. Rebecca judged Anthony impenitent, "smug and frightfully silly." They barely managed a conversation, carefully avoiding each other by staying in different rooms most of the time. Anthony got blind drunk and cried on the shoulder of one of Vita's uncles, telling him in copious detail how nasty his mother had been to him. Rebecca later lunched with Anthony, who was "all smiles," having just signed a lucrative book contract with McGraw-Hill.

At the end of the summer, Rebecca received Edmund and Vita at Ibstone. This would be the first of several visits. Every time they came, there seemed to be a new secretary, new staff, including a Portuguese butler who served meals with one arm tucked behind his back, with Henry at the other end of the table pontificating—or was he being funny? Vita could not tell. One of his disquisitions was on that humble fruit, the tomato. Perhaps he peeled an orange for her, as he had done for other female guests. He cut it around the top, and then he'd slice the peel in segments. It avoided the messiness.

6

THROUGHOUT THE AUTUMN OF 1965 Rebecca worked fitfully on the last two chapters of her Russian novel. She had succeeded in resurrecting it after a twenty-year interval, presenting it to Viking's "invaluable

Gwenda." Gwenda David read it on the train after a weekend at Ibstone and "practically wept." It was no good. What should she tell Rebecca? Henry called, "You haven't let Rebecca know what you think of the novel." "I will in a few days," Gwenda replied. Then Rebecca got on the phone, and Gwenda decided to be honest, if tactful. She told Rebecca it was slow, it was forced, and gave her a detailed reaction to the draft. "Right," Rebecca said, as she sat down to rewrite it.

By the end of March 1966, Rebecca sent her Russian novel, originally titled *Cockcrow*, then retitled *The Shoot*, and finally titled *The Birds Fall Down* to Viking, telling Tom Guinzberg, Harold's son, it was fascinating history but "rum" fiction. She doubted that she had brought her characters to life. Later she thought the novel her most accomplished work of fiction. She explained to Tom that the double agent, Kamensky, was based on the famous Azeff, who had simultaneously been the chief spy for the Tsarist government and head of the battle organization of the Social Revolutionary Party. In contemporary terms, it would be like discovering that J. Edgar Hoover was actually head of agit-prop for the Soviet Union.

Rebecca set the novel in 1900 to avoid dealing with the failed revolution of 1905 and the rise of Lenin and the Bolsheviks. She based some of her other characters on historical figures, and a few on Russians she remembered visiting her father in turn-of-the century London. There were "two shoots" in the novel: Kamensky destroyed himself, his plans, and his surroundings because in him "two systems, equally intricate, collide." Kamensky, Laura Rowan (the novel's heroine), and her father Edward are all blind to their circumstances and work at cross-purposes. Edward is of no use to his daughter because he is having an affair with his wife's best friend. Laura does not realize that Kamensky is in love with her because she "wants her father back."

Rebecca had been wanting all her life to wind a plot so tight that it would be impossible to sever the individual from the group, private life from history. Her father, Slavic-featured, and completely enmeshed in the public and political issues of his time, had deserted his family. His youngest daughter wanted him back, and like Laura, had to learn how to survive without him in the cross fire of history.

In the novel's first version (abandoned in 1944), Rebecca got stuck over how to develop Laura's later career after Kamensky's death. Rebecca finally realized that the whole novel could be a triangulated plot pivoting on a moment of pre-revolutionary history, with Laura as the apex of contending forces. In the dialogue between Nikolai and his revolutionary adversary, Chubinov, Laura finds herself literally caught in the middle—as she is caught in the estrangement between her Russian mother and English father. Laura straddles a divide between nations, ideologies, and personalities. Her grandfather Nikolai regards the Tsar as the representative of God the Father. Nikolai himself behaves with a sense of omnipotence founded on his profound religious beliefs. He is opposed to the modern idea of government as a human and historical construct, amenable to the pressures of change and the cataclysms of history. His death is the irrevocable demise of divinely sanctioned government, and of the idea that human authority can have a transcendent source. After him, there is only history, the process of unregulated change. In acting to save herself, Laura must deceive Kamensky and play the role of double agent herself. Her moment in history is thus a forecast of the betrayals and treacheries yet to come.

CHAPTER 35

Survivors in Mexico
1966–1967

I

THE VERDICT ON *The Birds Fall Down* at Viking: a winner. They immediately prepared for publication in fall 1966. Macmillan concurred, and the Book of the Month Club adopted the novel as a main selection, netting Rebecca $37,500. Royalties from book sales came to nearly that much, for it became a best-seller. Rebecca's royalties from *The New Meaning of Treason* topped $60,000 for the 1967 and 1968 tax years. Henry's large losses as an underwriter at Lloyd's, and the smaller losses of Ibstone's farm, were used to offset this high income.

Reviews of *The Birds Fall Down* were good to excellent, with a few notable exceptions; some reviewers seemed irritated by the book's long conversations and the hoopla surrounding its publication—an author's tour in October and several flattering notices and interviews. V. S. Pritchett, the most perceptive reviewer, observed that Rebecca's Russians "majored in being Russian." He admired her beautiful evocations of the French countryside, through which Nikolai and Laura travel—a product of Rebecca's reverence for things French. As she told several interviewers, she had had a French career, combining journalism and fiction in a way that seemed natural to her Gallic colleagues but foreign to the British. Similarly, her novel reflected a continental blend of ideas and action, characters and arguments. She pointed out that the exchanges some critics found improbable were commonplace in 1900. For her, dialogue, much more than description, revealed character. In her *Sunday Telegraph* reviews she chided novelists such as Iris Murdoch for talking too much about their characters rather than letting them talk.

2

REBECCA FOLLOWED her author's tour of America in October 1966 with her first visit to Mexico, telling an interviewer: "I've always promised myself I'd see the Mayan ruins before I died." *The New Yorker*'s editor, William Shawn, agreed to finance the trip, hoping it would produce several articles. Mexico City astounded her—a jumble of nineteenth-century French villas, skyscrapers, garden city houses, sixteenth-century churches, and hovels. She thought its modern architecture made everything in Europe or the U.S. "weak and indecisive." An hour from this "formidable capital" she found mountains and lakes that reminded her of Switzerland, another hour away, subtropical weather and gorgeous flowers. She found an Aztec pyramid abutting a railroad siding. The museums and the food were fabulous.

Mexico City had the usual urban congestion; it provoked Rebecca to contrast the present and the past: "The Indians had a genius for running, they hunted down the deer on foot, for sport. Today a tortoise could race a Mexican in his automobile at rush hour." The "architectural carnival held on snippets of sites" astounded her:

> the tiny balconies of a villa making an enthusiastic though mistaken reference to Venice is squeezed up against a neo-classical edifice rubbing pillars with the product of what someone remembered of an article about Le Corbusier seen in a doctor's waiting-room. Street after street raised questions in the indelicate mind. How does one make love here without being congratulated by the neighbours in the morning? How can one groan as one dies without making public one's private death, like a poor lost French king? How does one have diarrhoea and go to the bathroom in the night without feeling that one's intestines have been nationalised?

The mixtures of people of Spanish and Indian descent made Mexico "a seething sum of arguments." Compared to the ebullient, cross-pollinated Mexicans, Rebecca imagined that she and Henry appeared as characters out of the Forsyte Saga—Old Jolyon and Aunt Amy, perhaps, "lumbering and thick-blooded and dreamless creatures, able to hold our own in the cash nexus but not much good for anything else, though well-meaning and not entirely unlovable."

Each day, from the glassed-in top floor of their hotel, Rebecca and Henry watched the sunsets, the skies catching fire "as solid objects do," the mountains black against the crimson end of day, purple clouds rushing from horizon to horizon, fusing with the crimson, becoming "mulberry flecked with rose," and then "bleached and floated as white phantoms on a greenish firmament, studded with stars larger than they had been" the week before in New York. Watching the lights twinkling from the city below, Rebecca calculated that the change from sunset to full night had taken twenty-five minutes.

She thrived on the high altitude; Henry developed a harrowing cold and cough. He wore his thickest clothes on the hottest days. She would later regard this trip as a portent. She had always admired his tall and well-built physique; as a young man he had won several cups for his prowess as a welterweight. He had always moved with elegance. His slight lameness, due to an injury in the Ruhleben prison camp, only added to his charm; it was the equivalent of a "shy stammer." Now in his middle seventies, he had an "encumbered, girt look, as if his suits were made of a stiffer material than is customary, and when he moved it was with a hieratic delay, he might have been keeping his place in a slow procession." His face had changed. Rebecca compared his nose, which now resembled the beak of a big bird, to the sculptures of Aztec priests. Her once robust image of him dematerialized. He resembled a dying man-god; he looked unnatural and yet, "in a sense more natural than before." He had always projected the aura of a "collected person with no particular reason to be puzzled by life"—a misleading effect now replaced by a body "giving some clue to its contents," and to its genetic connection to a "suicidal gypsy clan" with a knack for settling in the "middle of the main highways of history," from Burma to Hamburg to Ruhleben. His head injury in that last destination contributed to the "desert," the desiccation of his mind and body. Henry's brain, starved of its blood supply, sapped him even as she studied the sites of the Aztec blood sacrifices.

They traveled to Yucatán, where Rebecca investigated the local politics and archaeological sites in a twenty-square-mile area, regretting that there were so many unexcavated ruins, and that the jungle encroached on the excavated ones. She loved the pale gold color of the stones. Out in continuous rain, seventy-four-year-old Rebecca confined herself to climbing the smaller ruins, observing, "I doubted if Yucatán bone surgery would be the best." She was guided by a friend, Romney Brent, a native of Mexico and an actor who had changed his name many years before. He seemed bored by her obsession, one of several Mexicans who did not seem to know how to join themselves to their country's past. Romney's native name was long and difficult to pronounce. As Alexander Woollcott once said to Rebecca, "I lost interest after the fourth syllable."

3

REBECCA AND HENRY returned home to Ibstone in December 1966. Refreshed from the pampering she received from Viking in New York and exhilarated with the idea of Mexico as a new subject for her writing, she planned to write an article on Leon Trotsky's stay in Mexico (she had visited his house and talked with his grandson). But eventually her fascination with the country developed into an idea for a book as grand in scope as *Black Lamb and Grey Falcon,* an evocation of a culture and a vision of history. It would include her patented dialogues with Henry, digressions on his family background and hers, a detailed interpretation of the Aztecs, Mesoamerican art, the Spanish conquest, and a discourse on Cortes and other great men, including Napoleon. She made detailed notes on Aztec social structure, read copiously on the pre-Columbian civilizations, consulted scholars. There would be a section on the artists Diego Rivera and Frida Kahlo. To refresh her memory and to gather new material, Rebecca returned to Mexico twice, in 1967 and 1969. She began her book at the age of seventy-four; it would have taken at least five years to finish at a time when she also wanted to complete *Cousin Rosamund,* her fictional saga of the century, and to write short stories. It was an enormous, astonishing pyramid of a book to consider scaling at this late stage in her career. It is not surprising that she did not complete it; what is remarkable is that some of the sixty-thousand plus words she produced approach the level of *Black Lamb and Grey Falcon.* In her mid-seventies, Rebecca emerged from Mexico with new breadth, a stunning recovery of energy and ambition that seemed to have deserted her in the long stretch between the completion of *The Fountain Overflows* (1957) and *The Birds Fall Down* (1966)—the latter work really the fulfillment of a novel almost completed by the end of 1944.

In some ways, her truncated Mexican epic is even more fascinating than her published work, because its multiple drafts reveal how hard she worked at achieving her autobiographical/historical/psychological effects. The false starts, the repetitions, the occasional confusions in the ordering of words and phrases—even the illegible words—have a mournful, cryptic fascination. They are her own Mayan ruin. All the rigging has been maneuvered into place for a might-have-been masterpiece.

In the human sacrifices of the Aztecs, Rebecca found a worthy parallel to the scene of the black lamb on the rock. In both cases, the gods had to be appeased, and human beings were haunted by the need to sacrifice, to atone for their very existence. The sculptures of the angry, hideous-looking Aztec gods overwhelmed Rebecca, for in them she saw the malign faces of fate that she had always believed was against her, and a metaphor for this, one of the bloodiest of centuries. She put the argument of the Mexican book in the form of a liturgy or set of moral axioms, which fit together like a chant:

> The human race wishes to die: to kill is to offer up a substitute
> It wants to live (but not much)
> It wants to be moral
> It wants a moral excuse for killing
> It kills if that is to remove something likely to make it die
> It is happy if it can find a creed which sanctifies killing
> It is happy if it can find a creed which kills but does not appear to.

She was impressed with the Aztec belief that blood renewed the universe and that copious amounts of human blood might prevent the world from self-destructing as it came to the end of the fifty-two year cycles in the Aztec calendar. What looked like a ritual of death actually contributed to salvation. She rejected this logic, but she saw it operating everywhere, East and West, among the Aztecs and their Spanish conquerors.

This is perhaps why Trotsky receives her sympathy. He is one of the slain modern gods, a victim of a revolution that fed on the blood of its makers, a renegade priest of a contemporary creed. As Henry puts it to Rebecca in her notes, Trotsky and Stalin "quarreled over a matter of faith." Rebecca portrays Trotsky as a king-in-exile. To be sure, he is a usurper, a Macbeth, the revolutionary whose genius entitles him to power even as it provoked him to traffic in evil. Trotsky, like Napoleon, opposes hereditary power, and stands for the human effort to transform ideas into action.

Rebecca admits that her love for Trotsky is "irrational," although she does not explain this emotion. Surely one reason for her love is what she calls his "Shakespearean character," his ability to observe "exactly what was happening round him, and put its essence into language." Another clue to her affinity with Trotsky is that he is named as one of the survivors, one of the many exiles welcomed to Mexico, a land seeking social justice, no matter how elusive this ideal has proven. Trotsky is one of those whom history is bound to get, yet he eluded Stalin's blood lust for more than ten years.

Rebecca's Mexican epic contains riveting scenes that fuse history, art, and politics. A friend shows her a photograph of Frida Kahlo and Diego Rivera, great artists who had a troubled marriage, followed by a divorce and a remarriage. They are standing in Frida's garden, near her creation of a thatched pyramid with a four-tiered altar on which idols are staked in a "congestion which, granted the fiery nature of Aztec gods, should have led to a seismic disturbance." Rebecca compares the look the couple gives each other to "that look of a slow pneumatic expansion always displayed by lovers in opera, which suggests that, like balloons, they have to be subject to a certain degree of inflation before they can get off the ground." History as theater, artists with a sense of their historical mission, wrests from Rebecca some of her most startling figures of speech.

Rebecca does not downplay the cruelty of the Spanish conquest, but she admires Cortes's audacity and political genius; her narrative encompasses both his esurience (one of her favorite words) and his piety, his lust for gold and his promise to win souls for his church. She relates the Spanish gifts to Mexico "beyond counting": wheat, barley, rye, oats, bananas, oranges, limes, apples, pears, sugarcane, horses, mules, hogs, sheep, goats, cattle, and the introduction of the wheel. History suggests to her that it is futile to blame the Spanish for empire-building when Ferdinand and Isabella were themselves just managing to push back Islam and needed colonies to make their economy grow. Her anti-Turk bias shows when she suggests that it would have been worse if the Turks had occupied Mexico as they had the Balkans, making a "mess that brought on us the turbulence of Europe and the two World Wars." Instead of Our Lady of Guadalupe, she asks us to imagine a mosque, and women in veils, revealing not faces but "black snouts," the men "looking their worst in that most unbecoming of male headgear, the fez," a fashion that "might have been running up all over North America." She admired Ataturk because he made Turkey modern, outlawed the veil and the fez, and turned his country's face westward.

The Spanish exploitation of the Indians, Rebecca recognizes, is an appalling record, but it ranks no worse than what the Egyptians, Greeks, and Romans did to their slaves—especially the miners, who in every culture seem to excite a peculiar sadism from their masters. Although she concedes that Freudian and Jungian explanations of history often seem detached from reality and incapable of verification because they are founded on a faith in the unconscious, she is attracted to the notion of mining as a raping of mother earth and the association of metals dug out of the ground with excrement. She notes that the Aztecs had a conception of gold as the excrement of the gods. She ponders why miners who extract such treasure from the earth should receive punishment rather than reward. She speculates that miners violate some fundamental taboo so widespread that it has been adopted by peoples as different as Afrikaners and Mormons. But Rebecca does not press her point so much as she reveals the sheer inadequacy of any rational explanation for the miners' harsh treatment. Teasing meaning out of history, her prose becomes almost incantatory.

Montezuma is presented as Cortes's equal—in some ways as his superior, for the Aztec emperor sensitively encountered an unknowable figure in Cortes. Was he the ferocious god, Quetzalcoatl, returned to earth as Aztec religion prophesied, or was he simply a man? Montezuma put several delicate, tactful questions to the Spaniard, intended to establish his true identity, but nothing in Cortes's replies could satisfy the Aztec emperor, who was loathe to offend a god or to put himself at a disadvantage with a man. The Aztecs, Rebecca points out, had founded their civilization on the remains of several others—the Mayans, the Olmecs, the Toltecs, the Miztecs, each of which had perished from some unknown cause, perhaps for some grave sin that the Aztecs feared they might themselves commit. Thus isolated, they could be compared to the British, if they had experienced not only the Norman conquest, the fall of Rome and Byzantium, but also (before the sixteenth century) the annihilation of France, Germany, Spain, and the Low Countries. In effect, Montezuma's position would be like a British or American government suddenly faced with "phenomena which might be either a hostile expeditionary force of spacemen or the Second Coming of Christ."

Rebecca's epic fragment on Mexico is a congeries of brilliant narratives broken up by sections of notes, sketches of argument and character, and bald statements of theme. How the Trotsky section would have been hooked to Cortes, Mexico to Spain, Rebecca and Henry to the history they confront, and that history to Rebecca and Henry, is not clear, but their potential nexus impregnates her text as she walks us through her visit to Trotsky's house, her conversation with his grandson, her dialogue with her driver, her tour of the Archaeological Museum in Mexico City. One of her working titles for the book, *Survivors in Mexico,* alluded to the linkage she never finished forging between her characters, who are, like herself and Henry, doomed on the main highways of history, and yet survivors nonetheless.

4

REBECCA WORKED fitfully on her Mexico book through the first part of 1967. She kept going over the same sentences. Even writing letters seemed difficult, and she sought relief in composing "rather odd poetry" about Mexico. She was troubled by a recurring virus and worried over the muddle Henry made of things. Deafer than ever, he now added new terrors to his driving: increasing speed and blackouts.

Ibstone seemed empty without her labrador, Albert, who had died the previous year of cancer of the bowel. He had been Rebecca's constant companion on walks, for although Henry adored his land, he almost never walked it—as Rebecca did almost daily when she was not ill. She had not been so affected by a pet's death since her beloved Ginger Pounce's passing. She had wrapped Albert in one of her best sheets and buried him alongside her cat, Mr. Briggs, in a nice grave at the bottom of Ibstone's hill. She would think of Albert, and even write about him, for years to come.

5

At the end of 1967, Rebecca wrote to William Shawn at *The New Yorker* to say she did not think she could complete her article on Mexico, and he generously told her to forget about the money the magazine had advanced to her. Rereading what she had written, she thought it good but disorganized; she could not construct the joints. Henry's newest cantrip had been pointed out by a young man, who said Henry no longer knew where he was putting his car. Rebecca worked up a facsimile of her tombstone:

HERE LIES REBECCA WEST
DIED   19
Dear Henry had no idea where he was putting the car.

Away from Ibstone for a Christmas trip to her nephew Norman and his family in Edinburgh, Rebecca and Henry returned home to discover that their home had been burgled and was swarming with reporters, police, and insurance agents. Some jewelry but none of her precious pictures had been taken. Henry felt the loss of an exquisite jade collection carefully assembled over the past thirty years. The whole household came down with flu. Rebecca had also lost Vyvyan Holland, an old friend from the 1920s whose son Merlin she and Henry had helped educate, and Harriet Cohen, the pianist who had served as the lively model for Harriet Hume. To Rebecca, at this time of year it always seemed as if she had just barely endured. Writing her Mexico book took extraordinary will power, good fortune, and enormous labor. As long as she kept at it, she was one of the survivors.

CHAPTER 36

Love Without Content
1968–1969

I

HER MEXICO BOOK stalled, Rebecca worried that she had wasted a year on it and noted that Anthony had written a piece on the country, surely meaning to scoop her. She pampered herself in March 1968 with a two-week trip to Monte Carlo, escaping from one of Henry's hyperactive, "overengined" phases, and hoping to get on with a new novel, tentatively titled *Mild Silver, Furious Gold*. It would feature characters modeled on Anthony, on Henry, and on herself. Caspar is brilliant but spoils his chance of succeeding at Oxford. The son of a distinguished Oxford don, an art historian, Caspar is afraid of failure and of "using any of his gifts. He cannot latch onto life anyhow, and he becomes fiercely envious, of everybody. He marries, but that does not help." Martin, Caspar's mother's second husband, becomes fond of Caspar, and Caspar expects Martin to leave him his money. When Martin becomes ill, Caspar hopes to hasten his death by telling him he has cancer, for Caspar has often heard Martin say that he would kill himself if he contracted cancer. Caspar even intimates to Martin that his wife and doctors have kept the knowledge of this fatal disease from Martin. But Martin discovers that Caspar is lying.

Rebecca began at least six versions of the novel, never getting much beyond a riveting scene in which Aminta, Caspar's grandmother, fires a rifle at him. He has been prowling near her home. Aminta is the only one in the family whom Martin has told of Caspar's lie, the only one aware of how ruthlessly Caspar will pursue his perfidy. She observes: "Twice he has plotted against me and everybody I care for, and I have to take precautions. There may be a third time." Caspar represents not merely a family's bad seed but the principle of evil itself, working through other people. Aminta remarks: "Again and again stupid people had said to me,

'But, you know, he really loves you all the time,' and there was always cruelty in their voices, and sometimes, repellently, in their smiles, a cruelty which was cleverer than themselves. It was as if their stupidity was a glove-puppet of a wicked hand." In one of her letters to Anthony, Rebecca had asked him how he would feel if she had attacked him in her work as he had attacked her in *Heritage*. To go on with her novel would have meant portraying him as evil incarnate. Once again, she stalled, unable to find a unifying theme for a novel that would have linked up with the *Cousin Rosamund* trilogy and her short story, "Parthenope," sharing with them some of the same characters and settings.

2

REBECCA RETURNED from Monte Carlo to Ibstone for a dispiriting summer and autumn. Henry, always a poor manager of the farm, now seemed almost entirely incapacitated. She wrote to his accountants, Spicer and Pegler, acknowledging that the farm losses had been useful in offsetting the profits from her literary career, and the farm had given Henry "an interest in life," but it had been a nuisance, disrupting other housework and her writing. Now the farm was in poor shape, the buildings filthy. She was determined to persuade Henry to give it up and move out of the "House of Usher."

Visitors found neither Ibstone nor its occupants in danger of disintegration. During this period, Merlin Holland came for a break from his college work. Henry met him at the Stokenchurch bus stop and drove him to Ibstone for a late-morning chat over coffee and newspapers. They would have lunch with distinguished guests, and around three or four Merlin would tour the gardens with Rebecca. Merlin saw no marked change in Henry's slow, deliberate, Germanically precise mind. Grateful because Henry had been so generous with his time and money, Merlin listened patiently to his advice.

Merlin realized he was a kind of substitute for the recalcitrant Anthony, whom Rebecca referred to as "my dreadful son." On one of his last visits to Ibstone, Merlin pleased Rebecca by telling her she had a "wonderful motherly face." She said she was relaxed with him and did not feel as though she had to be on her "best behaviour." She had a similar relationship with Justin Lowinsky, her darling Ruth's son—a "no-nonsense, say what you like" companionship.

3

ON OCTOBER 2, 1968, complaining of severe stomach pains, Henry was hospitalized. X-rays showed an obstruction in the bowel; an immediate operation removed a small cancerous tumor—caught early, the surgeon said. At first, Henry responded well to the operation. But he had had trouble before with high levels of uric acid; now he was diagnosed with uremia. The doctors thought him strong for his age (seventy-four), but he recovered slowly, hampered by weak kidneys. Rebecca cherished his gallant behavior and sweet temper, his expressions of gratitude for the attention he received. He sent her out one day to buy lipsticks for the nurses. In bed herself for three days with the flu, she wrote to several friends, asking them to send Henry cards. She also initiated plans to sell the house and farm, dreading Henry's protest.

By October 10, the doctors advised Rebecca that Henry might have no more than a week to live. One kidney had completely failed, and the other had also been damaged by the uremia. He was shaky but serene, with a special kindness that reminded her of the first years of their marriage. Only a month earlier she had shrieked into his deafness: "We cannot go on living here, we must give up the farm and sell the house, we must go to London." Now he greeted her, "How glad I am you convinced me that we have to go to London. I am looking forward to it so much, where shall we live?" He smiled and her heart ached. Later delirium set in. Henry imagined himself at a farm sale. During lucid periods he nettled her by dwelling on the minutiae of the farm business and the house. At one point, in "an agony of love," she knelt beside his bed. He turned to her and said, "Now, you must hurry up and make sure about ordering the Christmas cards." She sighed, knowing he would not live to see the holidays. Twitching with vexation, Henry declared to his incredulous wife: "All my life I have had to drive you to get things done." But later he apologized for the times he had interrupted her work, and he could not think why he had done so. It reminded her of poor Albert, who had killed some hens shortly before he died and then sat among them, seemingly wondering why he had done it.

Rebecca wrote long letters to Edmund and Vita, to friends such as Emanie Arling and Evelyn Hutchinson, giving them detailed accounts of Henry's condition and her worries. She took comfort in Justin Lowinsky and Merlin Holland, who were like family to her. She reflected bitterly that she could not count on Anthony to be at her side, or to appreciate all Henry had done for her. Heartened by Caroline's visit to Henry, Rebecca hoped she could begin to bridge the gulf between herself and her granddaughter. (Rebecca had been dismayed by Caroline's summer in America helping Anthony with research for a book.)

Henry rallied briefly. At midnight on November 1, the date of their thirty-eighth wedding anniversary, Henry stirred, and Rebecca gave him an exquisite fifteenth-century lapis lazuli cloisonné plate. He took it in his hands, spoke of its beauty, and thanked her lovingly. It was the last time he recognized her or was able to speak sensibly about anything. Shortly afterward he collapsed and Rebecca summoned her cousin, Ian Barclay, a medical doctor, who helped to make Henry comfortable. Sally, Ian's wife, served as a calming presence at Ibstone. Rebecca sat in Henry's hospital room and watched him rest in peace, noticing his finely shaped hands, indeed thinking how his spectacles had always hidden his classical features, and listening to his heavy breathing, a sort of "surf-break noise."

On November 3, 1968, Henry died in his sleep. A relieved Rebecca said that the manner of his passing was fortunate. Her last years with him had sometimes been intolerable, but she now thought it right that she had stuck by him. Life with him had been "nearly utterly all right and far better than most things anyway." Rebecca mourned the disintegration of Henry's gifts, hastened by the early onset of the cerebral arteriosclerosis, which (with the uremia) ultimately killed him, and which may have begun as early as the mid-1930s, when (as one doctor speculated) he may have suffered a stroke. She had resented Henry's philandering, yet she wondered now responsible he had been for his erratic behavior when a doctor asked her if Henry had not been behaving strangely for some years. She felt guilty about having treated him as being fully responsible for his actions. She regretted the times she had boxed his ears, made a scene, said frightful things. She should have known better, she thought. But how could she have known better? she wondered. The doctors had not presented consistent diagnoses. Ibstone seemed a desert, and she was more determined than ever to leave it.

Rebecca's secretary, Thea Bent, acted with superb good sense and compassion throughout this last ordeal, practically becoming Rebecca's maid. There had been a scene: Rebecca in hysterics over the black funeral clothes on her bed. At such times, Rebecca's voice rose like a bell. Ian and Sally watched Thea calm her. They knew Thea had to put up with a great deal, but Thea said she was dealing with a sensitive genius, subject to these fits. Later, Ian and Sally were sad to see Rebecca turn against Thea; they knew it was difficult to serve someone who could make unfair demands and blame the help for things beyond their control.

Rebecca was buoyed by many letters remembering Henry's kindness and generosity. Henry took immense trouble over people, continuing a conversation the next day by a letter, or writing out an apt quotation on a postcard, "a master of those small actions that warm the heart in the way that his own was always warm." One of Henry's Oxford classmates, Sir John Russell, observed that college friends feared for the gentle Henry in the "buffets of life," but were impressed with his exploits as a "prince of finance." Henry had played the fond uncle to the children of Rebecca's nephew Norman, and his wife Marion wrote Rebecca reminding her that Henry had once advised little Fiona about her choice of a husband. He listened patiently to her problem and remarked: "Well, my dear, who would you like to have breakfast with every morning?" Fiona knew the answer to that question and was delighted to have an adult treat her dilemma with such gravity. Merlin Holland remembered how Henry liked to play "the truant," picking up Merlin in his car after Rebecca had expressly forbidden him that pleasure. "Naughty old man," she called Henry. "I suppose it's silly really but I never forgot how much that showed me that you loved him," Merlin told her. Emanie Arling wrote: "There was something touching and kind about Henry in his good moods, and he was fundamentally so wrapped up in you." He was the "knowing and joyous priest of your cult," another of Rebecca's correspondents affirmed. Beverly Nichols remembered that at parties, during a break in the conversation, Henry would gaze across the room at his wife and say, "Isn't Rebecca looking splendid tonight?"

Marshall Best, recalling the glorious period at Viking when they were readying *Black Lamb and Grey Falcon* for publication, revealed to Rebecca that Henry had secretly offered to back the book if Viking deemed it a commercial risk. This news seemed to her like a delayed wedding present. "I often feel I was not really the right wife for Henry, that I should have had more of an understanding of Central European mysteries," she told Douglas Woodruff, another of Henry's Oxford classmates and close friends, to whom she explained the details of Henry's "odd background."

She thought it wonderful that Edmund and Vita came to Henry's funeral in the Saxon church in Fingest at the bottom of Ibstone's hill. Rebecca had Henry's favorite John Donne prayer read, an English vicar for the service, and a Russian Orthodox Priest to deliver the Blessings of the Dead. After the funeral service, everyone stood in the pouring rain, listening to the trumpeter perform the *Trumpet Voluntary* by Jeremiah Clarke. Then they went up to Ibstone House for a splendid party, which Rebecca regarded as both a send-off for Henry and a farewell to her home. Edmund and Vita accompanied her a week later on a visit to Henry's churchyard grave. She had a viral infection and whooping cough (caught from her cook's baby). Her cousin Ian Barclay and his wife Sally stayed at Ibstone and helped see her through the first days after the funeral.

Rebecca immediately set about straightening up Henry's estate and starting a new life. She was surprised to learn that his will failed to acknowledge certain friends who had stood by him, and she arranged for them to receive various sums. Henry's correspondence dismayed her— all the time he put in on his inferiors. She was determined to get on with her writing, spurred on by Marshall Best, who had just read with great enthusiasm five chapters of *This Real Night,* the sequel to *The Fountain Overflows.* By November 12, 1968 Rebecca had sold Ibstone for fifty thousand pounds (having paid six thousand for it in 1939). Henry had been plagued in his last year with the thought that he had no money, but his accountants at Slaughter & May estimated that his estate should be worth at least fifty thousand pounds after taxes and expenses.

Rebecca thought of removing to London to live in a "dolly-sized flat" or "rabbit-hutch," where she would finish her Mexico book and turn out novels. But she got "gummed up" with lawyers and a panoply of professionals—specialists in dealing with the affairs of the dead. Her accountants advised her to keep her valuable collection of pictures together to avoid trouble with the tax authorities; this in itself entailed purchasing a large property. Then Rebecca discovered that large flats were not so much more expensive than smaller ones. By mid-December, she had found what she wanted in Kingston House, on the edge of Hyde Park, just a five-minute walk from Harrods. Her rooms looked south over gardens. In the distance, she could see the garden she had in mind when Laura Rowan overheard her parents' conversation in the first chapter of *The Birds Fall Down.* A Russian Orthodox Church was nearby. Rebecca felt confident, realizing she had over one hundred thousand pounds in securities, plus what remained from Henry's estate.

Although Rebecca took great comfort in Henry's funeral and in the messages of condolence, it would take her years to work through her ambivalent feelings about him. "What did I mean to him?" she asked. "I know he had a feeling that I was the White Goddess, but I am not that, what did he care for me?" She was bitter because he had left five thousand pounds to one of his mistresses. He had invited several of them to Ibstone. The papers he left behind made clear these were not "innocent crushes." How could she square these brute facts with the evidence of his devotion to her? Had Henry been laughing at her all the time, and just treating their marriage as a convenience? She blamed him for being another unreliable man. The male attitude toward women, she lectured

Charles Curran, was "mean, silly, and dirty." She found "something so desperately unlovable, even unlikable, about the male sex," although she made an exception for Charles and a few others. Of course Henry had his sweet side, but his second-rate women proved him a squalid character. She was outraged to discover in Henry's papers a photograph of one of them taken in Amiens, which Rebecca had always regarded a special place for her and Henry alone. "But why did I have to marry at all?" she asked Charles. "Men are not good companions or allies on a long haul." Rebecca's vehemence on the subject of men startled Marjorie Hutton, who saw a good deal of Rebecca when she moved to London. At a party Rebecca overheard her agree with someone's comment that men were better than women. "Marjorie, don't be silly, you know as well as I do that all men are trash." One of Rebecca's *Sunday Telegraph* reviews begins, "There is, of course, no reason for the existence of the male sex except that one sometimes needs help in moving the piano." She loved Henry, but sometimes it felt like "love without content."

Rebecca consulted Evelyn and Margaret Hutchinson, one of her idealized couples. How would they explain Henry's behavior? Evelyn believed that Henry treated Rebecca as an "all wise mama who was supposed to clean up after the party." While Henry had acted immaturely, Evelyn did not believe that he meant to ridicule Rebecca. Evelyn's wife, Margaret, had sensed a "sexual psychopathic element" in Henry's character, but neither of them doubted the goodness of Henry's sane side.

4

BY THE AUTUMN OF 1969, Rebecca had her pictures hung in her new flat and felt ready to receive visitors and hold small parties. During a luncheon, a "King Kong sort of person in jeans" carrying a huge wrench entered the dining room. After exchanging stares with Rebecca, he bent over her, put up an enormous hand, and said in a hoarse whisper: "Understand that you have been having trouble with your lavatories." This was Ibstone transplanted. She began to feel Henry's presence when funny things happened.

5

ANTHONY WROTE to Rebecca about Henry, acknowledging his stepfather's many kindnesses and admitting, "I wouldn't have been so powerfully jealous of him if I hadn't known how much there was in him to love and like." He knew she had waited a long time for him to grow up, but he believed he had almost made it. He said that he remained quite fond of her, signing one of his letters "Comus"—her old nickname for him.

Rebecca rejoiced in Anthony's affectionate letters. She commiserated with him over six-year-old Sophie's terrible sledding accident, which had split her nose, fractured a cheek, and required extensive plastic surgery. Rebecca gave Anthony an uncommonly calm explanation about his exclusion from Henry's will. She admitted that Henry had originally intended to make Anthony his heir (an admission she later revoked), but Henry had not received the companionship from Anthony that he had expected, and "then there was one thing and another," as she put it with uncharacteristic delicacy. Shortly after the war Henry had become dedicated to helping his relatives, several of whom had become displaced persons. She promised that Anthony's children would receive money from the filming of *The Bird Falls Down*, and shipped him several precious items from Ibstone.

Tensions between mother and son did not entirely slacken. Aspects of Rebecca's life with H.G., which had been threatening to leak out since his death in 1946, saw print in Lovat Dickson's Wells biography. Dickson—known to his friends as Rache—had been Rebecca's editor at Macmillan and had secured her reluctant cooperation. He had done so by means of an apparently self-defeating strategy: he had offered to remove all mention of Rebecca from his book. His American colleague, editor Michael Bessie, was shocked. How could Rache write about H.G. without mentioning Rebecca? "That is the most effective way to get her to come round," Rache replied. Although she practically rewrote his book so far as the details of her own life were concerned, the fact that any connection with H.G. had to be discussed upset her. When she saw Rache's account of the Gatternigg affair (when a woman had tried to commit suicide in his London flat), she suspected Anthony had been his informant. Anthony denied it, but Rebecca could not suppress her suspicions. She reported to Edmund and Vita that she and Anthony were on another of their eighteen-month cycles of reconciliation and recrimination.

6

In the autumn of 1969, Rebecca returned to Mexico in hopes of levitating her foundered epic. She stopped over in New York for an unsatisfactory meeting with Anthony. She found him fat (dragging along several chins) and untidy: "It is a hard thing for a mother to say of her son but he looks like Margaret Rutherford." Anthony's agent, Lois Wallace, had the distinct impression that he took an adolescent glee in grooming himself to outrage his mother. His tight pants and long hair looked to Lois like a deliberate provocation.

In Mexico, Rebecca found a second family in the home of Kit and Thew Wright. Kit gave Rebecca a pampered sanctuary, with servants and luxurious accommodations. Rebecca responded by entertaining the whole family and making everything into a game. She would take an incident and elaborate it into such a vivid story that it became part of family lore, or she would regale the Wrights for days with her inventions about people she had just met and disliked. Rebecca had only one complaint about life with the Wrights: too much socializing, too much interruption of her concentration when she was at the typewriter working on her Mexico book. Kit, an enthusiastic hostess, awakened Rebecca at six in the morning to see the sunrise over a volcano.

Rebecca had come to love Mayan sculpture even more than the Greek. She described the pyramids in the Yucatán jungles as skyscrapers twenty-five hundred years old amid a sea of green treetops. She loved the Mexicans she met—so cheerful and derisive about politics (including rigged elections), people after her own nature. She wanted to stay, but saw no niche for her.

In Cuernevaca, on December 21, Rebecca celebrated her birthday with the Wrights. They had mariachis come to sing to her at dawn, and they brought her balloons. She sent a Christmas card to friends: "I am sitting in the Wrights' garden very happily browning in the sun. . . . My constant annoyance is that Henry is not here to see such things, and to tell me everything I have forgotten or never knew."

Kit watched Rebecca depart the country in mid-January 1970, walking with difficulty across the tarmac carrying a heavy camera and a bag: "I was too young to understand how brave she was. I think she had just had her sixtieth birthday." In fact, Rebecca had just turned seventy-seven.

CHAPTER 37

The Willy-Willies
1970–1971

I

IN JANUARY, Rebecca began keeping a diary, recording her physical aches and mental agonies, her nightmares, her premonitions, her pleasures and apprehensions, her writing goals, achievements, and disappointments. She had kept journals sporadically, but Rebecca West as diarist amounted to a new career, an effort to fix the dramas of each day with her memorable stamp, a salvage operation for a devastated soul. The queerest things could happen—right in her flat: "Tidied kitchen cupboard and found huge heavy saucepan I *never* bought containing blonde wig! . . . Poltergeist in operation . . . found one of my new earrings . . . gone from dressing table, no trace." Her troubles with pilfering and incompetent staff (secretaries and housekeepers) continued. As she aged and suffered the indignities of failing health, recounting how she got through the ordeals of days and nights became a writer's triumph over vicissitude.

Rebecca regularly visited Henry's grave. Retrieving his underwriter's deposit from Lloyd's, clearing his estate of debts and paying taxes, and other postmortem business exasperated her. "I could not have believed that the mere fact of being left a widow could take up so much of one's time." She had become intrigued with Henry's family background—traveling to his ancestral home in Berwick-on-Tweed. His family had become entangled in her Mexico manuscript and in her family memoirs (just begun) as another example of rootless survivors who spread history into tantalizing networks of human relationships. On her last trip to Mexico, she had detoured to Dayton, Ohio, to visit Irene Garthwaite, the daughter of Henry's cousin, Louis. Irene was another Andrews survivor, caught in a German camp for displaced people during the war, suffering through a troubling relationship with a stepmother, and making a life for herself in America. Rebecca admired not only Irene's endurance but her independence. Henry and Rebecca had been generous to her, but she never asked for money and did not want to be their ward.

Rebecca gained weight and fretted over her futile diets. She saw herself on television looking "frightful. Like a dull Mae West." She loved walking, especially in Hyde Park, but now even short strolls proved painful: "My legs are turning into wood—I'm dead from my knees down." She no longer had the stamina of earlier years. She deplored how "slow and stupid" she was in the kitchen. She watched the "idiotic TV," especially dramas. She thought the scripts poor but the acting superb.

Rebecca read voraciously, pulverizing contemporary gurus such as Marshall McLuhan and Herbert Marcuse. She did not believe in revolution for the hell of it, damn the consequences (her sketch of Marcuse), and McLuhan's notion of the medium as the message excited her contempt. To McLuhan, the world might seem a smaller place, but it was decidedly not a global village. If anything, people felt more remote from each other. She thought her friends stupid to think that Nixon's approach to China would accrue benefits to the West. She created rows at parties, condemning Black Power and expressing no sympathy for American radicals like Angela Davis. She said nothing good would come of the student protests. She attended a performance of *Hair* and claimed the nudity and the dancing had been done better in 1920s Berlin. In January 1970, she had watched good-looking young women walk down Manhattan streets hand in hand with much less attractive men unconscious of the beauties they had won. The young women looked submissive. Other feminists shared Rebecca's anxiety. In 1971 Gloria Steinem founded the National Women's Political Caucus, and the next year *Ms.* magazine.

Rebecca took therapeutic excursions to Kent to stay with the Hodges, and to Wiltshire, where her cousin, Ian Barclay, and his wife, Sally, had recently settled. In both cases, Rebecca contributed to the downpayments on houses. She loved the unassuming and undemanding manners of the Hodges and the Barclays, and they enjoyed her wit, which, in their comforting homes, showed its benign side. A restless sleeper, Rebecca would sometimes spend a day in bed at the Barclays writing letter after letter. When she had recharged herself, they could see she was eager to leave them for London. At the Hodges, she would sit outside in the garden or inside near the fire and write her diary, usually in red ink—the painful passages made it seem as though she were spilling her blood. She would occupy an entire weekend working on a *Sunday Telegraph* review, taking immense trouble with it. Her insatiable curiosity might fix on virtually anything—say the history of Porterhouse steaks—and the Hodges would scurry to supply her with every reference book in the house. After one of her visits, they might very well be sent a gift of several reference books.

She liked treating her friends to jaunts to foreign places, where she seemed to know everybody. She took John and Margaret Hodges to Venice, where they had tea with royalty. She warned them not to be surprised at the paucity of food—sandwiches the size of postage stamps, elaborate but tiny cakes. You were offered one or two tiny items and asked to sign a book. Because of currency regulations, Rebecca could not take as much money abroad as she wished. She solved her cash flow problems by having *The New Yorker* wire her money. On another junket, Justin Lowinsky commiserated with Rebecca hobbling on swollen legs in elastic bandages through customs. "Shut up, you bloody fool, those are dollars," she said, claiming to have stuffed the bills inside her stockings.

On a wet and cold expedition with the Hodges to North Wales, Rebecca decided she needed a vest. Dressed in a cape thrown over an old mackintosh and supported by a walking stick, Rebecca ventured into a general store. Her arthritic legs prevented her from mounting the stairs to the clothing department, so the staff brought her an array of vests. She then essayed the photography department, getting into a long, intricate argument with a bloke at the counter who thought he knew about cameras. A crowd formed around her, appreciating this debate of aficionados. A woman said, "you know, my son's a photographer." Well, this was just up Rebecca's street; they had a long conversation about him, a professional photographer living in Cheltenham. This interlude took about two hours and it made John Hodges observe: "She liked people. She really did." Back at the hotel Rebecca tried on her vests. They proved to be enormous long ones stretching down to her knees. She thought it a marvelous joke.

2

IN THE SPRING OF 1971, Rebecca and Thelma Holland traveled to Lebanon on a visit to Thelma's son, Merlin. There on business for a year, Merlin appreciated the attention of a benefactress to whom he had become close. Fond of Merlin and pleased with the results of his education, Rebecca had given him (just before his departure from England) her annotated set of Proust, saying "I know you love books." She wanted him to come around one day and pick out others, saying "I'm not going to last forever, you know." But taking more of her books seemed like burying her.

The Lebanese trip was Rebecca's idea and her expense, for she knew that Thelma missed her son but could not afford the fare to the Middle East, and that it would be quite expensive for him to journey home. Rebecca loved Thelma for her devotion to Merlin and for taking care of her much older husband, Vyvyan, in his last years. The two women did not have that much in common, and traveling with virtually anyone would get on Rebecca's nerves, but she judged Thelma "good hearted and affectionate."

Nearly eighty, Rebecca's energy and curiosity impressed Merlin as he watched her climbing all over a Crusader castle just inside Syria. She also wanted to know about the workaday life of Beirut. She had introductions to people in the smart set, but the mundane side of things fascinated her. Like Merlin, she found the Lebanese kind and generous, with a flashy Parisian side. They loved glitz, huge rooms with imposing chandeliers, and pseudoreproductions of eighteenth-century French furniture. In a house full of this ersatz grandeur, Rebecca turned to Merlin and said, *sotto voce*, "Oh, wonderful Louis Soisant-Quatorze."

Rebecca savored the "wild, inconsequent jam of divine buildings," with the congestion and zest of urban life in a non-western capital, a Mexico City on a much smaller scale but with a similar history of welcoming "wave after wave of refugees." Driving in Beirut resembled a medieval tournament; the ordinary rules of the road had been abrogated. Yet accidents were no greater here than anywhere else, and the city's drivers had evolved their own survival code.

Rebecca had trouble adjusting to the climate, which alternated from damp cold to burning heat, and included a week of torrential rain, floods, and three mild earthquakes. In Syria she found the people dour and the bathrooms abominable. In fact, her trip to the ancient ruin of Palmyra became an Arabian Nights tale, crossed with the "dottier works of William Faulkner." At one hotel, she encountered a "darkness that seemed not part of the natural conditions, but to be laid on, like the electric light which did little to disperse it." A tall one-eyed waiter served her, assisted by a companion in a perpetually crouching position, "as if he was going to excavate something out of the floor."

Rebecca and Thelma found their adjoining bathroom covered with an inch of water, a hand basin at one end with taps as high as Rebecca's head. The tap water shot past the basin and splashed up from the floor. Drops of rusty water on the ceiling fell on everything, including Rebecca's suede shoes, leaving ineffaceable marks. When Thelma pulled the toilet chain, the toilet broke away from the wall and fell on the floor. The next morning they moved to another room and found it clean and neat. She had her driver ask for an explanation from the saturnine landlord (wearing a costume that reminded her of a bookmaker in Saratoga Springs at the beginning of the century). The landlord said that he had given them a waterlogged room because they were English and probably anti-Communist. Then the one-eyed waiter entered the room, crying out sentiments that sounded to her like some famous slogan from Patrick Henry ("Give me liberty or give me death") or Stephen Decatur ("My country, right or wrong"). In fact, he was claiming that the old lavatories were better than the new ones. A day later, their lavatory broke down and they had to use one in the restaurant. Thelma braved it with a cigarette in one hand and a deodorizing spray in the other. In locking horns with the stench, Thelma saw a jug she imagined must contain water, and she emptied it where she thought it would do the most good. But it contained a large amount of crude ammonia, which pervaded the restaurant with fumes. With everyone coughing and choking, Rebecca and Thelma headed for the car, delayed momentarily by a "venerable Moslem," who paused with such a solemn air that they came to a respectful halt. Rebecca expected him to prophesy. Instead he blew his nose on his fingers.

Rebecca was seeking once again the meaning of civilization and its religious basis. She had come to see the Druse, a sect which had drawn its creed from both Islam and Christianity. She was attracted to their view of an undefinable God who had sent to earth perhaps as many as seventy incarnations of himself before deciding that mankind had rejected salvation—just like a body which repulses a vaccine. She had located a Druse town on the map and wanted her driver to take her there. He refused, pointing out that the town was in an area contested by Jews and Arabs. Did Rebecca think that her driver, a Lebanese Jew, would be welcomed by the Arab guerrillas? Would a Lebanese get a better welcome from the Israelis? he asked her. Another survivor, he fascinated her as part of the history she wanted to investigate.

In the Syrian desert, Rebecca found an image of what she called in *Black Lamb and Grey Falcon* the mystery of existence. "Look," said her driver, bringing the car to a stop. At first he seemed to be pointing at no more than a little whirlwind, "a puff of smoke, no, a huge round cobweb, of the same substance as the gossamers we see hanging on hedges on autumn mornings, but tall as a man," Rebecca observed. "In Australia, we call them 'Willy-Willies,'" Thelma said. Rebecca watched the ghostly dance of these skeletal figures. It was difficult not to believe they had emotions, joy or rage, for they moved with seeming purpose like human beings executing a command, grumbling or exalting in it. The pale maroon desert and a huge cumulus cloud cast a shadow over the scene, while the sun appeared a golden bar behind it, falling straight from the heat-bleached blue sky. Five minutes later she saw a giant amber Willy—perhaps thirty-feet high—turning and twirling its dancer's body, vanishing and reappearing, apparently in a frenzy, struggling to free its swathed arms, rising from the ground, with a head covered with red-gold, curling hair. It pivoted wildly until a long curl whipped out and its feet sank to the earth. This figure kept reconstituting itself, dense and evanescent, like the materialization of a human being, tussling for some knowledge denied it.

The scene recalled to Rebecca an upended desert on a mountain range in Mexico. Every few yards on a hillside she saw a

> masterpiece of modern sculpture: a variation of the human form expressing some emotion, nearly always painful. They warned. They lamented. They declared that nothing good would come of it, had ever come of it. What was it? Why, everything. At the times when the sun was sinking in
> . the west and the moon was rising in the east, these gesticulating figures pointed to both. Not anywhere would things go right. That was not the direction in which time was progressing. Inanimate objects seemed, regarding this one point, animate.

To Rebecca, the willy-willies and the Mexican sculptures struck attitudes that evoked the tragic vision she had explored in *Black Lamb and Grey Falcon*. (She had it in mind to copy out a passage from that book at this point in her Lebanon manuscript.)

At Palmyra, where the Romans had crushed Queen Zenobia's power, Rebecca admired the "glorious austerity of the colonnades." She had seen nothing as beautiful except Palenque, a city the Mayans mysteriously abandoned virtually intact in the jungle. But the Romans had ruined Palmyra, wrecking a worthy civilization they thought they could rebuild on their terms, not realizing that they were extending their government beyond the bounds of effectiveness, making the mistake of all imperial powers (like the Habsburg monarchy in Central Europe) of taking on more territory than they could properly administer. The Romans had made the same mistake with Cleopatra in Egypt. Both Zenobia and Cleopatra had suffered the same fate, transformed by male historical painters into luscious, rounded figures, whose fulsome breasts "appear more fruity to the male mind when exhibited by females in a state of defeat by the flat-chested male. We see the two great queens at moments when they are not throwing their bras away but [when] their bras are throwing them away, and leave them bulging and unprotected." Rome's triumph over these women was humanity's loss, for even as Rome prevailed over Zenobia and Cleopatra, it was beginning to disintegrate, leaving a large part of the world vulnerable to centuries of chaos. The fate of Zenobia and Cleopatra alone shows why women's liberation should not be ridiculed, Rebecca concluded.

On an "absolutely beautiful day" Merlin guided Rebecca up one of the low hillsides flowering with wild cyclamen to pay her respects at the grave of her avatar, Lady Hester Stanhope, a great nineteenth-century traveler. She had adopted male dress and a religion confected of Christianity and Islam, settling among the Druses, where the local population regarded her as a prophetess, a role she gradually accepted.

Part of what Rebecca struggled with in her trip to Lebanon and in her account of that journey was her age. In a review of Simone de Beauvoir's book on ageing, she called Simone the Mrs. Gummidge of France, and deplored her "blubbing over the lines on her face." That was as sensible as regretting one was not a horse and could not win the Kentucky Derby. "The real trouble about growing old," Rebecca countered, was the accumulated load of knowledge and experience and how to bring it to bear on current circumstances. Exhaustion set in. For example, how should she view the Vietnam War? she asked herself. She had known so many wars, and her mind rebelled against assimilating the complicated details of this new one; she found her focus blurred, one tragedy blended into another. The Arab-Israeli conflict was another case in point. Of course, she knew its origins, how the Balfour Declaration had neglected to provide for the Palestinians. Yet she had looked at a map and blindly asked her Lebanese driver to take her into a war zone. She found she no longer had the power to visualize a war; it had been easier to set her sights on pleasing Merlin and his mother. She felt the moral obligation to do better than that; she also felt the urge to give her mind a holiday. It was as if the ageing mind could stand only so many shocks; how different it was when she had been a child and observed her parents' agitation over the Dreyfus case in France, which had opened her mind to history.

Even more than the Mexico manuscript, the Lebanon draft is a shambles (pages and pages of fragments, passages compulsively rewritten, palimpsests of her restless, questing imagination). It is a brilliant wreck of a work—shards of it are like the suggestive ruins Rebecca liked to pick her way through for her aperçus. Her literary remains are her Romantic relics; if we did not know they were never completed, we might take them as her Tintern Abbey, imagining how the parts once fit into a whole. Thelma took Henry's place as companion, but his death meant the loss of that vital other half that could second and challenge her. She needed friction to ignite her prose.

3

REBECCA RETURNED from Lebanon in May 1971 and began writing about it. When she got stuck, she turned again to her family memoirs, deciding in early September 1971 to accompany Lettie on a two-week tour of Ireland, exploring the Fairfield roots. They arrived in Dublin on September 4 with Rebecca in a foul mood, grumbling about what a lout James Joyce was and Yeats a "crystal-gazing fortune-telling nut." She had never warmed to the Irish and had never visited Ireland, although A. L. Rowse, a friend of her later years, thought her character and wit Irish. Lettie's own closeness to Irish Catholics put Rebecca off, as did her father's Anglo-Irish arrogance. "It is a Man's Lib country," she once wrote. "They won't wear bras." She felt the Irish always made their relationship with England more difficult than it had to be, excusing Irish faults and blaming the English for their inability to get on with governing themselves.

Lettie mislaid her handbag, woke Rebecca early in a panic about getting started on their tour, jabbered and interrupted, prodded and poked at her, and generally (according to Rebecca) transformed the trip into a reenactment of Rebecca's childhood hell. Rebecca felt her bowels rumble. She ate mostly brown bread and butter. She came down with diarrhea. Lettie lectured her: "Well, it is the sort of thing that happens in these circumstances. You have had a succession of rich meals."

But Rebecca found parts of County Kerry as beautiful as Yugoslavia and Mexico. She felt at home in the old houses, and she enjoyed chats with distant cousins who filled her in on Fairfield lore. She felt ambivalent about her family's role in Ireland's economy, taking a lot of money out of the land but also improving it with "bits of civil engineering" that fostered trade. In one draft of her family memoirs she concluded: "The history of Ireland is one of continuous disorder. Mexico is Quakerish by comparison." She jousted with Lettie about the family tree, and penned for her niece Alison her versions of family genealogy, almost always signing herself Auntie C.

4

REBECCA CONTINUED her *Sunday Telegraph* reviewing, her lifeline: "Where would I be without Rivers Scott?" He was her new editor at the paper. They had dined together, and Rebecca was taken with his charming, graceful wife. Rivers seemed to appreciate everything "like a happy child." Rebecca thought, "how disappointed he will be when he grows up." But then she joyfully realized he had grown up and was not disappointed.

People like Rivers astounded Rebecca—as did her great friend, Marie-Noel (Lady Kelly), described in *The Meaning of Treason* as "gay and intelligent, a resourceful woman who could take anything that came her way." Rebecca often stayed at Marie-Noel's country home in Smardon. One day Marie-Noel spoke with touching regret about her life, admitting, "I am not a gentle person." Rebecca felt ashamed, for she suddenly realized, "I should be saying that to myself all the time. And it has never occurred to me to say it, never once in my whole life." Rebecca confessed: "I am not gentle." But she gave in to self-pity: "I have had my dignity cut away from me, *sawn off,* by all the people I have ever had anything to do with."

Lady Kelly, a diplomat's wife, loved Rebecca and her powerful vision; she also had a shrewd sense of what Rebecca required in friends who got close enough to become a second family for her. "She always called me her niece," Lady Kelly said of Rebecca, adding, "Because she liked dependants." Marie-Noel watched Rebecca work through her phases— up and down, up and down—anxious about the state of her soul. She was susceptible to the idea that younger friends like Marie-Noel could move her in and out of her moods. They were like drugs, stimulants and depressants to the system. She expected to have your whole attention, and she got angry if she did not get it. Marie-Noel was not an adoring friend, and she was not afraid of Rebecca, but she knew how to negotiate the heavy weather of Rebecca's moods. She knew that if Rebecca liked you, she would give her soul for you—but she would also recapture it. Tête-à-têtes were like a séance, lasting the whole afternoon or evening. It took all the skills of a diplomat for Marie-Noel to extract herself from these sessions, to prevent herself from being put into one of those nooks where Rebecca kept her pet friends.

5

THE GOLDEN AUTUMN OF 1971, the rosy sunsets she could contemplate from her windows over the garden, lovely—if painful—walks by the Serpentine in Hyde Park—tranquillized Rebecca. Driven out to Fingest in November to put flowers on Henry's grave, she felt her anger at him vanish, replaced by a melancholy desire for them to be on better terms. She drafted his death scene in her memoirs. As she bent over his bedside, she realized that he had never ceased playing (even in private) the perfect banker, the perfect husband, looking out for her comfort and security. Yet he had made a mockery of both roles. "In the same way," she reasoned, her ancestor Anthony Denny had looked down at his master, King Henry VIII, who had "after being for some time a good king, became a bad king, but so perfectly the image of *the king.*"

At any moment her delicate equilibrium could be upset by the willy-willies, or some other supernatural phenomenon. On December 6, for example: "A strange awakening about 4 in the morning. A poltergeist. The side of my bed drenched in water." A week later, she experienced a nightmare in which Anthony attacked her with a knife. She began to tell confidants that she feared her son might do her a physical injury, even murder her.

The growing weight of the past, an incipient ulcer, increasing deafness, and failing eyesight, owing to a cataract in her left eye, combined to depress Rebecca, and she admonished herself: "I must pull myself together. My life is too nearly at an end." In a rare self-critical mood she asked: "Why do I spoil things by noisiness and impulsiveness?"

CHAPTER 38

"The Real Right Beginning"
"Biography Is a Blood-Sport"
1972–1974

I

IN THE NEW YEAR, Rebecca recovered the joy of writing, happily researching and drafting her family memoirs, treasuring her solitude at home and her visits to the London Library. By January 20, she had thirty thousand words (exploring the experiences of her ancestor Anthony Denny in Ireland)—a breakthrough, she thought, because she had abandoned several projects after reaching the ten-thousand word mark. She had also begun writing fiction again, husbanding her time at home, and using shopping at Harrods and walks in Hyde Park as her recreation.

Her productive rhythm broke in late April. Anthony called. "Is anything wrong?" Rebecca asked. He said no. He had come to visit Caroline, recently married to Osei Duah, a Ghanian. She planned to settle with him in Africa. Anthony wanted to see Rebecca. She said she did not want to meet him; he had insulted the memory of her mother and sisters in his recent novel, *David Rees, Among Others*. He replied that a novelist must find his material where he could. Anyway, she had spread around shameful things about him—including the lie that he had been in "Nazi hands." Just before they hung up on each other, she managed to say "he was the most disgusting creature ever born."

Rebecca went through her usual cycle of illness, despondency, and recovery—writing so hard in June that she found it difficult to stop, relapsing in July when she had to supply memoranda for Gordon Ray's book on her and H.G. She had decided to give Gordon access to her papers at Yale, hoping that with her guidance this distinguished scholar would scotch Anthony's lurid accounts and present her side of the story. But it was agonizing to have her affairs raked over. During one of their

380

luncheon conferences, as she was getting up a full head of steam over H.G.'s cruelty to her, Gordon had irritated her with his interjection, "But wasn't it *great fun.*" "Good God" she remarked in her diary.

Rebecca was getting a double dose of H.G.: Norman and Jeanne Mackenzie were querying her about him for their biography. They had met with her and had agreed she could vet their manuscript, but they ran foul of her obsession with Anthony. She grilled them about him. They had seen him only twice. But she kept interrupting them: "When are you going to see Anthony?" To Norman, it seemed as though she wanted them to act as go-betweens. They told her Anthony had been "very cagey" but also "gentle and warm." An outraged Rebecca confided to her diary, "that icy hearted monster."

Her *Sunday Telegraph* reviews deplored the modern taste for cutting up lives, rendering the bloody data of biography that made subjects seem pathological. When she received a published copy of the Mackenzies' H.G. biography, she was aghast that they made him seem dull and hateful, revealing too many details of his private life, which were serialized in the *Sunday Times.* But she tempered her barbs in *The Sunday Telegraph,* saying what good company most of his friends found him. She fretted over how Anthony would react to this new book. Her frustration increased when he visited her without revealing what line he would take. As she feared, he used the occasion of the Mackenzie biography to write an article for the *Hampstead and Highgate Express,* airing his version of why he had not been able to write his father's life. She felt sure he was positioning himself to come out with his own biography.

2

ON AUGUST 8, 1972, the anniversary of her mother's death, Rebecca got up from her breakfast table and fell. Nothing seemed stable anymore, and how "mentally outraged" she felt about such accidents! It was her fifth heavy fall in the last year; this time she injured her good leg. Then Edmund and Vita cabled the distasteful news of Anthony's arrival in London, which he intended to make his home.

In early September, Rebecca suffered a devastating blow: Charles Curran died. He had suffered two heart attacks, and for the past year she had been worried about his ghastly appearance. Now that he was lost to her, she ached with misery, missing the "rough soft quality of his voice." It was as bad as losing her mother, Winnie, and Ruth Lowinsky. Rebecca wept. Alison touched her by saying she had the feeling that Charles used to knock at the back door and say, "Can Cissie come out and play." Rebecca thought about him all the time, about the "unfinished business" between them and her failure to tell him that he meant nearly everything to her. Their dodging of the sex question, however, had made it difficult for her. She alternated between periods of weeping and gratitude for his sweet sensibility.

Autumn brought an awful depression, increasing deafness, blindness in her left eye, inability to work, and a morose calculation that she had accomplished no more than a tenth of the writing she had projected. A visit to Charles's grave on a lovely golden day in late October soothed her and, she thought, Charles as well. Contented, she opened a new vein in the writing of her memoirs.

On December 21, 1982, Rebecca's eightieth birthday, *The Times* published Bernard Levin's tribute, "The Light That Never Failed." He considered her the greatest reporter in the language, with Orwell as her only rival for that distinction, and the greatest woman since Elizabeth I. Her publisher, Harold Macmillan, attended her party at the Reform Club, becoming the first Tory prime minister to enter the premises. She had always liked him as a publisher and politician, and took his presence as a special sign of favor.

Rebecca had little time to savor her moment of glory, because she learned that her granddaughter Caroline had become gravely ill in Ghana, overwhelmed by trying to adjust to the new country, learning its difficult language, and finding her equilibrium in her husband Osei's large and prominent family. Rebecca expressed her concern to Anthony, offering to do what she could to help. But that was precious little, since she was so far away from Caroline. Rebecca had to content herself with reports of Caroline's recovery from Anthony and Kitty, and sometimes from their friends. At such moments, Rebecca felt her family pursued by some modern equivalent of the Greek furies.

3

FOR THE FIRST HALF OF 1973, Rebecca struggled to write a new novel, *The Only Poet* (begun as a short story in the fall of 1962). She liked the dialogue—there were quite remarkable scenes between Leonora Morton and her lover Nicholas, a probing of the sex and love nexus that went considerably beyond what had been essayed in *Sunflower*. Indeed, in some ways, *The Only Poet* rewrites that abandoned novel, for it too is haunted by the figure of Max Beaverbrook, now called Gerard March, who woos Leonora, then abruptly drops her. "He used you," Nicholas remarks, "as a cover for something. Either he's a pederast or impotent." More than any other of Rebecca West's work, *The Only Poet* focuses on the physicality of lovemaking, of the one unique thing (it is never described) that Leonora is able to do for Nicholas. Yet he cannot remain faithful to Leonora, and she cannot accept his plea that she is more important than any of his other women. Eighty, and sensing her imminent death, Leonora ranges over their affair, still trying—as Rebecca continued to do in her diaries and letters—to fathom the male psyche.

Leonora lives in London but longs for her country home, which bears some resemblance to Ibstone. She misses her walled garden, the change of the seasons, her labradors, who are "like the ideal family solicitor, chasing the woodland smells as if they were getting concessions out of the Inland Revenue." But London is convenient for Leonora, as it was for Rebecca—especially for its indoor swimming pools. "One got something of what one had got from love-making, from that first thrust into the water, the surrender of the whole body to an unusual element." Leonora shares her creator's worries about physical appearance, fearing that she looks ridiculous, as "people did when they were old." Like Rebecca, Leonora still yearns for a lover "who is strong as men are, who gives a sense of protection." But obedience is not the word for Leonora's attraction to the powerful Nicholas: "For a woman to obey a man is horrible, to surrender her will, her sense of right and wrong, it is the sort of thing a prostitute does to curry favour with a man."

How Leonora was to die baffled Rebecca. "It has to be seen whether I have still the physical strength necessary for the exercise of the imagination," she confided to her diary. She had "wonderful notes" for the novel, but she feared she had lost her "capacity for fiction." When she wrote, however, she felt happy and hopeful, feeling Leonora hopping around in her mind, a figure "not unlike myself," but part of a work that seemed to Rebecca "unlike anything else I have written."

Dying was a natural preoccupation in Rebecca's life and fiction. One of her dreams had her hurrying away from a train leaving her baggage—"a symbol of death," she supposed. Her agent, A. D. Peters, Noël Coward, and G. B. Stern had recently died: her own physical problems (cataracts in both eyes now) made it difficult to swim in indoor pools. Sometimes she was too stiff to dress herself. Rebecca's poor eyesight meant she often could not find things—including her glasses. She would ask her hairdresser, Joan White, to look for them. Inevitably, Joan brought the wrong pair, a new search would begin, usually resulting in the location of the right pair in absolutely filthy condition. When Rebecca mislaid things, she upturned her Kingston

House flat in an uproar of frustration. One day on a mad reconnaissance for her lost lower plate, Rebecca asked her cook Rosie to help find it. Rosie pointed to the edge of the bed table, adding for good measure: "I wonder they didn't fall into bed and bite your bottom." Rebecca thought it was worth retaining Rosie for her dialogue. Yet Joan White found that Rebecca always knew *exactly* where things were on her writing desk, making it easy for Joan to fetch whatever her employer needed.

It had become an agony for Rebecca even to walk across the road from Kingston House to Hyde Park, and no doctor could tell her exactly why. She persisted in her outings, craving contact with nature, dwelling on the beauty of the trees, thinking how she would have liked to be a landscape painter, then brooding on Anthony's abandonment of painting. Kitty had faulted his brushwork, but his writing, in Rebecca's opinion, was merely imitation Rebecca West. She had now obliterated almost any happy memory of him. Even Vita, her grandson's wife, who felt great sympathy and rapport with Rebecca, remarked to Kitty: "I think she dislikes Anthony so much that the price of membership in her exclusive club is that you must do the same."

4

IN APRIL 1973, a hospital stay interrupted Rebecca's writing, prompting Margaret Hodges to write her: "I do wish you weren't quite so thorough. Surely pneumonia *or* pleurisy would have been quite enough!" Jenny Moncrieff, Rebecca's secretary, thought she had exhausted herself with work on *The Only Poet.* But Rebecca exclaimed, "it will take a lot more than a silly complaint like this to kill me!"

After her hospital stay, Rebecca continued her recuperation for a fortnight with the "inventively kind" Hodges, working again on her novel but bedeviled by nightmares—one a heartrending episode involving her return to Ibstone in the company of New York gangsters. Two large Irish tombs of basalt had been built and she found herself being taken away before she could say good-bye to her friends or visit her animals' graves. She woke up weeping, associating the gangsters with Anthony and the tombs with her own death. John Hodges would see her sitting in a chair, "like a soul in distress," suddenly erupting in shouts "Anthony, oh Anthony!" She was frightened of him, John remembered. Yet when Anthony called in August saying he wanted to spend his birthday with his mother, Rebecca relented, and invited him for lunch—an uneasy affair, for she simply could not trust him, though she felt sorry for him.

He could not get a novel going, found it hard to get steady journalistic assignments, and was troubled by Lily's desire to move back to the U.S.

Such meetings shook Rebecca. She calmed herself by watching television, finding a "nice idiotic" episode of *Star Trek,* "a good fairy tale." She followed the Watergate hearings, pronouncing them lugubrious and futile. She made progress on *The Only Poet,* but of a curious kind, announcing that she had achieved "the real right beginning." She sought the same perfection of origins in her memoirs. Nearly every ambitious project she attempted in her last years showed the promise of a brilliant beginning, which was constantly rewritten. She would go back, go back, go back to first causes, never clinching her arguments or developing her notes for the later parts of her novels. Her dreams followed the same pattern of reversion: a combing over of the past, then an abrupt halt, like her heroine Leonora, who dies still sorting out her history.

Rebecca tired easily and her book drafts sputtered. It is why the *Sunday Telegraph* reviews were so rewarding; she could treat them like little gems. She worried when an article in the paper attacked her. Did it mean she would be sacked? She suspected a plot somewhere. "Who would want to write a preface to my work today?" she asked herself. "The CP has done its work." The Viking Press wanted to do a *Portable Rebecca West.* William Shawn had declined to write the introduction, and Rebecca vetoed several other candidates.

5

IN THE AUTUMN OF 1973, Rebecca spent hours rereading drafts of her memoirs, writing poetry, mulling life over in her diaries. Her daily jottings do not have that composed air of passages meant for publication; they are raw, ragged, and repetitious, with the same issues endlessly cycling through her consciousness. She would take hold of a subject and not let go, shaking and ripping away at it until it had no life left. Her secretaries often observed the process: each day a new topic, a new evisceration—it was a method of purging herself.

Rebecca drew faces (one of Norman Mailer as a fat old lady) and invented whimsical cartoons (two angels are looking down at creation, one saying to the other: "He doesn't get any better at it, does He?"). Occasionally she struck off eloquent verse. "Where would these purple roses grow were there not the statue there?" begins a poem about the statue of a goddess in roses in a Wiltshire garden. A stone girl flowers on her plinth:

Offering the stems the long stem of her leg,
Offering them the freedom of her blossoming hip,
The hard buds of her breast, her spreading arms
That are like creepers fed by human milk . . .
Oh, stone girl, listen to the blackbird on the branch above you
He hymns the part you play.
His sweet note says you are the cause of causes.
Prop to the absolute, the stopper in the vial of the essence
That would dry up if you did your note seal this spot in space.

6

BY EARLY 1974, Rebecca had to suspend reviewing for *The Sunday Tele-graph* pending an eye operation; she could no longer read. Then Edmund wrote to say he and Vita had separated. Rebecca lacerated herself with worry over this attractive couple she had cossetted. She had spun a romance around them—he, the handsome, sensible, and loyal grandson; she, the beautiful, hard-working Italian immigrant child (the antithesis of Anthony, Kitty, and Lily). Rebecca had sent them dozens of letters addressed to "Dear Animals," often signing herself with a tiny drawing of a cat. Edmund and Vita had been sympathetic to her trials with Anthony. Now her image of them shattered just when she feared a new attack from her son. He would undoubtedly dispute the picture of her life with H.G. in Gordon Ray's book, perhaps even claiming he had been slandered, even though lawyers had carefully vetted Gordon Ray's manuscript.

Gordon had been most respectful of Rebecca's views—so much so that Gip Wells objected, pointing out that while Rebecca may not have told deliberate falsehoods, her picture of his father and mother was so coarse that he could only suppose that she had over many years reshaped the story to satisfy her emotional needs. A conscientious scholar, Gordon amended his text to meet several of Gip's reasonable criticisms—though he thought Gip very protective of his mother and less so of H.G. In the process Gordon aggravated Rebecca, who referred to the bulky Ray as a "retarded rhinoceros" with a name inappropriate for "one with no association whatsoever with brightness."

Gordon Ray was not the problem; it was Rebecca's conflicting feelings about exposing her life with H.G. and about biography itself. She believed in a decent interval between a person's life and his or her biography, so that family and friends would not be hurt and the subject's life could be seen in historical perspective. But Anthony had already published details of her family and personal life in articles and stories. She had been given no respite. She knew that he would look on Ray's book as her revenge; she saw it as her recompense for the sorrow, anger, and indignity he had thrust upon her. In order to steel herself for the publication of Gordon Ray's book, Rebecca wrote many letters to friends announcing its imminent arrival, entrusting copies of the manuscript to her confidants, and justifying its existence "now that biography has become a blood-sport."

Rebecca reminded herself that Anthony was a villain. (One projected version of *The Only Poet* centered on Martin, Leonora's wicked son who successfully breaks up his parents' marriage. Martin, like Anthony, illustrated the "reality of evil.") She discredited Anthony's various attempts over the years to become reconciled with her, concluding that he came to her with resentments he could not overcome. But she could not afford to acknowledge that, however awkwardly, her son did make some effort at reconciliation. She gave Anthony no advance notice of Ray's book. Indeed, she behaved precisely as he had done in 1955, when he visited her just before the publication of *Heritage*.

In March, Anthony phoned, warmly inviting her to his house in Hampstead to see Caroline, now recovered from her illness. The call and invitation mystified Rebecca. What did Anthony intend by it? It unnerved her that she ended up enjoying the visit. She found the living room beautifully designed. She admired Caroline's good looks, and Anthony's attractive younger children, Sophie and Adam. Even Lily "looked better" to Rebecca. Why were they being so nice to her? Had they heard of Gordon Ray's book, and was this some kind of retaliatory plot? Yet Rebecca could not help observing: "There is something marvelous about these people, which are my people. Lily's mother's pictures were on the wall. They were superb." The scene did not meet expectations. Girded for war, Rebecca found peace.

Rebecca had arranged with Rivers Scott to collect her at the end of her visit. When he arrived, he found them all together engaging in rather stilted conversation. Anthony escorted his mother to the door, paused, and asked Rivers to give his mother a hand down the steps. That Anthony did not do the natural thing and assist his mother struck Rivers as strange. It surely conveyed to Rebecca the breach that remained between herself and her son. She did not speak of it to Rivers, but she appreciated his sensitivity. Later she would write in her diary: "Rivers is one of the people that I like best of all those I have got to know since I came to London after Henry's death."

Rebecca's tantrums over Anthony alarmed Gwenda David, Viking's

London representative; they came at the moment when plans for a *Portable Rebecca West* began to gel. A critic, Samuel Hynes, had been found to introduce the volume. His superb *Times Literary Supplement* review of Peter Wolfe's book on Rebecca's writing would do with only slight modifications, because Hynes had uncannily emphasized precisely those pieces chosen for *The Portable*. Selecting Hynes ought to overcome her "neuroticism about critics," Marshall Best thought. It did.

The patient Gwenda soothed Rebecca, who basked in a beautiful spring, writing her memoirs on her balcony, and returning to *This Real Night*, the opening chapter of which would figure in Viking's anthology of her writings, now retitled "A Celebration." Gwenda David, impressed with the novel's quality, urged Rebecca to complete it.

Then Rebecca had a cancer scare. She discovered blood in her rectum. Tests revealed diverticulitis (an inflammation of the intestine), a chronic disease. Nothing much could be done, she was told, except to increase her dietary fiber. Agitated over reading an installment of Gordon Ray's book "whitewash[ing]" H.G. and Jane, Rebecca grumbled: "I ought to be sent to the vet to be put down." She relieved her aching legs under an electric blanket and slept as much as twelve hours a day. Gwenda accompanied her on a drive to Brookwood cemetery to "shop for a grave."

7

IN MAY 1974, Rebecca received a charming letter from Major Tony Redd, a professor at The Citadel, a military academy in Charleston, South Carolina. He had just completed his Ph.D. dissertation on her work. She was the twentieth-century writer he most admired. He taught her work regularly, and he thought she might like to know that she had "acquired a small, but devoted, group of young male readers." He enclosed a copy of his study, entitled "Rebecca West: Master of Reality." She responded warmly to his request for a July visit, liking his chronological, straightforward approach to her career and asking him for copies she wished to give to friends.

When they met, he was impressed with her clear golden brown eyes. Although she complained of blindness, a magnifier had made it possible for her to resume reading and reviewing. She had gone through several ophthalmologists (none of them satisfactory), who kept putting off an operation. One had never wearied of "doing the wrong thing," such as prescribing the wrong glasses; another was usually away from the office shooting grouse or yachting. How could she characterize the next one? "a blank, my lord, as Viola says in *Twelfth Night*." Number four: "a bounder," five "catatonic," and six: "had all the quiet and respectable air of Sammy Davis Junior." Seven might actually be her lucky number, a man in good physical trim who got on with the job.

Tony came to hear Rebecca talk, but she wanted to know all about him. Redd—was that a Cornwall name? Tony admired her flat, especially the paintings by Dufy and Bonnard, the white porcelain and Wedgwood pieces, and the tossing green branches of the tree seen through her tremendous picture window. Everything seemed immaculate and sparkling. Rebecca adopted a confidential tone with Tony almost immediately. She told him about her trouble sleeping, of dreams she had of giant butterflies in her room and rehearsing for the lead role in a musical comedy. He noticed her nervous mannerism of twisting her thumbs.

Their first dinner was a sumptuous event with the Scotts (Rivers and Christina) and the Huttons (Graham and Marjorie) at the Capitol Hotel Restaurant in Basil Street. Marjorie helped Rebecca with ordering courses and choosing wine. Rebecca talked about how she was always being asked to blurb books; she acceded to one importunate publisher, puffing an author with the line: "A veritable Watergate of a person." Her comment was left out, Rebecca laughed. Tony wanted to know why she had not finished the sequel to *The Fountain Overflows*. Rebecca traced the trouble back to 1960, when she had left the country to get away from Henry and an abominable secretary. Afterward, she had lost energy and interest in the project. Then to her dinner guests, Rebecca pronounced on Tony Redd: "He's all that we thought he would be." She later took to giving him a fanfare: "This is Tony Redd. He teaches Marines!"

At their second meeting, they embraced and kissed, sealing their rapport. They would see each other almost every summer for the rest of her life, going to the theater, to the zoo (where Rebecca loved to watch and draw the giraffes), and to her favorite restaurants (The Empress, The Capitol, the Carlton). Rebecca would say, "When you're in London you ought to let me entertain you—the old should entertain the young." In her chauffeur-driven car she would identify points of interest along the way. She took him to a reception at PEN for V. S. Pritchett and introduced him to several writers. They dined at her flat with Lady Antonia Fraser and novelist Rosamond Lehmann. Tony appreciated the way she began to relax in his presence, asking him to serve more raspberries and coffee, to find her glasses or the pills she would take after lunch. They talked about everything. Rebecca might give him an intricate account of her family background, her troubles with Anthony, then sympathetically analyze the fortunes of the Wilson government, then recall how Bertrand Russell chased her around a table but could not catch her, then give an imitation of the American writer Mary McCarthy. "You know, she snorts," said Rebecca, starting to snort à la McCarthy. "The truth of Sylvia Plath's poetry is so very obvious," Rebecca concluded. "She simply didn't like to wash up." At one lunch Tony observed her miss her cup when adding sugar to her coffee. "You can't win them all," she announced placidly. Later he noticed that she poured the milk quite perfectly.

Tony saw how difficult it was for Rebecca to walk on her swollen legs. Yet during intermission at the theater she got up from their front row center seats to powder her nose. He worried that she would never make her way back, but he was reluctant to accompany her and give the impression that he was watching over her that closely. He was much relieved to see her return without any apparent problem. She got along amazingly well, considering—as she said—all the "spare parts" (such as several pairs of spectacles and hearing aids) she had to lug around.

Arriving late at the Capitol Restaurant, Tony spied Rebecca seated in a little nook, looking very jaunty, Bloody Mary in hand. She made a witty comment about the arrival of the Southern gentleman, complimenting him on his tie, and lowering her voice to an intimate level when she called him Tony. The expression on her face was that of a woman waiting for a man, expectant, excited. As usual, they devoured everything except the silverware. Tony looked at Rebecca's hands; they were not those of a woman past eighty.

8

As THE AUTUMN 1974 publication date for Gordon Ray's H. G. Wells and Rebecca West loomed, Rebecca succumbed to days and nights of depression, diverticulitis, and insomnia. She imagined Anthony killing her because of the truth the book would reveal. Accompanied by her former secretary, Timmie Richardson, Rebecca tried to divert herself with a short trip to Venice, but she suffered another upset when she felt rudely rejected by Peggy Guggenheim. Why did people repudiate her? It often made her feel hounded by a supernatural force. Back home at the end of September, she scanned the Sunday papers for the first reviews. In spite of a reassuring letter from her nephew Norman, Rebecca dreaded her family's reaction.

October brought a flood of reviews. To Rebecca, the worst one appeared in the influential New York Times Book Review. Lillian Hellman, a staunch Stalinist, then at the height of her fame as a feminist heroine, asked some pointed questions: "why did Mr Ray trust the memory of a lady who is over eighty? And who trusts anybody's memory of a love affair?" She reviewed the careers of the lovers, praising Rebecca's early journalism and *Black Lamb and Grey Falcon,* but belittling the treason books, calling them examples of what happens when "good straight journalism begins to theorize in a manner too big for its pants or skirt." Rebecca had become too "high-blown" and "musical" in her prose—and worse, a hypocrite, wanting H.G. to leave his wife but saying that it was not what she really wanted; marrying a banker, becoming a member of the establishment, but still parading her socialist principles, all the while living a well-servanted and well-fed life. But leave that aside, and to hell with the scholarly rationale, concluded tough-talking Lillian. In truth, lovers had no right to make "an easy buck" out of the publication of love letters; it constituted not only a "betrayal of what two people were together, but of what one is alone."

Lillian Hellman's last sentence, with its emphasis on betrayal, hit Rebecca hard. Running a high temperature, she took to her bed and threatened suicide. Gwenda David had tried without success to keep this review—and others—away from her overwrought author. Rebecca worried that Viking would drop its plans for an anthology of her work. This had all occurred because she had tried to set the record straight, to show Anthony how much she had suffered during his earliest years. This is what it must feel like, she told herself, to be the "mother of anti-Christ.... Why did God deliver me into the power of this devil. What can have happened. Was H.G. the little fat sex god and really supernatural?"

But Rebecca did not give up the game. In mid-October, she wrote to Arthur Schlesinger, now married to Lily West's sister, Alexandra. Rebecca alluded to her troubles with Anthony, explained her efforts to help him, his wives and his children, and asked Arthur if he would consider becoming trustee for a legacy she wished to bestow on Anthony. Arthur responded warmly, congratulating her on the *Sunday Telegraph* reviews, and speaking fondly of a visit he had made to Ibstone in the late 1950s (they had quietly dropped the argument over McCarthy). He hesitated about accepting the trusteeship, since he had no expertise in such matters. Perhaps her solicitor could send him a description of his duties? Arthur wanted to do what he could for Rebecca and Anthony, knowing that whatever the problems were between mother and son, Anthony was fond of his mother. "What a stupid, callous lie," Rebecca confided to her diary and abruptly cancelling her initiative—though she continued to write the Schlesingers to keep them abreast of her opinion of Anthony's antics.

Anthony snidely reviewed Gordon Ray's book twice, suggesting it was a put-up job, with the biographer getting access to the letters for the price of playing Rebecca's tune. Anthony noted he was mentioned several times in the narrative, but the biographer had not consulted him— no doubt at Rebecca's request. He ridiculed the portrait of Rebecca's impoverished childhood. She and Gordon countered with published letters of rebuttal. In his annotated copy of *H. G. Wells and Rebecca West*, Anthony pounced on exaggerations and falsehoods, calling Rebecca's claim that for three months she hardly left the Holt Hotel near the sanatorium where he was treated for tuberculosis "a flat lie." He had a lesion on his left lung, but his case was not particularly serious, and Rebecca was merely inflating her concern for him. Behind the scenes Anthony gave Gordon Ray's publishers (Yale and Macmillan) grief over H.G.'s drawings, which H.G. had given him but which had somehow remained in Rebecca's Yale papers. The publishers had unlawfully reproduced his property, Anthony claimed, and he demanded sums which kept increasing each time the publishers delayed settling the issue. Finally, at Rebecca's request, Yale University Press sent the originals back to Anthony, and that ended the matter—legally, that is. The accusations of mother and son continued to escalate. Joan Haslip, who had known Anthony in the 1920s and 1930s and had remained Rebecca's friend, offered to intercede. But Rebecca believed a reconciliation impossible.

Most reviewers found *H. G. Wells and Rebecca West* fascinating and did not condemn Rebecca. She characterized the American reaction as "fair" and the English "sterling." Indeed, reviewers were impressed with how well she had held her own with the formidable H.G. They lamented the loss of most of Rebecca's letters and the narrative's lopsided reliance on H.G.'s. If anyone got blamed, it was H.G. As one reviewer put it, his name should not have been Jaguar, but "skunk."

Rebecca ventured out in public, even consenting to appear at the opening of a new bookshop in Tunbridge Wells, owned by a young friend of hers, Baron Nicolas van den Branden, whose family she had known for many years. With Nicky, as with other attractive young men, Rebecca recovered her humor. She enjoyed staying with him and his friend, Terence Davis. She used to say, "Now I am going to tell you a story, it's rather a long story, so you better pull up a chair." She was racy, telling the boys about an obscene phone call. A male voice asked, "Are you wearing anything?" She replied: "Actually, I'm wearing a tam-o'-shanter." The caller put the phone down, thinking, she was sure, that he had a nut on the other end of the line.

The calls on December 21, 1974, Rebecca's eighty-second birthday, were reassuring. She wanted more, more, more—which startled her, since usually she disliked such interruptions. She felt young the day of her impromptu birthday party, organized by an old Ibstone neighbor and friend, Marjorie Parr. It seemed like the 1920s again, with everyone innocent and sparkling.

For the prior few months, Rebecca had been revising her estimate of Henry, overcome suddenly with the certainty that she loved him, that he had been good to her, even if his brain disease marred their later years. She announced on December 24 her complete reconciliation with him.

Rivers Scott visited her on the 29th. They drank weak gins in the kitchen and she recorded her satisfaction: "a most companionable man." He often stopped by with a book for her to review, and to cheer her up. She nearly always rose to the occasion, shooting off remarks that rivaled Dr. Johnson's range, Rivers thought.

A. L. Rowse, one of the few Oxford dons Rebecca had any use for, and with whom she had a mildly flirtatious relationship, wrote her a joshing letter, remarking he would have been a much nicer lover for her than H.G., if not as good a sexual performer. But was H.G. really that good? the seventy-two-year old Rowse wanted to know. From his ancestral home in Cornwall, he sent a provocative New Year's message: "Remember it is a sin to despair—as does your father confessor, who loves you too much to inflict a penance—though I've a wicked one in mind." Intrigued, she wrote him for specifics on the penance. He deflected her query with a mock expression of shock over her affair with H.G. "Don't dare to cross the Devon frontier into Cornwall," he warned her. "I'll turn the key in the door and not let you go back over it again."

CHAPTER 39

"The Abnormality of My Life"
1975–1978

I

ON FEBRUARY 1, in the London Clinic, Rebecca's cataracts were finally operated on. She recovered her sight slowly, reading at fifteen-minute intervals. Her days were considerably lightened by a new friend, Stanley Olson, "a nice, spontaneous grateful creature." He had interviewed her in the spring of 1974 for his biography of the poet Elinor Wylie. One of the few people who had liked Elinor and felt she had been badly used by the press, Rebecca regaled Stanley with anecdotes. His questions recalled to her the 1920s, and she became quite tender, almost tearful. On subsequent visits, he proved to be the perfect confidant: He had as much gossip to give as she had the capacity to receive. Rather like her, he was a self-invented figure, carefully transforming himself from a midwestern American into an Edwardian gentleman; a perfectionist about his clothes and his food, he grew flowers especially for her. She came to rely on him and was once observed at a party in a panic after he had left her side: "Where's Stanley! I'm frightened without him." Stanley later became an invaluable source of information about Kitty and Caroline. Rebecca fretted over what she deemed their inattention to her, and Stanley, close to Frances Partridge, Kitty's friend, was often able to fill the gaps in Rebecca's knowledge.

Like Tony Redd, her other American consort and Boswell for a season, Stanley kept a diary, jotting down Rebecca's Johnsonian ripostes. To an intrusive guest: "Thank you for coming; it was extremely kind of you, especially as you are so busy, and as you were not asked." She had memorable ways of discarding people, speaking of their "instinct for failure." Stanley read Rebecca's work assiduously and aspired to be her biographer—a role several people would audition for in her last years.

Rebecca doubted that any biographer could capture the "abnormality of my life," the way Lettie, H.G., Anthony, and others had hounded her. No one would believe it: her key witness, Winnie, had died. Who could tell the truth about love affairs? Not even the principals, she declared—unconsciously echoing Lillian Hellman, of all people.

Victoria Glendinning came courting in the summer of 1975. Over lunch a cagey Rebecca entertained the possibility of a biography, but suggested it would have to be a "long-term project," with Victoria settling for visits and note taking on their sessions. Victoria wanted authorization to look at the Yale papers, but Rebecca put her off with the assurance that it would be forthcoming when she needed it. Rebecca looked forward to Victoria's visits. They got on well, and Rebecca thought her "highly intelligent." But Victoria remembers ringing Rebecca's doorbell, her heart pounding, and then after the visit feeling exhilarated because Rebecca had not chopped off her head. She could be so scathing; there was no telling how a conversation might go. Expressing a liking for someone whom Rebecca despised made one feel like a leper. Rebecca also became forgetful about appointments and would sometimes shuffle into the room barely dressed. She seemed touching and lonely.

Rebecca did not warm to Victoria in quite the way she did to Stanley. Victoria was a down-to-earth person, not attuned to the rather baroque fancies of Rebecca and Stanley. Victoria once said to him, "Of course Rebecca is the most awful liar." Stanley admonished her: "Don't you ever use that word about her." He did not mean that Rebecca always told the truth, but that she believed in her way of telling things. Victoria was not unsympathetic to this idea; it was just that she did not have his psychic feel for it. Stanley recognized that the so-called lies were part of the story's structure, its purpose.

2

FOR ALL HER COMPLAINTS, Rebecca did write. She had almost completed a version of the first chapter of *This Real Night*, for *Rebecca West: A Celebration*, Viking's anthology of her writings. She had also resumed her *Sunday Telegraph* reviewing. At dinner, her editor, Rivers Scott, broke it to her that her latest review was not "good enough." A crushed Rebecca admitted "it wasn't" and promptly rewrote it. She felt grateful for the sweet way he had put it to her; he had spoken out of the conviction that a writer, however formidable, wants a first reader to respond critically, as long as that writer knows that "whatever you're giving is for them, and you're not trying to show how smart you are." It was also easier to take criticism from a man who "loves all of the nicer gossip, however old." Rivers had said to her, "Rebecca, how on earth do you remember all these wonderful tidbits?" She said, "Well, you see, some people only have noble minds and they just remember the frightfully elevating things. I have a rather frivolous and scandalous mind and I remember all the naughty things about them."

Rebecca felt lonely, but she had the attention of another young man, Justin Lowinsky, the son of her dear friend Ruth. Justin came by frequently to chat and to advise Rebecca on business. He was absolutely loyal and even joked that for Rebecca he had taken the place of her faithful Albert. (She referred to Justin as her "dogsbody"—just as Gwenda David was her "lady-in-waiting.") On more than one occasion, she had employed him to sack one of the household staff at Kingston House. He also served as an audience for her stories—like the one about the obscene caller whom she had told, "I'm eighty-one and bored with it," slamming down the phone. She would ring Justin: "Time we had fish and chips." At Wheelers she enjoyed playing with the restaurant cat and perfecting her meow.

3

On November 10, 1975, Rebecca got a phone call from her grandson Edmund. He had not written to her for several months, and she had spent the time fretting over his divorce—still blaming Kitty for his choice of an expensive American medical school and for relying on the financial support of Vita's mother to obtain a house in Stonington, Connecticut, which complicated the divorce settlement. Now he was in London and wanted to visit and to introduce her to a friend. "By all means," Rebecca replied, "do bring him." Edmund said, "It's a she." Rebecca tried to respond warmly, saying "certainly, certainly," but with her "heart in my boots" thought, "Oh God," it was that nurse that Vita and Kitty had mentioned in less than enthusiastic terms. Rebecca questioned Edmund's motives. Perhaps he favored Anthony in ways she had never suspected? Was this to be a meeting with his future wife? Still attached to Vita, Rebecca simply could not adjust to the new arrangement. She had idealized Edmund and Vita's marriage. The image of married love strongly appealed to her. In her diary she mourned the death of Lionel Trilling, because he and Diana had seemed the perfect couple. That Edmund and his "friend" were staying with Kitty was a mark against them.

When Edmund and Cheryl visited Rebecca two days later, she had developed the direst suspicions. She liked nothing about Cheryl. Her looks, her voice, her manners, her clothes, her vocabulary, her posture—all were found wanting. Cheryl wore culottes, a cross between bermuda shorts and a skirt—a fashion Rebecca deemed vulgar. At dinner, Rebecca began to vilify Anthony and was miffed that Edmund did not pitch in. She switched to more neutral subjects, and when Cheryl excused herself for a moment, Rebecca asked Edmund if he meant to marry her. Taken aback by her abruptness, Edmund was noncommittal. Rebecca understood him to say no. When Cheryl returned, Rebecca and Edmund returned to the subject of Anthony, and Edmund outraged her by repeating his father's view that Gordon Ray's book had been unfair to H.G. Rebecca spied Cheryl nodding sympathetically at Edmund's remarks (in Rebecca's more colorful language it became a "pantomime of disapproval"), and damned Cheryl as an insolent, conniving intruder. "I will never see him again," Rebecca announced in her diary, deciding to cut him out of her will, even though her attorney, Riou Benson, advised caution, pointing out that Edmund would have heard mainly Anthony's side of things, and Cheryl would naturally see things Edmund's way. Edmund's position in the family could not have been happy or easy, Riou speculated. Even if Anthony had been a bad father, Rebecca should not be so quick to take it out on his son.

Riou Benson's shrewd assessment did not please Rebecca; he assured her that he had not meant to criticize her. To Rebecca, Edmund had joined up with H.G. and Anthony. When he later realized the vehemence of her reaction, he was baffled. He had kept his distance from Rebecca's and Anthony's quarrel, while remaining on good terms with both of them. He now became part of a drama without having been briefed for his role.

Rebecca reviewed the past. Surely Edmund had deserved her affection, or had she been a fool about him? She discussed her ambivalent feelings with a sympathetic Gwenda David, who nevertheless realized that Rebecca had overreacted and had brought this disastrous rupture on herself. Rebecca speculated that Edmund saw some advantage in joining Anthony's side, although what it could be puzzled her. Reverting to her fears of Anthony, she half expected to be murdered, and she warned Ian and Sally Barclay, her relations in Wiltshire, that she might die in suspicious circumstances. Suicide was not an option; she would never give Anthony that satisfaction.

In February 1977, Edmund (unaware of Rebecca's hard feelings) wrote to her announcing his marriage to Cheryl. He hoped the ceremony would be in England and that Rebecca would be able to attend. Kitty also wrote, saying Anthony and Lily would be at the wedding. Rebecca had complained of not hearing from Edmund; now she thought him mad and in the power of Kitty and Anthony. They were trying to get hold of her in order to . . . what? She could not imagine, but she shrank from them in fear. She felt like a pussy being stroked before she is "popped into a sack." She asked Emily Hahn to investigate. Was Edmund in some kind of trouble? Rebecca had heard from a friend there was some holdup in his medical certification. Is that why she was getting her "callup papers." It was an odd delusion—even for Rebecca—since she knew Edmund had been a first-class student. A letter from Emily effectively exploded this particular misgiving. When Edmund called inviting Rebecca to his wedding in Dorset, Rebecca "declined with the single monosyllable 'No.' "

It seemed to Rebecca that losing Edmund meant losing everything. Her mind seemed to stop. In a depression she took sedatives and dozed for hours, then tried to reckon with Marshall Best's selections for *Rebecca West: A Celebration*. Gwenda David struggled with her tired and confused author, who once again thought Viking had dropped the project (actually it awaited her final approval of the selections). Rebecca could not get free of her lethargy. Feeling separated from her body, she watched her life stretch out on a Hieronymus Bosch canvas; she was tortured by grotesque animals no one else could see.

Rebecca had pains (ischemia) that cut right down her cleavage, and frequent recurrences of diverticulitis dovetailed with Anthony's articles in *The Observer*, "Life with Aunty Panther and H.G." and "My Father's Unpaid Debts of Love." Rebecca busied herself contradicting Anthony, writing to Gip Wells and to her friends, threatening a libel suit. (A *Sunday Telegraph* lawyer convinced her to drop the idea of legal action, emphasizing that it would take years to get the case into court.) Rebecca's rebuttals called far more attention to the articles than they might otherwise have received. As Rivers Scott put it, "She never knew when to stand back and play it cool. In spite of her knowledge of psychology, she wasn't a tactician."

Anthony capped off his campaign with the publication of *Mortal Wounds*, a savage assault on Madame de Staël, Benjamin Constant, George Sand, Marcel Proust, and other writers, who together constituted Rebecca's literary pantheon. He not only attacked their achievement, he refuted *The Strange Necessity*, without mentioning either the book or its author. Using Eric Berne's popular book of psychology, *Games People Play*, Anthony relentlessly exposed fiction as a species of game playing—almost a transparent extension of the writer's biography, which dooms literature to acts of revenge and manipulation, with every book becoming, like *Heritage,* a roman à clef or a roman à these. Rebecca read *Mortal Wounds* with horror, because it so neatly and brutally reversed her position. She would often begin her literary studies with biography, insisting on the relationship between literature and life, but then show how Proust, for example, transcended his sources. Anthony denied this transcendence, and thus confirmed Rebecca's view that he had never become a complete writer, capable of the imaginative leaps that made literature more than autobiography. As one critic concludes, *Mortal Wounds* might have been titled, "Let's Make Mother Sorry."

It did not surprise Rebecca to learn from Gwenda David the story of Anthony's exorcism in Hampstead, since Rebecca had believed all along that an evil spirit possessed him. But Anthony had gone to an exorcist (officially sanctioned by the Church of England) thinking he could relieve the curse Rebecca had cast on him, although his own family were uncertain how seriously he took the matter. At any rate, the result, in Lily's West's words, was "occluded."

4

IN THE LATE SUMMER OF 1977, Tony Redd returned for his annual round with Rebecca. After one of their dinners, they returned to Kingston House for what became a painfully long conversation. He confessed he was amazed at the conspiracy of silence about her work. His students all liked, even loved her books, which got good reviews and sold better than those by many well-known writers. Yet her books seldom received significant, sustained treatment and major critics never lectured on them. He said he had been to lunch with the novelist Francis King, and Neville Braybrook was there, and they both praised her books but had never written anything seriously about them. Francis King said he had been asked to write an article on her for *The Spectator,* but he could not spare the time to go over her work and read it again. So did Paul Scott. Tony touched on what had often distressed Rebecca: Even in the memoirs of people who were beholden to her she was not mentioned. He always looked in the index, and she was not there. H.G. he observed, always was, though nothing memorable he did or said was mentioned. Tony said it appeared to be something supernatural, as if an invisible power were sealing the lips of those about to speak of Rebecca. This was indeed true, Rebecca thought, but it was so terrible, so frightening, that she could hardly bear to hear it spoken of even with the sympathy and affection that were Tony Redd's characteristics. (Diana Trilling, who thought Rebecca one of the greatest figures of the century, once confessed: "I always wanted to write something about her, and I never did, because I didn't think I knew enough . . . she was too big.")

Rebecca broached the idea of Tony writing her biography. He realized that it would be a long, complicated project, but he was interested, for he felt almost like a close blood relation, perhaps a lost grandson. Rebecca told him about Victoria Glendinning and asked him if he knew Stanley Olson. (He did not.) Tony realized that Stanley had impressed her. Gordon Ray's stock, on the other hand, had fallen. One summer he had been "that sweet man," now he was "that awful man"—or worse, "the great white whale."

Rebecca talking with Tony Redd provoked several dreams, the most vivid one putting her at the mercy of two people holding her head, forcing her to look at a board with stenciled phrases, and commanding her to make anagrams of them or she would be bastinadoed. She felt them tickling her feet and woke up in a sweat.

5

ON OCTOBER 10, Lettie made one of her garrulous visits to Kingston House. As usual, Rebecca bridled at the talk, but she noticed a peculiar childish quality in Lettie's words and became alarmed, especially after her sister said, "Do you know, Cousin Jessie died when she was the age I am now. She died when she was 91." Rebecca urged her sister to take a taxi home and later discovered that as usual Lettie had walked part of the way and boarded a bus. The next morning, Vera Watson, Lettie's neighbor, called to say Lettie had had a stroke; her right arm and leg were paralyzed and she was on the way to hospital. Rebecca resisted the seriousness of the case, calling Lettie a hopeless hypochondriac who had summoned Rebecca to bedside dramas when she imagined herself stricken with cancer, heart disease, and emphysema, without even having a temperature.

As Lettie's hospital stay lengthened, Rebecca began to notice her family's extraordinary attachment to her sister. At Lettie's bedside, she met her cousin, the "brilliant and good looking" Christine Byam Shaw (Aunt Sophie's granddaughter). Christine visited Lettie every day and had an "alert eye" for Lettie's well being. Rebecca asked her nephew Norman why he and Alison felt such respect and affection for Lettie. Norman startled her, saying everyone loved Lettie. She was so lively and had such a sensitivity to children; his own children adored her. Could it be true? Rebecca asked herself. She let Norman know that she regarded Lettie as a fool and a bore. It was his turn to be astonished. Rebecca thought it was sinister of Lettie to deceive Norman and Alison as to her true character, because Rebecca was certain that Lettie did not care for her family at all. This fuss over Lettie brought home to Rebecca all the "fears of my childhood."

Rebecca's diverticulitis worsened. She called Lettie's illness a ploy to soak up the family's attentions. Lettie would linger on and on, sucking Rebecca's blood, claiming to be poor, and inflicting various family members on Rebecca, urging her to do something more for her sister. Rebecca saw them grouped around Lettie like a medieval picture of the Assumption of the Virgin. Rebecca announced she was dying. Her physician, Dr. Ferguson, told her she was not.

Lettie remained in the hospital, deteriorating, becoming confused; the end seemed near. She asked Rebecca: "Have they any idea when I'm likely to disappear?" Rebecca said, "Well, they haven't said anything about that. I think we can't say more than that they expect you to go some time during the present century." Lettie fell asleep. Rebecca returned home feeling so arthritic that she had to climb out of the car on all fours. She slept badly and cried out in her sleep.

Lettie's approaching death, and Anthony's attacks, confirmed for Rebecca the abnormality of her life. She recalled instances in which she had been rejected or attacked, beginning with Lettie's earliest treatment of her. It had deprived Rebecca of empathy: "I am so appalled by not being able to love someone who is dying," she confessed to her diary. She had attempted to probe this disgust with her own feelings in a short story, "The Man Who Liked Strangers," started shortly before Lettie's stroke. Now, awaiting her sister's death, she returned to it, focusing on the life of Alix Morton, a middle-aged woman who has never recovered from her love affair with Murrough Macarthur (another Max Beaverbrook stand-in), who suddenly dropped her at the very moment when their lovemaking seemed at its best. Thirty years later Murrough is dying and summons her to his bedside. She is afraid of being hurt by him again, but she is also obsessed with the hope of learning from him why he rebuffed her.

"The Man Who Liked Strangers" has the same compulsive, obsessive feel as *The Only Poet*, and a wonderful sense of suspense, because Rebecca keeps delaying the moment of Alix's final meeting with Murrough. When it arrives, the encounter seems anticlimactic, since Murrough tells Alix nothing. But their exchange deepens the mystery, for Alix does discover that Murrough is troubled by a conversation he suspects took place between his daughter and Alix. He believes (erroneously) that Alix has been handed a secret about him and his family, and it is Alix's knowledge that Murrough cannot abide. Alix is aware that Murrough's daughter disapproved of her love affair with her father, but it only gradually occurs to Alix how the daughter has treated her as a rival for her father's affections.

The story swelled to twenty-five thousand words, with more and more autobiographical elements. People tell Alix, as they told Rebecca, that she has the mind of a man. To Murrough, then, Alix may seem especially threatening because she is both a lover and competitor, to whom he is afraid to submit, because she may overcome and master him. That she is also perfectly feminine only makes their relationship more insidious to him. As an equal and as a lover, Alix feels humiliated and defenseless. Like a Kafka character, she observes, "everybody in the world might turn on me, and I might be imprisoned without trial." Men suffer this fate as well as women, Alix concedes, but women seem particularly vulnerable to this form of rejection.

"The Man Who Liked Strangers" is a fascinating development of Rebecca's punishment dreams, in which she is bastinadoed not for what she has done but for what she is, a thinker and a lover who must be publicly humbled—by H.G., by Anthony, by Henry, by Lettie, by the world, which will not let her live, a world that plans her murder.

As Rebecca worked on her story in June of 1977, she reported in her diary a conversation with her niece Alison, who said: "Oh, Lettie has said the most extraordinary thing to Cathy [Alison's daughter]. She told her that her father beat her about the time you were born, and she thinks that she must have connected the two events, and that was the reason for her resentment of you." For Rebecca, Lettie's remark was like the shattering of a pose: Lettie admitted her hostility, a fact Rebecca wanted to savor. Lettie had wanted to beat her as she had been beaten. But Alison went on to quiz Rebecca about Charles Fairfield. Did Rebecca think he had beaten Lettie? An exasperated Rebecca dismissed the question, saying only that if Lettie had been beaten, Rebecca was sure she deserved it. Having to wait so many years for a deathbed confession eerily echoed the events of Rebecca's short story and her sense of the abnormality of her life—a fact no one could see, apparently, except Rebecca herself, who had struggled for so many years, like Alix, in perplexity. Rebecca expected no sympathy from Alison; she was on Lettie's side and shared Lettie's hostility. But to Alison, Lettie's remark had meant something much more innocuous: not that she was making some devastating admission of a lifelong campaign against Rebecca, but merely an acknowledgment that as an older child she had been jealous of the arrival of a new, petted family member.

Rebecca worried that because of her upset over Lettie, she would not be able to complete "The Man Who Liked Strangers." She was right, for the story's plot was as unresolved as her own feelings. Although she envisioned an ending, she admitted, "I don't really know how it is going to work out." A curious subplot had to do with Alix's friend, a man who preferred inviting strangers to his parties and whose character no one feels they have really fathomed. He stood for Rebecca's strong convictions about the inscrutability of reality: Certain people did not want to be known for what they really were. People did not know Lettie for what she really was; neither did they Henry, whose true character was anything but that of a reliable banker.

Another curious subplot involves Murrough Macarthur's daughter married to a Jewish writer, Himmelfarb, "a sort of Norman Mailer." In a sketch of the story, Rebecca has Himmelfarb learn (perhaps from his wife) that Murrough has committed incest with her and that Alix had seen her leaving her father's bed. In fact, the daughter has lied about Alix, Murrough realizes on his deathbed. Of this projected ending, Rebecca commented that it was better not to know what people are. She believed that her advantage had been to divine their true characters, and that she had been punished cruelly for that knowledge.

A surprising feature of "The Man Who Liked Strangers" is Rebecca's sympathetic portrayal of Himmelfarb, for she had little use for his true-life counterpart. They had met only once (at the Edinburgh Festival). Afterwards she had voiced her disapproval. But Mailer remembered that Rebecca had treated him to an account of her lovers—which suggests she saw something more in him than her attacks imply. Himmelfarb has Mailer's thick and heavy physique and an "inexhaustible kindness that is found only in certain Jews." Rebecca had an oblique connection with Mailer through his third wife, Lady Jeanne Campbell, Max Beaverbrook's granddaughter. Diana Trilling, who did not know of Rebecca's liaison with Max during her friendship with Rebecca, remembers what a keen interest Rebecca took in Jeanne ("almost that of a mother for a daughter"), wanting to know all about her activities and how she was faring in America. Diana was also a friend of Mailer's then and may have conveyed an enthusiasm for him that would have impressed Rebecca. Lady Jeanne had a streak of wildness that complemented Mailer's. Less well known is the fact that her aristocratic background (she was the daughter of the Duke of Argyll) appealed to his own yearning for dignity and his desire to exercise his exquisite good manners—a quality of the man rarely acknowledged. From afar, Rebecca seems to have latched on to this alter-Mailer, endowing him in her fiction with a virtuous receptiveness so that he became yet another example of a person whose true character is completely misconceived. One further aspect of Lady Jeanne's biography appears to have made a contribution to the short story, for Lady Jeanne is reported to have once told a friend that she suspected that she was actually Max Beaverbrook's daughter, not his granddaughter.

Halfway through Rebecca's writing of "The Man Who Liked Strangers," Lettie suddenly broke through her delirium, became very affectionate with Rebecca, looked at her baby sister and said: "Haven't we had strange lives?" What an understatement, Rebecca thought. She felt isolated, "the way I belong to nobody, nobody belongs to me."

On February 1, 1978, Lettie died. It horrified Rebecca that her sister's death provoked only her wonderment at how someone so "absolutely marmoreal" had gained a reputation as a kind woman. Lettie had chosen to be buried next to her mother, which Rebecca felt sure would annoy Mrs. Fairfield. Rebecca relented when Elizabeth Jenkins, one of Lettie's friends, phoned. Perhaps Elizabeth's love for Lettie, her appreciation of her friend's vivid personality and sense of humor disarmed Rebecca; she found herself enjoying the call much more than she expected, although it made no lasting dent in her determined defamation of her sister. Even Lettie's dying words, "I have always loved you," were said with the "immense condescension" of a Renaissance Pope, Rebecca alleged.

At the funeral, Alison watched Rebecca behave abominably, "sighing noisily with boredom and impatience." Rebecca had resisted any sort of gathering afterward, claiming that Lettie had few friends. Rebecca knew better from the letters of condolence, some of which she annotated with waspish corrections. One of Lettie's friends wrote in fond memory of a wet rainy evening when Lettie had announced she was setting off to take her younger sister to the doctor. "Lettie never took me to a doctor in her life. This is typical of her very provoking line of fantasy," Rebecca rejoined. Another friend proposed that Rebecca write a life of her sister. Rebecca did not deign to comment.

Rebecca received a letter of condolence from Anthony. He admitted never liking Lettie, but he felt sorry for his mother's loss. The letter touched her and she reciprocated his warm gesture by sending him some of H.G.'s books which he had inscribed to her. She phoned Anthony, and he mentioned that his daughter Sophie would like to see her grandmother. Lily also sent a note of sympathy, telling Rebecca a little about Sophie. Rebecca prayed for a "little time of peace with Anthony." A few months later, she had another one of her edgy, unsatisfactory visits with Anthony and his family. His overweight and graying appearance disturbed her. This time he helped her down the steps, and she stumbled, blaming her slip on his weak support. Her driver, who had come running to help, said to her in the car: "The old gentleman should have come with us to see you got into your flat safely." This made Rebecca "laugh and choke."

"If a play were written about my life," Rebecca said, "the stage direction 'Enter a lunatic' would be included time after time."

CHAPTER 40

Celebrating Rebecca West
1977–1980

I

THE PUBLICATION OF *Rebecca West: A Celebration* in the autumn of 1977 did not lift her spirits much. She enjoyed the publisher's party, wearing a new Yuki dress and surrounded by her friends, but the book's bits and pieces reminded her of so much she had left unfinished. To her, it seemed a little pretentious to issue the anthology in hardcover; it made her fingers and toes "curl up."

Reviewers echoed Samuel Hynes's introductory remarks on Rebecca's extraordinary range and quality and what he called her "intellectual toughness," in which she surpassed virtually all of her contemporaries. The austerity of her moral code reminded Hynes of St. Augustine, and he believed her engagement with that great figure had done much to shape her finest achievements. Yet he acknowledged that her work had not "fused in the minds of critics, and she has no secure literary status." Hynes believed that the multiplicity of her interests and her resort to several different genres explained this neglect—as did the defects of her novels (excepting *The Return of the Soldier* and *The Birds Fall Down*), which had not matched the superiority of her nonfiction or the fiction of her greatest contemporaries.

Hynes's introduction, a superb critical piece—still one of the few first-rate assessments of Rebecca West's career—was highly complimentary. Nevertheless, it exposed faults that reviewers emphasized. Like Hynes, Angus Wilson in *The Observer* celebrated Rebecca, yet he drew back from her severe "witch-hunting puritan" strain. Nicholas King, a little more cranky about her judgmental manner, complained in *The National Review*, "she never lets well enough alone." (Rebecca regarded this review as a personal betrayal of the magazine's editor, William F. Buckley.) In *The New York Times Book Review*, Robert Towers alluded to her "compulsion to milk every incident, every detail, until they have yielded not only their full significance but some rather ambiguous secretions as well." Martin Green lamented her lack of "autobiographical curiosity, the self-questioning and self-doubt that is an important ingredient of the sort of writing that she has practiced." Not surprisingly, he liked *Black Lamb and Grey Falcon* best, which does contain self-analysis. Several reviewers suggested the fiction failed because it was too tightly wound with Rebecca's ideas: her characters were not given enough latitude; her narratives became essayistic, lacking the spontaneity of great fiction. The conventional frame of the novel was never broad enough for Rebecca's imagination, which only became truly engaged with the actualities of history, concluded Mollie Panter-Downes in *The New Yorker*.

2

SAMUEL HYNES puzzled over the fact that Rebecca West had received such scant attention from the "partisans of women's liberation." One of his students, Jane Marcus, set out to rectify Rebecca's reputation, discovering in her early articles an extraordinary brand of feminism, still fresh sixty years after their publication. Jane wrote and visited Rebecca, consulted with Rebecca's friend, Jill Craigie (writing a history of feminism), and teamed up with the editors of a new press, Virago, interested in republishing Rebecca's work.

At their first meeting, Rebecca and Jane endeared themselves to each other. Jane arrived at Kingston House soaking wet, having neither an umbrella nor a raincoat. What a way to have to introduce herself to Rebecca West! But Rebecca made her feel at home, got a towel and dried Jane's hair, saying to her "It's so sexy to be wet." To Jane, Rebecca had the aura of an eagle. Age had crippled and speckled her hands with "spots like a good country egg," but her fingers were thick and powerful, hardly the hands Jane had imagined "for the author of such elegant prose." Impressed with Jane's articulate and confident manner, Rebecca was soon referring to her as "big, beautiful" Jane. Rebecca confided in her about Anthony: "History never forgives a woman who has been called a bad mother by her son." She met and liked Jane's husband, a mathematician. Did he think of himself as a triangle when he did mathematics? Rebecca asked. "No," he replied, "an infinite-dimensional space." "Sorry for thinking so small," she said.

Jane watched Rebecca's jousting with Michael Foot. Rebecca had never approved of his brand of Labor politics (he was then leader of his party in the House of Commons), thinking some of it foolish. But they enjoyed each other. Rebecca was taken with him and his extraordinary respect for her work, especially *Black Lamb and Grey Falcon,* which he called a "hymn to patriotism." "He thinks he's far Left but he isn't really—he's just a sweet woolly-wit," Rebecca told a friend. One night she sat on the living room floor of his Hampstead house looking up at him as he read Byron's poetry beautifully, obviously enjoying herself and denying Byron's greatness all the while. Editor Cornelia Bessie, sitting at Rebecca's feet, looked at her and suddenly saw in the eighty-five-year old woman a young girl.

Jill, Michael Foot's wife, became one of the strong connections in Rebecca's life: "I was just out to make as much of a fuss over her as I could and see that other people did. I think it did cheer her up," Jill recalled. Rebecca wrote in her diary: "I love her dearly." When Jill sought Rebecca out, Rebecca gave her a scrapbook of her early articles, many of which were reprinted in *The Young Rebecca.* Rebecca and Jill rejected a programmatic feminism, although both could be eloquent on the limitations of men. Michael had known H.G. and knew something of H.G.'s powerful appetites. At their first meeting H.G. said to him, "It isn't true that making love saps a man's energy. I've always found I work better if I've had more sex." H.G. made the point to Michael at Max Beaverbrook's home, when Michael was a Beaverbrook journalist. But neither Michael nor Jill knew anything about Rebecca's affair with Max.

Jill and Rebecca drew closer when Jill mentioned meeting Anthony in 1972, before she knew Rebecca. During his Hampstead house search, he called on Michael and Jill and noticed she was reading Andre Maurois's biography of George Sand. Jill mentioned Sand's daughter, Solange, and Anthony said: "It's not the daughter that's horrible, it's the mother." In a long harangue he defended the daughter as absolutely splendid and the mother as a consummate bitch. Jill did not know then the story of Anthony and Rebecca, but she wondered at his vehemence. Surely the mother had not got it quite as wrong as all that. Anthony referred to his troubled relationship with Rebecca, claiming he had a letter from her in his pocket that he was afraid to open. Rebecca later said it was probably a letter he had forged.

The attentions of Jill and Jane redirected Rebecca's view of her career. A year earlier, she had rejected Marshall Best's request to reprint *The Judge,* remarking that it was not good enough. Now she agreed to collect and reprint part of her enormous output. Primed by Jill and Jane, Carmen Callil and Ursula Owen of Virago Press arranged a meeting with Rebecca, approaching Kingston House almost as if it were a fortress.

(Interviewer Ann Leslie offended Rebecca by writing that she lived in "almost night-marish, mortician luxury; discreet commissionaires, concealed lighting, formal flower arrangements, a lobby hushed with reverential carpeting. It looks like the laying out room in an Evelyn Waugh funeral-home for Very Distinguished Remains.") Ursula regarded Rebecca as deeply daunting—even frightening. Rebecca could almost literally take your breath away, Ursula remembered, in the way she condemned people. She had recently reviewed Tolstoy's letters, calling him a "man who was inferior to all but a small section of the criminal population." But she proved to be charming and excited about their plans. "Nice girls," she told Alan Maclean, her Macmillan editor, "lesbian, of course"—a misapprehension that made Ursula laugh.

In the autumn of 1980, Virago Press began its program of reprinting Rebecca West's work in handsome, sturdy paperback editions. Rebecca seemed especially pleased to see *Harriet Hume* republished, and she complimented the publishers on the "charming format" chosen for her books. She looked forward to updating the last chapter of *The Meaning of Treason* and expanding her foreword. Two critical studies by Harold Orel and Motley Deakin were in the works as well as *The Young Rebecca* and Rebecca's last completed book, *1900*. In her final years, reviews would salute her with headlines such as "The Indomitable Dame Rebecca" and "A Woman of the Century." Marina Warner interviewed her for *The Paris Review*, an essential step in the canonization of contemporary literary figures.

3

REBECCA DID NOT feel canonized; indeed, her diaries recorded her dread of impending tragedy. Her chief worry was her granddaughter Caroline, who had had a difficult pregnancy in Ghana and had returned to England in her eighth month to have her baby. Rebecca had never felt quite comfortable with Caroline, finding her silences unnerving, but now she was shocked to find how deeply she cared abut her and the new baby, Barnabas, born without complication on September 7, 1978. Caroline continued to ail; she looked ghastly pale at Barnabas's christening, and Rebecca fretted that neither Kitty nor Anthony had looked after her properly, although Rebecca realized that Osei, Caroline's husband, was everything that could be desired in an attentive and loving husband. Rebecca complained a good deal that she was not kept informed of Caroline's condition, and she craved news of the baby, whom she found beautiful and intelligent. She had never seen a "more ravishing creature . . . and obviously sensible." She went on and on to friends about the baby's "bronze skin, fine features, radiant eyes, a very expressive cry, usually commanding rather than plaintive, and very happy."

The news of Barnabas's sudden death in late February 1979 rocked Rebecca as badly as any event of her life; indeed his death confirmed her belief in a supernatural nemesis. Now Barnabas seemed like a "creature from another and a better world. He was more like Ariel than I've ever seen. I am sure he would have been sweeter and more of a genius every year he lived." In his perfection, Barnabas resembled Richard Quin, the idealized brother of *The Fountain Overflows* and *This Real Night,* a character modeled after Joey, Rebecca's mother's sweet-natured brother described in *Family Memories.* Rebecca extolled Barnabas's "melodious way of crying, it was like running water, the lovely air of completeness about him, all his faculties seemed visible like buds. I instantly loved him."

Rebecca never really recovered from this calamity. Brokenhearted, she withdrew even further from her family, refusing to take an interest in the birth of her niece Alison's grandson, or in the arrival of her grandson Edmund's daughter, Clarissa. Instead, Rebecca turned more and more to Justin Lowinsky and Stanley Olson. Stanley had called Justin when he heard of the baby's death from Frances Partridge, Kitty's confidant. It had been Justin, not Kitty, who had sat with Rebecca and told her what had happened. It pleased Rebecca to see that Justin and Stanley had become good friends. She had known Justin since he was a little boy, and he had never failed her. (He had now taken her business affairs in hand, finally helping to settle Henry's estate, the complications of which had dragged on for an incredible decade.) Stanley seemed quite as indispensable, another one of her celebrants—like the Hodges, the Hutchinsons, and the Barclays, to whom she wrote constantly, giving them seismic readings of a life she often characterized as a train of horrors; she suffered now from dizziness, nausea, and migraines.

Yet Rebecca carried on with "undiminished fervour." She liked nothing better than a good argument, which Alison's ex-Communist husband, Jack Selford, usually gave her. He and Alison were the only ones who called her Becky. Becky could be sharp, saying to Alison on the phone: "Your idiot daughter and her idiot husband want to call their child Ivan." When her nephew Norman's daughter Fiona (a science student at Cambridge) came for a visit, Becky pounced, afterward blackguarding Fiona as a drunkard for accepting a second glass of wine, and an ignoramus for not having read Iris Murdoch. Alison, aggrieved on Fiona's behalf, got into a shouting match with her venomous aunt.

Rebecca attacked her family at precisely those times when her own household was in disarray. The menagerie of daft housekeepers and errant secretaries that bedeviled her life at Ibstone had been recreated in Kingston House, although on a smaller scale. When Rebecca did manage to secure good staff, misfortune intervened, and a beloved secretary, Elizabeth Leyshon, had a riding accident, forcing her to leave Rebecca's employ. During Christmas 1979, Rebecca called on Gwenda David to help sack her drunken housekeeper. Then Rebecca and Gwenda spent the holidays in Brighton, where Rebecca fumed about her family. Gwenda noted that Rebecca could not "appreciate that we all have trouble, more or less, with sons and daughters. That's part of life."

April Edwards, who served as Rebecca's secretary for thirteen months (from late 1979 to late 1980), found her employer exhilarating and awesome. At her job interview Rebecca drew herself up and asked: "What are your speeds?" April answered: "Well, Dame Rebecca, I did say I was not a qualified secretary. I haven't got any speeds." Somehow, the plain, direct answer sufficed. April remembered Rebecca working in a maelstrom of books and papers that often turned finding a particular item into an elaborate search. But April was intrigued: "She was such an actress. She could say one word and it enveloped a whole story and had you laughing. And one gesture, it would be a whole play. She would say, 'I don't know anything about wine.' And then she would tell me more about wine than I am sure most wine buffs could. She knew about gardens, architecture. She was completely formidable in what she knew."

If Rebecca expected company, April would help her to dress and to do her hair. Often Rebecca would prepare herself with vitriolic remarks about her callers. But the visit itself would go off splendidly—always lots of talk and laughter, with Rebecca giving a sensational performance. Afterward she would collapse, completely exhausted, once again defaming her guests. Victoria Glendinning, visiting Rebecca in late April 1980, remarked afterward, "for someone who was not well, you were being prodigal with your vitality."

The longer April worked for Rebecca the longer April's days with her became. For all her high spirits, Rebecca seemed hugely unhappy and did not want to let April go. She needed someone to share her anguish. She talked to herself, suddenly breaking out in a lament, often over Anthony. (In the early summer of 1980 she was devastated to learn that he had prostate cancer. It did not cancel her hostile feelings, yet it was agony for her to think of his suffering.) She had a great will to live, raging at interruptions—like the phone calls that took her away from writing. She was also at that stage when the body becomes a burden. "It hurt her to get out of a chair. She was so hampered," April recalls.

4

IN MARCH 1980, Rebecca and Dora Russell were filmed together as witnesses to history for Warren Beatty's *Reds,* the story of writers John Reed and Louise Bryant and the making of the Russian Revolution. Rebecca had known Louise Bryant in New York during Louise's marriage to pro-Bolshevik diplomat William Bullitt. Warren wanted Rebecca because she was of the period and had known Emma Goldman. Illuminated in an otherwise pitch-black funereal setting. Rebecca spoke for posterity through thick glasses, her head tilted slightly upward. Warren had become fascinated not merely with what she had to tell, but with her personality, which revealed itself in a characteristic digression. Rebecca punctured the reverential atmosphere of reminiscence by remarking on the curious phenomenon of the "loony" who wrote to one about that lovely week they had spent together years ago, when, in fact, they had never met.

Warren's casting director, Noel Davis, had arranged the initial meeting between Warren and Rebecca. Noel had met her through the actress Margaret Rawlings, and Rebecca had been charmed by Noel's anecdotes and mimicry. They had been friends a good ten years. Warren wanted to take Rebecca out to lunch. Noel thought a Kingston House tea a more likely possibility. When he called and told Rebecca about the film, she replied: "Yes, I remember John Reed and Louise Bryant very well. She was a stupid, silly woman. She was only interested in hats, really. Who's playing her?" Noel said, "Diane Keaton." Rebecca said, "Oh, ludicrous casting, *ludicrous!* She was a very pretty woman, Louise, no brain, of course, but a very pretty woman. That Keaton woman is too plain. Why did you cast her? I'm very disappointed in you." Noel said, "I didn't cast her. She's a star." Rebecca paused. "Oh, I see. Well, I will do anything if it will help *you.*" Noel ventured, "Well, I'd like you to receive him for a cup of tea." Rebecca groaned, "Ohhhhhh . . . ohhhhhh." Noel countered, "Well, the alternative was to have lunch with him at the Dorchester." She said, "Tea! Tea! Bring him here." On the way to the flat, Warren asked Noel, "Does she still do it?" Noel said, "She's over eighty." Warren said, "I didn't ask for her age." Noel said, "She's an old widow woman. She doesn't do it anymore."

At lunch Warren charmed her. He asked her about her sex life. "Well, I have some time free on Thursday afternoons," she replied. She called him "beauty boy," marveling at his "doll-like good looks," but wondering if his perfect body might not be made out of plastic. Warren told Noel, "She's an attractive woman. I don't care how old she is. She's sexy."

Rebecca liked the way he handled the *Reds* interview. He had an "eager mind," his questions were sharp, and he knew his stuff about Trotsky. She also liked her £186 check for three hours of filming.

Getting Rebecca to the studio proved no easy task. Noel picked her up in a limousine. It was then that he broke the news to her about Dora Russell. Rebecca said, "Oh God, I hope I don't have to meet her. Oh, I can't stand her. Dreadful, stupid woman! Oh! I went to interview Bertie about putting my son under his care and he made a pass at me. Really appalling when I had come in a professional capacity." At the studio, Noel shepherded Rebecca on to the stage, where Dora already sat. A horrified Noel watched Rebecca hobble on two sticks toward Dora. The two women looked at each other. Dora got up, held out her arms, and Rebecca held out hers, nearly toppling over. They both said each other's name. They touched. Noel thought they were going to kiss. But Rebecca said, "Oh, the trouble we had with our silly husbands. Ha ha ha!"

Released in 1982, *Reds* brought Rebecca many flattering notices, and she loved it. She even softened on Diane Keaton, saying she had done a creditable job.

5

ON APRIL 30, 1980, at about 11 A.M., April Edwards happened to look out of Rebecca's big picture windows, which had a view of the back of the Iranian embassy. In the garden, a man was lying on his stomach with a gun in his hand. An incredulous April wondered what to do. She kept looking at the man. What should she tell Rebecca? She was concerned about frightening her old and ailing employer. But as soon as Rebecca got word, she raced to the window, tremendously excited at the drama enacted not more than fifty yards away. She sat there all day, fascinated with the magnificent coolness of the police. She watched a conversation between a policeman and a gunman (one of the anti-Ayatollah Party who wanted ninety political prisoners in Iran released). The gunmen held hostages and threatened to kill them and to torch the embassy. The standoff continued through a second day, when Kingston House was evacuated—much to Rebecca's irritation, for she did not want to leave the scene of the crime. April first took Rebecca to her home and then to Rebecca's club, the Lansdowne. Threading their way through police cordons (April had to do it twice to retrieve Rebecca's medicine, which had been forgotten in the excitement), April was petrified, Rebecca electrified. "She was practically looking after me," April recalls. When

Rebecca's extraordinary account of the siege appeared several days later in the *Daily Telegraph.* April discovered that Rebecca had not missed a thing. In spite of her eye trouble, Rebecca saw what she wanted to see well enough. On the phone she sounded as if she had had a "whale of a time," her niece Alison noted in her diary. Yet Rebecca admitted the incident had shaken her. Would an explosion at the embassy destroy her home? But that was her "small anguish"—not much really compared to what others had suffered through the ages. More important was her proximity to people just yards away who might lose their lives; it caused "a sensation in the stomach and bowels which is similar to the kind of sea sickness that does not relieve itself by vomiting. This is a malaise that can only descend on one in peace. War prepares one's nerves for horror. In peace it comes to one uncooked." Just a hundred yards from her gate a Libyan lawyer had been shot dead.

Rebecca returned to Kingston House after a week of suffering without her familiar things. Her new doctor, Randolph Rowntree ("known to the house as Randy Candy") discovered a "hiatus hernia"—which sounded to her like an Edgar Allan Poe short story. Nothing kept her from resuming work on a new book, *1900,* which publisher George Weidenfeld had persuaded her to do. She had come nowhere near finishing her memoirs, although she had written hundreds of pages and variant drafts.

1900, a big picture book with a short narrative, provided the opportunity to salvage some of her autobiography by weaving it into a portrait of turn-of-the-century London and the emergence of the modern world. But finding the right tone, beginning in the right key, frustrated her. She tried at least eighteen different openings, many beginning with the premise of her as a "noticing child." She evoked her memories of Richmond-on-Thames on the outer edge of London, described the period clothes, the Boer War. One draft began with an allusion to the turmoil in contemporary Afghanistan and Iran. Another referred to her old age and sitting in her "invalid chair." Still another discoursed on the vagaries of history, assessing the differences between past and present. In Proustian fashion, she evoked the sights and smells (the burning of gas jets, for example), the aura of another age. She returned to the themes of her first book, portraying Henry James and John Singer Sargent (both Americans) as the "two butlers" to the English upper classes. They were the aliens, the outsiders, who could see "most of the game." Thinking of herself and Lettie, she emphasized the hostility between Henry and his older brother William.

6

By the summer of 1980, Rebecca had reached one of her peaks of frustration. Encumbered by multiple drafts of *1900* and more trouble with her domestic staff, she had to hire a new secretary for the six-week period April would be on holiday. On July 2, Diana Stainforth arrived at Kingston House for an interview. Diana wanted a job that would help support her while she tried to write her first novel for the popular market. The agency warned her that Dame Rebecca could be difficult; she was very deaf and did not suffer fools. Shown into the study, Diana saw a small, tubby white-haired woman sitting in a white plastic chair watching the television news, the volume turned right up. Diana shouted to get Rebecca's attention. Then Rebecca focused her bright, very dark eyes on Diana, and after a few words, signaled her approval.

Two weeks later, Diana was typing drafts of *1900*, which also required a good deal of fact checking. Diana handled Rebecca's many heavy reference books, although Rebecca always did the reading. Diana would arrive at 10 A.M. Sometimes Rebecca was having breakfast; sometimes she was in bed reading the newspaper. Usually, she was at work, having read her morning's mail, which remained opened on her desk or bed. Every other day or so, when Diana spotted a break in Rebecca's writing rhythm, they would go over the letters and Rebecca would dictate replies. Rebecca still handwrote some letters—not just to friends, but to anyone whose letter impressed her. Payment of bills was always prompt; she could not abide the idea of outstanding debts.

Rebecca stopped for tea about 11 A.M., watched the news with her lunch, returned to writing in the afternoon, when she might also have a weak gin with lemon and no ice. After four o'clock tea, she worked until 5:45, when she watched the evening news. The only interruptions in this schedule were for visitors and phone calls. She read review copies of books at a rattling pace, making notes on the front and back covers and in the margins. Most reviews went through two drafts; spelling and grammatical errors were rare. Even a final draft went to the *Telegraph* with a few last-minute changes. Rebecca kept to this arduous discipline until early 1981, when she completed *1900*.

Diana enjoyed Rebecca's chatty brightness. Rebecca would open the paper and exclaim: "Oh, he's died, and about time too. Wretched man! The old rake! He should have been shot! Communist! Nazi!" Diana would inquire: "Who?" and Rebecca would reply, "Never you mind, dear." Then she'd go on, "Oh, he was appalling." Sometimes Rebecca favored Diana with the whole story, admonishing her: "Well I'll tell you but you're not to repeat it." Like April Edwards, Diana found that Rebecca was never rude. Difficult, yes: "Oh God where is it, oh hell, Christ!" Then somebody would ring the doorbell. She'd say at the top of her voice, "There's someone coming, I don't want to see them. Oh God!" Then she would dress, come up to a visitor and say something like, "Oh my dear Mr Rollyson, how nice to see you. Do come in. New York's one of my favourite towns." If you arrived early, she'd say "Oh hell's bells. Why don't they let me alone." Sometimes they would hear her. Diana once said to an arriving guest, "Dame Rebecca will only be a few minutes." Then Diana heard her saying "Oh damn. God, I loathe people." But Rebecca would apologize to Diana: "I'm sorry, dear, I've been a difficult old bear." Some visitors could do no wrong—like Stanley Olson, arriving on his tricycle (specially ordered from Harrods) and looking the "epitome of a very tidy Oscar Wilde in his little red bowtie."

Rebecca liked to reminisce about the 1920s. She took out her paste jewelry and gave it to Diana, along with a black crepe evening dress (full length with a sweetheart neckline), saying she would look lovely in it. Diana noticed Rebecca's preference for women who made the most of themselves. She would comment on Diana's clothes with an expert eye: "You shouldn't wear that colour, dear." Diana thought Rebecca was hard on her niece Alison because she did not pay attention to her appearance. When Alison did, Rebecca remarked: "I am enchanted by your new looks! You are quite beautiful."

Diana once used the phrase "under the circumstances." Rebecca shouted at her, "In the circumstances you ignoramus." During one of Diana's holidays, a friend of hers took over. She wrote all right as one word and Rebecca screamed at her, "Where did you go to school?" She said, "With Diana." And Dame Rebecca said, "I might have guessed." It was meant and taken as a funny remark. Yet Rebecca never made Diana feel like an idiot; on the contrary, to share Rebecca's company was to feel intelligent and clever too. Rebecca could behave like one of the girls in the powder room, giggling about the men. Emily Hahn came for a visit, and Rebecca herself thought they behaved like schoolgirls. As for Diana, Rebecca recorded in her diary that she liked her "more and more. She could not be working harder."

When April Edwards told Rebecca she was expecting a child and would not return to work, Rebecca asked Diana to become her permanent secretary. Diana agreed and remained with Rebecca until the end. Diana explained that she worked only part-time so that she could finish her novel and was amused to discover that Rebecca had made up a story about her, supposing that Diana's days off were spent carrying on with a married man. Now Rebecca altered her tune, saying, "Ah, here comes my competition."

One day Rebecca learned that Diana was dog-sitting for a friend and had a golden labrador in her car. "You can bring him up," Rebecca said. "But he will have to be tied." Named Harry, he reminded her of the faithful Albert. The sight of Rebecca aroused Harry and he jumped her. Diana had to drag him off. Rebecca thought it hilarious, afterward making up the line, "Lord Harry advanced upon Dame Rebecca exposing his great concern."

CHAPTER 41

"To the Last Breath"
1981–1983

I

REBECCA SLEPT more than she used to, sometimes nodding off in her television chair. She had been growing forgetful, sometimes telling stories with interchangeable names and mixing up the details. Sometimes she confused her correspondents, sending a letter to her friend Terence Davis meant for Terence de Vere White, the Irish journalist. In another instance Eugene Weintraub of New York City had a very pleasant and prolonged correspondence with Rebecca because she mistook him for a Professor Weintraub she had met many years earlier. Eugene (a good letter writer) enjoyed himself so much that he did not clear up the confusion.

Rebecca realized she was slowing down. She feared that her mind was failing. She was beginning to shrink; all her dresses were too long. She supposed she had little more time to write or to live, the two things being virtually synonymous in her mind. One day she said to Joan White, her hairdresser, "I've made arrangements for my funeral." She told Joan all about what it would be like and then asked: "You will come, won't you?" Of course Joan would come. Rebecca thoughtfully put her on the list, and when the time came Rebecca's favorite driver, John Molloy, was sent to pick Joan up for the drive to Brookwood Cemetery.

Rebecca had decided to will her literary rights to her nephew, Norman Macleod, and on June 7, 1982 she wrote a brief statement expressing her wish that Victoria Glendinning write a short and Stanley Olson a "full" biography of her, with the cooperation of her literary executors.

Rebecca worried about her granddaughter Caroline starting a new life in London, while maintaining her ties with Osei in Ghana. Caroline sometimes called or wrote, but tensions between Rebecca and Kitty increased because of Rebecca's continuing hostility toward Edmund. Caroline had been upset by seeing a photograph of Vita's child by her second husband, especially because Rebecca displayed no picture of Edmund's daughter, Clarissa.

Alison's daughter, Cathy, wondered why her great-aunt did not take more of an interest in the Macleod clan. Except for Rebecca's nephew Norman, and her cousin Ian Barclay and his wife Sally, no family members seemed satisfactory. When Alison proposed a headstone for Lettie's grave (situated next to her mother's), mentioning Lettie as a "benefactress to children," Rebecca raged against Alison's "lyrical outpouring," and accused her of belittling Rebecca's mother and ousting her from her own gravestone. Lettie never gave anything to anyone, Rebecca declared. Yet for decades Rebecca had written letters blasting her older sister for giving all her money away to friends and family members. Any of Alison's or Norman's children could have refuted Rebecca on the subject of Lettie, but Rebecca's vehemence isolated her and alienated them.

Rebecca behaved like a Victorian matriarch, recalibrating her will, explaining in lengthy letters why she was not as wealthy as people supposed and her many obligations to friends and to Henry's relatives. She thought she was worth (between her art collection and her securities) in the neighborhood of two hundred thousand pounds. And this was not counting a literary estate which proved to be worth even more. But actual sums were immaterial, for no amount would have sufficed. She was always projecting some new incredible drain on her resources, worrying about the depredations of the Inland Revenue, the doubling of her maintenance at Kingston House. She thought Anthony's friends (chiefly the Schlesingers) had come to visit her in London to wheedle money for Anthony. All his life, she complained, he felt she owed him a living. All her life, he complained, she had schemed to deprive him of his birthright and blackguarded him to editors and his friends. Thus mother and son savaged each other.

Elizabeth Furse, who had first met Rebecca in 1934, when Elizabeth was a young communist helping the politically persecuted escape from Germany, sympathized with Rebecca and expressed Rebecca's view that since the advent of Freud mothers had been blamed too much for their children's psychological states. Elizabeth's former husband, Peter Haden-Guest, had been to school with Anthony, and Elizabeth had had her troubles with her own son, also named Anthony. Elizabeth greatly admired Rebecca's writing. They conferred at Kingston House. Elizabeth concluded that Anthony was one of those children who always found excuses for their cruelty to their mothers. Rebecca was the kind of parent who did not like herself and did not like her child because he was so like herself. Elizabeth doubted that Rebecca had the capacity to love.

Elizabeth called on Anthony in New York and asked him why he hated his mother, extracting a blunt admission: "Yes. We don't like each other because we are so much alike." Then he said to her, "Elizabeth, why do you ask me that?" Elizabeth said, "Your mother is very close to death as I am and there comes a time in one's life when one has to face facts, one is not cruel to people." Elizabeth found Rebecca quite prepared to admit she had been a bad mother. But when Elizabeth tried to console her, she found Rebecca's vanity an impediment to friendship. Witty and clever Rebecca was somehow not intelligent enough to have built up a relationship with her son, Elizabeth concluded.

2

BY MARCH 1981, Rebecca had sufficiently recovered from the ordeal of completing *1900* to enjoy another spurt of memoir writing. She kept odd hours now, sometimes sleeping all morning and writing in the afternoon. Diana would listen to her enthralling discourses on family history, picturing Rebecca's mother as "bright but not very pretty," and her father looking like Rhett Butler. The image of Charles Fairfield kept softening as Rebecca talked and rewrote her memoirs.

Rebecca had a marvelous new companion, her Scottish housekeeper, Tessa Monro, a law school graduate and widow of a South African Presbyterian clergyman. Like Diana, Tessa had come as a temporary and stayed as a permanent staff member. She and Rebecca often did crossword puzzles together. Sometimes Tessa sat in on Rebecca's meetings with guests. Writer Rhoda Koenig visited and soon she and Rebecca were sharing their enthusiasm for detective stories. Rhoda recommended Ruth Rendell's *A Judgment in Stone*. Rebecca asked what it was about, and Rhoda said, deadpan, that it had to do with an ostensibly respectable housekeeper who goes mad and murders the entire family. Both Rebecca and Tessa burst into shrieks of laughter.

3

REBECCA STILL WENT OUT for rollicking restaurant meals, but less frequently. Her high blood pressure kept her in bed. Yet she kept making new friends, many of whom visited her at Kingston House. The writer Martha Gellhorn wrote to Rebecca and was invited for sessions of reminiscence, Martha keeping her own end up quite well, describing her great scoop, meeting and conversing in French with Chou-en-Lai when he was still in hiding in China in the 1930s. No one raised the subject of Ernest Hemingway—a touchy one for Martha—but Rebecca had no doubt that the brute had abused Martha. If they discussed H.G., there is no record of it. Would Rebecca have been upset or amused to learn that the feisty Martha had also been H.G.'s mistress?

Doris Lessing came calling after Rebecca had praised her work on a radio program. Rebecca liked her as much as Martha but Rebecca's deafness made it difficult to converse, and that saddened Doris: "all that wit and brilliance and fire in prison." Doris sat and grieved over the ravages of age, watching Rebecca sit with food stains on her front and with a stick close at hand if she should want to get up. Yet Rebecca seemed on top of everything, her mind as bright as ever, and Doris departed warmed by Rebecca's assertion that Doris was the novelist of her generation.

Doris reread *Black Lamb and Grey Falcon* and found her state of mind resembled Rebecca's on the eve of World War II. Doris believed that the threat of nuclear war immobilized people; they were succumbing to a kind of death wish. Even the antinuclear protestors thought little about how people could protect themselves in the event that peace efforts failed. Almost no one wanted to confront the reality of war and Rebecca's warning that, in Doris's words, "human life has never been anything other than precarious, shifting, cataclysmic." In fact, at the age of eighty-nine, Rebecca had just completed a draft of a story, "Edith," about the survivors of a nuclear attack. For Rebecca, like Doris, believed that the human will to live should be asserted even in the bleakest circumstances, and that it was incumbent on the writer to imagine the human effort to survive a holocaust.

In the early spring of 1982, Rebecca received a troubling visit from her granddaughter Sophie, who spoke in such a soft mumble that Rebecca heard virtually nothing of what she had to say. Sophie came calling out of sympathy for her grandmother. More than anyone else in Anthony's family, she felt an affinity with Rebecca. Sophie had tired of the line that her father's every shortcoming was traceable to his terrible childhood. She empathized with Rebecca's struggle to raise a child and to make a name for herself. Unfortunately, this meeting had been put off too long. Rebecca, receptive but still wary, and Sophie, overwhelmed at attempting a relationship with her formidable grandmother so late in the day, found communication difficult. To her Rebecca was a sort of living icon.

Rebecca's great niece, Helen Macleod (Norman's daughter), also came calling. The exuberant Helen relished padding down the carpeted corridors of Kingston House, checking her reflection in the glass of the fire escape, before ringing the bell at Rebecca's elegant front door. The entrance hall lounge gave her a "tranquil misty green feeling." Contented with herself, she sat down in one of the chairs with gold lion arms, her favorites since childhood, because they breathed out the "sense of yesterday, of tradition and security."

Helen paid tribute to Rebecca: "Sometimes you seem like some magnificent island in the sea of blank bland faces which surround me 80 percent of the time." After a visit to Rebecca, Helen wrote, "It is nice to know that I can still relate in some way to an older relative. It gives me hope for breaking through to some semblance of adulthood (even if I do dye my hair and wear bright yellow socks)." Helen addressed her letter to "Aunt Rebecca," which stressed more than their family connection. Helen's mother, Marion, addressed her letters to Auntie Cissie. Helen had a cocky and full-throated self-confidence reminiscent of Rebecca.

Rebecca was also buoyed by a visit with Caroline, whom she called "seraphically beautiful." Rebecca admired her perfect skin and simple dress. It did Rebecca good to see that Caroline had recovered from a long illness, speaking confidently about herself and others. "Oh I must keep this going," Rebecca said to herself, agonizing over the estrangement that had made such occasions rare. Although she still lashed out at familiar targets such as Lettie and Aunt Sophie, she chastised herself for "blundering remarks that have offended people." How foolish she had sometimes been. How generous friends like Lady Kelly had been to her; "how little I have given her," Rebecca regretted.

Rebecca felt she was "nearly at the end." The Falkland Islands war contributed to her gloom. "Isn't it exciting?" Diana Stainforth asked. Rebecca's reply was so sharp that Diana almost felt as if she had been hit: "It isn't exciting, and you wait until the first disaster happens, you will be so upset. It's exciting until someone is killed." A few days later the British sunk the *Belgrano,* and Diana said, "I just can't believe it. How could we do this awful thing? All those poor conscripts." Rebecca remarked: "Remember what I told you. War is not like that. It's ten minutes of terror to fifty minutes of boredom. It's people being killed." The only redeeming feature for Rebecca was Mrs. Thatcher's steadiness in the crisis.

Rebecca exploded when *The New York Times Magazine* published Leslie Garis's profile of her on April 4, 1982. It began with a quotation from Anthony about his terrible childhood and half the piece featured the mother-son contest. It was a superficial, inaccurate account. Garis is the only person ever to describe Rebecca's eyes as "*cold* brown" (my emphasis). She completely missed the comic rapport between Rebecca and her housekeeper, Mrs. Monro, who was depicted as a dour, authoritarian Scot monitoring Rebecca's every word.

Rebecca retaliated with dozens of letters to friends and acquaintances, disputing the article point by point, calling it a "very characteristic production of Anthony." She was especially incensed at the treatment of Mrs. Monro, whom Rebecca regarded as a lifesaver. Always, in such instances, Rebecca could not resist going over old ground. She ignored advice from friends and colleagues, like Rivers Scott, that she should forget about the inept efforts of a journalist to jazz up a story, but she accepted her lawyer's advice not to take legal action. Diana Trilling and others sent protests to *The New York Times,* but nothing could convince her that the article would not do her great harm. Her only consolation was that she would be dead soon. When writer Babette Rosmond visited Rebecca, they discussed ways of doing away with Leslie Garis (renamed "Miss-Mud-and-Prussic-Acid"), deciding finally on a public drawing and quartering, with perhaps the liver and other precious parts being distributed to winning ticket holders. Babette was pleased to see that Rebecca's admirers had filled her flat with flowers.

On one of her last outings, in late June 1982, Rebecca encountered the kind of scene that still fed her avidity for experience and the power to write about it. She and Mrs. Monro were being driven out of Tunbridge Wells after a visit with her friends Nicholas van den Branden and Terence Davis. Rain came down like bullets, and they halted at a beautiful sight. In a pasture with a number of trees at its edge, a sort of bracelet seemed to be forming around the trunks near the ground. Lines of lambs were being huddled in a circle by "two sheep Mammas" sheltering their young and making sure none of them ran away. This tableau of pathetic and fragile lambs and sheep looking like widows reminded her of a Greuze painting. Her description then turned into an elaborate comment on the way she felt protected and cherished by Terence and Nicky in a style she deemed not sentimental, but "sensitive and classical," like their home and garden.

When Sophie visited again in early July, a terrified Rebecca expected violence, imagining Sophie strangling her as part of Anthony's malevolent plot against her. But the visit was pleasant and Rebecca liked her very much. To Sophie, Rebecca seemed much less the dragon lady, and Sophie was able to relax and tell a few jokes. When Rebecca offered Sophie a present, Rebecca was delighted to learn that she wanted an autographed copy of *The Young Rebecca,* which had just been published, along with *1900.*

The reviews had been superb, many of them consisting of strings of quotations from her ebullient prose. Although Rebecca had initially resisted reprinting her early work, saying "I hate reading my old stuff," it was, she admitted, "cracking good." Jessica Mitford extolled the "amazing modern style" of *The Young Rebecca,* as fresh and provocative as "today's New Journalism." Patricia Beer found Rebecca's language so contemporary that she began to wonder "if we really were going to get the vote." Anne Tyler captured the way Rebecca had readers doing double takes. In *1900,* there was a passage about Colonial Secretary Chamberlain, explaining that he was the descendant of a boot manufacturer. Then Rebecca added, "by a curious coincidence he himself looked like a single, highly polished boot." Tyler gulped, "Like a *what?*" "West ought to be declared one of the treasures of our century," she concluded. Peter Keating noted that Rebecca's historical approach in *1900* was "almost entirely through personalities," because she believed that ideas were "inseparable from the people who formulated or enacted them." Like other reviewers, male and female, he took issue with her sweeping judgments—such as "Men and women do not really like each other very much." Well, in the long run, they did not, Rebecca told an interviewer. Terence de Vere White marveled at the continuity of Rebecca's seventy year career, observing that she had appeared at nineteen, "armed at all points." She was a writer first, he emphasized, and proved capable of criticizing both her allies and her enemies. V. S. Pritchett called Rebecca's account of turn-of-the century Europe a "sportive essay . . . individual, even eccentric, but always telling."

4

DURING HER LAST SUMMER, Rebecca tired herself out (but with delight), starting a new short story, "The Heiress." She was also writing a piece for her ninetieth birthday. Both story and essay went through several false starts. The story had to be abandoned, the essay kept swelling with Rebecca's laments over her physical deterioration, her nostalgic evocations of walking in the Pentland Hills of Scotland, exploring the ruins of Mexico and the churches of France, her childhood haunts in South London (much of it bombed in the war) and walks with her father, a funny lunch with Charles Curran and Mae West—in which a bumbling intruder mistook Henry for Mae West's husband. Much of the material got cut and the published piece did not render the wonderful, spontaneous, meandering, stream-of-consciousness quality of her drafts.

In September, Rebecca saw the historian Martin Duberman, working on a biography of her old friend, Paul Robeson. They had a pleasant, wide-ranging two hours, somewhat strained by her inability to hear all of his questions. Her failing memory was evident, but her wicked wit did not desert her. Paul had such beautiful manners, Rebecca recalled. What were his parents like? she asked Martin. "His father had been a slave," Martin replied. "What?" she asked. Martin repeated himself. "That's good for the manners," Rebecca said. It was a joke that both knew would get her into trouble.

The interview exhausted Rebecca. For the past two years, she had had periodic collapses, with each recovery becoming a little weaker. Her final book review had taken four drafts with many corrections—an unheard-of struggle for Rebecca. When Diana arrived on the morning of Wednesday, September 29, she found a distraught Rebecca in bed. She had been up much of the night rereading and trying to correct a book review. She searched wildly through her papers for the new draft, knocking books off her bed. Diana tried to calm her, saying she would look through everything systematically. Suddenly Rebecca, in tears, sank back on her pillows, clutched Diana's hand, and said, over and over again, "I can't go on. I'm too tired. I can't go on." It was the first time Diana had seen her cry.

On Monday October 4, Justin Lowinsky arrived at the flat. He had Rebecca's power of attorney and would see to the household bills. Her mind was clear, but she tired very easily and stayed in bed. All appointments were canceled. Stanley Olson realized Rebecca was dying, and he saw the wisdom of establishing an unvarying routine. Any interruptions, no matter how kindly meant, would serve only to disturb her.

A week later, Alison was allowed a twenty-minute visit. Rebecca would not let her go. Alison tried to be soothing, but Rebecca wanted to start a family row by attacking her great-niece Fiona. Alison said that in fact Fiona was much adored by her young male friends. "Nobody," Rebecca stormed, "could adore Fiona." Was Rebecca dying, Alison wondered, or would she the next moment leap out of bed and go to a party?

Rebecca had her good days, when she came out of her confusion and bouts of hostility, but she appeared pale and fragile. On November 5 she fell and broke her hip. She had been trying to get out of bed—as usual, wanting to do things on her own. (She went through several "brainstorms" when she hit out at her attendants.) Screaming with pain she was taken to hospital and operated on the next day, staying there three weeks.

On sedatives, Rebecca had trouble reading her mail and recognizing people. On one of Alison's visits, Rebecca looked at her and asked pointedly, "Who engaged you?" There were periods of paranoia and disorientation, when Rebecca became delusional and could be placated only by cooperation with her fears of being kidnapped. She called out for her parents and sisters or Henry. Justin Lowinsky stayed with her during one long night. Some days she sat up and quoted Shakespeare by the yard, read the newspapers, and resisted the medication that would put her into a drowse. She grew steadily weaker but had moments when she seemed to snap into her old self. She still enjoyed long chats. Her nurses adjusted to her belligerent periods, writing notes about her delightful, playful conversation. They seemed downcast when Rebecca gave way to depression and cried. One day Rebecca told a nurse that she was an ugly little boy and ought to get out of her room. When the nurse told Rebecca she was a little confused, Rebecca replied that the nurse was disoriented. On one rather typical day Rebecca exclaimed, "I wish I wasn't half dead and half alive it's not good for one's style!"

On November 25, she returned home. Her condition changed little, although her spirits rose after visits with her nephew Norman and Stanley Olson. To Stanley, she talked about the basis of their friendship: "Mutual esteem and malice toward all." About a week before her birthday she took a bad turn, sleeping almost constantly, stirring occasionally to call out for Lettie. Most of the time she was comatose. On December 22, her nephew Norman caught a lucid moment. She grabbed his hand and exclaimed, "Oh, that wicked, wicked boy!" and burst into tears.

During one bright moment Rebecca said to Diana Stainforth, "I'm not going to need you for much longer, dear. I'm going to die. Mind you, I might need a secretary in the afterlife, so perhaps you'd better come with me." Both Diana and Tessa Monro remained with Rebecca, on one occasion helping her to pack for an imaginary trip. Dr. Rowntree did not believe Rebecca could recover; she had succumbed to old age.

In January, Rebecca renewed her argument with Alison about family history—now a hopeless enterprise because Rebecca had invented another husband for herself (after Henry), and Alison kept changing into different people. "You're a blockhead," she said to Alison, feebly knocking her knuckle against Alison's brow. "Solid wood," she claimed. "You're stupid, stupid, and I curse you." The sight of Rebecca rising from her pillow to curse her with her dying breath terrified Alison, although she realized Rebecca had her mixed up with someone else—probably Lettie—since Rebecca said: "You made my childhood a misery."

Gwenda David visited and thought Rebecca wanted to talk about Henry. "Oh don't talk about him. He bored me," Rebecca rasped. The next day Alison was overcome with her aunt's cheerful welcome, asking about what was in the newspapers. Rebecca said of Anthony, "He's a bad boy, but he's the love of my life." Alison asked Rebecca if she wanted to see him. "Perhaps not, if he hates me so much," she replied. Then she tried to write a note to H.G. about their son. During another confused period she asked, "Where's my little boy?" Tessa told her that he had grown up, and Rebecca seemed to lose interest.

On February 7, Rebecca lamented: "I'm dying so slowly, so slowly." Mrs. Monro spent a day fielding Rebecca's questions about heaven and hell. Ten days later, another exchange with Alison: "I don't regret anything except H.G.," Rebecca confessed. A staggered Alison asked Rebecca what she meant. How could she say that about a man she had loved for ten years? Winnie had told Alison that H.G. was the funniest man she had ever met. "He was all of that," Rebecca agreed. Alison then described a day when H.G. had taken an umbrella, blown inside out on a windy day, and wobbled about pretending to be drunk. Winnie said H.G. was funnier than Chaplin. "Oh, he was," Rebecca conceded, but life was ridiculous. What was the point? It was so like the old Rebecca that Alison thought she had returned from the dead.

In March, Rebecca developed pneumonia and lost her hearty appetite. Tessa Monro sat beside her and prayed silently for a quiet, painless, death. At the end of the prayer Rebecca said "Amen!" The last words Alison heard Rebecca say were "I'm lost. It's wrong." Her pulse became weak and rapid, her breathing shallower, then labored and erratic, a result of the congestion. Unconscious, she expired at 11:35 A.M. on the Ides of March. Diana, Tessa, and her nurse, Phillipa Thorp, watched her go.

Phillipa felt as if a chapter in her own life had ended. Phillipa's mind had been "saturated with laughter and intrigue." It got so that even on her day off she did not want to leave Rebecca. It had been hard to nurse her. Rebecca raged, cried, and resisted her sedatives. Phillipa had never experienced such determination in a person, and she was a little afraid of her powerful patient. Rebecca had been so recalcitrant at times that Phillipa dreaded the death scene. But it was as if Rebecca's battle to live and her fear of death had been a great drama resolved on her last comfortable and peaceful day—like a rest earned after a magnificent fight.

Rebecca liked to quote Charles Dickens on the "fundamental belief of living things in life." Dickens had said that "whatever power gave us life, and for whatever purpose, he was sure it was given to us on the understanding that we defend it to the last breath."

Epilogue

THERE WAS A MEMORIAL SERVICE at St. Martin-in-the-Fields. Michael Denison read from Rebecca's work as well as from that of John Donne, Robert Louis Stevenson, and D. H. Lawrence. Bernard Levin, who had steadfastly regarded her as both a great writer and woman of the century, gave the eulogy. He saluted her courage, her wit, and her grace, the way she made herself into a Rebecca West who bettered Ibsen's original by living, working, and acting—a symbol of the vital principle of life itself.

Most of the obituaries singled out *Black Lamb and Grey Falcon* and *The Meaning of Treason* as her greatest works. The best reminiscence came from Edward Crankshaw, who called her a "fantasist. Unable to accept the routine irrationality of human behavior she invented reasons where there were none—not only in her commentaries on public affairs but also in her personal relationships." She had not attained the first rank of novelists because "she was too much concerned with tearing open the pretenses and disguises with which her characters covered themselves to look closely enough at the small, real person under the mock-emperor's clothes." Yet Rebecca hewed closely to the truth, he concluded, because she had a vision that transcended her faults.

A paradox is at work here. A writer whose novels were not great had a great novelist's vision, an imagination that soared beyond the imperfections of individual works. The vision overwhelmed her characters, her plots, her life—but it could be leashed to history, to great accounts of courtroom scenes and travels, where she could measure her expansive mind against great landscapes and the law. In such cases, she submitted herself to the discipline of learning reality, of observing it from the outside; the fiction, both finished and unfinished, needed more characters with internal springs and Dickensian tics like Mr. Morpurgo and Beatrice Beevor in *The Fountain Overflows* and *This Real Night*.

Sunflower, This Real Night, and *Cousin Rosamund,* which appeared in the years immediately following Rebecca's death, did not significantly improve her reputation as a novelist. The novelist Anthony Burgess, echoing H.G. Wells on *The Judge,* complained there was not enough plot to *This Real Night,* which took the Aubrey family from the eve of World War I to its end. It had the feel of a memoir, he thought. Hilary Spurling regarded the continuing attack on Cordelia (Lettie's stand-in) tiresome, whereas Lorna Sage found Cordelia's awfulness supplied a good deal of the novel's interest—a counterweight to the sanctification of Rosamund, a cloying symbol of goodness. A. S. Byatt recommended *This Real Night* for its brilliant set pieces, though it lacked the "thingness and pace" of *The Fountain Overflows.* Several critics acknowledged that the whole trilogy, including the posthumous *Cousin Rosamund,* seethed with intellectual life, with a family thinking and arguing and imagining, musicians whose art is threatened by the incredible violence of the twentieth century, but also minds, like Rebecca's, which created an impregnable world of their own. They are the artists uninterrupted, an enviable fate Rebecca never felt she herself attained.

Among the critics, *Family Memories* fared best of all—probably because it was a novel masquerading as memoirs. Reviewer Humphrey Carpenter was astonished at Rebecca's regency prose, which he regarded as worthy of Jane Austen. He quoted the passage on Rebecca's statuesque maternal grandmother, Arabella Rowan: "a Denny and a Blennerhasset, a Roper and a Massey, and much else beside. . . . After the loss of her husband she joined the Plymouth Brotherhood and passed into a state of quite noble religious mania." This is vintage Rebecca, this yoking of great families and mania in turns of phrase that reflect her wry amusement at the twists of her own history.

Victoria Glendinning provided astute afterwords to several of Rebecca's posthumous publications, and published her elegant biography in 1987, favoring Rebecca's early years, since she knew that Stanley Olson would write the massive life and works biography. He projected a work of 300,000 words that would take him ten years to complete.

Stanley sought out Anthony, who had received nothing from Rebecca's will, and who did not attend her funeral. The day Rebecca died, Alison had called Anthony's home. She had been wondering for weeks whether he should be notified about his mother's impending death, but Rebecca had not wanted it. Lily and Anthony answered the call. As soon as Anthony heard Alison's voice, he hung up. He had never got along with "wee Alison," as he used to style her. Later Justin Lowinsky called him, and Anthony said that he did not think his attendance at the funeral would be appropriate.

Stanley thought Anthony looked exactly like Rebecca and Anthony's desire to reckon with his mother "authentic and great." It depressed

Stanley to see this "hollow shell of a man eroded by hate, and a desire to love." He liked Anthony's humor; he detected the same obsession with the "spectral workings of villainy" that sparked Rebecca. Stanley assured the haunted Anthony he had no desire to continue Rebecca's fight. Anthony visibly relaxed. Stanley thought Anthony would never find peace.

Michael Coren, one of H.G.'s biographer's, interviewed Anthony shortly before the latter died. Michael formed the impression of a man near his end, nice but still emotional. Referring to Anthony's biography, *H.G. Wells: Aspects of a Life* (1984), in which Anthony savages his mother, Michael put to him a query many readers might have wanted answered: "Although your mother probably wasn't the greatest parent in the world, it seemed to me that she at least did try—at least she'd built a physical presence there. Your father often seemed to just bugger off. In your book we really get a different picture from that. Do you think you were too nice to your father simply because he wasn't around, and you idolized someone who was not present—an understandable reaction?" Michael presumed Anthony had been asked this question many times, yet he seemed surprised and upset. Michael never really got an answer; indeed, the query effectively ended the interview. Anthony never resolved his feelings, and he could not walk away from them. He acknowledged there might have been some gain in doing so, "but there was quite a richness in the conflict of personalities that I learned a good deal from." Just like his mother, he felt he had to fight for his view of the relationship.

Anthony died on December 27, 1987. A few years earlier, his son Edmund remarked that Rebecca had "left the field of combat but I doubt it puts an end to it. I think there's going to be several more rounds of this beyond the grave."

Rebecca left the bulk of her estate to her nephew Norman Macleod. She also remembered several other members of her family, friends, and employees. Justin Lowinsky, Merlin Holland, Ian and Sally Barclay, and Rebecca's two granddaughters, Caroline and Sophie, received shares in her estate. Small bequests went to Mrs. Monro, John Molloy, who drove her to many of her appointments during her Kingston House years, to Eloise "Timmy" Richardson (a former secretary), to Joan White (Rebecca's hairdresser for nearly fifty years), to Christopher Leiley, the Buckinghamshire policeman who winked at Henry's reckless driving and kept him out of jail, and to Robert Langford, Ibstone's last farm bailiff who faithfully tended Henry's grave. Rebecca also remembered several of Henry's relatives, especially Irene Garthwaite, Henry's cousin, whose struggles as a German refugee during and after the war won Rebecca's heart.

Acknowledgments

MY FIRST INTERVIEWS BEGAN WITH Anthony's side of the family, and with his friends. Kitty West and Lily West both gave several interviews and answered my phone calls, which sometimes required them to recall painful experiences. They never refused to answer my prying questions, and they generously supplied me with many of Anthony's papers and photographs. Kitty also wrote several letters to me about her relationships with Anthony and Rebecca. Similarly, Caroline West patiently responded to all my requests for information and supplied many valuable letters. Sophie West gave me an intimate view of her father in the later stages of his lifelong struggle with his mother.

Dr. Edmund West and his wife Cheryl West welcomed me and my wife into their home, patiently answering all of my questions and follow-up phone calls. Cheryl gathered together many of Rebecca West's letters and allowed me to peruse them before they were sent to the Tulsa archive.

Of Anthony's friends Jane Gunther was the first to describe to me his winning side and to detail how difficult it was to remain friends with both Anthony and his mother. Somehow Jane's husband, John, was able to do so, perhaps because he had known Rebecca since the 1920s and had had glimpses of Anthony's difficult transition into adulthood. John was able to sympathize with both mother and son. I am grateful to Jane Gunther for giving me permission to study her husband's extensive archive at the University of Chicago, and to reprint extracts from his diary and letters.

I am indebted to Ann Fuller, who in the late 1940s helped Anthony find a home in Stonington, Connecticut, and who regarded herself as his American mother. Through Ann Fuller, Joe Fox got to know Anthony. Joe told me he liked to think of the ungainly Anthony as "The Bear." He remembered a jolly Anthony who liked to laugh a lot. Joe later edited several of Anthony's books and was dismayed to observe his friend's attitude toward his mother gradually harden and embitter him. In the early

1950s, Anthony returned to Stonington after one of his visits to his mother sporting a bandage on his left arm. "Anthony, what happened?" Joe asked. Anthony explained that he had been in the kitchen of his mother's house and had said something that ignited her rage, prompting her to come at him with a carving knife. Anthony's stories were so persuasive and endearing that "you sort of wanted to hug him and pat him on the back," Joe remembered.

Anthony was full of such stories about Rebecca, some of which Alexandra Schlesinger (Arthur's wife and Lily West's sister) recalled for me. She had an especially vivid memory of Anthony's account of a bed which Rebecca and H.G. once shared, and which Rebecca had cut in half and made into a bed for Anthony. To Lois Wallace, Anthony's agent, I am indebted for the anecdote about a middle-aged Anthony dressed in tight pants and long hair preparing to aggravate his mother. I thank Elizabeth Furse for sharing with me an account of her attempts to act as Rebecca's and Anthony's go-between. Frances Partridge not only supplied me with a vivid account of her friendship with Anthony, she also gave part of my manuscript a searching and helpful reading, and gave me several of Anthony's letters to her.

In London, Alison Macleod invited me for several lunches, over which we discussed Rebecca's family life. Alison spoke of her own troubled relationship with Rebecca, as well as her early disturbing contacts with Anthony. Alison's husband, Jack Selford, also contributed some lively reminiscences to this biography. Alison was able to give me invaluable insights into her mother Winnie and her Aunt Lettie. I owe a deep debt to Alison for allowing me to photocopy and to use freely her treasure trove of family papers and photographs. I have also benefited enormously from her reading of several chapters of this biography. She has saved me from many (though I fear not all) errors. She patiently withstood my phone calls, my quizzing her over facts and asking her to repeat several stories as I tried to get things right. Alison introduced me to her daughters, Stella and Cathy, who described their hostile feelings about their great-aunt, and to her friend Rosa Beste, who recalled Rebecca's sociable, generous, and fun loving side.

Norman Macleod, Alison's younger brother, has been a great supporter of my project. He and his wife Marion have given me several interviews and read chapters of my book, making helpful suggestions. I am grateful to Norman Macleod for giving me permission to quote from Rebecca West's unpublished papers and for providing some of the photographs used in this biography. His understanding of not only his aunt's life but of her work has made a significant contribution to this biography.

With his support, I was able to interview several people who might otherwise have been unavailable. He also agreed that I should interview his children, Graham, Fiona, and Helen—all of whom have given me a later generation's view of their formidable great aunt. I thank them for seeing me and for being so forthcoming with their recollections. Like Alison, Graham, Fiona, and Helen helped me to see Lettie in ways Rebecca refused to recognize.

David Ogilvy, Rebecca's cousin, proved to be an invaluable resource, telling me about his grandmother, Rebecca's "odious" Aunt Sophie. David takes a skeptical view of many of Rebecca's stories. His careful reading of several chapters of this biography sharpened my sensitivity to both the factual and fictional elements of Rebecca's memories, although I cannot be sure that David Ogilvy believes I have achieved the proper balance.

Dr. Ian Barclay, Rebecca's cousin, and his wife Sally often had Rebecca to stay in their home. From them I learned what a wonderful guest she could be, and how much she treasured family members who sympathized with her troubles and gave her a valuable respite from her hectic and competitive life in London. Ian generously shared his significant collection of Rebecca West's letters.

At Peters Fraser Dunlop (Rebecca West's agent), I had a helpful meeting with Michael Sissons, who took over from a retiring A. D. Peters, Rebecca's agent for most of her career. Pat Kavanagh suggested I speak with Margaret Stephens, who assisted A. D. Peters. Ms. Stephens gave me an invaluable look at the enduring relationship between Rebecca and her agents. Leslie Smith, one of Rebecca's lawyers, provided helpful details of Rebecca's financial affairs during her last years. Bethel Solomons spoke to me as both Rebecca's friend and her dermatologist. I am most appreciative of his candid remarks. Harold Tomlinson, one of Ibstone's farm bailiffs, gave me a very shrewd assessment of Rebecca and Henry, as well as showing me several of her letters in his possession and providing me with an aerial photograph of Ibstone.

I wish to thank Sol Kurzner, the current owner of Ibstone, for giving me permission to walk the grounds and experience the sights that were so important to Rebecca during her years in Buckinghamshire.

Rosalind Burdon-Taylor and her husband Charles treated me to a delightful afternoon near Ibstone House. Over a pub lunch, Rosalind reminisced about Rebecca and about her mother Greta Mortimer, Rebecca's fellow student at the Academy of Dramatic Art. Rosalind also wrote a brief memoir of Rebecca for me and gave me copies of several Rebecca West letters. Joyce Seligman sent me Rebecca's correspondence and reminisced in person about Rebecca's Ibstone years.

John Hodges and his daughter Ann invited me to tea and regaled me with many fond memories of Rebecca and Margaret Hodges. I was deeply moved when he decided to share with me a large collection of letters which no other Rebecca West biographer has seen. Anne McBurney, Rebecca's secretary following Margaret Hodges, made Rebecca's correspondence available to me and answered several questions in an informative interview.

Merlin Holland gave me several of Rebecca's letters to his parents, Vyvyan and Thelma Holland; even better, Merlin sat with me and commented on the letters, as well as supplying firsthand insights into Rebecca and Henry Andrews.

The distinguished novelist, A. L. Barker, spent an afternoon reminiscing about Rebecca West's generosity and how she took up Barker's work and championed it almost as if it were her own. To Michael Denison and Dulcie Gray I am indebted for an especially loving portrayal of Rebecca in her later years.

Jillian Becker, Lulu Friedman's daughter, not only gave me two extensive interviews about South Africa and about her mother's friendship with Rebecca West, she also turned over to me Rebecca's letters covering her South African period and several years afterward. Jillian's comments on my manuscript saved me from several errors—as did those of Sydney Kentridge, who followed up our interview with an important letter commenting on my South African chapter. I wish to thank Nadine Gordimer for allowing me to quote from her letter about Rebecca West.

Two of Rebecca's *Sunday Telegraph* editors, Rivers Scott and Nicholas Bagnall, supplied important insights into her working methods and the seriousness with which she approached book reviewing. Rivers was also an extraordinary mine of information, helping me to locate several interviewees and making helpful suggestions on my work-in-progress.

Diana Trilling welcomed my plan to write a biography of Rebecca West, gave me an interview about their friendship, and generously allowed me access to her valuable correspondence with Rebecca. She made several improvements in the chapters I entrusted to her perusal.

My fellow biographers have been generous with their advice and papers. Jeffrey Meyers shared with me his reminiscence of meeting Rebecca West during his work on Wyndham Lewis. Brian Connon, the biographer of Beverly Nichols, sent me several of Rebecca West's letters. Philip Hoare, the biographer of Noël Coward, sent me many items I might otherwise have missed. Carole Klein, the biographer of Doris Lessing, reviewed several chapters of my biography and gave me the benefit of her superb study of mothers and sons. Michael Foot shared with me his memories of H.G. Wells while working on his own H.G. biography. With both Michael and his wife Jill Craigie, I had several discussions about Rebecca and Max Beaverbrook. Jill, writing a history of feminism, gave me important material, including Rebecca's scrapbooks, and read my early chapters with an expert eye. At an early, crucial stage in my research, Carol Easton, biographer of the now late Agnes de Mille, helped to put me in touch with her subject. J. R. Hammond, author of an insightful study of H.G. Wells and Rebecca West, read my early chapters and saved me from several errors. Norman Mackenzie and Michael Coren, both biographers of H.G. Wells, were encouraging and helpful in responding to my questions. Diana Raymond generously shared with me her unpublished biography of Pamela Frankau, a work which deserves to be in print; she also answered questions and reviewed parts of an early draft of my biography. Deirdre Bair sent me important Anaïs Nin material, the fruit of her Nin biographical research. Martin Duberman kindly made available the tape recording of his interview with Rebecca West for his biography of Paul Robeson. Phyllis Hatfield, Stanley Olson's literary executor and biographer, gave me access to excerpts from Stanley's diary and could not have been more generous in encouraging my work. Jay Pridmore shared with me his experiences in researching the life of John Gunther. Barbara Belford searched her files for certain Violet Hunt items that proved useful for my biography.

I owe a special debt to several Rebecca West scholars. Tony Redd, Loretta Stec, Ann Norton, Phyllis Lassner, and Bonnie Kime Scott read drafts of my biography and made helpful corrections and suggestions. Bonnie Scott, at work on an edition of Rebecca's selected letters, was especially helpful in pointing out sources of new correspondence. Our meetings have sharpened the focus of my biography. Tony Redd sent me his diary entries on meetings with Rebecca West and copies of her correspondence.

The Notes section details many of the other contributions my interviewees have made to this biography. I would like to acknowledge them here not only for their willingness to be interviewed, but also in supplying correspondence and, in some cases, reviewing chapters of my biography: Voya (Gavrilović) Adzemovic, Irene Garthwaite Andrews, Lord Noel Annan, Nicholas Bagnall, Ralph Bates, Michael and Cornelia Bessie, Vincent Brome, the late Cleanth Brooks, William F. Buckley, Jr., A.O.J. Cockshut, Jilly Cooper, Fleur Cowles, Arthur Crook, Gwenda David, Noel Davis, the late Agnes de Mille, Michael Denison, Mrs. Lovat Dickson, Leon Edel, April Edwards, Clifton Fadiman, June Head Fenby, Jill Fox, Lady Antonia Fraser, Pat Wallace Frere, Richard Freund,

Aleksa Gavrilović, Darinka Gavrilović, Kosara Gavrilović, Victoria Glendinning, Dulcie Gray, Tom Guinzberg, Carola Hahn, Emily Hahn, the late Joan Haslip, the late Marjorie Hutton, Samuel Hynes, Elizabeth Jenkins, Lady Kelly, Linda Kelly, Francis King, Rhoda Koenig, the late Leo Lerman, Doris Lessing, Bernard Levin, Mike Levitas, Justin Lowinsky, Edith Oliver, Sheila Macdonald, Jane Marcus, Anna Lee Nathan, Ursula Owen, Alexandra Pringle, Margaret Rawlings, Babette Rosmund, Martin and Merle Rubin, Jane Sacchi, Virginia Salomon, the late William L. Shirer, Diana Stainforth, Fritz Stern, Raleigh Trevelyan, Nicolas van den Branden, Tom Wallace, Joan White, the late Chester Williams, Lucy Williams, Peter Willis, Cheryl West, Vita West, Mia Woodruff, Kit Wright, Marjorie Wynne.

There are many people I did not interview but who provided valuable information: Anne Anable, the late Kingsley Amis, Isaiah Berlin, Robert A. Colby, James B. Courtright, Jonathan Lovat Dickson, Frances Donaldson, Molly Panter Downes, Faith Evans, Arnold Gates, Norman Gates, James Gindin, William Goldstein, Richard Harrier, Selina Hastings, Alfred Kazin, Bruce Kellner, Joseph Laitin, Marjorie Lowenstein, Kenneth S. Lynn, Norman Mailer, Jessica Mitford, Sylvia Morris, Lady Diana Mosley, Fredric Raphael, Paul Robeson, Jr., Robert Robison, A. L. Rowse, Pamela Sheingorn, G. Thomas Tanselle, Telford Taylor, Hugo Vickers, Martha S. Vogeler, Eugene Weintraub, Larry Wolff, Ruth Wood.

I made nine trips to London to interview people about Rebecca West and to consult various archives. Frank Cheevers at the Hotel 167 in South Kensington made my stays comfortable and convenient. He and his staff took numerous messages for me and performed other kindnesses for which I am deeply thankful. Dilys and Gordon Cowan provided not only hospitality but also a visit to sites of H.G.'s early life which helped make him come alive for me.

In its early stages, my book profited greatly from suggestions made by Richard Cohen, Erika Goldman, Ethan Casey, and John Wilson—all of whom read drafts of my biography.

Amanda Vail alerted me to an important archive of letters at the Viking Press. Kathryn Munday, writing a study of Rebecca West and Virginia Woolf, reviewed several chapters of my biography and sent me a valuable letter to her from Nadine Gordimer. Susan Shreibman helped me retrieve material from the Trinity College library in Dublin. I thank Bob Eisenbach for trying to pin down Warren Beatty for an interview.

Several libraries and archives held collections of material without which this biography would have been impossible. I wish to thank Sidney Huttner, Lori Curtis, and the whole staff of Special Collections at

McFarlin Library, the University of Tulsa, which houses the largest Rebecca West collection, preserved in immaculate order. I never received anything less than excellent assistance. Walt Mauer in University Housing made my stays on campus pleasant and troublefree.

Next in importance is the Rebecca West collection at the Beinecke Library, Yale University. I am grateful to the staff for responding diligently to all my requests. Vincent Giroud, Curator of Modern Books and Manuscripts at the Beinecke, was especially helpful in alerting me to the library's new acquisitions of Rebecca West papers.

In New York, at the Pierpont Morgan Library, Christine Nelson made available the newly acquired Gordon Ray papers at just the moment I needed them. Similarly, the staff of The New York Public Library supplied indispensable items from their recently acquired *The New Yorker* files. Other items from the Berg Collection also proved essential. While researching the Emma Goldman Papers, I had excellent assistance from the staff of Special Collections, Tamiment Library, New York University. At Columbia University, the staff helped me locate many letters concerning Rebecca West's dealings with editors, agents, and publishers. At The Viking Press, Alan J. Kaufman, Senior Vice President and General Counsel, gave me access to editorial files containing Rebecca West correspondence. Carolyn Davis and her Special Collections staff at Syracuse University Library helped me find key items in the Dorothy Thompson and Francis Biddle collections. Elaine Engst, Curator of Manuscripts at Cornell University Library, advised me on the use of the Violet Hunt Collection.

At the Harry Ransom Humanities Research Center, The University of Texas, Cathy Henderson, Research Librarian, and her assistants, Cynthia Farar and Richard Watson, searched both their catalogued and uncatalogued materials and found many items that proved useful for my biography.

At Boston University, archivist Karen Mix combed through the A. D. Peters collection for items on Rebecca West. The staffs of the Houghton Library, Harvard University, and the Schlesinger Library, Radcliffe College, drew my attention to several letters from Rebecca West and helped me examine the papers of her friends. At Howard University, Special Collections, Esme Bahn discussed the Paul Robeson collection with me and made available the tape recording of Martin Duberman's interview with Rebecca West. Charles J. Kelly, Senior Manuscript Reference Specialist, and Mary Wolfskill in the Manuscript Reading Room at the Library of Congress answered my queries about their holdings on Rebecca West. With the assistance of the Special Collections staff at

Georgetown University Library, I located some important items on Henry Andrews in the Douglas Woodruff Papers. I am thankful to Daniel Meyer and his staff at the University of Chicago Library, Special Collections, for their help with the John Gunther Collection. Saundra Taylor, Curator of Manuscripts at Lilly Library, Indiana University, retrieved several important items from the Emily Hahn Collection and followed up on several of my queries.

Margaret Sherry, Reference Librarian/Archivist at Firestone Library, Princeton, discussed with me the Rebecca West–Raymond Mortimer correspondence. The staff of Princeton's Seely-Mudd Library also supplied correspondence between Allen Dulles and Rebecca West.

Fiorella Superbi Gioffredi, Curator of Collections and Archives at the Villa I Tatti, made available the correspondence of Henry Andrews and Rebecca West with Bernard Berenson. Sara S. Hodson, Curator of Literary Manuscripts, The Huntington Library, San Marino, California, drew my attention to several letters I had missed in previous archival searches.

My thanks to Amy Hague, Assistant Curator of the Sophia Smith Collection, Smith College, for sending me copies of Agnes de Mille's letters; to Raymond Teichman, Supervisory Archivist at the Franklin D. Roosevelt Library for responding to my queries; to Nancy MacKechnie at Vassar College Library for sending me items from the William Kent Rose Papers; to Virginia Smith of the Massachusetts Historical Society for sending me Rebecca West's letters to Ellery Sedgwick Smith.

In London, several libraries kindly allowed me to examine Rebecca West letters. I wish to thank the staffs of the British Library (letters to Bernard Shaw); the House of Lords Record Office (letters to Lord Beaverbrook); University College Library (letters to Arnold Bennett and George Orwell); King's College, Centre for Military Archives (letters to Basil Liddell Hart).

Several libraries in the United Kingdom sent me copies of Rebecca West's letters. I wish to thank Helen Bickerstaff, Assistant Librarian, Manuscripts Section, The University of Sussex Library (letters to Kingsley Martin); J.G.W. Roberts, Chief Officer of Leisure Services, Humberside County Council Central Library (letters to Winifred Holtby); Stuart O. Seanoir, Trinity College Library Dublin (letters to Patricia Hutchins and Thomas MacGreevy); E. D. Yeo, Assistant Keeper, Manuscripts Division, the National Library of Scotland (letters to C. Sarolea, Erik Linklater, and Cyril Lakin); R. A. Story, Archivist, Modern Records Centre, University of Warwick Library (letters to Richard Crossman, Victor Gollancz); Hazel Wright, Departmental Librarian, Rare Books and Manuscripts, Glasgow City Council Libraries Department (letters to

Reverend Henry S. McClelland); B. S. Benedikz, Sub Librarian, Special Collections, The University of Birmingham University Library (letters to Francis and Jessica Brett Yount).

I am grateful to Michael Bott at the University of Reading Archive who helped me locate several items in British universities and who sent me copies of Rebecca West letters in the Reading archive. Gaye Poulton, Group Contracts Director of Random House UK Limited, gave me access to the splendid publisher's archive at the University of Reading. The staff at the British Library Sound Archive made available several recordings of Rebecca West reading from her work. No biographical researcher in England can do without the helpful staff of Somerset House, which provided me with copies of wills by H.G. Wells, Rebecca West, and Henry Andrews.

I have been exceedingly fortunate in having the support of several travel grants and fellowships while completing my biography. The American Philosophical Society, The City University of New York, and Norman Fainstein, Dean of Liberal Arts and Sciences, Baruch College, The City University of New York, funded several research trips. Dean Fainstein and the travel committee of Liberal Arts and Sciences responded to all of my requests for funding; their support helped to ensure that I had the opportunity to examine essential primary sources.

At Baruch, several research assistants made my task a good deal easier. I thank Anita Anthony, Robert Chantemsin, and Vijay Gupta. Baruch's interlibrary loan staff, particularly Eric Neubacher and Louisa Moy, provided indispensable help—as did Spencer Means in the Reference department.

During my sabbatical year, a grant from the National Endowment for the Humanities supplemented my salary and made it possible for me to devote my time to writing and travel for this biography. I believe I owe my receipt of this grant in large part to Alan Maclean, Rebecca West's editor at Macmillan, who had faith in my ability to produce the biography and recommended me for the NEH grant.

Professor Michael Millgate of the University of Toronto has written countless recommendations on my behalf since my days as his graduate student. Whatever is good in my work owes much to his guidance. Professor George Garrett of the University of Virginia, has also written many letters in support of my work. His confidence in this biography has meant a great deal to me.

I am also indebted to Eliana Covacich of the Baruch Grants office. She encouraged me to apply to the NEH a second time, after my first effort proved unsuccessful, and she provided much needed advice. I am also grateful to Provost Lois Cronholm of Baruch College. She established a new fund for scholars which helped me to cover the considerable cost of photocopying primary sources.

My American agent, Elizabeth Knappman, has been steadfast in her support and shrewd in her editorial advice. Her staff at New England Publishing Associates is the best. Rivers Scott and Gloria Ferris, who represent me in Great Britain, have provided me with all kinds of assistance, making my numerous trips to London enjoyable and profitable. Roland Philipps, my editor at Hodder and Stoughton, showed me many ways to make this a better book, as did Scott Moyers, my editor at Scribner.

I would like to thank Peters, Fraser and Dunlop for allowing me to quote from the unpublished writings of Rebecca West. I am also grateful to the H.G. Wells estate for giving permission to quote from H.G. Wells's unpublished letters. Thanks to Nadine Gordimer for allowing me to quote from her unpublished letter about Rebecca West; to Lily West for allowing me to quote from the correspondence of Anthony West and to Mrs. Jane Gunther for allowing me to quote from the unpublished correspondence and journals of John Gunther.

At every step of the way I have had the unfailing support of my wife, Dr. Lisa Paddock. She has read and reread drafts of the biography and discussed numerous points with me. This has often meant interrupting her own writing. The only solution I see to this problem is for us to write books together. Stay tuned.

Notes and Sources

Consult the bibliography for full citations of the sources referred to in the notes by author's last name, or by last name and short title if there is more than one work by the same author. The acknowledgments contains a complete account of interviewees. Letters quoted in the text not in public research collections have been given to me by their recipients unless otherwise specified. Quotations from the letters between H.G. and Rebecca (most of them undated) are at Yale. Typed copies are also available in the Pierpont Morgan Library. With a few exceptions, correspondence between Rebecca and her husband, Henry Maxwell Andrews, is at Yale.

MSN	Manuscript Notebook	RW	Rebecca West
MW	Marjorie Wells	RWC	*Rebecca West: A Celebration*
NM	Norman Macleod	SKR	S. K. Ratcliffe
NMZ	Norman Mackenzie	SM	Sally Melville
NR	*The New Republic*	ST	*The Sunday Telegraph*
NS	*The New Statesman*	TG	Tom Guinzberg
NV	Nicolas van den Branden	TS	Typescript
REV	Review	TT	*Time and Tide*
RL	Ruth Lowinsky	VW	Vita West
RM	Raymond Mortimer	WM	Winifred Macleod

ABBREVIATIONS: RESEARCH COLLECTIONS

BU	Mugar Memorial Library, Special Collections, Boston University
Chicago	John Gunther Papers, Special Collections, The University of Chicago Library
Cornell	Rare and Manuscript Collections, Carl A. Kroch Library, Cornell University Library
CU	Rare Books and Manuscripts, Butler Library, Columbia University
HH	Houghton Library, Harvard University
Indiana	Lilly Library, Indiana University, Bloomington, Indiana
IT	Bernard Berenson Collection, I Tatti
LC	Manuscript Division, Library of Congress
Lords	Lord Beaverbrook Papers, House of Lords Record Office
NYPL	The New York Public Library
PML	Gordon Ray Collection, Pierpont Morgan Library
PU	Special Collections, Firestone Library, Princeton University
Syracuse	Dorothy Thompson Collection, Francis Biddle Collection, Syracuse University Library
Texas	Rebecca West Collection, Humanities Research Center, University of Texas, Austin, Texas
Tulsa	Rebecca West Collection, McFarlin Library, Special Collections, University of Tulsa, Tulsa, Oklahoma
Viking	Viking Press Research Library
Yale	Rebecca West Collection, Beinecke Rare Book and Manuscript Library, Yale University, New Haven, Connecticut

PREFACE

11 **"as an admirer"**: 10.IX.31, Nicolson and Trautmann, vol. IV.

1: THE FAMILY ROMANCE

Unless otherwise specified, quotations are from RW's memoirs, published posthumously as *Family Memories,* a heavily edited volume piecing together drafts of an uncompleted work. I also quote unpublished drafts, all of which are at Tulsa.

I have consulted the papers of her sister, Letitia Fairfield, and conducted extensive interviews and correspondence with Rebecca's niece, Alison Macleod, the daughter of Rebecca's sister, Winifred. Born in 1920, Alison learned much of the Fairfield and Mackenzie family histories from her mother and from Lettie. Alison also corresponded with Rebecca and the two of them debated points of family history.

David Ogilvy, Rebecca's cousin, born in 1911, discussed with me Charles Fairfield's reputation within his family. Another of Rebecca's cousins, Dr. Ian Barclay, knew both Lettie and Rebecca and heard from them about their childhoods.

I have also had the benefit of Victoria Glendinning's biography, which judiciously and accurately threads its way through Rebecca's accounts of her family's past.

For family history I drew on AM to CR, 22.X.92, 28.VI.93; to AM, 21.VII.75; to KW, 15.IX.55, Tulsa; to LF, 4.VI.60, courtesy AM; to HMA, 29.IV.50; to Lionel Trilling, 15.III.52, CU. See also "The Art of Fiction," "The Novelist's Voice," 1900.

Secunda and Wolfenstein provided valuable insights on fathers and daughters, mourning and loss.

17 **"physical maleness"**: "Men as Fathers," BBC radio interview transcript, 12.IX.64, Tulsa. **"The cleverest"**: Thomas Pillans to RW, 15.XI.16, Tulsa. **"most fascinating"**: to HR, 17.I.46, NYPL.

18 **"Dublin snob"**: to George Bernard Shaw, n.d., British Library.

19 **"More and more"**: "I Regard Marriage." **"My mother"**: "I Regard Marriage."

20 **"unromantic and philistine security"**: "The Novelist's Voice."

21 **"molly-coddling"**: for examples of Charles Fairfield's writing see *The Argus*, 20.XI.84, 13.VI.85, VIII.86, 5.IX.85, 28.II.91, clippings of which are pasted in several large scrapbooks, Tulsa.

22 **"He puts me in mind"**: quoted by Faith Evans in notes to *Family Memories*. **"perhaps a little"**: A. Ewing to LF, n.d., Tulsa.

23 **"childish resentment"**: This quotation is from RW's autobiographical story, "Short Life of a Saint," in *The Only Poet*. **"personal sorrows"**: "The Novelist's Voice." **"Rebecca's muse"**: INT. AM. **"dreadful little hovel"**: to HMA, 29.IV.50, Yale. **"one of the drearier"**: "I Regard Marriage." **"fine points of a horse"**: AM to CR, 22.X.92.

24 rough idea: "My Father." **"first-person sagas"**: Ivor Herbert, "Profile 66," *Evening News*, 16.VIII.66.

25 **"a wildgoose chase"**: "People Today." **"anguish of a soul"**: Tulsa. Some readers question whether Rebecca could have written such a poem at the age of eight. No draft exists in her own handwriting, only a typewritten version which gives her age as eight.

2: THE YOUNG REBECCA (1901–1912)

Quotations from RW's *Freewoman* articles are from Marcus, *The Young Rebecca*, unless otherwise specified. Quotations from RW's letters to Dora Marsden, Grace Jardine, and Rona Robinson, are from the Dora Marsden Collection, Firestone Library, Princeton University. These are undated letters, but I have established their approximate chronology through internal evidence.

In addition to RW's letters and memoirs, Alison Macleod has provided me with an account of Rebecca's life in Edinburgh, as remembered by Alison's mother, Winnie.

27 **"prudent despondency"**: *The Judge*. For a later and sunnier memory of Edinburgh, see to Mr. Westwood, n.d., National Library of Scotland. **"rather old fashioned"**: Walker. **Isabella's anorexia**: to EHN, 21.XI.61, Indiana. **"dreary diet"**: to DR, 21,V.68, Tulsa.

28 **Aunt Sophie**: INT. David Ogilvy. **"daughter of an aged scoundrel . . . fantasy world"**: to AM, 21.VII.75. **"horrid rich relatives"**: autobiographical fragment, n.d., Yale. **"disconsolated at Chelt"**: to LF, n.d., courtesy of AM; to NM, 7.VI.60; Winnie's school record, courtesy of Janet Johnstone, Librarian and Archivist, Cheltenham Ladies College. **"out of it"**: INT. AM. **RW's early schooling**: "Of Saintly Headmistresses and Wicked French Governesses": Unidentified RW article in the collection of NV; Annie Robson Cathcart to RW, 18.III.56, Yale; Ann Lawson to RW, 12.III.56; "People Today"; "The Art of Fiction"; to EHN, 28.II.54, Indiana; Norah Richardson to RW, 28.V.75; to Miss Fleming, 1.XII.60; Miss Fleming to RW, 5.XII.60, Yale.

29 **"most unpleasant"**: to DR, 21.V.68, Tulsa. **"child of"**: "A Visit to a Godmother," RWC. **"It was rather dramatic"**: "The Art of Fiction." **"How is it that"**: INT. JS; see also "The World's Worst Failure II: The Schoolmistress," NR, 22.I.16. **"as there was no boy"**: Walker.

30 **"Thank God"**: Marcus, *The Young Rebecca*. **"We are just settling down now"**: 5.XII.09, courtesy of AM. **"Keep the Liberal Out!"**: to LF, n.d., courtesy of AM. **"Adela"**: *The Only Poet and Other Stories*. Rebecca essayed at least two other less polished pieces of fiction, fragments of which are preserved in a manuscript notebook [Tulsa]. Perhaps the earliest piece is "The Minx," by "Anne Telope," a story of sixteen-year-old Veronica Fawcett. She is ambitious and craves success, spurns a two hundred pound bursary and rejects her family. She swings down an Edinburgh street colliding with the young English architect, Arnold Ivory, who has a considerable reputation as a roué. He is dark-browed and slim, with the smirking assurance of Charles Fairfield. Veronica is susceptible to his charms but ultimately rejects him: "She glared at him savagely and pushed past into the chilled twilight. In the fraction of a second they had stood face-to-face he had not noticed her: she knew and loathed everything in him." Arnold is clearly a patch on Richard Yaverland, the hero of *The Judge*. Indeed, Rebecca's second unfinished early piece of fiction portrays Ellen Yaverland, a seventeen-year-old beauty in love with Richard (no last name is given). Ellen admires the stage actress, Emmy Marchant, the type of artist who had "all the virtues she lacked as a woman. On the stage her body was pure and supple and disciplined, an instrument of the soul. . . . On the stage she was without vanity—without class. Across the auditorium she spoke with another voice, an index of the spiritual splendor that she possessed in the field of her life's adventure." This florid evocation of an actress foreshadows the presentation of Rebecca's actress alter ego in her novel, *Sunflower,* as well as suggesting how appealing the theater became for the young Rebecca as an instrument of liberation and artistic fulfillment. See also "Indissoluble Matrimony," a short story Rebecca wrote shortly after leaving drama school, reprinted in Marcus, *The Young Rebecca.*

31 **"got hell"**: to EHN, 28.II.54, Indiana. **"pythoning about:"** "The Art of Fiction." **"bristling with asides:"** to LF, n.d., courtesy of AM. **On Fairliehope**: to LF, 20.III.10, courtesy of AM.

32 **"No"**: to LF, 18.IV.10, courtesy of AM. **"an irritating child"**: autobiographical fragment, n.d., Yale. **"revolted against all authority"**: "People Today." **RW at**

ADA: to EA, 8.V.52, Yale; to Jean Overton Fuller, 27.III.62, Tulsa; Dickson. **"playing Antonio":** Glendinning. **"no personality":** to GR, 13.VIII.73, PML. **curiously stiff:** INT. Catherine Macleod. **"a twitch":** WM to RW, n.d., courtesy of AM.

33 **"I do not think":** autobiographical memorandum, 28.I.58, Yale; see also MSN, Tulsa. **"Don't you think":** MSN, Tulsa. **"Oh, I think":** Moyers. **"like a ballet dancer":** "Shoulder to Shoulder." **"lukewarm":** "A Reed of Steel," Marcus.

34 **On the WSPU:** TT, 16.VII.26, Garner, Olson. **"glorious red-haired":** *The Freewoman*, TT, 16.VII.26. **"deeply shocked":** INT. AM; see also, *The Freewoman*, 16.VII.26; "Rebecca West," BBC Talks and Documentaries, Radio Three 24.III.83. **"existed it seemed":** *Joan and Peter.*

35 **"She'll never":** MSN, Tulsa." **RW's name change:** Vera Watson to RW, 20.III.43, Yale; to Mr. Martin, 30.VII.61, Tulsa; "Tonight—Dame Rebecca West," transcript of interview with Ludovic Kennedy, Tulsa; "Rebecca West," BBC Talks and Documentaries, Radio Three, 24.III.83, Tulsa; Curtis; Dickson; Marcus, "A Voice of Authority"; Stec.

36 **"Rebecca West born":** courtesy of Jill Craigie, to whom RW entrusted two of her scrapbooks.

38 **J. M. Kennedy:** to Jane Lidderdale, 8.III.67, to Mr. Martin, 20.VII.61, Tulsa. **"plump and sprightly":** Selver. **"darling girl":** n.d., Yale.

39 **"Fabian nursery":** Brandon.

3: The New Woman and the Old Man (1912–1913)

40 **"generous gesture":** *H.G. Wells in Love.* **"so commonplace":** journal of Mrs. C. A. Dawson Scott, 18.II.13, courtesy of Mrs. Marjorie Lowenstein. For a vivid description of H.G. see Brome. H.G.'s piercing blue eyes were often mentioned to Norman Mackenzie in interviews for his biography of Wells. [INT: NMZ] H.G. mentions his exceptionally smooth skin in *H.G. Wells in Love.* His honey scent and large penis were described to Norman Mackenzie by several of H.G.'s mistresses. He was eventually diagnosed as a diabetic, which may account for his sweet smell. See also Morgan: "Maugham once asked Moura [Budberg], a tempestuous and beautiful woman, with high cheekbones and expressive eyes, what she saw in the paunchy, played-out writer [Wells]. 'He smells of honey,' she said."

41 **"walk of the matador":** Dickson. **"immense vitality":** Glendinning. **"noblest work":** to Dora Marsden, n.d., Princeton. **"watching his":** to Dora Marsden, n.d., PU. By October 12, 1912, Rebecca was using H.G. as a reference in a letter to the editor of *Everyman.* "I enclose some cuttings and a note from Mr. H.G. Wells," she wrote in her effort to get the periodical to accept work from her, which it did. [to Dr Sarolea, n.d., Edinburgh University Library]. **"small nature":** Quoted in Brandon.

42 **"an innocent":** Usborne. **"loss of fortune":** MSN, Tulsa.

43 **"Our drawing room":** Quoted in Glendinning. **RW's pursuit of H.G:** to GR, 13.VIII.73, PML. I am indebted to Alison Macleod for the story of H.G.'s visits to the Fairfield home in Hampstead, and for Isabella Fairfield's reaction to him. **"commonplace lovemaking":** *H.G. Wells in Love.* **"greatly drawn":** *H.G. Wells in Love.* **nervous collapse:** to Dora Marsden, n.d., Princeton.

44 **"I hate Paris":** courtesy of AM. **The New Freewoman:** *The Freewoman* ceased publication in the middle of October 1912 when it lost its financial backer.

Rebecca herself had not skipped a beat, having been invited by Robert Blatchford, the energetic, witty, and down-to-earth editor of the socialist paper, *The Clarion*, to become a regular contributor. Her first article appeared on September 27, 1912. Blatchford had been amused by her attacks on antifeminists in *The Freewoman*, praising her aplomb: "It's like a ride on an aeroplane; so exhilarating, so breezy, it is also irresistibly funny." [Marcus, Introduction to *The Young Rebecca*] Although she had other outlets for her writing, Rebecca canvassed vigorously for a new financial backer for *The Freewoman*, advising Doris Marsden about a mission statement for the paper and agreeing to write for it when it resumed publication. **"tragic and ludicrous":** to Dora Marsden, quoted in Glendinning. **"an externalization":** to GR, n.d., draft of a letter, MSN, Tulsa. **"I think":** to GR in notes to Ray, *H.G. Wells and Rebecca West.* **"Dear H.G.":** RW's letter is quoted in Ray and copies can be found at Yale and PML. In 1891, Horatio Bottomley, a journalist and financier, defended himself against a charge of fraud and was acquitted. Acquitted a second time in 1909, he went bankrupt again in 1911 after squandering enormous sums of money. At Tulsa there is an RW manuscript dealing with Bottomley. She may have thought of him in connection with H.G. because she regarded Bottomley as having the "genius of personality," who cheered the eye. She never met him, but even across the room in a restaurant the sight of him exhilarated her.

48 **"I think":** quoted in Usborne.

4: PANTHER AND JAGUAR (1913–1915)

50 **"clear off":** Mackenzie.
51 **"sexual hiccups":** The details about Rebecca's sex with H.G. come from an interview with Dr. Bethel Solomons. He treated her skin problems, but he was also an old friend (she knew him and his family for more than thirty years). Like Rebecca, Bethel had an intense interest in Proust, and Bethel often discussed male sexuality with her. She would ask him exactly what it felt like for a man to have an ejaculation. They discussed homosexuality. Their conversations, as far as I know, were unique in Rebecca's experience. She did not like discussing her intimate moments with H.G., but with her doctor/friend she seemed to relax and let loose her natural curiosity and desire to discuss such matters. These talks took place in the 1970s, when the details of Rebecca's relationship with H.G. could no longer be kept a secret. She had many unresolved questions, and Bethel may have seemed like a trusted, urbane, and sensitive male to whom she could unburden her concerns and admit her joy in lovemaking. **S. K. Ratcliffe's role in RW's early career:** to Mr. Thompson, 24.II.32, Tulsa. **"fresh and silvery":** draft obituary of Sylvia Lynd for the *News Chronicle*, n.d., Tulsa. **Quotations and details of the RW, Violet Hunt, Ford Madox Ford relationship:** Hunt, *The Flurried Years*; RW's REV of *South Lodge, Reminiscences of Violet Hunt, Ford Madox Ford, and "the English Review" Circle* by Douglas Gouldring, MSN, Yale; Belford; King; Lewis; Mizener; to Arthur Mizener 16.IV.68 and 13.VI.68, Cornell; to Thomas Moser, 8.IV.75, Tulsa; ST, 7.V.72.
53 **"Fame!":** Quoted in Glendinning. **"slipped":** H.G. told his son Gip about the accidental pregnancy. See G. P. Wells to GR, 21.II.74, PML. See Smith for Jane's initial reactions to H.G.'s announcement of RW's pregnancy.
54 **"I found":** diary entry, 21.IV.75, Tulsa. **"discreet enough":** H.G. to RW, n.d., Yale.

56 **"playing scales"**: *Daily News*, 14.III.14. **"I am full of misery"**: PML.

57 **"Suckling is"**: Ray. **"Well, I'm a rich man"**: INT. AM. **"suddenly froglike"**: "Women of England." **Rebecca's reaction to childbirth and to Anthony**: "Women of England"; Ray; a memoir by Letitia Fairfield, courtesy of AM.

60 **"persistent inability to work"**: to Ellery Sedgwick, 25.VII.15, Ellery Sedgwick Papers, Massachusetts Historical Society. See also 15.XI.15 and 24.II.16.

5: Sons and Lovers (1915–1918)

My account of Anthony West is derived from interviews with his first and second wives, Kitty and Lily West, from his autobiographical novel, *David Rees, Among Others*, which closely corresponds to what he told both his wives about his childhood, from Rebecca's diaries for 1917 [Tulsa] and 1918 [Yale], from Letitia Fairfield's memoir and Isabella Fairfield's correspondence [courtesy of AM], and from RW's correspondence with Sally Tugander Melville, n.d., Yale.

For RW's Leigh-on-Sea period, see to SM, n.d., Yale, as well as her diaries for 1917 and 1918.

62 **"I hate domesticity"**: to Sylvia Lynd, n.d., BU. **"chumming"**: to SKR, 1916, Yale. **"one of the real"**: "Femininity," *Daily News*, 9.VIII.17, Marcus, *The Young Rebecca*. **"precipitous flirtation"**: Quoted in Glendinning.

63 **"buckets of blood"**: 4.II.16, Yale. **"Surely, never before"**: "Hands That Make War: Welfare Work," *Daily Chronicle*, 1916, Marcus, *The Young Rebecca*. **RW's reconsideration of socialism**: "Socialism in the Searchlight", *Daily Chronicle*, 1916, Marcus, *The Young Rebecca*. **"orgiastic loquacity"**: "Femininity," *Daily News*, 9.VIII.17, Marcus, *The Young Rebecca*. **"I ates"**: n.d., Yale.

64 **"swelling quality"**: "Arnold Bennett Himself," *The New York Herald Tribune*, 19.IV.31. **"gastric jewellery"**: Bennett, *The Journals of Arnold Bennett*.

65 **H.G. and Paul Reynolds**: H.G. to Paul Reynolds, 20.III.16, 30.IV.18; Paul Reynolds to H.G., 19.IV.16, 25.III.18, CU. **"Oh the sadness"**: Secor. **The air raids**: Stern, *Monogram*.

66 **"He is indulging"**: to Sally Tugander Melville, n.d., Yale. **"very sweet"**: APW to RW, n.d., courtesy of AM.

67 **"someone enormously buoyant"**: APW, "Life with Aunty Panther and H.G. Wells." **"spoiled it for others"**: LF memoir, courtesy of AM. **"You hurt me"**: to KW, 19.X.55, Tulsa. **"private world"**: APW, "Life with Aunty Panther and H.G. Wells." **"continual agonies"**: "The Younger Generation," *Daily News and Leader*, c. 1918, Tulsa. **"very cold reception"**: to HRG, 20.X.55, courtesy of TG.

68 **"Anthony always knew"**: to GR, 26.III.74, PML. Aggravated by Anthony's accounts of his terrible childhood, Lettie pointed out that "by the end of the First World War England was full of children who had never seen their fathers, and in his early childhood Anthony could not have seen himself as the only child without one." [LF memoir, courtesy of AM] She is right, of course, but Anthony's problem was that he knew he had a father he could not *name;* he was a son whom neither parent openly recognized. **"successful amorist's gift"**: APW, "Life with Aunty Panther and H.G. Wells." **"The Time Book"**: unpublished MS, "dedicated to APW," Yale.

69 **"I hope Major Melville"**: n.d., Yale. For details of publication and origins of *The*

Return of the Soldier: see diary (1917), Tulsa; Frederick Allen to RW, 16.I.16, Yale; "On *The Return of the Soldier.*"

71 **"small masterpiece":** Hynes, Introduction to RWC.

6: THE JUDGE (1917–1921)

72 **"one of my favourite":** to Ruth Butcher, 24.XI.81, CU.

73 **"I damned near":** Marcus, "A Voice of Authority." **While H.G. fretted:** *H.G. Wells in Love.* **"La Femme Shaw":** Max Beerbohm to George Bernard Shaw, Yale. **"how scared":** 17.IV.19, courtesy of William Goldstein. **"large, pure":** NS, 10.VII.20. **Shaw's lecture to RW:** 14.VII.20, Yale. **"It is diligent":** NS, 10.IV.20.

74 **"essential thing":** NS, 5.VI.20. **"a certain kind":** NS, 31.VII.20. **"is the one":** NS, 18.II.22. **RW's new flat:** to Henry James Forman, n.d., NYPL. See also APW, "Life with Aunty Panther and H.G. Wells." **RW's disastrous 1919–1920:** to SKR, 28.VII.[20], NYPL.

75 **"you must have had":** 7.IX.20, Yale. **"violent love"** to Janet Dunbar, 17.II.77, Tulsa; see also RW diary entry, 10.X.75, Tulsa. **"dead set":** Linklater. **"beautiful beyond belief":** to Janet Dunbar, 17.II.77, Tulsa. See also to James Pinker, n.d., NYPL; to SM, n.d., Yale; to Mrs. Brett-Young 8.VI.19, Special Collections, University of Birmingham Library; to Mrs. Fairfield, n.d., courtesy of A.M.

76 **"Why can't she":** AM to CR, 30.XI.93. When Alison was born in the spring of 1920, Rebecca told Anthony she was going to visit the new baby. He replied, "You're not to bring that baby here! If you bring it here, I'll kill it!." INT.AM.

77 **"exhausted and horrified":** to Janet Dunbar, 17.II.77, Tulsa. **"perfect angel":** to Violet Hunt, n.d., Cornell; see also Florence journal, Tulsa; "The Good German," *The Weekly Westminster Gazette,* 12.VIII.22, Yale; to Mrs. Brett-Young 8.VI.19, Special Collections, University of Birmingham Library. **"carefully good looking":** "Violet's Folie De Grandeur," ST, clipping file, Yale. **"only person . . . desperately unhappy":** Violet Trefusis to Pat Dansey, n.d., Leaska and Phillips. **"Elegy":** reprinted in RWC.

78 **"elongated elf":** to Violet Hunt, n.d., Cornell. **"paw":** to APW, postcard, n.d., courtesy of AM. **"hideous, with staring eyes":** LF memoir, courtesy of AM. In the late 1970s, near death herself, Lettie dictated to her niece Alison her memory of her mother's last days, because Anthony had provided a shockingly different account in his autobiographical novel, *David Rees, Among Others.* My account of Anthony's memories is drawn from this autobiographical fiction. I have closely paraphrased the novel, changing fictional names to the names of their factual counterparts. This is unorthodox, I know, but more than most writers, Anthony West argued that fiction was a species of autobiography. See his argument in *Mortal Wounds.*

79 **"contestants were more than just friends":** APW, "Life with Aunty Panther and H.G. Wells." **"Was his Panther":** LF memoir, courtesy of AM. **Lettie and H.G.:** Wells's biographer Norman Mackenzie remembers that Odette Keun, H.G.'s mistress while Anthony was in his teens, told Mackenzie of expressing concerns similar to Lettie's and H.G. brushed her aside with the remark: "What is this archaic attitude of yours?" INT.NMZ.

80 **"It must be awful":** to LF, n.d., courtesy of AM. **"Do be tender":** to WM, postmarked 8.II.23. **"When I've learnt":** H.G. to APW, n.d., Yale.

81 **"especially in moments":** Orlich. For a much more hopeful reading of the novel's

ending, see Scott, *Refiguring Modernism* and Thomas. **"a fashionable absorption":** to Raymond Mortimer, n.d., PU. **Reception of *The Judge*:** Somerset Maugham to RW, 1922, Tulsa; Virginia Woolf to Ottoline Morrell, 18.VII.22, Nicolson, Vol. 2; Robert Littell, "Rebecca West's *The Judge*," *The New Republic*, 15.IX.22;

82 **"illustrating the influence":** Christopher Ward, *The Triumph of the Nut, and other Parodies* (Holt and Company), 1923.

7: The End of My Youth (1922–1923)

RW's interpretation of H.G.'s character dovetails with his self-analysis in *The Secret Places of the Heart*. I quote from H.G.'s novel to reconstruct his feelings at the time of his Spanish rendezvous with Rebecca.

83 **Quotations from Rebecca's 1922 diary:** Yale. I have also relied on her letter to LF, n.d., courtesy of AM. **"raw, unfinished, striving":** *"The Good German," Weekly Westminster Gazette*, 12.VII.22, Yale. **"whimpering and squealing":** to LF, n.d., courtesy of AM.

84 **"very beautiful":** Quoted in Mackenzie.

85 **"very naughty":** diary entry, 30.I.22, Yale. **"buffer":** to APW, n.d. [unsent], PML.

86 **"Today there's a wind":** n.d., Yale.

87 **"furious riding":** to SKR, n.d., Yale. **"dramatic instinct":** to Louis Golding, n.d., Texas. **"He's naturally":** H.G. to WM, n.d., courtesy of A.M. **"lazy boy":** to Helen Corke, 22.X.22, Texas.

89 **Jane Wells:** On a draft of Gordon Ray's *H.G. Wells and Rebecca West*, RW commented: "I feel you present me as a gifted, eccentric, incompetent, perhaps rather hysterical girl, and Jane is the wise, calm, and practical good woman of the proverbs with whom H.G. was bound to stay if his interest were to be preserved. That is what H.G., for his own obscure psychological reasons, wanted everyone to believe. There was nothing to it." (It is also what Anthony West, in his biography of H.G., wanted to believe.) In a diary entry for March 17, 1974, Rebecca fretted over what she regarded as Ray's reverence for Jane. What was so noble about a woman who "knuckled under" while her husband hunted other women? "It is not just. Gordon Ray has some vulgar idea about jealousy. But what jealously would last 41 years? Not mine." Rebecca became so exercised over the misperception of Jane that she composed a seventeen-page handwritten memorandum [Tulsa] on Jane's perfidy. It seems to have been provoked by the appearance of Norman and Jean Mackenzie's H.G. biography. They treat Jane, in Rebecca's words, as the "ingénue of the Wells story." I draw many of the details of Rebecca's view of Jane from this memorandum and from her correspondence with Gordon Ray, PML.

Rebecca reveled in drama and conflict, and Jane gave her no opening for a direct engagement of wills. Frank Swinnerton, a close friend of Jane's, said she was discreet and never revealed the true state of her feelings. H.G. called her a "shy and elusive personality." [*The Book of Catherine Wells*] Jane gave everything a neutral tint. Yet one of H.G.'s early biographers is certain Jane "loathed losing her husband to other women." [Brome] A later biographer, inclined to accept H.G.'s view that he and Jane had reached a pleasant accommodation concerning his infidelity, nevertheless concludes, "one is still left with the feeling that perhaps, just perhaps, he is making the situation slightly better than it actually was between them. He

remained an author of fiction at all times." [Smith] Beatrice Webb, the prominent
Fabian who had been so exercised over H.G.'s affair with Amber Reeves, supposed
that Jane tolerated H.G.'s promiscuity because she herself had broken up his first
marriage and felt she had no right to be possessive. [Mackenzie] In his H.G. biography, Anthony West sees Jane as a wily figure with a vein of steel in her, determined to stick by H.G. no matter what. When Jane's friends relayed to her
Rebecca's announcement that she intended to make H.G. marry her, all Jane "had
to do after that was smile gently and look just a little bit martyred before changing
the subject. . . . She could safely leave it to my mother, who had not called herself
Rebecca West for nothing, to do herself any damage that the situation might
require." In a wonderful phrase that would have driven his mother mad, Anthony
concludes that she was no match for the "marching strength of a married couple."
Like Rebecca, each of these interpreters fills the vacuum in Jane's character with
plausible speculations, although they do not (with the exception of Anthony West)
come to the kind of closure on Jane's character that Rebecca required in order to
appease her aggravated memory.

91 **"marry me":** to GR, 29.VII.74, PML. I learned of Winnie's destruction of H.G.'s letters from her daughter Alison, who never once heard either Lettie or Winnie
speak in favor of Rebecca marrying H.G.—not even hypothetically. e.g. "It would
have been all right if . . ." or "it would have been so much better if . . . could have
persuaded H.G. to get a divorce and marry her." **Max Beaverbrook:** In later years
RW told several different stories about her abortive affair with him. I've chosen the
one she told in her autobiographical memorandum [28.I.58, Yale] which closely parallels her account in *Sunflower.* Rebecca told Gordon Ray that Gladys, Max's wife,
visited her, saying that Max was in love with her and would ask her to marry him.
But he made no proposal then, and Rebecca was wary: "The last thing I wanted was
to marry a man who had recently been divorced, for I would find myself again under
suspicion of breaking up a marriage which had in fact been fractured long before I
came on the scene. Also I had to consider whether it would be a good move from
Anthony's point of view." Much later, Winnie told her daughter Alison a different
story—that Max had invited Rebecca to be his maîtresse en tête. She was to have
a splendid allowance—every penny of which she was to spend on being beautifully
dressed—and she was to live in a splendid house somewhere within easy reach of
London where he could bring his more raffish friends such as he wouldn't wish to
introduce to his wife. On thinking it over Rebecca decided this was not her role in
life. See RW's comments on Beaverbrook [referred to as "X"] in Gordon Ray's manuscript of *H.G. Wells & Rebecca West* [PML]. Beaverbrook's biographers, Anne
Chisholm and Michael Davie, are doubtful that Gladys's visit actually occurred, citing Rebecca's tendency to reinvent her past. But there is no reason to question the
mutual attraction of Max and Rebecca, or her mixed feelings about it.

92 **"the Gatternigg horror":** diary entry, Yale; see also *H.G. Wells in Love;* Ray; APW,
H.G. Wells; Smith. I have also drawn on what Rebecca told Lettie [LF to NM,
14.VIII.69].

93 **"bright flashes":** *H.G. Wells in Love.*

94 **Anthony's behavior:** to Henry James Forman, 15.VI.23, Yale; INT. AM.; LF
memoir, courtesy of AM. **"people often":** autobiographical memorandum, 28.I.58,
Yale; see also diary entry: "Everybody told me he was a wicked child, but I would
not believe them," 21.I.76, Tulsa. **H.G.'s letters to RW, his behavior at Swanage
and her state of mind:** to SM, n.d., Yale, to Eric Pinker, 18.VIII.23, NYPL.

8: THE NEW WORLD (1923–1925)

95 **The details of RW's American tour:** Lee Keedick [lecture agent] to SKR, cour-
tesy of AM; to SKR, 25.XI.23, Yale; "Traveling in America," *New Republic*,
24.XII.24; to WM, 2.XI,23, courtesy of AM; to Sinclair and Gracie Lewis,
9.XII.23, Syracuse; to LF, 8.II.24, courtesy of AM; *Chicago Tribune* 10.XI.23; *New
York Times Book Review* 11.XI.23; Burton Rascoe, "A Gossip on Miss West and Mr.
Maugham," unidentified newspaper clipping, RW's scrapbook, courtesy of Jill
Craigie. **Physical description of RW:** see G. B. Stern, "The Young Novelist Who
Has Become a Legend," *Literary Digest International Book Review*, 22.I.24.
"extremely mobile face": Jack C. Thomas to RW, 26.IV.24, Tulsa.

96 **"What a moving"** INT. JS. **"an odd mixture":** Langner. **"Gothic angel":** to HR,
25.VIII.47, NYPL.

97 **"entertained to death":** to Ellery Sedgwick, 23.VIII.24, Ellery Sedgwick Papers,
Massachusetts Historical Society. **"vamped half California":** Tulsa. **"glorious
beyond one's dreams":** to LF, n.d., courtesy of AM. **"Do be careful":** Lawrence
Langner to RW, 10.IV.24, Tulsa. **"Bill, she was":** Matthau. **Alexander Woollcott:**
autobiographical notes, MSN, Tulsa; to Edwin Hoyt, 20.III.66, Yale; AW to RW,
4.II.40, Tulsa. **"the incomparable Rebecca":** Kauffman and Hennessey. **"a Jewess":** to LF, 8.II.24, courtesy of AM.

98 **F. Scott Fitzgerald:** to Andrew Turnbull, n.d., Tulsa; see also Milford. **"Rebecca
West":** to GR, n.d., PML. These words are Rebecca's reconstruction of a scene
that is supposed to have occurred nearly fifty years earlier. Because of her instinct
for the dramatic, it is difficult not to suppose she heightened her humiliation to
make a point, or even invented a speech that makes palpable what she feared.
There is no reference to it in the letters written during her American tour. **"much
anti-English feeling":** autobiographical notes, MSN, Tulsa. **"miles and miles":**
8.XI.23, Tulsa.

99 **"'funny' food:"** 23.XI.23, Tulsa. **"This is an Indian":** 3.XI.23, Tulsa. **"dearly
beloved Anthony":** HG to APW, 4.I.24, courtesy of AM. **RW's sarcastic reply:**
H.G. to WM, 13.IV.24, courtesy of AM.

100 **"It was torturing":** to FH, Texas. **"sweetheart . . . my pet lamb":** n.d., Lords.
"wicked newspaper proprietor": n.d. Beaverbrook Papers. House of Lords
Record Office. Rebecca almost certainly wrote this tawdry tale after visiting Salt
Lake City in April 1924. **Beaverbrook's reputation:** see the essay in Michael
Foot's *Debts of Honour*. I'm also indebted to Foot for speaking with me about his
memories of Beaverbrook, who employed Foot as a journalist for several years. **"it
must have been":** autobiographical memorandum, 28.I.58, Yale. **"centre of
things":** I've taken this phrase from William Gerhardie's *Jazz and Jasper*, a fictional
portrait of Beaverbrook as Lord Ottercove.

101 **"careless elegance":** Foot. **"a quaint Bloomsbury":** *New Republic*, 10.XII.24.
"The Magician of Pell Street": reprinted in *The Only Poet*. **"Two very pathetic":**
to LF, postmarked 7.III.24, courtesy of AM. **"Dear Panther":** APW to RW, n.d., Yale.

102 **"a picture":** "My Religion." **spiritual discipline:** see RW's comments in "The
Classic Artist," a chapter of *The Strange Necessity*. **"raise an awful dust":** to LF,
postmarked 7.III.24, courtesy of AM. **"Anthony's latest escapade":** courtesy of
AM. **"I felt a weight":** APW to LF, n.d., courtesy of AM. **"rationalist case . . . web
of relationships":** APW, "Life with Aunty Panther and H.G. Wells." **"Only twelve
more days":** APW to LF, n.d., courtesy of AM.

103 **"well groomed"**: *David Rees, Among Others*. The following passage evoking Anthony's memories is also based on his novel. **"cover story"**: APW, "Life with Aunty Panther and H.G. Wells." **RW's attitude to Anthony:** I have relied on Carole Klein's fine study, *Mothers and Sons*. She cites several studies of the mother-son relationship demonstrating that the majority of women feel guilt about failing their sons.

104 **RW's day with Max Beaverbrook:** to FH, n.d., Texas. **"HAVE FORGOTTEN"**: Tulsa. See also to DS, 23.III.25, Yale.

105 **"hounded by a malevolent fate"**: to WM, n.d., courtesy of AM.

106 **"solid thickset woman": to Sherry Kahan, 13.VIII.73, Tulsa. "reject a conclusion"**: Introduction to *My Disillusionment with Russia*.

107 **"flight into sentimentality"**: Introduction to *My Disillusionment with Russia*. **"Menshevik or Social Democrat"**: to Sherry Kahan, 13.VIII.73, Tulsa. **"is a Russian"**: Introduction to *My Disillusionment with Russia*. **"light but not warmth"**: Wexler.

108 **"I remember"**: JG to RW, n.d., Chicago.

9: SUNFLOWER (1925–1927)

109 **"curiously gentle"**: journal of Mrs C. A. Dawson Scott, courtesy of Mrs. Marjorie Lowenstein. **RW's feelings about her separations from Anthony:** to SM, 12.XI.25, Yale. man. INT. DO. **"incubus"**: to SKR, XI.25, Yale.

110 **"achingly painful . . . wow!"**: to JG, n.d., Chicago. **"I had very few"**: to LF, postmarked 12.III.26., courtesy of AM. **"Not that I'd mind"**: to JG, n.d., Chicago.

111 **"best and sweetest"**: n.d., courtesy of AM. **"dark loveliness"**: Morris. **"You are"**: 22.X.26, Chicago.

112 **"rather heroic treatment"**: to JG, 22.X.26, Chicago. **"I rather imagine"**: to LF, 2.XI.26, courtesy of AM. *War Nurse:* to Miss Stephens, 1.II.48, Tulsa; to LF, 2.XI.26; EA to RW, n.d., Yale.

113 **"just a dull man"**: to JG, n.d., Chicago. **"no town for a child"**: to LF, 2.XI.26, courtesy of AM: see also journal of Mrs. C. A. Dawson Scott, 21.XII.26, courtesy of Mrs. Marjorie Lowenstein. **RW and Greta Mortimer:** INT. Rosalind Burdon-Taylor.

114 **"My poor Steve"**: to JG, n.d., Chicago. See to CC, 6.XI.49, Yale: "I was extremely ill after having nursed Stephen Martin, whom I was going to marry, through his last illness." See also to FH about a story RW wrote, a "compressed biography of Steve." So little is revealed about him in her letters, however, that it is hard to say which story it was or even if she published it. "Everybody weeps copiously who reads it," she told Fannie about a lover who is largely a phantom, although his biography could have contributed to one of several stories she wrote in the 1920s about the country's volatile commercial culture, in which a man's whole life is defined by the ups and downs of his business. RW also gives a brief description of Stephen Martin in a letter to Lettie, courtesy of AM. **"Father Violation Memory"**: MSN, Tulsa.

115 **the railway carriage scene:** *Family Memories*. **"sleeper effect"**: Secunda. **"latent highly disguised"**: to GR, n.d., PML. I have also drawn on to LF, postmarked 3.V.27, courtesy of AM. In an autobiographical memorandum, 20.I.58, Yale, RW makes the oblique statement that her father had a "strange nature," which was "attracted to me and cruel to me."

117 **"My treatment"**: notes for *Sunflower*, Tulsa. For an excellent treatment of the novel which I read after forming my interpretation, see Stec; **abandoned *Sunflower*:** to William Gerhardie, 28.III.28, Yale; Gerhardie to RW, 30.III.28, Yale; G. B. Stern to RW, n.d., Tulsa. **Notes for Sunflower:** Tulsa.

10: THE STRANGE NECESSITY (1927–1928)

119 **RW's new flat:** Nell Murray, "Rebecca West at Home," *The Herald* (Melbourne), 6.X.28, clipping file, Yale. **"I feel marvellous":** n.d. [c.IX.27], CU.

120 **"the most fascinating":** journal of Mrs. C. A. Dawson Scott, courtesy of Mrs. Marjorie Lowenstein. **"terrible mother fixation":** to LF, postmarked 3.IX.27, courtesy of AM.

121 **"disreputable Sealyham":** to FH, n.d., Texas. **Rebecca's and Anthony's responses to his illness:** journal of Mrs. C. A. Dawson Scott, 20.V.28, courtesy of Mrs. Marjorie Lowenstein; to IVD, 15.VIII.28, LC; "My Father's Debts of Love"; to Emma Goldman, Emma Goldman Papers, Tamiment Library, New York University; Watts. **"fake cheerfulness":** to FH, n.d., Texas. **"angel of patience and pluck":** to JG, n.d., Chicago. **"three first-rate plays":** "A Commentary," *The Bookman*, IV.29. **"bathing in the Book":** "My Golden Playground," *The Looker-On*, 9.III.29; see also "If I had to Live My Life Again," *Daily Mail*, 18.VIII.28.

122 **"exceedingly handsome":** TS "Beverly Nichols," *Sunday Chronicle*, 17.IX [no year], Tulsa. **"I wasn't rude":** G. B Stern, "The Clown of Parnassus," no publication title or date specified, Yale.

123 **"It begins with":** n.d., Cape General Files, University of Reading.

126 **The reactions of Wyndham Lewis and Havelock Ellis to *The Strange Necessity*:** to LF, postmarked 27.VII.28, courtesy of AM. **"your too affectionate":** 13.VII.28, Tulsa. **"most of the reviews":** n.d., HH.

127 **"apt to strike people":** to Hugh Walpole, 19.IX.28, Yale.

11: SEX ANTAGONISM (1928–1929)

128 **Anthony's recovery:** to IVD, 15.VIII.28, LC. Rebecca said that his condition had been misdiagnosed and he had been suffering no more than a severe case of pneumonia. But in *H.G. Wells* Anthony maintains X-rays have always shown a scar from tuberculosis. **"poetic masterpiece":** 21.X.28. **"I can't tell you":** 10.XI.28, Tulsa.

129 **"nearest thing":** draft letter to GR, MSN, Tulsa. **"Ward of Court":** 15.I.29, Yale.

130 **"Every day":** These words are from Anthony's novel, *Heritage*, in which Richard Savage, a transparent surrogate for Anthony, describes Max Town, an equally transparent depiction of H.G. It is Richard's mother, Naomi Savage, who suspects Max is "up to something." My quotations from Anthony's reactions to Rebecca are also taken from *Heritage*. **"accomplice":** APW, "My Father's Unpaid Debts of Love." **"in response to":** to WM, 7.III.29, courtesy of AM.

131 **"set books":** Annan, *Our Age*. For a discussion of Stowe and Anthony's years there, I am indebted to Lord Annan. **"freedom in their daily lives":** Annan, *Roxburgh of Stowe*. **"about dress":** Annan, *Our Age*; see also to WM, 22.III.29, courtesy of AM. **"I have had":** n.d., Yale. Anthony's memories of Stowe were conveyed

to his first wife Kitty, who got the impression that Rebecca was "a sort of distant, patronizing parent. I can't believe there was any warmth." INT. KW.

132 **"Write to H.G.":** PML. **233 "Jewish gazelle . . . Bambi":** Glendinning. **"cleverest woman . . . above it":** Frankau, *I Find Four People.* **"passionate whirling":** Raymond. **"female republic . . . baking in the sun":** Glendinning; INT. June Head Fenby (Rebecca's secretary); INT. Diana Raymond (Pamela Frankau's biographer), see also "I Said to Me," *New York American,* 6.IX.32.

133 **"wonderful swims":** to LF, n.d., courtesy of AM. **"I doubt if":** to RW, n.d., Yale. **"peripheral bore":** INT. Pat Wallace Frere. **"burden by attempts":** to IVD, n.d., LC.

134 **"I cannot tell you":** Yale. **"He was . . . manifestly reactionary":** n.d., Yale. **"you are one of":** 27.IX.29, Yale. If RW had reasons for appealing to Russell that are not in her letter, they have not come to light. Years later she called him a "dreary womanizer" and said she never really liked him. When he asked her permission to reprint her letter to him without comment in the second volume of his autobiography, she refused, saying it would be unfair to H.G., who had become a dear friend to her in the last ten years of his life. See to GR, n.d., PML; to Donald Mclachlan, 5.XII.64, Tulsa; to Bertrand Russell, 16.VI.67, Yale; Morehead.

137 **"tight and affected":** Nicolson and Trautmann, Vol. IV.

12: REBECCA CICILY (1929–1930)

Interviews: Rosalind Burdon-Taylor, June Head Fenby, Pat Wallace Frere, Emily Hahn, Diana Raymond.

139 **"dogged":** RW's REV of *Testament of Youth, Daily Telegraph,* 4.IX.33. **"developed in him":** Britain. **"wonderful knack of":** INT. Kosara Gavrilović. **"greatest aesthetic emotion":** RW TS REV of *Is God A Frenchman, Daily Telegraph,* 13.XI [no year specified], Tulsa; see also to HMA, 15.XI.29, Yale. **"Elk Dame":** INT. June Head Fenby.

140 **"he was everything":** autobiographical memorandum, 28.I.58, Yale.

141 **"ineducable":** to WM, postmarked 29.III.30, courtesy of AM; see also diary entry 16.III.30, Yale.

142 **"odd to look at":** MSN, Tulsa. **pool their resources:** MSN, Tulsa.

144 **"It sounds like":** INT. Rosalind Burdon-Taylor. **"hopelessly rootless . . . tick over":** to Douglas and Mia Woodruff, 9.XI.68, Douglas Woodruff Papers, Georgetown University Library.

145 **"Seeing the boy":** Yale. **"state of hating":** to Mr. Thompson, 24.II.32, Tulsa. **"seared by":** "Mr. Henry Andrews Banker and Patron," obituary in *The Times,* 12.XI.68. **"My own time":** 25.I.19, Yale.

146 **"I am sorry":** 28.VI.19, Yale. **"He was the only man":** Douglas Woodruff memoirs, Douglas Woodruff Papers, Georgetown University Library. **"I wrote him":** 12.VII.20. Douglas Woodruff Papers, Georgetown University Library. **"for more than eight months":** 9.VIII.20, Tulsa. **"His [Henry's] Oxford friendships":** autobiographical memorandum, n.d., courtesy of AM.

147 **"essential clerical virtues":** Douglas Woodruff memoirs, Douglas Woodruff Papers, Georgetown, University Library. **"finest speech of the day":** TS "In Ruhleben," n.d., Tulsa. **"He says":** n.d. [c.VIII.30], CU. **RW's wedding:** Watts; Raymond Swing to JG, 9.XII.30, Chicago; Marion Fletcher to RW, 20.XI.30; GBS to RW, 31.X.30, Yale; EA to RW, n.d., Yale; identified newspaper clipping, Yale.

13: RIC AND RAC AND COMUS (1930–1933)

149 **"magnificent flat"**: draft letter to Jilly Cooper, MSN, Tulsa; see also "Lecture to London Literary Institute," TS, 8.XI.34, Tulsa. **"No words"**: Tulsa.

150 **"Anthony's reaction to Henry"**: see *Heritage*. **"bored for England"**: INT. EW, KW, LW.

151 **"Dear Mr Wells"**: n.d., Yale.

152 **"the best practising"**: quoted in Glendinning. **"He is high strung"**: Yale; see also Hanns Sachs to RW, 7.IX.32, Yale. **"Often he reminded me"**: n.d., Yale.

154 **"We are adept"**: n.d., Tulsa. **"Byronic humps"**: to AW, n.d., HH. **tensions between RW, HMA, and Anthony**: see *Heritage*; RW, autobiographical memorandum, n.d., Tulsa; RW diary entry 13.IV.33, Yale. **"very Russian"**: 28.IV.33, Yale; see to AW, n.d., HH.

14: ANTICIPATING THE APOCALYPSE (1933–1935)

156 **"all the foreign interests"**: "Notes on return from Berlin I.5.33," Yale.

157 **"Will you leave"**: n.d., Tulsa. RW wrote a great deal about Henry's courageous efforts to G. B. Stern, her friend and a Jew whom RW supposed would especially wish to know what Henry had done. Some years later, Rebecca was shocked and angered to learn that Stern had destroyed her letters, which Rebecca wanted preserved for her archive at Yale.

158 **"death dance"**: to FH, n.d., Texas; see also to Joseph Langner 2.VI.33, 13.XI.35, Yale. **"I can't serve."**: INT. Justin Lowinsky.

159 **"my husband"**: "The Second Sex," BBC transcript, 12.IX.64, Tulsa.

160 **"thrift in Comus"**: diary entry, 4.XI.33; see also diary entries 22, 25.IV.33, Yale. **"miraculously happy"**: n.d. [postmark 1934], PML. **seeing a psychiatrist**: diary entry, 9.IV.33, Yale.

15: THE RETURN OF THE FATHER (1934–1935)

161 **"Do you know"**: Stiehlmann. **"love of life"**: n.d., Yale.

162 **"formulas of conventional psychoanalysis"**: n.d., Yale. **"emotional shock treatment"**: Fitch. **"lived out his writings"**: Fitch. **"joy of her femaleness"**: quoted in Pierpont. **"prepare to be raped"**: Fitch. **"Violate me"**: memoranda section of 1935 appointment diary, Yale. **"R's great point"**: Nicolson and Trautmann, Vol. V. **"*encaustique* . . . abandoned us"**: Nin, *Incest*. In 1965, Anaïs showed Rebecca passages from her diary that she was readying for publication. Rebecca objected to the account of the spring 1934 visit, expressing her "amusement" that Anaïs should think Orchard Court was "palatial" and her flat luxurious—comfortable yes, but really Rebecca's friends would find Anaïs's view "eccentric . . . if the porter threw a red rug under your feet when you got out of your taxi it was a unique gesture, he never did it for anybody else." Even though the accuracy of Anaïs's diary has been attacked, the details Rebecca supplies tend to confirm rather than refute Anaïs's impressions. See to GR, n.d., PML; to Anaïs Nin, 4.XI.65, Tulsa.

163 **"You did not meet"**: n.d., Yale. **"as an author"**: Rupert Hart-Davis to ADP, 20.II.35, Texas; see also ADP to RW, 25.I.35, Texas.

164 **"extraordinarily good"**: 5.III.35, PML. **"Of course I must have been"**: Quoted in Raymond. **"Don't misunderstand"**: n.d., Tulsa.

165 **RW's dislike of homosexuality**: INT. Pat Wallace Frere. **Failure to sell "The Addict"**: see George Bye to RW: "Everyone likes it, but objects to its length." 15.XI.34, CU. **"You put that in"**: Frankau, *Pen to Paper.*

166 **"most important factor"**: n.d., Yale.

16: The Difference Between Men and Women (1935–1936)

168 **"HMA's sexual life"**: I am indebted to interviews with Agnes de Mille, Justin Lowinsky, Norman and Marion Macleod. RW wrote about Henry's infidelities in several manuscript notebooks containing draft versions of her memoirs [Tulsa].

169 **"He and I . . . mad with loneliness"**: 28.I.58, Yale. **"It was too much"**: INT. Pat Wallace Frere. **RW's depression**: Lloyd Morris to RW, 7.II.35, Yale; to Carl van Vechten, 18.II.35, NYPL.

170 **"Anaïs Nin"**: this paragraph derives from Deirdre Bair's research for a biography of Anaïs Nin. **"marvelous success"**: 7.IX.35, Yale. **"I did 20 km"**: n.d., Yale.

171 **"loved more than"**: "A Novelist's Dilemma," *The Book-lover,* Tulsa.

172 **"a clown possessed"**: Tulsa.

173 **"I do not"**: "A Novelist's Dilemma," *The Book-lover,* Tulsa.

17: Love and Marriage (1935–1936)

177 **"beautiful example"**: autobiographical fragment, n.d., Yale. **RW's Scandinavian and Baltic trip**: see her report to Colonel Bridge, British Council, 27.X.35, Tulsa. **"hard and narrow . . . the unexpected"**: A report to Colonel Bridge of the British Council, n.d., Tulsa. **"more picturesque"**: autobiographical fragment, n.d., Yale. **"overrun either by"**: "The Novelist's Voice."

180 **"Antoine Bibesco"**: On one of her Atlantic crossings, Rebecca's friend Mina Curtiss mentioned she had just been to Paris to meet Proust's friends. Rebecca brightened and asked if she had met Bibesco. "Not you, too, Rebecca," Mina said as they both broke up in laughter. See Curtiss; to J. G. [c.1927], 9.VII.62, Chicago; to LLF, 14.X.60, courtesy of JB. **"Tu es ni belle"**: to LB, 16.V.36, PU; Stanislav Vinaver to RW, 15.VI.36, Tulsa. **"He took me"**: to EA, n.d., Yale **"grim business . . . comfortably off"**: n.d., Yale. **"turning round and round"**: autobiographical memorandum, 28.I.58, Yale.

181 **"Anthony and Kitty West"**: INT. KW, KW handwritten memoir, courtesy of KW.

183 **"Anthony upped and married"**: to EA, n.d., Yale.

184 **"All my life"**: n.d., courtesy of AM.

18: Gone with the Balkans (1936–1938)

Interviews: Alison Macleod, Norman Macleod.

186 **"It is assumed . . . against the Reds"**: TS, 14.IX.36, Tulsa.

187 **"Vinaver will say"**: details and quotations from RW's second Yugoslav trip are from a manuscript notebook at Yale.

192 **"I suppose I'm tired"**: to LB, n.d., PU. **"snap book"**: n.d., Texas; see also to LB, 17.VI.37, PU. **"going very strong"**: 24.III.36, Texas. **"wretched, complicated"**: to EA, postmarked 30.VI.37, Yale. **"physical relations"**: autobiographical fragment, Tulsa. **"I don't believe it"**: AM to Victoria Glendinning, 19.VIII.86, courtesy of AM.

193 **"mild infatuation . . . anyone else"**: 8.XII.38, Yale. **"I am plowing"**: Texas. **"something near panic"**: n.d., Yale. **HMA to Anica Savic-Rebac:** 7.VII.37, Tulsa. **"poor darling Slavs . . . Balkans"**: to LB, n.d., PU.

19: WAR (1938–1941)

194 **"on the spot"**: HMA to Professor Henry D. Saurat, University of London, 28.IV.38, 38, Tulsa.

195 **"frightful Nazi . . . anywhere"**: HMA to Hugh Seton Watson, 7.VII.38, Tulsa. **"I hope"**: 24.IX.38, Yale. **"We have ordered"**: 29.IX.38, HH. On helping refugees, see the correspondence between RW and Ben Huebsch, 7.X.37, 14.XII.38 and 20.I, 17.II.39, LC.

196 **HMA's memoranda:** 19.XII.38, Yale. **"The country . . . to Neville Chamberlain"**: to LB, n.d., PU. **"stiffened . . . beyond repair"**: to DT, 21.XI.38, Yale. **"preserve any equanimity"**: to IVD, LC. **"in the meantime"**: to AW, n.d., HH.

197 **"She always knew"**: INT. KW. **Anthony's attitude to the war:** INT. KW, Frances Partridge; see also Partridge's *A Pacifist's War.* RW wrote several letters to friends about Anthony's activities during the war, but in none of them does she clearly explain the issues between her and Anthony. To Edward Glover, n.d, Yale, she gave an account of her son happily announcing he was going to avoid military service. Her interpretation of his behavior seems implausible; it probably stems from anger.

199 **"we have been rude"**: 13.X.39, HH. **"Anthony has"**: n.d., PML. **"Dear Rac"**: n.d., Yale. **"The Great"**: to AW, 21.X.39, HH. **"No matter"**: 10.XI.39, Viking. **Adjusting to wartime:** to AW, 21.10.39, HH. **"like a dog"**: to IVD, n.d., LC. **"Henry worried"**: 26.VI.39, Yale.

200 **"cheerful but"**: AW to RL, 9.XI.39, Tulsa.

201 **"They can't get"**: n.d., Tulsa. **"MEN ARE"**: 29.II.40, Yale. **"She always appears"**: 6.VII.39.

202 **"not an opportunity"**: n.d., Yale. **"Russian Communist State"**: "The First Fortnight." **"on the instructions"**: Ronald Kidd to RW, 16.V.40, Tulsa. **"cub is"**: 9.IV.40, PML. **"Anything that"**: to EA, 8.XII.38, Yale; see also to AW, 6.XI.40, HH.

203 **"We are all going"**: 22.V.40, HH. **"You can't think"**: 23. VII.40, LC. **RW's will:** Tulsa.

204 **Margaret Hodges:** INT. JH. **"halfwit"**: to Mary Andrews, 10.II.40, Yale.

205 **"an access"**: "Housewife's Nightmare."

206 **"an agreeable"**: to EA, n.d., Yale. **"looking like"**: to DS, 19.XI.40, Yale. **"complete explanation"**: to IVD, 23.VII.40, LC. **"I had meant"**: 20.XI.40, HH. **"breathers"**: Viking. **On Henry's contribution to Black Lamb:** HRG to RW, 14.V.41, Viking, Ben Huebsch to RW, 28.X.41, LC.

207 **"Yes, I am going"**: to Herbert Van Thal, 13.I.41, Tulsa. **"slightly larger"**: 9.II.41, LC. **"REBECCA'S OPERATION"**: LC. **"unusual concentration"**: HMA to HRG, 25.II.41, Viking. **"two set backs"**: Viking. **"She loves me"**: 17.IV.41, Texas.

"heartbreaking letter": n.d., Yale. **"provoking pessimism":** to EA, n.d., Yale. **"unbearable . . . futile act":** to AW, HH.
208 **"ultimate fate":** 14.V.41, Viking.

20: BLACK LAMB AND GREY FALCON: A MODERN SCHEHERAZADE

My subtitle is taken from Stanislav Vinaver's letter to RW [16.VI.37, Yale], in which he suggests that her stories must be infused with her personality and with the personalities of those who had told her the stories. The conflicting images would be unified by the "real love between the teller and the told."

212 **"But what was . . . of the universe":** to Clifton Fadimon, 10.XI.41.
214 **"pellucid":** "Two Kinds of War": *Sunday Times*, 9.VIII.42. **"strange mixture":** *A Personal History*; **"on the picture":** 19.III.42, Yale.
215 **"artlessness":** 22.V.42, Yale.

21: BLOCKED AND ABANDONED (1941–1945)

Quotations from "Cockrow" are from the notes and manuscript which date her work on the novel between 1941 and 1944. [Tulsa] **Interviews:** Aleksa Gavrilović, Darinka Gavrilović, Kosara Gavrilović, Voya Gavrilović. Parts of this chapter are based on Kosara Gavrilović's unpublished memoir.

217 **"Russian novel":** to EA, n.d., Yale.
219 **RW on Mihailović's dealings with the Germans:** MSN article, "Prospects in Yugoslavia" (Yale): "Now I think it very unlikely that Mihailović did not sometimes come to an understanding with the Germans and the Italians, that he didn't say on various occasions to the Italians that if they allowed him to do this he would allow them to do that. Such understandings are a recognized part of ancient warfare, and have always been carried on in places outside the Western convention."
220 **"You don't seem . . . not much chance for us":** 7.III [1942], Yale. **"too corrupt . . . people we are":** 16.III.[42], Yale.
221 **"Madame Sara's Magical Crystal":** published for the first time in *The Only Poet and Other Stories*.
222 **"You and I":** to Aleksa Gavrilović, 18.II.76. **"ordinary human beings":** 21.VIII.44, Tulsa.

22: "AND HOW I SEE THE DRAMA GO ON" (1944–1945)

Interviews: John Hodges, Justin Lowinsky, Margaret Rawlings, Joyce Seligman, Kitty West.

226 **"put in . . . voice of love":** to DS, 23.III.44.
227 **"I suppose . . . miserable and afraid":** diary entries, n.d. [c. April 1944], 5.VI.44, Tulsa. **Visiting HG:** to EA, 27.V.44, Yale. **"greatest of Nannies . . . tortured him":** diary entry, 5.VI.44, Tulsa. **"humming and hawing":** Mackenzie.
228 **"swollen and stupid . . . fifty years before you":** diary entry, 5.VI.44, Tulsa.

"loved like a daughter": to EA, 27.V.44, Yale. "shattering blow": 26.V.44, Tulsa. "I can't tell you": to RL, 1.VII.44, Tulsa. "so like . . . Ah yes!": diary entry, 5.VI.44, Tulsa.

230 "Rebecca, I must tell you": to EA, 27.V.44, Yale. "wise & kind": n.d., Yale.

231 "shiftless, queer": to EA, 27.V.44, Yale. "living his own life": diary entry, 5.VI.44, Tulsa. "Sometimes in Anthony's": to EA, 27.V.44, Yale. "maternal paradox . . . toward men": Klein. "I am having": 24.VI.44, Tulsa.

232 "appalling childhood . . . hang on": 20.V.44, Tulsa. "You're very independent": to Edward Glover, n.d., Yale. "There was a feeling": 20.IX.44.

233 "extremely ill": to LF, 20.IX.44, courtesy of AM.

234 Anthony's pacifist sympathies: to EA, 20.VII.44, Yale. "And by the way": Partridge, *A Pacifist's War.* "Oh, are you?": INT. DTR. "I just don't understand you": APW, *H.G. Wells.*

235 "woodnymph . . . happy": to EA, 20.VII.44, Yale.

236 "cold cruelty": 20.IX.44, courtesy of AM. "wracked and overwrought": 8.VII.44; MW to RW, 8.VII and 13.VII.44, Tulsa. "It is a letter": n.d., courtesy of AM.

237 "My dear": to EA, 20.VII.44, Yale. "But of course": Frankau, *Pen to Paper;* see also Pamela Frankau to RW, 25.VII.44, Yale. Rebecca wrote an unpublished story, "The Aftermath of a Divorce," [Tulsa] a transparent version of what she felt went wrong with her upbringing of Anthony. She pins much of the blame on the absent father, whom Anthony glorified and emulated. "H.G. was": to EA, 20.VII.44, Yale.

238 Visiting Anthony's garage flat: to LF, 15.X.44, courtesy of AM. blamed Kitty: to WM, 15.XII.44, 1944, courtesy of AM. "same capacity": to WM, n.d., courtesy of AM. "man of action": to WM, n.d., courtesy of AM. "amiable but cold": diary entry, 30.III.45, Tulsa. "twisted and dangerous creature": to EA, 6.VI.45, Tulsa. "A complete reconciliation": 29.V.45, Tulsa.

23: Retribution and Treachery (1945–1946)

Interviews: Alison Macleod, Kitty West. Quotations from RW's 1945 diary are from a single volume at Tulsa.

240 **RW's anti-Soviet writing** to Mrs. Cecil Chesterton, 21.VIII.44. Yale; preface to *Beyond the Urals* by Elma Dangerfield. London: British League for European Freedom, 1946. **RW's concern for personal safety:** to DS, 5.IV, 2.V.45, Yale. **RW on the Labor Party:** *Harper's,* IX-XI, 45; to EA, 6.VI.45, Yale.

241 "Ross's cable": 6.VI.45, Yale; see also to HR, 18.VI.45, Yale.

242 meeting the Queen: 15 III.44, diary entry, Tulsa. Rebecca attended an afternoon party at Buckingham Palace. She was writing an article for *The New York Times* ("Britain's Royal Princess Comes of Age") and had been invited to meet Princess Elizabeth. Rebecca had worried that the invitation would not be extended "on account of my past." She remembered once surprising her mother with her "passionate loyalty to the throne," cheering King George and Queen Mary on King Street in Edinburgh. Then she had become a Republican. Now she had returned to the idea of "kingship as an essential symbol, without which mankind cannot develop law and order." Republicanism, she thought, suited only people like the Americans, who laid the foundations of their traditions in the modern period, after the ages of myth and poetry. In her *New*

York Times article, she saw the task of the "limited monarchy" as embodying the status quo, to "make do with it until such times as the intellectuals have convinced the community of the necessity for a change." To her, a monarch should create an "impression of being as wholly exempt from liability to error as children imagine their parents to be. All the peoples of all states make this demand."

The Queen pleased Rebecca by saying she had read *Black Lamb and Grey Falcon* and had found it thrilling, especially the parts having to do with the governing of states. When the Queen expressed the hope that the royal family was really useful to the people, Rebecca replied: "Of course it is. Heads of the state are now far more important than they were thirty years ago." The Queen answered earnestly and wistfully, "Yes, the people seem to want it." Rebecca loved the simplicity of the Queen's remarks: "You see, I think it all helps the English to be English, and I do think England has something to give the world—something special. Or do you think that is wrong?" Rebecca said that she thought it was perfectly right, explaining Dostoevsky's theory of nationalism in *The Possessed*. Rebecca had articulated this theory almost ten years earlier in an essay, "The Necessity of the International Ideal." Each nation must be "fully aware that its gods are true gods, who can work miracles, and will in the end disclose all mysteries. We are obliged, if we are going to achieve anything valuable, to be proud of Britain." By the same token, "there could be no more hideous prospect imaginable than that there should be no other country than England." A "society of nations" depended on this paradoxical formula: they could work together only by recognizing each other's individuality, sovereignty, and independence. Rebecca feared a world where there would be no other country than the Soviet Union and its satellites. She was thinking precisely this thought as she spoke to the Queen.

The Queen then asked her about the future of Yugoslavia. Could it be revived in its old form? Could the Croats and Serbs be reconciled? Rebecca thought not. She compared the problem to the Irish. This conversation-stopper caused "some reserve" to cross the Queen's mind, and Rebecca was dismissed with a "most charming smile." **"kindly restore":** 26.IX.45, courtesy of AM.

244 **"God evidently":** 6.IX.45, Yale. **"they just seem":** 25.IX.45, Yale. **"little whippy":** 2.XII.45, Yale. **"You may not realize":** 28.VI.93.

245 **"I know of":** 28.IX.45, Yale. **John Amery:** to Mary Andrews, 2.XII.45, Yale. **"I gather":** C. M. Rolph in conversation with NMZ about his interview with RW, reported to CR by NMZ.

246 **"coterie of tomorrow":** 13.I.46, Tulsa; see also to Kingsley Martin, 6.VI.46, University of Sussex Library, to Richard Crossman, 25.XII.45, Modern Records Center, Warwick University.

24: THE TRIALS OF NUREMBERG (1946)

Interviews: Justin Lowinsky, Anne Charles McBurney.

247 **"citadel of boredom":** *A Train of Powder.*

248 **Biddle's good looks:** to WM, n.d., courtesy of AM. **Biddle's impressions of RW:** Francis Biddle to Katherine Biddle, 30.VII.46, Syracuse. **RW's shyness:** Francis Biddle to Katherine Biddle, 2.VIII.46, Syracuse. **"highly erotic":** to HR, 28.VII.46, NYPL.

249 **"What chance":** to EA, 13.VIII.46, Yale. **"amusing wench"** Francis Biddle to

Katherine Biddle, 8.VIII.46, Syracuse. **RW and HG:** to HR, 29.XI.46, NYPL; see also to DS, 18.X.46, Yale.

250 **Biddle's love letters":** in RW's collection at Yale.

252 **RW's meetings with Joseph Laitin:** memoir courtesy of Joseph Laitin.

253 **"not a smile":** to HMA, n.d., Yale. **"a Sabine woman":** to HR, 23.X.46, NYPL; see also to GBS, 7.X.46, Tulsa. **In Prague:** to DS, 10.X.46, Yale; to WM, 29.VIII.50.

254 **"knots of tenderness":** Monica Sterling to RW, 13.X.46, Yale; see also to care: to EA, 24.XI.46, Yale. **"greatest darling":** to Pat Frere, 7.X.46, Yale.

255 **"Men are all filth":** to EA, n.d., Yale.

256 **"By God!":** to EA, n.d., Yale. Did Henry know about Rebecca's affair with Francis Biddle? His close friend, Justin Lowinsky, believes so. He remembers hearing a story (perhaps from Stanley Olson, Rebecca's friend and biographer) that Henry somehow discovered the affair and pleaded with Rebecca not to leave him. She agreed. Then a short time later he went off on an affair of his own. I have found no written record of this episode.

25: "The Sibyl of Our Time" (1947–1948)

257 **"I suppose":** to HMA, n.d., Yale. **"lovely dark . . . out of the car":** MSN, Tulsa.

258 **"stay here":** to HMA, marked "received June 7, 1947," Yale. **Harry Ashmore:** to RW, 17.VI.47, Yale. **Southern response to RW:** HR to RW, 24.VI.47, Yale. **"absolutely amazing":** HR to RW, 8.VII.47, Yale.

259 **"What an ass":** 3.II.48, Tulsa. **English publication of *The Meaning of Treason:*** See to Max Beaverbrook, 21.XII.47, Lords and to HRG, I.I.48, Viking. Because the English law of libel made it easier to sue authors, RW's manuscript went through extensive vetting that held up publication.

260 **John Osborne:** to RW, n.d., Yale; see also RW to JG, 25.XI.47, Chicago. **Sales of** *The Meaning of Treason:* 19.XII.47, Viking.

261 **Theobald Mathew:** See RW's introduction to the Virago Press edition of *The Meaning of Treason.* **"hectic flush":** *The Nation,* 10.I.48. **"you are the major":** EH to RW, 9.VIII.48, Yale. **Republican convention:** *Evening Standard* and *New York Herald Tribune,* 21–26.VI.48. **Democratic convention:** *Evening Standard* and *New York Herald Tribune,* 12–15.VII.48.

262 **Progressive Party Convention:** *Evening Standard* and *New York Herald Tribune,* 24, 26.VII.48. **smear campaign:** to EH, 13.IX.48, Yale. **"sexy and sardonic":** INT. William L. Shirer. **"kindly nature":** to DS, 29.XII.48, Yale.

26: Richard III's Mother (1949)

Interviews: Anne Charles McBurney, Frances Partridge, Kitty West, Lily West.

263 **"good for nothing":** to HR, 16.XII.49, Yale. **"endless harm":** to GBS, 4.IX.49, Tulsa.

264 **"scotching rumors":** KW to MW, 10.II.[50], Tulsa. **"electrified us":** to EHN, 26.I.52, Indiana.

265 **"Why the hell":** 12.IX.49, Tulsa **"mother was ashamed":** n.d., Yale. See also APW, "Mother and Son."

266 **"exercise in literary composition"**: MW to RW, 5.IX.49, Yale. **"I understand"**: APW to G. P. Wells, 9.IX.49, Yale.

267 **"disgraceful document"**: to GBS, 12.IX.49, Tulsa.

268 **"difference between"**: 14.II.49, Yale.

269 **"When I catch"**: n.d., Tulsa. **"Spy out the land"**: Partridge, *Everything to Lose*, Yale.

270 **"long and horrid"**: n.d., Tulsa.

27: THE MEDUSA HEAD (1949–1952)

Interviews: Emily Hahn, Edith Oliver, Alison Macleod, Diana Trilling, Caroline West, Edmund West, Kitty West, Lily West.

271 **"I'm lucky"**: to EA, 28.XI.49, Yale. **"Illegitimacy does something"**: to EA, 31.I.50, Yale. **the controversy over Anthony's departure:** APW to MW, 24.I.50, Tulsa; MW to RW, 26, 30.I.50, Tulsa; LF to RW, 6.II.[50], Tulsa.

272 **"sanest person"**: DT to HR, 17.II.50, NYPL. **On Ross, Anthony and Rebecca:** HR to APW, 21.II.50, NYPL; HR to RW, 24.II.50, Tulsa; to EA, 28.II.50, 6.III.50, 14.IV.[50], Yale.

274 **"I just think"**: DT to RW, 18.III.50, Yale. In late November 1950, Rebecca became deeply involved in helping Mike Lewis extricate himself from a charge of assault brought against him by a woman he had slapped after having had too much to drink. Rebecca helped to minimize the publicity and put her attorney, Richard Butler, at Mike's service. See to Maxim Kopf. (Dorothy Thompson's husband) 28.XI.50, Syracuse; Richard Butler to RW, 28.XI.50, Tulsa; to Max Beaverbrook, 5.XII.50, Lords; to DT, 22.XII.50, Tulsa. **"pleasantly cynical"**: HR to RW, 4.IV.50, Yale.

275 **"Just be good"**: to JG, 6, 9.IV.50, Chicago; see also ADP to RW, 24.IV.50, Yale; EA to RW, n.d., Yale. **"emotional losses"**: diary entry, 18.IV.50, Tulsa; see also to EHN, 26.I.52, Indiana. **"arrested development"**: to John Morris, 6.XI.52, Tulsa. Rebecca told John and Jane Gunther that Anthony expected her to dance attendance on him: "If he had a plate or a cup he wanted to get rid of and there was a tray right in front of him, he wouldn't put it down on the tray, he would hand it to me to put down." **Kitty's attitude toward Anthony:** see several undated letters to RW at Yale; Partridge, *Everything to Lose*.

276 **"she creates"**: 24.IV.50, NYPL. **"I am not going"**: 24.IV.50, Syracuse. **RW and Caroline:** Rebecca once asked her American friend, Emily Hahn, what she thought of Caroline. Emily had married an Englishman, and in the late 1940s had settled in Dorset near Kitty and Anthony. Emily's daughter, Carola, played with Caroline, and they became lifelong friends. "Oh, Caroline's all right," Emily assured Rebecca. "They call her Mouse because she never speaks out." Rebecca said, "I always thought they called her that because she wants to make something of herself and draws attention to herself." Emily did not think so. [INT. EHN] Henry had a much more soothing impact on children. He liked to tell them stories, and Emily Hahn's daughter, Carola, remembers him looking about for her—the youngest of a party of children at Ibstone—and asking, "Where's the little one?" She thought he had a nice face; she liked the way he paid attention to children. [INT. Carola Hahn] Henry wrote a letter (9.I.51) to Ann Hodges, Margaret's daughter, referring to his face of "Roman gravity" which allowed him to play the "heavy uncle."

278 **"complex about"**: DT to RW, 9.V.50, Yale; to WM, 3.V.50, courtesy of AM; to DT, 17.V.50, Syracuse; DT to RW, 28.IX.50, Yale. **"I have no idea"**: 11.X.50, Yale. **"adopt a policy"**: Richard Butler to RW, 26.VI.50, Tulsa.

279 **"threat of ruin"**: to HR, 3.VI.50, NYPL. **"maddening, difficult"**: V. S. Pritchett to RW, 19.XII.50, Tulsa; see also APW to KW, 24.IX.50, Tulsa; to HR, 15.XII.50, NYPL.

280 **"*New Yorker* grade"**: to HR, 29.I.51, NYPL; see also HR to RW, 9.I.-51, Yale. **"first-rate stuff"**: to HR, 25.VI.51, NYPL; see also HR to RW, 20.VI.51, NYPL; to KW, 10.V.51, Tulsa; to CC, 10.V.51, Tulsa. **"head above water"**: ADP to RW, 7.V.51, Yale. **"fast friends"**: JG to RW, 2.VII.51, Yale.

281 **"so terribly like H.G."**: to WM, n.d., courtesy of AM; see also to John Morris, 21.IV.51. Yale; to GBS, 25.VIII.51, Tulsa. **"so very much to Ross"**: to DS, 8.XII.51, Yale; see also William Shawn to RW, 13.II.52, Tulsa. **"keeping a full diary"**: *Evening Standard*, 7.XII.51. **"The trouble is"**: 24.IV.50, NYPL. **"clear, hard classical"**: Grant. **"[Y]our writing constituted"**: 13.XII.51, Tulsa.

282 **RW's attacks on Anthony**: to DS, 8.XII.51, 24.II.52, Yale; to EA, 8.XII.51, 14.XII.51, Yale; to KW, 4.XII.51, 17.XII.51, Tulsa. **"Madame Vallentin's biography"**: to Madame Vallentin, 20.VIII.50, Tulsa; see also Richard J. Walsh of John Day Company to Victor Gollancz, 2.VIII.50, Tulsa. **Janet Flanner:** to EA, 3.III.52, Yale.

283 **"sort our family"**: 8.5.52, courtesy of AM. **"sullen, stupid"**: to EA, 8.V.52, Yale.

28: The Communist Conspiracy (1952–1953)

Interviews: Mike Levitas, Arthur Schlesinger.

284 **anti-Communist articles**: "Rebecca West Tells Spy's Story," *New York American*, 1.III.50; "The Terrifying Import of the Fuchs Case," *New York Times*, 4.III.51; her *Evening Standard* REV of *I Believed*, W. Douglas Hyde's story of his membership in the Communist Party; her profile of Whittaker Chambers in *The Atlantic Monthly*, June 1952; "The Hiss Case," *Sunday Times*, 8.V.53.

286 **"odd difference"**: "The Astonishing Career of Alger Hiss," *Evening Standard*, 23.X.50. **Hiss, Nixon and HUAC:** to EA, 20.II.50, Yale; to Countess Marion Durnhof, editor of *Die Zeit*, 21.VII.53, Tulsa; to EMH, 4.XII.53, Yale. Walter Gellhorn, *Harvard Law Review*, October 1947 details many of HUAC's outrageous procedures. **"Francis Biddle"**: 6.II.52, Yale.

289 **"uncouth individual"**: AS to RW, 29.V.53.

290 **"schoolmaster reproving"**: 7.VI.53. **"At a convention"**: Richard Rovere to RW, 21.VI.53, courtesy of AS.

291 **"One of the most"**: to Richard Rovere, 6.VII.53, courtesy of AS; see also to "My dear Margaret," 1.V.53, Tulsa; to BBG, 16.V.53, Syracuse; to EMH: 1.IX.53, Yale.

292 **"I agree"**: 8.V.53, Tulsa. **"Rebecca West admits"**: 25.V.53, Tulsa. **"The fear is irrational"**: EA to RW, 8.V.53, Yale.

293 **"united front"**: 27.VI.53, Tulsa. **"arrogant, intolerant"**: 26.VI.53, Tulsa; see also to Sol Levitas, 15.VI.53, Hoover Institution. Levitas sent fifty copies of Rebecca's letter to his friends, including Diana Trilling, who showed me one of the copies. See also DT to RW, 2.VII.53, Yale. **"able and balanced"**: 8.VII.53, Hoover Institution. **"ideologically dangerous"**: to Countess Marion Durnhof, editor of *Die Zeit*, 21.VII.53; see also to DT, 30.IV.53, Syracuse.

294 **"indeed responsible"**: to Nicholas Bagnall, 16.VIII.78, Tulsa.

29: THE KAFKAS AND THE BRONTËS (1952—1954)

Interviews: Emily Hahn, Frances Partridge, Kitty West, Lily West, Kit Wright.

295 **RW on Anthony and his marriage:** to DS, 17.XI.52, Yale; to EA, 9.XII.52, Yale.
  "smoldering look": 23.IV.53, Yale. **"Would Rebecca":** EA to RW, n.d., Yale. **"I
  cannot tell you":** to KW, 20.XI.52, Tulsa; see also to EHN, 26.I.53, Indiana.
296 **"fluttering movements":** to DS, 17.X.53, Yale; see also EHN to RW, 27.I.53, Indiana.
297 **"le coeur":** RM to RW, 24.I.54, Yale; see also to EA, 1.I.54, Yale. **"odd outfit":** to
  MH, 13.X.53, courtesy of JH. **"Oh yes":** RW to EMH, 4.XI.53, Yale; see also to DS,
  23.XI.53, Yale;
298 **"he ought to be valued":** to BB, 12.II.54, IT; see also HMA to BB, 31.I.54, IT; BB
  to RW, 16.II.54, IT. **"I don't know":** 13.III.54, Yale.
299 **"repudiated the Byronic man":** "The Role of Fantasy in the Work of the Brontes."
  Caroline Lamb: *New York Herald Tribune,* 22.XII.29. **"becoming all flashing
  white teeth":** Partridge, *Everything to Lose.* See Anthony's first novel, *The Vintage,*
  in which the hero is told: "You are too much the Byronic romantic figure. Who
  called upon you to put yourself under a curse?"

30: HERITAGE (1955–1956)

Interviews: Michael Bessie, Ann Fuller, Diana Raymond, Kitty West, Lily West.

300 **"laughed uncontrollably":** to Carmel Snow, 20.II.58, Tulsa. **RW's impressions of
  Anthony's and Lily's visit:** to David Ogilvy, 23.VIII.55, Tulsa; to APW, n.d., courtesy of LW; to KW, 15.IX.55, Tulsa; to HMA, 15.IX.55, Yale; to DS, 28.IX.55, Yale.
  "that dreary form": to EA, 7.V.55, Yale. **"glamorous actress":** to DS, 28.IX.55, Yale.
301 **"as if they were":** to EMH, n.d., Yale.
302 **"There is something":** to EA, 15.IX.55, Yale. **"Of course after that":** EA to RW,
  n.d., Yale. INT. Ann Fuller. **"nervous laugh":** EHN to RW, 8.X.55, Tulsa; see also
  to EH, 15.X.55, Yale; to Max Beaverbrook 25.X.55, Lords; Max Beaverbrook to
  RW 30.X.55, Lords; to EHN, 26.X.55, Indiana.
303 **Anthony and Communists:** to HRG: 29.10.55, courtesy of TG; see also "Rebecca
  West Probes the Case of the Treason Twins," *The New York American,* 2,4.X.55;
  Vera Watson to RW: 8.II.56, PML. Watson is one of several people who asked RW
  if Anthony's novel was a communist inspired attack. **"Not your mother":** John
  Van Druten to GBS, 3.XI.55, BU; see also EA to RW, 7.XI.55, Yale.
304 **"tender concern":** 11.IX.55, Yale. **"villainous mistake":** 5.XII.55, LC; see also
  Vyvyan Holland to RW, 20.I.56, Tulsa. **"You have always":** 7.XII. 55, Yale. **"Shall
  you":** in *Pen to Paper,* Frankau reports this conversation disguising the names with
  initials and changing sexes, so that RW is made into a male writer and Anthony
  into a female one.
305 **"low nastiness":** 8.XII.55, Chicago; see also to DS, 11.I.55, Yale; CC to RW, n.d.,
  Tulsa. **"My God . . . great and moody artist":** 28.I.56, Tulsa. **"if you were not":**
  1.II.56, Syracuse.
306 **"wicked book":** 4.IV.56, Tulsa; see also MW to RW, 10.V.56, Tulsa. **"This, of
  course":** 14.II.56, Yale. **"Maybe *Treason*":** DT to RW, 1.III.56, Yale. **"psychopathology of the left":** DT to RW, 17.III.56, Yale.

307 **"several skins":** CC to Sadie, 10.XI.55, Tulsa. **"I have been defeated":** 16.I.56, Yale. **"a monster":** to KW, 28.I.56, Yale **"Do you really believe":** 8.II.56, Yale. **"nothing he says":** 22.II.56, Tulsa; see also to RM, 21.II.56, Tulsa; RM to RW, 23.II.56, Yale.

31: THE FAMILY POLITIC (1956)

Interviews: Cleanth Brooks, Alison Macleod, Tom Wallace.

308 **"Shakespeare loathed":** to EA, n.d., Yale.
309 **Edmund Burke:** see to BB, 3.II.58, IT.
310 **"full pressure":** *The Spectator,* 25.VII.58. **"is too profound":** *The London Magazine,* XII.58.
312 **"Cordelia I think":** to EA, n.d., Yale.
313 **"more of the truth":** 19.VIII.57, Tulsa.
314 **"saw only":** MSN, Tulsa.
315 **"Of course":** to LF, 2.I.57, courtesy of AM; see also WM to RW, 5.I.[56], Tulsa.
316 **"Nobody in the family":** to EA, n.d., Yale; see also to J. G., n.d., Chicago. For Lettie's reaction to the novel, see Maboth Mosely diary, 1.II.57, PML. **"today's finest":** John F. Sullivan, *The Commonweal,* 11.I.57. **"the number of people":** to EA, n.d., Yale.

32: LAMENTATIONS (1956–1959)

Interviews: Emily Hahn, Caroline West, Edmund West.

317 **"white and shiny":** to DS, 15.IV.57, Yale. **"Why was I":** to HRG, n.d., Viking; see also HMA to BBG, 11.IV.57, Princeton. **"rose magnificently":** 19.VIII.57, Tulsa.
318 **"travesty of humanity":** to MH, 24.I.58, courtesy of JH. **RW's health:** to JG, n.d., Chicago; LF to NM, 16.V.58. **RW on Paul Robeson:** to HMA, n.d., Yale. **"Yes, wasn't":** 4.IX.58, Tulsa. **"something untrustworthy":** to EA, 30.XII.57, Yale. **"Rebecca's witchlike":** Monica Sterling to Margaret Rawlings, 4.VII.60.
319 **"Pamela cannot":** Monica Sterling to Margaret Rawlings, n.d., **"matey":** to EHN, n.d., Indiana. **"roley-poley":** to DS, 20.I.58, Yale. **"You have a terrible":** to MH, 24.I.58, courtesy of JH. **"willing to play":** to NM, 20.I.58; see also to EMH, n.d., Yale; RM to RW, 24.I.58, Yale. **"purswade":** to James T. Babb, 14.II.58, Yale.
320 **"The friends":** to DS, 14.I.58, Yale. **RW on her Yale archive:** to Mr. Hibbs, 28.I.58, Yale University Library, Yale. **RW on Anthony:** to Odette Arnaud, n.d., Tulsa; to DT, n.d., Syracuse. **"Publish and be damed":** INT. EHN. **"I never sought":** to Nicholas Bentley, 4.I.59, Tulsa; to NM, n.d. **"pretties":** to EMH, 14.II.59, Yale.
321 **"good work":** HMA to MRH, 1.IV.59, Tulsa; LF to NM, 14.II.59. **"THE AGONY":** Tulsa. **The origins of "Parthenope":** to William Maxwell, 27.IX.58, NYPL.
324 **"The first thing":** to William Maxwell, 9.VII.58, NYPL.
325 **"curiously ambivalent":** to Miss Galton (Caroline's headmistress) 28.IX.59, Tulsa; see also to EHN 28.IV.59, Indiana. **"horribly shadowed":** 21.IX.59. **"It is a**

feminist": 6.XII.59, Syracuse. **"motherhood is":** to EMH, 20.VIII.59, Yale. **"long and lacerating":** to EMH, 20.VIII.59, Yale. RW does not identify the letter's author. **"Let me be":** 2.X.59, Indiana.

33: IN THE CAULDRON OF SOUTH AFRICA (1960–1961)

Interviews: Jillian Becker, Sydney Kentridge, Harold Tomlinson, Alison Macleod, Norman Macleod.

326 **Rebecca's dervish dance:** INT. Harold Tomlinson.
327 **"a little overtired":** to MH, 16.XI.59, courtesy of JH; see also to HRG, 26.XII.59, 6.I.60, courtesy of TG; Julian S. Crossley to HMA, 28.XII.59, Tulsa. **"madness that has":** to EMH, 15.IX.59, Yale; see also to LF, 19.X.59. **"It will be all right . . . forty years before":** INT. NM.
328 **"piece of stretched . . . calm lake":** TS, "January 1960," Tulsa.
329 **"Now tell me":** to HMA, 10.I.60, Yale. **"deep, slightly":** Nadine Gordimer to Kathryn Munday, 26.V.93, see also to William Maxwell, 23.XII.59, NYPL.
330 **Meeting Sydney Kentridge:** INT. Sydney Kentridge; Sydney Kentridge to CR, 21.XI.94; see also to H. Hodson, 7.VI.60, Tulsa. **"modest and self-effacing":** Suzman. **"Johannesburg is as exciting":** journal, Tulsa. **"I really":** to HMA, 30.I.60, Yale. I have not located the telegram. **"terribly like":** to MM, n.d., courtesy of JH.
331 **"I am considering":** 1.II.60, Yale. **"divorced from reality":** 4.II.60, Yale. **"great lady":** Sweetman.
332 **"limpid observant":** Packer **"moth-eaten":** to HMA, 19.II.60, Tulsa.
333 **"Illegal":** journal, Tulsa. **"DAONT YEW":** to HMA, 2.II.60, Tulsa.
334 **"She said that":** Nadine Gordimer to Kathryn Munday, 26.V.93, see also HMA to EH, 30.III.60, Tulsa; to LLF, 18.IV.60, courtesy of JB; to HMA, marked "received 30 March 1960," Tulsa.
335 **"you can hardly":** 12.VII.60, LC; to NM, 25.IV.60.
336 **"Rac, darling":** 31.III.60, Yale. **RW's fight with Nadine Gordimer:** to Glen Wolfe, 9.VI.60, Yale. **"liars and intriguers":** RW to Mrs Brown, 25.V.65, Tulsa.
337 **Justice Kennedy's charges:** to H. Hodson (Editor of the *Sunday Times*), 9.IV.60, Tulsa; to Sydney Kentridge, 6.IX.60, 14.IX.60, Tulsa; to Richard Butler, 14.IX.60, 23.IX.60, 13.X.60, 26.X.60, 28.X.60, 21.XII. 60, 9.II.61 Tulsa; to L. A. Biddle (attorney for the *Sunday Times,* 1.I.61, 18.II.61 Tulsa; to Cyril Russell, 1.IX.60, 8.IX.60, 13.IX.60, Tulsa; Sydney Kentridge to RW, 26.X.60, Tulsa; Sydney Kentridge to CR, 21.XI.94; to Mr Biddle, 26.XII.60, Tulsa. In a later account, RW stated a court official had pointed to Justice Bekker and said he was Justice Kennedy; see to Sydney Kentridge, 28.II.61, Tulsa. **"Lettie":** INT. AM.
338 **"I got the impression":** INT. Sydney Kentridge; RW wrote to LLF, 9.II.61: "This is the most humiliating thing that has happened to me in all my professional life." See also to EHN, 8.XI.60, Indiana; to Theo Mathew 21.XI.60, Tulsa. **"a difficult lady":** to LLF, 9.II.61, courtesy of JB. RW writes: "Thomson said that he hoped I would not go on writing for them." The "not" is surely a typographical error, since her next sentence compares his invitation to bathing in a crocodile pool. See also to Sydney Kentridge, 28.II.61, Tulsa. **"Big Sister":** to LLF, 6.VI.60, courtesy of JB. **"refined beauty":** to Vera Watson, 15.VI.60, PML; see also to DS, 15.VI.60, Yale; AC to RW, 16.VII.60, Tulsa.

339 **"horrid streak"**: DT to RW, n.d., Yale. **"singularly composed"**: RW to BBG, 25.VI.61, PU; see also to JJG, 28.II.60, Chicago. **"lovely coiffures"**: to LLF, n.d., courtesy of JB. **"Let it pass"**: to HRG, 10.XII.60, courtesy of TG. **"crack and fly"**: to GBS, 28.I.61, Tulsa.

34: CROSS FIRE (1960–1966)

Interviews: Fleur Cowles, Gwenda David, Irene Garthwaite, John Hodges, Marion Macleod, Norman Macleod, Frances Partridge, Virginia Salomon, Harold Tomlinson, Diana Trilling, Lily West, Kitty West, Edmund West, Vita West.

340 **"solidly working through"**: to ISB, 4.X.60. **"apparently expressing"**: autobiographical fragment, n.d., Yale. **"very sentimental"**: to Mrs. Solomon, 20.II.61, Tulsa. **"For goodness' sake"**: to AM, 22.VIII.61; see Vera Watson to RW, 12.XII.60, 17.VIII.61, Yale; to Vera Watson, 19.VIII.61, PML; Vera Watson to RW, 9.IX.61, Tulsa.

341 **Henry's forgetfulness**: INT. Harold Tomlinson. **"a desperate effort"**: to MB, 28.XII.61, Viking; see also to EHN, 17.II.62, Indiana; to JG, 20.I.62, Chicago; to NM, 7.II.62.

342 **"like a piece"**: to MH, n.d., courtesy of JH. **"I see"**: to EMH, 28.I.62, Yale. **"[A]n awful man"**: to NM, 6.XI.63. **"Killer Joe"**: to HMA, 8.II.62, Yale; see also HMA to Virginia Salomon, 12.II.62, Yale; to Leo Lerman, 20.I.70, Tulsa. **"a giggling idiot"**: to EMH, 2.III.62, Yale. **"cultivating my acquaintance"**: to HMA 14.II.62, Yale. **"cracked"**: Brightman; see also to BBG, 2.IV.62, PU. **"warm liking"**: to Lawrence Babb, 7.V.62, Tulsa.

343 **"atrophy of the brain"**: to MH, 24.IX.62, courtesy of JH; see also to EMH, 25.IX.62, Yale; to EMH, 27.VI.62, Yale; to NM, 28.VIII.62.

344 **"My God"**: INT. Justin Lowinsky; see also to Richard Butler, 27.VI.62, Tulsa. **"reliable witchdoctor"**: to EMH, 15.VI.62, Yale. **"tour of"**: to JG, n.d., Chicago.

345 **"cross fire"**: to NM, 13.XI.64. **"an indescribable"**: to EMH, 25.IX.62, Yale; see also to John Calder, 24.VIII.62, Yale; David Carver to RW, n.d., Tulsa. **"odious old phony"**: to David Carver, n.d., Tulsa. **"wholesome farm boy"**: to AWP, 3.IX.62, Tulsa. **"oafish and ragging"**: to HMA, n.d., Yale. *Lolita:* See RW's review in ST, 8.XI.59. **"obscene at all"**: to J. Dillon McCarthy, 31.I.62, Yale.

346 **"Here were"**: to EMH, 19.VI.63, Yale. **"Nobody sensible"**: "We Must Bite the Bullet." **"fruition of sex!"**: to EA, 8.VI.63, Yale. **"only girls"**: INT. Fleur Cowles. **"vast sums"**: GD to MB, 14.VI.63, Viking.

347 **"God doesn't love"**: to MB, 30.XII.64, Viking. **AWP/RW rivalry:** When Anthony visited Frances Partridge in the summer of 1959, she noted that he was in "rather a provocative mood. Some of the characters he attacked may have been stand-ins for Rebecca—Madame de Staël and George Eliot, for instance." See Partridge, *Everything to Lose*; see also to JG, 6.VIII.61, Tulsa; to BBG, 28.VIII.61, PU; to JG, 28.VIII.61, Chicago, to LLF, 4.IX.61, courtesy of JB. **RW's draft letters to APW:** two undated, one dated 14.VIII.61, another 15.VIII.61, Tulsa; see also to NM, 13.IX.61.

348 **"Mr Chadband tone"**: 15.IX.61, Tulsa. **"Why did you"**: to HMA, 6.II.62, Yale. **"uneasy"**: to EMH, 1.IV.62, Yale; see also EA to RW, 3.IV.62, Yale.

349 **"As for Lily"**: to KW, 20.VI.62, Tulsa. **"If you had"**: see APW's three letters to

RW, one marked "received December 11th, 1964," one undated, one dated 23 December, Tulsa; see also to JG, 11.XII.64, Chicago; to Richard Butler, 12.I.65, Tulsa. **"Dear Rac":** Quoted in to KW, n.d., Tulsa. **RW on Vita West:** to HMA, 10.VI.65, 15.VI.65, Yale; to KW, 17.VI.65, Tulsa.

350 **"all smiles":** to KW, 24.VII.65, Tulsa. **Henry peeling an orange:** INT. Rosalind Burdon-Taylor. **"invaluable Gwenda":** to MB, 27.XI.65, Viking. **"You haven't":** INT. GD. **"practically wept":** INT. GD. RW gave a somewhat different view, downplaying Gwenda's influence on the novel. See to MB, 12.VI.66, Viking.

351 **"rum" fiction:** to TG, 29.III.66, Viking. **"two shoots":** to TG, n.d. **the Russians who visited RW's father:** to Clifton Fadiman, 10.VIII.66. **Nikolai:** He is described as embracing his daughter Tania like a "great beast of prey." Both Piers and Clare Aubrey are described as eagles in *The Fountain Overflows*. See Norton for a discussion of Nikolai as one version of the father Rebecca always wanted. Norton discusses Laura's dream of becoming an animal, of her wish that by some magical test, Nikolai "would speak to her in animal language and that she might understand and answer in the same tongue." The words hark back to Rebecca's fantasy (brought out in analysis) of consorting with her father as animals do with each other. For a more negative view of Nikolai, see Stec. Her reference to Nikolai's anti-heroic death in a "provincial French hotel" recalls Charles Fairfield's death in obscurity in a Liverpool hotel.

35: SURVIVORS IN MEXICO (1966–1967)

Interviews: Edmund West, Kitty West, Lily West, Vita West.

353 **Henry's losses:** HMA to MB, 19.VII.66, J. L. Wannen (Henry's accountant at Spicer & Pegler), 26.VII.66, Viking. See also the royalty statement attached to this correspondence. **"chided novelists":** See RW's review of Iris Murdoch's *The Red and the Green*, ST, 17.X.65.

354 **"I've always promised":** John Barkham, "Writing Just 'Function' for Rebecca West," *North Carolina Leader*, 26.X.66. **"weak and indecisive":** to AM, n.d., see also to EHN, 3.XI.66, Indiana, to EVW, 2.XI.66, to KW, 4.XI.66, Tulsa.

355 **RW on Henry:** to Kit Wright, 14.III.67; see also drafts of her Mexico book, Tulsa. **"I doubted":** to LF, n.d., courtesy of AM. **"I lost interest":** INT. Kit Wright.

358 **Ataturk:** "Triumph of a Proud Turk," 8.XI.64, ST.

359 **"rather odd poetry":** to Kit Wright, 10.VI.67.

360 **Ginger Pounce:** to LF, 24.IX.66; to Greta Mortimer, 22.IX.66, courtesy of Rosalind Burdon-Taylor.

36: LOVE WITHOUT CONTENT (1968–1969)

Interviews: Ian and Sally Barclay, Michael Bessie, William F. Buckley, Jr, Mrs Lovat Dickson, John Hodges, Merlin Holland, Marjorie Hutton, Joyce Seligman, Lois Wallace, Caroline West, Edmund West, Kitty West, Vita West, Kit Wright.

361 **RW on her Mexico book:** to EVW, 9.V.68, Tulsa. **RW on Anthony:** to KW, 16.VII.68, Tulsa. **"overengined":** to BBG, 23.VII.68, Tulsa. **"using any of his**

gifts": "Mild Silver, Furious Gold," TS, Tulsa; see also the description of the plot in to Alan Maclean, 12.VI.68, Tulsa.

362 **"an interest in life"**: to D. C. Evans (of Spicer and Pegler), 20.IX.68, Tulsa. **"House of Usher"**: to Peter Wolfe, 22.IX.68, Tulsa. **"wonderful, motherly . . . no nonsense"**: INT. Merlin Holland; see also Merlin Holland to HMA and RW, n.d. [c. October 1968], Tulsa.

363 **Henry's hospitalization**: to LF, 3,8.X.68 courtesy of AM; to EVW, 6.X.68, Tulsa; to ISB, 7.XI.68; to Merlin Holland, 7.X.68. **"We cannot go on"**: to EA, 8.10.68, Tulsa. **"agony of love"**: RW to Jonathan Mitchell, n.d. Yale; see also to EVW, 8.XI.68, 15.X.68, Tulsa, RW to EMH, 17.X.68, Yale; to BBG, 17.XI.68, PU.

364 **"surf-break noise"**: to EA, 16.XI.68, Tulsa. **"nearly utterly"**: to MB, 3.XI.68, Viking; to ADP: "I have had, as you know many and continual difficulties with Henry, but I would rather that things had gone well with us than anything in the world, and they often did." 8.XI.68, BU.

365 **"a master"**: Sybil Eccles to RW, 15.XI.68, Tulsa. **"buffets of life"**: 8.XI.68, Tulsa. **"Well, my dear"**: Marion Macleod to RW, n.d., Tulsa. **"the truant"**: n.d., Tulsa. **"there was something"**: 5.XI.68, Yale. **"knowing and joyous"**: Jonathan Mitchell to RW, 21.XII.68, Tulsa. **"Isn't Rebecca"**: BN to RW, 25.XI.68, Tulsa. **Marshall Best on Henry**: MB to RW, 10.XI.68, Viking. **"I often feel"**: to Douglas Woodruff, 14.XI.68, Georgetown. **"odd background"**: to Douglas and Mia Woodruff, 8.XI.68, Georgetown. **Henry's funeral**: to NM, 11.XI.68; INT. Joyce Seligman.

366 **"Henry's will"**: to Mr. Brydges (HMA's attorney), 11.XI.68, Tulsa; to AC, n.d. [November 1968]. **"dolly-sized"**: to Richard Church, 28.XI.68, The John Rylands Library, University of Manchester. **"gummed-up"**: to EA, 15.XII.68, Tulsa. **Kingston House apartment**: to EMH, 14.XII.69, Yale. **"What did I mean to him"**: to Jonathan Mitchell, n.d., Yale. **"innocent crushes"**: to EMH, 23.IV.69, Yale.

367 **"mean, silly"**: to CC, 18.XI,68, Tulsa; see also to EA, n.d., Tulsa. **"There is, of course"**: 28.VI.70. **"love without content"**: diary entry, 31.I.71, Tulsa. **"all wise mama"**: EH to RW, 26.IV.69, Yale. **"King Kong"**: to Kit Wright, 2.X.69. **"I wouldn't have been"**: APW to RW, n.d., Tulsa.

368 **"then there was"**: to APW, 31.V.69, Tulsa; see also to EMH, 3.V.69, Yale; RW to G. P. Wells, 15.VIII.69, Tulsa; to EVW, n.d. [c. October 1969], Tulsa. I have also drawn on LF to NM, 14.VIII.69.

369 **"It is a hard thing"**: to EVW, n.d. [c. X.69], Tulsa. **RW in Mexico**: to CC. 25.XI.69, Tulsa; to EVW, 14.XII.69, Tulsa; to LF, 3.I.70 [misdated 1969], courtesy of AM. **"I am sitting"**: to BBG, n.d., PU.

37: THE WILLY-WILLIES (1970–1971)

Interviews: Ian and Sally Barclay, Irene Garthwaite, John Hodges, Merlin Holland, Lady Kelly, Justin Lowinsky.

370 **"Tidied kitchen"**: 7.III.70, 18.X.71, Tulsa. **"I could not"**: to EA, n.d. [c. March 1970], Tulsa.

371 **"frightful"**: 18.IV.70, Tulsa. **"My legs"**: diary entry, 1.I.70, Tulsa. **"slow and stupid"**: diary entry, 2.II.71, Tulsa. **Marcuse**: to EMH, 27.V.70, Yale; **McLuhan**: "McLuhan and the Future of Literature."

372 **RW's Lebanese trip:** to EW, 20.V.71, Tulsa and drafts from her incomplete essay [Tulsa].

375 **"glorious austerity":** to EMH, 23.IV.71, Yale.

376 **"absolutely beautiful day":** INT. Merlin Holland. **Mrs. Gummidge:** "Meet France's Mrs. Gummidge," ST, 19.V.72.

377 **RW's Irish tour:** diary entry, 3.IX.71, Tulsa; to AM, postcard 13.IX.71; to EA. n.d., [c. X.71], Tulsa. **"crystal gazing":** diary entry, 5.IX.71, Tulsa. **"It's a Man's Lib":** to AM, n.d. [Autumn 1975]. **"Well, it is":** diary entry, 12.IX.71. Tulsa. **"bits of":** to EMH, 24.II.72, Yale. **"history of Ireland":** MSN, Tulsa.

378 **"Where would I be":** diary entry, 2.VIII.71, Tulsa. **"I am not":** diary entry, 26.VIII.71, Tulsa.

379 **golden autumn:** diary entries, 32.X, 1.XI, 3.XI, 71, Tulsa. **"A strange":** diary entry, Tulsa. **RW's fears of Anthony:** INT. JH, Bethel Solomons. **"I must pull":** diary entry, 27.V.71, Tulsa. **"Why do I":** diary entry, 24.VI.71, Tulsa.

38: "THE REAL RIGHT BEGINNING"
"BIOGRAPHY IS A BLOOD-SPORT" (1972–1974)

Interviews: John Hodges, Norman Mackenzie, Tony Redd, Rivers Scott, Nicolas van den Branden, Caroline West, Kitty West, Joan White.

380 **"Nazi hands":** diary entry, 29.IV.72, Tulsa.

381 **"But wasn't":** diary entry, 20.VIII.71, Tulsa. **"that icy":** diary entry, 25.X.71, Tulsa. See also NM to RW, 24.IX.71, 26.X.71, Tulsa. **RW on the Mackenzie biography:** diary entry, 16.V.73, Tulsa; "The Real H.G. Wells," ST, 17.VI.73. **"mentally outraged":** to Greta Mortimer, 22.VIII.72, courtesy of Rosalind Burdon-Taylor. **"rough soft":** diary entry, 21.IX.72, Tulsa. **"Can Cissie":** diary entry, 22.IX.72, Tulsa.

382 **"unfinished business":** to EHN, 18.IX, Indiana. **Harold Macmillan:** to EMH, 15.I.73 **RW's work on "The Only Poet":** diary entry, 12.II.73, Tulsa.

383 **"It has to be seen":** diary entry, 26.II.73, Tulsa. **"wonderful notes":** diary entry, 28.II.73, Tulsa. **"not unlike myself":** diary entry, 4.III.73, Tulsa. **"symbol of death":** diary entry, 19.X.73, Tulsa.

384 **"I wonder":** diary entry, 2.I.73, Tulsa. **"I think she dislikes":** VW to KW, 28.II.73. **"I do wish":** 9.IV.73, Tulsa. **"it will take":** Jenny Moncrieff to EH, 11.IV.73, Yale. **"inventively kind":** diary entry, 20.IV.73, Tulsa; see also diary entry, 17.IV.73, Tulsa. **Anthony's visit:** diary entries, 3,4.VIII.73, Tulsa.

385 **Watergate:** to EA, n.d., Tulsa; "There Are Plastic Gnomes in Washington," *New York Times*, 24.VI.73. **"the real right beginning":** diary entry, 28.IV.73, Tulsa; see also Jenny Moncrieff to EH, 2.V.73, Yale. **"The CP":** diary entry, 1.III.73, Tulsa; see MB to RW, 23.XI.73, Viking; diary entry, 29.IV.73, Tulsa. **"He doesn't":** Tulsa.

386 **"Offering the stems":** Both Yale and Tulsa have copies of RW's poetry. **RW on Edmund and Vita:** to EW, 17.II.74, Tulsa; diary entry, 10.III.74, Tulsa. **Ray's vetted manuscript:** Michael Rubinstein (of Rubinstein, Nash and Co., Solicitors) to Alan Maclean, 8.II.74, 10.II.74, 11.II.74, PML. **Gip Wells on Ray's book:** Gip Wells to GR, 27.I.74; see also GR to RW, 4.IV.75, PML. **"one with no association":** to EMH, 20.III.74, Yale.

387 **"now that biography is a blood-sport":** to Beverly Nichols, n.d., courtesy of Brian Connon. **"reality of evil":** notes for *The Only Poet*, Tulsa. **RW and Anthony:** diary

entries 18–19.III.74, Tulsa. Rebecca associated her repudiation of Anthony with her very survival; making character judgments, she contended, strengthened the self: "From the time we are children we know that the people round about us are good or bad. Cousin Jessie is good. Aunt Sophie is bad. We go on making judgments throughout life. It is our first source of self-help and self-defense of a psychological kind." **Rebecca's tantrums:** Barbara Burn to MB, 21.III.74, Viking.

388 **"neuroticism about critics":** MB to Alan Maclean, 5.II.74, Viking. **Gwenda on the sequel to *The Fountain Overflows:*** GD to MB, 24.VIII.74, Viking. **"white wash[ing]":** to EMH, 28.V.74, Yale. **"I ought":** diary entry, 12.V.74, Tulsa. **"shop for a grave":** diary entry, 13.VI.74, Tulsa. **Tony Reed:** INT. and Redd diary; see also Tony Redd to RW, 24.VIII.74, Tulsa.

390 **Peggy Guggenheim:** diary entries, 27,28.IX.74, Tulsa. **Norman's reassuring letter:** to RW, 4.X.74, Tulsa.

391 **"why did Mr. Ray":** "Love letters, some not so loving," 13.X.74. **RW's reaction to Hellman's review:** GD to Barbara Burn, 10.X.74, Viking; diary entry, 18.X.74, Tulsa. **RW on Anthony:** diary entries, 4.XI.74, 24.XI.74, Tulsa; to AS, 18.X.74; AS to RW, 6.XI.74. **"What a stupid":** diary entry, 11.XI.94, Tulsa. See RW's letters to the Schlesingers at Tulsa.

392 **Anthony's reviews of Ray: "Love and Mr Wells":** *Books and Bookmen,* 1974; "The Mystery of My Birth," *Harper's,* January 1975. **letters of rebuttal:** *Harper's,* April 1975. **"A flat lie":** APW's annotated copy of *H.G. Wells and Rebecca West* courtesy of LW; see also APW to Richard Garnett (Macmillan's), 8.VI.75, 4.VII.75; RW to GR, 5.VIII.75, Yale. **Joan Haslip:** diary entry, 17.XI.74, Tulsa. **"fair" "sterling":** diary entry, 6.V.75, Tulsa. **"skunk":** Ann Waldron, *Houston Chronicle,* clipping file Yale. **RW's birthday:** diary entry, 21.XII.74, Tulsa; to EMH, 22.XII.74, Yale.

393 **A. L. Rowse:** 4.XII.74, Tulsa. **"Remember":** n.d., Tulsa; see also to A. L. Rowse, 23.IV.75, Tulsa. **"Don't dare":** A. L. Rowse to RW, 4.V.75, Tulsa.

39: "THE ABNORMALITY OF MY LIFE" (1975–1978)

Interviews: Gwenda David, Emily Hahn, Victoria Glendinning, Phyllis Hatfield, Elizabeth Jenkins, Justin Lowinsky, Alison Macleod, Norman Macleod, Tony Redd, Rivers Scott, Diana Trilling, Nicolas van den Branden, Cheryl West, Edmund West, Kitty West, Lily West, Vita West.

394 **"a nice spontaneous":** diary entry, 1.IX.78, Tulsa. **"Where's Stanley":** Quoted in Hatfield; see also diary entry, 18.IX.74, Tulsa. **"abnormality of my life":** to DTR, 6.VI.75.

395 **"highly intelligent":** diary entry, 17.VII.75, Tulsa. **"loves all of the nicer":** diary entry, 23.VIII.75, Tulsa.

396 **"dogsbody":** to Greta Mortimer, 17.IV.7?, courtesy of Rosalind Burdon-Taylor. **"By all means":** diary entry, 11.XI.75, Tulsa. For Edmund's visit see also Riou Benson to RW 27.XI, 3.XII.77, 17.III.78, Tulsa. **Lionel Trilling:** diary entry, 11.XI.75; to DTR, 18.XI.75.

397 **"pantomime of disapproval":** to ISB, 16.XI.77. **"I will never":** diary entry, 12.XI.75, Tulsa; see also diary entry, 2.I.76, Tulsa. **fears of Anthony:** to ISB, 21.XI.75. **Suicide:** to ISB, 29.3.76. **Edmund's letter to RW:** diary entry, 7.II.77, Tulsa; see also to Victoria Glendinning, 7.II.77 [not sent], Tulsa.

398 **"popped into a sack":** to EHN, 9.II.77, Indiana, Tulsa. **"declined with":** to GR, 24.II.77, PML. **losing Edmund:** diary entry, 16.XII.75, Tulsa; see also diary entry, 29.XII.75, Tulsa. **"ischemia":** to ISB, 29.I.76. *A Sunday Telegraph* **lawyer:** to LLF, 8.IV.76; courtesy of JB. *Mortal Wounds:* diary entry, 3.IV.76, Tulsa.

399 **"Let's make":** Davidon. **Anthony's exorcism:** INT. Caroline West, LW, diary entry, 10.V.76, Tulsa. **"Tony Redd":** INT., Tony Redd's diaries, Tony Redd to RW, 25.V, 24.VIII.74, 12.V, 29.VIII, 76, 28.I.78, Tulsa. **Tony Redd returned:** diary entry, 2.VIII.76, Tulsa.

400 **"I always":** INT. Diana Trilling. **several dreams:** diary entry, 3.VIII.76, Tulsa. **"Do you know":** to ISB, 10.IX.76; see also diary entries, 11.X.76, 27.10.76, Tulsa. **"brilliant and good looking":** to ISB, 1.II.77.

401 **"fears of my childhood":** diary entry, 23.II.77, Tulsa; see also to EMH, 2.XI.76, Yale. diary entry, 6.XI.76, Tulsa. **Rebecca announced:** diary entry, 11.XII.76, Tulsa. **Assumption of the Virgin:** to EMH, 10.I.77, Yale. **"Have they":** diary entry, 20.V.77, Tulsa. **slept badly:** diary entry, 31.V.77, Tulsa. **"I am so":** diary entry, 1.VI.77, Tulsa. **"The Man Who Liked Strangers":** Tulsa.

403 **"I don't":** diary entry, 10.VI.77, Tulsa.

404 **"Haven't we":** diary entry, 11.VI.77, Tulsa. **"the way I belong":** diary entry, 18.VII.77, Tulsa. **"absolutely marmoreal":** diary entry, 1.II.78, Tulsa. **Elizabeth Jenkins:** INT. See also diary entry, 3.II.78, Tulsa. **"I have always":** diary entry, 3.II.78, Tulsa. See also to EMH, 26.II.78, Yale. **"sighing noisily":** diary entry, AM, 6.II.78. **"Lettie never":** RW comments on letter from Jean Lawrie, C.B.E., 16.II.78, Tulsa. **Another friend:** Priscilla Norman to RW, 8.II.78, Tulsa. **Lily also:** LW to RW, 21.II.78, Tulsa. **"little time of":** diary entry, 8.II.78, Tulsa.

405 **"the old gentleman":** diary entry, 5.III.78, Tulsa; see also to GR, 6.III.78, PML. **"If a play":** to EMH, 17.X.78, Yale.

40: CELEBRATING REBECCA WEST (1977–1980)

Interviews: Michael and Cornelia Bessie, Jill Craigie, Noel Davis, April Edwards, Michael Foot, Emily Hahn, Samuel Hynes, Alison Macleod, Fiona Macleod, Jane Marcus, Ursula Owen.

406 **"curl up":** to EMH, 25.X.77, Yale; see also GD to MB, 31.X.77, Tulsa; to ISB, 21.X.77. **"witch hunting":** 11.XI.77. **"she never":** 6.I.78.

407 **"compulsion to milk":** 10.II.77; see also diary entry, 27.IV.78, Tulsa. **"spots like"** Marcus, "A Speaking Sphinx"; see also Jane Marcus to RW, 2.III.79, Tulsa. "big, beautiful": diary entry, 25.II.78, Tulsa. **"hymn to patriotism":** INT. Michael Foot; see also Michael Foot, "My Country Right or Wrong?", clipping file, Tulsa.

408 **"He *thinks*":** to Virginia Salomon, n.d. **"I love her dearly":** 7.IV.78, Tulsa. **"It's not the daughter":** INT. Jill Craigie; see to GR, 25.IV.78, PML.

409 **"man who was":** "Tolstoy's Bad Habits," ST, 16.IV.78. **"charming format":** to Ursula Owen, 22.IX.80, Tulsa; see also to Carmen Callil, 19.IV.80, Tulsa. **"more ravishing creature":** to KW, 15.XI.78, Tulsa. **"bronze skin":** to EMH, 15.XI.78, Yale. **"more ravishing creature":** diary entry, 27.II.79, Tulsa. **"melodious way":** to EMH, 27.II.79, Yale; to MH, 27.II.79, courtesy of JH.

410 **"undiminished fervour":** AM diary, 29.VII.79. **"Your idiot daughter":** AM diary,

4.X.79. **"appreciate that"**: GD to MB, 4.I.80, Tulsa; see, for example, to NM, 12.I.80, Tulsa.

411 **"for someone"**: 4.29.80, Tulsa.

412 **"doll-like good looks"**: Mandrake, "Warren's good manners charm Dame Rebecca," ST, 7.II.82; see also diary entry, 29.III.80, Tulsa.

413 **"eager mind"**: Campbell, "Performance Art."

414 **"whale of a time"**: AM diary, 20.IV.80; see also diary entry, 30.IV.80, Tulsa. **"known to the house"**: to ISB, 5.VI.80. **"hiatus hernia"**: to ISB, 30.V.80. **"noticing child"**: manuscript draft, Tulsa.

416 **"I am enchanted"**: to AM, n.d. [c. autumn 1980]. **behaved like schoolgirls**: diary entry, 28.IV.80, Tulsa. **"more and more"**: diary entry, 6.I.81, Tulsa.

41: To the Last Breath (1981–1983)

Interviews: Elizabeth Furse, Rhoda Koenig, Doris Lessing, Justin Lowinsky, Alison Macleod, Cathy Macleod, Helen Macleod, Norman Macleod, Marion Macleod, Babette Rosmond, Rivers Scott, Diana Stainforth, Nicolas van den Branden, Sophie West, Joan White.

418 **Eugene Weintraub:** to Eugene Weintraub, 11.VI.82, Eugene Weintraub to RW, 12.VII.82, "The Wrong Man" Eugene Weintraub TS sent to CR; see also diary entry, 21.X.81, Tulsa; to EMH, 11.I.82, Yale. **"full biography"**: Tulsa.

419 **"lyrical outpouring"**: to AM, 29.IV.81, AM diary entry 28.IV.81: see also to NM, 29.IV.81, Tulsa.

420 **Rhoda Koenig:** Rhoda Koenig to CR, 15.III.93. **Martha Gellhorn:** H.G. describes Martha Gellhorn as his lover in a typescript draft of his autobiography, PML.

421 **"all that wit"**: Doris Lessing to RW, 6.II.82, Tulsa. **"human life"**: Doris Lessing, "These Shores of Sweet Unreason: Possible Protective Psychological Mechanisms?", Alfred A. Knopf Papers, courtesy of Carole Klein. **"Edith"**: TS, Tulsa.

422 **"tranquil misty green"**: Helen Macleod to RW, 27.V.82, Tulsa. **"Sometimes you seem"**: Helen Macleod to RW, 25.XI.82, Tulsa. **"seraphically beautiful"**: diary entry, 25.III.82, Tulsa. **"blundering remarks"**: diary entry, 4.IV.82, Tulsa. **"nearly at the end"**: diary entry, 14.IV.82, Tulsa. **Mrs. Thatcher:** to Virginia Salomon, n.d. **"very characteristic"**: to EHN, 20.IV.82, Indiana.

423 **Babette Rosmond:** Babette Rosmond memoir, Boston. **"Miss Mud"**: to Terence Davis and Nicolas van den Branden, 2.VIII.82, courtesy of NVB; see also to Rivers Scott, 2.VI.82, Tulsa. **"sensitive and classical"**: to Terence Davis and Nicolas van den Branden, 21.VI.82, courtesy of NVB. **a terrified Rebecca:** diary entries, 8,9.VII.82, Tulsa; see also to EHN, 9.VII.82, Indiana.

424 **"I hate reading"**: diary entry, 22.I.82, Tulsa. **"like a what?"**: The Saturday Review, IV.82. **"almost entirely"**: The Times Literary Supplement, 5.III.82. **"armed at all points"**: The Spectator, 8.V.82. **"today's 'New Journalism' "**: New York, 10.V.82. **"if we really"**: London Review of Books, 6–29.V.82. **"sportive essay"**: The New Yorker, 19.VII.82. **"The Heiress"**: fragmentary drafts, Tulsa. **piece for her ninetieth birthday:** fragmentary drafts, Tulsa; see also "There is Nothing Like a Dame," Vogue, II.83.

425 **Justin Lowinsky:** Simmons and Simmons (lawyers) memorandum, 4.X.82, Tulsa. **Stanley Olson:** diary entry, 4.X.82, courtesy of Phyllis Hatfield. **"Nobody"**: AM diary entry, 10.X.82. **"Who engaged"**: diary entry, AM, 14.IX.82.

426 **"I wish"**: Nurse's notes, 21.XI.82, Tulsa. **"Mutual esteem"**: diary entry, Stanley Olson, 9.XII.82, courtesy of Phyllis Hatfield. **"Oh, that wicked"**: diary entry, AM, 22.XII.82. **"I'm not going"**: Stainforth memoir. **succumbed to old age**: Diana Stainforth to Mr. and Mrs. Martin Rubin, 7.III.83, Tulsa. **"Oh, don't"**: diary entry, AM, 13.I.83. **"He's a bad boy"**: diary entry, AM, 19.I.83.

427 **"Where's my little boy"**: diary entry, AM. 19.I.83. **"I'm dying"**: diary entry, AM. **"Amen"**: diary entry, AM, 4.III.83. **"I'm lost"**: diary entry, AM, 6.III.83. **"highlights"**: Phillipa Thorp to ISB, 26.III.83. **resisted her sedatives**: Diana Stainforth to Eileen Farley, 7.III.83, Tulsa. **"fundamental belief"**: Quoted in *The Meaning of Treason.*

EPILOGUE

Interviews: Michael Coren, Lily West, Irene Garthwaite, Bernard Levin.

429 **"fantasist"**: *Observer*, 20.III.83. **Reviews of *This Real Night*:** Hilary Spurling, "The Fountain Clogs," *Observer*, 21.X.84; Lorna Sage, *"This Real Night,"* *New York Times Book Review*, 18.VIII.85; A. S. Byatt, "A good mind at work observing clever women," *The Times* 18.X.84.

430 **The day Rebecca died:** diary entry, AM, 15.III.83. **"wee Alison"**: INT. Lily West.

431 **"hollow shell"**: Stanley Olson's date book, 5.VI.84, courtesy of Phyllis Hatfield. **"but there was quite"**: William Goldstein, "Anthony West," *Publishers Weekly*, 20.IV.84. **"left the field"**: Deborah Fitts, "The Story H.G. Wells Didn't Write," *Westerly Sun* (Rhode Island), 3.VI.84.

Bibliography

Adamic, Louis. *My Native Land.* New York: Harper & Brothers, 1943.

Allen, Walter. *The Modern Novel.* New York: E. P. Dutton, 1964.

Ambrose, Stephen E. *Nixon: The Education of a Politician 1913–1962.* New York: Simon and Schuster, 1987.

Annan, Noel. *Our Age: English Intellectuals Between the World Wars—A Group Portrait.* New York: Random House, 1990.

——*Roxburgh of Stowe.* London: Longmans, 1965.

Beach, Joseph Warren. *The Twentieth-Century Novel: Studies in Technique.* New York: D. Appleton-Century Co., 1932.

Bell, Anne Oliver, ed. *The Diary of Virginia Woolf. Volume Four 1931–1935.* New York: Harcourt Brace Jovanovich, 1982.

Belford, Barbara. *Violet.* New York: Simon and Schuster, 1991.

Bennett, Arnold. *The Journals of Arnold Bennett 1911–1920.* New York: Viking, 1932.

——*Lord Raingo.* New York: Doran, 1926.

Bogan, Louise. *What the Woman Lived: Selected Letters of Louise Bogan.* New York: Harcourt, Brace Jovanovich, 1973.

Brandon, Ruth. *The New Women and the Old Men: Love, Sex and The Woman Question.* New York: Norton, 1990.

Brightman, Carol. *Writing Dangerously: Mary McCarthy and Her World.* New York: Clarkson/Potter, 1992.

Brittain, Vera. *Testament of Youth.* [1933] London: Virago, 1978.

Brome, Vincent. *H.G. Wells: A Biography.* London: Longmans, Green & Co., 1951.

Brown, Peter. *Augustine of Hippo: A Biography.* Berkeley: University of California Press, 1967.

Calder, Robert. *Willie: The Life of W. Somerset Maugham.* New York: St. Martin's Press, 1989.

Campbell, Beatrix. "Performance Art." *City Limits.* March 25, 1982. [Profile of Rebecca West]

Chamberlain, Lesley. "Rebecca West in Yugoslavia." *Contemporary Review.* 248 (May 1986): 262–266.

Clarke, Ann Jennifer. "Know This is Your War: British Women Writers and the Two World Wars." State University of New York at Stony Brook Ph.D. dissertation, 1989.

Cohen, Harriet. *A Bundle of Time.* London: Faber and Faber, 1969. [Rebecca West introduction]

Colquitt, Clare. "A Call to Arms: Rebecca West's Assault on the Limits of 'Gerda's Empire' in *Black Lamb and Grey Falcon*." *South Atlantic Review.* 51 (1986): 77–91.

Curtis, Anthony. "Dame Rebecca West talks to Anthony Curtis about social improvements and literary disasters." *The Listener,* February 15, 1975.

Curtiss, Mina. *Other People's Letters*. New York: Macmillan, 1978.

Cuthbertson, Ken. *Inside: The Biography of John Gunther*. Chicago: Bonus Books, 1992.

Davidon, Ann Morrisett. "The Case of Anthony West." *The Nation*. January 24, 1976.

Davies, Dido. *William Gerhardie: A Biography*. Oxford: Oxford University Press, 1990.

Deakin, Motley. *Rebecca West*. Boston: Twayne, 1980.

De Mille, Agnes. *Portrait Gallery*. Boston: Houghton Mifflin, 1990.

Dickson, Lovat. *H.G. Wells: His Turbulent Life and Times*. New York: Atheneum, 1969.

———*The House of Words: The Memoirs of a Publisher*. New York: Atheneum, 1963.

Drabble, Margaret. *Arnold Bennett: A Biography*. New York: Knopf, 1974.

Dragnich, Alex N. *Serbs and Croats: The Struggle in Yugoslavia*. New York: Harcourt Brace & Co., 1992.

Duberman, Martin Bauml. *Paul Robeson*. New York: Ballantine Books, 1989.

Ellman, Mary. *Thinking About Women*. New York: Harcourt Brace Jovanovich, 1968.

Ferguson, Moira. "Feminist Manicheanism: Rebecca West's Unique Fusion." *The Minnesota Review*. 15 (1980): 53–60.

Fitch, Noel Riley. *Anaïs: The Erotic Life of Anaïs Nin*. Boston: Little Brown, 1993.

Foot, Michael. *Debts of Honour*. London: Davis Poynter, 1980.

———"My Country Right or Wrong?" *Sunday Telegraph Magazine*. November 1987.

Ford, Ford Madox. *The Good Soldier* [1915]. New York: Vintage Books, n.d.

Foster, Margaret. "West's Country." *The Guardian*. October 25, 1980.

Frankau, Pamela. *The Devil We Know*. London: Heinemann, 1939.

———*I Find Four People*. London: Ivor Nicholson and Watson, 1935.

———*A Letter from R*b*cc* W*st*. Edinburgh: The Tragura Press, 1986.

———*Pen to Paper*. Garden City, N.Y.: Doubleday, 1962.

Fussell, Paul. *Abroad: British Literary Traveling Between the Wars*. New York: Oxford University Press, 1980.

Garner, Les. *A Brave and Beautiful Spirit: Dora Marsden 1882–1960*. Aldershot, England: Avebury, 1990.

Gellhorn, Walter. "Report on a Report of the House Committee on UnAmerican Activities." *Harvard Law Review*. October 1947.

Gerhardie, William. *Jazz and Jasper*. London: Duckworth, 1928.

Gilbert, Sandra. "Soldier's Heart: Literary Men, Literary Women, and the Great War." *Signs* 8 (1983), 422–50.

Glendinning, Victoria. *Rebecca West: A Life*. New York: Knopf, 1987.

Glenny, Misha. *The Fall of Yugoslavia. The Third Balkan War*. New York: Penguin Books, 1992.

Gould, Bruce and Beatrice. *American Story*. New York: Harper & Row, 1968.

Grant, Jane. *Ross, The New Yorker and Me*. New York: William Morrow, 1968.

Hammond, J. R. *H.G. Wells and Rebecca West*. New York: St. Martin's Press, 1991.

Hardwick, Elizabeth. *Seduction and Betrayal: Women and Literature*. New York: Vintage Books, 1975.

Hart-Davis, Rupert. *Hugh Walpole: A Biography*. New York: Macmillan, 1952.

Hatfield, Phyllis. *Pencil Me In: A Memoir of Stanley Olson*. London: Andre Deutsch, 1994.

Hayman, Ronald. "Rebecca West." *Books and Bookman*. March 1982.

Herbert, Ivor. "Rebecca West." *Evening News*. August 16, 1966.

Hicks, Jim. "Specialist in Traitors, Spies and Weeds: A Walk and Talk with Rebecca West." *Life*. September 30, 1966.

Hoyt, Edwin P. *Alexander Woollcott: The Man Who Came to Dinner*. Radnor, Pennsylvania: The Chilton Book Co., 1973.

Hunt, Violet. *The Flurried Years.* London: Hurst & Blackett, 1922.

Hutchens, John K. "Rebecca West, Novelist and Great Reporter." *New York Herald Tribune Book Review.* April 22, 1956.

Hutchinson, G. E. "The Dome." In *The Itinerant Ivory Tower: Scientific and Literary Essays.* New Haven: Yale University Press, 1953.

Jong, Erica. "The Miller's Tale." *The Times Literary Supplement.* June 25, 1993.

Judd, Alan. *Ford Madox Ford.* Cambridge: Harvard University Press, 1991.

Kaplan, Robert D. *Balkan Ghosts.* New York: St. Martin's Press, 1993.

Kaufman, Beatrice and Joseph Hennessey, eds. *The Letters of Alexander Woollcott.* New York: Viking, 1944.

Kennard, Jean E. *Vera Brittain and Winifred Holtby: A Working Partnership.* Hanover: University Press of New England, 1989.

King, James. *The Last Modern: A Life of Herbert Read.* New York: St. Martin's Press, 1990.

Klein, Carole. *Mothers and Sons.* Boston: Houghton Mifflin, 1984.

Kobler, Turner. "The Eclecticism of Rebecca West." *Critique.* 13 (1971): 30–49.

Kramnick, Issac and Barry Sheerman. *Harold Laski: A Life on the Left.* New York: Allen Lane, The Penguin Press, 1993.

Kurth, Peter. *American Cassandra: The Life of Dorothy Thompson.* Boston: Little Brown, 1990.

Lamb, Richard. *Churchill as War Leader.* London: Bloomsbury, 1991.

Langner, Lawrence. *The Magic Curtain.* New York: E. P. Dutton, 1951.

Leaska, Mitchell A. and John Phillips, eds. *Violet to Vita: The Letters of Violet Trefusis to Vita Sackville-West.* New York: Viking, 1989.

Pierpont, Claudia Roth. "Sex, Lies, and Thirty-Five Thousand Pages." *The New Yorker.* March 1993.

Pritchett, V. S. "The Climate of Paranoia." *The New Yorker.* December 12, 1966.

Ray, Gordon, *H.G. Wells and Rebecca West.* New Haven: Yale University Press, 1974.

Ray, Philip E. "The Judge Reexamined: Rebecca West's Underrated Gothic Romance." *English Literature in Transition 1880–1920* 31 (1987), 297–307.

Raymond, Diana. *Pamela Frankau: A Life* (unpublished manuscript).

Redd, Tony Neil. "Rebecca West: Master of Reality." University of South Carolina Ph.D. dissertation, 1972.

Reed, Jr., Robert. "Rebecca West." *Notes and Queries.* November 1957.

Rendel, Sir George. *The Sword and the Olive: Recollections of Diplomacy and the Foreign Service, 1913–1945.* London: John Murray, 1957.

Rowse, A. L. *Glimpses of the Great.* Lanham, MD: University Press of America, 1985.

Saint Augustine. *Confessions.* New York: Penguin Books, 1961.

Schorer, Mark. *Sinclair Lewis: An American Life.* New York: McGraw Hill, 1961.

Scott, Bonnie Kime. *The Gender of Modernism: A Critical Anthology.* Bloomington: Indiana University Press, 1990.

———*Refiguring Modernism.* Bloomington: Indiana University Press, 1995.

Secor, Robert and Marie Secor. *The Return of the Good Soldier: Ford Madox Ford and Violet Hunt's 1917 Diary.* University of Victoria, 1983.

Secunda, Victoria. *Women and Their Fathers.* New York: Delacorte Press, 1992.

Selver, Paul. *Orage and the New Age Circle.* London: Allen & Unwin, 1959.

Sherman, Susan, ed. *May Sarton, Among the Usual Days: A Portrait.* New York: Norton, 1994.

Showalter, Elaine. *A Literature of Their Own: British Women Novelists from Brontë to Lessing.* Princeton: Princeton University Press, 1977.

Smith, David C. *H.G. Wells: Desperately Mortal.* New Haven: Yale University Press, 1986.

Spark, Muriel. "Personal History: The School on the Links." *The New Yorker.* March 25, 1991.

Sparks, Allister. *The Mind of South Africa.* New York: Knopf, 1990.

Spender, Dale. *There's Always Been a Women's Movement in This Century.* London: Pandora Press, 1983.

Stec, Loretta. "Writing Treason: Rebecca West's Contradictory Career." Rutgers University Ph.D. dissertation, 1993.

Steel, Ronald. *Walter Lippmann and the American Century.* Boston: Little Brown, 1980.

Stern, G. B. *Another Part of the Forest.* London: Cassell, 1941.

———*Monogram.* London: Chapman & Hall, 1936.

Stetz, Margaret Diane. "Rebecca West and the Visual Arts." *Tulsa Studies in Women's Literature.* 8 (Spring 1989): 43–62.

———"Drinking 'The Wine of Truth': Philosophical Change in West's *The Return of the Soldier."* *Arizona Quarterly,* 43 (1987): 63–78.

Stiehlmann, Gunther, ed. *A Literate Passion: Letters of Anaïs Nin and Henry Miller 1932–1953.* New York: Harcourt Brace Jovanovich, 1987.

Stokes, Sewall. *Pilloried!* New York: D. Appleton and Co. 1929.

Suzman, Helen. *In No Uncertain Terms: A South African Memoir.* New York: Knopf, 1993.

Sweetman, David. *Mary Renault: A Biography.* New York: Harcourt Brace, 1993.

Swinnerton, Frank. *The Georgian Scene: A Literary Panorama.* New York: Farrar & Rinehart, 1934.

Taylor, A.J.P. *The Habsburg Monarchy 1809–1918.* [1948] New York: Penguin Books, 1990.

———*A Personal History.* London: Coronet Books, 1984.

Taylor, Telford. *The Anatomy of the Nuremberg Trials.* New York: Knopf, 1992.

Teachout, Terry. "A Liberated Woman." *The New Criterion.* 6 (1988): 13–21.

Thomas, Sue. "Rebecca West's Second Thoughts on Feminism." *Genders.* 13 (Spring 1992): 90–107.

Tillinghast, Richard. "Rebecca West and The Tragedy of Yugoslavia." *The New Criterion.* June 1992.

Todorovich, Boris. *Last Words: A Memoir of World War II and the Yugoslav Tragedy.* New York: Walker and Company, 1989.

Tusa, Ann and John. *The Nuremberg Trials.* New York: Atheneum, 1986.

"Twentieth Century Woman." M. D. October 1970. [Profile of Rebecca West]

Urie, Dale Marie. "Rebecca West: A Worthy Legacy." University of North Texas Ph.D. dissertation, 1989.

Usborne, Karen. *Elizabeth: The Author of Elizabeth and Her German Garden.* London: The Bodley Head, 1986.

Walker, Linda. Transcript of interview with Dr. Letitia Fairfield, March 28, 1976, courtesy of Alison Macleod.

Watts, Marjorie. *Mrs. Sappho: The Life of C. A. Dawson Scott, Mother of International P.E.N.* London: Duckworth, 1987.

Weldon, Fay. *Rebecca West.* London: Penguin Books, 1987.

Wells, H.G. *Ann Veronica.* London: Unwin 1909; Virago, 1984.

———*The Autocracy of Mr. Parham.* London: Heinemann, 1930.

———*The Book of Catherine Wells.* London: Chatto and Windus, 1928.

———*Boon, The Mind of the Race, The Wild Assess of the Devil, and The Last Trump Being a First Selection from the Literary Remains of George Boon, Appropriate to the Times Pre-*

pared for Publication by Reginald Bliss, with an Ambiguous Introduction by H.G. Wells. London: Unwin, 1915; New York: Doran, 1915.

————H.G. Wells in Love: Postscript to An Experiment in Autobiography, ed. G. P. Wells. London: Faber & Faber, 1984.

————Joan and Peter [1918]. London and New York: Macmillan, 1935.

————Marriage. London: Macmillan, 1912; The Hogarth Press, 1986.

————Mr. Britling Sees It Through. London, Casell, 1916; The Hogarth Press, 1985.

————The New Machiavelli. London: John Lane, 1911; Viking Penguin, 1985.

————The Passionate Friends. London: Macmillan, 1913; The Hogarth Press, 1986.

————The Research Magnificent. London and New York: Macmillan, 1915.

————The Secret Places of the Heart. London: Cassell, 1922.

————The World of William Clissold. London: Ernest Benn, 1926.

West, Anthony. David Rees, Among Others. London: Hamish Hamilton, 1970; New York: Random House, 1970.

————"H.G. Wells." Encounter. February 1957, 52–59.

————H.G. Wells: Aspects of a Life. London: Hutchinson, 1984. New York: Random House, 1984.

————Heritage. New York: Random House, 1956; London: Secker & Warburg, 1984.

————"Life with Aunty Panther and H.G. Wells." The Observer. January 4, 1976.

————Mortal Wounds. New York: McGraw Hill, 1973.

————"Mother and Son." The New York Review of Books. March 1, 1984.

————"My Father's Unpaid Debts of Love." The Observer. January 11, 1976.

West, Rebecca. "The Addict." Nash's Pall Mall Magazine. February 1935.

————"The Art of Fiction," The Paris Review 79 (1981). [Interview]

————Black Lamb and Grey Falcon: A Journey Through Yugoslavia. New York: Viking, 1941; London: Macmillan, 1942; reissued in Penguin Books paperback 1986.

————Cousin Rosamund. London: Macmillan, 1985; Virago 1986; Viking Penguin, 1986.

————"Deliverance," Ladies' Home Journal. August 1952. Reprinted in The Only Poet.

————"Elizabeth Montague." In From Anne To Victoria: Essays by Various Hands. London: Cassell, 1937.

————Family Memories. London: Virago, 1987; New York: Viking Penguin, 1988.

————"First Fortnight," Ladies' Home Journal. January 1940.

————The Fountain Overflows. London: Macmillan, 1956; New York: Viking, 1956; Virago Press, 1987.

————"Goodness Doesn't Just Happen." In This I Believe, ed. Edward P. Morgan, New York: Simon and Schuster, 1952.

————Harriet Hume. London: Hutchinson, 1929; New York: Doubleday Doran, 1929.

————Henry James. London: Nisbet & Co., 1916; New York: Henry Holt, 1916.

————The Harsh Voice. London: Jonathan Cape, 1935; Virago, 1982.

————"In the Cauldron of South Africa." The Sunday Times, March 27, April 10, 17, 24, May 1.

————"I Regard Marriage With Fear and Horror." Hearst's International. November 1923.

————The Judge. London: Hutchinson 1922; Virago 1980; New York: Dial, 1980.

————Lions and Lambs. With David Low. London: Hutchinson, 1928; New York: Harcourt Brace & Co., 1928.

————"McLuhan and the Future of Literature." The English Association. 1969.

————"The Man Who Came to Dinner." In London Calling, ed. Storm Jameson. New York: Harper & Brothers, 1942.

————"Margaret Thatcher: The Politician as Woman." *Vogue.* September 1979.

————*The Modern Rake's Progress.* With David Low. London: Hutchinson, 1934.

————"Mrs. Thatcher and Mr. Callaghan." *Washington Post.* April 26, 1979.

————"My Father," *Sunday Telegraph.* December 30, 1962.

————"My Journey into Television." *Sunday Telegraph,* October 8, 1978.

————"The Necessity and Grandeur of the International Ideal." In *Challenge of Death,* ed. Storm Jameson. New York: E. P. Dutton, 1935.

————"My Religion." *My Religion.* New York: D. Appleton, 1926.

————*1900.* London: Weidenfeld & Nicolson, 1982; New York: Viking, 1982.

————"The Novelist's Voice." BBC Broadcast, September 14, 1976, Tulsa.

————"Of Course Oswald Did It." *Sunday Telegraph,* December 27, 1964.

————*The Only Poet and Short Stories,* ed. Antonia Till. London: Virago Press, 1992.

————*Pablo Picasso: A Suite of 180 Drawings.* An Appreciation by Rebecca West. New York: Harcourt, Brace, 1954.

————"The Private and Impersonal Notebooks of Braque." *Harper's Bazaar.* November 1955.

————*This Real Night.* London: Virago 1987; New York: Viking, 1984.

————*Rebecca West: A Celebration.* London: Macmillan, 1977; New York: Viking, 1977.

————*The Return of the Soldier.* London: Nisbet & Co., 1918; New York: The Century Co., 1918; Carroll & Graff, 1990.

————On *"The Return of the Soldier." The Yale University Library Gazette.* 57 (1982): 66–71.

————"The Role of Fantasy in the Work of the Brontës." Haworth: Publications of the Brontë Society, 1954.

————*Selected Poems of Carl Sandburg.* New York: Harcourt, Brace, 1926.

————"Shoulder to Shoulder." *TV Guide.* October 21, 1975.

————*The Strange Necessity: Essays Reviews.* London: Jonathan Cape, 1928; New York: Doubleday Doran, 1928; Virago, 1987.

————*Sunflower.* London: Virago, 1986; New York: Penguin, 1988.

————*The Thinking Reed.* London: Hutchinson, 1936; New York: Viking, 1936; Virago, 1984.

————"Tradition in Criticism." In *Tradition and Experiment in Present-Day Literature.* London: Oxford University Press, 1929.

————"A Visit to a Godmother." *Writers on Themselves.* London: British Broadcasting Corporation, 1964. Reprinted in *Rebecca West: A Celebration.*

————*War Nurse: The True Story of A Woman Who Lived, Loved, and Suffered on the Western Front.* New York: Cosmopolitan Book Corporation, 1930.

————"Was It Really Like This in Dallas?" *The Reporter.* May 18, 1967.

————"We Must Bite the Bullett." *Sunday Telegraph.* June 26, 1963.

————"Who is to Blame for Dr. Ward?" *Sunday Telegraph.* August 4, 1963.

————"Woman As Artist and Thinker." In *Woman's Coming of Age: A Symposium.* Ed. Samuel D. Schmalhausen and V. F. Calverton. New York: Liveright, 1931.

————"Women as Brainworkers." In *Women and The Labour Party.* Ed. Dr. Marion Phillips. London: Headley Brothers Publishers, 1918.

————"Women of England." *The Atlantic Monthly.* January 1916.

————"Women Re Women." *Mademoiselle.* February 1970.

Wexler, Alice. *Emma Goldman in Exile: From the Russian Revolution to the Spanish Civil War.* Boston: Beacon Press, 1989.

Wineapple, Brenda. *Genet: A Biography of Janet Flanner.* New York: Ticknor & Fields, 1989.

Wolfe, Peter. *Rebecca West: Artist and Thinker.* Carbondale, IL: Southern Illinois University Press, 1971.

Wolff, Larry. "Rebecca West: This Time, Let's Listen." *The New York Times Book Review.* February 10, 1991.

Wolfenstein, Martha. "How Is Mourning Possible." *Psychoanalytic Study of the Child.* 21 (1966).

———"Loss, Rage, and Repetition." *Psychoanalytic Study of the Child.* 24 (1969).

Index